After the Civil War

CW00735374

The Spanish civil war was fought not only on the streets and battlefields from 1936 to 1939 but also through memory and trauma in the decades that followed. This fascinating book reassesses the eras of war, dictatorship and transition to democracy in light of the memory boom in Spain since the late 1990s. It explores how the civil war and its repressive aftermath have been remembered and represented from 1939 to the present through the interweaving of war memories, political power, and changing social relations. Acknowledgement and remembrance were circumscribed during the war's immediate aftermath, and only the victors were free to remember collectively during the long Franco era. Michael Richards recasts social memory as a profoundly historical product of migration, political events, and evolving forms of collective identity through the 1950s, the transition to democracy in the 1970s, and the bitterly contested politics of memory since the 1990s.

MICHAEL RICHARDS is Associate Professor of European History at the University of the West of England. His previous publications include *A Time of Silence: Civil War and the Culture of Repression in Franco's Spain, 1936–1945* (Cambridge 1998) and, as co-editor, *The Splintering of Spain: Cultural History and the Spanish Civil War* (Cambridge 2005).

After the Civil War: Making Memory and Re-Making Spain since 1936

Michael Richards

CAMBRIDGE
UNIVERSITY PRESS

CAMBRIDGE
UNIVERSITY PRESS

University Printing House, Cambridge CB2 8BS, United Kingdom

Published in the United States of America by Cambridge University Press, New York

Cambridge University Press is part of the University of Cambridge.

It furthers the University's mission by disseminating knowledge in the pursuit of education, learning and research at the highest international levels of excellence.

www.cambridge.org
Information on this title: www.cambridge.org/9780521728188

© Michael Richards 2013

First published 2013

Printed in the United Kingdom by Clays, St Ives plc

A catalogue record for this publication is available from the British Library

Library of Congress Cataloguing in Publication data

Richards, Michael, 1961–
  After the civil war : making memory and re-making Spain since 1936 /
Michael Richards.
    p.   cm.
  ISBN 978-0-521-89934-5 – ISBN 978-0-521-72818-8 (pbk.)
1. Spain–History–Civil War, 1936–1939–Social aspects.   2. Spain–History–
  20th century.   I. Title.
  DP269.8.S65R53 2013
  946.081′1–dc23

                                                              2012044101

ISBN 978-0-521-89934-5 Hardback
ISBN 978-0-521-72818-8 Paperback

Additional resources for this publication at www.cambridge.org/9780521899345

For Edward

and in memory of Robert James (1907–2000)

Contents

List of maps and tables

Preface

The origins of this book lie in an invitation several years ago to produce 'a social history of the Franco years'. There exists no broad such history and it seemed that a study of society during the Spanish dictatorship would fill a significant gap in the historiography and map a future agenda for research. Several substantial problems beyond the normal questions about the identification and selection of themes, the location of source material and the weighing of evidence quickly became obvious. The first problem was how to establish the chronological parameters of the project: at which point should the story begin and where should it end? The simplest solution was to begin with Franco's victory in 1939 and work forwards, more or less letting the civil war take care of itself as a looming but relatively undelineated backdrop to what came after. Both the dictator as focus and 1939 as starting point felt instinctively unsatisfactory, however, being essentially political points of departure for what was projected explicitly as a *social* history. This unease was significantly reinforced by the phenomenal surge in the recording of memories related to the civil war since the late 1990s and current debates in Spain over assimilation of testimonies of 'ordinary Spaniards' into the history of the country's often painful twentieth century. To many of the public it seemed that the civil war could not easily be left behind, primarily because much of the conflict's violence was intimate, occurring within communities and leaving a distressing legacy. It also seemed to many that this legacy had not been broached at the end of the Generalísimo's regime and therefore that Franco's death in 1975 marked a more problematic demarcation point than had usually been assumed. For these reasons, this study begins with an account of the Second Republic and civil war (the 'event' remembered) and includes a substantial final section on the era running from the transition to democracy in the late 1970s to 'the return of memory' since the 1990s.

The second problem was that although the regime and the state were not to be the primary area of concern, the weight of politics, particularly during the dictatorship itself, could not be ignored. Life under a non-democratic authoritarian regime is lived in relation to political power in a way which is different to that lived within a broadly free civil society, though the nature of this dictatorship–democracy distinction is complex and may not necessarily match up to popular images. Although there were several fundamental features of the Spanish dictatorship which were constant and repressive – and political change was stubbornly resisted – the relationship of state to society under Franco was not an unchanging one. Politics could therefore not be excised from any history of the post-war era, 'social' or otherwise. This would be confirmed by analysis of the memory 'boom' in recent years, an often avowedly political movement within civil society (producing a political counter response) which itself came on top of a historiography shaped in part by the politics of the war and its legacy.

Third, if it was therefore essential to incorporate questions of power and politics, how precisely was this to be done? The path chosen here is to explore the interweaving of war memories, political power, and social relations, through time, as a cumulative and combined process by which representations of the past have been created ('making memory') and power has been reconstructed ('remaking Spain'). Although the rupture of civil war was integral to the process, the intertwining through time of power and memory (and thus, simply put, of state and society) allows for a critique of the image of post-war Spain split apart along a single political fracture between two homogeneous collective identities: 'the victors' and 'the defeated'. This image has rarely been interrogated, but the testimony examined here suggests the more complicated reality. To begin with, the binary division originated in the ideological exigencies of fighting the war; Franco's victory then institutionalised the division by categorising everyone, in theory and often in effect, as part either of 'Spain' or of 'Anti-Spain'. In the aftermath this dualism expanded, both in terms of experience and of the representation of reality. Nevertheless, although they appeared simply to reinforce the dualism, the combined pressures of war memories, of finding ways to protect oneself from punishment (as an 'enemy' of the new power), and of the evolution of socio-economic relations, in fact obscured a more convoluted mesh of social and cultural responses made to survive materially, to attempt to make sense of the war and its aftermath, and to look to the future.

Whilst the labels ('victors' and 'defeated') and the political regime were static, society did not stand still. The rural poor, most significantly, began to migrate as a result of the war and its outcome. The war had represented a social watershed and, although by no means all migrants in poverty in the 1940s had been active Republicans, thousands responded to the political and economic repression imposed by early Francoism by leaving the past behind and embarking on an urban future, accepting the hard sacrifices which this entailed. That migrants were depicted (or 'constructed') by urban middle-class observers as 'the defeated' suggests much about the unspoken assumptions made and the relationship between war, memory, and post-war change. The experience of flesh-and-blood historical actors, the choices they made, and their commentary upon these actions, all reveal the nature of the assumptions inhabiting the post-war era. Strands of tolerance, conscience, compassion and reconciliation cut across demonisation, denunciation, the grasp for power and the exercise of war-related grievances, even as early as the 1940s and certainly during the rest of the Franco era and beyond. Although memory has been a dominant theme of cultural debate and political action since the 1990s, much of the story of civil war complexities, social fracture, marginal urbanisation, the Church's turn towards society, and the social context of the post-Franco transition to democracy and rapid modernisation has not previously been told and least of all in relation to the evolution since 1939 of the mythscape and social memory of the war. The chapters which follow seek to do this by integrating the dynamics of civil war with elements of continuity and change during all phases of the Franco regime and the later attitudes and assumptions of the democratic era.

Acknowledgements

This study was made possible by the support of various institutions and individuals. The initial research was carried out during a period of study leave during 2007–8 granted by the Humanities Faculty of the University of the West of England. I also have pleasure in acknowledging the financial support of the Arts and Humanities Research Council through a Fellowship held in late 2011 and early 2012 during the final stages of writing up. The attentive effort and generous commentary offered by the anonymous readers of the original proposal for the book, the AHRC application to support its completion, and the submitted manuscript were indispensable. I am immensely grateful to History staff and students at UWE for providing a supportive and stimulating environment in which the ideas presented here have developed, and especially to Martin Simpson with whom I have the pleasure of teaching comparative approaches to Europe in the 1930s and 1940s. I am also indebted to several other friends and colleagues for their advice, encouragement and practical assistance: Peter Anderson, Miguel Ángel del Arco Blanco, Richard Cleminson, Ignacio Fernández de Mata, Kate Flynn, Pamela Radcliff, Tim Rees, Francisco Romero Salvadó and Alison Sinclair. The arguments presented here have benefited from engagement with the work of three historians and colleagues in particular: Helen Graham, Paul Preston and Mary Vincent; to Helen, who generously read the entire manuscript and sharpened my wits throughout, I owe a special debt of gratitude. Any remaining errors in the text are, of course, my own.

Finally, I would like to acknowledge the love and encouragement of my parents, Ken and Diana Richards, and to thank my wife, Nancy Shelton, and our children, Edward, Eve and Anna. To my family I owe the greatest debt of all. Without their sacrifices while living with this book (and its author) during the past six years, it might never have materialised.

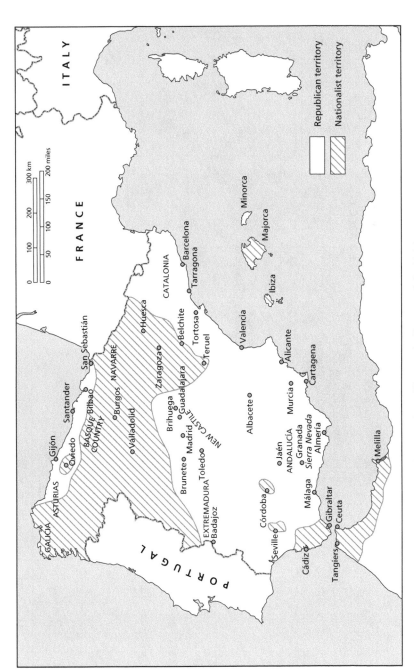

Map 1 The division of Spain following the military rebellion: 20 July 1936

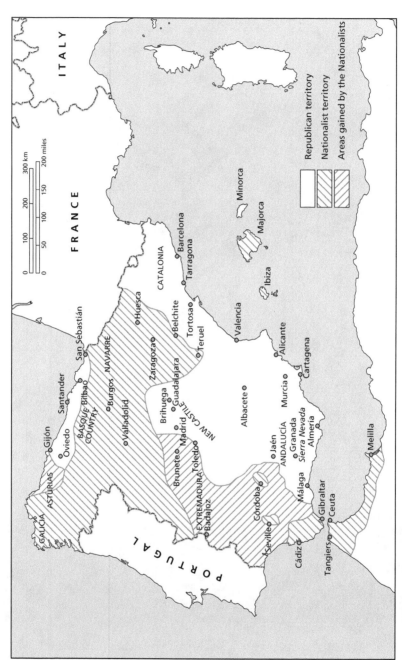

Map 2 The divisions at the beginning of February 1937

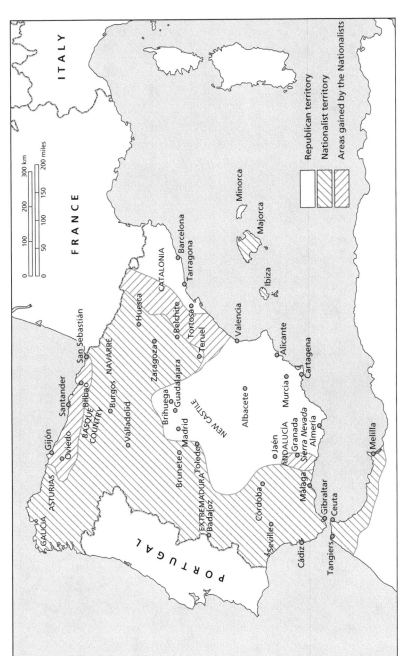

Map 3 The division of Spain, April 1938: Republican territory split in two

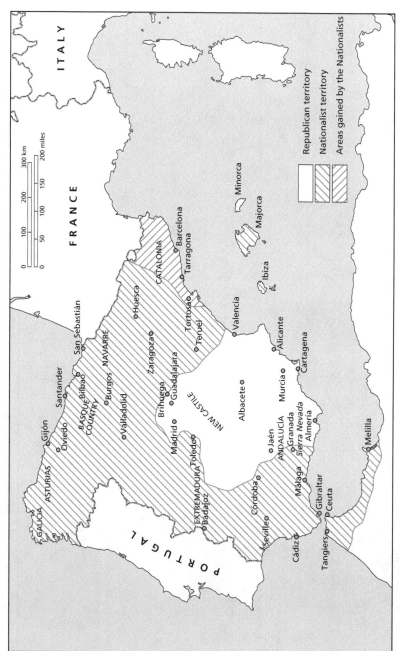

Map 4 The division of Spain, March 1939, towards the end of the war

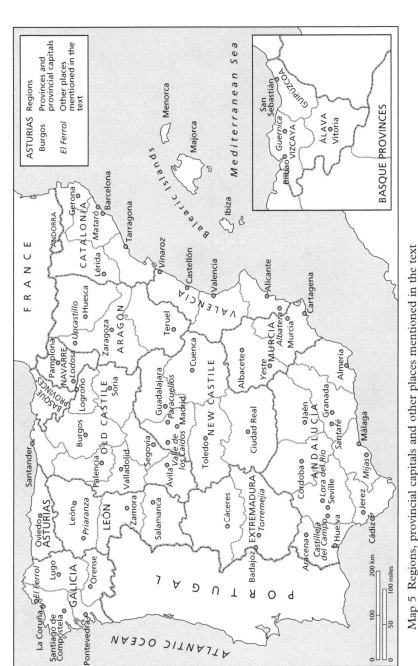

Map 5 Regions, provincial capitals and other places mentioned in the text

Introduction: cultural trauma in Spain

This book explores how the life-shattering ordeal of Spain's civil war and repressive aftermath has been remembered and represented during the post-war decades from 1939 to 2007, the moment at which the Spanish parliament passed a government-sponsored Law of Historical Memory. The principal aim is to place into historical perspective the recent pre-occupation with memory, which has been at the centre of Spanish political debate on justice and reparation since the late 1990s.[1] The legacy of civil war rupture and post-war violence was sustained and significant during the unprecedented social change from the 1950s onwards, as 'official' or doctrinal memory, personal testimony, and the constructed narratives of public figures attest. 'Master narratives' and mythscapes of the war persisted and overlapped, forming the background to the historical picture of the war constructed both by individuals and by identifiable communities of memory. Throughout the post-war decades, remembering the conflict and its victims was shaped and understood according to the shared qualities and objectives valuable to the formation of collective identities. Most recently, memorial activity, crystallised particularly through the excavation of wartime burial pits and the identification and dignified reburial of the mortal remains of Republican victims of wartime and post-war terror, has been stamped with the impression of a universal culture of human rights.

During the long Franco era (1939–75), those who were free to remember collectively and able to participate symbolically in the public replaying of the recent conflict were counted exclusively amongst the victors. These public representations formed the basis of officially encouraged claims to a collectively traumatic past. The concept of cultural trauma will be understood here as a tapestry of historical constructs depicting specific painful events which is shaped by the *post facto* interplay of political power, social relationships and agency, and shared

---

[1] In comparative terms, see István Deák, Jan T. Gross and Tony Judt (eds.), *The Politics of Retribution in Europe* (Princeton, NJ, 2000).

structures of meaning.[2] Whilst related materially and metaphorically to personal trauma (persistent damage caused to individuals who have lived through violent experiences which cannot be forgotten), *cultural* trauma is viewed here as something distinct. This remains the case even though it is essential to recount many individually traumatic experiences in order to make sense of and evaluate claims of collective trauma.

The individual–collective distinction can naturally be applied to the theme of memory in general (of which trauma is a particular form). The problematic concept of memory is treated here inclusively both as a faculty of the individual mind, which functions in the light of social and cultural influences, *and* as the production of images, representations and narratives of the past which are disseminated and shared in the public realm through active social agency. This way of working relies broadly on the celebrated theory of collective memory elaborated by the sociologist Maurice Halbwachs who, though he did not focus on trauma, maintained in his ground-breaking research of the 1920s that past events and experiences always formed a social or collective framework for present experiences and were drawn upon in making the present intelligible.[3] The analytical value of the concept of 'collective memory' has, in recent times, been diminished, however, by imprecise usage and the making of easy assumptions about the content of group memories with little or no critical analysis of the historical process and necessary social agency involved.[4] The concept of cultural trauma, though it can be related to that of 'cultural memory' (which refers too broadly to memory as a 'vehicle' which carries widely held suppositions about the individual and social world), is more precise in meaning because it insists on pinpointing particular negative events and instances, and the associated processes of memory construction, rather than general phenomena, allowing description and analysis of the ways in which pasts related specifically to suffering and sacrifice are actively contested and struggled over.[5] This angle of approach, particularly

---

[2] See, e.g., Patrick Finney, 'On Memory, Identity and War', *Rethinking History*, 6, 1 (2002); John R. Gillis, 'Memory and Identity: The History of a Relationship', in Gillis (ed.), *Commemorations: The Politics of National Identity* (New Haven, 1994); Wulf Kansteiner, 'Finding Meaning in Memory: A Methodological Critique of Collective Memory Studies', *History and Theory*, 41 (2002).

[3] Maurice Halbwachs, *Les cadres sociaux de la mémoire* (Paris, 1925); *La mémoire collective* (Paris, 1950); Halbwachs, *On Collective Memory* (ed. Lewis Coser) (Chicago, 1992).

[4] See Jay Winter, *Remembering War* (New Haven, 2006); Emmanuel Sivan and Jay Winter (eds.), *War and Remembrance in the Twentieth Century* (Cambridge, 1999).

[5] On cultural memory, see Michael Lambek and Paul Antze, 'Forecasting Memory', in Antze and Lambek (eds.), *Tense Past: Cultural Essays in Trauma and Memory* (London, 1996), pp. xi–xxxviii.

when presented within a chronological structure, allows for analysis of struggles for 'ownership' of cultural trauma and the evolution of post-war memory in relational and processual terms, an appropriate theme for social historians.[6]

The experiential and the representational require some level of separation in explaining cultural trauma. Although events may be catastrophic, dislocating and painful, affecting masses of individuals, they are not inherently traumatic: in its collective form, trauma is a socially mediated attribution. As the sociologist Jeffrey Alexander has written, 'events do not, in and of themselves, create collective trauma'.[7] At a collective and cultural level we know this is the case because similarly negative historical 'happenings' are not always followed by a traumatic legacy; in some instances events need not have happened at all in order for a case to be made to a potential community of memory and for a sense of identity to be considered compelling. Though this is generally not so in the case of Spain's civil war, the point forces us to consider the processes by which a multitude of individual experiences interact in their retelling with broader society-wide settings and developing group consciousness in the making of such claims, particularly when they are made by competing collective victims.[8] The active construction and mediation of claims of cultural trauma in Spain – their rise and fall over seven decades – and the dialectic of 'possession' of group trauma form a unifying thread throughout this study. Although recent historiographical focus has tended towards 'the memory of the defeated', especially since the 1970s, Francoists as well as Republicans made claims on political and social allegiance and group identity through the construction of collective trauma claims based on particular representations of the origins, experience and effects of the civil war. Since we are interested in social memory in its relational dimension and as a process, claims on both sides require evaluation, though the objective is not to look or argue for any 'equivalence of suffering'.

In the aftermath of communal violence, social groups often deny or dilute their responsibility by projecting blame for their own suffering

[6] On history and sociology in the study of memory, see Jeffrey Olick, *The Politics of Regret* (London, 2007), pp. 85–118.

[7] Jeffrey C. Alexander, 'Toward a Theory of Cultural Trauma', in Alexander (ed.), *Cultural Trauma and Collective Identity* (Berkeley, CA, 2004), p. 8. See also Ron Eyerman, *Cultural Trauma: Slavery and the Formation of African American Identity* (Cambridge, 2001), pp. 1–22.

[8] See Benedict Anderson, *Imagined Communities: Reflections on the Origin and Spread of Nationalism*, revised edn (London, 2006). On the role of constructions of the past in the Balkan conflicts of the 1990s, see for example: V. P. Gagnon, *The Myth of Ethnic War: Serbia and Croatia in the 1990s* (Ithaca, NY, 2004).

onto the demonised or 'othered' enemy: the hated group 'in our midst'.[9] In so doing they refuse to recognise the trauma of these others. Based on making claims of the indelible nature of the cultural and psychological scar left on group consciousness, a struggle ensues to create or reconstruct communities and political authority by denying legitimacy to other collective identities, especially of 'the defeated'. Commemorating Spain's war twenty-five years after its beginning, a leading member of the secretive Catholic lay organisation Opus Dei, who was an industrialist, banker, and veteran of Franco's 'crusade', justified his fears in 1961 that society might forget the war and its sacrality by suggesting that those who supported the left could not have been traumatised to the same extent as Catholics and conservatives because the left always undertakes collective endeavours in the name merely of social and material gains; it was the right which suffered for the sake of the nation, history and identity.[10] This association of trauma with identity, and as something sacred, though obviously reductive in its basic premise (since both left and right clearly later remembered their struggles as traumatic and essential to collective bonds at particular moments and for various reasons), is nonetheless essential in explaining the dissonance between diverse individual, collective and 'official' memories (the last, particularly during the Franco dictatorship of 1939–75), their varying levels of intensity, and their relation to both popular and governing myths of the past, throughout the post-war era of unprecedented social change.[11] The ambivalence of cultural trauma, the tension between avoidance of painful or shameful events and reliving or reconstructing them, is explicable only in terms of social process, including the formation of collective identities and generational evolution, and of finding solutions to the problems thrown up by change.

This does not mean that the events remembered are unimportant. Meaningful attribution of traumatic status to any collective claim can only be understood in relation to the nature of the originating events. The quantifiable aspects of a destructive social event are insufficient, however, in measuring its catastrophic status. The extent to which

---

[9] Neil J. Smelser, 'Psychological Trauma and Cultural Trauma', in Alexander (ed.), *Cultural Trauma*, p. 52.

[10] Lucas María de Oriol y Urquijo, 'Los horizontes abiertos en 1936', in Hermandad de Alféreces Provisionales, *Generación del 36* (Zaragoza, 1962), p. 39. For memory as claims of Catholic trauma at the hands of the Republic, e.g., Alfonso Bullón de Mendoza and Álvaro de Diego, *Historias orales de la guerra civil* (Barcelona, 2000), p. 106.

[11] For the individual–collective dissonance: Jeffrey K. Olick, 'Collective Memory: The Two Cultures', *Sociological Theory*, 17, 3 (1999), 333–48. On the politics of war and memory: e.g., Henry Rousso, *The Vichy Syndrome: History and Memory in France since 1944* (Cambridge, MA, 1991).

symbolic or sacred sources of collective identity are destroyed, leading to a common sense of disgust, shame or guilt, is vital, though the leap made from this historical reality to its construction as a defining collective tragedy into which the identity of certain groups often becomes 'locked' is dependent on many other factors.[12] Communal violence detaches groups and individuals from previous cultural moorings to the external world, and this displacement of identity often persists, is repeated and reacted to, long after the initial violence. The catastrophe, as Alan Mintz has argued, inheres in the event's 'power to shatter existing paradigms of meaning'.[13] In Spain, the vast majority of those killed on the home front, on both sides, had not been captured at the front but were rounded up, often from their homes, and frequently because they had been denounced from within the community to wartime authorities.[14] Social cohesion and solidarity were profoundly undermined in the Spanish case by massive disruption of organised social life and the extensive reach and intimacy of communal violence.

So radically against human nature did the violence seem to witnesses and subsequent observers (including historians) that it has been interpreted as inherently and collectively traumatic. This 'naturalist' approach, though persuasive as far as common sense is concerned, is not without difficulties, not least because there is an evident tension between individual and collective trauma, just as there is between individual and collective memory. Although the likelihood of painful events leading to cultural trauma is certainly high after protracted and wide-ranging internal wars, claims of cultural trauma are not automatic: social and political agency is required and it is this which forms the basis of the chapters which follow. The composition, structure, aims and representativeness of the 'collective victim' in question need in each case and in each period to be detailed and described.

We need, first, to turn to events, however. Individual memory and personal trauma are obviously and intimately related to events in the past. Collective memory and cultural trauma are also related to the

---

[12] On the 'sacrality' of memory of violence in recent years (and memory's implicit critique of History as 'secular' or 'sacrilegious'), see Tzvetan Todorov, *Hope and Memory: Lessons from the Twentieth Century* (New York, 2003).

[13] Alan Mintz, *Hurban: Responses to Catastrophe in Hebrew Literature* (New York, 1984), p. x, cited in Peter Gray and Kendrick Oliver (eds.), *The Memory of Catastrophe* (Manchester, 2004), p. 7.

[14] In psychological terms, it is frequently maintained that trauma is more severe if the originating event is one of 'human design'. E.g., American Psychological Association, *Diagnostic and Statistical Manual of Mental Disorders*, 3rd edn (Washington, 1980), p. 236.

past, though more problematically. Understanding post hoc collective representations of devastating events certainly demands careful historical consideration of such 'happenings'. The premise of chapters 2 and 4 is that without exploration of Spain's war and its polarised aftermath it is impossible to explain post-war memories. As Timothy Snyder has commented, 'our recollections are always recollections of something, and unless we have an independent source of knowledge about this something, we can learn nothing about how memory works'.[15]

The Spanish civil war was fought out on the field of battle and, more significantly in terms of memory and trauma, within communities, during the years 1936–9. In a country of some 23 million inhabitants, the conflict cost the lives of around 350,000 Spaniards and the exile of approximately half a million more. Throughout Spain, half of the total recorded deaths occurred through politically motivated violence away from the field of battle.[16] There were over 30,000 more registered deaths in 1936 (413,000) than the pre-war norm, though the actual number was certainly higher. In 1937 the total number of recorded deaths was 472,000, it rose to 485,000 in 1938 and was 470,000 in 1939; for each of the three years it was at least 20 per cent higher than the 1935 rate. The biological and demographic rhythm of society was irreversibly disrupted.[17] The birth rate declined by 100,000 in 1937 and 1938 and by 200,000 in 1939, and marriage was delayed, especially amongst 'the defeated'.[18] At least 100,000 'Reds' were executed by the rebel 'Nationalists' during the war years, and probably some 50,000 in the post-war purge.[19] Between 38,000 and 55,000 'enemies of the Republic' were killed in the government zone during the conflict, most in the first five or so revolutionary months from July to

[15] Snyder, 'The Memory of Sovereignty and Sovereignty over Memory: Poland, Lithuania and Ukraine, 1939–1999', in Jan-Werner Müller (ed.), *Memory and Power in Post-War Europe* (Cambridge, 2002), p. 40.

[16] For comparison: 19 per cent civilian deaths of total losses in the 1914–18 war; 48 per cent of the total in World War Two; 34 per cent in Korea; 48 per cent in Vietnam, and 40 per cent in the Bosnian war of the 1990s, though many of the victims in at least two of these wars died as a result of bombardment rather than political execution. The most recent and thorough account is Paul Preston, *The Spanish Holocaust* (London, 2012).

[17] See Jesús Villar Salinas, *Repercusiones demográficas de la última guerra civil española* (Madrid, 1942); Juan Díez Nicolás, 'La mortalidad en la guerra civil española', *Boletín de Demografía Histórica*, 3, 1 (March 1985), 42–5; Karl Mannheim, 'The Problem of Generations' [1928], in Kurt H. Wolff (ed.), *From Karl Mannheim*, 2nd edition (New Jersey, 1993), p. 365.

[18] E.g. George A. Collier, *Socialists of Rural Andalusia: Unacknowledged Revolutionaries of the Second Republic* (Stanford, CA, 1987), p. 183.

[19] Santos Juliá (ed.), *Víctimas de la guerra* (Madrid, 1999), pp. 410–12.

November 1936.[20] Approximately 7,000 of these victims were murdered priests and others belonging to holy orders. For the Spanish Church and the Nationalist faithful, the origin of the theocratic New State and of post-war cultural trauma was the blood tribute of its martyrs who had given witness to the grim reality of 'Godlessness'.[21] The death toll related to the political repression of defeated Republicans, and to hunger, disease and imprisonment during the first post-war years was almost as high as that in the period of the war, and the annual rate of deaths did not return to pre-war levels until 1943. There were as many officially recorded mortalities in 1941 (484,000) as there had been at the height of the war. In Catalonia, one of the country's most developed regions, the infant mortality rate was on average 40 per cent higher throughout the 1940s than in 1935, reaching levels unheard of since the influenza epidemic of 1918–19. Average general life expectancy in Catalonia in 1941–5 was lower by four years than in 1935; the number of widows under 30 multiplied by five times that of 1930.[22] This was probably related to the influx of rural migrants from the south during and in the aftermath of the conflict, where there was real starvation during the early 1940s, but the Barcelona middle classes also went hungry in this period.[23]

When we add the post-war recorded deaths above the pre-war norm (215,000 during 1940–2) to the wartime figure, therefore, we are able to estimate the total human losses on both sides attributable directly or indirectly to the civil war as approximately 565,000. We can also con-clude that some three-quarters of the total war-related deaths in the period 1936–44 were non-battle fatalities.[24] The scale of the suffering – the objective basis against which the status of culturally constructed collective trauma may be gauged – helps us to imagine the reasons for the silence in the aftermath of the civil war of those who considered themselves to be amongst the defeated.[25] Public memory was inhibited because the gulf which had opened up between the fragmented state and

---

[20] See, e.g., José Luis Ledesma, 'Una retaguardia al rojo', in Francisco Espinosa Maestre (ed.), *Violencia roja y azul: España 1936–1950* (Barcelona, 2010); Joan Villarroya, 'La vergüenza de la República', *La aventura de la historia*, 1, 3, January 1999, 32.

[21] See Antonio Montero Moreno, *Historia de la persecución religiosa en España, 1936–1939* (Madrid, 1961). Two features of this important book were later (from the 1980s onwards) evident in accounts of executions on the other side by rebel forces: (1) long appendices listing the names of victims; (2) use of the term 'extermination'.

[22] Borja de Riquer and Joan Culla, *El franquisme i la transició democràtica (1939–1988)* (Barcelona, 1989), pp. 27, 42.

[23] Francisco Candel, *Los otros catalanes* (Barcelona, 1965), pp. 115–17.

[24] Though much reduced in numbers, deaths through war-related violence continued significantly until 1948.

[25] See Michael Richards, *A Time of Silence: Civil War and the Culture of Repression in Franco's Spain, 1936–1945* (Cambridge, 1998).

society during the war had allowed a widespread form of collaboration with wartime authorities to take place in both war zones through denunciation of 'enemies' by individuals (see maps 1–4). This privatised form of complicity with violence was extremely widespread and grew in the aftermath. Within the context of the post-conflict political settlement and the constructed 'trauma' of the victors, denunciations impeded collective recognition of suffering and the processing of the pain of the war. Acknowledgement and remembering were circumscribed because the deep ideological and cultural divisions of the pre-war period had been perpetuated in the extreme violence of the conflict and widened, not resolved, by General Franco's total victory.

Part I sets the scene for analysis of post-war memory, first, by outlining the political, moral and social dimensions of war memories, and, second, by accounting for the crisis of the Second Republic, the erosion of state legitimacy in the 1930s, and the complex and intimately violent process accompanying coercive state reconstruction in both war zones during the civil war. In violent intrastate conflict, being precise about the historical 'happening' which forms the kernel of collective or cultural trauma is not as straightforward as it may appear. Two particular problems need to be posed: first, the difficulty of locating the primary 'traumatic' reference points and identifying more precisely than previously the associated collective victims of the conflict; and, second, critiquing the notion of the civil war and its violence as a singular, 'national' and 'unified' experience to be analysed most fruitfully at the macro level.

The chapters in Part II explore memories of the war during the Franco years, from the 1940s to the 1970s. (Map 5 shows the regions and other places mentioned in the text.) Each decade is explored in two chapters, first, through the production of state-supported myths, propaganda and politics of memory, and, second, through the shaping of 'social memory': recollection as reflected in pervasive cultural assumptions and social practices. Chapter 3 thus explores the use and renovation of religious symbolic resources in examples of the victors' commemorative ceremonial and the making of memory claims in the aftermath of the war and throughout the 1940s. Chapter 4 looks at the profound impact of the war within the tissue of the body social in the 1940s and the manner in which defeat was assimilated and social obligations, loyalties and solidarity were unmade. Moving to the 1950s, Chapter 5 demonstrates how the Cold War revivified memories of Franco's 'crusade' and assisted in maintaining the General's power, even though active commemoration was limited. Political neutering and the hypervigilance of the 1940s gave way gradually to a sense of resignation about the past and impulses towards future-oriented urban migration, often from the most fractured rural communities (Chapter 6). From the 1960s (discussed in chapters 7 and 8), there was a decline in collectively expressed affective reactions from many regime loyalists and Catholics to what they saw as the wartime profaning and pollution of sacred values. Political power had slowly evolved from reliance on charismatic authority towards more routinised bases of legitimation, and the state encouraged a vague generalisation of the trauma, cautiously, at the level of political rhetoric in the shape of a narrative of the war as a 'fratricidal' struggle. This narrative aimed (at a rhetorical level) to incorporate sections of society not previously encompassed by the victimised collective imagined by and associated with Franco and the wartime Nationalists. Amid unprecedented social change and pressure for modernisation, a unified and coherent sense of Catholic and conservative traumatic identity was no longer tenable, and the Church's turn towards public reconciliation by the early 1970s would be highly significant, though internally contested (Chapter 9).

Part III, dedicated to war memories after Franco, compares the variety of ways in which memory registered during the three decades or so since 1975. The shadow of the past during the tense era of transition to democracy in the years 1975–82 is explored in Chapter 10. This process was eased by concurrent macro development of the market economy and the Amnesty Law (Ley de Amnistía) of 1977, though the transition itself would come under threat from renewed political violence, not least from a section of the army. The relationship between modernisation, 'moving forward', and 'forgetting the past' during the tenure of the first post-Franco socialist government from 1982 to 1996 is discussed in Chapter 11. In Chapter 12, focused on the period from 1996 until the Law of Historical Memory of 2007, it is argued that the recent surge of war-associated memories is related to a critique of 'forgetting' after 1975, but also to a general fragmentation of contemporary forms of collective identity, the retreat of the nation-state, and the consequent dilution of national identity as the basis of memory. The march of global capital has created pessimism about the possibility of radical change through political action.[26] Whereas Spaniards embraced the future with enthusiasm from the 1960s to the 1980s, the novelty and coherence of modernity as an ideal began to flag towards the end of the millennium, and sustenance and authenticity were sought in eras of the past marked

---

[26] Charles Taylor, *Sources of the Self* (Cambridge, 1989); Charles S. Maier, 'Consigning the Twentieth Century to History: Alternative Narratives for the Modern Era', *American Historical Review*, 105, 3 (2000), 807–31; Tony Judt, 'The Past is Another Country: Myth and Memory in Post-War Europe', in Deák, et al. (eds.), *Politics of Retribution*, pp. 293–323.

by radicalism, commitment and sacrifice. In a fluid and inconstant world there was a renewed focus on the past as the basis of identity and political critique, though this has sometimes led to oversimplification, an emphasis on imaginative reconstruction, and the treatment of history as moral rhetoric.[27]

In each period, those who acted as 'meaning makers' in the public sphere, the often generationally defined collective agents of memory and cultural trauma who rose and fell with the changing times, are identified. The ever-evolving relationships of various 'traumatised' groups to political power and to the rest of society (the wider 'audience' for memory claims) are analysed, as are the ways in which each collective defines the fundamental injury done and identifies and depicts the perpetrators. The 'meaning' of the past was mediated within religious, aesthetic, legal, state-bureaucratic, and scientific (academic historical) institutional arenas and the channels of mass communications, a process of evolving social and political relations.

[27] E.g., Zygmunt Bauman, *Liquid Modernity* (London, 2000).

Part I

Setting the scene

1   War memories since 1936: political, moral, social

The past is not over there on the date it took place, but here, in me.[1]

On 1 April 1964 the principal Spanish national newspaper of the dictatorial era produced a lavish three-part souvenir issue with 120 heavily illustrated pages in commemoration of the twenty-fifth anniversary of the victory of General Franco. The three sections were dedicated in turn to 'the past', 'the present' and 'the future', with 1939 constituting 'Year Zero', the pivotal moment between 'then' and 'now'. Franco had, after all, insisted on unconditional surrender. The recent past was of course an essential and contested area of Francoist legitimacy, and in 1964 the past would be temporally compressed by imagining it exclusively through a critical and tendentious account of the Second Republic, the democratic regime which had been inaugurated after elections in April 1931 and later destroyed during the civil war. As was typical, the image of the Republic as chaotic would be further distilled by focusing on the tumultuous period of Popular Front government, from February to July 1936, when the state resorted frequently to its coercive apparatus to maintain order. The 1964 supplement's first part, on the past – 'from the Phrygian cap to the Hammer and Sickle' (a title symbolising what for Franco supporters had been an inevitable descent from 'liberty' to 'Bolshevism' in the 1930s) – thus illustrated the dictatorship's self-justification and issued a thinly veiled warning for the present.[2] The need to avoid a repeat of the conflict of the 1930s would form the backdrop to restricted political activity in the 1960s and the more open process of transition to

---

[1] José Ortega y Gasset, 'Historia como sistema' (1935), in Ortega, *Obras completas*, vol. VI (Madrid, 1964), pp. 44, 49.

[2] 'Del gorro frigio a la hoz y el martillo', *ABC*, 1 April 1964. The Phrygian cap, a symbol of liberty during the French Revolution, was associated particularly with the iconic figure of Marianne and the sans-culottes, and symbolised republicanism also in Spain, from the 1860s to the 1930s when it adorned allegorical images of the 1931 Republic as 'La niña bonita' ('the pretty girl'). Phrygian caps were distributed in April 1931 amongst the crowds celebrating the coming of the Republic: Marcos Ana, *Decidme cómo es un árbol* (Barcelona, 2007), p. 24.

democracy after Franco's death in November 1975.[3] In April 1964, officially sponsored representations of the Second Republic as 'socialising', 'leftist' and 'revolutionary' gave sense to such warnings, at least to the conservative readership of *ABC*.[4] Conflict and insecurity were accentuated as the essence of the democratic era. At a moment when the future was imagined in the shape of a monarchical succession to Franco, as predetermined by the Head of State himself, the past was therefore simplified. Officially, 1930s attacks upon the Republican state from within the army and the Catholic Church could be forgotten, as was any positive reflection on the modernising reforms introduced by Republican governments.

The civil war which would bring the Republic to a protracted and bloody end had been legitimated by the Church and the rebels themselves as a 'crusade' against atheistic and 'Asiatic' communism within weeks of the military rebellion which triggered the conflict on 17–18 July 1936. Amid executions, imprisonments and repressive surveillance, it would prove impossible to salvage a liberal or radical community of memory in the aftermath of the conflict. For Republicans, the progressive struggles of the past had been based upon idealised images of the future; it would largely be the men and women 'of ideas', however – both leaders and followers – who would be exiled or targeted during the post-war purge. Liberal associations and political groups and parties, libertarian meeting places and the social clubs and Casas del Pueblo of the socialist working-class movement were closed and trade unions were banned. Notions of redistributive and democratising change were brutally ended and a sense of collective resignation amongst those who had supported left-of-centre Republican governments would fade only gradually as collective protest was reconfigured in response to social change. Over the course of three decades of migration from the poverty-stricken countryside there would follow a shift from primary social relations to a predominantly urbanised, more complex and denser society, which Franco's 'New State' would seek to control.[5]

The war had created an irreparable rupture between the past and the future, and not only for those who had supported the Republic until the end. It would also represent an unequivocal demarcation between 'old' and 'new', becoming the founding political myth of the New State. At the same time, the war marked a broader social watershed to which

---

[3] Paloma Aguilar Fernández, *Memoria y olvido de la guerra civil española* (Madrid, 1996).
[4] Explicitly, *ABC*, 1 April 1964, p. 24.
[5] See, for example, Claudio Esteva Fabregat, *Industrialización e integración social* (Madrid, 1960), esp. pp. 21–9.

the increased power and presence of the state would respond.[6] The key collective subject of this profound change was non-elite society composed of those who possessed little cultural capital. Their ways of addressing the past are fundamental to the story of post-war defeat, hunger and migration, and oral testimony will be drawn upon to provide examples since extended written accounts of subaltern lives are rare. On the other hand, we have much fuller autobiographical reflections written by members of the cultural elite, largely those within the regime until the late 1950s, but also including varyingly tolerated opponents of the dictatorship thereafter. Their life trajectories are available to us and will be used in a different way, especially to trace the contours of generational evolution and to elucidate the relationship between social memory and power. These elites have usually been seen as public political figures, but they were also social actors and were influenced by collective experiences. We can legitimately use their memoirs to open up more than their own specific histories because they both reflected upon and reacted to social change and commented upon the way non-elite groups responded to and forced the pace of modernisation.

The politics of the civil war were determined by the dynamics of state building, involving violence on both sides: the war, beginning with the military rebellion, was instrumental in establishing a new system of political and ideological domination.[7] Recent historiography has begun to overcome the chronological dividing line of April 1939 by demonstrating the degree of continuity between war and repressive reconstruction.[8] The death toll of the civil war and public and private remembrance of 'the fallen for God and the *patria*' (as well as personal and private recollection of those killed in the name of the Republic) were nonetheless fundamental to a sense of historic rupture. 'The fallen', a term limited to martyrs of Franco's 'crusade', legitimated symbolically the myth of 'beginning' bound up with a new social order, their bodies presented in the official literature of the early 1940s as 'penitential material', the basis of a sacred memory which rhetorically bound the

---

[6] Mary Vincent, *Spain, 1833–2002: People and State* (Oxford, 2007), p. 158.

[7] Early Francoism, during and after the war, can be viewed as an example of 'extreme nation-statism'; a 'hyphenated fascism', where fascist tendencies were undercut by the army which yielded relatively little to paramilitarism, though the ideology was a feature common to both: Michael Mann, *Fascists* (Cambridge, 2004), p. 46.

[8] Santos Juliá, 'Últimas noticias de la guerra civil', *Revista de Libros*, 81 (September 2003); Michael Richards, 'The Limits of Quantification: Francoist Repression and Historical Methodology', in Julio Aróstegui and Sergio Gálvez (eds.), *Generaciones y memoria de la represión franquista* (Valencia, 2010), pp. 787–820.

victors together.[9] An evident tension therefore prevailed between the dictatorship's habitual practice during the 1940s and 1950s (and beyond) of tracing its birth to 18 July 1936 and use of the term 'Year Zero' to describe 1939, and there would be a constant and significant slippage in 1964 between commemorating 'the Rising' ('Alzamiento') and its 'victory' and celebrating 'peace'.[10]

Eleven years on from 1964, as the Franco dictatorship drew to a close in 1975, it seemed to some observers that the word 'reconciliation' was on everyone's lips. Franco loyalists rejected the need of such a notion, arguing that old antagonisms had long ago been transcended by the 'order' and 'prosperity' achieved by the regime. Seemingly with satisfaction, Gonzalo Fernández de la Mora, the General's Minister of Public Works during the period 1970–4 and believer until the end in a perpetual threat to the *patria* posed by a 'leftist-Masonic conspiracy', proclaimed what he perceived to be a widespread ignorance about the civil war: 'those Spaniards who do not even know the principal episodes of that epic achievement are legion' (this was an unwitting comment, perhaps, on the ineffectiveness of state propaganda and defective control of history during four decades of the military regime).[11] Fernández de la Mora's argument was that Spaniards *in Spain* were indeed reconciled while 'those in the exterior' (Franco loyalists avoided the term 'exiles') were not, an idea which had been born almost as soon as the war ended in 1939.[12] The image that those Spaniards outside Spain had of the war, influenced by 'brain-washed Europeans', was 'unrecognisable' and 'macabre' and ignored the peace enjoyed in the country 'for almost half a century'. Writing, in fact, thirty-six years after the end of the war, an era spanning at most two generations, Fernández de la Mora would accuse the opposition movements in exile of living in the past, of 'bunkerisation', a term normally aimed at anti-reform figures such as he: 'this painful spectacle, without doubt susceptible to psychiatric justification, inspires

---

[9] Michael Richards, 'Presenting Arms to the Blessed Sacrament: Civil War and Semana Santa in the City of Málaga, 1936–1939', in Chris Ealham and Michael Richards (eds.), *The Splintering of Spain: Cultural History and the Spanish Civil War* (Cambridge, 2005), p. 222.

[10] See Chapter 7.

[11] Gonzalo Fernández de la Mora, 'Reconciliación', *ABC*, 13 November 1975. On his insistence on the continued 'leftist-Masonic conspiracy', see José María Izquierdo, 'La muerte del Generalísimo', in Santos Juliá, Javier Pradera and Joaquín Prieto (eds.), *Memoria de la Transición* (Madrid, 1996), p. 67.

[12] For a certain reluctance to use the term 'exilio', in favour of 'exodus of the defeated', or 'migrants' or, occasionally, 'refugees', see, e.g., Vicente Marrero Suárez, *La guerra española y el trust de cerebros* (Madrid, 1961), p. 199. Similarly, on the extensive attempt to calculate the 'migratory balance' resulting from the war, see Ramón Salas Larrazábal, *Pérdidas de la guerra* (Barcelona, 1977), pp. 82–92.

more commiseration than repudiation'. The writing of history, largely under the state's control, had begun to move on, he maintained:

Historiography within Spain has made a brave effort not so much of neutrality but of magnanimity. A certain, almost masochistic, self-criticism has even become fashionable and an apologetic intention [towards] the defeated. Because of the snobbishness of the bourgeoisie, Republican partiality has become intellectually more beneficial. If the balance has inclined somewhat within Spain it has been towards the compatriots who were mistaken and who lost.

The belief that history had been written by 'the defeated' represented one position which has been resurrected in recent years by 'revisionists', though at the height of the anxious period following the death of Franco there existed a wide range of views about dealing with the past.[13] In 1976, the former Rector of Madrid University, Pedro Laín Entralgo, a one-time cultural official of the fascist Falange who had come of age politically during the tumultuous 1930s, published what he described as a confessional memoir, *Descargo de conciencia*, which in its broad scope and self-critical tone – and in the responses it provoked – is of interest in exploring the role of fear, myths, collaboration, denunciation, and state-society relations generally in the construction of post-war memory.[14] In the early 1940s, Laín had produced a notorious booklet in which he argued the case for Spanish support of the Axis cause and in which, at a time of fierce repression in the name of the 'crusade', he had legitimated 'the Christian value of just violence'.[15] Haunted by this position, Laín's 1970s 'Unburdening of Conscience' recounted his experiences of the war and its aftermath, including the death of his Republican father as a result of the strains of the conflict, the execution in Seville of his wife's father by authorities allied to the Falangist cause, and estrangement from his brother José, a member of the Communist PCE and a wartime Republican official. The aim of the book was to place these sources of personal emotional trauma alongside his wartime allegiance to the rebels who had precipitated Spain's tragedy. Laín was unusual in admitting to having been 'deficient' and guilty of 'civic cowardice', though he maintained that he had never written a single line which did not implicitly or expressly 'accord full human dignity to the defeated'.[16] Documented cases indeed exist which demonstrate several acts of his generosity

[13] For 'revisionism', see Stanley Payne, 'Mitos y tópicos de la guerra civil', *Revista de Libros*, 79–80, July–August 2003. E.g., Ramón Salas Larrazábal, *Los datos exactos de la guerra civil* (Madrid, 1980), p. 7.

[14] Pedro Laín Entralgo, *Descargo de conciencia* (Barcelona, 1976).

[15] Pedro Laín Entralgo, *Los valores morales del nacionalsindicalismo* (Madrid, 1941), p. 8; Herbert Southworth, *Antifalange* (Paris, 1967), p. 4.

[16] Laín Entralgo, *Descargo*, pp. 274–5.

towards academic colleagues who became victims of the Francoist purge after April 1939. More significantly, his intellectual and political trajectory from the late 1940s was shaped consciously by a need to explain and understand the country's historical divisions, which he saw as deeply rooted in history, and to find a way of transcending them.[17] These courageous endeavours, essentially based on the myth of 'two Spains' locked in conflict over centuries and their irreconcilability as the cause of catastrophe in 1936, were spurred on by a desire for reconciliation largely by ignoring questions of political culpability during the period immediately preceding the conflict as well as by overcoming personal wartime suffering and guilt.

Laín's self-examination attracted hostile criticism at the time and has continued to do so, particularly from the political left. When the book was presented to the press and public in May 1976 the atmosphere was likened to a judicial interrogation where accounts were to be settled.[18] Any individual who had publicly lined up in the ranks of the victors and afterwards built a successful career was bound to provoke criticism from those forced into exile, imprisoned or purged and made to earn a living on the margins of professional life. Many were content to believe that 'a fascist is always a fascist' whilst others accused the author of pretentiousness in setting himself up as a 'moral spokesperson of Spanish citizenship' as the transition to democracy dawned.[19] The problem for many fascist intellectuals was the limited extent of their acts of opposition to the dictatorship, or sacrifices made, and the mismatch between words and deeds, and between the public and the private.[20] One prominent intellectual, the philosopher Julián Marías, a contemporary of Laín, defended his academic colleague particularly publicly in 1976. Like Laín, Marías united modernist philosophy with Catholic faith: both had been

---

[17] See Pedro Laín Entralgo, *España como problema* (Madrid, 1962 [1949]). Also José Luis Abellán, 'Laín, filósofo de la cultura española', especially the sections 'El peso de la guerra civil en la vocación histórica y antropológica de Laín' and 'La antropología de la esperanza', in *Cuadernos Hispanoamericanos*, nos. 446–7, *Homenaje a Pedro Laín Entralgo*, August–September 1987.

[18] Juan Padilla, 'Trayectoria de Laín Entralgo', *Boletín de la Institución Libre de Enseñanza* 69 (June 2008), 115–30 (p. 115).

[19] One of Laín's sternest critics was the radical psychiatrist and anti-Francoist activist Carlos Castilla del Pino, who considered he had suffered the effects of Laín's pusillanimous attitude to the politicised process of academic promotion. See his withering critique of Laín's memoir: 'one of the most mendacious, grandiloquent and pretentious books that has been written in our country', Castilla del Pino, *Casa del olivo* (Barcelona, 2004), p. 385.

[20] Castilla del Pino compared Laín's trajectory with that of the ex-Falangist poet and open critic of Francoism Dionisio Ridruejo, who sacrificed more by confronting the regime and accepting exile. See also Dionisio Ridruejo, *Casi unas memorias* (Barcelona, 1976).

disciples of the moderate Republican, modernist and internationalist philosopher José Ortega y Gasset, and this, in the case of Marías, would become the pretext for his later victimisation. In 1976 he targeted Laín's critics, pointing to the hypocrisy, in many cases, of those who set themselves up to decide what should be remembered of the war in the wake of Francoism.[21] In defending Laín, Marías himself chose to forget some unpalatable truths, focusing instead on his friend's resistance to the dictatorship from a 'liberal' standpoint since the 1950s, depicting him as 'the reverse of the civil war, the negation of its spirit'.[22]

Marías had sided with the Republicans during the war and suffered the consequences, enduring a term in prison in the late spring of 1939 after being denounced by a former friend.[23] Afterwards he lived in a form of 'inner exile' under the dictatorship.[24] He had written pro-Republican newspaper articles during the civil war, necessary propaganda in favour of a state fighting for its life. In the last days of the conflict, one of these pieces – 'The Role of the Republicans in the Peace' – appeared on the front page of the Madrid edition of the newspaper *ABC*.[25] In late March 1939, amid the violent implosion of Republican power in the capital, Marías maintained defiantly, and optimistically, that the Republic's supporters would not leave the country and, implicitly at least, that peace could be constructed by both sides because all Spaniards wished to be saved at last from the mortal peril and unimaginable hardship of the war. The pressure to take sides had been enormous, though for many individuals the real choice had been whether to be 'in favour of or against *the war*', rather than each other. Much recent testimony supports the contention that many fell 'in-between' the contending factions, wanting primarily to be protected from the ravages of the conflict.[26] The hope of

---

[21] See, e.g., Julián Marías, 'La conciencia de Pedro Laín', *La Vanguardia Española* 25 June 1976; Marías, 'Los supuestos', *El País*, 29 June 1976, pp. 8–9; Ignacio Sotelo, 'El patriotismo de Pedro Laín', *Isegoría*, 25 (2001), 346.

[22] For the contradictions in Laín's political position since the 1950s, see Santos Juliá, '¿Falange liberal o intelectuales fascistas?, *Claves de Razón Práctica*, 121 (April 2002), 4–13.

[23] Marías wrote in 1989 that he 'did not care to remember' the friend's name: Julián Marías, *Una vida presente: memorias*, 2 vols. (Madrid, 1989), vol. I, p. 263.

[24] He was awarded a professorial chair only in 1979, four years after Franco's death. Marías's son, the writer Javier Marías, has produced an acclaimed multi-volume novel, the first part of which replays these experiences: *Tu rostro mañana: Fiebre y lanza* (Madrid, 2002).

[25] *ABC*, 25 March 1939.

[26] For the notion of 'three Spains', see, e.g., Paul Preston, *Las tres españas del '36* (Barcelona, 1998). The concept can be traced to the beginning of the nineteenth century, but was resurrected towards the end of the 1939–45 war when many people briefly hoped that 'the third Spain' might form the basis of reconciliation '*sin Franco*'. See, e.g., José Ferrater Mora, *Cuestiones españolas, Jornadas*, 53 (Mexico, 1945), pp. 26–8.

reconciliation at the end of March 1939 was expressed by Marías, however, before rebel forces had taken control of the city and begun to hold summary military courts and before the civil population had become mired, as in much of the rest of the country, in the officially encouraged spiral of denunciation of 'enemies of the *patria*'. The Francoist repression, as he saw it, was a great mistake and without it reconciliation would have been possible.[27] The *denuncia* against Marías had been read to him in a prison cell by a military lawyer whose own father had been killed during the wartime revolution in Madrid. The officer did not believe the claims made about Marías in the accusation and quietly confided to him that he was 'spiritually with you'. The father of an acquaintance of Marías, Salvador Lissarrague, had also been killed in the Republican zone. For this reason, as close relative of one of 'the fallen' and because of his links to the Falange, the son was accorded many advantages and political standing. When called upon to condemn Marías, however, he refused and gave an honest account. Lissarrague was no liberal; a Falangist intellectual and close associate of Pedro Laín, in 1940–2 he would reorganise the Madrid Ateneo along ideologically acceptable lines, apparently with gusto. He would also co-author a manual of political education – in effect, indoctrination against 'the Anti-Spain' – for university students,[28] and he became Professor of Social Philosophy in Madrid in 1955. A sense of conscience thus frequently coexisted with political opportunism within individuals. Other reactions reflected the stark ideological force of the violent politics of extreme nation-statism during and after the war.[29] When the mother of the man who had denounced Marías was confronted by a friend of the detained philosopher she defended her son's action by saying that, after all, 'the *patria* is the *patria*'.[30]

The brief account of the civil war produced by Marías thirty-seven years later in defence of Laín's *Descargo de conciencia* owed something to the sentiments expressed in his optimistic article at the end of the war. It skirted around the causes of the war, which might have disrupted the by now dominant public narrative of the war as a 'fratricidal conflict' for which an entire generation had been to blame, a new myth which

---

[27] Marías, *Una vida presente*, I, p. 265. This argument would be repeated, in effect, by the historian Javier Tusell around the time of the resurgence of war memories in 1997: *El País*, 22 December 1997. See also Chapter 12.

[28] Salvador Lissarrague, Luis de Sosa and Andrés María Mateo, *La esencia de lo español, su olvido y su recuperación* (Madrid, 1945).

[29] Mann, *Fascists*, especially p. 13.   [30] Marías, *Una vida presente*, vol. I, pp. 275–7.

by the 1970s had replaced the old narrative of Franco's 'crusade'.[31] The defence mounted by Marías made several assertions relating to historical questions, however, which had not been much discussed in public and which continue to be debated. First, that both belligerent sides had been connected to foreign totalitarian powers, so that minority political groups (fascist Falangists and Stalinist Communists) were catapulted into leading positions, producing a 'double deformation' of wartime politics.[32] Second, that political violence during the civil war – the killing of civilians, which (according to Marías) was 'more or less legalised' by both incumbent and rebel state organs – outweighed the violence at the front in its intensity, intimacy and long-lasting social effects. And, third, that the victors, far from halting the bloody struggle when Franco declared the war to have ended in 1939, prolonged its purifying spirit and consequences, virtually until 'the present' (1976), and that there remained a considerable fraction who, like Fernández de la Mora, 'wished to perpetuate it indefinitely'.

Taken together, Marías maintained, these three points provided an opportunity to deconstruct several myths. The post-war narrative of 'the defeated' depicted the Republic as a legal regime, enjoying broad legitimacy, a state of law beyond reproach, which was violently attacked in a rebellion by a fascist-military clique, producing a war which would become the first battle waged by Nazism and Fascism. This emphasis on democracy and the rule of law was not unjustified and, though not always able to achieve it, many Republican leaders, repulsed by the violence committed in the name of the Republic and fearful for its image internationally, would appeal to the imperative of legality.[33] The Socialist

---

[31] The new myth is summed up in the title of the war memories of the socialist Juan-Simeón Vidarte: *Todos fuimos culpables* ('We Were All to Blame'), first published in Mexico in 1973 and in Spain (Madrid) in 1978.

[32] While it is true that extreme parties were less popular in Spain until July 1936 than, say, France, on neither side was violent ideology and action merely 'imported'. On the complex political and social dynamics of the Republic at war, see Helen Graham, *The Spanish Republic at War, 1936–1939* (Cambridge, 2002), which overturns PCE-centred accounts which Marías was probably influenced by. For these, see, especially, Burnett Bolloten, *The Grand Camouflage: The Communist Conspiracy in the Spanish Civil War* (London, 1961), published in translation in Franco's Spain in 1961, almost uniquely for a foreign account of the war, because it could be read as reducing the Republic at war to 'Communism': *El gran engaño* (Barcelona, 1961). For Francoist assessment of Bolloten's book as 'great', see, e.g., Luis García Arias, 'Sobre la mediación o la denominada tercera España', Hermandad de Alféreces Provisionales, *Generación del 36*, pp. 55, 91. On political structures and violence on the rebel side: Joan Maria Thomàs, *La Falange de Franco* (Barcelona, 2001), pp. 97–111.

[33] E.g., Josep María Solé i Sabaté and Joan Villarroya, *La repressió a la reraguarda de Catalunya (1936–1939)* (Barcelona, 1989); Santiago Álvarez, *Negrín, personalidad histórica* (Madrid, 1994), pp. 43, 280.

wartime minister Julián Zugazagoitia, executed by a vengeful Francoist state in November 1940, had argued cogently for moderation in August 1936 and later expressed his fear that the violence of the war would poison the lives of future generations.[34] The Republic was indeed legally constituted, with an elected government, and its sovereignty was recognised internationally. At the same time, state incapacity was starkly revealed by the attempts at reform from 1931 to 1936, and the regime's popular legitimacy wavered precariously between parliament and the street for much of the period. By contrast, the rebel interpretation – still prevalent even amongst reform-minded Christian Democrats in the 1960s and regime loyalists even in 1975 – depicted the Republic in the hands of 'criminals', mired in blood-soaked chaos, the regime constantly on the verge of being dismembered by or submerged in revolution.[35] The only possible reaction, according to this view, which was maintained as the basis of legitimation by Francoists and others until the dictatorship's last days and beyond, was a 'guerra de liberación' in order to save the country from domination by the Soviet Union.[36] For Marías, these two irreconcilable narratives had some sense in 1936 but forty years later their truth value had dissolved amid the mass of differing vantage points from which the past was viewed, ranged along and in between the evolving social and political events and changes of the post-war era, though he remained clear that the military rebels had possessed no right to destroy the structures of the Republican state and 'multiply the violence by ten times'.[37]

Ultimately, Marías defended the 'fratricidal thesis' from a moral position, arguing that using the side which one supported – or found oneself on, often because of geographical accident rather than commitment – as

---

[34] E.g., Julián Zugazagoitia, 'Un imperativo legal', *El Socialista*, 23 August 1936, p. 1; also his prologue to Zugazagoitia, *Guerra y vicisitudes de los españoles* (Barcelona, 2001 (1940)), pp. 25–6.

[35] This thesis, as resurrected famously in José María Gil Robles, *No fue posible la paz* (Barcelona, 1968), deliberately reimagined the political crisis of the Republic as a collapse of the state. See the recent resurrection of this interpretation by so-called 'revisionists': e.g., Pío Moa, *Los orígenes de la guerra civil española* (Madrid, 1999); also his *Los mitos de la guerra civil* (Madrid, 2003).

[36] E.g., Luis Galinsoga and Francisco Franco-Salgado, *Centinela del occidente: semblanza biográfica de Francisco Franco* (Barcelona, 1956), especially pp. 189–206, 459–62.

[37] The myth of two irreconcilable 'Spains', espoused by left and right in 1936 and resurrected in many guises for years after the war, was debunked by Santos Juliá in an important article of 1981 coinciding with the fiftieth anniversary of the inauguration of the Second Republic. Juliá concentrated on the lack of a national civil power able to reshape society and institutions of authority, as had occurred, for example, in France after 1789, and the consequent undermining of the state by army and Church: 'El fracaso de la República', *Revista de Occidente*, 7–8 (November 1981), 196–211.

the basis for accusations forty years after the war was 'morally and politically monstrous'; 'sanctification' of either side amounted to 'a colossal falsehood'. This applied both to accusations against 'the defeated', as was done for decades during the Franco years, and, potentially, after 1975, against those who were 'the victors'.[38] The problem was that his call to recognise the complexity of the past carried with it a contradictory counsel of forgetting in the interests of peaceful political coexistence. Much of the rest of this book explores this contradiction in the political, moral and social questions posed over what to do with Spain's conflictive past, necessarily in part by moving away from grand narratives and structures.

Individuals, generations, and memory

First-person expressions of the experiences of flesh-and-blood protagonists and witnesses, whether in the form of pondered autobiography or as more scattered recollections of 'ordinary' witnesses, are related to processes of social change and ideological 'master narratives'. In Spain, the war was first glorified by the victors as a religious crusade (in the 1940s and 1950s), and later as a 'fratricidal struggle' (in the 1960s and 1970s) with the aim of relativising its significance at a time of economic modernisation. Individual stories of the self reveal the effects of historical change at a 'molecular' level; they present clues as to how memories are recalled, emerge, resonate and react with collective myths and grand narratives.[39] The prolific Catholic-Marxist writer and activist Alfonso Carlos Comín, a child of the civil war, born in 1933, exemplified new ways from the 1960s of relating the past to the present by tying religious conscience to individual experience and social engagement as he sought to diagnose the country's post-war maladies: 'I do not know how faith can be lived without consciously living one's own personal history as part of social history.'[40] Autobiographical texts, as rhetorical acts of pride, conscience, self-definition and memory, are not, however, free of problems. Retrospective self-representation of the subject in youth

---

[38] Marías, 'Los supuestos'.

[39] See, e.g., Gramsci, 'Justification of Autobiographies', in Antonio Gramsci, *Selections from Cultural Writings* (London, 1985), pp. 132–3. Also, Paul John Eakin, *How Our Lives Become Stories: Making Selves* (Ithaca, NY, 1999). 'Ordinary' people rarely leave us extended written accounts of their lives, but see, e.g.: David Vincent, *Bread, Knowledge and Freedom: A Study of Nineteenth-Century Working-Class Autobiography* (London, 1981); James S. Amelang, *The Flight of Icarus: Artisan Autobiography in Early Modern Europe* (Stanford, 1998).

[40] Comín, 'Fe en la tierra' (1975), in Comín, *Obras*, 7 vols. (Barcelona, 1986–94), vol. II, p. 288.

is as much a reflection of mature consciousness as it is a 'true' account of a youthful past. As with any historical document, however, it is partly this rootedness in a particular discursive context which makes autobiographical statements valuable and enlightening.[41]

As well as the reflections of Laín and Marías, a further case is that of their contemporary Cardinal Vicente Enrique y Tarancón, born in 1907, who, beside the new king, Juan Carlos, would play a pivotal role as a symbol of reconciliation during the transition to democracy after Franco, belying the sociological cliché of the Church as rigidly aligned with traditional power at all moments. While Tarancón's *Confesiones* (1996) recount his attitudes during the decline of the dictatorship, the 1984 memoir of his early life and career describes living through the years of the Republic as a young priest and surviving the civil war, and makes evident his belief in the legitimacy of Franco's Holy War and New State.[42] Tarancón does not reflect directly in his autobiographical writings on the problematic relationship of the remembering subject to the events of the past. In contrast, one of the aims of Laín's extended account of the period from the 1930s to the 1970s was candidly to think through the relationship of memory to notions of otherness, distance and identity. Drawing on the Ignatian Catholic tradition of spiritual exercises and his own medical training which influenced his implicit assumption that Spain suffered a form of 'sickness' from which he himself was not immune, he would employ the term *epicrisis* (a summing-up after a crisis of health) in judging his own past and examining his conscience.[43] These reflexive passages are constructed with textual contributions from voices identified in turn as 'the actor' (Laín viewed as immersed in historical events), 'the author' (Laín as storyteller, providing narrative structure and justification), and 'the judge' (Laín 'now', or 'outside himself', viewing both events and justifications and weighing them in the balance). Thus, Laín confesses to doubt when he asks himself whether he had felt sufficiently the gravity of the shedding of blood behind the 'heroism' of the victors and the 'mourning'

---

[41] E.g., Samuel Hynes, 'Personal Narratives and Commemoration', in Emmanuel Sivan and Jay Winter (eds.), *War and Remembrance in the Twentieth Century* (Cambridge, 1999), pp. 212–13. Although there are important differences to do with the role of the interviewer, something similar can be said of oral history. See, e.g., Ronald Fraser, 'Historia oral, historia social', *Historia Social*, 17 (1993), 131–9. Also, Anna Caballé, 'Biografía y autobiografía: convergencias y divergencias entre ambos géneros', in J. C. Davis and Isabel Burdiel (eds.), *El otro, el mismo: biografía y autobiografía en Europa, siglos XVII–XX* (Valencia, 2005), pp. 55–7.

[42] Vicente Enrique y Tarancón, *Recuerdos de juventud* (Barcelona, 1984); *Confesiones* (Madrid, 1996).

[43] Laín Entralgo, *Descargo*, esp. p. 444.

of the defeated, a question at once naïve and fundamental.[44] Self-referentially, and not unproblematically, 'the judge', according to Laín, represents the 'yo mismo' (the 'real I').[45] In one episode he imagines himself in 1936, on the platform of the railway station of Pamplona, in the early stages of the civil war, having sided with the rebels (and against his father and brother). The description of the crisis of the young man searching for himself is jarringly self-centred in the light of what we know of the violent purge of Republicans, summarily executed in large numbers in the area at the time, but revelatory, nonetheless, of the coexistence of barbarity and an evasive and individualist retreat into 'normality' and the self.[46]

Family relations and stories are central to Laín's framing of memory, as they have notably been in the reawakening of popular memory in Spain since the 1990s. The extent and speed of change brought about initially by the war and by painful adaptation to its outcome meant that collective experience was often radically different from one generation to the next, a keenly felt contemporary perception throughout the post-war era. Generational identity would therefore be a significant influence on looking back at the conflict, though cohort-specific perceptions were of course qualified by wartime allegiances and experiences, as well as by competing identities of social class and religion.

A venerable philosophical tradition exists in Spain which considers generations as fundamental to understanding historical change. It originates in the conjunction of rapid change and the collapse of empire at the end of the nineteenth century, as explained by the intellectual and literary 'Generación del '98', and later by the new intellectual vanguard of 1914, led by José Ortega y Gasset.[47] Ortega argued that each new generation – referring both to intellectuals and the broader society – had its own internal distinctiveness, displacing previous orthodoxies, thinking in new ways, and establishing the tempo of change.[48] What is

---

[44] Laín Entralgo, *Descargo*, p. 263.

[45] Laín Entralgo, *Descargo*, p. 176. For a more directly historico-psychoanalytical search for the self which, nonetheless, explores notions of otherness, distance and identity, see Ronald Fraser, *In Search of a Past* (London, 1984).

[46] On violence, see Javier Ugarte Tellería, *La nueva Covadonga insurgente* (Madrid, 1998). For a critique of such political rationalising, see Santos Juliá Díaz, 'La Falange liberal o de cómo la memoria inventa el pasado', in Celia Fernández Prieto and María Ángeles Hermosilla Álvarez (eds.), *Autobiografía en España: un balance* (Madrid, 2004), pp. 127–44.

[47] See, e.g., Pedro Laín Entralgo, *La generación del noventa y ocho* (Madrid, 1947).

[48] Ortega, *En torno a Galileo* (1933), in Ortega, *Obras completas* (Madrid, 1964), vol. V, pp. 11–164. See Chapter 11 for application of this idea to the 1980s. More controversially, Ortega linked intellectual generations to a need, as he saw it, of a 'select minority' to lead society in the 'age of the masses' (the era of the 1890s to the 1930s), an idea taken up by fascist intellectuals. See Ortega y Gasset, *La rebelión de las masas* (Madrid, 1976 (1929)).

interesting here for historians is that this theory views social structures and events primarily as temporal phenomena: 'human life is successive, it consists of happenings; nothing human can be understood without telling a story'.[49] Similarly, Ortega's contemporary the Hungarian sociologist Karl Mannheim famously held that shared experience, stories and myths, collective forms of behaviour, binding customs, silences in common, and other methods adopted in order to 'move forward' were all constitutive of and constituted by generational identity.[50] Maintaining that the common experiences of those born within a chronologically bound cohort have a dominant and determining weight in structuring experience, this conception of the relation of generation to memory can be criticised as overly essentialist. Mannheim's contention that, because youth lacks direct experience of events in the past, there is 'a lightening of the ballast for the young [enabling] them to live on in a changing world' is, however, worth consideration.[51] Here there is a contrast (though not incompatibility) with Halbwachs's presentist understanding which stresses how past events and experiences are drawn upon and shaped by memory in making the present intelligible. What makes the theories of Mannheim and Ortega valuable is their insistence that generational identity is conferred by determining influences embedded in change through time and socio-historical process.[52] Although Ortega was not specific about the historical process involved in identity formation, he did maintain that the 'historical reality' of a society is grasped only when it is conceived as a collective drama (or, in some cases, 'collective trauma') constituted by the trajectories of individual human lives: 'there is no drama without characters and without a plot', just as cultural trauma also requires both actors and a narrative, constructed as it is through a continuous dialogue between generations. Whilst distinguishing between generational succession within groups of intellectuals or public figures and broader socio-generational groups, and keeping the political and psychological role of the civil war in view for each case, the chapters which follow explore these evolving dialogues as part of

---

Initially, in 1931, a strong supporter of the modernising Republic, Ortega was exiled during the civil war, only returning (controversially) in 1948, seven years before his death.

[49] Ortega, *En torno a Galileo*. Also, Julián Marías, *El método histórico de las generaciones* (Madrid, 1949); *España inteligible: razón histórica de las Españas* (Madrid, 1985), pp. 28, 37. The argument is redolent of E. P. Thompson's understanding of social class, also traceable to Durkheimian sociology and to Halbwachs.

[50] Mannheim, 'Problem of Generations', pp. 356–7.

[51] Ibid., pp. 369–70. Generational determinism in at least some ways seems highly likely in terms of direct experience of wars and revolutions and their aftermaths.

[52] Ibid., p. 367. For a critique of 'essentialism', see Olick, *Politics of Regret*, p. 8.

continuous processes of identity formation, decade by decade, from war, through state building and social change, towards modernisation, democracy and the globalising influences of the present.[53]

Ortega's most influential protégé was Julián Marías, who we have already met in the context of the end of the war in 1939 and the aftermath of the dictatorship in 1976 and who developed his mentor's ideas in his work about the life course of individuals and generations. Each generational 'zone', according to this theory, has a span of fifteen years; Ortega, writing in 1933, labelled these zones (in a notably gendered way, based on a masculine model of 'the heroic') as follows: 'childhood' (from birth to 15 years), 'youth' (15–30), 'initiation' (30–45), 'dominance' (45–60), and 'old age' (from 60). For the purposes of historical analysis, cohorts can be 'fixed' in relation to these 'zones' and to watershed moments ('event horizons') to produce what Ortega called, in his schematic way, 'decisive generations', from which distinctive attitudes and behaviour can be measured, testing the hypothesis that generations at different phases of the life cycle experience the same events in different ways. We could simplify this relationship between generations and history by citing Alan B. Spitzer: 'young soldiers fight and die while older cohorts mourn and rule', a suggestive point, though too simple in relation to *civil* wars where civilian deaths are invariably high. It is clear, however, that successive generations, in several cases, entered a different world to that of their predecessors.[54] Mannheim's distinction between personally acquired memories and appropriated memories, arguing that the first has greater 'binding power' for generations, is important, though the manner and context in which memories are 'handed down', through generational and other forms of dialogue, is always complex and varying.

An important 'moment' in terms of national and genuinely social impact was defeat in the 1898 Spanish-American war (*el Desastre*), but a series of subsequent 'event horizons' in Spain's contemporary history can be suggested against which the experience of eight generations can be correlated. These include the advent of the military dictatorship of Primo de Rivera in 1923, the coming of the Second Republic in 1931, the

[53] On self-designated and evolving post-war generational identity amongst political prisoners, see Carles Feixa and Carme Agustí, 'Discursos autobiográficos de la prisión política', in Carme Molinero, Margarida Sala and Jaume Sobrequés (eds.), *Una inmensa prisión* (Barcelona, 2003), pp. 204–11.

[54] Alan B. Spitzer, 'The Historical Problems of Generations', *American Historical Review*, 78 (1973), 1,353–85 (p. 1,363). See also Robert Wohl, *The Generation of 1914* (Cambridge, MA, 1979). On Spain, see, e.g., Juan Goytisolo, *Disidencias* (Barcelona, 1977), p. 289; Marrero, *Trust de cerebros*, parts 2 and 3; Rafael Borràs Betriu, *Los que no hicimos la guerra* (Barcelona, 1971), particularly pp. 61, 84–6, 123, 153, 274, 313, 451, 527.

start of the civil war in 1936 (and its end in 1939), the denouement of world war in 1945, the student unrest of 1956, commemoration of the twenty-fifth anniversary of Franco's victory in 1964, the death of the dictator in 1975, the electoral victory of the PSOE in 1982, the coming to power of the Partido Popular in 1996, the new millennium, and the 2007 Law of Historical Memory. If we accept the key correlation as the coincidence of a cohort's gaining of maturity (between 'youth' and 'initiation' according to the Ortega-Marías schema) with a significant historical event, those particularly influenced by the war of 1898 would have been born during the period 1864–78 (being 20–34 years old in 1898).[55] In public life, this cohort included the polymath writer and philosopher Miguel de Unamuno (1864–1936); the Catholic-nationalist ideologue Ramiro de Maeztu (1875–1936); and the liberal poet Antonio Machado (1875–1939), all of whom retained prestige at the time of the Second Republic but were overtaken by the events of the 1930s and perished as a result of the civil war.

Moving fifteen years forward, those born during the period 1879–93 reached active maturity in the aftermath of empire, during the years of the Primo dictatorship and the Moroccan wars of the first decades of the twentieth century. This cohort included many of the military and political leaders of the civil war, among them Manuel Azaña (born in 1880), Juan Negrín and Francisco Franco (both born in 1892).[56] In relation to the civil war, we could call this cohort the 'generación rectora', the generation which governed in the lead up to and during the conflict. When related in broad social terms to analysis of post-war memory, we will see in chapters 3 and 4 that the framework for memory of this generation, on both sides, was based on political idealism and justifications for fighting the war and redeeming the sacrifice, and on internalisation personally and collectively of the notions of 'crusade' or 'liberation' on the one side, and 'democracy' or 'revolution' on the other. This first post-1898 generation was also one within which death, repression and exile registered significantly during the war.

---

[55] For this methodology, see Julián Marías, 'La actitud religiosa de siete generaciones españolas', in Joaquín Ruiz-Giménez, *Iglesia, estado y sociedad en España, 1930–1982* (Barcelona, 1984), pp. 325–33. Detlev Peukert in *The Weimar Republic: The Crisis of Classical Modernity* (Harmondsworth, 1991), cites work on generations relating to Germany in the era of modernisation, war and Nazism: pp. 14–18, 292.

[56] Though younger, this group was of course far from untouched by past events and Azaña might well be temporally (and temperamentally) located more fittingly alongside Machado and 'los del 98'. For the effect of 1898 on the child Franco and, indeed, on General Mola (b.1887), see Michael Richards, 'Constructing the Nationalist State: Self-Sufficiency and Regeneration in the Early Franco Years', in Clare Mar-Molinero and Ángel Smith (eds.), *Nationalism and National Identity in the Iberian Peninsula: Competing and Conflicting Identities* (Oxford, 1996), pp. 198–225.

A third generation incorporates those born between 1894 and 1908, aged between 28 and 42 in 1936. We may call this cohort 'the mobilised generation': men and women who had matured politically with the struggles of the Republic, took up arms in its defence or with the aim of preventing reform and resisting social change, or, at least, were conscripted to fight for one cause or the other. As a whole, the 'mobilised generation', which in terms of experience converges with the cohort which followed, suffered grievously during the war. Those who were amongst the victors, including Tarancón (b.1907) and Laín Entralgo (b.1908), had opportunities to share in power and wield influence, nationally or locally, after 1939; the defeated would live much of their adult years in the shadow of the war.[57] Many significant public figures of the next generation, including the Falangist Dionisio Ridruejo (b.1912), who after the war would recant his associations with rebel violence, and the Christian Democrat Joaquín Ruiz-Giménez (b.1913), who would become a minister of Franco in the early 1950s, came to identify to some degree with the defeated, preached tolerance, and allied with otherwise marginalised figures who had supported the Republic, such as Marías (b.1914). Those of both cohorts were likely to promote ideological justifications for war when they recalled it afterwards, though there was also greater willingness to question the degree of sacrifice imposed by the conflict than was often the case amongst the 'generación rectora'. Translating this approximate survey of public figures into social terms, the violence of the war and its aftermath was concentrated on those aged between 25 and 45 years in wartime Republican areas, where large numbers were killed, for example in Málaga, La Coruña, Aragón, Valencia, Badajoz and Huelva.[58] At a social level, as chapters 5 and 6 show, many who had been mobilised militarily and ideologically before and during the war focused in the aftermath, either willingly or under pressure, on the values of public order, peace, even a desire for authority and a reverence for national symbols – part of what some recalled as 'an era of respect' rather than allegiance to the regime – and on achieving a

---

[57] Helen Graham, *The War and Its Shadow: Spain's Civil War in Europe's Long Twentieth Century* (Eastbourne, 2012), especially, pp. 53–73.

[58] In Badajoz the most affected group was that aged between 30 and 34 and in Huelva, that aged between 35 and 39. Francisco Espinosa Maestre, *La columna de la muerte: el avance del ejército franquista de Sevilla a Badajoz* (Barcelona, 2003), p. 243. See also Antonio Nadal, *Guerra civil en Málaga* (Málaga, 1984), p. 192; Matilde Eiroa San Francisco, *Viva Franco: Hambre, racionamiento, falangismo. Málaga, 1939–1942* (Málaga, 1995), p. 248; Luis Lamela García, *A Coruña, 1936: memoria convulsa de una represión* (La Coruña, 2002), p. 130; Vicente Gabarda, *Els afusellaments al país Valencià (1938–1956)* (Valencia, 1996), p. 215.

sense of normality which eschewed ideology and politics because these were associated with the pain of war.[59]

It should be noted that there was no necessarily identical response according to age cohort, as we can see in the post-war evolution, for example, of the lives of two other figures, both born in 1922. The radical psychiatrist Carlos Castilla del Pino (1922–2009), who produced two lively volumes of autobiography towards the end of his life, and the Francoist minister Manuel Fraga Iribarne, author of a less-than-revealing political memoir, published in 1980, both experienced the war during their own personal transition between 'childhood' and 'youth'. Reaching political maturity in the aftermath of war (though not having fought in it), they both located themselves temporally as part of a 'generación puente' ('bridge generation') between the era of war and that of peace. Whilst Castilla del Pino would rebel against the war and all it stood for, Fraga accepted and promoted the conflict as the legitimating 'moment' of Franco's rule and of the subsequent developmentalism of the 1960s, and made a long and prominent political and academic career for himself.[60] In social terms, masses of the youthful mobilised, or those slightly younger, who reached adulthood in the first few post-war years, suffered the hunger and discrimination of the 1940s. They would form the nucleus of the first post-war migrants from rural areas to urban centres in the period from the 1940s to the 1960s.[61] From opposite ends of the political spectrum, Castilla del Pino and Fraga, beginning in the late 1950s, would thus engage with the hungry generation and their migration, the former directly in consultations in his clinic in Córdoba and through oppositionist politics (see Chapter 8) and the latter less directly by adopting a sociological analysis of the country's past and its evolution and problems (see Chapter 6).

A fifth cohort, born during the approach or tenure of the Second Republic in approximately the period 1924–38, would become the children of the war (the oldest being 15 in 1939), who developed a particularly strong, though not uniform, collective self-identity in the post-war period. One child of the war, born in 1924 and from a conservative family, noted seventy years later that

---

[59] E.g., Joseph Aceves, *Social Change in a Spanish Village* (Cambridge, MA, 1971), p. 31; E. C. Hansen, *Rural Catalonia Under the Franco Regime* (Cambridge, 1977), pp. 140–1; Víctor Morales Lezcano and Teresa Pereira Rodríguez, *Memoria oral de una transformación social* (Madrid, 1997), p. 125.

[60] One contemporary of Fraga's 'bridge' generation was Gonzalo Fernández de la Mora, born in 1924, who would preach continuity in the early 1970s with less 'openness' than Fraga.

[61] See, e.g., Jesús García Valcárcel, 'Causas de la emigración española, interior y exterior', in Semanas Sociales de España, *Los problemas de la migración española* (Madrid, 1959), p. 95.

ever since I was a child all my memories have been conditioned, behind a curtain of familial and personal circumstances, by the sequence of the future civil war and by the idea of having always lived under a dictatorship, or almost always, as if you were born and lived with an inevitable predestination: me and my whole generation.[62]

The material and psychological effects of the war and the immediate post-war years, marked for many Republicans by demonisation and the struggle to rebuild lives, were felt acutely by children of the war.[63] As with their predecessors, many of this cohort would be amongst the migrants of the first post-war decades. The work of the social realist writers of the 1950s, the majority from middle-class families which had supported the military rebels, would attest to the political and material impulses behind this process of migration.[64] The children of the war were also socialised as witnesses to the persecution and the impotence of their parents. Later, they would experience directly the silencing of the wartime violence as the past receded gradually into the background. In rural communities, young people lacked political frames of reference for political action, while in the cities it became possible to discover more about the recent past and this generation would start to shape the future political and social struggle. The writings and political conscience of the activist Alfonso Comín emerged from a Catholic dissident movement, for example, which developed particularly after the Second Vatican Council of the early 1960s. At the same time, some of those born in the later 1930s would have little if any direct memory of the war and no sense of responsibility for it; many in urban middle-class society would later join the student protests of 1956, a dramatic product of the gulf between generations which had opened up as the young rejected their parents' past and which would have profound ramifications for the Franco regime.

Fifteen years later, those born between 1939 and 1953, representing in social terms the impetus behind the biggest post-war wave of mass

---

[62] Antonio Jiménez Blanco, *Los niños de la guerra ya somos viejos* (Madrid, 1994), p. 27. See also Borràs, *Los que no hicimos*, pp. 27, 49, 61–2, 84–6.

[63] On the repressive process of adoption of children of Republicans: Ricard Vinyes, Montse Armengou and Ricard Belis, *Los niños perdidos del franquismo* (Barcelona, 2002); Michael Richards, 'Ideology and the Psychology of War Children in Franco's Spain, 1936–45', in Kjersti Ericsson and Eva Simonsen (eds.), *Children of World War II: The Hidden Enemy Legacy* (Oxford, 2005), pp. 73–101. On children evacuated to the Soviet Union: Marie José Devillard, Álvaro Pazos, Susana Castillo and Nuria Medina, *Los niños españoles en la URSS (1937–1997): narración y memoria* (Barcelona, 2001). On childhood trauma in the Republican zone, e.g., Bullón and Diego, *Historias*, pp. 102, 161–2; in Nationalist Vigo: pp. 183–4.

[64] There were many interesting male writers; several women are especially relevant and important, however, e.g., Josefina Aldecoa (b.1926), Ana María Matute (b.1926) and Carmen María Gaite (b.1925).

migration in the 1960s, would be seen as central to the nature of 'Franco's peace' and the regime's notion of normality when the twenty-fifth anniversary of the victory was celebrated in 1964. While those who had been born before the civil war spoke of a 'bridge generation', participating in a form of social transition from backwardness to modernity, the young who were growing up in the 1950s have looked back and described themselves as a 'parenthetical generation', living a repressed existence between the sacrifices of the war, which still cast their shadow, and the relative freedoms of the consumer society which remained beyond reach. Increasingly there was a focus on making a life for the future, although an intangible sense of fear, isolation and guilt has often been recalled. In political terms this cohort included, amongst the oldest, the trade unionist and Communist Party activist José Luis López Bulla (b.1943), who migrated from rural Andalucía to industrial Barcelona in 1965 (see Chapter 8), and the former labour lawyer and, two decades later, first post-war Socialist prime minister Felipe González (born in 1942), who matured as the 'economic miracle' of the 1960s and urbanisation brought in their train new social and cultural bases of identity and political struggle.[65] Amongst the younger members of this generation born as the shadows of war began to recede is José María Aznar (b.1953), grandson of a prominent Francoist diplomat and propagandist and in 1996 the first post-dictatorship conservative to be democratically elected as prime minister. In 2004, Aznar would be succeeded as prime minister by José Luis Rodríguez Zapatero (b.1960), leader of the PSOE and another 'grandchild of the war', whose own grandfather, Juan Rodríguez Lozano, a military officer loyal to the Republican government, was executed by the rebels in August 1936. Those who since the late 1990s have led the movement for the 'recuperation of historical memory' have largely been 'grandchildren of the war', though some on the political left, such as the PSOE's deputy prime minister in 2004, María Teresa Fernández de la Vega (b.1949), the architect of the Memorial Commission which would draw up the 2007 Law of Historical Memory, were related to former Francoist officials.[66] For several decades, as we will note, many opponents of the dictatorship had come from conservative, pro-Nationalist family and cultural backgrounds.

---

[65] José López Bulla, *Cuando hice las maletas: un paseo por el ayer* (Barcelona, 1997). On the generational coordinates of PSOE resurgence in the late 1970s and early 1980s: Abdón Mateos, 'La política de la memoria de los socialistas hacia la guerra civil y el exilio en la España democrática', in María Dolores de la Calle Velasco and Manuel Redero San Román (eds.), *Guerra civil: documentos y memoria* (Salamanca, 2006), pp. 66–7.

[66] María Teresa Fernández de la Vega, 'Lo hecho y lo por hacer', in Julio Aróstegui (ed.), *España en la memoria de tres generaciones* (Madrid, 2007), pp. 19–25.

The official memory of the war as a 'crusade against communism' would be maintained for two decades or more as the basis of the political legitimation of Franco's state. Demonising the modernisers of the Second Republic and use of 18 July 1936 as the founding moment of the state and of 1939 as 'Year Zero' relied on sustained commemoration of 'the Fallen' and on simplification of the past, a form of legitimacy which denied reconciliation and which would gradually became untenable. The civil war had nonetheless represented a social watershed because, although modern ideas were purged in the process of building the authoritarian state, the conflict, discrimination and polarisation of its aftermath produced the beginning of a demographic movement away from rural backwardness; this shift in turn confirmed the necessity of a greater presence of the state in daily life, which would not relent until the 1970s. From the 1950s there had emerged a significant, though relatively isolated, movement for greater tolerance (not least amongst Catholics of the post-1930s generation), in favour of grappling morally and politically with the past and motivated, in part, by this convergence of rural and urban worlds. The complex dynamics of the war, the violence produced, and the subsequent discriminatory settlement were the origins of incalculable trauma. Much of this suffering could not be brought into the public sphere which was monopolised by the self-legitimating myths of the victors until the 1960s. The more complex reality can be explored only by moving away from myths and the grand narratives – some of which have been recycled uncritically by historians. A different emphasis would be towards the experience of individuals and groups actively involved in conveying memories and constructing stories about the war and its violence and, in some cases, expressing sentiments to do with conscience and reconciliation. These activities attempted to make sense of the past, to understand changing circumstances, and to form or reconstitute meaningful collective identities. The point of departure remains, however, the nature of the civil war and its violence.

2 Democracy, civil war, and intimate violence in the 1930s

> I belong to a generation which has always called itself apolitical, which committed the grave mistake of seeing only the negative aspect of politics, of ignoring the fact that politics could one day become an absolutely essential activity, an activity for our *patria*, of life and death [...] There is nothing strange in the fact that it is a man who is not part of my generation, but of a later one, Doctor Negrín, who today has the glory of interpreting, in the midst of war, the political will of Spain.[1]

Antonio Machado, the Republican poet of the people in the 1930s, born in 1875 and therefore a contemporary of President Manuel Azaña, was requested in September 1938 to comment over wartime national radio on the thirteen-point programme for peace devised by the prime minister, Juan Negrín, the consummate political pragmatist of the 1930s, born in 1892, the same year as Francisco Franco. Machado's words were prophetic, pronounced just a few months before his death in exile in February 1939 and the Republic's defeat. The apoliticism before 1936 to which he referred in 1938 had been based on republicanism's intellectual bent and Machado's own tacit rejection of Spanish politics, his civic critique of a political life which he perceived as revolving around mere clientelism and the naked struggle for power rather than consent. Machado's creative sense of what politics ought to be would make his ideas important again in the 1970s, during the expansion of civil society which accompanied post-Franco democratisation, but as the war drew to an end he could only regret bitterly that the country had proved to be 'a land of lamentable negligence', of political failure, leading to catastrophe.[2]

Myths about the Republic's political failure were bolstered by the catastrophic depths of the defeat, of course, and the victors' propaganda until 1975, and have often been suffused with a sense of inevitability. The

---

[1] Antonio Machado, 'Glosario de los trece fines de guerra', in Julio Rodríguez Puértolas and Gerardo Pérez Herrero (eds.), *Antonio Machado. La guerra: escritos, 1936–1939* (Madrid, 1983), pp. 288–9.
[2] Manuel Azaña, *Los españoles en guerra*, 2nd edn (Barcelona, 1977 (1939)), pp. 7–8.

alleged continuity between the paramilitary street violence of early 1936 and the bloodletting in the context of civil war after 18 July 1936 allowed responsibility for the war to fall upon politicians and their decisions rather than the time-honoured weaknesses of the state itself, the fragmented nature of civil society, and the actions of the rebel generals who would construct Franco's New State with the support of the Catholic Church.[3] The pre-war social and political crisis had been a modern one, comparable to – and in some respects less severe than – those experienced in other European states of the era attempting rapid modernisation. It was largely the historical peculiarities of the Spanish situation and especially the reliance of the state upon the army and the Church as national bureaucratic organs and as political arbiters which limited responses to the multiplicity of social demands made in the period from 1931 to 1936. Popular mobilisation against the July 1936 coup both indicated that the Republic had brought about some level of social and political coordination and, however, made the seemingly archaic outcome of bloody civil war unavoidable once the rebels gained vital assistance from foreign fascist powers.[4]

As Paul Preston has shown, the violence which ensued after the military rebels' declaration of a state of war on 18 July 1936 was possible because the pre-existing state's monopoly of legitimate force was rent asunder.[5] A powerfully backed challenge leading to intrastate war is one of the commonest ways by which state power has historically been disrupted; another is foreign military intervention.[6] The level of fragmentation in such situations varies according to the salience of the combat. In Spain, this was no merely local insurgent challenge; the rebellion had erupted from within the state's own apparatus of coercion, both central and local, and affected practically all regions, demanding responses from state institutions, local power brokers and ordinary citizens. The distinction between state action to maintain order and popular, or 'privatised', criminality thereby became confused; a vacuum opened within which intimate civil violence could occur.[7] Support for the rebels from Nazi Germany and Fascist Italy rapidly followed the coup and, coupled with French and British non-intervention, placed the incumbent government

[3] Juliá, 'Fracaso de la República'; Vincent, *Spain*, pp. 119–34.
[4] Julio Aróstegui, *Por qué el 18 de julio . . . y después* (Barcelona, 2006).
[5] Preston, *Spanish Holocaust*, Part III. In general terms: Anthony Giddens, *The Nation-State and Violence* (Cambridge, 1985), p. 121.
[6] Theda Skocpol, *Social Revolutions in the Modern World* (Cambridge, 1994), p. 229.
[7] For Negrín on the problem of distinguishing between common and political crimes in 'a savage civil war as ours has been', see Santiago Álvarez, *Negrín, personalidad histórica* (Madrid, 1994), p. 152.

in a position of inferiority from the beginning, dependent on aid from the Soviet Union which was given primarily to further Stalin's own interests, and allowing the Republic little time or means to claw back control of social order through legitimised force. The rapid involvement of the international powers enlarged the fighting capacity of the belligerent sides, turning a relatively small-scale military rebellion into a full-scale war. Nazi and Fascist involvement saved the military coup from outright failure, giving the rebels the means to wage war.

In a situation of fragmented sovereignty, when individuals within civil society feel in danger of becoming stateless, a sense of insecurity and fear becomes pervasive. Such wars are fought within communities; they become conflicts of identity, the violence apparently inexorable, and the metaphor of civil war as a 'sickness' ('one fights almost against oneself') or an 'epidemic' has often seemed appropriate.[8] The Catalan psychiatrist Emilio Mira, looking back on the conflict, would write in the early 1940s that 'all wars are terrible, but the Spanish war was one of the worst, because it was no simple war of invasion. At times an individual had more fear of a family member living in the same space than of the bombs dropped by the enemy aeroplanes.'[9] This sense of the intimacy of civil war violence had not diminished many years later: 'nobody who has not lived through a civil war can have any idea, any idea at all, what it is like, nobody'.[10] The intimacy of civil war violence, both that in the name of the rebels' 'crusade' against 'Godless' democracy and that which emerged as part of the inchoate social revolution in areas defended by Republicans, forms the basis of the post-war memories discussed in this study.

The Second Republic, 1931–6: reform, obstruction and legitimacy

The complex origins of the civil war are to be found in Spain's historic evolution on the margins of European social transformation and in the harshness of Spanish life which the Second Republic, inaugurated through elections in April 1931, sought to alleviate. The most important areas of contention by 1931 were land ownership and agrarian relations of production, the uneven growth and politicisation of the revolutionary rural and urban working class, and regional identity,

[8] Charles King, *Ending Civil Wars* (Oxford, 1997), p. 26.
[9] Emilio Mira y López, *La psiquiatría en la guerra* (Buenos Aires, 1944), p. 16.
[10] Castilla del Pino, *Casa del olivo*, p. 380. Also testimony, Carlos Gil Andrés, *Lejos del frente: la guerra civil en la Rioja Alta* (Barcelona, 2006), p. 443.

especially in Catalonia and the Basque Country. The often unmediated dependency of the state on the bureaucratic and public order apparatus of Church and army would limit the effectiveness of reforms aimed at these myriad points of social fragmentation. Against the wishes of conservative and traditionalist groups, including sections of the peasantry and economic, military and cultural elites, a new constitution was passed in December 1931 which declared and celebrated the sovereignty of the people ('workers of all social classes'), called for increased wages for the poorly paid, a programme of land reform, a level of autonomy for the regions, the separation of Church and state, and depoliticisation of the army. This was an unprecedented break with the past and, according to social and political conservatives, an attack against 'the most sacred sentiments of the people', which would form the background to the constructed Catholic memory of the Republic itself as a traumatic attempt to destroy the nation and of the war as justified resistance to a tyrannical state.[11]

The rise and fall of democracy and the nation-state in Europe during the years between the two world wars relied on the capacity of states and political movements to absorb and channel the economic and political demands of modern mass society. The coming of the Republic raised collective hopes and expectations of modernisation and democratisation amongst substantial sections of the middle and lower classes, depicted problematically by the regime's liberal leaders as a unitary 'pueblo republicano'. The new government simultaneously challenged the material and institutional interests of property owners and, equally important, was perceived as threatening the collective identity of those of religious faith ('el pueblo católico'). Sections of the urban high bourgeoisie, agrarian traditionalists, and monarchists, as well as many rural Catholics, would mobilise politically against these threats. The Republic faced the challenge of these tensions and conflicts within a political culture which had not been developed for popular participation and was unaccustomed to compromise, negotiation and policy implementation.[12] All of these factors contributed to the highly public nature of political contention during the period 1931–6. Popular demands were imperfectly met as politicians and their followers sought to use the limited resources of state power to achieve reform in the broad spheres of morality, economics,

---

[11] E.g., José Orlandis Rovira, 'Veinticinco años después', in Hermandad de Alféreces Provisionales, *Generación del 36*, p. 12.

[12] For analysis of the notion of citizenship during the Republic as contested between competing images of 'the people', see Rafael Cruz, *En el nombre del pueblo* (Madrid, 2006).

religion and intellectual life.[13] Although overhaul of the key institutions of army and Church was set in train, the Republic aimed primarily at a transformation of society. The envisaged transformation neglected the interests of specific, though broad, social groups (especially middle-class Catholics) upon which its ability to function partly rested.

In urban society especially, the private sphere of the family merged with the political sphere in struggles, for example, over marriage and divorce, the birth rate and population policy, and the growth of leisure. Modernity clashed meanwhile with the hard though seemingly harmonious rural life of Catholic society in much of central Spain and the north which revolved around the local priest, the medical doctor and the schoolteacher, figures perceived as sponsoring the 'healthy life' of organic, spontaneous and unselfconscious collective memory. In contrast, the urban preference of 1930s Republican politics and culture was overtly laic and anti-clerical and actively discouraged public religious devotions.[14] It was widely claimed by the 'carriers' of traditionalist norms – priests, politicians, conservative intellectuals – that a significant popular culture was in the throes of destruction at the hands of modernism and forgotten by liberalism.[15]

Initiatives introduced during the Republic, such as civil marriage, discouragement of baptism of newborn children, and laicisation of cemeteries, were enthusiastically seconded by many 'popular' sections of society, but also heightened the cultural gulf and generational differences, which in turn influenced mobilisation through acts of collective affirmation, political meetings, laic festivals, and civic ceremony.[16] As exhortations were made to the masses to consume both goods (more difficult in the 1930s compared to the boom of the previous decade) and ideas, politics became 'massified' and quasi-theatrical, often taking place in the street, beyond the reach of parliament and with different objectives. At a time of economic slump and faced with the obstruction of entrenched elites, the radicalisation of young adults in the 1930s was founded on the incapacity of state institutions in reacting to popular demands. Politics

---

[13] Michael Richards, 'The Popular Front', in Gordon Martel (ed.), *A Companion to Europe, 1900–1945* (Oxford, 2006), pp. 375–90. For comparison with the Weimar Republic, see Stanley Payne, *Spain's First Democracy: The Second Republic, 1931–1936* (Madison, 1993), p. 372.

[14] E.g., Leandro Álvarez Rey, *La derecha en la II República: Sevilla, 1931–1936* (Seville, 1993), pp. 215–35.

[15] See, e.g., Alfonso Iniesta, *Garra marxista en la infancia* (Burgos, 1939), pp. 267–8, 282. The urban focus is reflected in citizenship itself: Cruz, *Pueblo*. On the political effects of uneven, rural–urban, development, see Graham, *Spanish Republic at War*, pp. 1–21.

[16] Ana Aguado and María Dolores Ramos, *La modernización de España (1917–1939)* (Madrid, 2002), pp. 153–221.

increasingly became a struggle to stand in for the state through direct action, by the left to enforce change and by the right to prevent it.[17]

From April 1931 until the autumn of 1933 a programme of reforms was introduced by a coalition of liberal republicans, led by Manuel Azaña as prime minister from October 1931, and the largely social democratic PSOE. In part as a result of the electoral divisions of the left, particularly between the anarcho-syndicalist CNT and the PSOE (which had its own revolutionary wing), a conservative government was elected in November 1933, including the Catholic CEDA, considered by the left to be of dubious democratic credentials, though it had built mass support amongst the middle classes and at the expense of the avowedly fascist Falange Española, founded in 1933.[18] Both the PSOE and the CEDA were prone to factionalism which made consistency of aims and practice difficult, pushing both towards radical and confused positions. When a new cabinet was announced in early October 1934 it included three *cedistas* in the key ministries of Labour, Agriculture and Justice. It seemed to the left that Spanish democracy was going the same way the German Weimar Republic had in early 1933. The general strike mounted to unite Republicans' desires to re-establish the basis of popular citizenship with the determination of the left wing of the PSOE to bring about a social and political revolution indicated the fragmented nature of the workers' movement. The move largely failed except in the northern mining valleys of Asturias where a Workers' Alliance united socialists, anarchists and communists. The resultant localised revolutionary commune lasted a fortnight before succumbing to bloody suppression by the Army of Africa, to which the ostensibly Republican government resorted all too easily, under the ultimate command of Francisco Franco. The violence of the October rebellion, including the murder of priests, terrified the middle classes, and its subsequent brutal suppression included the imprisonment of thousands of leftist activists and liberal political leaders. Asturias and 6 October would become important reference points of the political propaganda and imagery of both left and right during the civil war.[19] Although the Franco dictatorship would later glory

[17] See, e.g., Sandra Souto Kustrín, 'Y ¿Madrid? ¿Qué hace Madrid?' Movimiento revolucionario y acción colectiva (1933–1936) (Madrid, 2004), particularly, pp. 86–101; Vincent, Spain, pp. 131–4; Sid Lowe, Catholicism, War and the Foundation of Francoism: The JAP in Spain, 1931–1939 (Eastbourne, 2010).

[18] Paul Preston, The Coming of the Spanish Civil War: Reform, Reaction and Revolution in the Second Republic, 2nd edn (London, 1994).

[19] For an example of a minute's silence (in Málaga), see Vida Nueva, 6 October 1936; La Publicitat, 6 October 1936; La Batalla, 6 October 1936; La Vanguardia, 6 October 1936; Núñez Seixas, 'Nations in Arms', p. 54; Cruz, Pueblo, pp. 79, 262.

in the July 1936 military rising as its founding moment, it would blame the left's rebellion of October 1934 for the war, depicting this as the beginning of the country's social and political problems and thereby 'explaining' the conflict by reference to 'communism'.[20] The rebellion had in fact been a badly coordinated product of the weakness of the working-class organisations which resulted in highly localised actions in pursuit of ill-defined goals. Later, a relationship between October 1934 and the early months of the civil war would become clear in the execution of Republicans who had participated in the October revolt. In the Aragonés pueblo of Uncastillo (Zaragoza), for example, of the 110 men who had attempted to gain control of the Guardia Civil post in the town in 1934, 44 were to be executed in the summer of 1936. The tally would probably have been higher had others not been fighting at the front.[21]

In the aftermath of the October 1934 rebellion, a more united political direction was sought; strategy turned to rebuilding the Republican–Socialist coalition of 1931 to win back power and refocus popular support. Progressive liberals optimistically believed that demands from below could be directed through enlightened 'tutelage'.[22] Azaña's efforts, in tandem with those of the leading moderate pragmatist of the PSOE, Indalecio Prieto, would culminate in the construction of an electoral coalition, the Frente Popular, to bring liberal and working-class parties together. A key moment of the rallying of the 'pueblo republicano' was Azaña's open-air speech at Comillas (outside Madrid) in October 1935, delivered to the largest crowd that any European politician had mobilised at that time without recourse to paramilitary methods.[23] Between 200,000 and 400,000 supporters heard the former prime minister call for a democratic 'redemption of the Republic' based on resistance to authoritarianism and fascism. Azaña recognised explicitly the great potential power of the masses as a positive moral force: 'I have no fears of the popular torrent, or that it will overwhelm us; the question is to know how to guide it so that we do not allow this enormous popular force

---

[20] On 'the state of 18 July', see, e.g., 'De cara al futuro' (Franco interview), *ABC*, 1 April 1964; Gonzalo Fernández de la Mora, review of Azaña, *Obras completas* (ed. Juan Marichal), 3 vols. (Mexico City, 1966–7), *ABC*, 7 March 1968, in which Azaña's idea of the modern (laic) state was again critiqued. Also Marqués de Valdeiglesias, *ABC*, 30 January 1970; post-war declarations of Nationalist civil war volunteer officers in Hermandad de Alféreces Provisionales, *Generación del 36*.

[21] Víctor Lucea Ayala, *Dispuestos a intervenir: Antonio Plano Aznárez: socialismo y republicanismo en Uncastillo (1900–1939)* (Zaragoza, 2008), pp. 388, 391. For the local polarisation associated with October 1934, see, e.g., *ABC*, 4 April 1935. See also Gil, *Lejos*, pp. 145–8.

[22] E.g. Ortega y Gasset, *Rebelión de las masas* (1929).

[23] Santos Juliá, *Orígenes del Frente Popular en España (1934–1936)* (Madrid, 1979).

to lose its way or be wasted or ruined.'[24] Later, in the wake of Franco's civil war victory, because of their symbolic significance to the Republic the fields of Comillas would become a contested site of memory.[25] The masses, many favouring socialising measures which would radically alter the balance of economic power and gravitating towards the rhetoric of the Marxist wing of the PSOE, were drawn to the Russian Revolution of 1917 as a model, rather than to the bourgeois revolution of 1789, and were not always willing to be guided. In an era of economic crisis and social tumult, and with a weak state as backdrop, the basis of cross-class alliance imagined by Azaña, no advocate of proletarian revolution, would be severely challenged.

The intensity of cultural and political activities during the years of the Second Republic, beginning with the new regime's democratic and historic electoral victory in 1931, was thus very real, though certain associated images have endured longer than others. Even allowing for an understandable sense of nostalgia, the often festive atmosphere that pushed for a popularisation of 'the political' (and, up to a point, the politicisation of 'the personal') has been recalled in many post-Franco testimonies. There was undoubtedly a growth of women's expectations, as expressed by one woman from Málaga who was in her twenties in the years before the civil war:

the Republic changed customs, people had more open minds, there was a rapid intensification; one could tell in the way people expressed themselves, in communication between people, we simply spoke more and about more things, about politics; when there were informal meetings in the canteen, women went along too.[26]

Once war came, the siege mentality in the Republican zone, the struggle there to secure basic material needs, and internal political arguments would all interact with spontaneous resistance and ideological commitment in reshaping the new patterns of social and cultural practice initiated in 1931.

Until July 1936, political action at the level of the village, town or municipality reflected both local conditions and state initiatives, both varying according to the pendulum swing of national politics. Frequent recourse by citizens to the state, through the law, in order to make local office-holders responsible for their actions suggested an acceptance of the notion of institutionalised authority and, at the same time, uncertainty

---

[24] Azaña, *Obras*, III, p. 292.   [25] See Chapter 3.

[26] María José González Castillejo, 'Realidad social de la mujer: vida cotidiana y esfera pública en Málaga (1931–1936)', in Pilar Ballarín and Teresa Ortiz (eds.), *La mujer en Andalucía*, 2 vols., vol. I (Granada, 1990), p. 427.

about the capacity and legitimacy of state intervention in public life. Collective action was above all local, however much some observers, both during and after the Republic, laid the blame for actions against the old order on instructions emanating directly from Madrid.[27] Both implementing and obstructing reform were attempted through the evolving and contested legal framework of relations between proprietor and employee, landowner and tenant farmer or labourer, and Catholic believer, Church and state. For mobilised Catholics, symbols of inherited identity based on the sacred unity of nation and religion were struggled over, as demonstrated by the withdrawal of crucifixes from state schoolrooms in 1932 in line with laicising measures which were popular with those who blamed the Church's domination of education for illiteracy, cultural repressiveness and material poverty.[28] The withdrawal of crucifixes would later, during the civil war, be portrayed crudely as a prelude to the murder of priests. The ritualised return of school crucifixes as an element of 'liberation' during the war would become central to the construction of the cultural trauma claimed by pious Catholics. The crucifixes' restitution was accompanied by the purging of Republican teachers.[29] Memories of the 'gente de orden', middle-class upholders of order, were thus often of attacks against religion during the Republic, though worker strikes also figured prominently, often blended with stories of crime, disorder, and generally irreligious behaviour, remembered in part to justify the 1936 military coup retrospectively.[30] Performative actions which had symbolised radical political change, such as the burning of churches and images of the saints, were recalled by all sections of society, however, including those who supported change and claimed to understand the motives. In July 1936 when news broke of the military coup in working-class Valencia, the bonfires consumed images and furniture removed from churches and convents and, 'with irreverent and blasphemous gestures', groups of individuals removed bells from

[27] See, e.g., on Vinaroz, in Castellón, Enrique y Tarancón, *Recuerdos de juventud*, pp. 78–9. Also, Vincent, *Spain*, pp. 141–2.

[28] On the period 1931–6, e.g., William A. Christian, *Visionaries: The Spanish Republic and the Reign of Christ* (Berkeley, 1996).

[29] On crucifixes, civil war and purge of teachers, see, e.g., *Diario de Navarra*, 30 August 1936, p. 1; 2 September 1936, p. 1; 6 September 1936, pp. 1, 3; *El Ideal Gallego*, 28 August 1936, p. 1; *El Correo de Andalucía*, 5 September 1936, p. 5; *Heraldo de Aragón*, 3 September 1936; *La Vanguardia Española*, 1 August 1939, p. 1; Eugenio Vegas Latapié to Ronald Fraser, in *Blood of Spain* (Harmondsworth, 1979), pp. 204–5. For Catholic historiography stressing the 'inevitability' of the civil war 'purge' of priests because of laicisation from 1931, see, e.g., Vicente Cárcel Ortí, *La persecución religiosa en España durante la Segunda República, 1931–1939* (Madrid, 1990).

[30] E.g. memories of an officer of the Francoist Brigada Social in Gijón, Carlos Elordi (ed.), *Los años difíciles* (Madrid, 2002), pp. 248–9.

churches and threw sacred images from the windows of convents.[31] Testimony suggests how war children in both zones experienced a feeling of 'insecurity in the people around us [...] A vague sensation of fear and humiliation' at times, mixed with a sense of uncomprehending excitement, when they witnessed intracommunal violence. Making sense of their memories is complicated by the emotional and psychological legacy which was in part created by the post-war Francoist imposition of guilt.[32]

While Catholic and pro-Franco memories stressed continuity between the sporadic violence of the pre-war years of the Republic and that of the war, to the swathes of society imbued with the culture and spirit of the Republic, the pre-war years of reform were shaped by active citizenship, though this unprecedented popular activism could easily be idealised in contrast to the catastrophic 'afterwards' of the civil war. The hope of a 'new world' revolved around popular representation and solidarity and associated sites of collective identity, including the socialist meeting places (Casas del Pueblo) where laic schools were often established. These were supported by progressive elements of the fractured middle classes, many of the younger among them active in the PSOE youth militia. Family events, such as workers' picnics on Sundays, celebrations of May Day, with red flags flying, affirmed these values and there were frequent clashes with other middle-class youths, mobilised by Catholic organisations such as the JAP, which represented those with property to whom power would return with the war.[33]

The politics of civil war, 1936–9

Civil war can be defined as violent conflict between parties subject to a common authority at the outset of political crisis and 'of such dimensions that its incidence will affect the exercise or structure of authority in

---

[31] Francisco Marcos Hernández, *La generación perdida: Murcia, Valencia y Barcelona (1926–1950)* (Barcelona, 2005), pp. 60–1.

[32] Richards, 'Ideology and the Psychology'. On children remembering church burning, see also Morales and Pereira, *Memoria*, p. 127; Borràs, *Los que no hicimos*, p. 127. See also Josefina Rodríguez Aldecoa, *Los niños de la guerra* (Madrid, 1983), p. 12; Jesús Fernández Sánchez in Aldecoa, *Niños*, p. 66.

[33] Francisco de Luis Martín and Luis Arias González, 'Los "templos obreros": funciones, simbología y rituales de las Casas del Pueblo Socialistas en España (1900–1936)', *Cuadernos de Historia de España*, LXXVI, 2000, 273–300; Francisco de Luis, *Cincuenta años de cultura obrera en España, 1890–1940* (Madrid, 1994), pp. 263–83. For an idyllic pre-war (often childhood) vision, see e.g., Elordi (ed.), *Años difíciles*, pp. 302–5. Also, pp. 33, 38, 273–4; Arturo Barea, *The Forging of a Rebel: The Clash* (London, 1984 (1946)), p. 87.

society'.[34] The regime crisis precipitated in Spain by the rebel military coup in July 1936 was only imperfectly resolved by arming the masses, to be rapidly and loosely grouped under the banner of Workers' and Peasants' Anti-Fascist Militias. The incumbent government retained the largest cities with their substantial working-class populations, but this advantage was only relative because the urban centres were also strongholds of the Popular Front's main ideological opponents, rightist monarchists and Catholics, many linked by profession to the institutions of the pre-1931 state, who were suspected of undermining the Republic. The government's defenders in Madrid were diverted towards bloody purges of 'enemies', and the Republic's own divisions made protection of the citizenry in general difficult. Civil servants, judges, the police, all seen as representatives of bourgeois order, became suspects, and the judicial corps was virtually dismantled after the military uprising.[35] Many judges were arrested, killed or fled in fear. Even in the Basque Country, where there had been no revolutionary outburst, an order was announced to replace judges who were suspected of being anti-Republican with those who were loyal to the regime.[36] In order to ensure the security and defence of the besieged state, the police were reorganised by a decree issued on 5 August 1936. An earlier edict announced the dismissal of civil servants who had cooperated with the 'subversive movement' or were 'enemies of the government'.[37]

The first few months of the conflict witnessed proportionately the greatest incidence of communal violence during the three years of war. Power devolved towards political militias in both loyalist and rebel zones, though a crucial distinction must be made. In areas where the military rebellion quickly took control, right-wing militias were supplemented by insurgent armed forces and police who shared the same 'purifying' objectives and participated in ad hoc violent repression. This contrasted with loyalist zones where the relation between state forces and militias was fraught with mistrust and confusion of aims. The impact of the coup here was to diminish or even to paralyse state organs of public order and

[34] Andrew C. Janos, 'Authority and Violence: The Political Framework of Internal War', in Harry Eckstein (ed.), *Internal War* (New York, 1964), p. 130. See also Peter Waldmann, 'Societies in Civil War', in *Sociologus*, 49, supplement 1 (1999) *Dynamics of Violence*, ed. Georg Elwert, Stephan Feuchtwang and Dieter Neubert, p. 61; Stathis Kalyvas, *The Logic of Violence in Civil Wars* (Cambridge, 2006), p. 5.

[35] Testimony of wartime public prosecutor in Madrid, Fraser, *Blood*, pp. 177–8.

[36] Germán Rueda Hernanz, 'Suspensión de jueces y fiscales municipales por ideología política, Vizcaya, 1936', in Ministerio de Cultura, *Justicia en guerra* (Madrid, 1990), pp. 167–9. See decree on municipal judges, 15 August 1936, *Gaceta de Madrid*, 229, 16 August 1936.

[37] *Gaceta*, 220, 7 August 1936, p. 1,108; *Gaceta*, 204, 22 July 1936, p. 770.

their capacity to control violence against those deemed to be supportive of the military rebellion. The short-term objective of the rebels was to secure territory and pacify the potentially hostile rearguard; longer term, and developing out of this immediate aim, the desire was to exorcise, once and for all, the threat posed by leftist and liberal ideas and to purge society of their associated organisations, leaders and activists. Selective violence on a mass scale, designed to cower the population and gain control of regions and cities, took the form of a collective liquidation of the Republican rank and file, as witnessed, for example, in the massacre in the bull ring of Badajoz in mid August 1936.[38] Officers of the rebel army, used to colonial war, viewed prisoners not as producers but merely as a hindrance to be liquidated. A more covert strategy at a 'micro' level was based on privately generated intelligence through denunciation and was seen as equally rational since it would 'cleanse' communities and create such fear as to deter defections to 'the enemy' (in local terms, a category effectively created by the coup itself).[39] At a local level, the civil war presented the opportunity for a violent backlash against Republican legislation on, for example, land redistribution (including reclamation of usurped rights to common land) and education. In many communities, kinship relations would be fractured by political mobilisation and class conflict.[40] In a small town in rural Valladolid, the visiting son of a locally noted Republican, a member of Azaña's party, Izquierda Republicana, was executed by Falangist militiamen in August 1936 largely because his father had helped enforce the laws introduced by the Republican government relating to communal taxation.[41] His was by no means a unique case.[42] The son of an executed Republican mayor in a small Badajoz village recalled in the late 1970s from 'cultured' Barcelona, where there was an organised working-class movement boosted by thousands of rural migrants, how 'in a community without culture many people changed sides: "Ah, I'm a socialist, or I'm this, or I'm that"'. When villagers wanted to kill the parish priest, his father the mayor had intervened, arguing for maintaining a legal sense of order. Later, however, his father would be killed by 'the same *señores* he had served all his life'.[43] Amid fear

---

[38] On 'exemplary' violence, Francisco Espinosa Maestre, *La justicia de Queipo* (Seville, 2000); and on Badajoz, see Espinosa Maestre, *Columna de la muerte.*

[39] On defections: Gil, *Lejos*, p. 150.

[40] Recollection articulated in 1979: Jaume Botey Vallès, *Cinquanta-quatre relats d'immigració* (Barcelona, 1986), p. 69; Gil, *Lejos*, p. 448; Collier, *Socialists*, p. 31.

[41] Personal testimony, Sabina de la Cruz, 'Una familia rota; una sociedad truncada', in Emilio Silva (ed.), *La memoria de los olvidados* (Valladolid, 2004), pp. 79–80.

[42] See also Lucea Ayala, *Dispuestos a intervenir*, pp. 372–98; Preston, *Spanish Holocaust*, *passim.*

[43] Botey Vallès, *Relats*, pp. 74–6.

and hunger, opinion in an amorphous town or village which had formerly been superficially 'Republicanised' could just as rapidly accommodate and even support the newly imposed order which superseded the Republic.

In loyalist zones, many militiamen and women and those who favoured social improvement believed the moment had come to overthrow the old regime and its pillars of support. The violence of local revolutions would therefore be accompanied by appropriation and collectivisation of property, beginning with the land and goods of absentee property-owners. In urban centres, the feeling of strength of the masses became intoxicating and the sense of compression of time and space, noted at the time by psychologists, would later be recalled by participants: 'Revolutions move fast [...] Days are like hours, and months like days.'[44] Doubts were swept away as 'the people' took control of public space. Everyday symbols of the social and political status quo became the focus of the theatre of revolution. Street names and dress codes were changed: the former invoked Republican heroes and ideals, while the latter banished hats and neckties, replacing 'bourgeois' apparel with 'egalitarian' overalls and red revolutionary neckerchiefs. Revolutionary gestures were often violent: the imperative of display (sometimes of human bodies, dead or alive), the desire for desecration, the revolutionary purification of public space, and the carnivalesque inversion of Catholic values and rituals were performative expressions which dramatised the corruption of the old order.[45] More rationally, in Republican cities the churches were closed to worship and were put to use as shelters for refugees, storehouses, or blood donation centres.[46] In early October the mass meeting of the JSU in Málaga attracted a large number of young militiawomen who had been discouraged from fighting at the front but who played a prominent public role in giving talks on educational and health matters as well as on politics and mobilisation.[47] At the first PCE rally for women in the city, only weeks before its fall in February 1937, emphasis was placed on shared sacrifices for the benefit of combatants and on justification of the struggle. One female activist of the JSU declared how 'bourgeois

---

[44] A POUM activist in Fraser, *Blood*, p. 141. See also Emilio Mira, 'Psicología de la conducta revolucionaria', *Universidad de La Habana*, September–December 1939, 43–59; Richards, 'Biology and Morality in the Spanish Civil War: Psychiatrists, Revolution and Women Prisoners in Málaga', *Contemporary European History*, 14, 1, 2001, 418–21.

[45] Bruce W. Lincoln, 'Revolutionary Exhumations in Spain, July 1936', *Comparative Studies in Society and History*, 27, 1985, 241–60.

[46] For the case of Málaga: *El Popular*, 12 January 1937, p. 4; *Vida Nueva*, 12 September 1936, p. 1; *Julio*, 22 January 1937, p. 1; 25 January, p. 3.

[47] *Eco Popular*, 5 October 1936, p. 3.

humiliation' of women had been aggravated by the Church, even though 'Christ had been the first socialist in the world'.[48] There was a popular perception of what constituted the genuine word of Christ and that this was not preached by the Spanish Church.[49] The extent to which the Church might favour progress and social improvement (according to Christ's teaching) would become clearer for some when as migrant labourers they left rural Spain for the city in the war's aftermath and were ministered to by 'worker priests'.[50] Whether fundamentally an act of faith as part of a critique of the Church or not, the bonfires of devotional objects and the desecration of churches were imprinted in memory in ways which could not be controlled. Once communities were divided by the process the coup had set in train, the performative aspects of Republican anti-clerical identity which had signified a sense of change after April 1931 became signifiers of 'us and them' boundaries to those who were resistant to greater freedom and modernisation and led to violence against those who had supported violent acts against the Church.

In cities, towns and villages which remained in Republican hands, the boundary effect operated in the opposite direction. Religious images and literature kept in the home became incriminating and would often be destroyed by those who possessed them to avoid discovery. Allegiance to one side or the other was not uniformly correlated to social class, and many were uncommitted, but there quickly arose a generalised sense of fear, and people became used to speaking in a low voice. A working-class woman who was a child in Madrid in 1936 recalled the sense of insecurity: 'in those days everything made you scared'.[51] Many people avoided leaving their homes in the besieged capital at night in dread of the *paseos* – 'being taken for a ride', a euphemism for extra-legal execution – and during the day for fear of the shelling, and in Madrid it was difficult to move between neighbourhoods without a pass issued by the militias.[52]

---

[48] *El Popular*, 12 January 1937, p. 4.

[49] On popular anti-clericalism, see, e.g., Manuel Delgado, 'Anticlericalismo, espacio y poder: la destrucción de los rituales católicos, 1931–39', *Ayer*, 27 (1997), 149–80; Julio de la Cueva, 'Religious Persecution, Anticlerical Tradition and Revolution: On Atrocities against the Clergy during the Spanish Civil War', *Journal of Contemporary History*, 33, 3 (1998), 355–69; Mary Vincent, 'The Keys of the Kingdom: Religious Violence in the Spanish Civil War, July–August 1936', in Ealham and Richards (eds.), *Splintering*, pp. 68–89.

[50] E.g. Morales and Pereira, *Memoria*, p. 128. See also chapters 6 and 8.

[51] Elordi (ed.), *Años difíciles*, pp. 40–1. See also pp. 92, 170; Javier Cervera, *Madrid en guerra: la ciudad clandestina* (Madrid, 2006); Pedro Montoliú Camps, *Madrid en la guerra civil* (Madrid, 1999), pp. 35, 183, 224, 282, 431; Valencia, see Marcos Hernández, *La generación perdida*, p. 62; Rioja, Gil, *Lejos*, p. 169.

[52] Carlos González Posada, *Diario de la revolución y de la guerra (1936–1939)*, ed. Miguel Ángel del Arco Blanco (Granada, 2011).

While public authority was undermined first by the July 1936 coup and then by the inchoate popular revolution, the threat to those perceived to be fifth columnists would be greatly intensified by the military onslaught of the rebel forces. Francoist air raids which killed civilians in Bilbao, Málaga, Valencia, Cartagena and Madrid itself produced a violent popular backlash in the form of uncontrolled mob executions of rightist prisoners who, in spite of protests from Republican authority figures, were taken from their prison cells and murdered as retribution. In the capital this reaction was given added impetus as information filtered through about rebel atrocities in other parts of the country. During the night and early morning of 22–23 August 1936 several dozen rightist military men and political figures held in the city's Modelo (Model) prison were executed when militiamen, buoyed up by the crowd's anger at news of the massacre of hundreds of Republicans in the bullring of Badajoz a week before, took control of the gaol.[53] The Modelo killings, widely reported in the Nationalist zone and later constructed as 'martyrdom' by the Franco regime, would become a focus for memory in the post-war years.[54]

In November 1936 the incapacitated Republican government left the capital for Valencia, certain that Madrid was about to fall to the insurgents, although the city would not in the end succumb until March 1939. Inhabitants of the predominantly working-class neighbourhoods to the south-west of the city, upon which the rebel advance was aimed, believed that the defence was being mounted by 'Russians', a reference to the prominence of Soviet aid, amid growth of the PCE and the significance of the International Brigades in the capital's defence.[55] Madrid had been left in the hands of the remnants of the army, the political militias, and Soviet military advisers, including the NKVD, which would play a significant role in persuading some of the Madrid Defence Council that ruthless measures were necessary and which would be implicated in the notorious mass killing of political prisoners at Paracuellos del Jarama and Torrejón de Ardoz during November and December 1936.[56] The approximately 2,700 victims, viewed as a potential fifth column should

---

[53] Some of those killed in the Modelo prison were conservative Republicans, several of whom had been imprisoned by the Republican authorities in an attempt to protect them from the revolutionary violence. See, e.g., Fraser, *Blood*, pp. 175–6; *Guerra y vicisitudes*, pp. 128–30.

[54] See, e.g., G. Arsenio de Izaga, *Los presos de Madrid: recuerdos e impresiones de un cautivo en la España roja* (Madrid, 1940). See also Chapter 3.

[55] See, e.g., Elordi (ed.), *Años difíciles*, p. 94; Xosé Manoel Núñez Seixas, *¡Fuera el invasor!* (Madrid, 2006), pp. 143–5.

[56] Ángel Viñas, *El Escudo de la República* (Barcelona, 2007), pp. 35–87.

the invaders enter the city, were largely middle-class monarchists and Catholics and included several important political figures and more than a thousand soldiers, deemed to be a threat in the event of the collapse of the city's defence.[57]

Whilst rumours about these murders spread, optimism about the Republic's survival was expressed through the iconography and myths of Communism. The revolution adopted the rhetoric of others, as all such inchoate socio-political movements do, particularly at a moment when these 'others' were able to depict themselves as the only lifeline of the revolution, becoming signifiers of unity and survival, as well as expressing specifically political objectives. During the siege, a demonstration of two hundred thousand women took place in November 1936 calling for the mobilisation of the population in the city's defence; portrait placards of Marx, Lenin and Stalin, as well as the hammer and sickle, were vividly to the fore. As in other cities, images of the PCE leader Dolores Ibárruri were also carried aloft: the defiant stance of La Pasionaria would be invoked for years after in people's homes as an example to children of 'the decency of labour' and 'the struggle for liberty' by parents who had lived through the war.[58] Gradually, and especially from May 1937, in order to maintain public order the Republican government, in uneasy alliance with the PCE–PSUC, clawed back control of its monopoly of coercion from trade union militias and revolutionary committees, and the level of violence against right-wing 'enemies of the revolution' declined dramatically. The war was thereby prolonged by organised military resistance, though by this point the rebel state had begun to establish itself militarily, domestically and, in contrast to the Republic, internationally.[59]

In the government zone, even as the social revolution itself was reined in, the symbols of the Republic were increasingly supplanted by revolutionary myths of, for example, 'the Proletariat of the *Patria*', 'Petrograd', and '1917', which surrounded increasingly rationalised military organisation ('the People's Army') and state-building political aims ('the National Revolution'). Those fighting for the rebel side, meanwhile, were

---

[57] Preston, *Spanish Holocaust*, pp. 341–80; Ian Gibson, *Paracuellos: como fue* (Barcelona, 1983).

[58] E.g., a daughter's memories of her mother, a Vizcayan fish seller, killed in an air raid during the war: Elordi (ed.), *Años difíciles*, pp. 119–20. Also María de la Luz Mejías Correa, *Así fue pasando el tiempo: memorias de una miliciana extremeña* (Seville, 2006); Ángela Reñones, 'Un crisol para mis recuerdos', in María Guadalupe Pedrero and Concha Piñero (eds.), *Tejiendo recuerdos de la España de ayer* (Madrid, 2006), p. 147. For wartime use of the Pasionaria image in Málaga, see *El Popular*, 8 November 1936, p. 3.

[59] Graham, *Spanish Republic at War*.

assured in devotional booklets designed for the trenches that their struggle was a religious crusade: 'You are enlisted in the Army of Christ. And you are fighting against the Anti-Christs of today.' The mothers of Nationalist soldiers were emulating the Mother of Christ and the soldiers themselves were sustained by comparison with his ordeal: 'Meditate upon the various scenes of that night and that day in which Christ wished to purify all suffering before taking leave of his mortal life. Meditate on the flagellation, the beatings, the way of the cross, the dreadful torment, the hunger, the fatigue, the thirst.'[60]

Beside what were for some of those who fought for the rebels the consoling aspects of the war as 'crusade', including Catholic mass prayed for the souls of those lost, there was also a decidedly threatening consequence for 'the other side': Republicans who found themselves in zones 'liberated' by the insurgents. Here, ideology played an important role in a coalescing of collective resentment of the political and moral transgressions of an enemy now imagined as 'the infidel'. Justification of the 'holy war' to 'save Spain' would allow the rebels to depict themselves as the Catholic nation in arms as well as making violent activation of preexisting social cleavages between believers and unbelievers, or good and evil, easier. The symbolism of the 'crusade' would combine with the demands of conservative society (both elite and humble) to legitimate the terror of conquest. In Seville it was reported that the mineworkers of Rio Tinto who had attempted to attack the city had 'died in a Christian way, assisted spiritually'. In conquered Santiago de Compostela a great procession was arranged in which the silver reliquary reputed to contain the remains of Saint James was carried upon a Nationalist gun carriage. The 'crusade' also produced conversions: it was reported with some satisfaction that a young Muslim amongst the Moroccan troops fighting with the Carlists in Pamplona had asked to receive baptismal waters.[61]

Christian charity and acts of conscience were not unheard of, though they were swamped by the repressive essence of the 'crusade' and what were perceived by the nascent Nationalist state to be the exigencies of power. As a young priest, Vicente Enrique y Tarancón, who would later become figurehead of the social and political realignment of the Spanish Church during the 1970s, had believed unhesitatingly in the 'crusade' and, during the conflict's aftermath, in reconciliation through the New State. His closest

---

[60] Karl Stahli, *Cristo en las trincheras* (Bilbao, 1938), pp. 25–6, 51–2. For Nationalist soldiers' wartime idolisation of their mothers, e.g., Bullón and Diego, *Historias*, p. 84. Comparison with Republican zone: p. 94. Also Mary Vincent, '"The Martyrs and the Saints": Masculinity and the Construction of the Francoist Crusade', *History Workshop Journal*, 47 (1999), 90.

[61] *El Correo de Andalucía*, 4 September 1936, p. 10; 8 September 1936, p. 4.

colleagues had been amongst the murdered priests and his own devout father had been destroyed psychologically by the war. The first priest to enter the town of Vinaroz (Castellón) following its 'liberation' in 1938, Tarancón would be required to administer to prisoners awaiting execution, which he and colleagues carried out with sensitivity.[62] Many years later he had not forgotten the words of one of the executed, an educated man, who accepted the company of the priest but warned that nothing would be achieved by his administering to him and issued a profound and tragic condemnation of the Church: 'I have lost the faith with which my blessed mother inculcated me, by word and through example.'[63] The Church had been incapable of being a mother in the most difficult times, though it would enjoy a privileged position in the 1940s and 1950s, despite the fact that many, then and later, considered it to share responsibility for the war and its violence. During the most conflictive moments of his later life, particularly in the early 1970s when Tarancón would be vilified by some intransigent Catholics who considered his support for democratisation a betrayal, he would recall the condemned man of 1938 who in the end had received communion 'with devotion' before he was executed.

Intimate violence and memory

Following the military rebellion in the summer of 1936, there had been intense mobilisation in rural Castile and Navarra, as well as in other parts of the country, for the assault upon the central state; large numbers of Catholic and conservative tenant farmers and smallholders became militiamen or were incorporated into various ad hoc public-order columns and forces of occupation which were active in the home-front process of 'pacification', often of 'neighbours'.[64] The mobilised were likely to have been associated formerly with anti-Republican political organisations: the fascist Falange, the Carlist Requeté, the monarchists of Renovación Española, or the CEDA and its violent youth movement (JAP), which had been at the heart of opposition to the Republic's reforms. Their

---

[62] Enrique y Tarancón, *Recuerdos de juventud*, pp. 262–72.   [63] *Ibid.*, pp. 268–70.

[64] See, e.g., Ugarte Tellería, *Nueva Covadonga*, pp. 145–49; Martín Jiménez, *Guerra civil en Valladolid*; Francisco Cobo Romero and Teresa María Ortega López, *Franquismo y posguerra en Andalucía oriental* (Granada, 2005), pp. 106, 117, 125–6; Santiago Vega Sombría, *De la esperanza a la persecución: la represión franquista en la provincia de Segovia* (Barcelona, 2005); Isaac Rilova Pérez, *Guerra civil y violencia política en Burgos (1936–1939)* (Burgos, 2001); Ian Gibson, *Granada en 1936 y el asesinato de Federico García Lorca* (Barcelona, 1986), pp. 107–18; interview with Raimundo Fernández Cuesta, 'Los falangistas realizamos el trabajo sucio: fusilar', in *Diario 16*, supplement *Historia del Franquismo*, 1 (1984–5), 23; Dionisio Ridruejo, *Escrito en España* (Buenos Aires, 1962), pp. 91–8.

earlier political education was paramilitary, and myths of violence were prominent in their ideology. Violence was exalted as a 'mission', as sacrificial and as instilling 'national vitality'.[65] It was recalled that the founder of the Falange, José Antonio Primo de Rivera, executed by the Republican authorities in November 1936, had insisted that the young who repudiated the party's collective objectives 'will be excluded from our generation, as microbes are excluded from a healthy body'.[66] The violence employed by the insurgents during the 'liberation' of communities would be greater than that committed in the name of the Republic and the revolution which had preceded rebel capture in many communities where often there had been no armed conflict as such.[67] In Aragón, as far as the available sources show, some 8,500 men and women were killed during the period 1936–46. The majority of the victims fell during the first months of the war in areas where there had been little or no fighting. Looking at small rural communities, which were typical of sites where violence was unleashed, the example of Los Olivos (Huelva) illustrates how Republican violence as a response to the military rebellion – in this instance, the burning of the church – was greatly outweighed by the violence of the rebel occupation of the pueblo when 12 per cent of adult males were killed during the first year.[68]

The struggle for loyalty following the initial fracturing of legitimised authority in July 1936 was thus fought out between armed parties to the conflict producing pressure on civilians to demonstrate their allegiance. Territorial boundaries were fluid, running through communities rather than around them. Crossing these sinuous lines, or finding oneself on the wrong side when the balance of power shifted, was dangerous and likely to activate violence self-legitimated by reference to ascriptive 'us and

[65] Richards, *Time of Silence*, p. 28.   [66] *Arriba España*, 14 February 1937.

[67] Ignacio Martín Jiménez, *Guerra civil en Valladolid* (Valladolid, 2000), p. 182; Vega Sombría, *De la esperanza*, esp. pp. 388–91; Julián Chaves Palacios, *La represión en la provincia de Cáceres durante la guerra civil (1936–1939)* (Cáceres, 1995), pp. 32–6, 317–21; Antonio Hernández García, *La represión en La Rioja durante la guerra civil* (Logroño, 1984), vol. I, pp. 25, 28–9.

[68] Collier, *Socialists*, p. 146. Also, e.g., Francisco Espinosa Maestre, *Guerra civil en Huelva* (Huelva, 1996), p. 16; Julián Casanova et al., *El pasado oculto: fascismo y violencia en Aragón (1936–1939)* (Madrid, 1992), pp. 42–66, 91–115, 135–50, 175–92. See also Altaffaylla Kultur Taldea, *Navarra, 1936: de la esperanza al terror* (Tafalla, 1986; 2nd edn, 2003); Alicia Domínguez Pérez, *El verano que trajo un largo invierno: la represión político-social durante el primer franquismo en Cádiz (1936–1945)*, 2 vols. (Cádiz, 2005), vol. I, pp. 74–103; Luís Lamela García, *A Coruña, 1936: memoria convulsa de una represión* (La Coruña, 2002), pp. 118–21; Jesús María Palomares Ibañez, *La guerra civil en Palencia: la eliminación de los contrarios* (Palencia, 2002), pp. 121–44; Rilova Pérez, *Guerra civil y violencia política en Burgos*; Luís Castro Berrojo, *Capital de la cruzada: Burgos durante la guerra civil* (Barcelona, 2006), pp. 211–22.

them' categories. Those who were the targets of the violence were in effect placed forcibly outside the new-state-in-embryo, in a condition of what would become legal limbo. Public behaviour according to political conscience in the era before the war could have fateful consequences once the conflict was raging. Republicans 'with ideas', those who had been politically active or who supported measures of social improvement, became particular targets.[69] Chances of survival as communities were overcome by the rebels and the extent to which the targeted were ostracised or reincorporated into communities depended on the dynamics of the local rebuilding of authority in the wake of 'liberation' in the name of the Francoist *patria*. In these areas, pre-war elites, linked through networks of economic and social power, collaborated in the elimination of Republican authorities, class enemies, liberal intellectuals, 'troublemakers', and recalcitrant employees, those on landowners' 'blacklists'.[70] Regaining political sovereignty was complemented by the recapturing of land collectivised during the wartime revolution; for powerful landowners this represented a localised or regional regaining of territorial sovereignty.[71]

Violence therefore depended on the dynamic relationship between pre-existing elites, military power brokers and social collaboration. In many communities, those who had access to weapons and were able to use them with impunity effectively *became* the state.[72] A Falangist activist in Granada complained in December 1938 that the 'most elemental norms of justice are violated [because] elements have come to power thinking that the enjoyment of their authority is the ultimate purpose of the Movement'.[73] The clearest case of rebel 'warlordism' was produced in Seville under the commander of the army of the south, Gonzalo

---

[69] E.g. Richard Barker, *El largo trauma de un pueblo andaluz* (Seville, 2007), pp. 109–10; Gil, *Lejos*, pp. 220–1; Castilla del Pino, *Casa del olivo*, pp. 106–7; Fraser, *Blood*, pp. 163–5. Particularly amongst women, it was possible to attend Mass and actively to support the Republic, though this did not necessarily save one from insurgent retribution.

[70] See, e.g., Ángela Cenarro, *Cruzados y camisas azules: los orígenes del franquismo en Aragón, 1936–1945* (Zaragoza, 1997); Antonio-Miguel Bernal, 'Resignación de los campesinos andaluces: la resistencia pasiva durante el franquismo', in Isidro Sánchez Manuel Ortiz and David Ruiz (eds.), *España franquista: Causa General y actitudes sociales ante la dictadura* (Castilla-La Mancha, 1993), pp. 146–8.

[71] Guzmán de Alfarache, *18 de julio: historia del Glorioso Alzamiento de Sevilla* (Seville, 1937); Rafael de Medina, Duque de Medinaceli, *Tiempo Pasado* (Seville, 1971), pp. 31–44.

[72] For a comparable wartime example, see Jan T. Gross, *Revolution from Abroad: The Soviet Conquest of Poland's Western Ukraine and Western Belorussia* (Princeton, 1988), and for the particular point: p. 119.

[73] Letter to Julián Pemartín (Sub-Secretaria de FET, Burgos), 21 December 1938, AGA, SGM, Secretaría Política, Vicesecretaria General, sig. 52/46, caja 12.

Queipo de Llano, who ruled the region more or less autonomously during and after the war through ruthless violence and populist rhetoric, both in pursuit of personal power and in the interests of suppressing liberalism.[74] Through the issuing of certificates of good conduct, relatively lowly individuals could also become the arbiters of people's lives, though they could only do so by reference to the pre-existing ideological patterning of collective identities mapped out by political conflict between 1931 and July 1936.[75] The division of those who were 'supporters' (*adictos*) and those who were 'suspect' was nonetheless often determined by private initiatives and opportunism which involved denunciations of neighbour by neighbour.[76] Few families, especially in rural areas, remained unaffected by the fear of this intimate violence.

Political denunciation – the volunteered provision of information by the population at large about instances of disapproved behaviour[77] – became a key means of co-opting support for the rebels. In the extreme circumstances of a fractured state and a powerfully repressive ideology,

---

[74] Manuel Barrios, *El ultimo virrey* (Barcelona, 1978). On warlords, David Keen, *The Economic Functions of Violence in Civil Wars* (London, 1998).

[75] The cultural anthropologist Mary Douglas labelled as 'grid' characteristics the social distinctions applied to individuals according to accepted community roles, rules, rights and duties. These she contrasted with group boundaries, where 'group' is defined on immutable bases of collective identity, such as race, region or religion, which overlaid grid characteristics. Mary Douglas, *Natural Symbols: Explorations in Cosmology* (London, 1996 (1973)), pp. 54–64. 'Grid' patterns in Spain were destabilised in the 1930s by attempted social and legal reform, accelerated modernisation, and political mobilisation. Obstruction of these processes caused political polarisation and tension. When the military coup triggered civil war, 'group' distinctions defined boundaries and, combined with reference (often by denouncers) to pre-war grid violations and recriminations, fuelled the violence. The structure of group cleavages was also primarily 'cumulative' rather than 'cross-cutting': the principal group divisions, based on religion and social class, reinforced one another closely. Roland Paris, *At War's End* (Cambridge, 2004), pp. 170–1.

[76] For 'privatised' power, see, e.g., Alfonso Lazo, *Retrato de fascismo rural en Sevilla* (Seville, 1998), p. 59.

[77] For definition of denunciation: Robert Gellately, *The Gestapo and German Society: Enforcing Racial Policy, 1933–1945* (Oxford, 1990), p. 130. For reports of lawlessness and denunciations leading to violence in the early weeks of war in the Republican zone, see, e.g.: on suspicious movement of individuals noticed by doormen in Barcelona, *La Vanguardia*, 22 July 1936; Valladolid, *ABC*, 28 July 1936; unfounded, *ABC*, 1 August 1936; calls to denounce (from the Republican teaching union), *ABC*, 4 August 1936; on formal restriction on militia investigation of denunciations through a political organisation, not individuals, *ABC*, 25 August 1936; similar, in Barcelona, *La Vanguardia*, 30 July 1936, 21 August 1936; calls to denounce abuses of authority of militias in Barcelona, *La Vanguardia*, 23 July 1936; denouncing economic exploitation, *La Vanguardia*, 25 August 1936. For theorisation in case of civil war: Kalyvas, *Logic*, esp. pp. 176–83. See also Sheila Fitzpatrick and Robert Gellately (eds.), *Accusatory Practices: Denunciation in Modern European History, 1789–1989* (Chicago, 1997); André Halimi, *La délation sous l'Occupation* (Paris, 1983).

this led easily to violence.[78] Alignment with the occupiers by taking advantage of the direct access to the coercive apparatus of the state during the repression placed an individual above suspicion. For the rebels, this social reinforcement of the terror was the beginning of a mobilisation of consent through active negation of Republicanism.[79] This political context was essential: denouncing 'enemies' was very publicly encouraged by the 'liberating' authorities and was depicted as a civic duty, as it had also been from an early stage in the Republican zone.[80] Incitement to denounce was a function of regional and local politics. The Head of Public Order in Lérida (Catalonia) published an order in July 1938, as the region was occupied, which succinctly reinforced this: 'Whoever does not denounce those not worthy of forming part of the New State will be considered a poor citizen.'[81]

Not all information came from ordinary citizens; much of it was of a more codified type, including blacklists drawn up by employers and the 'intelligence' (ubiquitous index cards) of rightist political groups, often drawing on quasi-official records. Informal denunciation was, nonetheless, as divisive of community cohesion as the class revenge taken by local pre-war wielders of power and was often a way of positioning for power and other rewards: direct economic gain, and profiting in terms of employment or status.[82] Authorities sought information knowing that what came back was based, in part, on their own doctrine and propaganda: the pathological perceptions constructed by the rebels. In spite of pre-war polarisation, for many victims the extent of the violence and of civil collaboration in it could not have been predicted. Many of the victims had remained in their town or village believing that, although they supported the legally constituted Republic, they had done nothing to be punished for.[83]

One way in which a sense of responsibility for violent acts could be deflected or denied, even many years later, was by locating blame with agents outside the community: 'A man was denounced by people from

---

[78] On the rebel zone: Ángela Cenarro, 'Matar, vigilar y delatar: la quiebra de la sociedad civil durante la guerra y la posguerra en España (1936–1948)', *Historia Social*, 44, 2002, 65–86.

[79] See, e.g., Cobo Romero and Ortega López, *Franquismo*, p. 125.

[80] As such, in the Republican zone, see, e.g., *La Vanguardia*, 22 August 1936.

[81] Mercè Barallat, 'La repressió en la postguerra civil a Lleida', in *El primer franquisme a les terres de Lleida (1938–1950)* (Lérida, 2002), p. 69.

[82] E.g., Francisco Espinosa Maestre, *La guerra civil en Huelva* (Huelva, 1996), pp. 374–8; Gabarda, *Els afusellaments*, pp. 44–50; Francisco Sevillano Calero, 'Consenso y violencia en el "Nuevo Estado" franquista', *Historia Social*, 46, 2003, 159–71.

[83] E.g., Collier, *Socialists*, pp. 154–5; *Imperio* (FE-JONS, Zamora), 6 March 1938; *Noticiero de Soria*, 16 June 1938. Franco's apparently magnanimous term 'those whose hands are not stained with blood' would often appear to be used to refer only to those who fought on the rebel side. E.g. *Imperio*, 2 March 1940.

his own village, but it was always men from another village who seized him and performed the execution';[84] 'outsiders were responsible for the reign of terror, but not without collaboration from within the village'.[85] Another witness suggests the collaborative nature of the purge: 'the first (to be involved) were from outside, but those from here joined in straight away'.[86] When in the early 1970s the historian Ronald Fraser conducted interviews for his masterly oral history of the civil war he found that those who spoke about violent loss of life placed themselves very deliberately at a distance from the killing. Carlists blamed the 'Blue Shirts' (Falangists); right-wing prisoners were killed not by local labourers but by 'a few men, possibly outsiders, who managed to escape during the night'; aristocratic Francoists were 'opposed to the repression' and 'did what (they) could to prevent it'. A witness who had supported the right was typical: 'our situation was precarious; had there been any weakness, etcetera [...] It is a sad law of war.'[87] Violence and denunciation unleashed by the coup saw the breaking of taboos in small communities and this was one reason for the enveloping silence in the war's aftermath. For decades the truth was obscured by perpetrators, with the complicity of many others, partly to safeguard impunity but also for fear of the psychological and moral consequences of revisiting the past.

From an early stage of the war, rebel authorities took the lead in expropriating the property of the enemy. It was not unusual for the homes of those killed in the repression to be appropriated, and forced political 'donations' and the imposition of 'fines' by Falangists were common.[88] As state power was established, informal punishment based on privatised local power interacted with formal law in the shape of dictatorial decrees. The Franco state created an archive in the aftermath of the war by one such decree of 26 April 1940, to collect and collate evidence as the foundation of a collective lawsuit against those deemed responsible for Republican wartime 'crimes against Spain'.[89] The

---

[84] Aceves, *Social Change*, p. 9.

[85] Collier, *Socialists*, p. 20. See also pp. 152, 162–3; Gil, *Lejos*, pp. 152, 438, 443; Jan Mansvelt Beck, *The Rise of a Subsidized Periphery in Spain* (Amsterdam, 1988), pp. 46–8.

[86] Lucea Ayala, *Dispuestos a intervenir*, p. 385. Also José Sánchez Jiménez, *Vida rural y mundo contemporáneo* (Barcelona, 1976), pp. 242, 248.

[87] Fraser, *Blood*, pp. 122, 132, 158, 161, 167–70, 202.

[88] See, e.g., Vega Sombría, *De la esperanza*, pp. 153–5, 157–60; Ian Gibson, *The Assassination of Federico García Lorca* (London, 1979), pp. 166, 170, 240; Graham, *War and Its Shadow*, p. 60; on wealthy Falangists, Gerald Brenan, *The Face of Spain* (Harmondsworth, 1965 (1950)), pp. 84–5. On the opportunistic purge of rent collectors in Barcelona: Fraser, *Blood*, p. 152.

[89] *Boletín del Estado* (*BOE*), no. 125, 4 May 1940. For published findings: Ministerio de Justicia, *Causa general: la dominación roja en España. Avance de la información instruída por el Ministerio público* (Madrid, 1943). The Causa bolstered the founding myth of the

procedure of this so-called Causa General became a formalised means by which the language of negative emotion applied to the Republic became the common currency of officials and sympathetic social and political beneficiaries. The effect in such a deeply fragmented society was a virtual hysteria of suspicion; many accusations in the Causa files were based on vague stories, vengeance and rumour and there was of course no such opportunity for accounting for the crimes committed against Republicans by the rebel side.[90]

The standard of evidence in cases against supporters of the Republic was invariably low. In the city of Málaga, which fell to the rebels in February 1937, the calls for denunciations played on emotions as well as the familiar trope of 'purification'. Appealing to instincts of revenge and fears of difference, the local Falange called for 'the criminal lowlife' and the 'badly born' who had caused the streets of the city to 'flow with blood' to be exposed, and the Civil Governor threatened to impose a fine on any person who dared to intervene on behalf of prisoners. In an era of martyrdom there was no place for 'sentimentalism'.[91] Mere opinions were perceived as threats. One young domestic servant was denounced by her well-off employers because, although her behaviour had been 'normal' before the war, during the revolution she 'became an anarchist' and, as was alleged in a written denunciation following 'liberation', had declared that her employers would probably be killed like many others because 'if the situation had been the other way around, they would have been doing the killing'.[92]

Another working-class woman received a prison sentence of 6 years for 'revolutionary excitation' after being denounced as a 'leftist' and for having supported anti-clerical incendiary assaults on her parish church in the Republican years prior to the civil war and later 'displaying happiness' at killings and, like other women, 'celebrating' the expulsion of religious personnel from convents and ecclesiastical residences. Scant evidence had been produced to support these alleged thought crimes. In a sign of the discrimination along the faultlines between 'victors' and 'defeated', this woman was also suspended from holding any public or

---

Franco state, facilitating the purge but also intended to reflect Rousseau's notion of 'the general will'. See George L. Mosse, 'Fascism and the French Revolution', *Journal of Contemporary History*, 24, 1 (1989), 5–6.

[90] Cobo Romero and Ortega López, *Franquismo*, pp. 124, 126.

[91] *Sur-¡Arriba!*, 10, 11, 12 and 19 February, 13 March 1937; *Arriba Española*, 13 February 1937, p. 4; Gil Gómez Bajuelo, *Málaga bajo el dominio rojo* (Cádiz, 1937), p. 51. Also, e.g., Juan Ortiz Villalba, *Sevilla '36: del golpe militar a la guerra civil* (Córdoba, 1998), p. 147.

[92] Archivo de la Prisión Provincial de Málaga (APPM), Expedientes Personales (EP), no. 259, C3, L2. For similar fear (Seville), Barker, *Largo trauma*, p. 87.

private employment, any office or right to aid or social assistance, and, for good measure, the court had noted that she ought to have dedicated herself to 'women's work' rather than involving herself in political matters. Her case, as was automatic for political convicts until 1942, was referred to the Court of Political Responsibilities for the possible order of reparations and confiscation of her property and that of her family.[93] A thirty-year-old woman with four children, and married to a man at the front with government forces, was denounced for showing support for the Republican fighters as they passed through in lorries bound for the front. When the city fell, she left and did not return voluntarily thereafter, behaviour perceived as an unequivocal sign of guilt. Her case typified the way an individual's unexplained absence presented an opportunity for others to 'prove' their loyalty or gain economically through denunciation: a potentially 'victimless' accusatory practice.[94]

While wartime denunciation was a relatively covert form of individual participation in power politics, cathartic rites of conquest were directed publicly (and felt intimately) against individuals who had transgressed the ethics of the idealised 'integrated' community. Gender perceptions were frequently essential to the process. In Spanish tradition, the Virgin Mary was viewed as the ideal of womanhood and women were envisaged in roles which were culturally purifying and socially unifying; social cohesion was perceived by traditionalists as relying on the harmonising (and subordinate) role of women as wives and mothers who were called upon by this doctrine to restrain the political protest of husbands and sons. The transgressions of Republican women therefore made them targets for the violence of rebel state construction during and after the war. The image of the patron of Navarra, Santa María la Real, was publicly processed at the end of August 1936 as a symbol not merely of religious adoration but of harmony between earthly motives and sacred ideals.[95] This idealised function of women was clear in the exhortation of the military governor in Málaga to the Falange's Sección Femenina following the city's liberation in February 1937: 'Educate the next generation, so that our children will suckle purity of the race; so that when you part with them, as the *patria* requires, you will be able to declare with

---

[93] APPM, EP, no. 300, C3, L2.

[94] APPM, EP, no. 262, C3, L2. Also Francisco Moreno Gómez, 'La represión oculta: el gran tabú de la democracia', in Arcángel Bedmar (ed.), *Memoria y olvido sobre la guerra civil y la represión franquista* (Córdoba, 2003), pp. 21–37.

[95] *Diario de Navarra*, 30 August 1936, p. 4. For similar examples, see also 2 September 1936, p. 1; 8 September 1936, p. 6; *El Correo de Andalucía*, 4 September 1936; *Diario de Burgos*, 14 August 1936, p. 2.

pride to the four winds that you are true Spanish women and true Andalusian women.'[96] When individuals were deemed to have transgressed this ideal, cathartic violence targeted on women was publicly acted out in purifying the 'contaminated' community.[97] Influenced by the rebels' nationalist ideology and seeking justification in the collective trauma suffered during the Republic and revolution, previously displaced conservative sections of the community, or opportunists seeking to benefit, turned on Republican neighbours in ritualised displays of violence; this was punishment 'performed', a dramatisation of the ideology of nation building which in the process imposed upon the punished a silence which would last for years.[98]

As towns and villages were occupied by advancing rebel forces, many women who had supported the Republic (or associated with men who had) were singled out, usually by Falangists and local landowners, for punishment which included administering castor oil (as a 'purgative'), head shaving and ritual procession through the streets, including those in mourning or with babes in arms, for public vilification. The intention was that the community would be brought together, at the expense of Republican scapegoats, by implicitly projecting its own collective commitment to the national ideal and sense of guilt or shame for having allowed cohesion to break down.[99] Falangists would often insist on attendance to witness the spectacle and the Sección Femenina and youth and children's movements would take part. The rituals of violence reinforced the urgency of demonstrating loyalty. Child affiliations to the Falange youth movement were reported to have increased markedly following collectively witnessed executions of Republicans in one southern town on the feast day of the patron saint of the pueblo, the Virgen de las Virtudes. Decades later, people would recall such scenes though none

---

[96] *Sur-¡Arriba!*, 17 February 1937.

[97] On catharsis in its original medical sense – as a physical purging of the body after poisoning or sickness – see Pedro Laín Entralgo, *Therapy of the Word in Classical Antiquity* (New Haven, 1970), pp. 187–9; Andrzej Szczeklik, *Catharsis: On the Art of Medicine* (Chicago, 2008).

[98] René Girard, *Violence and the Sacred* (London, 1988).

[99] E.g., Vinyes et al., *Niños perdidos*, pp. 90–1; Botey Vallès, *Relats*, p. 75; Jordi Roca i Girona, *De la pureza a la maternidad: la construcción del género femenino en la postguerra española* (Madrid, 1996), p. 30; Bullón and Diego, *Historias*, pp. 154, 178, 189–90; Francisco Moreno Gómez, *Córdoba en la posguerra* (Córdoba, 1987), p. 304; Sánchez Jiménez, *Vida rural*, p. 247; Giuliana Di Febo, *Resistencia y movimiento de mujeres en España, 1936–1976* (Barcelona, 1979), pp. 96–7. For comparative cases, see, e.g., Fabrice Virgili, *Shorn Women: Gender and Punishment in Liberation France* (Oxford, 2002); Monika Diderichs, 'Stigma and Silence: Dutch Women, German Soldiers, and Their Children', in Kjersti Ericsson and Eva Simonsen (eds.), *Children of World War II: The Hidden Enemy Legacy* (Oxford, 2005), pp. 151–64.

would admit to participation.[100] The personally traumatic nature of memories of these events was considerable, and many scapegoated victims were among those who moved away to the relative anonymity of the city during the early post-war years.[101]

The experience of the town of Lodosa in the area of Estella (Navarra) which fell to the rebels rapidly after the military rebellion was one where gender and re-establishment of state power came together. Composed of Carlist militiamen (*requetés*), these volunteers understood 'liberation' as a process of social regeneration, an amalgam of 'Christian charity' and 'terror and panic'.[102] The local head of the Requeté, lauded as 'an exemplary patriot, good Christian and valiant soldier', had overseen 'extraordinary and admirable works of apostleship and redemption' combining 'rigorous punishment' and 'convincing with tenderness'.

Many old and young women who have had long tongues [been gossips], and have created uproar amongst the communist crowd, have had their hair completely cut off and been made to walk through the streets followed by the people and the gibberish of that infantile flock was forcibly replaced by cries of 'Viva España!', 'Down with the traitors!', 'Spain yes, Russia no!'

Similar punishments were inflicted in other nearby towns and the area of Estella saw 761 individuals killed in the repression that accompanied 'liberation'. Afterwards, 'visits' were made to 'communist' men and women to persuade them to live 'peacefully and honourably'. The result had been an increase in attendance at Mass and Catholic marriages and baptisms, some of the recently born being sponsored as *padrino* (god-father) by the Requeté leader. The rural tradition of a local *señorito* being given this role, usually at the suggestion of the priest, was thus more blatantly politicised than ever.

Years later, some of those who had lived through the ordeal of the war recalled particular individuals who had dared to protest against ritualised violence. Josefa Casalé Suñén was an educated mother of four children from the town of Uncastillo (Aragón) who gave reading classes in the

---

[100] Magdalena González, 'Un nuevo significado para los viejos tiempos: Interpretación de la guerra civil y el primer franquismo en Conil de la Frontera', 'Todos los nombres' project website, CGT de Andalucía and Asociación Memoria Histórica y Justicia de Andalucía: www.todoslosnombres.org/php/generica.php?enlace=objetivos, accessed 18 May 2010; 'La generación herida: La guerra civil y el primer franquismo como señas de identidad en los niños nacidos hasta el año 1940', *Jerónimo Zurita: Revista de Historia*, 84 (2009), 99.

[101] E.g., Gil, *Lejos*, pp. 218–19; Fraser, *Blood*, p. 150; Morales and Pereira, *Memoria*, pp. 39, 79, 107, 120–2; Carlota Solé, *Los inmigrantes en la sociedad y en la cultura catalanas* (Barcelona, 1982), pp. 66, 78–84, 97; Barker, *Largo trauma*, pp. 119–20. See also chapters 4 and 6.

[102] *Diario de Navarra*, 30 August 1936, p. 4.

evenings to the illiterate men and women who worked in the fields. The bitterness of the pre-1936 conflict over laicisation of education spilled over into the war resulting in purges of teachers in both zones.[103] Josefa Casalé had openly supported the Republic in 1931 and the popular demands for land redistribution in the 1930s.[104] The land workers had resisted the rebellion in July 1936 and in the process had killed five right-wing inhabitants of the village.[105] Following occupation of the town, the Socialist mayor, Antonio Plano Aznárez, was publicly and brutally executed in October 1936, on the second anniversary of the popular revolutionary rebellion of 1934. After being beaten and pumped with castor oil he was paraded, insensible, before the populace, and shot as the impotent and humiliated majority watched while others expressed satisfaction. The anger of those supporting the conquerors was then vented on the body of the victim in what was described as a 'ceremony of shame'.[106] When the daughters of local Republicans were paraded through the streets, with shaven heads, to be condemned, Josefa had protested, thereby threatening to disrupt the cathartic intentions of the violent ritual. As a result of her protests, for which she was denounced, she was executed in the prison of Ejea de los Caballeros at the end of August 1936, one of at least seventy victims in Uncastillo. Her brother was killed the day after her execution.[107] Many of the wartime victims, including a substantial number of women, were buried in common, unmarked, graves.[108] The intimacy of the violence in a small community where

---

[103] For the purge of liberal teachers, see, e.g., Francisco Morente Valero, *La escuela y el estado nuevo: la depuración del magisterio nacional (1936–1943)* (Valladolid, 1997); Wenceslao Álvarez Oblanca, *La represión de postguerra en León: depuración de la enseñanza, 1936–1943* (León, 1986); Jesús Crespo Redondo, *Purga de maestros en la guerra civil: la depuración del magisterio nacional de la provincia de Burgos* (Valladolid, 1987), esp. pp. 71–7; Espinosa Maestre, *Columna de la muerte*, pp. 244, 507; Barker, *Largo trauma*, pp. 42–4, 111.

[104] On land conflict in Uncastillo, see, e.g., *ABC*, 19 December 1931, p. 27; 20 October 1933, p. 32.

[105] See José Luis Ledesma, *Los días de llamas de la revolución: violencia y política en la retaguardia republicana de Zaragoza durante la guerra civil* (Zaragoza, 2003), p. 340.

[106] Lucea Ayala, *Dispuestos a intervenir*, pp. 388–9; Pedro Torralba, *De Ayerbe a la 'Roja y Negra'* (Barcelona, 1980), pp. 356–60. The significance of shame (*vergüenza*) will be discussed in Chapter 4.

[107] Elordi (ed.), *Años difíciles*, pp. 182–7. Surviving sources of the Registros Civiles differ from the prison record in indicating that Josefa was killed on 1 October 1936. There were many administrative irregularities in record-keeping: the cause of death was recorded merely as 'consecuencia guerra'. See Casanova et al., *Pasado oculto*, p. 398. On civil war executions in Ejea of those who attended the Comillas rally to hear Azaña in October 1935: Henry Buckley, *Life and Death of the Spanish Republic* (London, 1940), p. 183.

[108] At least 17 women from the town were killed in the repression. For other regions, see, e.g., 185 women executed in Huelva (Espinosa Maestre, *Guerra civil*, p. 436); also at

everyone knew everyone else was intensified because the family of Josefa's husband had supported the rebels.[109]

Whilst the shape and development of the war of fronts in Spain are clear enough to historians, the complexity of the intimate violence triggered by the military coup of July 1936 behind the lines was obscured in the postwar years and only began to be recognised publicly by a few isolated commentators as the Franco era drew to a close. This has become the primary object of public memory since the 1990s. The weight of insecurity and the desire for self-preservation or advancement created a broad acceptance and subsequently, in a situation where talking about politics was unwise, memory became internalised. A liberal Republican chemist commented in the 1970s of the situation in Falangist Castile shortly after the rebellion, when the wave of executions was at its height, that 'only by acting as though everything is perfectly normal can you show that you are above suspicion'.[110] The fact of conscription and 'loyalty' to one side based merely upon geographical accident seemed to count for little in the aftermath. One retired captain of the Civil Guard who was employed as second in command of a Francoist concentration camp in Valencia wrote to Franco himself in June 1939 about his concerns. The Caudillo's pledge that only 'those with blood-stained hands' would be punished was not being adhered to since Falangists in particular were denouncing all leftists:

There are hundreds and hundreds of Falangists and persons of the constituted authorities who maintain the belief that all, absolutely everyone, who belonged to parties of the left, and even those who, never having belonged to said parties, found themselves obliged by circumstances to lend their services to the Red cause, are and will always be unworthy of coexisting with the rest of their compatriots. Knowing as I do the psychology of the (loyal) townsfolk [...] this will not seem strange to them and they will easily accept it.[111]

*

least 482 in Badajoz (Espinosa Maestre, *Columna de la muerte*, p. 242); on Murcia, Carmen González Martínez, *Guerra civil en Murcia* (Murcia, 1999), p. 148; on Segovia, August 1936, Vega Sombría, *De la esperanza*, p. 277; at least 40 women killed in Rioja, Gil, *Lejos*, pp. 212–16; at least 165 women in Madrid, in the aftermath of 'liberation', Fernando Hernández Holgado, *Mujeres encarceladas: la prisión de Ventas* (Madrid, 2003), p. 118; 79 recorded in Teruel, Cenarro, *Fin*, pp. 80, 89–90.

[109] The killing in Uncastillo was not restricted to the first days or weeks; the process continued into 1937, although some 85 per cent of the victims were killed in the period from 21 July 1936 to 29 October 1936. The final recorded victim died on 29 May 1939.

[110] Fraser, *Blood*, p. 168.

[111] Informe, Comandancia del Campo de Concentración de Porta Coeli, Emilio Tavera Dominguez to Franco, 21 June 1939, AGA, Vicesecretaria General, 17.02, sig. 52/46, caja 228.

Divisions of religion and social class in the 1930s had reinforced each other closely, adding potency to the clash.[112] Both socially conservative and progressive conceptions ascribed particular cultural meanings to the key political identities of the 1930s and this process was intensified once the state was fractured by the military coup in July 1936.[113] There was genuine political commitment and idealism on both sides, but the spectacular rise in affiliation to political parties, trade unions and, as state or local functionaries, to the bureaucracy owed much to calculations made to avoid suspicion or gain advantage or protection. The preoccupation of many had been to defend themselves from the ravages of the war.[114] The struggle for individual sovereignty revolved around a link to, or collaboration with, political actors who had access to resources and to embryonic state forces on each side. The most personally difficult memory of the war and its aftermath for many, as will be seen, is related to the ramifications of such difficult choices, retrospective justification of them, and dealing with the consequent trauma and the effects of intimate violence on pre-war social relationships. A Francoist officer of the state political police, the Brigada Social, in a moment of contrition at the end of a memoir written in the 1960s, made a point of emphasising the dilemma of choices and opportunities: 'in the first place I would set down in my own defence the cases of all those, on one side or the other, who for lack of a patron or a protector lost their lives or their property. I pray to God for them, for their families, and also for myself.'[115]

The extent of post-war isolation or sense of collective identity and solidarity related to the conflict shaped the process by which individuals pieced together a coherent story from fragments of their past and social groups constructed competing narratives of collective trauma. The case of the murdered son of a Republican local councillor in rural Valladolid was typical in the intimacy of the violence and of the trauma of relatives left to make sense of the catastrophe. When Falangists came to the family home for Miguel, the father of five young children, they were led by a cousin and by two priests, one of whom had baptised Miguel as a child. The wartime 'mid-night knock on the door' would become part of

---

[112] See 'cumulative group cleavages', note 75. Also Smelser, 'Psychological Trauma', p. 38.

[113] See Douglas's 'group' and 'grid' characteristics mentioned in note 75.

[114] For the choice to espouse the cause of the Republic and subsequent lives lost, humiliation, and loss of property, see Collier, *Socialists*, pp. 23, 32–6, 42. On seeking conferment of official position, however lowly, as a means to protection: e.g., García Valcárcel, 'Causas de la emigración', p. 97.

[115] This officer had cousins who suffered on the other side: one was killed and another exiled. Elordi (ed.), *Años difíciles*, pp. 244, 250–1.

post-war folklore.[116] Women and children often felt responsible; sometimes they had opened the door to the armed patrols and were pressured
into revealing the whereabouts of their husbands, sons or fathers and they
remember these details vividly and painfully.[117] Miguel's eldest daughter,
who had been six years old in 1936, had pieced together the events of that
night over many years, in spite of the resistance and fear of the community about speaking of it, and during the surge of war memories since the
1990s began to share the story publicly with others who had had similar
experiences. Reconstructing personal war memories depended on a
shared framework, mutually constructed by the children and grandchildren of 'the defeated'.[118] Not even the closest relatives of Miguel would
dare to go to the house after the war: 'my little brother of three could not
go out because the children in the street would say to him: "We're going
to kill you like your father."'[119] Miguel's place of burial was never found.

The nature of post-war memory has depended over decades on the
radically different treatment of Nationalist and Republican victims.
Wartime record-keeping of rebel killings was not thorough; judicial
and extra-judicial executions carried out by the Franco state and its
supporters were not systematically entered in civil registries or were
entered only years later and often listed with misleading causes of death.
Common burial pits across the country concealed the remains of wartime victims of the embryonic dictatorship. For decades the vast majority of these would remain unexcavated. The death on 19 August 1936,
from 'war wounds', of the republican poet Federico García Lorca was
not entered in the civil registry until 1940. As in thousands of other
cases, Lorca's body was buried in an anonymous pit.[120] In contrast, once
territory was 'liberated' by the rebels or during the early 1940s, the
Franco regime decreed that the sites of burial of victims of the revolutionary violence in the Republican zone be located and sanctified, and
some level of dignity was accorded them through a process of public
mourning. In homage to the 'martyrs of our crusade', an Interior Ministry order of 4 April 1940 called on local authorities to ensure that the
places of burial of victims of the 'revolución marxista' be temporarily
granted the status of sacred ground, in collaboration with the ecclesiastical authorities, until human remains could be transferred by families
to cemeteries or to the planned 'pantheon of the fallen' (what would

---

[116] E.g. Aceves, *Social Change*, p. 9.
[117] See, e.g., Castilla del Pino, *Casa del olivo*, p. 505; Collier, *Socialists*, p. 158.
[118] See, in general, David Middleton and Derek Edwards (eds.), *Collective Remembering* (London, 1990).
[119] Sabina de la Cruz, 'Una familia rota; una sociedad truncada', pp. 79–80.
[120] Gibson, *Assassination*, pp. 161–7.

become the Valley of the Fallen – Valle de los Caídos).[121] Through religious services of consecration conducted across 'liberated' Spain in the aftermath, the bodies of the Nationalist 'fallen' were claimed as penitential and redemptive material and their sacrifice became the basis of the mythologies of various post-war communities of suffering and of memory.[122] Those who died fighting for the Republic could not be publicly remembered, and to mourn openly for the executed was to risk social sanction both during the war and in its aftermath.[123]

---

[121] *Boletín Oficial del Estado*, 5 April 1940.
[122] E.g. in Málaga, see Francisco García Alonso SJ, *Oración fúnebre predicada en la Santa Iglesia Catedral de Málaga* (Cádiz, 1942), pp. 9, 13, 32, 36.
[123] E.g. Moreno Gómez, *Córdoba en la posguerra*, pp. 63–4. See also, e.g., Barker, *Largo trauma*, p. 100; Collier, *Socialists*, pp. 158, 161.

Part II

Memories of war during the Franco years

3 Repression and remembrance: the victors' liturgy of memory

> Caudillo of Spain: [...] Thousands of companions during the captivity were brutally dragged away from our cells and knew how to face death, looking only at Spain, and repeating your name so that our tormentors would recall it at the moment of justice which has now dawned [...] Dignified by the bloody persecution perpetrated by the enemies of the *patria*, treated without pity for thirty-two months, the ex-captives are distinguished as a select group of Spaniards to be singled out for missions of leadership and vigilance. They, as no other group, know the value of our victory [...] They will remind us of those fallen on the battlefield and in the innumerable immolations which were decreed by the Red terror [...] They will translate the words of the dead and pass on their mandate.[1]

In January 1940 the recently founded National Association of Ex-prisoners ('ex-cautivos'), constituted by those who had suffered imprisonment in the Republican zone during the civil war and led particularly by captives in the Modelo prison in Madrid, produced an emotive public message of loyalty directed personally to General Franco which conferred charismatic status upon him and summarised the special claim on memory of the conflict made by those who were able to portray themselves openly as its victims.

The civil war lacerated the lives of the defeated and of many of the victors, though recognition of this in the aftermath varied greatly depending on opportunity and capacity to partake of the spoils of victory. The wartime experience has been explored in the previous chapter and the aftermath for the defeated will form the main theme of the next. Here, the ways in which the nascent state encouraged associations of ex-captives, ex-combatants and the families of 'martyrs' to remember, and how various groups of 'memory activists', including Falangists and Catholics, came to construct a sense of collective trauma, will be explored. Many set themselves up as moral witnesses to the tragedy, and they employed the familiar tropes of collective memory after war: 'redeeming

---

[1] *ABC*, 24 January 1940.

the sacrifice'; 'the spirit of a generation'; 'blood irrigating the growth of a new nation'; rebirth and regeneration; the 'moral values of the victory': austerity, discipline, vigilance and intransigence.[2]

After 1 April 1939 'the fallen' in Spain meant those who fought and died on Franco's side or were killed by groups or organisations linked to the Republic. Those who suffered imprisonment and the families of 'the fallen' were also represented in the public memory of the first two post-war decades, a public memory which had a relatively fixed doctrinal and ritualised form, a liturgy shaped by overlapping sets of ideas and practices originating in the Catholic Church and in fascism and made concrete in monuments, ceremonies and prescriptive language. For devoted Catholics, it was natural that personal memory would fit with a greater, bigger, religious story. Ways of remembering were entwined, therefore, with two means to redemption and purification in the name of the wartime sacrifices: 're-Christianisation', on the one hand, and punishment and coercion, on the other.

Public space between family and state would be severely circumscribed, and there was without doubt a great swathe of 'passive' or unwitnessed memory of loss amongst those who were in some way connected to the cause of the civil war rebels. In public, Spanish nationalist prescriptions were adhered to. Regional cultures, as exemplified in linguistic difference, had blame for the catastrophe of the war heaped upon them. The Castilian language was lauded in the 1940s; centuries before it had been 'the vehicle of the crusade against Islam' and now it became 'the axis of the spiritual politics of the Spain reborn with the Rising of July 1936'.[3] These claims originating in conquest and the energetic ideology of 'Spain' and 'anti-Spain' were affirmed in the austere virtues defined and proffered in the ex-captives' message to Franco cited at the beginning of this chapter: rectitude of conduct; unlimited spirit of sacrifice ('selfishness and comfort cannot exist amongst us'); blind discipline; 'intransigence and intolerance with the internal and external enemies of Spain'; being 'ever watchful'; displaying 'unshakable unity, as firm as iron, as in the union which the hatred and crimes of our enemies brought about, as our crusaders, more fortunate than us, demonstrated in the trenches and at the front against the common enemy'.[4]

---

[2] For Laín Entralgo explaining his allegiance to the regime in the 1940s through the utopian hope that 'blood can at times become a seed', see *Descargo*, p. 265. He admitted later (1975) that national tragedy did not become 'fecunda', but 'in spite of all ... I hoped and I continue hoping' (p. 266).
[3] Luis de Galinsoga, 'Grandeza e hipoteca del Castellano', *Arriba*, 29 May 1946, p. 4.
[4] *ABC*, 24 January 1940.

The experience of wartime imprisonment and living in fear of death would have important personal and political consequences. Wartime experiences barbarised the lives of many of those who became significant political protagonists in the post-war years.[5] The same can be said, in fact, of much of society in Spain during the early post-war years. For now, in the context of the victors' liturgy of memory in the 1940s, it is enough to point out that several communities of memory in the aftermath played a significant ideological role based on a well-publicised alignment with suffering. By the 1950s, memories of such wartime experiences would begin to produce glimpses of a cultural and political opening up (*apertura*). In the first post-war decade, however, this ideological role was politically instrumentalised largely through the agency of various associations linked to the Falange and orthodox Catholic lay groups which would obstruct any trace of a movement towards reconciliation.

Reconciliation denied: the politics of victory

The history of Spain since 1939 is the history of a mediated, negotiated and often reluctant process of reconciliation, a process which has been seen at various moments as incomplete. State building and stability in the 1940s were bound up with total victory and thus with a continuation of physical and symbolic violence. There would be no peace-keeping force, no negotiation process enforced by outside bodies, and no neutralised zone as refugees fled towards France in early 1939 and few military and political limitations were placed upon the victors.[6] The relationship between the violence and post-war reconstruction of political authority can be traced to the civil war itself, to its beginning, indeed, on 18 July 1936, though wartime and post-war violence were not identical: two often chaotic states had been replaced by a single more coherent set of institutions. What is certain, however, is that in several instances – Navarra, Zaragoza and Burgos, for example, in the north and centre, and substantial regions of the south – the conflict ended within weeks or even days of the initial rebellion, almost three years before the formal cessation of war, and the 'purge' of society began instantly.[7] In early 1942

---

[5] Javier Tusell, *Franco y los católicos: la política interior española entre 1945 y 1957* (Madrid, 1984), p. 440.

[6] On civil wars in general, see King, *Ending*, pp. 35–6. On celebration of total victory and what it made possible in Spain, e.g. García Arias, 'Sobre la mediación', in Hermandad de Alféreces Provisionales, *Generación del 36*, especially, p. 90; Luciano de la Calzada Rodríguez, 'El espíritu del 18 de julio, como realidad histórica y proyección hacia el futuro', in *La guerra de liberación nacional* (Zaragoza, 1961), pp. 601–43.

[7] Richards, 'Limits of Quantification'.

Franco described the purpose of the purge as 'cleaning the site ready for our structure'.[8] The violence and divisions of the war left a society which was deeply fragmented as groups and individuals sought to align themselves with the new power, to gain materially from the polarised situation, or, at the very least, to survive the ordeal of defeat.[9]

The victors, at state level, settled easily on punishment and expiation rather than reconciliation. No general amnesty was to be granted until the wartime revolutionary killings had been expiated.[10] The partial amnesty of January 1940 referred only to some of those political prisoners serving twelve years or less, and the vast majority of prisoners accused of 'military rebellion' had been sentenced to longer periods or were awaiting the death penalty.[11] The rupture of civil war thus became the political point of departure of the post-war and of the search for justice and retribution by those who counted themselves amongst 'the victors'. The extensive and violent purge of liberal schoolteachers was a case in point.[12] On average, between a quarter and a third of teachers throughout the country were 'purged' for alleged political crimes, receiving some sanction, ranging from suspension for a limited period to banishment to another geographic region (internal exile), a financial penalty, imprisonment, or, in hundreds of cases, to execution. Many were replaced by Nationalist veterans, the relatives of Francoist wounded, or those imprisoned or maltreated by 'the Reds'.[13] The phrase used in the recollections of teachers and other public employees is telling: 'afterwards I was purged (depurado) for many years'.[14] The long-lasting effects on the lives of individuals and their families of denunciation and punishment of teachers were considerable.[15]

Another case was the power given to the Public Prosecutor of the Supreme Court in April 1940 to collect the testimony of citizens, in the interests of the state lawsuit, known as the Causa General (General Cause). Denunciations made to the Causa by activists of the fraternity

---

[8]   Speech in Barcelona, 24 January 1942, *ABC*, 29 January 1942, p. 1.
[9]   See Chapter 4.
[10] Richards, *Time of Silence*, pp. 152–6. E.g. Franco, 'Discurso pronunciado con motivo de la entrega, a los comisionados de Jaén, de la reliquía del Santo Rostro', Jaén, 18 March 1940, *Palabras del Caudillo, 19 abril 1937 – 7 diciembre 1942* (Madrid, 1943), p. 157.
[11] *Anuario Estadístico, 1943* (Madrid, 1944), p. 1,100, *1948*, vol. I, p. 1052.
[12] E.g. Álvarez Oblanca, *La represión de postguerra en León*; José María Lama, *La amargura de la memoria: República y guerra en Zafra (1931–1936)* (Badajoz, 2004); Morente Valero, *La escuela y el estado nuevo*.
[13] Circular, 31 August 1937, *BOE*, no. 324, 9 September 1937; *Diario de Navarra*, 30 August 1936, p. 3.
[14] E.g. Elordi (ed.), *Años difíciles*, p. 250; Morales and Pereira, *Memoria*, pp. 74, 122.
[15] E.g. Reñones, 'Un crisol', p. 140.

of ex-captives, many of whom were well-known pre-war Falangist plotters against the Republic, became one of the primary sources of evidence for the post-war persecution of Republicans.[16] Although so-called 'witnesses to events' might often have been no such thing, the 'crimes during the Red domination' were annotated in detail, resulting in publication of a weighty report in 1943 which drew together the stories of wartime violence in the Republican zone, giving a sense of the magnitude of the 'criminal' revolution which was inflated but perfectly believable to many Spaniards willing to support Franco. Legal cases arising from this continued throughout the 1940s.[17]

Further discriminatory examples were the related questions of war pensions and public employment. It was only the widows and children of men who had fought for Franco who received compensation and a war pension; there was no financial recognition for the families of those who died on the other side. A Republican league of war-wounded had been established during the war and held its first meeting in Madrid in May 1937 and a congress in Valencia in August of that year, but the association disappeared with the defeat.[18] By contrast, several decrees were announced within months of the end of the war to favour Nationalist ex-combatants and their families. Civil servants and local authority workers dismissed for rebellion by the wartime Republican government were able to claim the salaries lost since 18 July 1936.[19] In August 1939, one such decree required that 80 per cent of public appointments be controlled according to wartime service for the rebel side. At the same time, a thorough purge of Republican sympathisers from public employment was carried out. Some 25,000 were dismissed from the public administration in Catalonia alone, a measure effected by politically reliable and non-Catalanist municipal and provincial authorities.[20] Distribution of posts was to be divided equally between four categories: the 'official war-wounded' (those who served with the Nationalists); temporary junior officers brought into the rebel army during the war (*alféreces provisionales*);

---

[16] See, e.g., the case of the Republican academic and psychiatrist Emilio Mira y López: Josep María Solé i Sabaté, 'La psiquiatría de postguerra contra la ciència analítica d'Emili Mira', *La Vanguardia*, 24 February 1987, p. 43.

[17] *ABC*, 22 August 1943, p. 10; 21 October 1943, p. 12; Ministerio de Justicia, *Causa general*. The 4th edition was republished, unedited, in 1961 and has recently reappeared (2008 and 2009). E.g. declarations of Cipriano Rivas Cherif; see Antonio Manuel Moral Roncal, *Diplomacia, humanitarismo y espionaje en la guerra civil española* (Madrid, 2008), p. 29.

[18] Pedro Vega, *Historia de la Liga de Mutilados* (Madrid, 1981).

[19] On compensation, see the decree of 25 August 1939, *BOE*, no. 239 (27 August 1939).

[20] Riquer and Culla, *Franquisme*, pp. 26, 55. See also Vega Sombría, *De la esperanza*, pp. 197–219.

other rebel ex-combatants and ex-prisoners from the war period; and war orphans or dependants of 'national victims'.[21] It has been estimated that by the end of 1942 some 50,000 ex-combatants had benefited by finding jobs through the endeavours of their association.[22]

Wartime propaganda had made no distinction between war aims and the public declarations and image of the Caudillo, and Franco's personal commitment to retaining power and his own accumulation of symbolic capital during the conflict were important factors of continuity from brutal war to repressive post-war. Heroic memories and the propaganda of anti-communism conferred a charismatic authority which was felt and expressed in society and within government paternalistically, both in public and privately. The liturgical guide for affiliates of the Sección Femenina declared 1 October (the anniversary of the General's elevation to Head of the Nationalist state in 1936) the day of 'the Holy Angel of the Guardian of Spain', with its own particular Mass: 'from our faith we know that the Lord created a legion of angels; among them he has chosen for us one protector [. . .] the custodian of our *patria*'.[23] Franco thus became a reincarnation of heroic warriors, mystics, ascetics and monarchs of the past, condensing centuries of Spanish glory.[24] This ethos seeped into society. Instructors of the Francoist youth organisation, the Frente de Juventudes, were often Nationalist ex-combatants, and some of them were war-wounded. Their primary aim, according to a manual on moral training, was 'to make fertile the seed of our dead', and an ascetic sense of sacrifice was paramount, for both boys and girls.[25] The saints turned into military heroes in Spanish National Catholicism, as in images of the 'warrior saint', James the Apostle (Santiago), became the template for the crop of equestrian sculptures of Franco situated in public squares and streets which carried his name or that of other heroes of the crusade. His purifying sword would be blessed by the Cardinal Primate of Spain in

[21] Decree 25 August 1939, *BOE*, 259, 16 September 1939. See also José Manuel Sabín, *Prisión y muerte en la España de postguerra* (Madrid, 1996), pp. 45–6.

[22] José Luis Rodríguez, *Reaccionarios y golpistas: la extrema derecha en España* (Madrid, 1994), p. 102.

[23] Delegada Nacional de la SF, *Guía litúrgica* (Madrid, 1945); *El Correo de Andalucia*, 9 October 1937, p. 10.

[24] On this teaching of history under Francoism, see, e.g., Esther Martínez Tórtola, *La enseñanza de la historia en el primer bachillerato franquista, 1938–1953* (Madrid, 1996); Gregorio Cámara Villar, *Nacional-Catolicismo y escuela: la socialización política del franquismo (1936–1951)* (Jaén, 1984).

[25] Servicio Nacional de Instructores, *Bases para la educación moral del Instructor del Frente de Juventudes* (Madrid, 1945?), p. 10; Delegación Nacional de la Sección Femenina, *Plan de formación de las juventudes* (Madrid, 1945?), p. 109.

a quasi-sacramental coronation in May 1939, becoming part of a symbolic tapestry of sacred objects which alluded to historical precedent and continuity in sacred struggles against 'infidels'.[26]

The potency of Franco's authority, blended with reasons of state, is evidenced in the commitment even of members of the wartime generation who would later have doubts about the direction of the country in the post-war era. In 1949, for example, when the time came to debate a new concordat between the state and the Church of Rome, Joaquín Ruiz-Giménez, as ambassador to the Vatican, declared to a group of visiting cardinals that 'Franco embodies the heartbeat of all of the youth which was mobilised behind basic Christian principles'.[27] There was some doubt, indeed, that such a confirmation of Spain's Catholic commitment was even necessary because, it was argued, the religious character of the state 'is today fundamentally guaranteed by the profound Christian spirit of our Generalísimo'.[28] When in May 1947 the Caudillo made a visit to Saint Ignacio Loyola's cave retreat at Manresa, the most sacred site of the Ignation Company of Jesus, it was, according to the *Revista de San Ignacio*, testimony to 'the affection that the General has for the sanctifying work of Ignatian [Spiritual] Exercises and proof of his deep-rooted piety'.[29] The image of Franco as 'saviour of Spain' and 'father of the nation' was bolstered by his 'adoption' of several war-ruined towns, with the intention that they become shrines. The idea possessed some resonance with the political reality in Brunete, near Madrid, or Belchite, in Zaragoza, but in 'adopting' the Basque town of Guernica, not only were the delusions of power clear, but divisions within the Church were highlighted.[30] Resentment towards the New State would emanate, not least, from within Basque Catholicism. Falangist intelligence officers reported in the early 1940s that 90 per cent of priests in the province of Guipúzcoa, for example, were Basque nationalists at the orders of the exiled former bishop of Vitoria Mateo Múgica, in spite of fear of denunciation in such places as Guernica.[31] According to the local

---

[26] E.g. Luis Carrero Blanco, *La victoria del Cristo de Lepanto* (Madrid, 1948).

[27] *Ecclesia*, 3 November 1949.

[28] Ruiz-Giménez to Martín Artajo, 16 September 1949, cited in Tusell, *Franco y los católicos*, pp. 238, 241.

[29] Francisco J. Carmona, *Cambios en la identidad católica: juventud de Alfonso Carlos Comín* (Madrid, 1995), p. 65.

[30] See 'Estudio de un pueblo adoptado: Guernica', *Reconstrucción*, 1 (April 1940), 22–7; Dirección General de Regiones Devastadas y Reparaciones, *La reconstrucción de España: résumen de dos años de labor* (Madrid, 1942); 'Ley de Adopción', in José Moreno Torres (Director General de Regiones Devastadas), *La reconstrucción urbana en España* (Madrid, 1945).

[31] Delegación Nacional de Investigación e Información (DNII), bulletin no. 633, 30 April 1942, caja 16, 17.04, sig. 52/35, Vicesecretaria General, SGM, AGA. María Jesús Cava Mesa, *Memoria colectiva del bombardeo de Gernika* (Bilbao, 1996), pp. 266, 281.

Falange, the purge had not gone far enough and local nationalism constituted a danger to state security: mass was being prayed in the Basque
language, some people persisted in using the Basque form of their names,
and collections were made in churches for those who had been exiled.[32]
When the allied powers failed to intervene against Franco after 1945 this
defiance declined, but Basque resentment would remain and grow
throughout the Franco years and beyond.

With the 1936 coup, the democratic constitution of the Republic of the
1930s had been permanently suspended in rebel-held areas and officially
the state of war would prevail until 1948. In legal terms, defence of the
previous constitutional order became 'military rebellion'.[33] Constitutional
guarantees were replaced by military justice applied to a broad range of
activities, including the expression of opinions inimical to the new power
and the new moralism. Those put before the military courts had to prove
themselves innocent, a reversal of the legal maxim *onus probandi*, and in
many cases the court went no further than hearing the charges and the
political antecedents of the accused.[34] Some post-war liberals would
maintain that the Francoist Consejos de Guerra had been 'relatives' of
the Tribunales Populares of the wartime Republic, but the military courts
were part of a very different context: of an unchallenged peacetime
dictatorship.[35] The civil Law of Political Responsibilities, announced in
early February 1939, had the function of imposing primarily economic
sanctions against Republicans whose political support for the former
government (or, in fact, lack of active support for the rebels) was seen as
encouraging the social revolution and the material damage it had caused.
The Provincial Political Responsibilities tribunals would be composed of
a high-ranking army officer, a Francoist member of the judiciary, and a
local Falangist. By the end of 1941 some 100,000 cases had been heard
specifically under this legislation. The Law of Responsibilities covered
political affiliations which were in contravention of no legal statute before
July 1936. In sum, the state under Franco was thus more present in daily
life than before the war but in the 1940s represented only an *embryonic*
rule of law where politics and criminality remained intertwined and

---

[32] DNII bulletin no. 545, 15 March 1942; no. 541, 28 February 1942, cajas 17/18, 17.04,
sig. 52/35, Vicesecretaria General, SGM, AGA.

[33] Manuel Ballbé, *Orden público y militarismo en la España constitucional* (Madrid, 1985),
p. 402.

[34] See, e.g., Martín Jiménez, *Guerra civil*, pp. 199–208, Solé i Sabaté and Villarroya, *La
repressió*, pp. 102–4. Also Julius Ruiz, *Franco's Justice: Repression in Madrid after the
Spanish Civil War* (Oxford, 2005); Peter Anderson, *The Francoist Military Trials: Terror
and Complicity, 1939–1945* (London, 2010).

[35] E.g. Marías, *Una vida presente*, vol. I, p. 273.

beneath which corruption was normal practice. Judicial procedures in the wake of the civil war and for many years thereafter were poorly legitimated, measures were applied arbitrarily and personal issues, rather than general principles, had undue influence, and there continued to be great confusion for many years between de jure and de facto legality.[36]

The process of military demobilisation and integration of Republican soldiers, many of them conscripts, would begin with centres for classification, such as the notorious camp at Albatera, near Alicante, holding some 30,000 Republicans for investigation and categorisation in 1939, and Porta Coeli in Valencia, where control of 'classification tribunals' in 1939 depended on vague criteria, personal influence and denunciations.[37] Official reckoning suggested that more than 430,000 prisoners had been captured by the Nationalists during the fighting (over and above those disposed of summarily by firing squad). By mid March 1939, some 180,000 of these were 'awaiting classification'.[38] In addition there were thousands of political prisoners: by the end of 1939, according to regime figures, the total had reached some 270,000, and by 1940 the authorities were troubled by the extent of overcrowding and disease.[39] Three concentration camps were established in Valladolid, for example, and local newspapers in 1938 produced long lists of prisoners detained who had been 'saved' by the rebels. In the cells for political detainees, six individuals occupied the space designed for one.[40] The provincial prison still had 3,000 wartime inmates in 1940, and more than 100 prisoners died there in the squalid conditions during the period from December 1940 to June 1942.[41] In the provincial

---

[36] Manuel Ortiz Heras, *Violencia política en la Segunda República y el primer franquismo* (Madrid, 1996), p. 391; Vega Sombría, *De la esperanza*, pp. 182–96.

[37] Informe, Comandancia, Porta Coeli, 21 June 1939, AGA, Vicesecretaria General, 17.02, sig. 52/46, caja 228. On Albatera, see Javier Rodrigo, *Cautivos: campos de concentración en la España franquista, 1936–1947* (Barcelona, 2005), pp. 202–4. It had previously been a Republican labour camp for detained 'fascists'. See Glicerio Sánchez Recio, *Justicia y guerra en España: los Tribunales Populares (1936–1939)* (Alicante, 1991), pp. 181–2.

[38] Inspección de Campos de Concentración de Prisioneros, report: 15 March 1939. Archive of Ministerio de Asuntos Exteriores, Madrid, Archivo de Burgos, R1067, exp. 6.

[39] *Anuario Estadístico* (Madrid, 1942), p. 1,099. The official average for the period 1930–4 was 9,403. At the end of 1940 there were officially 240,916 prisoners, of whom 7,762 were awaiting a death penalty: 8 May 1940, Fundación Nacional Francisco Franco (FNFF), *Documentos inéditos para la historia del Generalísimo Franco*, vol. II (Madrid, 1992), pp. 176–7; 5 November 1940, FNFF, *Documentos*, II, pp. 386–7. By the end of 1942 the official prison population remained almost 125,000 and at least 38,000 by 1948. *Anuario Estadístico* (Madrid, 1948), vol. I, p. 1,052. 'Nota del Director General de Prisiones', May 1940, FNFF, vol. II, 1, pp. 76–7.

[40] Martín Jiménez, *Guerra civil en Valladolid*, pp. 196–7.

[41] Jesús María Palomares Ibáñez, *El primer franquismo en Valladolid* (Valladolid, 2002), pp. 105, 109–13.

prison in Huelva, where at least 3,040 lost their lives in the rebel repression, many who were awaiting trial, serving political sentences or waiting to be transferred elsewhere died during the early 1940s as a result of the conditions. Most of the victims were land workers, though many were miners of the Rio Tinto company. Thirty died in the prison in March 1942 alone.[42]

Political prisoners and unfavourably classified Republican combatants were subjected to prison labour. A law of early September 1939 provided for the establishment and regulation of militarised prison labour colonies, and the period 1942–4 was the high point of the use of captive labour in militarised industries, including coal, iron, mercury and pyrite mining. Between 1939 and 1946, prison labourers worked more than 20 million work days in such enterprises.[43] A period in a labour battalion or penal detachment was designed to punish past political affiliations and explicitly to remind Republicans of the damage caused by the war. The Dirección General de Regiones Devastadas put prisoners to work on the reconstruction of battle sites such as Teruel, Belchite and Brunete as a way of allocating culpability and enforcing memory of 'the futile destruction wrought by communism'.[44] Ruins were preferred to museums: 'stained with blood', they were a 'living' testimony of the sacrifice.[45] These sites would also have monuments to those 'Fallen for God and for the *patria*'. Ruins also represented the physical presence of both the threat of violence and the catastrophic results of war.[46]

The deaths of many prisoners were recorded in cemetery records as caused by typhus, influenza, tuberculosis, enteritis, bronchial pneumonia, and other conditions. There were indeed high levels of disease, but violent deaths were often recorded euphemistically. The high number of deaths substantiated in state records in the period 1937–40 from heart attacks amongst young adults, for example, seems difficult to account for.[47] The fragmentary records for the province of Burgos show that 6

---

[42] Espinosa Maestre, *La guerra civil en Huelva*, pp. 676–80.

[43] Isaías Lafuente, *Esclavos por la patria* (Madrid, 2000), pp. 179–80, 327–30.

[44] See, e.g., *Reconstrucción*, Año 1, no. 1 (April 1940), 6–16 on the 'destruction' and 'heroism' of Belchite.

[45] 'Ruinas que ennoblecen', *Arriba*, 21 August 1941, in Gabriel Ureña, *Arquitectura y urbanística civil y militar en el periodo de la autarquía (1936–1945)* (Madrid, 1979), pp. 124–5. On reconstruction of churches in Asturias: *Reconstrucción*, I, 2 (May 1940), 5–17.

[46] Antonio Bonet Correa, 'Espacios arquitectónicos para un nuevo orden', in Bonet, *Arte del franquismo* (Madrid, 1981), p. 13.

[47] *Anuario Estadístico de España 1943* (Madrid, 1944), p. 1,286; Souto Blanco, *La represión franquista en la provincia de Lugo*, p. 247. Also Vega Sombría, *De la esperanza*, pp. 374–5. On disease, eg: *Anuario Estadístico de España, 1943*, p. 1,286; *1950* (Madrid, 1951), p. 780.

political detainees died in 1936, 16 in 1937, 28 in 1938, 35 in 1939, 60 in 1940, 91 in 1941, 95 in 1942 (including 41 from tuberculosis and 31 from 'avitaminosis'), and 28 in 1943. It has been calculated that at least 293 were executed in Burgos, 386 were 'disappeared', and 359 died in prison: 1,038 documented deaths, in sum, and this in an area dominated from the first day of the war by the rebels and where there had been no fighting.[48] As we will see in subsequent chapters, migration of those targeted by the authorities from rural Burgos to urban centres such as Barcelona began to take place amid the repression following the war.[49]

While Burgos had been controlled by the rebels, Valencia had been under the authority of the Republic for most of the war and there were some 2,800 killings of those politically of the right or suspected of being fifth columnists.[50] Following the fall of the region, the violence of retribution by the new and unchallenged regime was systematic and far-reaching. Written records have been collated for 4,714 executed in the area and a further 1,165 deaths in prison: a total of 6,087 deaths from 1938 to 1956, as recorded in civil registries.[51] In Zaragoza, 447 prisoners were executed in the period from the formal end of the war in April 1939 until 1946, in addition to the many executed during the war.[52] In Badajoz, the majority killed by the Nationalists died in 1936 (4,661) but 565 were killed in 1940 (3.5 times more than in 1937), 232 in 1941 (more than in any of the years 1937, 1938 or 1939), and 122 in 1942 (more than in 1939 (112)). The killing of a 32-year-old land worker on 19 January 1945 signalled the end of a cycle of executions in Badajoz which had begun in July 1936 and where 6,600 executions were recorded.[53] At least 4,700 executions took place in Málaga between 'liberation' (early February 1937) and the end of the war (1 April 1939), but there were a further 710 recorded killings between then and the end of 1942. Another 35 prisoners were killed in 1943 and 1944, and the last recorded execution in Málaga took place in May 1948.[54]

The process of classification of detainees was open to corruption from the beginning, and some individuals were able to secure their freedom through a guarantee provided by a relative with political influence or the means with which to bribe prison authorities, although reconciliation within families was often difficult. Substantial sums had sometimes to

[48] Rilova Pérez, Guerra civil, p. 271.   [49] E.g. Botey Vallès, Relats, p. 75.
[50] Vicente Gabarda, La represión en la retaguardia republicana: país Valenciano, 1936–1939 (Valencia, 1996).
[51] Vicente Gabarda, Els afusellaments al país Valencià, pp. 215–16.
[52] Casanova et al., Pasado oculto, p. 221. There had been some 190 killings in Zaragoza during the period of Republican authority.
[53] Espinosa Maestre, Columna de la muerte, pp. 241, 253, 320–1.
[54] Eiroa, Viva Franco, pp. 246–7, 276–87.

be raised by selling land or homes.[55] There was also conflict amongst the authorities over which class of Falange affiliate had the right and economic standing to grant a political guarantee allowing for releases from the camps.[56] The brother-in-law of the Falangist intellectual Pedro Laín Entralgo had been a political commissar of a Republican military unit during the war and was captured in Alicante and sent to Albatera in 1939. When, in order to secure his release, Laín went to Albatera to locate him amongst the thousands of men held there, he was able to do so only because of his personal influence. He would hide his brother-in-law until arranging a safe conduct with a false name to enable him leave the country, though only after paying a considerable sum of money to a black-market operator to get him across the French border.[57]

Securing widespread working-class support for Franco's New State by appealing to 'the spirit of our generation' was no more likely in the aftermath of bloody civil war than was mobilising Catalan or Basque nationalists behind the regime.[58] The war had been fought partly over reform of the economic system, and the 1938 outlawing of trade unions would maintain a low-wage economy in an era of hunger. Falangist reports bemoaned the collective attitude of industrial workers, shaped by the expectations, memories and culture of the Socialist Casas del Pueblo of the pre-war years.[59] A system of rewards for workers was initiated to commemorate auspicious days related to the conflict: the bonus marking 18 July and the day off on 1 October (Día del Caudillo) commemorating Franco becoming Head of the Nationalist state in 1936.[60] In spite of this, and the Falange's revolutionary rhetoric, the state system of *sindicatos verticales* (vertical unions), given over to the Falangist Movimiento as recognition of the party's contribution to victory in 1939, was viewed with suspicion.[61] The National Delegate of the

---

[55] E.g. Collier, *Socialists*, pp. 162, 166; Cava Mesa, *Memoria colectiva*, pp. 283–5.

[56] Letter from Secretaría Nacional de la DNII to Secretaría General de FET-JONS (Burgos), 27 July 1939, AGA, SGM, Vicesecretaeria General, 'asuntos políticos', 17.04, sig. 52/35, caja 7.

[57] Laín Entralgo, *Descargo*, pp. 259–60. On the black market in safe-conducts, see also Morales and Pereira, *Memoria*, p. 179.

[58] For the speech of Minister of Acción y Organización Sindical, Pedro González-Bueno, on the occasion in 1939 of the annual Fiesta de la Exaltación del Trabajo (18 July), see *Información* (Bilbao), XXVI, 598, 29 July 1939, 399–400; *Boletín Minero e Industrial (BMI)* XVIII, 7 (July 1939), 125–35.

[59] See, e.g., Boletín Informativo de Empresas Ferrocarriles Españoles del Norte (no. 440), DNII, FET-JONS, 29 January 1942, AGA, SGM, 17.04, VCG, caja 21, pp. vi–x.

[60] The naming of 'model companies' coincided with the Fiesta de la Exaltación del Trabajo (18 July). See *BMI*, September 1941, pp. 243, 259; *BMI*, July 1945, pp. 290–2.

[61] An official internal report of the DN de Sindicatos in 1946 found that the purchasing power of the peseta had declined to one-third that of 1936, though it was admitted that

sindicatos explained the lack of improvement in 1946 by stating that at the end of the war a period of 'convalescence, to staunch the flow of blood from moral and material wounds', had been required. It had been necessary for the government to 'take hold of the reins of power with firm hands, improvising a stage of energetic interventions'.[62]

Although many pre-war Falangist affiliates were lost in the civil war, and the weight of radical Falangism was depleted, the party grew vertiginously in its aftermath as ex-combatants, ex-captives and public functionaries who emerged unscathed from the process of *depuración* were granted membership. This influx provoked resentment among the outnumbered 'Old Guard'.[63] In Barcelona these Falangists 'of the first hour' numbered less than 1 per cent of the membership in 1939, and of the 34,000 affiliates in Vizcaya, in the industrial Basque country, in 1941 only 724 were militants from the pre-war days of José Antonio Primo de Rivera, and more than 9,000 had joined after the war.[64] Later, the numbers of radical 'Old Shirts' were further thinned as the volunteer Blue Division dispatched by Franco to the Eastern Front to fight for Hitler lost numbers. Some who volunteered and were feted as heroes in the early 1940s had done so because they had been too young to be active in the 1930s and to fight in the Spanish war.[65] Some observers believed the political aim of the regime all along had been to dismember radical elements in the Falange.[66] Increasingly, the Movimiento would be swamped by *arrivistes* eager to participate in the spoils system, to protect economic interests, or joining merely out of fear of being implicated with the Republic.

The political background of ordinary individuals continued to follow them around. In each province, employers were required to provide the authorities with a sworn list of all employees.[67] The government decreed in October 1940 that unemployment registration would be dependent on production of a certificate from the previous employer.[68] There were

the real situation was worse. 'Informe sobre desequilibrio entre precios y salarios', October 1946, AGA, 17.02, sig. 52/46, SGM, SP, caja 41, p. 4.

[62] Fermín Sanz-Orrio, *Arriba*, 19 March 1946, p. 4.

[63] On the 'Old Guard', see Emilio Romero, *Los papeles reservados*, 2 vols. (Barcelona, 1985), vol. I, pp. 119–30.

[64] Report on Jefe Provincial (Granell), Vizcaya, February(?) 1941, AGA, 17.10, SGM, DNPC, caja 67.

[65] E.g., *Pueblo*, 5 January 1943, pp. 1–2; *Juventud*, 5 August 1943, p. 2. See also Xavier Moreno Juliá, *La División Azul: sangre española en Rusia, 1941–1945* (Barcelona, 2005).

[66] On 'disarticulation', see, e.g., Marías, *Una vida presente*, vol. I, p. 317.

[67] For Barcelona, see *La Vanguardia Española*, 3 August 1939, p. 3.

[68] R. Garrabou, J. Lleixà and O. Pellissa (eds.), *Franquisme: sobre resistència i consens a Catalunya (1939–1959)* (Barcelona, 1990), p. 65.

thousands of dismissals of employees from private companies and public offices, although re-employment could be gained with a certificate of good conduct signed and issued by a regime insider.[69] Those unable to obtain the necessary certificate, if they were unable to work at their own trade for years, would likely suffer great hardship.[70] The political purging of the workforce quickly became a source of confusion, however, in the reincorporation of combatants into the workplace and even created shortages of skilled labour.[71] The sixteen thousand men who had migrated to Bilbao with the 'liberating army' were keen to remain, although some Falangists predicted that the future consequences of uncontrolled migration to industrial centres would be 'terrible': the Castilian or Navarran farmer was 'completely overturned materially' in Vizcaya and would have to be obliged to return to run the family farm if a living could still be made there.[72] Larger industrial companies in areas where the Falange was relatively weak independently announced amnesties for workers who fell within the category of those to be 'purged', however. Inconsistencies were pointed out:

If it is accepted as a good criterion that he who abandons his place of work to join up as a volunteer in the Red militia has no right to reincorporate himself in his workplace, then it is indispensable that he who abandons his job to flee abroad or to the Red zone should find himself in the same position. To sanction the first and not the second is inadmissible. The first at least have a guarantee in their hands of having fought in the ranks of the National Army (some of them as conscripts), while the second have no moral or legal excuse with which to protect themselves.[73]

None of this meant that Franco's single state party (the Movimiento, based on the Falange) was unimportant since it represented a sense of continuity in a regime which owed its very existence to the civil war. When threatened by a resurgent monarchist movement in the late 1940s which appeared to promise political reforms, the Falange played a part in conjuring up apocalyptic images of the years of the Second Republic in order to stave off notions of an amnesty for Republicans, freedom of the press, or democratisation, and to ensure that the war memories of the mass of conservative feeling would support this intransigence. Monarchism was associated with a discredited past, with outdated

[69] Josep Solé i Sabaté, 'La justicia catalana franquista y sus fuentes', in Sánchez et al. (eds.), *España franquista*, p. 90.
[70] E.g., Valladolid, Elordi (ed.), *Años difíciles*, p. 238; Collier, *Socialists*, p. 177.
[71] See, e.g., *Información* (Bilbao), 15 May 1939, p. 252.
[72] CNS, Delegado Provincial, 'Informe sobre el paro', Vizcaya, 5 October 1939, AGA, 17.10, SGM, DNPC, caja 23.
[73] CNS, Delegado Provincial, 'Informe sobre el paro'.

traditions which it was believed had led to catastrophe. Franco's ambassador to the Holy See, Ruiz-Giménez, commenting on the visit to Rome in 1949 of the legitimate heir to the Spanish throne, Don Juan de Borbón, insisted privately that, rather than considering a monarchical return, it was more important to reform the state with 'its organic institutions and with the juridical norms which channel the spirit of our generation'.[74]

If monarchism was discredited and Falangism repressive, Catholic non-elite lay groups would provide a consistent outlet for discontent and associational life from the 1940s onwards, in spite of the ecclesiastical hierarchy's close association with the 'crusade'. The Catholic workers' association, the Hermandad Obrera de Acción Católica (HOAC), founded within Acción Católica (AC) in 1946, pressed for greater freedom for union activity and would give cautious support to the first major strikes which took place in 1951, though AC leaders warned against any return to the past and the regime suppressed many of HOAC's activities.[75] One regional AC dignitary in Madrid expressed caution: 'I believe that our workers' leaders must never cease to be workers [...] They must habitually be in their workshops, factories or centres of work [...] The socialists did the opposite and those of us who had to wrestle with them reproached ourselves for it.'[76]

At the same time, young, educated and socially aware Catholics, including the intellectual, activist and child of the war Alfonso Carlos Comín, would establish relations with elements of a socially oriented Catholic past which pre-dated the war. Comín was also influenced by the French Catholic intellectuals who had been critical of Franco's crusade and by the social Catholicism preached by some Spanish Church leaders (such as Ángel Herrera, who would become Bishop of Málaga in 1947), and put into practice by parish priests in workers' missions by the 1950s.[77] The 1940s, as Comín described them, were 'the dark years of Spanish Catholicism', the period when his mother would recount anecdotes to her youngest son about his Carlist father who had died in the war and when the content of religious faith did not matter as long as it had been demonstrated that you were a Catholic.[78] He was also much affected

---

[74] Tusell, *Franco y los católicos*, pp. 183, 187.
[75] Michael Richards, 'Falange, Autarky and Crisis: The Barcelona General Strike of 1951', *European History Quarterly*, 29, 4, 1999, 543–85.
[76] Letter of Emilio Enciso Viana, 4 May 1951, Archivo de Acción Católica General de Adultos (AAC), caja 95, carpeta, 95–1–1.
[77] See, e.g., Ángel Herrera, *La palabra de Cristo*, 10 vols. (Madrid, 1952–8), a vast collection of sermons and homilies.
[78] Comín, 'Fe en la tierra', *Obras*, vol. II, p. 302.

by the work of the Republican poet Antonio Machado, and based his faith on a Christ who came from and belonged to the humble classes.[79] Comín would later move to the Málaga slums to work and live amongst the poor.[80] Herrera's critique was more restrained and came from within the Church. When he greeted the papal nuncio, Tedeschini, in Madrid in June 1949, he evoked the civil war not so much as a crusade, however, as a trial sent from above which resulted from a failure 'to give appropriate attention to instructions from Rome and the consequent and tremendous offence to God who sent us the punishment we deserved'. The country had responded to the test by sacrificing 'much of its youth in the trenches'. Spain would continue to act as 'the right arm of the Catholic Church, because so much heroism, so many prayers, such martyrdom, could not be lost'.[81] When his criticism risked sanction, however, Ruiz-Giménez advised him so, suggesting that his reference to 'the totalitarian reality' might be misunderstood and that the 'right to rebellion', which had been argued for justifiably to legitimate the rebel generals in 1936, could not be spoken of in the post-war era for fear of encouraging opposition to the regime. Alberto Martín Artajo, Catholic Minister of Foreign Affairs and former president of AC, also urged caution in relation to Catholic dissent, commenting that such exceptional circumstances as those pertaining in 1936 (eliciting rebellion) were not likely to be repeated 'during this generation'.[82] Ruiz-Giménez, whose views would become far more radical after 1956, maintained that Catholic unions, like the HOAC, made no sense in Spain because the official *sindicatos* had a 'genuinely Christian inspiration' and the existing system could be reformed 'from above'; granting freedom to trade unions would amount to 'opening the door again to the Marxist enemy'. A series of papers presented to participants in a Catholic mission in Bilbao in 1953, including one on the possible legitimacy of strike action, was accordingly suppressed by the government, and Carrero Blanco, chief of the political general staff, sent a warning to Martín Artajo about 'Marxist proselytising', insisting that, as a consequence of the war, it fell to the state to 'organise society upon foundations distinct from liberal and anarchic ideas'.[83]

---

[79] See chapters VI, XV, XXXIX of Antonio Machado, *Juan de Mairena. 1936*, ed. José María Valverde (Madrid, 1972). Also José María González Ruiz, *La teología de Antonio Machado* (Madrid, 1975).

[80] His extended study of the social and economic development of Andalucía, first published in 1965, was a form of tribute from an urban middle-class northerner (from a Francoist family) to the working class of his adopted region from where so many migrants to Barcelona had come: Comín, *España del sur*, in *Obras*, IV (Barcelona, 1987).

[81] *ABC*, 9 June 1949, pp. 6–7; *Ecclesia*, 11 June 1949; Tusell, *Franco y los católicos*, p. 237.

[82] Tusell, *Franco y los católicos*, pp. 290–1.   [83] Tusell, *Franco y los católicos*, pp. 212, 360–1.

Sacred and performative memory

The Holy War was the founding myth of the post-war Franco state. The narrative of religious crusade, emphasising martyrdom, ascetic values, a cyclical conception of time, and social stasis, dominated the official war memory objectified in the many shrines dedicated to the sacrifices of the war. The early Franco years saw the sacralisation of political discourse and of public and performative memory, which conjured up the suffering of the war.[84] The 'crusade' had many martyrs, first identified as such by Pius XI during the conflict, and a protracted process of beatification began in October 1944 with nine of the religious killed in Mieres during the Asturian revolution ten years before, confirming a sense that the war was begun by the left before 1936.[85] Such activities relied upon mutual support between the political regime and the Church. Franco had explicitly given encouragement to Acción Católica in April 1940, many of whose members had been killed during the civil war: 'the greater part of the people needs to be re-Christianised [. . .] Go forward with the assurance that you may count on all of the confidence and all of the support of the New State.'[86] The 1941 agreement signed between Rome and the Spanish state granted control of education and a monopoly of public devotional symbolism to the Church, although this created friction with Falangists who were also responsible for propagandising. When in 1942 the Bishop of Málaga wished to use the radio to publicise an AC campaign to re-Christianise Sundays and devotional festivals, for example, the national President of AC, Alberto Martín Artajo, felt compelled to write a letter to the Falange's Delegado Nacional de Propaganda in Madrid for permission.[87]

A crusading memory was persuasive to Catholics even though it was imposed coercively on the defeated, as witnessed in the symbols of domination: the fascist-style raised-arm salute and memorial crosses to 'los Caídos' ('those fallen for God and for *patria*'), with lists of names

---

[84] On collective memory as performative – 'as only coming into existence at a given time and place through specific kinds of memorial activity', see Nancy Wood, *Vectors of Memory: Legacies of Trauma in Post-War Europe* (Oxford, 1999), p. 2. For agency in social memory, see Paul Connerton, *How Societies Remember* (Cambridge, 1989), particularly pp. 41–104, on recollection and bodies brought together through performative acts.

[85] See Pedro Chico González, *Testigos de la escuela cristiana: beatos mártires de la revolución de Asturias* (n.p., 1989). The eight holy brothers and one priest were not finally beatified until 1990. Some 34 religious personnel were killed in Asturias in October 1934: Montero, *Persecución*, p. 44.

[86] *ABC*, 13 April 1940, p. 8. See, e.g., note dated 5 May 1941, on the killing of the director and staff of the AC anti-Marxist newspaper *Trabajo* in 1936: AAC, caja 93, 93–2–2.

[87] Letter to Patricio G. Canales (1942), AAC, caja 208, carpeta 208–1–2.

(especially of Falangists) displayed on the walls of parish churches, to which, in some places, it was expected that passers-by would make the salute. When people declined, and some did resist, they were likely to be denounced and punished with a beating or a prison cell.[88]

Popular religiosity, focused on expectations of the Mother of Christ to intercede in earthly and heavenly matters in times of trial, seems to have permitted a degree of collective and controlled unburdening of collective emotions related to the war, but the simultaneous use of coercion casts considerable doubt on the achievement of a generalised spiritual reconstruction. The moving words contained in a final letter to her family from a socialist woman executed in 1941 nonetheless suggest the complexity of religious faith: 'I ask only that you take my daughters along the right road in life, that they are good, that they turn out to be honourable women as their mother has been [...] and that they turn often to the Virgin [...] [She] will be mother of my children; she will protect them and defend them from all danger.'[89] The cathartic potential of Holy Week processions, the re-enactment of suffering through Christ's Passion, and the annual devotional procession of a released prisoner on the festival of the Virgin of Merced (24 September) remained limited even in the first post-war years, largely because of the lack of a political will and legal framework of reconciliation. Too often the rituals reinforced rather than de-activated wartime and class boundaries, and the official refusal to recognise publicly the wartime sacrifices made by the defeated continued throughout the Franco years.[90] In contrast to the catharsis (though limited) offered by such popular devotions as Holy Week, when the image of the Sacred Heart, associated with the middle classes and social elites, was processed in Málaga in June 1940, attended by military and Movimiento authorities, a sense of conquest was evoked:

Málaga, when it cast the image of Christ from the streets of the city, made way for the multitude which became owner of lives and property. Now it views the beautiful image of the Heart of Jesus through tears of emotion and memories of tragedy, as again He becomes master of a Málaga purified by fire, beautified by the crown of the martyr and watered by the noble blood of its sons.[91]

To a limited degree, the 'families' of the regime – most significantly Catholics, representing traditionalism and much of the middle class, and

[88] See testimony from pueblo in Jaén: Elordi (ed.), *Años difíciles*, p. 286. Also pp. 86–7.
[89] Cited in ibid., p. 228.
[90] On ritualised release in Málaga, see, e.g., *Sur*, 29 March 1945, pp. 1, 3. On Holy Week: Richards, 'Presenting Arms'.
[91] *Málaga y el corazón de Jesús* (Málaga, 1940), p. 12.

Falangists, imbued with a populist zeal – disagreed about reconciliation, as is clear from a passage from the 1946 Falange press:

Spain, after a century of divisions, landed up in the terrible adventure of the civil war. Dozens of cities destroyed, a million deaths [sic] and several million defeated and resentful have been the final tally of this trial. We have glorified our dead and rebuilt the devastated pueblos. But the spiritual reconstruction of Spain awaits: the rebuilding of the national conscience.[92]

But even the most radical Falangists feared a resurgence of liberalism and an organised working class. For the same writer the solution lay not in practical measures but in the metaphysics of National Catholicism: a restructuring of individual conscience, requiring an influx of new priests into the Church: 'the furrows have been opened by the victorious sword of our Caudillo. But we require individuals able to sow the seeds.' In practice, the memorial activities of the social and political groups which most actively supported the regime would be predicated on what they saw as their own collective trauma rather than on an inclusive process of bringing society together.

The neo-pagan Falangist cult to the dead, including the display of names of the fallen on the exterior walls of churches, was not welcomed by all clerics and would be roundly criticised by the maverick Cardinal Segura of Seville who refused to allow memorial inscriptions to appear on the walls of his cathedral. But during the civil war and its aftermath there was no generalised move to prevent the mixing of representations of Catholic saints and martyrs with the Falangist 'fallen'.[93] Gradually, after April 1939, public war memories were appropriated by the Falange, a process which produced usable rhetoric and memorial ceremony in the interests of the state.

As the state was reconstructed there was a shift therefore from mourning and overcoming loss towards evocation of the horror and the targeting of accusations against the Republic and Republicans. Urban spaces where violence had been visited upon those who supported the rebellion and which had been shaped by the conflict became sites of memory. This rapid politicisation of memory can be traced in the construction of the memory of the wartime killing of rightist prisoners in Madrid, particularly those who had been held in the Modelo prison during the early months of uncertain Republican rule when the capital was besieged by rebel forces.[94] In the aftermath of the military rebellion

---

[92] Jesús Suevos, *Arriba*, 19 March 1946, p. 8.
[93] Tusell, *Franco y los católicos*, p. 341. Also, e.g., Claudio Hernández Burgos, *Granada azul: la construcción de la 'cultura de la victora' en el primer franquismo* (Granada, 2011).
[94] G. Arsenio de Izaga, *Los presos de Madrid: recuerdos e impresiones de un cautivo en la España roja* (Madrid, 1940).

against the government, General Fanjul, instigator of the revolt in Madrid, had been executed in the precinct of the prison. The wartime population of the Modelo would rapidly grow as hundreds of middle-class residents of the city, including large numbers of military officers and several prominent political figures, including Falangists and leading figures of the CEDA, were arrested as possible 'fifth columnists' in a somewhat indiscriminate process driven by both ideology and panic. The revolutionary violence also saw many ad hoc killings, known as *sacas* ('being taken out') or *paseos* ('being taken for a ride'), carried out by the leftist militias.[95] Some of those taken prisoner, including young Catholics like Joaquín Ruiz-Giménez and his two brothers, had been detained at the instructions of the Republican authorities to protect them from the militia patrols. Others were moderate Republicans, including Melquiades Álvarez, leader of the Partido Reformista, who would be one of those murdered during the night and early morning of 22–23 August 1936, when thirty or so prisoners were killed, probably as popular retaliation for the mass killing of Republicans by rebels in Badajoz a week before.[96]

The effects of the executions on the Republic, both internally and abroad, were significant. Fearing the reaction of foreign governments, the moderate PSOE leader Indalecio Prieto declared that 'with this brutality we have lost the war' and applied pressure on the Left Republican prime minister José Giral to establish popular courts (Tribunales Populares) in order to curb excesses and channel revolutionary justice through some form of legal process.[97] Melquiades Álvarez had been a political mentor and friend of Manuel Azaña who had become President of the Republic in May 1936 and who suffered a profound personal and political crisis on being informed of the August killings. His close associate Ángel Ossorio y Gallardo, a convinced Republican but also an avowed Christian and conservative, was contacted to speak with the President, and argued that responsibility for outrages rested ultimately with the military rebels who had produced the dreadful situation of civil war and that Azaña must remain to do his duty. Ossorio also evoked 'the logic of history': a 'new civilisation' was being created. The President felt unable to accept these latter arguments – he failed to see how the brutal reality

---

[95] See, e.g., Cervera, *Madrid en guerra*, p. 52; González Posada, *Diario de la revolución*, p. 16; Montoliú, *Madrid*, pp. 19–23.

[96] The first 'saca' from the prison in Málaga occurred on the same day as that in Madrid: Francisco García Alonso, *Flores de heroísmo* (Seville, 1939), p. 94.

[97] Gabriel Jackson, *Breve historia de la guerra civil española* (Barcelona, 1986), p. 73; Zugazagoitia, *Guerra y vicisitudes de los españoles*, pp. 128–31.

had anything to do with a 'new civilisation' – but he complied with his duty, nonetheless, and did not resign.[98]

The first mass held in memory of those killed in the prison in August 1936 took place on 22 April 1939 and was celebrated by a priest, José Palomeque Flores, who had himself been a wartime captive.[99] Open-air masses were prayed within the ruined precincts of the prison.[100] The idea of an association of prisoners had been born during captivity, spoken about as a way of strengthening morale. With the celebration of the first mass in the name of the martyrs, an association of survivors (the Asociación de Supervivientes de la Primera Galería de la Cárcel Modelo) took concrete form. In the initial declaration Father Palomeque focused on the need to heal the pain of the ordeal rather than evoking the horror: 'the aim of this Association is not to recall criminal acts nor to produce rancour, but to ask for God's pity for the souls of the victims who gave their lives for Spain'. Making reference to the pain suffered during the period of captivity, he also called for forgiveness 'for all persecutors'.[101] Thoughts of anger or revenge were not sustaining, he maintained; spiritual resources, including personal examination of conscience, had made survival possible and the predicament in the aftermath had to be offered up to God in order to make peace with oneself.[102] The principle that only forgiveness could bring peace was contradicted, however, by the dominant imperative towards expiation, punishment for the suffering created, and penance, and an inexorable will to define the power of the new state consciously in contrast to 'enemies'.[103]

The most notorious episode of mass killing in the Republican zone, however, had been the execution at Paracuellos and Torrejón of some 2,700 rightist prisoners from the prisons of Madrid who were 'liquidated' with the connivance (at least) of Soviet NKVD agents in early November and December 1936.[104] The process of according the victims the status of martyrs of the 'crusade' began as soon as the city was occupied. Newspaper notices began to appear requesting information about loved ones who had been imprisoned. The Minister of Interior, Ramón

---

[98] For Azaña's association with Álvarez, see Santos Juliá, *Vida y tiempo de Manuel Azaña, 1880–1940* (Madrid, 2008), pp. 51, 107–116. For his crisis, see pp. 392–3. For documentation: Juliá (ed.), *Manuel Azaña: Obras completas*, 7 vols. (Madrid, 2007), vol. VI, pp. xv, 259.

[99] *ABC*, 21 April 1939, p. 8.   [100] *ABC*, 29 April 1939, p. 10; 30 April 1939, p. 5.

[101] *ABC*, 25 April 1939, p. 18.   [102] See also, in Málaga, García, *Flores*, p. 25.

[103] See also Richards, 'Presenting Arms'. On the analogous case of German army officers ('the front generation') on returning from the front in 1918 as the subject of 'trauma' constructed politically through 'the stab-in-the-back' thesis, see Richard Bessel, 'The Great War in German Memory', *German History*, 6, 1 (1988), 20–34.

[104] Viñas, *Escudo de la República*, pp. 35–87. Also Gibson, *Paracuellos*.

Serrano Suñer, who had been much affected by his own brief wartime imprisonment and the loss of two brothers at Paracuellos, publicly related the events of August 1936 at the Modelo prison within days of the Nationalist entry into Madrid at the end of March 1939.[105] On 11 April 1939 the first plea for information appeared in the conservative newspaper *ABC*, requesting news of a Nationalist airman who had been held in the Modelo but 'disappeared' during the first weeks of November 1936.[106] Further such requests appeared during the next few weeks and the basic facts of the dreadful events gradually emerged, though no precise account of responsibility was offered.[107] By the end of April it was clear that those who had disappeared during this period had been victims of the *sacas*; their martyrdom could now be confirmed and the first death notices began to appear in which the killings were described using the ubiquitous wartime labels employed by the rebels: 'victim of the Marxist fury', or of the 'Marxist and foreign hordes'.[108]

With the city's 'liberation' it was possible to search for victims' remains, though this was a relatively protracted process. The body of the medical doctor José María Albiñana, founder of the Partido Nacionalista Español, and one of the Modelo victims, was identified in early 1940, in the cemetery of La Almudena, and taken amid some political ceremony to his birthplace in Valencia for burial.[109] Other martyrs' bodies were claimed. The mayor of Vitoria, for example, visited Madrid in January 1940 to express to the widow of Ramiro de Maeztu the desire that the mortal remains of the founder of the right-wing organisation Acción Española might be laid to rest in the city of his birth.[110] An Asociación de Familiares de los Mártires de Paracuellos de Jarama y Torrejón de Ardoz was quickly established, later broadened to become the Asociación Oficial de Familiares de Mártires de Madrid, including those of the Modelo, and functioning in conjunction with the Hermandad Nacional de Ex-cautivos and the Falange to catalogue the victims and issue certificates once documents of identification of 'the

---

[105] *ABC*, 8 April 1939, pp. 19–21. On Serrano's escape and his brothers, see Moral Roncal, *Diplomacia*, pp. 118–19, 129. For earlier wartime propaganda based on prisoner testimony, see, e.g., Julio F. Guillén, *Del Madrid rojo: últimos días de la cárcel Modelo* (Cádiz, 1937).

[106] *ABC*, 11 April 1939, p. 29.

[107] *ABC*, 13 April, 1939, p. 28; 14 April 1939, p. 22; 16 April 1939, p. 27.

[108] E.g., *ABC*, 14 April 1939, p. 20; 16 April 1939, p. 29; 26 April 1939, p. 27; 11 May 1939, p. 20.

[109] *ABC*, 26 April 1940, p. 10; 28 April 1940, p. 14. Violent squads associated with Albiñana's party were responsible for purges in Castile. On Burgos, see, e.g., Castro, *Capital*, pp. 211–22.

[110] 'Actos piadosos en memoria de los Caídos', *ABC*, 7 January 1940.

sacrificed' ('*los inmolados*') had been presented by relatives. Plans were put in place for a subscription to construct a monument at Paracuellos to those killed 'by the hordes of the Popular Front' which would become the primary site of memory of the massacre with funerals for the fallen each year, beginning in 1940 and coinciding with the Catholic festival of All Souls.[111] A state grant of 100,000 pesetas was presented in June 1939 by General Franco, and in early 1940 the disinterring of bodies at Torrejón began, for transferal to Paracuellos, which became a sacred site with its monument in the form of a Via Crucis and chapel.[112]

With gradual politicisation, public interest became oriented towards the origins of the massacre and responsibility for it. Details of subsequent Consejos de Guerra (military court hearings) were publicised as part of a general recounting of atrocities committed 'in the name of the Popular Front'.[113] In August 1939, on the third anniversary of the Modelo killings, a multitudinous ceremony was held within the ruined site in memory of 'the fallen' with a procession of forty thousand affiliates of Falangist organisations at its centre, including boys and girls of the youth movement, amid fascist salutes from those present.[114] A field mass was held on one of the inner courtyards before a large 'Cross of the Fallen': the blood which had been shed would 'fertilise the National Movement'.[115] In contrast to the first masses of the immediate post-liberation period in April, and although this was only some four months later, the accompanying rhetoric was shrill and the dominance of the Falange was marked. The sense of an approaching European war and of Falangist sympathy for the anti-communism of Hitler and Mussolini is palpable in the newspaper reports which relay how it had been 'the Asiatic frenzy irradiating from Moscow' which, in the civil war killings in the Republican zone, had cut down 'the true Spain'. The officiating priest, on exalting Franco, urged all those present to 'pray to God to guard his life for the good of the *patria*'.

By the summer of 1940 and the fourth anniversary of the August 1936 killings, the complicity of the Republican authorities attracted greatest attention: the Popular Front government had 'decreed' the killing and, by 1942, the claim was that a metaphorical 'death sentence' had been

---

[111] *La Vanguardia Española*, 20 August 1939, p. 12; 7 December 1939, p. 6; 7 November 1943, p. 12; 8 November 1953, p. 3.

[112] *Arriba*, 9 April 1941, p. 3; *ABC*, 16 June 1939, p. 41.

[113] E.g., on responsibility for the Modelo killings, *ABC*, 2 May 1939, p. 17; on the Bellas Artes 'Cheka', *La Vanguardia Española*, 20 April 1940, p. 1.

[114] By the end of 1936 the prison had been virtually destroyed because of its proximity to the battle front.

[115] *ABC*, 23 August 1939, pp. 1, 4, 11; *La Vanguardia Española*, 25 August 1939, 3.

passed on the victims as early as April 1931 when the Republic had been inaugurated. The government had 'handed over the victims to the horde', and foreign states, those at war with the Axis powers in 1942, had made no protests.[116] The commemorative narrative would indeed be shaped by responses to the European war, and by August 1943, the seventh anniversary of the Modelo killings, the tide had begun to turn against the Axis war effort and public memorialisation was more muted.[117] In the relevant section of the report of the Causa General, published in 1943, it was nonetheless taken for granted that the legitimacy claimed by the Republican government implied a capacity to control all political groups within its orbit and that the government, in 'deciding' not to rein in the killers, was responsible.[118]

In the 1940s, therefore, Madrid had become a source of memories of violence associated not with the shelling and bombing of the city by the rebels but with particular sites where Republican atrocities had been committed. Rather than becoming a sacred site, however, the Modelo prison was represented as a place of contamination. Although it had been a place of sacrifice of 'the fallen', there would be some ambivalence about its memory as a result of the victors' denigration of the polluted city. The leading Francoist journalist, Manuel Aznar, declared bluntly towards the end of May 1939 that 'Madrid is repugnant to us [...] We appeal to the heavens that a new city be born upon the blood-stained ruins [...] And that the physical and moral centre can break through the cordon of vileness and squalor created during the last few decades by the Madrid of the Reds.'[119] There would be no new prison as replacement for the Modelo on the same site, close to the centre of the city. The desire was to push the gaol, those detained within it, and all of the connotations of the 'degenerate' Republic to the margins of Madrid, to the working-class district of Carabanchel, in the south of the city, where families lived amid war ruins and where a new penitentiary would begin to take shape in 1940, built by a thousand Republican prisoners and to be opened in June 1944. It was not that the Modelo was painfully identified with the murder of rightist prisoners, but that an opportunity was presented to 'cleanse' the city and replace it with a statement in stone about the permanence and power of the new regime. A huge new building to house Franco's military Air Ministry, inspired by Philip II's palace and monastery, El Escorial, and the Nazi Reich Chancellery in Berlin, would be erected on the site of the

---

[116] *ABC*, 22 August 1940, p. 1; *ABC*, 23 August 1942, p. 7.

[117] *ABC*, 22 August 1943, p. 10; 21 October 1943, p. 12; Ministerio de Justicia, *Causa general*. For the section on the Modelo prison, see pp. 215–29.

[118] Ministerio de Justicia, *Causa general*, pp. 217–18.   [119] *ABC*, 25 May 1939, p. 3.

old prison. A space for a 'cross or monument' was to be left free on the prison site to 'perpetuate in that place the suffering and martyrdom of the prisoners who were taken from there to be murdered by the Red horde'.[120] As the prison building was dismantled, stones from the ruins were used in other war memorials in the region.[121] On the other main site of civil war killing within the city, the Montaña barracks, also destroyed during the conflict, a monumental Falangist Casa del Partido, another Escorial, was planned, occupying 70,000 square metres. This became one of several grand projects of the 1940s to be abandoned for lack of resources, and the site eventually became a public park.[122]

It would be Paracuellos, however, which would become synonymous with the crimes of 'los rojos', the name itself part of the official and daily discourse of war memories and accusations against the Republic for decades. One of the several homes established in Madrid after 1939 for war orphans was named after the place, for example.[123] Other children's institutions in the city, all still functioning into the 1970s, recalled the battles of Brunete and the Jarama. In February 1940 an emergency housing settlement was established in Madrid, built by political prisoners, as part of a network of *campamentos provisionales* set up under the auspices of the technical services of the Falange. The location was the Campo de Comillas, on the war-ravaged proletarian outskirts of the city, site of a famous rallying speech made by Manuel Azaña in October 1935 in the process of re-creating the Republican–Socialist alliance which would fight and win the Popular Front elections of February 1936. The prisoners were part of a labour battalion including those from the Miguel de Unamuno Prisoner Classification Centre.[124] Some 700 units, with

---

[120] *BOE*, no. 178, 15 June 1939; *ABC*, 17 October 1940, p. 6; 26 November 1941, p. 17. The new ministry was created by a law of 8 August 1939 and its functions were decreed on 1 September 1939. For influences, see, e.g., *Vértice*, June 1942; Alexandre Cirici, *La estética del franquismo* (Barcelona, 1977), p. 128.

[121] E.g., the 10-metre-high Monument a los Caídos positioned by the Carretera de Aragón in 1943 at the entrance to Madrid's Ciudad Lineal and the rotunda with cupola begun in 1954 in the Plaza de Moncloa but never completed. *ABC*, 23 October 1943, p. 5; Javier Fernández Delgado, Mercedes Miguel Pasamontes and María Jesús Vega Gonzalez, *La memoria impuesta: estudio y catálogo de los monumentos conmemorativos de Madrid (1939–1980)* (Madrid, 1982), pp. 385–90.

[122] Francisco José Portela Sandoval, 'El eco del Escorial en la arquitectura española de los siglos XIX y XX', in Francisco Javier Campos and Fernández de Sevilla (eds.), *El monasterio del Escorial y la arquitectura* (San Lorenzo, 2002), pp. 341–2. A monument to the fallen was established by a memorial commission in 1972. Fernández Delgado et al., *Memoria impuesta*, pp. 168–9.

[123] See Carlos Giménez, *Todo Paracuellos* (Barcelona, 2007).

[124] Sixto Agudo González, 'Comunicado sobre los campos de concentración franquista', in *Los campos de concentración y el mundo penitenciario en España durante la guerra civil y el franquismo* (Barcelona, 2003), pp. 934–45.

capacity for 4,140 homeless people, were put up in forty days, 'thanks to the initiative of the Caudillo', without electricity or water and with floors of sand, though inaugurated with conspicuous religious and political ceremony. Such occasions were opportunities to recall the sins of the revolution, and in Madrid this invariably signified references to Paracuellos. In his inaugural speech, the provincial head of the Falange, Jaime de Foxá, did not spare his words, claiming the rudimentary housing development to be 'our response to that great falsehood of [Azaña's] meeting at Comillas four years ago [sic] which begat in the mind of the greatest monster of the century the dreadful preparation of the murders [paseos] of the revolution in Madrid'. With a peculiarly Falangist emphasis, Foxá identified three 'glorious dates' upon which the 'new Spain' affirmed itself through remembering: the birth of the Falange (29 October 1933); the unification of all the 'combatants of Spain under the flag of rebellion' (13 July 1936), and 7 November 1936, 'a sacred day for Madrid, when the best of the city's youth was lost in the terrible common grave at Paracuellos'.[125] Sternly administered by Falangists, most of the inhabitants of the emergency housing were war widows, the mothers of prisoners, or the wives of those in hiding. Those who infringed the regulations, including the night-time curfew, would be taken to the authorities for castor oil to be administered or for a punitive shaving of the head.[126]

Demonising language would continue in newspaper reports about commemoration of the Paracuellos killings throughout the 1950s and the early 1960s.[127] The alleged culpability of the PCE leader, Santiago Carrillo, which would become a controversial issue during the transition to democracy in the 1970s, was 'established' and made public in the early 1940s.[128] The massacre and the killings more broadly in wartime Madrid and elsewhere in the Republican zone affected several generations of elite society, constituted through influence and intermarriage by established aristocratic families and the new Francoist political caste. One example was the well-connected Navarran family of María Arteta y Goñi, whose daughter was married to the prominent Falangist minister José Luis de Arrese (in 1932). María Arteta's husband, Gregorio Sáenz de Heredia, brother-in-law of General Miguel Primo de Rivera and uncle of the founder of the Falange, José Antonio, was killed at Paracuellos, as were

---

[125] *La Vanguardia Española*, 27 February 1940, p. 1; *ABC*, Seville, 27 February 1940, p. 3.
[126] Elordi (ed.), *Años difíciles*, pp. 99–100; José López Diaz, 'Vivenda social y falange: ideario y construcciones en la década de los 40', *Scripta Nova*, 7, 146, 1 August 2003.
[127] See chapters 5 and 6.
[128] On Carrillo, see *La Vanguardia Española*, 9 November 1945, p. 3. On the persistence of the myth of Carrillo signing death sentences: e.g., Bullón and Diego, *Historias*, pp. 160, 164.

two sons. She would later be awarded the Medalla de Sufrimientos Por la Patria. When she died in 1965 the obituary tribute described her in terms which reflected the new focus on peace after 1964: 'one of the heroic Spanish mothers who contributed with her sorrow and sacrifice to the Spanish peace of today'.[129]

Public memory in the aftermath of the civil war was articulated by specific staunchly pro-regime groups. Although a discourse of healing could be glimpsed at times, the emphasis in the 1940s was certainly upon evoking and condemning the horror of the war which was laid exclusively at the door of Republicans. Organised civil associations which were energetically pro-Franco but not part of government, as such, transmitted and sustained recollections of particular experiences and sacrifices from which they constructed the case for having suffered collective trauma. There was a high degree of interchange between these associations and governmental state institutions. The motivation of those who were mobilised in such groups may not have been primarily political or ideological, but collectively to remember lost family members fighting on the rebel side; they were concerned both with redeeming the sacrifice and with the construction of a new moral community. Their commemorative actions and the language employed were inevitably bound up with the politics and guiding principles of the regime which excluded the defeated.

This process of collective remembering constituted an embryonic associational activity within the public space between family and state; at this time the dynamic was neither broad nor autonomous of absolute rule, but it would later connect with more critical forms of remembering the conflict. A few of the youngest men during the war who entered the restricted political sphere in the 1940s and 1950s would be amongst the first to seek reform in the mid 1950s. But militant Catholicism, fascism and military hardliners largely followed the lead of Franco, the symbolic embodiment of the victory; they believed in the constructed truths and certainties of the 'crusade'. Building the state thus precluded reconciliation: the country would be subjected materially and symbolically to the power of the victors.[130] Although in the immediate aftermath some priests and Falangists expressed a need for a more developed sense of national conscience, this would be drowned out in the 1940s by political imperatives: the war and the heroism and sacrifice exclusively of the

---

[129] *La Vanguardia Española*, 30 May 1965, p. 44. A plaque to Navarran martyrs was unveiled on the day of Saint Francisco Javier in December 1941 at the church of San Fermín de los Navarros in Madrid.

[130] Richards, *Time of Silence*, p. 69.

victors conferred sufficient political capital upon them to make their power unified, permanent and unquestioned. Exclusion, discrimination and repression were therefore the essence of the post-war state-building process which responded to calls for justice and retribution; any conflict between the 'families' of the regime could be resolved by invoking the war and its traumatic legacy. Memory thus also contributed to punishment of 'the Reds', of 'the enemy within', and of so-called 'Marxist families'. The truth value of the rhetoric of anti-communism found apparent confirmation and a logical outlet once Hitler began to wage war on the Soviet Union, and it would do so again after 1946 during the first stages of what would become the Cold War. This again meant conjuring up images of the violence of the revolution in the Republican zone. Whilst the regime and its support base thus harked back for many reasons, the social memory of the defeated, though barely discernible beneath the surface of political rhetoric and officially sanctioned commemoration, was both repressed and paradoxically less tied to social stasis, as the next chapter will seek to demonstrate.

4 Repression and reproduction: social memory in the 1940s

> If all this bloodshed is washed away and forgotten it will be not only a triumph for General Franco but a miracle.[1]

> Times are bad; we are living among people any one of whom may have murdered our father or our brother, and yet we have to treat them as if they were our friends.[2]

That the immediate post-war years in Spain were marked by social fragmentation should not seem surprising. Even from the cloistered surroundings of Salamanca, Franco's temporary headquarters in 1937, the Rector of the Irish seminary recognised that the horror would not be easily forgotten. A year later he had not altered his view: 'those [who] remember our tiny civil war in Ireland, and what it cost the country, will understand what the recent war must have cost Spain'. When, a decade later, in the spring of 1949 Gerald Brenan called on a family in rural Granada he had first known years before the war he found that the horrors of the executions which had followed the military rising of 1936 were as present in their minds 'as though they had happened yesterday'. Perhaps they felt able to talk about the war to someone who was an outsider, as had the officer of the Civil Guard cited above, more sensitive than most to fears about an 'enemy within'.[3]

Appalled by the violence on both sides, the wartime President of the Second Republic, Manuel Azaña, had made an impassioned plea in July 1938 for a future reconciliation, though it was to be in vain:

Although hatred and fear have played such an important role in the incubation of this disaster, this fear will have to be dispelled and the hatred will have to be concealed, because however much Spaniards are killing each other now there will still remain plenty who will need to resign themselves – if that is the correct term – to continue living together, if the nation itself is to carry on living.[4]

---

[1] Rector of the Colegio de Nobles Irlandeses, Salamanca, Annual Report (S46), 1937–8 (p. 5), 1938–9 (p. 4), Salamanca Papers, Maynooth University, Dublin.
[2] Brenan, *Face of Spain*, pp. 121–2.   [3] Ibid., pp. 133–4.
[4] Manuel Azaña, 'Discurso en el ayuntamiento de Barcelona', 18 July 1938, in *Los españoles en guerra*, pp. 122–3.

General Franco's total victory, consummated eight months after Azaña's speech, signalled the death knell for hopes of reconciliation. There would be no intervening peacekeeping force as thousands of refugees fled towards France. Azaña, who would become the most demonised public figure of Francoist propaganda after 1939, would be amongst them. Though there was no active policy of reconciliation, a semblance of 'normality', widely understood as a return to peace, order and authority, was in the aftermath of the exhaustion and bloodletting of the war appealing to much of society.

Memories of the internal life of areas where the war was directly and violently felt suggest a generalised avoidance in the 1940s of politics or discussion of anything related to social class, division and conflict. Convinced Republicans who would have insisted that the violence had been instrumental in crushing lower-class demands for reform were repressively silenced. For many of the uncommitted it made sense to explain violent conflict as the result of private vendettas or quarrels which could be seen plausibly in personal terms. Thus, a narrative of the war at the micro level usually became accepted if it was sufficiently vague. For decades, those with responsibility for the wrongdoing of the past remained unidentified, a mystical 'other', partly because there was no consensus over who bore responsibility, but also because of fear: 'we were told [in the 1960s] that the only event of the civil war was that "they" had burned the church and that "we" do not talk about politics because that is why people kill one another'.[5] This way of making sense of the situation fitted the discourse available to those who were raised and lived in such communities. Remembering was painful and ultimately offered few benefits, so a tacit agreement to 'forget' was entered into. Though the atmosphere was socially less stifling, something similar can be said of urban society. In his memoir about a constrained middle-class life in Barcelona during the early post-war years of the 1940s, published in 1975, the year of General Franco's death, the poet and liberal publisher Carlos Barral described the motives for this general acceptance of the predominant way of 'remembering' the war:

Not only were virtue and shame imposed, and orthodox thinking and fear of God, but all record of a different life was wiped from consciousness. Nobody felt obliged to understand those who had been mistaken. All the older people I knew in those days had either lived under the wing of the Nationalist army or had suffered the unrepeatable privations and humiliations of the war. In my family any allusion to Republican relatives was scrupulously avoided: influential people

---

[5] Collier, *Socialists*, pp. 6–7, 179. See also Morales and Pereira, *Memoria*, pp. 125–6; Barker, *Largo trauma*, pp. 209–12, 214. Also Chapter 7.

who had shared our table and were now on the other side of the frontier or had committed suicide in some political prison. And everyone, including the maidservants, who the day before yesterday had shouted '*no pasarán*', took part in the enthusiasm for the new era and wrapped themselves in the folds of delirious religiosity.[6]

The reduction by those who were not convinced Francoists of dissonance associated with the war's legacy made life easier but there was a moral and psychological cost: dictatorship required that such everyday compromises of conscience also be forgotten. This chapter explores how this avoidance of the past related to the rebuilding of power and daily reproduction of society in the 1940s through a combination of violence, accommodation and active support.

Social fragmentation and networks of advantage

For many, even for those who were not strictly refugees, the end of the war began a period which was darker still than the conflict itself. The political dynamics of wartime, shaped locally by privatised power and intimate violence, were carried over into the era after 1 April 1939. In addition, the conflict provoked a significant economic regression. After a civil war it is rare indeed that any foreign power can be held responsible and forced to indemnify the victors. Who, then, was to pay for reconstruction in post-war Spain? Economic repression was complex, but it originated in Franco's regime handing socio-economic power back to pre-war elites and in a pervasive sense that 'the defeated' within the country must bear the cost.[7]

All wartime refugees were ordered by the authorities to return to their place of origin, although many did not adhere to this order, knowing that returning would probably lead to a process of 'classification' and punishment. When the city of Málaga was occupied in February 1937, thousands had fled along the coast, eastwards, towards Almería. Many would continue, eventually reaching Barcelona, and some of them finished up in French concentration camps after escaping the Francoist advance on Catalonia in the winter of 1938–9. The perception of the conquerors was that those who fled must have had 'uneasy consciences' and were 'probably implicated in murder', an accusation which would be attached to refugees long after the end of the civil war.[8] Without a guarantee from

---

[6] Carlos Barral, *Años de penitencia* (Barcelona, 1975), p. 18.

[7] On this specific point, see Moreno Torres (Director General de Regiones Devastadas), *Reconstrucción urbana*. Also Richards, *Time of Silence*.

[8] Luís Bolín, *Spain: The Vital Years* (London, 1967), p. 252.

a regime insider, any individual coming from a previously 'Red' zone would be submitted to a process of political purging, risking deprivation of liberty and of future employment. Only for those with an unimpeachably rightist background was the process a formality. Many others were left to languish in prison. The Falangist provincial head in the Balearic Islands wrote directly to Franco in March 1942 suggesting that the magnanimous granting of freedom to ten leftists imprisoned in the penal colony of Formentera in August 1936 as a precaution, though they had committed no crime, would be a dignified way of celebrating the third anniversary of the Victory.[9] Those who were released through Libertad Vigilada (Conditional Liberty) and the families of those executed or still in prison were watched, and often socially and economically marginalised.[10] For many, 'conditional freedom' restricted the public sphere to daily work and attending Mass.[11]

The violence of occupation and the instituting of a nationwide system of military trials against the Republican population, a repression which was socially reinforced through denunciation by 'ordinary Spaniards', bound the insurgents and their supporters together during the civil war. Wartime refugees who returned to communities at the end of the war often faced the humiliation of a witch-hunt, and scapegoating became part of the rites of legitimation of triumphalist authorities and neighbours. The occupants of posts in local government were named by these 'liberating' forces. The new local bureaucracy, and those with economic power, composed of pre-war elites and *arrivistes* who would benefit from the divisions of the war, played on war memories to cement their authority. The town of Mijas (Málaga) was typical: the influential shopkeepers and professionals, who were committed to the new regime by background and personal experience, took advantage of the opportunities. Their allegiance was publicly displayed in a plaque set in the wall of the *ayuntamiento* (town hall), celebrating the village's liberation from 'the Marxist Hordes' by 'Franco's Imperial Crusade'.[12] The counterpoint to this process was the disappearance of the revolutionary culture of the left, for which elites were grateful. The anti-state objectives of the 1930s' rural and semi-urbanised working class had met with a historic defeat and their organisations, unions and clubs, as well as the slogans about

[9] Declaración del Jefe Provincial de FET-JONS, Baleares, 24 March 1942, AGA, SP, 17.02, sig. 52/46, caja 8.
[10] Report of DGS, Toledo, 29 April 1942, Fundación, *Documentos* (FNFF), vol. III, p. 425.
[11] DNII bulletin no. 627, Oviedo, 15 April 1942; no. 679, Granada, 15 May 1942; both AGA, 17.04, VCG, caja 16; Morales and Pereira, *Memoria*, p. 126.
[12] Ronald Fraser, *The Pueblo: A Mountain Village on the Costa del Sol* (London, 1973), p. 120. Also Sánchez Jiménez, *Vida rural*, p. 245.

redistribution of land and work, would never re-emerge again in the same way. Under the pressure of war memories and real and threatened state repression, a form of self-silencing seemed inevitable.[13] The psychiatrist Carlos Castilla del Pino recorded how difficult it was in the late 1940s to break the silence even in the privacy of his consulting room in Córdoba. Fear 'paralysed' those who related their stories. It was unusual, at the same time, for a day to pass when he did not run up against problems derived from the war. The typical dialogue he recalled ran along these lines: 'Are your parents still alive?' 'No, my father died twelve years ago now.' 'From what did he die?' 'In an accident.' 'How did it happen?' 'Well, it was in the war.' 'But what kind of accident?' 'The things that happened then.' 'And brothers and sisters, how many of you are there?' 'There were six of us, but the two eldest also died during the war.'[14] Other testimony, many years after the war, was often equally oblique: 'I was left without a father almost as soon as I was born'; 'he was left without parents and I raised him. God wanted it that way.'[15]

An element of this pressured and partial 'return to normality' involved the willingness of fearful people in rural communities who had supported the Republic to allow the language of politics to be replaced by idioms of honourable personhood; the avoidance of shame (vergüenza), the culturally constructed perception in a community of what was moral, remained an imperative in such communities well into the 1960s and even beyond.[16] Although formerly fear of shame may have acted as an integrative factor, the reforming and educating ethos and legislative action of the first governments of the Republic had threatened to detach social groups from dependency on custom-based external moral sanctions. The events of the 1930s and the intimate violence of the war undermined integration: reimposition of vergüenza, external moral sanction by the community (as distinct from individual conscience, which refers to internal moral sanction), played a role in the dynamics of victory and defeat in rural communities (as discussed in Chapter 2). Moral judgements, seemingly about women's 'looseness' or a young man's homosexuality, when the targets were related to previously left-wing families could obscure the political dimensions of the social critique aimed at them.[17] In particular,

---

[13] E.g., Abdón Mateos, 'La contemporaneidad de la izquierdas españolas y las fuentes de la memoria', in Alicia Alted (ed.), *Entre el pasado y el presente: historia y memoria* (Madrid, 1996), p. 96. Also Esteva Fabregat, *Industrialización e integración*, p. 22.

[14] Castilla del Pino, *Casa del olivo*, p. 125.   [15] Botey Vallès, *Relats*, pp. 60–1.

[16] See Aceves, *Social Change*, pp. 65–8.

[17] Collier, *Socialists*, p. 183; Gil, *Lejos*, pp. 272, 397; Stanley H. Brandes, *Migration, Kinship, and Community: Tradition and Transition in a Spanish Village* (New York, 1975), pp. 149–51; Julian Pitt-Rivers, *People of the Sierra* (London, 1954), p. 113.

the defeat – and the hunger which went with it – produced migration on a considerable scale in the immediate aftermath of the civil war, creating shanty towns on the outskirts of the main cities (earlier than is usually recognised), where the scrutinising gaze typical of the pueblo could be avoided. To officials, this process, which would carry on during the 1950s and become a flood in the 1960s, was marked enough in the 1940s to have had an 'asphyxiating' effect on urban municipalities.[18] By the late 1950s, a new industrial working-class way of life would develop, based on large-scale factories, and militancy would be focused on improving wages and conditions through collective bargaining and furthering democratisation.[19]

Economic production and consumption depended on the inefficient and often vengeful rural elite. State legislation formalised the return of wartime collectivised agricultural land, 'redeemed from the Reds', to former owners.[20] Combined with state intervention, this created scarcity and resource hoarding, a huge black market and great hunger. Personal memories of the 1940s make frequent reference to this situation at the micro level of fractured politics and primitive accumulation. Examples were the forced depositing of staple products – grain and olive oil, particularly – with local state authorities in exchange for a certificate of political reliability.[21] Elements of the Castilian peasantry who had supported the rebels believed that their sacrifices, 'born in the hard years of our war', entitled them to greater rewards, though the majority of humble Catholic peasants ultimately received scant tangible benefit.[22] Nonetheless, such was the extra value extracted from basic necessities, wheat, flour, and other primary products, through the manipulation of scarcity by 'food-controllers' linked to social and political elites and their control

---

[18] See José Antonio Martín Fernández to Ministerio de Gobernación, 'Informe – Valores municipales', May 1944, AGA, SGM, Vicesecretaria; sig. 17.04, 52/35, caja 41. Also, e.g., Solé, *Inmigrantes*, pp. 66, 97; Morales and Pereira, *Memoria*, p. 126; José Antonio Ortega and Javier Silvestre, 'Las consecuencias demográficas', in Pablo Martín Aceña and Elena Martínez Ruiz (eds.), *La economía de la guerra civil* (Madrid, 2006), pp. 87–96.

[19] See, e.g., Santos Juliá, 'Obreros y sacerdotes: cultura democrática y movimientos sociales de oposición', in Javier Tusell et al. (eds.), *La oposición al régimen de Franco*, 3 vols. (Madrid, 1990), vol. II, pp. 147–59.

[20] 'Ley de 23 de febrero 1940 sobre devolución a sus propietarios de la fincas ocupadas', *BOE*, no. 66, 6 March 1940. In spite of appearances to the contrary, propaganda suggested that, with the victory, agriculture had seen a resurgence. *La Vanguardia Española*, 31 August 1939, p. 2; Miguel Primo de Rivera in *Hechos*, November 1942.

[21] E.g. Lazo, *Retrato*, p. 60. On memories of food exports from Bilbao in early 1940s, e.g., Elordi (ed.), *Años difíciles*, p. 90.

[22] Richards, *Time of Silence*, pp. 134–43. AGA, SP, 17.02, sig. 52/46, caja 3, letter from Abastos, 20 March 1942; Informe, Abastos, 21 March 1942; Informe, 1941, AGA, SP, 17.02, sig. 52/46, caja 8.

of local tax levies, that a great concentration of capital and landholding was possible.[23] Charles Tilly sees this 'opportunity hoarding' during war situations as operating when members of 'a categorically bounded network' ('the victors') acquire access to a resource that is 'valuable, renewable, subject to monopoly, supportive of network activities, and enhanced by the network's *modus operandi*' (the daily control of staple necessities by 'the victors').[24] Capital accumulation, aided by the state's regressive and corrupt tax system, would be invested in the new economic opportunities offered by tourism and the construction industry in the 1950s and 1960s.[25]

It is significant that denunciation and financial reward were related: one individual in rural Seville, for instance, having recently allied with property owners in his village, was able to save a younger brother from execution, the arbitrary use of official standing which also permitted the imposition of economic penalties for petty infringements of the new moralism, such as using irreverent language, buying a black-market loaf of bread, or defying the curfew.[26] Under such acute conditions of dependency it was easy to make acceptable social and political behaviour the condition for granting a supplementary ration.[27] It was not that there was a deliberate Francoist policy to starve 'Reds', but clearly there was widespread lack of concern among authorities about hunger, itself founded on a prior ideological schema reinforced by the war, and countless opportunities to profit materially at the expense of 'the defeated'. Some officials registered the extent of the suffering and attempted to relieve the situation. In an October 1941 report which reached General Franco's future *éminence grise*, Admiral Luis Carrero Blanco, the Civil Governor in Cádiz related how,

the extremely grave situation of food shortages which this province, one of the most undersupplied in Spain, finds itself in, because of underproduction, has

[23] Carlos Barciela, 'El mercado negro de productos agrarios en la posguerra, 1939–1953', in Josep Fontana (ed.), *España bajo el francismo* (Barcelona, 1986), p. 200. Also Ridruejo, *Escrito en España*, p. 98; Pitt-Rivers, *People of the Sierra*, p. 21; Collier, *Socialists*, p. 176. Also DNII bulletin no. 552, 15 March 1942, AGA, VCG, 17.04, caja 16.

[24] Charles Tilly, *The Politics of Collective Violence* (Cambridge, 2003), p. 10.

[25] A 1951 report by several procurators of Franco's pseudo-parliament (led by the future Minister of Finance Navarro Rubio) was devastating in criticising the disproportionate burden placed on 'the modest classes' by a fiscal system essentially unreformed since 1849: Proposed amendment to 1952–3 budget, AGA, SGM, Secretaría Política, 52/46, sig 17.02, caja 72, November 1951.

[26] E.g. Lazo, *Retrato*, p. 52. Also Vega Sombría, *De la esperanza*, p. 251; Gil, *Lejos*, pp. 394–6.

[27] E.g. Botey Vallès, *Relats*, p. 81; Francisco Alburquerque, 'Métodos de control político de la población civil', in Manuel Tuñón de Lara, *Estudios sobre historia de España* (Madrid, 1981), p. 427; Joan Serrallonga Urquidi, 'Subordinación, abastos y mortalidad: La Montaña Catalana, 1939–45', *Historia Social*, 34 (1999), 45–66.

culminated in an appalling elevation in the number of deaths [...] As the winter approaches, with all of the severity of that season, it is to be expected that the index of mortality will continue its upward spiral.[28]

The plight of the countryside was, in the end, the result of the civil war and the victors bore some responsibility. In August 1939, a doctor from Huesca felt compelled to write to the then Secretario-General of the Movimiento, Agustín Muñoz Grandes, to complain that when a child in Altorricón had died of hunger the local authorities had been 'indifferent'.[29] This sense of economic control as an element of repression, in the face of suspected organised financial aid (Socorro Rojo) collected by left-wing sympathisers, is plain in the declarations of a Falangist intelligence officer from Murcia in February 1942:

the fact that numerous families of those who have fled in order to elude the weight of justice (including those on conditional release or an attenuated prison regime) carry on their lives normally, even though they lack known sources of goods and income, and get on well from an economic point of view, suggests that the Socorro Rojo is functioning within the province.[30]

While officials acted freely, informal justice was employed by landowners and their political agents in punishing economic crimes, such as petty theft of foodstuffs and poaching.[31] One young lad from rural Lérida who was sixteen in 1939 explained how 'people lacked all solidarity, because a deep fear had taken hold of what remained of that society'. The reforms of the Republic had permitted his family to work some land in order to make a living, but in 1939 they were denied cultivation there because they were seen as opponents of the regime. His father was in exile and the young men of the family were forced to become muleteers to make ends meet, undergoing feudal conditions, sleeping with the animals and being contracted to the employer twenty-four hours a day.[32]

Exclusion was fuelled by demands for justice and retribution based not merely on ideological persuasion but also on a sense of entitlement from aggrieved sections of society which saw it as the state's duty to respond. Long-standing social or personal issues of contention which pre-dated 1936, usually to do with land ownership or tenancies, were

[28] Cited in Ángel Viñas et al., *Política comercial exterior en España (1931–1975)*, 3 vols. (Madrid, 1979), vol. I, p. 318.
[29] Letter, 17 August 1939, AGA, VCG, Correspondencia, 17.04, caja 1.
[30] DNII bulletin no. 501, 28 February 1942, Murcia, AGA, 17.04, VCG, caja 16.
[31] E.g. Luis Miguel Sánchez Tostado, *La guerra no acabó en el 39* (Jaén, 2001), pp. 455–6; Fuensanta Escudero Andújar, *Dictadura y oposición al franquismo en Murcia* (Murcia, 2007), pp. 175–6.
[32] Elordi (ed.), *Años difíciles*, pp. 288–9. See also Collier, *Socialists*, pp. 212–14; Barker, *Largo trauma*, pp. 216–23 (including political confiscation of property).

stoked up by war divisions and post-war profiteering and political favouritism. Rebuilding political authority was begun by purging society, as is borne out in the sentiments expressed by local representatives of the New State at the end of the war. After almost three years of turmoil, there was an understandable preference for stability, and many accepted that this would be achieved in part coercively. A captain of the Civil Guard in the province of Cáceres expressed this desire for a return to 'daily life' and 'tranquillity', where 'the honourable' could pursue their rights protected by the law. At the same time, the conquering authorities would carry out 'an extensive cleansing'.[33] The popular journalist Wenceslao Fernández Flórez, who had been obliged to seek refuge in a foreign embassy in Republican Madrid before being evacuated to the rebel zone, reflected similar sentiments in June 1939:

We lived [before the victory] without justice, which is the greatest torment that a man can suffer. But now we have justice, rapid, pure, perfect. It is the bread of the soul [. . .] Everything is going well. The criminals are falling: the sacrilegious, the instigators, those who steal, those who kill [. . .] But you and I and everyone still has to do something [. . .] Nothing violent [. . .] but to do with the ethic of good citizenship, a healthy policing of morals. The Caudillo has spoken: 'the war is finished, but good Spaniards must stay alert'.

Although the courts of law were not perfect, according to his observations, 'the conscience of honest, decent, people (was) itself like a court of law which must begin to function immediately'.[34] The privately expressed affirmations of the provincial head of the state party in Toledo, outlining problems and aims to Madrid in October 1939, echoed this sense of justice based on a framework of shared ideals:

The first moral problem is to carry out rapid and energetic justice; the families of those killed [by the Republican side in the war], who are the most solid moral mainstay that the province and the Cause possesses, become demoralised if they see weakness. The province has approximately 20,000 killers who must urgently disappear; these people have never worked and they never will, they have never been grateful and they never will; assuming that each one costs only 2 pesetas daily, that is still 40,000 pesetas a day; 15 million per year! With that I could sort out this province economically.[35]

---

[33] Chaves Palacios, *Represión en la provincia de Cáceres*, p. 101.

[34] *ABC* (Seville), 1 June 1939, p. 3. Fernández Flórez confirmed his loyalty to the new regime of 1939 by publishing a novel based on lurid tales of the blood-thirsty multitude of Madrid: *Una isla en el mar rojo* (Madrid, 1939). On post-war executions seen popularly as legitimate: e.g. Bullón and Diego, *Historias*, p. 198.

[35] 'Problemas de la Provincia de Toledo', 25 October 1939, AGA, VCG, 17.02, sig. 52/46, caja 228.

Hunger forced the poor to resort to the feeding stations of the Movimiento, particularly Auxilio Social, the Falange's rudimentary social aid organisation, giving propaganda opportunities and reinforcing social control. Among those forced to live in shacks (*chozas*) or caves on the margins of communities were many who were subject to the process of conditional liberty, imposed because of wartime antecedents, which demanded that they report regularly to the police and account for their whereabouts, so that a prisonlike atmosphere was created in small communities.[36] Networks of power, formed of old elites and 'new' opportunists who had joined the Falange, coalesced through patronage and clientelism and the agencies of 'purification' and law enforcement charged with 'liquidating' the 'crimes' of the civil war.[37] These included local Commissions of Libertad Vigilada which enforced conditions of release and other formal bodies for the regulation of Nationalist ex-combatants' benefits (in pay and employment). Many towns set up their own commissions to take evidence for the Causa General (the state-sponsored lawsuit against Republicans), to inform the authorities about civil war violence, church burning and collectivisation. This activity was conducted through networks of advantage in which political and economic gain were often inseparable. The publicising (or invention) of war heroism and personal or group wartime adherence to the Glorioso Movimiento Nacional and donations to the organisations of the Falange established unimpeachable political credentials with the likelihood of future economic benefits, at the expense of 'the defeated'. One woman from a rural community recalled many years after the event how her family had discovered that their home had been sacked by people in her pueblo and another family moved in. A provincial Falangist decree of August 1936 in Huelva encouraged occupying forces to appropriate and sell property to pay for alleged political crimes; both Republican and rebel forces 'requisitioned' in this way 'for the war effort'.[38] The 'us and them' boundary between Republicans and rebels was confirmed by habitual use of the term

---

[36] Testimonies: rural Seville: Botey Vallès, *Relats*, p. 92; Elordi (ed.), *Años difíciles*, p. 320.

[37] On local networks, see, e.g., Escudero Andújar, *Dictadura*, p. 38; Miguel Ángel del Arco Blanco, *Hambre de siglos: mundo rural y apoyos sociales del franquismo en Andalucía Oriental (1936–1951)* (Granada, 2007); Joan J. Adriá, 'Los factores de producción del consentimiento político en el primer franquismo', in Ismael Saz and A. Gómez Roda (eds.), *El franquismo en Valencia: formas de vida y actitudes sociales en la posguerra* (Valencia, 1999), esp. p. 140.

[38] E.g. Pilar de la Granja Fernández, *Represión durante la guerra civil y la posguerra en la provincia de Zamora* (Zamora, 2002); Southworth, *Antifalange*, p. 3; Ortiz Heras, *Violencia política*, pp. 395–9; Collier, *Socialists*, pp. 152, 162.

'rojo' ('Red') which was carried on from the wartime generation to the children of the war:

They shot my grandfather in August 1940 for being a Red. When he died my grandmother was only 35 and had three children to look after, as well as her mother and mother-in-law. It is impossible to imagine what she had to go through in order to bring up that family, and even more so in a pueblo in which she was marked out for being the wife of a Red. They put her in prison for this reason, they searched her house and took away the few items of value that she had. And they did it more than once.[39]

The home of Pedro Laín Entralgo's family, in rural Aragón, had twice been sacked during the war, first in 1936 by anarchists, who assumed that those who absented themselves were likely to be enemies of the cause, and then, after his Republican father's death, by Nationalist neighbours as the pueblo was occupied with the advance of the Francoist army towards the Mediterranean coast in 1938.[40] For many years afterwards, and in spite of his Falangist connections, Laín was looked upon with suspicion in the town of his birth.

Economic repression functioned beneath the rhetoric of a moral economy of the state based doctrinally on the mythical model of the ascetic agrarian family as primary unit of production, where men and women understood their roles and industry and the city were mistrusted.[41] The austere Castilian peasantry had been subjugated cruelly, it was argued, to the 'citizen ideology' of liberalism since the late nineteenth century.[42] This rural idealism can be summed up in the description of the industrial economy and urban life in the leading publication of the Francoist youth movement in 1943 as 'a general offence against the family economy which inevitably causes the degeneration of our own customs into impurity'.[43] There were, of course, conservative rural communities where life continued to be based on unchanging customs and traditions, usually in areas where there had been little or no political conflict during the Republic and civil war and which instinctively welcomed the military rebellion from the first moment. Here, indeed, winter family evenings in the first post-war years might have been spent gathered around the fireplace to exchange stories about the village, about the land, work, courtship, and marriage. The children were perhaps persuaded to demonstrate their scholarly

---

[39] See, e.g., Elordi (ed.), *Años difíciles*, p. 268. See also Solé, *Inmigrantes*, p. 70; Morales and Pereira, *Memoria*, pp. 35, 122–3.
[40] Laín Entralgo, *Descargo*, p. 299.   [41] See Richards, *Time of Silence*.
[42] Iniesta, *Garra marxista*, p. 278.
[43] J. R. Serra, 'Hay un enemigo', *Juventud*, 5 August 1943, 2.

abilities and the family would pray the rosary together. This form of life existed somewhat outside of time even in the aftermath of the war when this became the ideologically constructed ideal. 'History', we could argue, intervened in such households only when the father, as head of the family, imposed ritually that everyone listened in reverence as the Himno Nacional was broadcast each day by Radio Nacional.[44] As paternalist official doctrine encouraged a focus on family and domesticity, the private sphere became a place where traditional fatherly authority was perpetuated but also a site of refuge from public glare.[45]

Rural tranquillity often existed in relation to bouts of intense violence. When one woman whose Republican father and uncle had been imprisoned returned home with her mother to Los Corrales de Buelna in the province of Santander from a place of safety, they were advised to take refuge in her grandparents' house and to run there and not to stop until they arrived. The same night some residents of the pueblo came to their door accusing them of being 'rojas comunistas' and saying that they ought to have left when the 'liberators' had come 'to rescue the *patria* from communism'. Her mother was taken away for interrogation and was ordered to present herself to the local Falange so that she could participate in celebrating Franco's victory. The daughter understood that this would entail ritualised humiliation and she determined to go to the Guardia Civil to protest: 'the majority of the pueblo knew that we were good people, but at that time nobody dared to speak up for us'. Her own family had also been victims of the other side: 'the Reds' had killed two of her mother's cousins in reprisal for the first Nationalist air raid on Santander in 1937. Finally, she pointed to the crucifix which hung on the wall of the Civil Guard office – 'I asked him if the crucified Lord would approve of what was being done to us' – and this had some effect.[46] Like many others throughout the country in the aftermath of 'liberation', the family could not continue to live within the community and ultimately escaped with the help of friends who offered them shelter in Catalonia, a region which from the time of the war until the 1970s would attract masses of Spaniards, many of them fleeing persecution: 'it should not seem strange that my family loves Catalonia so much, because

---

[44] E.g. Xosé Chao Rego, *Iglesia y franquismo* (La Coruña, 2007), p. 474; María Guadalupe Pedrero Sánchez, 'Las cartas de tío Eusebio', and Josefa Buendía Gómez, 'Peinando recuerdos', both in Pedrero and Piñero (eds.), *Tejiendo recuerdos*, pp. 98, 110, 122–3, 165.

[45] Pilar Folguera, 'La construcción de lo cotidiano durante los primeros años del franquismo', *Ayer*, 19 (1995), 165–87.

[46] E.g. Elordi (ed.), *Años difíciles*, pp. 308–10. For the conflictive background and wartime violence in the municipality of Los Corrales, see Jesús Gutiérrez Flores, *Guerra civil en Cantabria y pueblos de Castilla* (Buenos Aires, 2006), pp. 79–81, 88–101.

it opened its arms to us in those moments in which our own land [*tierra*] offered us only hatred'.[47] During the Catalan floods of October 1940 she would meet her future husband, a political prisoner held in Barcelona who was assigned to help with reconstruction work. In Barcelona she would become one of many in the immediate post-war years who had arrived in the city as political detainees, or to be close to detainees and remained. The forced movement of young men through obligatory military service of two years (introduced in August 1940), was also to become a significant factor in post-war migration.[48] Many of them were also put to labour on public works projects. Virtually all those called up were deliberately stationed outside their home regions. This meant that many lost whatever civil employment they had secured, but it also opened the possibility of making a new start far from home.

Resistance and networks of survival

The brutality of the wartime violence meant that many leftists and supporters of the Republican government had little option but to flee into the hills, woods and mountains as villages, towns and cities were occupied by rebel forces. Avoiding the obligatory post-war process of classification and punishment, they became outlaws so far as the state was concerned.[49] The end of formal hostilities thus merged with the onset of sporadic underground wars, or *guerrillas*, which would last throughout the 1940s. Later the remnants of Republican groups were supplemented by escapees from Francoist prisons and concentration camps and those avoiding military service. By the time of the liberation of much of France in October 1944, many Republican exiles, organised by the PCE, had become hardened veterans of the French resistance movement, the so-called *maquis*, and would bring greater discipline and politicisation to the Spanish resistance. The political aim of the movement was to keep the ideals of the Republic alive and to hold out in the hope of an allied victory against Hitler and Mussolini, which it was believed would mean the end of Franco.

---

[47] See also the testimony of a 1950 migrant who 'owed everything to Catalonia': Solé, *Inmigrantes*, pp. 83–5 and 65–9.

[48] See María González Gorosarri, *No lloréis, lo que tenéis que hacer es no olvidarnos: la cárcel de Santurrarán y la represión franquista contra las mujeres* (San Sebastián, 2010), pp. 119–24; López Bulla, *Cuando hice*, p. 21; Botey Vallès, *Relats*, p. 99; Candel, *Otros*, p. 118; Miguel Siguan, *Del campo al suburbio: un estudio sobre la inmigración interior en España* (Madrid, 1959), pp. 89, 101; Collier, *Socialists*, p. 191.

[49] See José Antonio Vidal Castaño, *La memoria reprimida: historias orales del maquis* (Valencia, 2004), pp. 23–5, 30, 42.

In practice, the guerrilla groups concentrated largely on survival, and the struggle became entwined in resource-related violence and political activity. The resistance campaigns would see a return of the repression, particularly in areas where Republican ideas had held sway and revolutionary violence and collectivisation of land had been introduced during the civil war. A renewal of collaboration between local Falangists and the Guardia Civil reasserted the principle of authority in remote areas, even though the imposition of siege tactics alienated many and contrasted with the regime's general accent on 'normality'. The spreading of rumours and 'falsehoods', which were catalogued by Falangist intelligence agents in weekly reports, was explicitly associated in state propaganda with civil war enemies and with 'bandits', 'Masons' and 'Communists'. Gendered language was used to describe the covert threat: 'the rumour is like a procuress who drags the purest and healthiest intentions down towards the mire of evil [and] shows no respect for the roots of Spanish life, a life purified by the generous and heroic blood of its very best. We will separate the wheat from the chaff.'[50]

The generalised use of repressive force on a local scale in response to what the regime called 'bandolerismo' was symbolic of the state's reclamation of the monopoly of coercive force, though state forces of order rarely acted with general popular consent. Because the *guerrilleros* relied on communities of support in the villages and towns, the civil population became implicated and would suffer the worst of the violence.[51] Counter-strikes by the state following assassinations and sabotage were often impossible to direct against those responsible, and repression was therefore focused on civilians.[52] The authorities and their brokers could control locally generated resources upon which the population was dependent and, as 'war zones' were decreed by the regime, a 'pact of hunger' would be imposed to ensure that the families of fighters had no work and went hungry.[53] The relationship of the guerrilla fighters to communities was complicated still further by denunciations, a continuation of the sense of insecurity of the war. Thus, guerrilla violence

---

[50] F. Ferrari Billoch, *Andanzas del bulo: Apuntes para su historia* (Madrid, 1942), pp. 34–5.

[51] See J. Prada Rodríguez, 'La mujer y los escapados: aproximación al papel de la mujer como soporte material de la resistencia antifranquista', in Ministerio de Cultura, *Las mujeres y la guerra civil, II Jornadas de estudios monográficos, Salamanca, October 1989* (Madrid, 1991) pp. 218–23; Tomasa Cuevas, *Cárcel de mujeres 1939–1945* (Barcelona, 1985), p. 16; Collier, *Socialists*, p. 160; Agustina Monasterio Baldor, 'Cuando los árboles caminan: memoria oral y guerra civil en el valle del Miera', unpublished paper, New York University, 2010.

[52] Sánchez Tostado, *La guerra no acabó*, pp. 33–7.

[53] Di Febo, *Resisténcia y movimiento*, pp. 76–86; Barker, *Largo trauma*, pp. 223–8.

would be aimed not only at key local or regional political figures but later also at those found guilty of treachery.

Daily freedom of action in these areas would be constrained. Peasant farmers and land workers required a pass in order to reach their fields, making daily productive work problematic to such an extent that it was a further factor which concentrated rural wealth and pushed country people towards migration.[54] The tactic of starving out 'Reds' and the forced clearance of cultivated land and crop burning were used, subjecting entire villages to martial law and curfew regimes and even alienating some conservative peasant farmers who had previously supported the wartime 'crusade'.[55] Villagers or townsfolk were caught in a dilemma: if they failed to tell what they knew they risked violence from the authorities (including beatings and other forms of torture), but if they succumbed and provided information, they were also in danger from the resisters.[56] As an example to others, 'denouncers' could pay the ultimate price, according to the *ajusticiamientos* (quasi-judicial pronouncements) of the *guerrilleros*. The PCE leadership also feared that the movement might be infiltrated, that its 'purity' might be diluted, and was consequently ready to be brutal.[57]

The complexity and long-lasting political and psychological effects of this struggle for survival are suggested by the case of a young man from Córdoba whose father had been executed by the Nationalists during the civil war.[58] In 1950 he had been persuaded to join the *maquis* in the sierra, although he had quickly become disillusioned, especially by the brutal treatment of those who 'repented' and wished to return to town.[59] Dedicating himself only to cooking for the group, he had not participated in actions which he believed might later compromise him, and when he received a message from his betrothed to the effect that he could return since 'he did not have blood on his hands', he did so but was arrested and sentenced to imprisonment; in detention he was ostracised by other

---

[54] E.g. from Almería to Terrassa (Barcelona) in 1942: Botey Vallès, *Relats*, p. 78.

[55] See Hartmut Heine, 'Tipología y características de la represión y violencia política durante el periódo 1939–1961', in Tusell et al. (eds.), *La oposición al régimen*, p. 316.

[56] Sánchez Tostado, *La guerra no acabó*, pp. 427–30, 452; J. P. Chueca Intxusta, 'Mujeres antifranquistas en la retaguardia nacional: el caso de Navarra', in Ministerio de Cultura, *Las mujeres y la guerra civil*, pp. 224–8.

[57] Mercedes Yusta Rodrigo, *La guerra de los vencidos* (Zaragoza, 1999), pp. 74, 78–9, 146; Fernanda Romeu, *Más allá de la utopía: agrupación guerrillera de Levante* (Cuenca, 2002), p. 283; Hartmut Heine, *A guerrila antifranquista en Galicia* (Vigo, 1980).

[58] Carlos Castilla del Pino, *Un estudio sobre la depresión: fundamentos de antropología dialéctica* (Barcelona, 1966), pp. 117–20.

[59] For the post-war guerrilla movement in Córdoba, see Moreno Gómez, *Córdoba en la posguerra*, pp. 347–533.

prisoners because of his desertion of the cause. He began to feel persecuted and feared for his family, and under this pressure he began to see
'signs' in the form of crucifixes. After release, and on returning to his
pueblo, he suffered a similar ostracism, both by *las personas de derechas*,
because of his association with the guerrilla struggle, and by those of the
left, because he had forsaken the movement. At first, he closed himself
away, but later he escaped to Barcelona where he had a sister who had
migrated with her husband some years before. Deprived of human contact, he again became delusional, haunted by 'people who made the sign
of the cross with their fingers and arms', symbolising the threat of death.

Surviving the guerrilla resistance was intertwined with the daily
struggle for material survival of those recently traumatised by the war.
To exist in such straitened economic and political circumstances as an
excluded individual, without a network of supportive social relations, was
hardly to survive at all. Some of those who were persecuted clearly
achieved some sense of solidarity, however, through micro-level networks of survival by which 'the defeated' made a bare living; in a few
cases, after long years of sacrificial labour, some level of prosperity was
possible, though this was rare in the 1940s. Eventually some were able to
recall and talk with a sense of idealism rather than victimisation about the
post-war era.[60] A form of resistance to the imposition of scarcity, through
ingenuity, daring and hard work, often of women in particular, was
possible via the black market which operated at several levels.[61] Many
of the wives of men who had been killed or imprisoned, or were in hiding
or exile at the end of the war, practised small-scale commerce which,
because of government controls on all economic activity, had become
illegal.[62] It is not coincidental that during the very worst of the hunger in
the winter of 1941 there was a surge in the number of women in prison as
a result of sentences for small-scale illegal buying and selling.[63] The wife
of Manuel Cortes, the Socialist official who spent thirty years in hiding in
his own home from 1939 until Franco's general civil war amnesty of
1969, survived through such activity and managed most of the time to
evade the police.[64] With a friend whose husband had been killed in the

---

[60] E.g. Monasterio Baldor, 'Cuando los árboles'; Barker, *Largo trauma*, p. 249.

[61] See, e.g., Encarnación Barranquero Texeira and Lucía Prieto Borrego, *Así sobrevivimos
al hambre: estrategias de supervivencia de las mujeres en la postguerra española* (Málaga,
2003), esp. pp. 221–52.

[62] Based on his extended visit in 1949, Gerald Brenan noted this possibility of rising out of
poverty: *Face of Spain*, pp. 79–80, 105.

[63] Encarnación Barranquero Texeira et al., *Mujer, cárcel, franquismo* (Malaga 1994),
pp. 39–42.

[64] Ronald Fraser, *In Hiding: The Life of Manuel Cortes* (London, 1972), pp. 36–41.

repression, Juliana became an egg seller (*recovera*), buying produce from country people and walking on foot all night to the city of Málaga, where there was great scarcity, to sell them eggs, sleeping at her sister's home in the migrant zone of rudimentary dwellings which had grown up on the outskirts of the city since the civil war.[65] This practice flouted conventions of domesticity, and remaining within the parameters set by the community of what was shameful was not easy: 'people were envious of me, of the money I'd got; they talked about me because I was a woman alone'. Others were more charitable:

once in a while someone might say, 'Here, take this for your child,' and give me a bit of bread. But it was very rare [...] I didn't go round telling them my troubles, I kept them to myself. Because there were some who might be willing [for me] to share my troubles with them, but there were others who would say, 'let her look out for herself. He [her husband] shouldn't have got mixed up in politics; that was their fault.'[66]

The concurrent upsurge in urban migration from the rural south to the largest cities and a burgeoning of the shantytown dwellings on the margins, called *chabolas* (in Madrid and elsewhere) and *barracas* (in Barcelona), also originated with the war, the intensity of its violence and subsequent repression, and the failure of a political will to seek reconciliation. One migrant, interviewed many years later, put it simply: 'we came from the war [...] from the prisons'.[67] In attempting in 1941 to explain that year's epidemic of typhus in the country, Franco's post-war Director General of Health, José Palanca, reflected the great demographic disruption of the war and its aftermath by describing it as 'the dance of the Spaniards'.[68] In the ten-year period from 1935 to 1945 the population of Spanish cities had grown hugely: for example, Las Palmas grew by 25 per cent, Valencia and La Coruña by 40 per cent, Salamanca by 44 per cent, and Albacete by 56 per cent, and this according only to official statistics which understated the shift.[69] The refugee problem during the war, added to by the repression, the fracturing of rural communities, and the guerrilla conflict, all became impulses towards

---

[65] For the black market and war widows, see also Barker, *Largo trauma*, pp. 305–7, 310.
[66] Fraser, *In Hiding*, p. 40.
[67] Morales and Pereira, *Memoria*, p. 154. Also Candel, *Otros*, pp. 115–17; Carmen Martín Gaite, *Esperando el porvenir: homenaje a Ignacio Aldecoa* (Madrid, 1994), p. 93.
[68] José Palanca, 'Hacia el fin de una epidemia', *Semana Médica Española*, 4, 2 (1941), 432.
[69] Pedro Bidagor Lasarte, Jefe de la Sección de Urbanismo de la Dirección General de Arquitectura, *El futuro Madrid* (Madrid, 1945), p. 48. Similar claims can be made for other cities in Andalucía, for example Seville, Granada, Málaga and Almería. *Anuario Estadístico* (1943), 44. On urban migration generally in the 1940s, see Jesús García Fernández, *La emigración exterior de España* (Barcelona, 1965).

the post-1939 process of urbanisation. In the small town in Huelva studied by the anthropologist George Collier in the 1960s some 35 per cent of those on the defeated side in the civil war had migrated in the period 1937–50 compared to 25 per cent in the town at large. Life expectancy was also lower for the defeated survivors of the war who had still been young in the 1940s.[70] When depopulation was recalled it was remembered that many of those who left in the 1940s and 1950s had earlier been imprisoned and that most did not return. If many of the civil war defeated were forced to sell up, some descending on the social scale, from being traders, for example, to become wage labourers, others who were not politically compromised found their position reaffirmed and some, even those previously without land, were able to become land-owners by acquiring property from neighbours who had been 'on the wrong side'.[71] Nonetheless, it was often through some act of familial support or social solidarity, as well as personal sacrifice over a long period, that migration was possible.

Local statistics collected by Catholic lay organisations as early as 1943 revealed a marked migration from the rural areas of Burgos in Castile to the provincial capital, the population of which had grown by 50 per cent since 1935, much of it as a result of refugees fleeing the violence.[72] The burgeoning shanty towns on the outskirts of many cities were viewed optimistically by the underground Communist opposition as a possible focus of political resistance which would provoke a coordinated state response.[73] By contrast, the Falangist press alluded to migration as a form of Calvary, describing the slums of Madrid in 1950 as the city's 'crown of thorns' which threatened 'the brilliant, happy and confident centre'.[74] By the end of 1947 it was estimated that in seventeen large cities there were 797,992 individuals living in these informal migrant

---

[70] Collier, *Socialists*, pp. 171–2, 175. See also Morales and Pereira, *Memoria*, pp. 79, 107, 120, 122.

[71] E.g. Francisco Lara Sánchez, *La emigración andaluza* (Madrid, 1977), p. 193; Collier, *Socialists*, pp. 9, 23–4, 41–4.

[72] *Ecclesia*, 29 May 1943, 10. See also, for similar cases, Roque Moreno Fonseret and Francisco Quiñonero Fernández, 'Guerra civil y migraciones en una ciudad de retaguardia: Alicante (1936–1940)', paper presented to the seminar 'Jornadas sobre Movimientos migratorios provocados por la guerra civil española', University of Salamanca, 15–17 December 1988; Moreno Fonseret, 'Movimientos interiores y racionamiento alimenticio en la postguerra española', *Investigaciones Geográficas*, 11 (1993), 309–16; González Martínez, *Guerra civil en Murcia*, pp. 128–34; Josep Maymi Rich, Josep Ros Nicolau and Xavier Turró Ventura, *Els refugiats de la guerra civil a les comarques del Gironès i el Pla de l'Estany* (Barcelona, 2006); Ortega and Silvestre, 'Las consecuencias demográficas'.

[73] E.g. *Nuestra Bandera*, May 1950, pp. 413–14.

[74] *Arriba*, cited in *Nuestra Bandera*, January 1950, p. 12.

communities, including 60,000 families in Barcelona and 40,000 in Valencia, with few basic services (see Map 6). For each individual a police file was initiated but there was not a commensurate political will or resources to resolve the causes of *chabolismo*.[75]

Such were the conditions in parts of the countryside that those who fled hunger and unemployment were encouraged by local officials with the offer of free transport, even though this was in the form of filthy and evil-smelling train wagons intended for livestock, which took days to reach their destination. At a time when levels of health had plummeted because of hunger, migrants were vulnerable to suffer the consequences. One woman, a child in 1939, vividly recalled years later how, on arrival at Getafe station (on the outskirts of Madrid) 'they took us out of the cargo wagons and put us in third-class carriages so that the spectacle of our arrival in Madrid would not appear as shameful as it had in Getafe. My mother was eight months pregnant and when she jumped from the wagon the foetus became dislodged and the child was still-born.'[76] In several towns in the province of Córdoba the authorities presented labourers with a train ticket and 10 pesetas in return for the promise that they would leave and not return. Many travelled to Valencia, where they were not particularly welcome, and, in desperation, occupied the remnants of dwellings which had been bombed during the war.[77] It was in these areas that typhus first appeared in the city.

The travails of leaving the past behind were thus not over once migrants arrived in the city. Both men and women migrants worked long hours, the younger women often as domestic servants, those who were older employed occasionally as seamstresses in the houses of the well-off. It was particularly difficult for the families of prisoners to make a living, and many became dependent on Auxilio Social. One woman, whose husband was 'redeeming' his political crimes through hard labour in a penal work detachment, gave up one child to the local *junta* (committee) for the protection of minors for adoption and sold half of her own meagre food ration on the black market enabling her to buy enough basic necessities for her other children. She had come into contact with Auxilio Social and its Central Department for the Protection of Mothers and Children by attending daily at one of its public kitchens.[78] Children also

---

[75] *Libertad Española*, 7, 16 August 1956, p. 8; Batista, *Brigada Social*.

[76] Elordi (ed.), *Años difíciles*, pp. 98–9. Also p. 242; Howard Kershner, *Quaker Service in Modern War* (New York, 1950), pp. 86–7; José Palanca, 'Las epidemias de la postguerra', *Gaceta Médica Española*, 17, 5 May 1943, 205, 208.

[77] Marcos Hernández, *La generación perdida*, pp. 46, 71.

[78] José J. Piquer y Jover, *El niño abandonado y delincuente: consideración etiológica y estadística* (Madrid, 1946), pp. 231–2. Also Elordi (ed.), *Años difíciles*, p. 221.

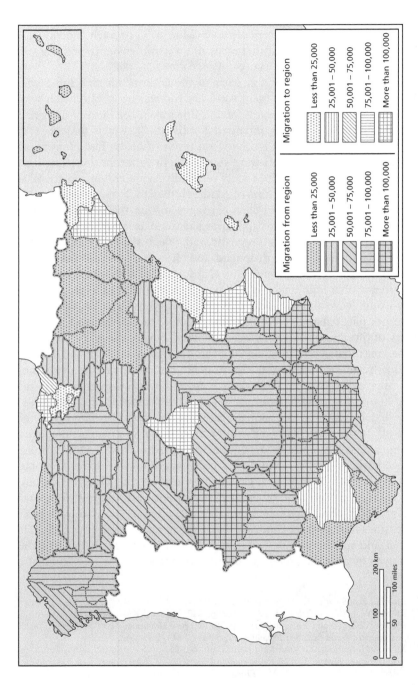

Migration from region

	Less than 25,000
	25,001 – 50,000
	50,001 – 75,000
	75,001 – 100,000
	More than 100,000

Migration to region

	Less than 25,000
	25,001 – 50,000
	50,001 – 75,000
	75,001 – 100,000
	More than 100,000

Map 6 Internal migration, 1941–60

worked in factories and in domestic service, particularly if the principal breadwinner had been lost in the war, as was the case of the girl of fifteen from Galicia who became a domestic maid in Madrid after her father had died in prison and her mother was imprisoned in the former convent in Santurrarán (Guipúzcoa) where many women and children died and there were again forced adoptions: 'They were such painful years that I'll never be able to forget.'[79] The family of one woman from rural Huelva, whose father had been a moderately successful farmer and businessman, had supported the Republic and became involved in local politics in order to contest the power of the village cacique. One brother had been executed by Falangists in 1936 and his sisters and mother had suffered the public humiliation of head shaving. Those with political power now confiscated the family assets, and the family had little choice but to sell their land to pay for the release of a brother in prison for his political affiliation. His sister, who explained the story many years later, became one of the village poor and was reduced to labouring in the fields and later to domestic service. Her children would offer her an escape route when she followed them to industrial Catalonia at the end of the 1950s.[80] Later it was possible for younger migrant women to escape the life of the domestic maid for the more independent lifestyle of factory work, but this was not the case until the later 1950s. In Bilbao, domestic servants still constituted 35 per cent of paid female employment in 1960; 75 per cent were migrants. Many had left repressed smaller towns, including Guernica.[81] When women from the countryside arrived in towns and cities and went seeking positions in the houses of the wealthy middle classes, whether in Madrid, Barcelona, Bilbao, or elsewhere, they would be asked to produce papers to see whether there were reports of previous moral and political behaviour. Gaining a certificate of good conduct was difficult, and some women were accused of being 'Reds'

---

[79] See Elordi (ed.), *Años difíciles*, p. 204. Also Iñaki Egaña, *Los crímenes de Franco en Euskal Herria, 1936–1940* (Tafalla, 2009), pp. 243–8; González Gorosarri, *No lloréis*; Gutiérrez Flores, *Guerra civil*, p. 353; Feixa and Agustí, 'Discursos', pp. 206–7. On low-cost factory labour of women and children in Valencia, see, e.g., report of J. R. Cotton, British foreign mission, February 1952: TNA/FO371/102024/WS1105/2.

[80] Collier, *Socialists*, pp. 33–7, 41, 161.

[81] Cava Mesa, *Memoria colectiva*, p. 282. Corresponding 1970 figures were 28.27 per cent and 84 per cent. José Antonio Pérez, 'Trabajo doméstico y economías sumergidas en el gran Bilbao a lo largo del desarrollismo', in José Babiano (ed.), *Del hogar a la huelga* (Madrid, 2007), pp. 77–136 (p. 87). See also Pilar Díaz Sánchez, *El trabajo de las mujeres en el textil madrileño* (Malaga, 2001), pp. 56–71. Some 12 per cent of a sample of 100 maids in Madrid in the 1950s had experienced the death of both parents: Jesús María Vázquez, *El servicio doméstico en España* (Madrid, 1960), cited in María Ángeles Durán, *El trabajo de la mujer en España* (Madrid, 1972), p. 141. Of the total, 52 per cent were from the countryside.

and the door was slammed shut, as a woman from Murcia remembered: "'They're Reds, they're Reds!" They said this to everyone who tried ... everyone who went looking for work, if you didn't carry reports with you.'[82]

Migration was inexorable, so much so that the regime's peasant-orientated, anti-urban, ideology was contradicted by the reality of the 1940s. Even for those who could demonstrate some allegiance to the regime, reality failed to measure up to the image constructed by the official doctrine.[83] In December 1944 the theme of the Third Industrial Congress of the Falangist syndicates was the desire to dissipate the dangerous proletarian concentrations of Barcelona and the Basque Country in favour of developing industrial enterprises in rural provinces.[84] But as early as 1946, other Falangist agrarians were to be found criticising the government's attempt to prevent migration. The head of the Falangist olive-growers, syndicate would point to the contradictions:

the government having considered social migration an evil and a social calamity has contributed to an aggravation of the economic and social situation of Spain [...] The liberation from the countryside of a section of the agricultural population constitutes precisely one of the indexes of the social-economic progress of a nation [...] Far from making migration from the countryside difficult, a reasoned political economy must favour it as far as possible, above all in those provinces where it is not produced spontaneously in the right proportions.[85]

Paternalist state support to ameliorate the situation existed side by side with charitable assistance. The Catholic diocese in Málaga was hopeful in 1946 of raising money for medicine for the sick, many of the affected being transient migrants from the countryside, and was managing to supply clothing produced by the women of Acción Católica to a few of the many unclothed poor.[86] The Catholic Church urged the well-off to

---

[82] María Encarna Nicolás Marín, 'Actitudes de la sociedad murciana en la etapa 1936–1978', in José Manuel Trujillano and Pilar Sánchez Díaz (eds.), *V Jornadas Historia y Fuentes orales. Testimonios orales y escritos. España, 1936–1996* (Ávila, 1998), p. 123. Also Emilio Silva and Santiago Macías, *Las fosas de Franco: los republicanos que el dictador dejó en las cunetas* (Madrid, 2003), p. 325.

[83] E.g. Letter of Jefe, Hermandad Provincial de Labradores y Ganaderos, 19 May 1945, AGA, SP, 17.02, caja 36.

[84] See Alberto Ribas i Massana, *L'economia catalana sota el franquisme* (Barcelona, 1978), pp. 118–24, 135–42; *Boletín Minero e Industrial*, November 1944, 457. For mining as the harsh midway point between rural hunger and urban factories, see Botey Vallès, *Relats*, p. 80; Armando López Salinas, *La mina* (Madrid, 1960).

[85] Cristóbal Gómez Benito, *Políticos, burócratas y expertos: un estudio de la política agraria y la sociología rural en España (1936–1959)* (Madrid, 1996), p. 240.

[86] 'Acción Católica de la diocesis malacitana: memoria', November 1946, AAC, caja 208, carpeta 208–1–2.

contribute more, particularly during the 'time of penitence' at Lent: 'It cannot be tolerated that, while some people entertain and enjoy themselves and feast and squander immense fortunes on caprices and luxuries, so many of the wretched and starving live by their side, half naked, lost, without a home where they might live with the minimum of decency and hygiene which basic human dignity demands.'[87] Free bread had to be distributed regularly in 1946 to prevent starvation, as to the 1,500 needy in Úbeda (Jaén), an area blighted by terrible violence on both sides during and immediately after the war.[88] Already, in the autumn of 1939, the lack of employment or of public works had been noted and investment was needed urgently if hunger and drought were not to 'ravage' the countryside.[89]

The widespread outbreak of typhus, which had its roots in the period of the civil war but reached alarming proportions in 1941 and did not abate until the second half of the decade, was partly created by the demographic movement to flee poverty and marginalisation. Anxieties about wartime antecedents, uncontrolled migrants and disease all accentuated middle-class fears; in explaining the epidemic, 'enemies' were further demonised. The first major outbreak of typhus had occurred in Granada, in early 1940, infecting some three hundred prisoners interned in a deserted sugar factory in the town of Guadix; a year later, hunger had provoked an exodus from the province, taking the disease with it. It was here that popular stories began to circulate about the 'piojo verde', literally the 'green louse', a term used generally to refer to typhus itself. By June 1941, more than 1,200 victims were in hospital in Madrid, though many more were thought to be suffering in their homes, and there had been some two hundred deaths. One of the first acts of the Junta de Epidemias set up in 1940 was to institute a campaign for cleanliness to tackle what one doctor declared to be the 'lamentable panorama in which a whole section of society, of dubious educational formation, torments us daily with its unhygienic habits and nauseating customs'. There was no justification, it was argued, for people's 'reprehensible abandon': 'it is coarse habits and low culture which are the origin of the lack of cleanliness and deplorable inter-social

---

[87] Carta Pastoral de los Secretariados de Caridad, in *Fuego: Órgano de Acción Católica de Málaga*, February 1945, p. 1.

[88] E.g. *Arriba*, 13 March 1946. See also a 1950 complaint to Raimundo Fernández Cuesta about profiteering 'while the Andalusian countryside dies of hunger': AGA, SP, 17.02, sig. 52/46, caja 71, signed 'Varios amigos del campo'. On the wartime killing, see Preston, *Spanish Holocaust*, pp. 270–1; Carlos Ramón Martínez, *La represión franquista en la comarca de la Loma de la provincia de Jaén* (Jaén, 2010), pp. 22, 57–63.

[89] 'Problemas – Toledo'; Report of Civil Governor, Almería, 28 January 1942, FNFF, vol. III, p. 182. See Fundación FOESSA, *Informe sociológico sobre la situación social de España: 1970* (Madrid, 1972), p. 162.

mixing which we too frequently observe'.[90] The epidemic would spread far and wide, however, and in rural Zaragoza the daughter of a Republican woman who, with the connivance of right-wing locals, had been executed with others who had supported the reforms of the 1930s remembered how the notion of disease became part of the language of ostracism within communities:

In the pueblo, which was right-wing, they reproached us [...] They called us 'Reds'. They even asked me, smiling to themselves, who it was who had killed my mother. I answered them that it had been the Guardia Civil, but if I'd known I would have said it was the fascists of the pueblo [...] They would take us Reds to school in procession because they said that we were infected with *el piojo verde*. Later they took us to the infirmary to cut and wash our hair, they disinfected us just for being Reds, to destroy us, knowing all the time that we did not have the *piojo verde*.[91]

One cause of the spread of typhus was overcrowding in the migrant slums such as the settlements of Puente de Vallecas on the perimeter of Madrid which had a census population of 60,000 in 1940, though the real figure was thought to be much higher (see Map 7). (By the early 1950s the population would grow to more than 220,000, an increase of 270 per cent in the course of little more than a decade.)[92] A 1941 study of the conditions of 100 poor families there revealed that the adults were absorbing only one-third to one-quarter of the basic necessary calorific intake and that the children had as little as one-fifth: the extent of underfeeding 'had to be studied on the spot to be believed'.[93] The Director General of Health recognised that the level of physical development of working-class children was about one-half to one-third of that of the children of the 'comfortable class'; the effects of hunger were suggested also in the 'apathy' of the children and a 'loss of memory' in the adult population.[94] Defective physical growth of 1940s working-class children would become a reminder of the consequences of the war.[95] Elements

---

[90] A. Gómez Jiménez, 'La ingenuidad y la limpieza', *SER: Revista Médica-Social, FET-JONS*, 9 (October 1942), 100–2.

[91] Elordi (ed.), *Años difíciles*, pp. 187. For the folklore of the 'piojo verde', see, e.g., Laín Entralgo, *Descargo*, pp. 364, 376.

[92] This represented almost one-quarter of the capital's population growth in this period. Juan Mayoral, *Vallecas: las razones de una lucha popular* (Madrid, 1976), p. 30.

[93] William D. Robinson, John H. Janney and Francisco Grande Covián, 'An Evaluation of the Nutritional Status of a Population Group in Madrid, Spain, during the Summer of 1941', *Journal of Nutrition*, 24 (1942), 557–84. For memories of 1940s Vallecas, see Morales and Pereira, *Memoria*, pp. 148–54.

[94] José Alberto Palanca, *Importancia social de la sanidad pública* (Madrid, 1944), p. 12.

[95] William D. Robinson, John H. Janney and Francisco Grande Covián, 'Studies of the Physical Characteristics of Selected Children in Madrid, Spain, in 1941', *Journal of Pediatrics*, 20, 6 (June 1942), 723–39. Also Escudero Andújar, *Dictadura*, p. 172;

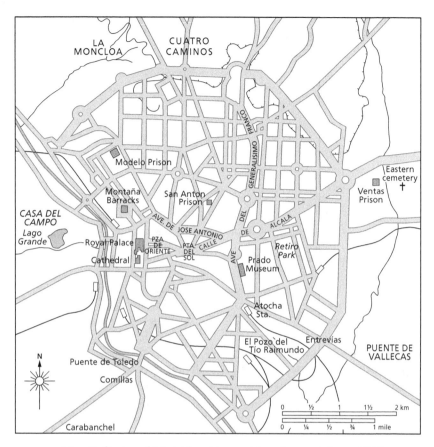

Map 7 Centre of Madrid and its working-class periphery, 1940s

close to the regime attempted to encourage charity to relieve the 'terrible municipal ulcer' of migration in Madrid, drawn in by the 'false light' of the city, leading to its assumed corollary of crime, begging and prostitution.[96] In 1956 the writer Carmen Martín Gaite would publish an evocative short story, based on her own 1940s experiences of Catholic missionary work in Vallecas, exploring post-war social conscience faced with the migratory influx. The story describes how a Madrid doctor,

Barranquero and Prieto, *Así sobrevivimos*, pp. 101–26; Michael Richards, 'A memoria da fame e a historia do tempo presente', *Grial*, 44, 170 (2006), 26–35.
[96] See, e.g., 'Falsa luz de la ciudad', *ABC*, 2 December 1949, p. 7.

influenced by the prevalent image of migrants, is summoned to the *chabolas* to treat a young girl of a migrant family from Jaén:

> he knew above all that there were so many of them, swarms, which multiplied with each day, emigrating from even poorer places and that they spread, hidden in the backstreets, like a contagion, their dwellings of earth and sun-dried bricks [...] They were so many that they advanced towards the better part of the city, invading and contaminating it.[97]

Martín Gaite thus situated the darkness of the rudimentary, itinerant, community on the margins between urban culture, which was future-oriented and represented enlightenment, and the rural void which had been left behind.

Generations and post-war memory: children of the war

The war produced a fear within conservative Catholic society particularly of general moral abandonment and reinforced belief in a 'congenital' disposition of 'the masses' towards uncontrolled behaviour and violence. Official doctrine sought to confirm this: 'Marxist' and 'liberal' ideas had caused a threatening 'relaxation of decency', deliberately aimed at 'destroying the Christian family'.[98] The Republic's laic and mixed-sex education had possessed no 'ethical formation', it was argued, and no way of instilling a sense of 'an interior life' in children. Article 436 of the penal code, which would be frequently invoked after 1939, stipulated that 'doctrines contrary to public morals' constituted an offence. These fears are notable in perceptions of the children of the enemy in the aftermath of the war, viewed as part of a formless and unstructured mass, possessing little culture and without consciences. The coeducation and secular teaching encouraged by the Republic had been morally damaging; the 'crisis' of the Spanish family had political origins:

> The head of the family and the schoolteacher were, in the years before the civil war, the leaven that in certain social classes fermented hatred of the rich, the noble and the virtuous [...] Democratic ideas have had the unhappy ability of inculcating in children the idea of certain rights, uprooting the principles of traditional morality and fomenting depravity, and opposing the notions of subordination and hierarchy.[99]

---

[97] Carmen Martín Gaite, 'La conciencia tranquila', in Martín Gaite, *Cuentos completos* (Madrid, 1981), pp. 309–24 (citing pp. 314–15), originally in *Destino*, January 1956.

[98] E.g. *Disposiciones penales sobre inmoralidad pública* (Madrid, 1943), p. 5.

[99] Antonio Vallejo Nágera, *Niños y jóvenes anormales* (Madrid, 1941), p. 62. Also Piquer, *Niño abandonado*, p. 41.

The children of Republicans, it was claimed, had not only lost a sense of 'feeling Spanish' but, in the wake of the revolutionary violence, lacked respect for human life. Many repatriated evacuees, it was pointed out, had been renamed by foreigners:

the lives of enormous masses of people and no few children, lived in the foreign concentration camps, as in the slums of big cities, were so distressing and so full of deprivation as to carry [those affected] back to the prehistoric phase of instinctive tendencies, without any control at all. It should not seem strange that children in such conditions had not the slightest notion of moral understanding.[100]

In the case of repatriated children, physical and spiritual reintegration into the *patria* would be required to guard against 'contagion', though little attempt would be made to repatriate children from Russia and the Ukraine in the 1940s since they were believed to have been 'Sovietised' and would be both politically and sexually dangerous, in need of a form of moral 'disinfection' which was difficult to achieve. The 'abandoned and delinquent child', partly because of 'scarce intelligence', had 'an extraordinarily overdeveloped tendency to imitate', and given the 'unhealthy' moral conditions of the environment 'automates behaviour through a multitude of bad habits and acquired vices'; these theories led easily to recommendations for segregation of children from 'Marxist' families.[101] Migration heightened these fears. According to psychologists, eager to align themselves with the new power, 'while many individuals and indeed entire families maintain the appearance of an honourable religious and social life, once they lose themselves in the cosmopolitan world of the great city they give themselves over to all manner of licentiousness'.[102]

Religion played an important role in the attempt at regeneration, and Catholic baptisms surged in the aftermath of the war, godparents and patrons being found, in many cases, within the local Delegations of Auxilio Social and the Falange, especially the Sección Femenina. In Madrid, in August 1939, 150 children born during the period of 'Red domination' in Vallecas were sponsored by Auxilio Social and baptised collectively. In Barcelona, 34 Auxilio children aged from ten to thirteen

---

[100] Piquer, *Niño abandonado*, p. 240. For psychological effects upon individuals of becoming known as a child of 'Reds', see, e.g., Silva and Macías, *Fosas*, p. 325.

[101] Antonio Vallejo Nágera, *La locura y la guerra: psicopatología de la guerra española* (Valladolid, 1939), p. 52; *Divagaciones intrascendentes* (Valladolid, 1938), p. 105; *Niños y jóvenes anormales* (Madrid, 1941), pp. 47–8; Francisco Marco Merenciano, 'Nuevas orientaciones sobre higiene mental', 1942 (reprinted in *Ensayos médicos y literarios: antología*, Madrid, 1958, pp. 98–9).

[102] Piquer, *Niño abandonado*, p. 240.

years and 'all belonging to Marxist families' were 'reintegrated' in this way in the same month under the guidance of the New State.[103] Catholic lay missions in urban areas were thus able to claim a working-class religious resurgence. Campaigns were launched to proselytise and give instruction through courses of spiritual exercises to 'those without God' in the growing city suburbs, to domestic servants, and in the larger factories. Careful use was made of local devotions, and the Virgin Mary became 'the principal missionary'.[104]

The Falange of the 1940s echoed Catholic warnings about morality, although it couched its faith in terms of concerns about the dilution of the 'values of the war' and 'defence of the *patria*'. While war in Europe was raging, these ideas echoed Nazism: the nation's youth was increasingly prey to 'Americanism', behind which lurked 'Judaism', as represented by modern dancing, for example, which 'grossly excites the lowest appetites and deadens youthful vitality with flabby and melancholic listlessness, quite inappropriate in the hard times in which we live'.[105]

The long-lasting sense of shame and confusion of the children of sanctioned Republican parents was often profound, though this has only begun to be discussed openly in recent years. The loss of a mother or father painfully reshaped an individual's world.[106] According to the dominant public doctrine, if fathers or mothers had been executed or imprisoned it must have been for some good reason, and the propaganda pointed to the culpability of those who became 'mixed up with politics'.[107] A statistical survey conducted by psychologists in the early 1940s in Barcelona on the damage the war caused to children tutored in state homes was based on their expressed attitudes towards their own parents and found that while many 'disapproved' of the 'immoral lives' of their mothers and fathers during the war and revolution, many others were prone to imitate such acts (see Table 4.1).[108]

---

[103] *La Vanguardia Española (Suplemento Gráfico)*, 11 August 1939, p. 2; 12 August 1939, p. 2; 16 August 1939, p. 4.

[104] Aurelio Orensanz, *Religiosidad popular Española, 1940–1965* (Madrid, 1974), p. 10. On the last sacraments and mass in working-class Madrid, see, e.g., *Ecclesia*, 31 January 1942, 9–13; 'Catequesis de suburbios', *Ecclesia*, 23 January 1943, 10; 29 January 1942; 30 January 1943, 7; 24 April 1943, 17.

[105] *Juventud*, 5 August 1943, p. 2.

[106] E.g. testimony of José Agustín Goytisolo, in Juan F. Marsal, *Pensar bajo el franquismo* (Barcelona, 1979), p. 161, and the memoir of his brother Juan Goytisolo, *Coto vedado* (Barcelona, 1985). Also, Teresa Pàmies, *Los niños de guerra* (Barcelona, 1977); retrospective testimonies (in 1970) of wartime children in Borràs, *Los que no hicimos*.

[107] E.g. Vega Sombría, *De la esperanza*, p. 274.

[108] See Richards, 'Ideology and the Psychology of War Children in Franco's Spain, 1936–45', in Kjersti Ericssohn and Eva Simonsen (eds.), *Children of World War II: The Hidden Enemy Legacy* (Oxford, 2005), pp. 73–101; Richards, 'From War Culture to Civil

Table 4.1 *Republican children's attitudes to parents' (alleged) support of religious persecution, according to Barcelona psychologists (%) according to Barcelona psychologists*

Attitudes to parents	Wards of juvenile courts	Children in state institutions	Children of parents in prison	Repatriated evacuee children
Indifference	22.45	18.23	10.14	14.46
Simple approval	20.1	26.3	17.45	28.19
Imitation	43.6	35.43	49.13	56.05
Disapproval	13.84	20.06	23.27	1.3

Control of schooling and welfare initiatives allowed the state, Church, and charitable activities of the wealthy a presence in daily life and sought to ensure the internalisation of shame.[109] The widows of men executed for their political ideas and activism were faced with bringing up children in a hostile environment. The solution found was usually to instruct children, whatever they might hear about 'the Reds', to remain silent in public about politics and the war, but at the same time to maintain faith in the absent father and the ideals fought for.[110] Later, in adulthood, those who recalled such situations frequently focused on the sacrifices made by parents and their avoidance of politics in favour of 'honest' and 'respectable' hard work.[111] Others were persuaded that Francoist vilifications of the Republic were justified. There were some young Falangists who attempted to 'get on', even to the extent of occupying a local position in regime politics – the only politics and the only state bureaucracy available – in spite of the sacrifices and beliefs of their parents and even in some instances when a parent had been imprisoned or executed by the rebels.[112] A short story about the 1940s, 'Cassette', by Rafael Azcona, penetrates the emotionally tainted world of intergenerational hostility in the aftermath of the conflict; in the same vein the writer

Society: Francoism, Social Change and Memories of the Spanish Civil War', *History and Memory*, 14, 1/2 (Fall 2002), 110–12. More broadly on possible psychological implications, see Castilla del Pino, *Estudio sobre la depresión*, especially, pp. 61–125.

[109] Agnes Heller, *The Power of Shame: A Rational Perspective* (London, 1985), p. 5. E.g., on nuns teaching the children of the 'fusilados', Brenan, *Face of Spain*, p. 56.

[110] E.g. Castilla del Pino, *Casa del olivo*, p. 127; Barker, *Largo trauma*, pp. 112, 227–8.

[111] See, e.g., Magdalena González, 'La generación herida: la guerra civil y el primer franquismo como señas de identidad en los niños nacidos hasta el año 1940', *Jerónimo Zurita: Revista de Historia*, 84 (2009); Morales and Pereira, *Memoria*, pp. 34, 39.

[112] See, e.g., a young Falangist colleague of Castilla del Pino in the 1940s: *Casa del olivo*, p. 110.

Josefina Aldecoa commented memorably on the phenomenon of war children who, as she saw it, rejected their parents' pasts in the interests of material profit: 'at times, the children of the defeated [...] turned their backs on the example of their fathers and closing their eyes they united with the plundering mob'.[113] Rejection of parents also worked the other way. Many testimonies suggest that for the young middle class who were children of Francoists the containment of desires and the pressure of obligations and responsibilities, as preached by the Church, produced a sense of moral conscience, though it also forced a premature transition from childhood to adulthood.[114] In many cases on both sides, mothers and fathers had been rendered powerless by the war, their extreme fear obvious to children during the conflict. In the difficult aftermath the authority of which they had been partially divested had somehow to be remade: 'one had to go on living. Slowly, lifelessly, in an ordered methodical rhythm [...] Perhaps out of desperation, perhaps necessary for survival, parents became strict again: you have to study, you have to work hard, you must stay at home, you have to obey, obey, obey.'[115]

Silence in the aftermath of Spain's tragedy was a product in the first place of memories of the emotional and material turmoil of civil war which erupted into the daily life of family, work and social reproduction, in many cases destroying the essential basis of coexistence. The intimate violence of the war was continued after 1939 at the behest of the state; reassertion of its authority was supported by certain groups and individuals who actively collaborated. Many others were complicit to the extent that they complied out of a profound yearning for peace, order and 'normality'. Accommodation with the new power has been seen as the basis of a working social consensus.[116] This chapter has discussed three elements of this early post-war situation through which war memories were mediated: the violent rebuilding of political power through profiteering networks; the daily process of material reproduction through micro-level strategies of survival – and, in many cases, the resort to migration – in a context of unprecedented economic regression; and

---

[113] Rafael Azcona, 'Cassette', in Aldecoa, *Niños*, pp. 107–22. The Aldecoa citation is on p. 121.

[114] *Senectud (Madrid)*, 47. See also Ana María Matute and Josefina Aldecoa, 'Las niñas de la guerra', in Miguel Munárriz (ed.), *Otra mirada sobre el mismo paisaje* (Oviedo, 1995) p. 62.

[115] Aldecoa, *Niños*, p. 12. Also Borràs, *Los que no hicimos*, pp. 160, 513.

[116] Saz and Gómez Roda (eds.), *Franquismo en Valencia*, pp. 9–35; Pere Ysàs, 'Consens i dissens en el primer franquisme', in Giuliana di Febo and Carme Molinero (eds.), *Nou estat, nova política, nou ordre social* (Barcelona, 2005), pp. 161–88.

the depiction and treatment of 'war children' as a factor in generational post-war social memory. Whilst there was a pervasive attempt to impose a new moralism shaped by the war and its sacrifices, such an imposition carried a material price for Republicans; the resistance of the defeated was constrained by the circumstances, but ranged from aiding *guerrilleros* or participating in small-scale black-market activity, to migration. Such was the willingness of 'the victors' to extract benefits from the outcome of the war that many people expressed an almost overwhelming perception of general moral degradation. Social fragmentation nonetheless redounded to the benefit of those forming networks of advantage which saw pre-war elites (including local caciques) subsumed into Francoist state-building with those newly endowed by the war with political and economic capital. Resistance required immense sacrifices and risks, either by joining the guerrilla struggle or participating in micro-level networks of survival, usually held together by formally illegal black-market trade. The social fracturing of the war and its aftermath profoundly affected rural communities, triggering the initiation of the great post-war migration, a fleeing from the countryside and all that the recent past represented. The city became a refuge. The response of the state, urban elites, and institutions of authority to migrants was ambivalent. They were seen primarily as a product of war and revolution and were often demonised, a tendency legitimated by psychologists who suggested that revolutionary desire was an inheritable trait. Parallel to this imposition of shame a slowly developing sense of conscience to do with the war began to emerge, though this was less evident in the 1940s than negative discrimination. This would grow more significant during the 1950s, although even then, amid resurgent anti-communism, the notion of reconciliation was officially frowned upon and repressed as the regime consolidated its control.

5   Memory and politics: from civil war to Cold War

I belong to a generation which lived neither through the war nor the later privations. We lived parenthetically, in a form of limbo in the transition between the post-war and today's society. We have no battles to talk about, nor the great hardships, although, yes, there were some, but we lived our time as well as we could.[1]

Between two wars: generations in the 1950s

As elsewhere, the 1950s in Spain have often seemed in historiographical terms to constitute a lost decade.[2] All periods of history are transitional, but the 1950s, situated temporally between catastrophic war and its harsh aftermath and the consumer society and the 'economic miracle', beginning in the early 1960s, seemed peculiarly parenthetical in retrospect. For more than a decade after 1945, Europe lived in the shadow of death, and the relationship between war and post-war would be at the heart of collective representations of the continent's twentieth century.[3] The effects of Spain's war extended into the 1950s when much of Western Europe was in recovery, perpetuating a feeling of political and social stasis: the institutionalisation of the victors' power, the long-lasting implications of intimate violence, the great hunger of the 1940s and ambivalence about reconciliation. The economy returned to depressed pre-war levels of production only in 1954, six or seven years later than other states which had participated in the 1939–45 war, and the effects of this limited Spanish recovery were in any case geographically uneven.[4] Time moved forward

---

[1] Isabel Magan, born Recas, Toledo, in early 1950s, testimony (2002), Elordi (ed.), *Años difíciles*, p. 336.
[2] Heiko Feldner, Claire Gorrara and Kevin Passmore (eds.), *The Lost Decade? The 1950s in European History, Politics, Society and Culture* (Cambridge, 2011).
[3] See Richard Bessel and Dirk Schumann (eds.), *Life After Death: Approaches to a Cultural and Social History of Europe during the 1940s and 1950s* (Cambridge, 2003); Tony Judt, *Postwar: A History of Europe since 1945* (London, 2005).
[4] Jordi Catalán, *La economía española y la segunda guerra mundial* (Barcelona, 1995), pp. 23–9.

at a snail's pace. The Secretary General of the Falange, Raimundo Fernández Cuesta, referred to the vanquished in stark and brutal terms in 1951: 'between their Spain and ours there is an abyss that can only be crossed by repentance and submission to our doctrine. Otherwise, may they remain on the other side of the abyss, and if they attempt to cross it surreptitiously, may they perish.'[5]

Collective and personal experience of conflict, repression and division, and the ways in which these events and processes are recalled, is essential for understanding the era since 1945, a period still within the grasp of living memory in the early twenty-first century. Periodisation is difficult, however. Although 1959, when a strategy of economic liberalisation was adopted by the Franco regime, has often been seen as a pivotal moment between past and future, the social reality was complex, and beneath the political stasis society was on the move well before the end of the 1950s as 'ordinary' Spaniards became active protagonists in the process of modernisation through migration.[6] The dominant ascetic doctrine which called for expiation of the guilt of war and revolution through suffering had been used to justify government priorities benefiting agriculture and rural society rather than cities, but the strategy had failed and, indeed, had helped force the pace of migration. The cities would grow and consumer demand, repressed since the civil war, would eventually take off, boosted by the liberalising policies of the 1960s. This 'miracle' would pave the way for a narrative of the civil war which departed from the 'crusade', one based on the notion that guilt and responsibility for the war were shared, in effect another myth which would come into its own during the transition to democracy in the 1970s.[7] For now, in the 1950s, there was resistance to any new such narrative.

Virtually the entire Francoist political class of the 1950s had been affected by close personal loss during the civil war. This experience became a force of intransigence and contributed to unquestioning adherence to the glory of the Holy War doctrine. This suffering in the past also shaped more nuanced, even critical, conservative views of the past. The war had pushed individuals who were instinctively or by background conservatives (rather than fascists) towards the Falange. Many, Javier Tusell has argued, would have been more at home in a Christian

---

[5] Cited in International Commission of Jurists, *Spain and the Rule of Law* (Geneva, 1962), p. 65. Also, Jacques Georgel, *El franquismo: historia y balance, 1939–1969* (Paris, 1971), p. 149.

[6] The problem of delimiting sub-periods in Francoism is implicit in a recent collection of essays: Nigel Townson (ed.), *Spain Transformed: The Late Franco Dictatorship, 1959–75* (Basingstoke, 2007).

[7] See Víctor M. Pérez Díaz, *The Return of Civil Society: The Emergence of Democratic Spain* (Cambridge, MA, 1993), p. 24.

Democratic party than in a military dictatorship, although many other conservatives or traditionalists, it is clear, felt quite at home as part of a totalitarian regime, and most never strayed beyond the political parameters of Francoist orthodoxy.[8] The moderate Catholic Joaquín Ruiz-Giménez and the ex-Falangist Pedro Laín Entralgo, both of whom appear frequently in these pages, are of particular interest because of their open espousal of reconciliation, although they would only adopt this position unequivocally once they were disentangled from the official doctrine of National Catholicism during the second half of the 1950s.[9]

The dominant doctrine of the 1950s, however, remained that of guilt and expiation which was in part expressed in the particular form and influence which Spanish anti-communism was to have in response to international developments. At the height of National Catholicism, many Church leaders were content to rail against the legacy of pre-war liberal teachings whenever and wherever they occurred. Bishop Zacarías de Vizcarra, Consiliario General of Acción Católica, blamed 'materialist' philosophers for Spain's war, and principally José Ortega y Gasset, because he had advocated 'a theodicy without God' and 'a psychology without the soul'. Ortega, an admirer of such 'laic saints' as the socialist Pablo Iglesias and the liberal educational reformer Francisco Giner de los Ríos, had been a great influence on key 'reconcilers', such as Laín, Ruiz-Giménez, and, from the Republican side, Julián Marías, and had returned to Spain from foreign exile at the end of the 1940s to a far from unqualified welcome from the regime. According to Vizcarra, 'religious liberalism' was the ideological product of an entrenched 'laic mentality' amongst intellectuals of the generation educated by the Institución Libre de Enseñanza in the 1930s, and he denounced the 'exaltation' of 'intellectual idols' (including also Unamuno), who had 'played a part in the incubation' of the war 'which cost the lives of a million Spaniards' (*sic*).[10] He cited colleagues, one of them Head of Theology of the CSIC, who professed to know of individuals for whom 'Ortega's spiritual breath had passed through as a cyclone, devastating their religious beliefs'.[11] Later, in 1955, Vizcarra would take particular exception to the full-page

---

[8] See, e.g., ex-CEDA leaders such Ramón Serrano Suñer and Luciano de la Calzada and several of those who in the 1930s contributed to the rightist intellectual review *Acción Española*.

[9] Another reformer who had suffered grievously during the civil war was Joaquín Pérez Villanueva, Ruiz-Giménez's Director General of Universities in the Education Ministry of 1951. Tusell, *Franco y los católicos*, p. 310.

[10] *Ecclesia*, no. 658 (1954), cited in Feliciano Blázquez, *La traición de los clérigos en la España de Franco* (Madrid, 1991), p. 101.

[11] Citing General Franco, laicism had the 'stench of freemasonry': Vizcarra, *Ecclesia*, no. 758, 21 January 1956, 9–11.

announcement of the death of Ortega in the review published by the
Congreso Nacional de Escritores Jóvenes, with the unadorned tribute
'Filósofo liberal español'.[12] Shortly afterwards, the Young Writers' Congress would be suspended by the government following student protests
in 1956 and the end of Ruiz-Giménez's term of office as Minister of
Education. The crisis would come to a head in 1958, several years after
Ortega's death, with an exchange of articles and books amongst priests
and intellectuals over the compatibility or otherwise of his philosophy
with Catholicism and, therefore, of modernity with Spain.[13] It is significant that some twenty years later Laín Entralgo would recall Ortega
when remembering a scene he had witnessed in Pamplona during the
early days of the civil war in 1936. Called upon to pay homage to a
recently killed soldier, Laín found the famously bizarre commander of
the Spanish Foreign Legion, General José Millán Astray, at the feet of the
body of the young martyr of the cause, surrounded by doctors, nurses,
holy sisters and a number of mourning soldiers. The general's disturbing
eulogy to death itself was followed by a raucous rendition of the Hymn
of the Legion, of which, at this stage of the war, none of those present
knew the text so that Millán sang alone, the others listening in silence,
several of them sobbing. Although we cannot know what Laín felt at
the time, the recollection years later was symbolic for him of the 'Two
Spains' thesis through which he understood the conflict as a clash
between backwardness and modernity: 'for as long as I live I will remember the sense of stupor and chill fear that invaded my soul'. Ortega's
question about the nature of the country and its culture seemed appropriate: 'My God, what is Spain?'[14]

Away from the intellectual conflicts, however, the 1950s would see the
maturing of the first post-war generation within society, too young to
recall the worst of the repression in the early 1940s, sheltered by their
families from the recent past, and developing in a broader atmosphere
which advocated leaving the past behind. During the 1950s, indeed, the
interaction of several generations defined in relation to the civil war and
with diverging priorities and attitudes comes clearly into focus. A long-
lasting post-war suspicion of politics was noted in a study of one Castilian

[12] As Rector of Madrid University, Laín had been involved in the difficult organisation of a
homage at the university; *Descargo*, pp. 412–14.

[13] See José Andrés-Gallego, Antón M. Pazos and Luis de Llera Esteban, *Los españoles entre
la religión y la política* (Madrid, 1996), pp. 134–5.

[14] Laín Entralgo, *Descargo*, pp. 178–9. Ortega's rhetorical question is found in his
Meditaciones del Quijote. So symbolically significant was Ortega, Laín believed, that
one's pre-war attitudes to him were a reliable marker of corresponding post-1939
political attitudes. E.g., *Descargo*, p. 290.

town at the end of the decade, for example, which found that 'the "declining" generation, which felt so politically minded and optimistic in its middle age and whose Republican wing was decimated in the first days of the civil war, today hates with a deep-rooted hatred the word "politics" and all that it involves. It is a word held in absolute discredit.'[15] A decade or so later, in rural Catalonia, where regional nationalism had been strong in the 1930s, it would be observed that 'the political muteness of the young stands in sharp contrast to the sophistication of their elders'.[16] Many of the young would only begin to learn about the war (albeit in a still limited way) once they migrated with their parents because there would be freer access to social interaction in urban surroundings. The burden of 'liturgical memory' would gradually be supplanted by that of 'fratricidal conflict' (a 'war between brothers'), representing a 'lightening of the ballast for the young' in what was becoming a changing world, though this new sense of historical consciousness was itself deficient, the result of a compromise between society and the regime.[17]

The majority of those born in the early 1920s had been too young to be mobilised to fight, though too old to be considered afterwards as 'children of the war', defined broadly as those born during the second half of the 1920s and the 1930s. In reality, those of the so-called 'bridge generation' – between preceding and succeeding cohorts, the first clearly shaped by the tragedy of war, whether at the front or in the rearguard, and the second the 'parenthetical generation', which grew up in the 1950s – were as much victims as the 'war children'.[18] The dark shadow of the war extended for several years in the many homes torn apart for reasons which were largely incomprehensible to the young.

The childhood experience of war and post-war was far from uniform: much depended on geographic location or whether intimate violence was directly experienced and whether a family had been forced to flee from home. Social class played a part because the poorest had fewer connections and options for recovery. Examination of the fragmentary traces of memory in letters, diaries and testimonies suggests that the silence which surrounded children's lives in the 1940s was both stubborn

---

[15] Carmelo Lisón-Tolosana, *Belmonte de los Caballeros: A Sociological Study of a Spanish Town* (Oxford, 1966), pp. 189–90. On the discrediting of and silence about politics in the 1960s and 1970s, see also, e.g., Stanley H. Brandes, *Migration, Kinship and Community: Tradition and Transition in a Spanish Village* (New York, 1975), p. 29; Susan Friend Harding, *Remaking Ibeica: Rural Life in Aragón under Franco* (Chapel Hill, 1984), p. 181; Juan Martínez Alier, *Labourers and Landowners in Southern Spain* (New Jersey, 1971), pp. 221–34.

[16] Edward C. Hansen, *Rural Catalonia under the Franco Regime* (Cambridge, 1977), pp. 140–3 (p. 143).

[17] Mannheim, 'Problem of Generations', pp. 369–70.   [18] See Chapter 1.

and intangible, producing an unfathomable sense of instability and pervasive feelings of stigma, frustration and anguish.[19] War children thus came to see themselves as part of an 'obedient generation' in the face of a 'monolithic conspiracy of silence'.[20] Elements of the stifling 'closure' (*clausura*) of the immediate post-war years carried on into the fifties and even the sixties. We could interpret this feeling as resulting from both a transplantation of a 'small-town mentality' to wider society and a pressured privatisation of identity. Prudence, born out of fear and adhering to the motto 'one must not get involved in anything', led to a passive consent, which was not quite the same thing as 'forgetting'.[21]

Silent compliance in the 1950s and 1960s was thus widespread, motivated by fear of repression, as such, and of opening up superficially healed fractures within communities by revisiting events which could not be resolved or mastered. It became accepted that one had to keep quiet and hide opinions not only about politics but about certain individuals and past behaviour. The psychiatrist Carlos Castilla del Pino, speaking with the authority of amassed case histories from the period, claimed that '*prudencia*' was the key. Making careful judgements about what was permissible and what could not be done was part of daily life: 'the Spanish citizen acquired a subtle perception of the reality and refined his or her sense of this to adapt to the rules of the game of the existing socio-political context'.[22] This prudence was easily absorbed into the stifling 'normality' of the era, at times with the assistance of specialised medical discourse. Behaviour which in the early years would be considered '*desafecto al régimen*' ('hostile to the regime') was later, especially in the 1960s, incorporated into daily life as 'failure to adapt', as social self-marginalisation or abnormality.[23] Although this silencing was inevitably felt by many as repression of a sense of self and of collective identity, it would make possible a passive acceptance of the reconfigured official narrative of the war as a fratricidal conflict.

[19] E.g., Carles Santacana i Torres, *Victoriosos i derrotats: el franquisme a l'Hospitalet, 1939–1951* (Barcelona, 1994), p. 113; Feixa and Agustí, 'Discursos', pp. 208–9; Borràs, *Los que no hicimos*, pp. 7, 74, 154, 204, 487, 527.

[20] Borràs, *Los que no hicimos*, pp. 160, 513.

[21] On consent, see, e.g., Saz and Gómez Roda (eds.), *Franquismo en Valencia*. For testimony referring to '*clausura*', of 'confinement and sadness', see, e.g., Borràs, *Los que no hicimos*, pp. 83–5, 135, 198, 207.

[22] Carlos Castilla del Pino, 'Problemas psicológicos de una generación', *El País*, 'Extra', 20 November 1985, p. 18. Also Castilla del Pino, *Casa del olivo*, p. 370. See also Luis Martín Santos, *Tiempo de silencio* (Barcelona, 1961); Dolores Plá Brugat, 'La experiencia del regreso: el caso de los exiliados republicanos catalanes', in José Manuel Trujillano and José María Gago (eds.), *Historia y memoria del franquismo, 1936–1978* (Ávila, 1997), pp. 84–7.

[23] Castilla del Pino, 'Problemas psicológicos'.

The self-censoring ethos would be critiqued by the social realist literary movement of the 1950s, composed of young writers, 'children of
the war', born in the period 1925–8. These mainly middle-class cultural
critics were largely the offspring of those who had fought for, or at
least supported, Franco's 'crusade', but they witnessed the war and
revolution and their repressive aftermath as children and adolescents.
They felt generally compelled to reject the official liturgy of memory.[24]
The literature produced by such writers as Ignacio Aldecoa, Carmen
Martín Gaite, and Ana María Matute was widely consumed and had an
influence on the way in which the younger generation thought about the
war and its legacy.[25] These 'children of the crusade' were affected by the
plight of the defeated in the aftermath of the conflict and the hardships of
migrants of the 1940s and 1950s, and they drew on war memories to
make sense of them, as did political dissidents and analysts emerging
from the milieu of student unrest in Madrid and Barcelona in 1956. The
Catholic-Marxist writer and political activist Alfonso Carlos Comín was
representative of this activity. Born in 1933, he had been only six when
his father, Jesús Comín, who had been a Carlist parliamentary deputy
for Zaragoza during the Second Republic, died on active service for the
rebels in early 1939. There had often been conspiratorial political meetings against the government in the family home, and the term 'Red' was
heard constantly 'to refer to this or that person', Alfonso recalled.[26] He
would be left with ambiguous feelings about the country's divisions and
conflicts. In much of this literature, both fictional and analytical, there
was a sense of suppressed rage and guilt about a country seemingly split
in two, a feeling of internal isolation, where the resident population
lived 'as much in exile from the expelled segment as the latter does from
the former'.[27]

The sense of regret about a society split in two also affected Joaquín
Ruiz-Giménez, who would become, in effect, an anti-Francoist dissident, from a liberal Catholic perspective, by the early 1960s. He would
relate his calls for reconciliation, in fact, to his own war memories
and to individuals associated with 'the Anti-Spain'. He had maintained,

---

[24] See Chapter 6.
[25] We should include the important novel of youthful alienation *Nada* (1944), by the less
overtly critical Carmen Laforet, who was not part of this informal movement. E.g.,
Piñero Valverde, 'Mi viejo álbum', in Pedrero and Piñero, *Tejiendo recuerdos*, p. 59.
Some were ex-Falangists and, though not part of the movement or the war child
generation, the realist novels of Camilo José Cela, who was associated with the regime,
were influential. Aldecoa, *Niños*, p. 20. Also, Martín Gaite, *Esperando el porvenir*.
[26] Alfonso Carlos Comín, 'Fe en la tierra' (1975), in Comín, *Obras*, 7 vols. (Barcelona,
1986–94), vol. II, p. 302.
[27] See Paul Ilie, *Literature and Inner Exile* (Baltimore, 1980), p. 2.

for example, a correspondence with Ángel Galarza who had held cabinet office under the PSOE in the 1930s and was wartime Director General of Security and Interior Minister of the Republic, whose humane action in 1936 had saved the imprisoned Ruiz-Giménez and his brothers from execution in Madrid. The two men shared certain ideas about the political future and in 1949, from his exile in Paris, Galarza expressed the view to Ruiz-Giménez (who was by no means yet in opposition to the Franco regime) that in order to transform Spain from its ruinous post-civil-war condition, and in the aftermath of world war, a 'grand Catholic Party, profoundly oriented towards social policy and tolerance' was needed.[28] In spite of the apparent sympathy of Ruiz-Giménez, soon to be Minister of Education, the existence of a Republican government-in-exile, which, as the Cold War was developing, could easily be linked in Francoist propaganda to Communism, presented the dictatorship with an opportunity to argue that Franco represented the best option in guarding domestic and international stability. Many Catholics who had supported the Francoists associated their own personal experiences with the perceived threat, a fear heightened by propaganda and by a level of social unrest in the early 1950s and the threatening migration to towns and cities (see Chapter 6). Memories of Franco's anti-Communist crusade would therefore prove indispensable in resisting any moves towards an *apertura*.[29] When Ángel Galarza died in exile, seventeen years later, in 1966, a rather changed Ruiz-Giménez, amid a somewhat different political and social context, would take the opportunity in the pages of the barely tolerated opposition publication *Cuadernos Para el Diálogo* to critique the nature of official war memory and its effects on political culture in Spain:

In relation to the death in Paris, where he resided since 1939, of the distinguished socialist Ángel Galarza (r.i.p.), the majority of the newspapers have inserted a short biographical note taking care to avoid anything beyond the merest ephemeral description, as has become normal in these kinds of obituary notices [. . .] What we want to emphasise here is the serious lack of respect for a deceased individual and for history committed by one newspaper which finished its brief reference with this judgement: 'he tolerated and protected the checas.'[30] How much longer will hatred and resentment last? How much longer the retrospective

---

[28] Tusell, *Franco y los católicos*, p. 448. On Galarza in wartime Madrid, see Cervera, *Madrid en guerra*, esp. pp. 68, 72.

[29] For this propaganda, see, e.g., Galinsoga and Franco-Salgado, *Centinela del occidente*.

[30] The term used for the secret police organisations of the political parties of the Popular Front which operated freely in acts of repression from July to December 1936. Part of post-war Francoist mythology, the term was derived from Tcheka, the first Soviet political police after 1917.

spitefulness which does not even respect the peace of the grave? In Madrid there are many people who owe their lives to Ángel Galarza, who managed on more than one occasion to prevent precisely that act which the newspaper attributes to him. But in any case, his memory, and that of any person, demands greater charity than that demonstrated in that anonymous biography. That is not the way of Christian reconciliation nor the attitude required for the future.[31]

War memories amongst Republicans were also complex. Both personally and collectively a sense of loss had to be dealt with. In political terms – though distinctions between personal and political could not be rigid – many on the left continued to believe in the ideals for which they had fought and suffered. Many influenced by Marxism, for example, continued to believe in the Soviet Union which had represented an essential symbol of hope during the conflict. They and others probably understood the official Francoist post-war myths of the war for what they were, though demonstrating this was impossible under the dictatorship. In any event, a life had to be made somehow, particularly in the interests of children. In the Cold War atmosphere of the early 1950s, and as the United States offered much-needed financial assistance in return for pledges of support for its own crusade, it remained difficult for those who had supported the Republic to transmit objective knowledge of pre-war Spanish democracy to subsequent generations. For the post-war generation, as the extract at the head of this chapter indicates, there were neither battles to talk about nor, in many cases, the great hardships of the war's aftermath. For those born in the 1950s it often proved difficult to relate to the ways of thinking of parents and grandparents because the conflicts and losses had not been shared directly and because the war seemed less relevant when other issues were pressing. In a fast-changing world the terms of reference which would have allowed the young to understand the idiom of their elders' memories were largely absent, though the question of collective trauma associated with the war would arise for many of their own children forty years or so later.

The politics of memory and the Cold War

The Franco regime's resurrection of the crusade narrative and recovery from the disdain directed towards the dictatorship by foreign governments between 1945 and 1947 went hand in hand with the West's anti-Soviet

---

[31] 'Respeto a los muertos', *CPED*, 35–6, August–September 1966, 2. On Galarza's in fact rather mixed record on wartime security, see, e.g., Preston, *Spanish Holocaust*, pp. 292–3. In contrast to other notices, *La Vanguardia Española* respectfully reported the burial and the coffin wrapped in the colours of the Spanish Republic: 2 August 1966, p. 13.

crusade as Stalinism increased its sphere of influence. The Cold War interacted with civil war memories in the motivations and activities of anti-communist Catholic groups, and veteran, ex-captive, and war victim associations originating in Franco's war. Through acts of remembrance, analogies were made with various acts of persecution in the late 1940s and 1950s. Analysis of these various associations of memory reveals the extent of collaboration between them in the face of fears of 'forgetting'.

The anti-communist legacy had already been abundantly clear from the Caudillo's frequent declarations during the Second World War. A month after Hitler's invasion of the Soviet Union in June 1941, the General's speech to mark the fifth anniversary of the 1936 military rebellion against the Second Republic had recalled in glorious terms how 'the first battles against communism' had been won during Spain's war. He had also been confident that the Allies were more or less defeated already and that a repeat of his own victory over Stalin was 'absolutely inevitable'.[32] Apart from the propaganda of Franco's 'crusade' as a war against 'Asiatic barbarism', his government's tacit support for Hitler once Germany had invaded the Soviet Union in June 1941 was symbolised by the sending of a Spanish military force, the so-called Blue Division, largely consisting of Falangist volunteers accompanied by army officers, to fight for the Axis on the Eastern Front, confirming the 1941 policy shift on the war in Europe, from non-belligerency to 'moral belligerency' in favour of the Axis. Several hundred men of the Blue Division who were captured by the Soviets would be repatriated to Spain after Stalin's death during the 1950s. Serrano Suñer, the Spanish Foreign Minister, had reminded Falangists from the balcony of Falange headquarters in Madrid on 24 June 1941 that the moment for the Falange to 'dictate its sentence of condemnation' had arrived: 'Russia is guilty! Russia is guilty! Guilty of our civil war [...] Guilty of the murder of so many comrades and so many soldiers who fell in that war brought on by the aggression of Russian Communism. The destruction of Communism is a necessary condition for the survival of a free and civilised Europe.'[33] In this atmosphere, direct comparisons were made between the notorious mass killing of Nationalist prisoners in November and December 1936 and later massacres carried out in the name of Soviet power and the communist threat. Paracuellos, already a symbol of martyrdom, thus became a prototype, in this view, for the later massacre of Polish military officers by Soviet forces at Katyn in 1940 and the later mass killings in Korea

---

[32] *ABC*, 18 July 1941, pp. 21–3.   [33] *ABC*, 25 June 1941.

which would receive much attention in the national press.[34] The comparison had been made earlier in the 1940s, but the political significance during the onset of the Cold War in the 1950s was all the greater.[35]

A further justification for the resurgence of 1950s' anti-communism was the claim that Stalin's Russia held captive Spanish children who had been evacuated by the Republic with their parents' support to Russia and the Ukraine during the civil war. Anti-Soviet hostility was stoked up in the propaganda, which even claimed, for example, that many of the '6,000 Spanish children' had been the 'orphans of parents killed by the Reds' during the civil war.[36] A resurrection of wartime attitudes can be witnessed in the 1950s campaigns to repatriate Blue Division prisoners and Spanish-Soviet children and the collections by Catholic organisations to aid peoples persecuted by communism. In fact, a total of 3,000 or so children had been evacuated from the Republican zone to the ports of Yalta and Leningrad between March 1937 and October 1938 to escape Nationalist bombardment and, in most cases, because of the idealistic commitment of their parents to the Republic and apprehension about the consequences for them of a Franco victory.[37]

After Stalin's death and the re-instatement of informal Soviet-Spanish relations, many politically active Republicans who had fled the country as adults at the end of the civil war returned with their own children born in exile. Many of the children as adults would have to confront the political and cultural discrimination and negative perceptions as returnees during the 1950s. Only a minority of the contingent of more than four hundred of those returned from Odessa in January 1957, for example, were said by the Spanish authorities to be 'normal'.[38] Among them were the ex-Communist José Laín Entralgo and his wife and child, who returned not because of the clichéd rationale of 'choosing freedom' peddled by the Franco regime, though many were deeply disillusioned by Stalinism, but because of nostalgia for their homeland. The Spanish intelligence services, which resented his protection 'because of his family name', categorised José Laín as 'dangerous' nonetheless and kept him and his family under close scrutiny.[39]

---

[34] E.g. *La Vanguardia Española*, 4 December 1953, p. 11.
[35] E.g. Ernesto Caballero Giménez, *La matanza de Katyn (Visión sobre Rusia)* (Madrid, 1945). For a recent revival of this thesis, see César Vidal, *Paracuellos-Katyn: un ensayo sobre el genocidio de la izquierda* (Madrid, 2005).
[36] *Fotos*, 5 July 1941.
[37] See, e.g., Marie José Devillard, Álvaro Pazos, Susana Castillo and Nuria Medina, *Los niños españoles en la URSS (1937–1997): narración y memoria* (Barcelona, 2001).
[38] Virginia Ródenas, 'Así se interrogó a los españoles repatriados de la URSS', *ABC*, 6 December 2009. For press coverage, see *ABC*, 23 January 1957.
[39] Laín Entralgo, *Descargo*, pp. 453–4.

Even before this, during the second half of the 1940s, Spain, embodied politically on the international stage by General Franco, had undergone a dramatic and fortuitous change of image. The shift from Axis-supporting pariah – a status symbolised particularly by the United Nations decision of December 1946 to impose diplomatic sanctions and the withdrawal of foreign ambassadors – to ally in the Cold War was confirmed gradually by the return of ambassadors between 1947 and 1950. This change in fortune was the result of international developments, but could be fruitfully exploited. The official politics of memory played increasingly on Soviet aid to the Republic, perpetuating the myth of the civil war as an attempt by 'Asiatic bolshevism' to destroy Christian civilisation. This filtered down as far as the Catholic middle classes, reigniting civil war memories. Catholic organisations made collections of money to aid Catholics persecuted by Communism in Central and Eastern Europe, and the Soviet Union was demonised in all possible ways, including depiction of it as a place where 'violations of womanhood' were commonplace.[40]

In February 1946 the French government had unilaterally closed its border with Spain, and in March the British, French and US governments condemned the Franco regime, although they also declared their unwillingness to intervene directly to bring about its downfall. The political committee of the UN echoed these criticisms. Spain protested that the UN lacked the legitimacy necessary to make such a judgement, and the regime's defence against the alleged international ('Jewish–Masonic') campaign would be based on a programme of propaganda and Falangist mobilisation founded in part on memories of the Republic and war. Within the country, for example, the controlled press began to publish lists of state political institutions, Falangist provincial delegations, religious confraternities, city and rural local authorities, as well as individuals, across the country, which publicly declared their 'adhesion' to the Caudillo.[41]

In March, the Falangist press went to work systematically on conjuring up analogies between the Spanish Republic, its post-1939 government-in-exile, and the communist regimes emerging from the debris of the Second World War in Eastern Europe. The civil war was implicitly invoked, for example, in reporting on and criticising Tribunales Populares set up to try alleged collaborators with Nazi Germany (militants of the Ustasha) in Tito's socialist Yugoslav state and the executions resulting from the deliberations of these courts. At a somewhat lower pitch, the Falangist press continued to associate Spain positively with

---

[40] E.g. Pla y Deniel in *Ecclesia*, 6 January 1951, 20; 20 January 1951, 9–10; 10 February 1951, 15.

[41] E.g. the long list in *La Vanguardia Española*, 13 February 1946.

the Axis powers because their war had been against the Soviet Union. Göring's testimony at Nuremberg, for example, was admired since he had defended 'the principle of Caudillaje' in Germany when Hitler had grasped power and was against free political parties which opened the door to communism: 'Democracy ruined Germany [just as it had] ruined us.'[42] The 'squalid' exiled Republican government, led by José Giral, was associated with the 'enemies of our history' and was blamed for whipping up feeling against the Motherland.[43] The programme of Giral and the exiles for 'transformación social' in Spain provided useful propaganda material for the Franco regime because it could be publicised as a plan by the 'Reds' in exile to wreak revenge should they ever return. The regime played on a common will to avoid a repeat of the horrors of the past: the civil war and the preceding years of the Republic were 'etched in our painful and wounded memory'.[44]

In December 1946, as a prelude to UN sanctions, the US government recommended that Spain be excluded from all international organisations. The immediate response in Madrid took the form of a mass demonstration on 9 December in the Plaza de Oriente against the UN agreement, mobilised in defence of 'national honour' and sovereignty, and composed of a cross-section of the public amenable to the political designs of Falangist-dominated civil war ex-combatant and ex-prisoner associations. There was a popular dynamic to the demonstration, though many took advantage of the day off from work decreed by the FET *sindicatos* in the city and the largely conservative surrounding rural areas.[45] General Franco's centrepiece address to the multitude incited memories of the war, as did the slogans of the assembled masses, and restated the significance of the conflict as a crusade against communism. The claims of Spanish independence, as defended in the city in 1808 against Napoleon's forces, were evoked, as was 'the cry of hope given out from within the Red zone (during the civil war), the fervent dedication to the destiny of Spain during the most horrific moments of the Soviet terror'. The address to the huge crowd amounted to an appeal to a perpetual anti-communism as well as an attack on those who

speculate vilely with your loyalty and with our internal peace. Those who attempt to do us injury, with impunity, wishing to steal away the glory of the victory of the Spanish (much applause) and the value of your sacrifices, to force us back to

---

[42] *Arriba*, 19 March 1946, 3, 8.
[43] On the divisions and errors of the government-in-exile, see Miguel Ángel Yuste, *La II República Española en el exilio en los inicios de la Guerra Fría (1945–1951)* (Madrid, 2005).
[44] E.g., *Arriba*, 29 May 1946, p. 1; 13 March 1946, p. 1; 19 March 1946, p. 8.
[45] *Hoja del Lunes*, 9 December 1946; *Imperio* (Zamora), 10 December 1946.

precisely our most hated handful of enemies [...] What has happened in the UN cannot seem at all strange to us as Spaniards: when a wave of communist terror lays waste to Europe and violations, crimes and persecutions – of the same order as those you yourselves witnessed and suffered – preside over the life of twelve formerly independent nations (in Eastern Europe), it should not seem strange that the sons of Giral and La Pasionaria are tolerated there.[46]

Many of the demonstrators carried placards, most ideologically or politically inspired, though some were more simply suggestive of the desire to avoid another war. Somewhat in contradiction with much of the daily reality of the country in the 1940s, one such legend declared that 'There are no Reds, nor Whites here. We are all Spaniards.' Another was a call to protect specifically Christian civilisation: 'the Crucifix in our homes and in our schools', reflecting war memories of the conflict over powerful symbols of identity during the Republic and civil war. Most of the slogans lauded Franco explicitly in recalling the war, a feeling which had been passed to a new generation, it was believed: 'we fought in the trenches and we will fight again wherever you direct us'; 'the sons of the martyrs are standing here to defend their saviour'.[47] There was clearly a Falangist input into the choreography, but many of the sentiments were also popular amongst sections of the middle class and provincial and rural Castilian society.

After Franco's speech, the multitude solemnly and deliberately made its way past two of the key sites of wartime ruins marking places of martyrdom and imprisonment, a procession tracing the route to the Montaña barracks and the Modelo prison. Both the ruined barracks and the site of the prison were symbols of what the press called 'our Alzamiento' and of collective suffering; some of those marching past had been imprisoned in the Modelo under threat of death, and the propaganda recalled how the victims of Paracuellos and Torrejón had been taken from there and other Madrid gaols. At the same time, participants could marvel at the monumental Air Ministry building which, though still incomplete, could be seen rising from the debris, an image of emergent power to replace that of the 'polluted' prison.

Spain did not win immediate concessions from the international powers, but in spite of considerable domestic problems the solidity of the regime in the global circumstances towards the end of the 1940s had been underlined. At the end of March 1947 the so-called Law of Succession was formulated, a further propaganda salvo, particularly for

---

[46] *Arriba*, 10 December 1946, p. 1. There were smaller demonstrations organised by FET and ex-combatant associations in Barcelona, Seville, Valencia and other cities.

[47] *Arriba*, 10 December 1946, p. 6. Also, *ABC*, 10 December 1946; 11 December 1946.

international consumption, defining the form of regime born out of the civil war and formalising its continuity as 'a Catholic and social state, constituted as a kingdom'. In spite of the protest of the exiled Juan de Borbón, declaring his own claim to the throne, the law provided for a military interregnum under Franco as Head of State; moreover, the future monarch, whoever it was to be, would undertake to swear an oath of loyalty to the fundamental laws of the Francoist state and nation, beginning with the fascist-inspired Labour Charter of 1938 and culminating with the Ley de Sucesión itself. Demonstrating the country's unique variant on 'organic democracy', a state-controlled referendum on the succession was prepared amid a renewed anti-communist propaganda campaign, the Church and the press recommending a 'Yes' vote, which was duly secured. On the eleventh anniversary of the 1936 rebellion, in July 1947, the press maintained the anti-communist momentum, mobilising international and domestic support by evoking the civil war as a conflict caused by 'the same stratagems [as those] at work today in Greece and in Hungary, Poland or Czechoslovakia'.[48] By November 1947 the Cold War atmosphere had in fact created a sense of international accommodation towards Spain, and ratification of the moral condemnation of Franco by the UN failed, making the return of ambassadors inevitable. The wave of strikes in France in December were depicted in the Spanish newspapers as the work of 'professional agitators' in the pay of international communism, which it was claimed remained the main threat to peace in the world; liberal governments were depicted as insufficiently strong to counteract the threat.[49]

The political capital accrued by Franco during his own 'crusade', accentuated by propaganda giving credit to his 'genius' in keeping the country out of the world conflict, was therefore consolidated in the Cold War atmosphere of the late 1940s and early 1950s. The charismatic dimension of the Caudillo's power would be confirmed by the quasi-sacred status accorded to objects related to his military command during the civil war displayed in the Museum of the Army in the Palacio del Buen Retiro in Madrid, where amid glorification of the Nationalist cause, Franco had opened new galleries in March 1946 only days after the declaration by foreign governments against Spanish membership of the UN.[50] Several large equestrian portraits of the Caudillo in the style

---

[48] E.g., Torcuato Luca de Tena, 'La justificación del Movimiento Nacional', *ABC*, 18 July 1947.

[49] See, e.g., *Ya*, 2 December 1947.

[50] Paul Preston, *Franco: A Biography* (London, 1933). p. 555. On the museum: Selma Reuben Holo, *Museums and Identity in Democratic Spain* (Liverpool, 1999), pp. 82–5.

of those of former monarchs were hung, and other were pieces displayed, both in the galleries devoted to the 'Guerra de la Cruzada' and throughout, amongst relics from the national past, including the sword reputedly used in battle by El Cid, and (according to legend) that of Cervantes, and the marble triptych before which the Holy Roman Emperor, Charles V, had prayed during his reclusive and meditative retirement at the monastery at Yuste. The Army Museum also housed commemorative material relating to wartime martyrs such as those killed at Paracuellos.[51]

By the turn of the decade, the regime had ridden the storm; much had been protected and even gained by evoking the civil war. In his speech at Las Palmas towards the end of October 1950, Franco evoked both the Asturian rebellion of 1934 – 'carried out at the orders of the Comintern' – and its corollary, as he saw it, the civil war: 'in the first anti-Communist reaction in Europe, Spanish hearts and Spanish arms stood up for the defence of the faith and of civilisation, fourteen years before the world had realised the necessity'.[52] Shortly afterwards, on 31 October, the UN resolution against Spain was overturned, though Franco's state would not be permitted membership of the organisation until 1955. The following day was the Feast of All Saints, a national holiday, marking the beginning of a period of remembrance and on this occasion coinciding fortuitously with Pope Pius XII's proclamation of the dogma of the Assumption of the Virgin, celebrated with a 21-gun salute in Madrid, ordained by Franco, when the church bells of the city were also rung simultaneously in celebration.[53] Later, in September 1953, the US-Spanish alliance would be cemented with an accord by which the US would supply Spain with substantial technical and financial assistance in return for the stationing of US airforce bases in Spain. Sealed only weeks after the Concordat signed between the government and the Vatican, the agreement with the United States was hailed in the press as guaranteeing national sovereignty and placing Spain 'amongst the leaders of the western alliance [for] the maintenance of peace'.[54]

The bombast of asserting 'national honour' through anti-Soviet alignment in the Cold War was accompanied by parlous economic conditions. Monuments to particular groups of martyrs were established in the 1950s and 1960s, but the political apogee of Francoism, between 1953 and 1956, would not be impressively crowned with physical

---

[51] E.g., *La Vanguardia Española*, 16 May 1953, p. 3.   [52] *ABC* (Seville), 27 October 1950.
[53] *ABC* (Seville), 2 November 1950.
[54] *ABC*, 27 September 1953. For the Concordat see Tusell, *Franco y los católicos*.

national monuments to the 'crusade' and to the regime's perpetuation.[55] Resources were still being ploughed into Franco's pantheon of the fallen at Cuelgamuros, the grandiose mausoleum of the Valley of the Fallen, which would be inaugurated in 1959. Although the Valle de los Caídos was represented by the regime as a perennial homage to the martyrs and heroes of the 'crusade', the monument would be used largely for minor state occasions and was never viewed popularly as a national monument.[56] Further expenditure was lavished on the grand Arco de la Victoria in Madrid, first planned in 1939 as part of the reconstruction of the war-damaged University City. The monumental arch was first planned as one element of a grander and largely Falange-inspired scheme to include a 'Museum of the Revolution' and other buildings dedicated specifically to the combatants, war prisoners and war-wounded. The plans gathered dust for lack of resources, however, and were reinvigorated only in 1946 in a scaled-down plan to erect the Victory Arch as an act of 'national affirmation' in defiance of the internationally imposed isolation of the country, though the arch was not finally finished for another ten years.[57] The 9-metre-tall bronze equestrian statue of the Caudillo designed to be situated in front of the arch, also much delayed, was finally placed in the interior patio of the Ministry of Housing in 1959.[58]

The community of memory related to the singular event of the Paracuellos massacre, which had emerged in the aftermath of Madrid's 'liberation' in 1939, continued to prosper. To commemorate the twentieth anniversary, in early November 1956 the Church of San Manuel y San Benito in central Madrid was filled with the relatives of those 'murdered by the Red hordes', as it had been at this time in previous years. Following the practice begun during the war, it was still claimed that there were some 20,000 such martyrs at Paracuellos, though this exaggerated number was cited less frequently from the 1960s and subsequent research suggests

---

[55] For particular monuments, see, e.g., that with an image of the Virgen del Asedio (1954) commemorating those killed in the 'Red fury' at the Ciudad Universitaria (Madrid); the Falangist monument to the 'Caídos de Chamartín de la Rosa' (1946); see also those to José Calvo Sotelo, Plaza de Castilla (Madrid), inaugurated on 13 July 1960; to executed Carmelite fathers, Carabanchel cemetery (1961); to martyrs of the confraternity of la Sacramental de San Isidro (1943); and to murdered priests at Solsona (Lérida), *Ecclesia*, 27 January 1951, p. 17. Fernández Delgado et al., *Memoria impuesta*, pp. 141, 171, 173–5, 271, 397.

[56] For the official ideology, see, e.g., Gregorio Marañón Moya, 'El alférez definitivo', in Hermandad de Alféreces Provisionales, *Generación del 36*, p. 101.

[57] Fernández Delgado et al., *Memoria impuesta*, pp. 404–9.

[58] A few years later it was moved to the Plaza de San Juan de la Cruz where it remained until 2005.

that some 2,700 had been killed.[59] As remained customary two decades after the events, the families of the dead proceeded after the requiem mass to the sacred site at Paracuellos, known as the 'cementerio patri- ótico', which had been sanctified after the civil war, where the remains of the martyrs were at rest and where a monument was constructed. While the language of the war as a 'Cruzada de Liberación' indicated the broadly national-Catholic nature of the culture of memory amongst conservatives, use of such terms as 'la horda roja' to describe the perpet- rators was typical of an equally generalised demonising language; the language also avoided any necessity for precision in allotting respo- nsibility for the murders. Certainly, the broad 'us and them' discourse of the civil war and its aftermath remained a part of public and official linguistic currency into the 1960s.[60]

Reconstruction of the monumental image of the Sacred Heart of Jesus at the Cerro de los Ángeles, site of pilgrimage and symbolic throne of Christ located at the geographic heart of Spain, to which the monument had been consecrated in the presence of Alfonso XIII in 1919, was much delayed. This was in spite of the fact that the 'Calvary' of the Sacred Heart at the hands of Republican militiamen in August 1936 had been depicted as a desecration which synthesised all other acts of sacri- lege. The public subscription organised to support the work would be protracted and difficult, however, and the architectural and financial challenge of the monument, with its basilica beneath, was only overcome in 1965. In compensation, the Immaculate Heart of the Virgin at the Basílica del Pilar in Zaragoza would be formally consecrated in the name of the Francoist nation on the Día de la Raza (12 October) in 1954, the act of consecration being celebrated in the cathedral at the monument to the civil war fallen, which served as an altar, with General Franco presiding, accompanied by his wife, Doña Carmen, both seated on thrones beneath a regal canopy.[61] During such protra- cted commemorative spectacles there were opportunities to legitimate national sanctification by publicly evoking leftist critiques of the unity of Church and state made in the past by political figures associated with the Second Republic.[62] One of these was the moderate socialist Julián Besteiro who had been openly critical of national consecration to the Sacred Heart in 1919 from a rationalist and secular position.

[59] *La Vanguardia Española*, 8 November 1956, p. 19. See Jorge Martínez Reverte, *La batalla de Madrid* (Barcelona, 2004).
[60] E.g., *La Vanguardia Española*, 2 November 1962, p. 7; *ABC*, 4 April 1963, p. 65.
[61] *ABC*, 13 October 1954.
[62] See 'La deuda de España en el Cerro de los Ángeles', *Ecclesia*, 9 June 1951, p. 9; *ABC*, 25 June 1954, pp. 37, 41.

As the official Francoist discourse on the civil war changed course in the 1960s – and within a decade of being identified as a dangerous advocate of the destruction of the national essence – Besteiro would begin to be praised somewhat by the regime as an isolated example of 1930s' Republican moderation and reason. At the inauguration ceremony of the new monument to the Sacred Heart in 1965 the tone was different to that of the early 1950s, and although many military uniforms could be seen and many of the spectators were diehard Francoists, public references to the civil war were measured and a prominent place was accorded to Prince Juan Carlos, representing a younger and forward-looking Spain.[63] As though to underline the sense of a new era dawning, the Catholic mass during the blessing of the basilica was prayed in Spanish, rather than Latin, in accord with the recent guidance emerging from the reformist Vatican Council.

Aside from financial incapacity, constructing a genuinely national monument was a problem also because of the fragmented nature of nation and society, in spite of official claims to the contrary. Instead of a single monolithic memory of victory and conquest, there was in reality a plurality of collective memories even amongst the victors.[64] During the 1940s these had been merged in the public expressions of the officially sanctioned crusade narrative and the focus of responsibility for the catastrophe was firmly placed with Republicans. By the 1950s, the Nationalist wartime coalition had begun to fragment at subgovernmental level and distinct communities of memory fell away from the rigid control of the centre of political power occupied by the most loyally Francoist elements of army, Falange and Council of Ministers. Many of the memories and ways of thinking of these various 'communities' were, of course, shared, but they were also shaped by adherence to a particular sense of place, a geographic region, or a temporal or cultural 'map' of the past, which diverged to some degree from the constructed regime ideal. In the organised commemoration of the Paracuellos killings there was a dominant hard core of ideologically orthodox 'memory activists' who decided on how memories should be sustained, but the many dedications to the largely middle-class victims show how they hailed from many parts of the country and were therefore commemorated in different places and in a variety of ways. The small group of 'protected dwellings' ('viviendas protegidas') built in 1958 for the

---

[63] 'Consagración de España al Corazón de Jesús', *Blanco y Negro*, 3 July 1965. Also, *ABC*, 26 June 1965.

[64] E.g., on Falangist intellectuals, see Laín Entralgo on the Burgos 'ghetto': *Descargo*, pp. 231–2, 237.

humble classes in Lérida, Catalonia, for example, were opportunistically named after two martyred brothers, one of whom had been murdered at Paracuellos, as part of a localised memory and sense of identity, albeit one linked to the regime.[65]

With post-war state centralisation, even Carlism, the movement from which the language of crusade had first emerged in the summer of 1936, did not present Francoism with unqualified support or unambiguous collective memory after 1939.[66] Another example were the *mandos* ('leading cadres') of the Sección Femenina (SF), the women's section of the state party, of whom there were some 15,000 at national and local level.[67] The SF leadership worked to keep memory of wartime sacrifices alive, particularly those of Falangist martyrs killed in action or executed who were in many cases relatives of particular *mandos* and also gave unqualified public loyalty to Franco as a father figure. On the ground, however, the daily activities of the SF, concerned with charitable work and welfare, were not conducive primarily to memory making. Although some of the women of the SF doubtless produced a dour or melancholic impression in conveying traditionalist ideas, the extensive tasks given to the women of the SF involved them in active social roles, something that contradicted the official discourse about the public passivity of the ideal woman, condemned only to mourn.[68] At times, there were unintended consequences and much depended on individual characters. When urban and educated women of the SF visited small rural communities they might impress girls and young women by virtue of their apparent independence and more open way of speaking than those in the pueblo, where everyone knew everyone else. The ideological messages that activists conveyed to women while giving advice on child health to working-class families could not always be controlled by other

[65] *La Vanguardia Española*, 4 May 1958, p. 10. Also Roberto Germán Fandiño Pérez, *Historia del movimiento ciudadano e historia local* (Logroño, 2005), p. 63.

[66] Francisco Javier Caspístegui, *Navarra y el carlismo durante el régimen de Franco: la utopía de la identidad unitaria* (Pamplona, 1997); Cándida Calvo, 'Franquismo y la política de la memoria en Guipúzcoa. La búsqueda del consenso carlista (1936–1951)', in Alicia Alted Vigil (ed.), *Entre el pasado y el presente: Historia y memoria* (Madrid, 1996), pp. 163–82.

[67] Kathleen Richmond, *Women and Spanish Fascism: The Women's Section of the Falange, 1934–1959* (London, 2003).

[68] E.g., María José Ruiz Somavilla and Isabel Jiménez Lucena, 'Un espacio para mujeres. El servicio de divulgación y asistencia sanitario-social en el primer franquismo', *Historia Social*, 39 (2001), 67–85; Inmaculada Blasco Herranz, *Armas femeninas para la contrarrevolución: La Sección Femenina en Aragón (1936–1950)* (Málaga, 1999); Matilde Eiroa San Francisco, 'Trabajo asistencial: El Servicio Social de Sección Femenina', in María Teresa López Beltrán (ed.), *Las mujeres en Andalucía*, 2 vols. (Málaga, 1993), vol. II, pp. 301–13.

(often male) authorities, such as priests.[69] They could, in effect, give an impetus to personal affirmation and aspirations to do with education which went beyond traditional life as hymned in the official ideology.[70] For urban middle-class women with time to comply with the 'Servicio Social' obligations of the SF, there were more opportunities and less of a weight of Catholic tradition upon them. They may well have been shocked when confronted with the poverty virtually on their own doorsteps; for some, activism in the public sphere heralded a loss of innocence which might ultimately contribute to a desire for greater social reconciliation. This ambiguous cross-class communication, which tended to place greater social equality and liberty at the heart of reconciliation, was nonetheless often at odds with the limitations of the regime's social policy and continued ideology of crusade and the dominance of National Catholicism.[71]

Fissures were also present within the state party, based on the Falange, and there were genuine expressions of dissidence from so-called Old Shirts, those who had joined the party during the pre-war days, usually because they naively believed in the fascist rhetoric of 'revolution' propounded by the leadership of the 1930s. A leading radical from Valladolid, Luís González Vicén, wrote in June 1956, for example, to his friend José Luis de Arrese, Secretary General of the Movimiento, suggesting, in effect, that far from achieving reconciliation, the regime had perpetuated the division and mentality of the civil war:

at this very moment, the difference between being a Red or a non-Red [. . .] between conquerors and conquered, is a reality in national life and in the administrative decisions of the government. The accessibility of power [. . .] the treatment of citizens in which the difference is equally marked, the chance for social influence and many other factors, clearly indicate that this most grave problem still lacks solution. If this is so obvious from our camp you can easily imagine how it appears from the other side. They not only regard themselves as defeated and politically unsatisfied; they see themselves treated as second-class Spaniards and exaggerate the injustice which they receive, building up hatred against the other half whom they think the cause of this evil.[72]

So-called 'radical' Falangists, many of whom wished to reduce the power of the army and the Church and even the arbitrary personal rule of

---

[69] E.g. Victoria Lorée Enders, 'Problematic Portraits: The Ambiguous Historical Role of the Sección Femenina of the Falange', in Enders and Pamela Radcliff (eds.), *Constructing Spanish Womanhood* (Albany, 1999), pp. 375–97.

[70] E.g., Piñero Valverde, 'Mi viejo álbum', p. 61; Buendía Gómez, 'Peinando recuerdos', p. 159.

[71] E.g. Castilla del Pino, *Casa del olivo*, pp. 337–8.

[72] Cited in Stanley Payne, *Falange* (Stanford, 1961), p. 253.

Franco, were a minority, however, though they believed themselves to be the genuine ideological heirs of the party's founders. They had taken the lead in the wartime militia and later saw their maintenance of guardianship over the values of wartime sacrifice as their right, becoming, effectively, a 'warrior community' with its own unique claim to legitimate expressions of memory. Amongst Nationalist veteran Brotherhoods (*Hermandades*), volunteering, rather than conscription, was an important part of the currency of community loyalty and reward, the allocation of which provoked internal divisions.

By no means all of these veterans were 'radicals', however, even in the circumscribed terms of the Falangist Old Shirts. A great many were dyed-in-the-wool Francoists and constantly preached the need to safeguard the victory in the spirit of the 'crusade'. Commemoration fluctuated according to the times, generational change and political requirements. We have already seen how important Falangists were in setting the public parameters of early post-war commemoration, but this role was shared by Nationalist wartime junior officers (*alféreces provisionales*), though many joined the state political Movimiento and thus also became Falangists. The majority were student volunteers who had still been at university in 1936. They were trained by German and Italian military instructors in dedicated wartime academies, which also gave religious instruction. In middle age, they formed their own association (April 1958) with the aim of recuperating memories which, as limited political reform and economic liberty were on the cards, were deemed to be in danger of being lost.[73] The founding ceremony of the *alféreces*' association took place at the battleground of the Cerro de Garabitas in the Casa del Campo on the outskirts of Madrid, where in 1937 the life of the Conde de Mayalde, then an *alférez provisional*, who would become Director General of Security in the 1940s and mayor of Madrid, was saved 'through divine intervention' and a monument to the Sacred Heart had been erected.[74] Both Falangists and *alféreces* were encouraged to believe that under Franco's command they, virtually alone, had been instrumental in winning the war, and both groups received many privileges in the aftermath, including preferential entry into the legal and teaching professions and university. More than a hundred *alféreces* were to become members of the Cortes, Franco's pseudo-parliament, more

---

[73] Xosé Manoel Núñez Seixas, 'Los vencedores vencidos: la peculiar memoria de la División Azul, 1945–2005', *Pasado y Memoria*, 4 (2005), 85; José María Garate, *Alféreces provisionales: la improvisación de oficiales en la guerra del '36* (Madrid, 1976), p. 335; Bullón and Diego, *Historias*, pp. 41–3.

[74] Fernández Delgado et al., *Memoria impuesta*, p. 130. It was also from here that bombing raids on the city were launched.

than thirty were Civil Governors, at least twenty became mayors of large cities, and several were appointed as government ministers.[75]

The radical critique from within the Falange was therefore largely drowned out, but it remains important because the critiques draw our attention towards the continuation of wartime divisions into the later 1950s. Nonetheless, as a public body parallel to the state, the association of *alféreces* became highly politicised in defence of the memory of what most affiliates, including the less intransigent element, continued to call the Cruzada de Liberación de España, which members saw as the foundation of their collective identity and of the meaning of Spain itself, a meaning they sought to explain to the young.[76] The associations of both the ex-combatants and the *alféreces* were to become the preferred audiences for the bellicose and anti-communist post-war speeches of Franco and other leading figures of the regime who habitually conjured up wartime memories. At the inauguration of the Valley of the Fallen in April 1959 there were, for example, some ten thousand former *alféreces provisionales* present, in addition to twenty-five thousand Falangists.[77] The *alféreces'* new association had been welcomed by the Primate of Spain, Pla y Deniel, in Toledo in June 1958, when he repeated the Holy War thesis in giving thanks to 'the healthy [*sano*] people of Spain', led by the *alféreces*, who waged the war as a crusade against 'terror and anarchy' and for 'the common good'. The Church, he assured his audience, 'would never have blessed a mere military pronouncement'. Evoking the memory of the murders of hundreds of religious martyrs in Toledo reinforced the message.[78] It was a 'just war' because it was necessary to restore order, though it remained subject to legal norms which, 'if violated in a particular case, must be condemned', as the executions of resisters against Communism in Hungary since the Soviet invasion of 1956 were to be condemned. At the same time, Joaquín Ruiz-Giménez, the former Minister of Education, a wartime volunteer officer himself who was beginning a philosophical journey towards Christian Democratic opposition, argued a different case: that war should always be subordinated to the highest human values, and that if a war were 'just' then achieving

[75] Rodríguez, *Reaccionarios y golpistas*, p. 104.
[76] See, e.g., Hermandad de Alféreces Provisionales, *Generación del 36*; Julio Busquets, 'Las alféreces provisionales hasta la creación de la hermandad (1936–1958)', *Historia 16*, 119 (March 1986), 44–55. Also Castro Berrojo, *Capital de la cruzada*, p. 206. A modest monument 'to the Alférez Provisional', following the tradition of commemorating 'the unknown soldier', was erected in Madrid in 1965.
[77] *ABC*, 2 April 1959.
[78] The killing of priests came after the military coup and, in Toledo, during the ten-week siege of the Alcázar. The term 'sano' indicates wholesomeness and goodness, as well as health or sanity.

a just peace ought to be possible.[79] Neither Pla y Deniel nor Ruiz-Giménez spoke of the Francoist executions during and after the civil war, though they were of course aware of them, as was the Cardinal's eventual successor, Enrique y Tarancón. Neither did they discuss the military aid proffered to the rebels in 1936 by Nazi Germany and Fascist Italy.[80]

The veterans of the Blue Division, sent five years later to fight for Hitler on the Eastern Front, constituted another community of memory based doctrinally on anti-communism which perpetuated the culture of the civil war. Altogether, during the period from July 1941 to February 1944, there were some 45,000 Spaniards (6,000 of whom were professional soldiers) in the so-called Spanish Voluntary Division, officially part of the German Wehrmacht, with probably 20,000 on the Eastern Front at any one time. As in the case of the *alféreces*, many of those who volunteered for the División Azul were young Falangist university students who had been too young to fight in the Spanish war; many had lost family members and felt they had 'accounts to settle with Communism'. Approximately 4,300 would be killed, some 500 were taken prisoner in Russia, and the number of wounded was high, many being permanently disabled.[81] With the assistance of the Red Cross at the end of March 1954, in the aftermath of the death of Stalin, 248 prisoners of war were returned from Odessa to Spain amid emotional scenes, to be lauded as idealists and 'héroes de la Madre Patria'. The first state-produced newsreel film to be shown in colour, two weeks later, featured coverage of the celebrations which were heightened as the return coincided conveniently with the 1 April Victory Day parades, the biggest of which was held in Madrid where recently received US armaments were paraded.[82] The repatriated Blue Division veterans were presented with medallions bearing a representation of the Virgin Mary, Saviour of Captives, while in Barcelona a solemn service of thanksgiving was held and prisoners were able to kiss the sacred image of Our Lady of Mercy. During the celebration of Holy Week, shortly after, some of the repatriated prisoners of war would be amongst the processing penitents. In the blanket press coverage for the next few days, Franco was given credit for the prisoners' return but there was little focus on the political aspects of the story of the Blue Division, largely because of its association with the Axis powers,

---

[79] Joaquín Ruiz-Giménez, 'Guerra y paz en el alma del hombre español', address given at the University of Zaragoza, 1959, in Ruiz-Giménez, *Del ser de España* (Madrid, 1963), pp. 102, 108, 111.

[80] *La Vanguardia Española*, 18 July 1958, p. 4. Enrique y Tarancón, *Recuerdos de juventud*, pp. 262–72.

[81] Moreno Juliá, *División Azul*.   [82] *ABC*, 2 April 1954.

and the Caudillo played no role personally in the celebrations. The sympathy felt for Hitler and National Socialism by many of those Spaniards who had joined the expedition was an element of the past which the dictatorship wished to play down in the era of *rapprochement* with the United States. In the shadow of the Cold War, however, the Caudillo could not help but draw attention to the anti-communist significance of the Blue Division. During his visit to Cáceres in May he would praise 'our brave combatants of the División Azul' and, harking back to the civil war, he warned how they 'will tell you exactly what the so-called "communist paradise" consists of'.[83] Thereafter, in contrast to the bellicose pro-Axis tone of the early 1940s, which depicted the Russian population as semi-barbarian, the tone of remembrance of the Blue Division was sacrifice, naturally, and anti-communism. The profile of the veterans' brotherhood, established months after the return of ex-prisoners in 1954, and of the relatives' association, may not have been as high as that of the civil war ex-combatant and ex-captive groups which could be linked unproblematically in the 1950s to the Francoist founding myth of the 'crusade', but there was a high level of collaboration between all such associations.[84] Veterans of the Blue Division, in company with ex-combatants and militants of the Frente de Juventudes, took turns during the early 1950s to mount guard over the tomb of the martyred founder of the Falange, José Antonio Primo de Rivera, for instance, at Philip II's monastery of El Escorial.[85]

After 1954, several of the veterans published memoirs which focused largely on military campaigns and reinforced the official myth of the Division as merely anti-communist rather than pro-Nazi. They kept silent about difficult questions related to their treatment of Russian civilians and the execution of partisans.[86] The episode also formed a significant part of the collective imagery of sections of the Spanish army, often in ways which distorted history. The anti-communism demonstrated by the Blue Division, it would be claimed at the end of the decade, marked an important point in the development of a 'Europeanist sentiment' which imagined either Russia itself or, at least, the ideology

---

[83] *La Vanguardia Española*, 12 May 1954, p. 3.
[84] José Luis Rodríguez Jiménez, *La extrema derecha española en el siglo XX* (Madrid, 1997), pp. 361–4.
[85] See, e.g., *La Vanguardia Española*, 7 February 1954, p. 6.
[86] See, e.g., Gerardo Oroquieta Arbiol and C. García Sánchez, *De Leningrado a Odesa* (Barcelona, 1958), awarded the Premio Nacional de Literatura 'Francisco Franco'. Both authors were former *alféreces provisionales* of the Spanish civil war, and Oroquieta had been a prisoner for eleven years in Russia. Xosé Manoel Núñez Seixas, '¿Eran los rusos culpables? Imagen del enemigo y políticas de ocupación de la División Azul en el frente del este, 1941–1944', *Hispania*, 66, 223 (2006), 695–750.

of communism as 'Asiatic'.[87] Memory of Franco's volunteers was inscribed in the names of many streets, public works projects and schools, but not to the same extent as the memory of the civil war 'fallen', and there were few public monuments to the Blue Division in Spain's main cities.[88] The political culture of Francoism, particularly at a provincial and local level, was nonetheless shaped by the ideals of the 'crusade' and of anti-communism, as espoused through veteran, youth and student organisations, and by the conferment of prestige and status upon veterans through awards, decorations and political posts as mayors, as town hall officials and in public administration, a process which was heightened in the case of the División Azul veterans in the aftermath of the return of prisoners.[89] At a national level, several political posts were held by veterans, most famously, perhaps, by Fernando María Castiella, who had sworn allegiance to Hitler and been awarded the Iron Cross, and who became Minister of Foreign Affairs in 1957.[90] After Franco, there was a surge of publications relating to the División Azul, including that of the Falangist 'dissident' Dionisio Ridruejo, published in 1978. These accounts maintained the central myth of anti-communist motivations. As in the case of Pedro Laín Entralgo, the dalliance with National Socialism in the early 1940s remained a problem. In the spirit of post-Francoist reconciliation, Ridruejo's 'notebook' did, however, include a brief observation recounting how the capture in 1941 of the first Spanish Republican fighting with the partisans in Russia had been greeted by the men of the Blue Division with 'unheard-of joy', suggesting to him that 'the excitable rancour of our civil war' was, at that time, 'still throbbing'.[91]

Gradual diminishment of the crusade narrative would be sponsored by certain individuals, such as Ruiz-Giménez, Laín Entralgo and Manuel Fraga, who possessed varying degrees of influence within the Franco regime, though from somewhat different positions. In part this was because they recognised that the crusade's resonance in binding together successive generations was fast reducing by the middle of the 1950s. In line with the anti-communist tone of the times, demystification of the civil war would rely increasingly from the end of the 1950s on the

---

[87] E.g., Emilio Esteban-Infantes, *La División Azul (Donde Asia empieza)* (Barcelona, 1956); Ramón Serrano Suñer, 'Hacia un patriotismo europeo', *ABC*, 29 September 1959, p. 3.

[88] Núñez Seixas, 'Los vencedores vencidos', pp. 83–113.

[89] See, e.g., *ABC*, 13 August 1954, p. 21; *La Vanguardia Española*, 21 March 1954, p. 4; 8 August 1954; 11 September 1954, p. 3; 23 September 1954, p. 24. On veterans trading on the past in leading the Frente de Juventudes: e.g., Aceves, *Social Change*, p. 34.

[90] Preston, *Franco*, p. 604; Payne, *Franco Regime*, p. 452; Tusell, *Franco y los católicos*, pp. 429–32.

[91] Dionisio Ridruejo, *Los cuadernos de Rusia* (Barcelona, 1978), p. 152.

achievement of peace and security since 1939 rather than on the triumph itself. Increasingly, propagandists would avoid conjuring up wartime effigies. Nevertheless, although modernisers, such as Fraga, liked to depict themselves as apolitical, they remained part of the Movimiento and were quite prepared to compare the alleged 'chaos' of the years of the Second Republic with the 'order' of Franco's post-war peace.[92]

A generational clash of attitudes between backward-looking National Catholicism which blamed liberal laicism for the war and a future-oriented concern with social modernisation which seemed to be contradicted by exclusion of 'the defeated' became evident in the 1950s. This preoccupation would begin to be revealed both amongst elites (political figures who were part of the regime and those who were somewhat marginalised because of their 'liberal' views) and within society, particularly as urban migration gathered pace (the theme of the next chapter). Gradually, questions to do with the marginalised, with social conscience, and with the nature and extent of what was seen as internal exile would be raised.

This process coincided, however, with the high point of the Cold War, and memories of Spain's war were reinvigorated by the East–West struggle of ideologies. While young writers and activists strained against the rigours of authoritarianism and self-censorship, the anti-communism of the victors appeared vindicated by history, and orthodox Francoists saw little reason to give up their ideology or concede political ground. The Cold War also caused the several groups which constituted the 'families' of the regime, including intransigent Catholics, to cling to each other, thus strengthening the Caudillo's hold on power. The country's international change of fortune in the 1950s was based, indeed, on the anti-communist legacy of the civil war. The 'Communist threat' also seemed to justify the watchfulness of the state as social unrest began and migrant shanty towns swelled on the perimeter of the large cities. For those who had supported the losing side in the civil war, both the exiled and those remaining in the interior, the situation seemed hopeless since international tension made the case for the Republic difficult to sustain. There remained difficulties for the state, however, with expressions of a genuinely national memory of the war. Increasing social diversification and demands for the delivery of charitable and rudimentary state welfare would test the regime's ability to impose its unitary ideology, a problem

---

[92] For Fraga's political position between those (Opus Dei) who stood for continuing with National Catholicism and others who persisted in the idea of the Falangist 'revolución pendiente', see Ismael Saz, 'Mucho más que crisis políticas: el agotamiento de dos proyectos enfrentados', *Ayer*, 68, 2007.

magnified by mass migration, begun in the 1950s and growing vertiginously in the 1960s. Communities of memory often had a local or regional focus, most obviously in areas with a strong regional nationalist identity, such as Catalonia and the Basque Country. The weakness of Spanish nationhood had not been resolved by the war and authoritarianism. An added factor was that much of the war's violence had been intimate and remembering, to a substantial extent, was also intimate. The geographical displacing of this social memory is the theme of the next chapter.

6 Memory and migration: flight from the countryside in the 1950s

What customs! Such a different way of life! In the countryside we live always dependent on the harvest, forever looking to the heavens and calling on Divine Providence. I've always believed in God, but since I arrived in Madrid, I've felt so bewildered that I no longer know what to think.[1]

The displacement of war memories

We can refer to the displacement of memories in the first twenty years or so of the post-war era in two principal ways. First, it is necessary to discuss the violent uprooting of the rural poor which was engendered by the conflict and its repressive aftermath. Although migrants were reluctant to give details and often wished not to talk about their towns or villages of origin, oblique references to 'denunciation', 'shaming', loss of 'honour', 'falling into disgrace', and the often unbearable 'harsh criticisms' or 'sanctions' of neighbours, which made 'remembering past events upsetting', would all seem to confirm that fleeing from rural pueblos, as one confided, 'separated them from a sorrowful past'.[2] The most economically humble classes of the Spanish countryside were far from being the only section of society to suffer the consequences of the war, but they bore the brunt collectively more than most other social groups. At the sharp end of state repression, the masses in rural poverty who possessed little or no social or cultural capital would become central actors, though silently, of the historical social change which was to follow. Migration led them to the margins of urban life, often to subhuman conditions, an existence determined by little else than material survival: 'poverty diminished their faculties, reduced their horizons, and erased their initiatives. Many, since childhood, have developed in an atmosphere of hatred [and], despair [...] deceived by those who treated

[1] Castilian miller, Madrid 1958, cited in Siguán, *Del campo*, p. 141.
[2] Siguán, *Del campo*, pp. 76–80, 114.

156

them badly in their place of origin and compelled them to leave.'[3] After the pervasive stasis of the 1940s it begins to become clearer when we look at the succeeding decade that the civil war had represented a social watershed as well as marking a deep political fracture. For the landless poor who had been amongst the most solid supports of the Republic, the war had destroyed the revolutionary myths of the 1930s, a blow which would provide the impulse for a flight from the countryside. The dream of overturning social and political power had died with the war, and the precarious balance in much of the rural south between the honour of manual labour and rejection of the primitively exploitative system was extinguished during the polarised aftermath.[4] This socio-psychological rupture reinforced a dissociation with the past more broadly as links with the culture and forms of identity of the pueblo and with previous generations were broken.

Second, although much of this chapter will discuss migration resulting from the war as a violent displacement specifically of the largely defeated rural lower classes, it is also necessary to account for social memory by moving away from such broad categories as 'the defeated' and 'the victors'. These are relatively meaningful terms in describing divisions in the aftermath of civil war, but their meaning was shifting and imprecise, and such terms were frequently used as shorthand to describe the social and political landscape rather than as an accurate reflection of a less homogeneous binary reality incorporating the entire population socially or ideologically. Many people, whatever their political opinions or background, felt equal revulsion at the violence on both sides. In many cases after the war – or, given wartime conscription, even during it – it was no easy matter to locate individuals simply within one or other supposed 'group', thus labelled, though state-led coercion after 1939 arose from attempts by those vested with authority to do precisely that. When, the former Republican state lawyer Ramón López Barrantes returned to Madrid in 1951 after eleven years in exile, he would express the sense of discrimination experienced by stigmatised 'Reds', a term still commonly hurled at Republicans: 'the abyss that separated the victors and the defeated continued to be implacable [. . .] Even though twelve years have passed, the waves of incomprehension and rancour still pressed down heavily upon the wracked body of the defeated.'[5] Nonetheless, alongside

---

[3] Florentino del Valle, 'La inmigración en Madrid', Semanes Sociales, *Los problemas de la migración*, pp. 375–92, p. 390.

[4] Martínez Alier, *Labourers and Landowners*, esp. pp. 31–2, 234–8; Bernal, 'Resignación', in Sánchez et al. (eds.), *España franquista*, pp. 145–59.

[5] Ramón López Barrantes, *Mi exilio* (Madrid, 1974), pp. 375–6. López Barrantes had been a member of the Madrid College of Lawyers in the 1930s and of Izquierda Republicana and was *asesor jurídico* to the Consejo de Ministros during the Azaña years.

the geographic-cultural displacement of memory through migration, which itself complicated matters, there was a gradual shift away from wartime categories. Some public commentators began cautiously to admit that the political allegiances of the 1930s had been more complex than was suggested by the 'us and them' categorisation required by war mobilisation. There was also a slowly broadening social consciousness and desire to forget the past which was entwined with a critique of the Franco regime from a minority who had formerly been amongst its natural social support base.

Those who were connected in some way to the 'crusade' (particularly, in the 1950s, the maturing sons and daughters of enthusiastic wartime rebels), and others who were content with what they perceived to be a return to 'normality' under Franco, can be distinguished both from each other and from Francoist activists and propagators of the triumphalist mentality. The emergence of a numerically significant part of post-war society, located politically between those who were obviously amongst 'the defeated' (a category which would come to be used synonymously with 'the poor') and those who were 'active victors' (those who enthusiastically participated in civil violence or directly benefited politically or materially from it), is discernible through their 'interior' (or semi-public) reflections in the form of literature, coded published opinions, and cautious acts of protest, some of them sharpened by witnessing the urban–rural encounter that mass migration inevitably produced.

In contrast to these relatively privileged figures, the half-starved rural populace which faced the hardships of migration would leave little trace of their reflections on this process, though some sense of the ways in which the experience was internalised has come to light in sociological surveys and, especially, in their bearing witness through oral history projects many years later. Survival and finding opportunities for children, who represented the future, became more important than dwelling on the past:[6] 'we came, the two of us, with six children, the smallest only a month old, in the wagon of a train, squeezed in on the ground, with other families who also came to Madrid seeking a way of life'; 'in the pueblo with so many daughters what were we to do? At least here we can give them an occupation and they will be able to earn a living.' The effects and memories of the war and the violence lived on, as migrant testimony attested: 'all of this was because of the war'. The older generation, those who stayed put, reflected on ways in which the outcome of the war determined change: 'modern youth are so ambitious and reckless

[6] See, e.g., Esperanza Molina, *Los otros madrileños* (Madrid, 1984), p. 15.

that they do not resign themselves to this kind of life'.[7] The social significance of the war, representing the defeat of democratic modernisation, thus became evident in the great migration which had begun in the 1940s and would gather pace in the 1950s. Government and state would be forced to react to the crisis of hunger the war had created and to which the regime's corrupt practices and inefficiency (described in Chapter 4) had failed to respond. Migration would fuel the widespread protests against the cost and conditions of living in Barcelona, Madrid, Bilbao, and other parts of the country in early 1951, forcing a resort to foreign aid and the naming of a new Council of Ministers in July 1951, on the fifteenth anniversary of the start of the civil war.[8]

For rural migrants, the search for education, 'culture' and health depended on a sacrificial struggle in the shanty slums which spread around the margins of the cities, a way of life which in material terms was similar to the life left behind. The differences were that discrimination was more generalised, less intimate in the city than in tradition-bound rural communities, and the level of hunger was more sustainable because wages were regular. Beneath the surface, spatially segregated existence on the urban margins and new patterns of employment, much delayed in European terms, would become part of the process by which a new class-based sense of collective identity coalesced, though of course urban work was itself alienating.[9] There were remnants of the former understanding and representation of rural protest in latifundist agriculture – factory organisation might occasionally be depicted as a *'caciquist* plan' – but the popular rural culture of labour protest and its political ideas would inevitably decline in the new conditions.[10]

There were limits at this stage to this public reconfiguring of identity. The decade of the 1950s was an era when attention was directed inwards, towards family and the private and personal, a reaction to the constraints upon other forms of solidarity and the constant scrutiny exercised by political and moral agencies – regime and Church – and fear of association with 'the defeated', though this internalisation was not a reaction exclusively of ex-Republicans. The tendency can be associated with the

[7] Siguan, *Del campo*, pp. 59, 70, 73, 105, 140. Also, on conditions, Botey Vallès, *Relats*, p. 107; Lara, *Emigración andaluza*, pp. 194–5.

[8] Richards, 'Falange, Autarky and Crisis'.

[9] Xavier Domènech Sampere, 'La otra cara del milagro español: clase obrera y movimiento obrero en los años del desarrollismo', *Historia Contemporánea*, 26 (2003); José Babiano Mora, *Emigrantes, cronómetros y huelgas: un estudio sobre el trabajo y los trabajadores durante el franquismo* (Madrid, 1995); Siguán, *Del campo*, pp. 236–7.

[10] E.g., Botey Vallès, *Relats*, p. 132; Solé, *Inmigrantes*, p. 69. For one rural migrant living on the margins in the shanty town and labouring in urban construction, the city was 'like the mountain' from which you had to 'extract food'. Siguán, *Del campo*, p. 233.

production of consent to the victors' regime: those who had suffered the consequences of the leftist revolution and the war, or denunciation in their name, were not about to question the legitimacy of the Franco regime. For many who had suffered during the tumult of the war without being directly political and who were not among the masses in poverty it seemed possible to re-establish a level of control and 'normality' in the 1950s. 'Morality' and 'decency' became accepted elements of discourse – an emphasis derived from Catholicism – because they related to a striving for a coherent existence in contrast to the fear and uncertainty of the conflict. Among families which had suffered the effects of the revolution, myths of the civil war circulated which inevitably reinforced the official narrative. Personal loss was made sense of by superimposing upon it the ideological and cultural 'grid' of the 'crusade'. The daughter of one devout conservative from the pueblo of Campos del Río (Murcia) remembered how her father had believed in good faith that Franco was 'an instrument chosen by God'. During the war, when the dominant landowner and ex-mayor was killed, the woman's father had been denounced to the Republican authorities by a neighbour and spent some months in prison, leaving her mother with two children to feed. His generally positive view of Franco and the regime can therefore be explained by a conservative predisposition which was confirmed by his proximity to the suffering: 'I'm sure my father, as the vast majority of Spaniards of the time, was never conscious of the historical implications or of the consequences for many Spaniards of Franco's authoritarian and fascist state.'[11] In the 1950s, recollections of the war could not be described as 'historical'; some social groups (such as rural migrants) were, however, tied to historical change more than others (paradoxically, those whose interests appeared to be safeguarded by Franco and his 'historic mission', such as small and middling landowners). For now, however, war memories were shaped by direct experience and by the myths which framed collective perceptions.

Telling stories about the war within families would not, therefore, achieve much enlightenment for younger generations about its causes or explain the violence. To victims, part of the essence of intimate violence was precisely that it is inexplicable. Constructed largely to perpetuate a sense of identity based on suffering, such stories were constructed within an environment where information was restricted; more to the point, they were not relayed in order to develop historical

---

[11] Buendía Gómez, 'Peinando recuerdos', p. 156. On conflict in Campos del Río, see González Martínez, *Guerra civil en Murcia*, pp. 165, 187, 194, 207.

understanding.[12] These stories were interwoven with phrases indicating the desire to forget: 'that all happened a long time ago'; 'it is better not to look back'; 'one has to turn over a new page'.[13] One woman remembered how all the pupils in the school she attended in the province of Seville in the early 1950s had been directly affected by the war. Another child's parents came from families on opposing sides, which was not unusual. The maternal grandfather had been summarily executed by '*los nacionales*' following an anonymous denunciation.[14] But the children of those who fought the war were not generally encouraged to interrogate their parents about their attitudes and role in the conflict.

It is difficult to be precise about possible 'lessons' handed down, beyond a generalised anti-Marxism in conservative Catholic families and a sense of a lost democratic legacy in those which were Republican (though far from all families were simply in one or the other camp). Some conservative parents preached tolerance and reconciliation. There were households where the Franco cause had been supported but where exaltation of the triumph and acts of intolerance towards 'the defeated' were frowned upon: 'If we ever let slip a criticism or less than respectful allusion to a neighbour my father always corrected us: "all individuals must be treated with respect and referred to by their real names not by the nicknames given them in the neighbourhood"', a sign perhaps that identity derived from one's community of origin had become diluted by conflict. For some, forgiveness from the mid 1950s seemed to require a new level of formality and respect.[15] Whether it was because of this upbringing or out of a sense of rebellion against parents, however, by the middle of the decade amongst the younger generation of the relatively well-off there would be a sense of rejection of the bourgeois normality or 'respectability' founded on the legitimacy of the war and the consequent ostracising of the defeated.

As we saw in Chapter 5, the policy of forced return of migrants and the ideology surrounding it were challenged by several social commentators. They were also countered by some of the younger, university-educated generation who were usually the children of veterans of the 'crusade', as

---

[12] See Jesús Izquierdo Martín and Pablo Sánchez León, *La guerra que nos han contado* (Madrid, 2006).

[13] See, e.g., Ignacio Fernández de Mata, 'El surgimiento de la memoria histórica: sentidos, malentendidos y disputas', in L. Díaz Viana and P. Tomé Martín (eds.), *La tradición como reclamo: antropología en Castilla y León* (Salamanca, 2007), pp. 195–208. Also Bullón and Diego, *Historias*, p. 17; Castilla del Pino, *Casa del olivo*, p. 212.

[14] E.g., Piñero Valverde, 'Mi viejo álbum', pp. 58, 62.

[15] Pedrero Sánchez, 'Las cartas', p. 113. Also, Bullón and Diego, *Historias*, p. 201. On nicknames, identity and power: Pitt-Rivers, *People*, pp. 7, 31, 168–9.

witnessed in such events as the so-called Conversaciones Cinematográficas, held at Salamanca University in 1955, and the Congreso Universitario de Escritores Jóvenes in Madrid in 1956, both linked to nascent dissident activities among former Falangist students and intellectuals, both of which were repressed by the authorities.[16] This awakening of a critical consciousness was evident in the social-realist literary movement of the 1950s, in Madrid and Barcelona, which was an expression of the shared memory of the 'war child' generation, incorporating leftist writers including Juan Goytisolo, Antonio Ferres and Armando López Salinas, and political thinkers, most notably Alfonso Carlos Comín and Manuel Sacristán, all born during the second half of the 1920s or early 1930s. Several were formerly attached to the Falange through the SEU or to lay Catholic working-class organisations, and a few were from working-class backgrounds.[17] Many would join the clandestine opposition movement of the PCE in the 1960s.[18] Studies of migration at this time by sociologists and social psychologists informed these writers and the nascent opposition movement.[19] While for some, especially Comín, radicalisation took place in a context of attachment to Catholic organisations and to religion, others rejected Catholicism and felt repugnance towards the world which the generation of the 'crusade' had imposed through destruction of the Republic and through the harsh, grey reality of military dictatorship. They developed, in effect, a 'vicarious memory' based on the myths and images of what Spanish democracy in the 1930s had been: 'nostalgia for a Republic we had never known and about which we had never heard one single objective judgement, turned us into pseudo-Marxists or anarchists'.[20]

---

[16] See, e.g., Roberto Mesa (ed.), *Jaraneros y alborotadores: documentos sobre los sucesos estudiantiles de febrero de 1956 en la Universidad Complutense de Madrid* (Madrid, 1982), p. 214.

[17] From Barcelona, see particularly the early novels of Juan Goytisolo (*Duelo en el paraíso*; *Fiestas*; *La resaca*; etc.) and Ana María Matute (*Los Abel*; *Los hijos muertos*; *Los soldados lloran de noche*). From the left, Juan García Hortelano, José María Caballero Bonald and Alfonso Grosso. From working-class backgrounds: Antonio Ferres (b.1924, from a landless Andalusian family; see, e.g., *La piqueta*, 1959); Armando López Salinas (b.1925, e.g., *La mina*, 1960 (written in 1959)). On the novelist Rodrigo Rubio, a migrant from rural Albacete, see Borràs, *Los que no hicimos*, pp. 312–15. Similarly, on migrants from Jaén to Madrid *chabolas*: Ramón Nieto, *La patria y el pan* (Barcelona, 1962). See also *Ecclesia*, 25 April 1964, p. 27.

[18] See, e.g., Ana, *Decidme*, pp. 37–8.

[19] These included the social psychologist Miguel Siguan: Castilla del Pino, *Casa del olivo*, p. 353. See also, e.g., Jesús Iribarren, *Introducción a la sociología religiosa* (Madrid, 1955).

[20] Barral, *Años de penitencia*, pp. 33–4, 235–6. Barral was born in 1928. On 'mythology' of the Republic, see Jordi Gracia, *Estado y cultura: El despertar de una conciencia crítica bajo el franquismo, 1940–1962*, 2nd edn (Barcelona, 2006), pp. 31–2. On Josep María Castellet, see Juan F. Marsal, *Pensar bajo el franquismo* (Barcelona, 1979), pp. 83–93. For Marxism,

The poet Dionisio Ridruejo led the disillusioned, though somewhat isolated, critique of the Falange's marginalisation by the regime. The less radical Laín Entralgo, Rector of Madrid University during the student protests of 1956, was of a similar mind. Ridruejo, more outspoken in his dissent, would be subjected to a process of internal exile and gaoled for his support of demonstrating students, while Laín, who had favoured liberalisation in the universities, would lose his post for what was seen as tacit encouragement. Since the late 1940s he had clashed with leading regime loyalists associated with Opus Dei who through the CSIC maintained a firm grip on cultural institutions and orthodoxy from a Catholic traditionalist position. The political career of Joaquín Ruiz-Giménez, Minister of Education since 1951, was also ended in the aftermath of the student unrest.[21] In the face of doctrinal rigidity, Falangist dissent was thus limited to a small section of the intelligentsia and isolated 'revolutionaries'; by the 1950s, Falangism was shaped in practice by the many provincial political opportunists who were the local mouthpieces of orthodox Francoism and guardians of narrow economic interests, a situation which further encouraged migration to the cities.

It is in this context of ambivalence about the immediate past amongst several social classes, combined with living the direct effects of the civil war, that this chapter recounts the social and political conditions of life in rural society which motivated migration. Looking particularly at the south, the Andalusian province of Jaén forms a case study for analysing the causes, interpretation and consequences of the migratory process. This chapter also explores the urban reception of migrants from the point of view of the state and Catholic organisations in order to assess how the migrant–host relationship related to memories of the recent conflict. State repression of demographic movement was resisted by the rural poor and interpreted in a variety of ways by those who commented upon the grim reality of migration. The official doctrine insisted that 'the city' was a source of danger and impurity. Whilst the 1951 film *Surcos* ('Furrows'), made by the Falangist director José Antonio Nieves Conde followed this official argument, for example, it managed to depict the plight of those who fled rural life in search of redemption with some sympathy. The censor ensured that the story of the migrant family at the film's heart ended with a fall from grace, however, followed by harmony achieved only through return to the countryside. But the epigraph of the final frame of the film summed up a slightly more ambiguous conclusion:

see, e.g., Joan Benach Xavier Juncosa and Salvador López Arnal. (eds.), *Del pensar, del vivir, del hacer: escritos sobre 'Integral Sacristán' de Xavier Juncosa* (Barcelona, 2006).
[21] Pablo Lizcano, *La generación del 56: la universidad contra Franco* (Barcelona, 1981).

'these *campesinos*, who have lost the countryside and have yet to gain the difficult objective of civilisation, are as trees without roots'.[22]

Migration

During the 1950s and 1960s the rate of rural depopulation in Spain was higher than anywhere else in Western Europe. The percentage of the total workforce employed in agriculture plummeted from 50 per cent in 1950 to around 20 per cent in 1970. Whereas in 1950 one in every ten working Spaniards was a landless labourer employed seasonally on great estates, according to official reckoning, by 1966 the proportion was one in twenty. Only two decades after the end of the civil war, much of the agrarian population had rejected both the myths and reality of rural life. Migration to the cities was directly or indirectly motivated by the experience, outcome and memory of the civil war. A migrant inhabitant of industrial Barcelona (Sabadell; see Map 8) explained it thus:

What kind of people came here? All the disinherited, those who did not even have a place to drop dead in their town of origin. We were people who had a restlessness [*inquietud*] and a tendency towards the left because we had been obliged to leave our homelands [*nuestras tierras*] [...] Sabadell was an epicentre for the reception of people from all parts, from every place, and naturally very few fascists came because they were well accommodated in their place of origin.[23]

Franco's victory was legitimated in part by maintaining rural property and a myth of idealised peasant life. According to a 1950 speech of the Caudillo, Spain was 'much more than the frivolous story of its cities'.[24] The official doctrine declared that mechanical pseudo-civilisation threatened the world with its brutalising force. By contrast, the rural world was valued as the social, cultural and political cradle of family, religion and nation. The imagined *patria* was thus embodied by the small property-owning rural lower class which had been the backbone of the Nationalist army during the civil war. In language redolent of Miguel de Unamuno and other turn-of-the-century regenerationists, as well as their more conservative French contemporary ideologues of race such as Maurice Barrès, the virtues of thriftiness, selfless stoicism, and faith in

[22] A similar morality tale would be told in relation to coastal tourist towns, in Josep María Forn's film *La piel quemada* (1967).

[23] Cited in Domènech Sampere, 'La otra cara del milagro', 96. Also, e.g., on 'Los Olivos' in the Aracena valley in Huelva, Collier, *Socialists*, p. 20; Sebastian Balfour, *Dictatorship, Workers and the City: Labour in Greater Barcelona since 1939* (Oxford, 1989), pp. 31–2.

[24] *ABC*, 28 May 1950, pp. 15–16.

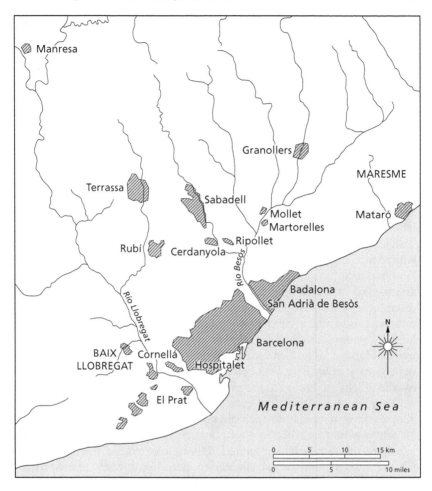

Map 8 Province of Barcelona with industrial suburbs, 1960s

primordial loyalties were 'sedimented' in the 'warrior-like' and 'victorious' Castilian peasant.[25] The reality did not match the rhetoric and, though compensated doctrinally, the peasantry of the post-war era possessed little power as the Falange became marginalised at state level.

[25] See, e.g., Joaquín Arrarás Iribarren, *Historia de la cruzada española*, 6 vols. (Madrid, 1939–41), vol. V (Madrid, 1941), pp. 52, 69; Emilio Mola, *El pasado, Azaña y el porvenir* (originally published 1934), in Mola, *Obras completas* (Valladolid, 1940), p. 1,177; Vallejo Nágera, *Divagaciones intrascendentes* (Valladolid, 1938), p. 139. On Franco: Iniesta, *Garra marxista*, p. 282.

Beneath the 'sovereignty of the peasantry' and the ideal of 'familial patrimony', partly disseminated to persuade the rural population to stay put, political and administrative practice moved away from fascistic populism and adopted a more pragmatic rural strategy which tacitly (and often grudgingly) accepted social change. Small-scale agricultural production and the way of life that went with it would decline dramatically, and approximately half a million farms were swallowed up in the decade after 1962.

The historically 'defeated' (the rural landless) were first to be ruined by Franco's victory; later would come these poor Castilian farmers who also could not make ends meet in the new economic times. The social ills of small-scale family-based production paled, however, in comparison with those of the low-wage seasonally employed masses of landless labourers concentrated particularly in the southern half of the peninsula. The latifundist form of agricultural production and social reproduction which the Republic of the 1930s had pledged to end was based on labour dependency, overseen by a pre-democratic political machinery and backed historically by frequent deployment of state coercion.[26] The disciplining effects of primitive accumulation on the vast monocultural estates, producing a rigid and uniform social structure and endemic hunger, were maintained by rebel victory in the civil war and thereafter by Francoism.[27] The Communist activist Marcos Ana, who spent more than twenty years in a Francoist prison cell, was motivated politically by the plight of his own parents who had scraped together a living working on one of the great estates of Salamanca as 'noble and simple people, slaves to the land which did not belong to them'. In January 1937 his father would be killed in a rebel bombing raid on Alcalá de Henares to where the family had migrated. His mother would feel responsible for the tragedy and 'cried silently to herself for years afterwards'.[28] Another landless labourer, born in 1917, who fought for the Republic and migrated from Badajoz to Barcelona in 1956, explained the system as 'feudal' and the workers as 'the slaves of the powerful', the *caciques*, who had long controlled the situation politically. The desire to challenge this situation had been a root cause of the war in which he had fought, been captured and imprisoned, and in which his father was killed.[29] By the 1960s, the system would be increasingly deprived of its labour force;

---

[26] Pascual Carrión, *Los latifundios en España* (Barcelona, 1975 (1932)).

[27] See, e.g., Eduardo Sevilla Guzmán and Manuel González de Molina, 'Política social agraria del Primer Franquismo', in J. L. García Delgado (ed.), *El Primer Franquismo: España durante la Segunda Guerra Mundial* (Madrid, 1989), pp. 135–87.

[28] Ana, *Decidme*, pp. 21, 48–9.

[29] Botey Vallès, *Relats*, pp. 49–50. On deserted '*caciques*', p. 53.

the change sought by the wage labourers of latifundia Spain, who described themselves commonly as 'the disinherited' rather than the defeated, would come to pass through migration, one of the main social consequences of the war.

For all that Francoism had fought a war with the intention of imposing a traditional work discipline on the rural landless, social crisis in the countryside was unavoidable precisely because of economic processes that the military dictatorship encouraged. The social instability inherent in seasonal unemployment was at the forefront of thinking about 'the social question' in the 1950s. According to Falangist critics, the roots of rural unemployment were 'the characteristics of particular cultivations' (monoculture in olive production in Jaén, for example), 'the regime of property' (ownership by landed grandees), and industrial underdevelopment. The state-initiated Badajóz and Jaén Plans, launched in the early 1950s and later incorporated into the broader Development Plans unveiled in 1964, were based on grand irrigation schemes. Although results were unspectacular, the regime did not spurn opportunities to herald the achievements of rural irrigation, for example when commemorating in 1961 the twenty-fifth anniversary of the start of military rebellion and 'the state of 18 July'.[30]

For Francoism, the creation of a mesocracy, a society based on a numerous property-owning middle class, as a source of social stability, seemed possible only through social engineering, but reforming the landowning structure was politically impossible, and opening the safety valve of mass migration of excess labour became the only possible alternative. Urbanisation in the end depended heavily on growth of the service sector boosted by tourism which became a substantial part of the national economy in the 1960s and which culturally and physically obscured much of the recent past, in some instances by building over the bodies of those executed by the regime. At the same time, foreign investment, integrated with domestic capital accumulated partly from the large-scale black-market monopolies of the 1940s and 1950s, was used to develop hotel-strewn resort towns on the south coast such as Marbella and Torremolinos.[31] This tertiary sector growth and the gradual and patchy industrialisation which the regime settled on by the mid 1960s

---

[30] 'Eficacia de una revolución política', *ABC*, 25 April 1961.
[31] E.g., Barral, *Años de penitencia*, pp. 83–4; Brenan, *Face of Spain*, pp. 100–1. On the Torremolinos concentration camp established in 1938: Rodrigo, *Cautivos*, p. 198. For wartime burial pits on Málaga coastline, *Sur*, 29 December 2010; *El País* (Andalucía), 25 September 2011, p. 5 (remembered by prisoner who later migrated to Barcelona). See also recollections of Catalan coast: Norman Lewis, *Voices of the Old Sea* (London, 1984), pp. 52, 96, 123–4, 136–8, 140–3, 175–8.

became the centrepiece of propaganda celebrating what the government described as 'the most exceptional agrarian reform of all time', whilst at the same time it grappled with seemingly uncontrollable population shift, in part by exporting unemployed labour en masse to Northern Europe.

The process of spontaneous urbanisation had begun a decade earlier: by the early 1950s there were many thousands of families living a rudimentary existence in the shanty towns of the biggest cities. The state could not keep pace: in 1957 the housing deficit was estimated to be 1,067,452 family units.[32] The Spanish term *suburbio* referred to an outlying area on the edge of the city, often occupied by a lower-class population of recent arrival, living in self-made dwellings, known as *chabolas* or *chozas* in much of the country, including Madrid, and as *barracas* in Barcelona. The majority of residents were rural migrants, though some inhabitants had come from the inner city, forced out by black market rents. At the same time as Franco was meeting with US financial advisers (who confirmed that restrictions on food distribution were hampering Spanish economic development), a British diplomat reported in June 1950 that there were 50,000 people living in the squalid outlying slums of Madrid 'in caves and hunger and disease-ravaged "*chabolas*"', to the south of the city, in such zones as Puente de Vallecas, La Ventilla, Pinos Altos, La Elipa, Entrevías, and the grey, dust-ridden, wasteland of El Pozo del Tío Raimundo.[33] Dwellings in these spontaneous communities with no officially registered street names were self-constructed, made from found or cheaply produced materials. Most had no floors, electricity, water, or sanitation, though the corrupt tenancy system for plots of privately owned terrain, if 'system' it can be called, was hugely exploitative. The effects on the physical growth of children born in the shanty towns compared even with those who remained in the poverty-stricken southern countryside were dramatic, as a 1966 bio-typological study of teenage factory workers born during the period 1948–53 on the margins of Barcelona to migrant parents (themselves born in the era of the war) demonstrated.[34] The misery of these conditions could only be put up with because in most cases migrants had little to return to.[35] Diocesan Catholic institutions calculated that there were 439,000 individuals living in these conditions

[32] Valle, 'Inmigración', p. 382.
[33] British Embassy report, 9 June 1950, TNA, FO371/89612; 'Madrid, ciudad de contrastes', *Cultura y Democracia*, no. 2, February 1950.
[34] José María Basabé Prado, 'Efectos del ambiente suburbial sobre el biotipo del inmigrante', *Estudios geográficos*, 27, 105 (1966), 579–605.
[35] Botey Vallès, *Relats*, p. 99.

in Madrid as early as 1952 and up to 600,000 by the end of the decade. The estimation in 1940 had been 10,000.[36]

Seen by some observers as a kind of rebellion, these informal and illegal communities were, perhaps, the only form of resistance possible for rural migrants 'ruined by Francoism'.[37] They were permanently vulnerable because they were prone to be cleared forcefully by the police at any moment and the residents returned to the countryside. A government decree of August 1957 reinforced a similar edict four years earlier in railing against 'uncontrolled emigration' and 'systematic constructions' made possible by black market speculation in land. A more open-minded sociologist preferred to reflect the active agency of migrants through their 'clandestine building' and 'spontaneous urban-isation'.[38] The Dirección General de Regiones Devastadas, set up by the Interior Ministry (Gobernación) in 1938 to rebuild war-damaged settlements, had for some years enforced the destruction of *chabolas*, even though many families had paid substantial sums for a tiny plot to build on.[39] This destruction was justified as part of the DGRD's remit to submit all new constructions to authorisation and its control of urban planning, partly with the aim of repressing rural 'absenteeism and immigration'.[40] Besides allowing for the immediate destruction of constructions and expulsion of residents, the 1957 decree permitted state expropriation of the plots of land and required would-be migrants to notify the Civil Governor in their province of origin of their intention to arrive, giving details of a pre-arranged residence in the capital.[41] Newcomers were entered onto the census and any political allegiances or criminality could be checked; as a result, according to the criminali-sing language of the authorities, 'some subjects lost their lairs'.[42] This process of destruction and control was not confined to Madrid: some nine thousand individuals were expelled from Barcelona in the 1950s, and many more whose dwellings had been destroyed were placed in temporary barracks put up by the authorities or in the castle-prison of Montjuich. This site of wartime and post-war political executions

---

[36] *Libertad Española*, 7, 16 August 1956, p. 8; Valle, 'Inmigración', p. 377.

[37] Candel, *Otros*, p. 121; Solé, *Inmigrantes*, p. 65.   [38] Siguán, *Del campo*, p. 245.

[39] 'El pueblo "sin permiso" desapareció ayer', *ABC*, 16 July 1955. See also Siguán, *Del campo*, pp. 59, 69, 94, 98.

[40] José Moreno Torres, *La reconstrucción urbana en España* (Madrid, 1945), section on 'aspecto social'. Much of DGRD's effort was directed towards rebuilding ecclesiastical and religious sites (churches, memorial crypts, seminaries, cemeteries) and buildings which housed state offices (civil and military government, Civil Guard barracks, town halls), which had been targeted in the conflict.

[41] *BOE*, 21 September 1957. Also Siguán, *Del campo*, p. 246.

[42] 'El pueblo "sin permiso"' desapareció ayer', *ABC*, 16 July 1955.

reminded people who were sent there of periods spent in wartime and post-war concentration camps.[43] Migrants continued to be viewed as an inferior category, just as they had been in the 1940s. The Falangist newspaper *Arriba* maintained that 'the *chabola* suits some individuals better than a proper living space'.[44] The illegal communities were viewed by the authorities as sites where 'epidemics were cultivated like a fungus' and their destruction was part of a 'humanitarian offensive against infiltration'.[45]

The conditions in the shanty towns, though dire, were superior to the absolute poverty and discrimination of the immediate post-war years in many rural homes where hunger verging on starvation had been constant. In some areas 'bread' was made with stolen acorns, and ears of corn left after reaping were much sought after. These conditions were remembered later as inferior to the extremely hard life of the shanty towns.[46] This was part of the cumulative effect of memories of repression and hunger: the difficulties of life could be borne because the recent past had been unbearable. Anything could be endured because you could not let those who had reimposed such conditions see how you suffered. From a Madrid *chabola* one woman in the 1950s explained this: 'of course, we are full of misery here, but nothing could compare with what we have lived through in the pueblo. Disease, hunger, cold, and each year another child [...] Return to the pueblo? Not even if you tied me up and carried me back!'[47] This was a strong part of the ethic of 'the defeated' working class of the post-war years. A woman whose grandfather had been executed in 1940 recalled how in the 1950s her relatively petty suffering had been placed in relation properly to the past by her grandmother, using a graphic metaphor to suggest extreme pain: 'when I was small and I cried for some silly reason, she would say to me: "Child, even if your insides are hanging out, you don't cry. You pull them back inside yourself, put your hands over the top and carry on, without anybody ever seeing you cry."'[48]

The economic rationale of migration is clear in 1950s testimonies: 'We were very backward, we lived through such hunger and hardly had clothes to wear; we were so desperate when the season of olive gathering

[43] Molina, *Los otros Madrileños*, p. 24; Botey Vallès, *Relats*, pp. 97–8.

[44] Cited in *Libertad Española*, 7, 16 August 1956, p. 8.

[45] See, e.g., 'Contra las inicuas expulsiones en los suburbios', *Mundo Obrero*, año XXIII, 19, August 1954; 'El pueblo "sin permiso"'.

[46] E.g., Botey Vallès, *Relats*, pp. 58–9.

[47] 'María', aged 45, arriving in 1952; 'Avelina', 24, arriving in 1955. Siguán, *Del campo*, p. 59. (Also p. 101.)

[48] Personal testimony, Elordi (ed.), *Años difíciles*, pp. 268–9.

came upon us that the little we earned then made hardly any difference.'[49] This structural poverty, in isolation from the particular material and psychological conditions of the aftermath of the civil war, is not sufficient, however, in understanding the post-war migratory process. The peculiar economic hardship of the 1940s and 1950s could not be separated from the conflict. In his testimony, the son of a family from rural Granada recalled that at the time of fleeing the countryside in 1950 (when he was fourteen), his mother had invoked a particular heritage and sense of identity as a way of expressing her feeling of segregation. References to the war, the violence and the polarisation took the form of an omnipresent threat expressed through metaphorical allusions and historical imagery:

My brother [after he found work in Catalonia] wrote to us that another brother should go and then my father; a little while after, the rest of us went: my mother (who had suffered a strange illness, leaving her bed like a skeleton), my younger brothers and me [. . .] All of this was because of the war; as a family we had got by working a few plots of land, but after the war things went from bad to worse; for us it was like a black shadow, a monster that passed over our home and created the situation which obliged us to emigrate to Catalonia [. . .] When we left [the pueblo] it was still dark [. . .] On reaching the highest point of the ridge from where you could make out the pueblo, my mother made a cross in the air and pronounced a kind of curse towards the town which she was leaving at that moment, where she had suffered so much sadness. We were all around her. My mother looked towards the land where she had been born, which she would never see again, to where our *morisco* forebears had settled after fleeing from Granada. She said a few words and then told us to continue on our way; her eyes were wild and her mouth was tightly closed with sadness and fury. She did not curse the land but the system which had forced her to abandon it, because her family had lived there for many generations; they were amongst those who formed the village when it was populated by peasants and the *moriscos* from the mountains.[50]

Other migrants recalled much later how the war had changed everything. One who remembered thus was the granddaughter of a Republican woman from rural Aragón whose execution by rebel authorities in August 1936 was discussed in Chapter 2. The grandmother had been killed because she had encouraged the illiterate working men and women of the village to learn to read and spoke up publicly in defence of local women who were ritually punished as part of the wartime 'liberation' process. The grandfather had also died during the conflict

---

[49] Siguán, *Del campo*, p. 60.
[50] Testimony related in Lara, *Emigración andaluza*, pp. 193–4. *Moriscos*: Muslims, often of European descent, converted forcibly to Christianity and repressed as heretics following expulsion of Islam at the end of the fifteenth century.

as a result of the loss of his wife. After the killing, their daughter had been taunted as the child of 'rojos' and suffered great discrimination. Her daughter would view her own fleeing from the pueblo as a form of escape:

When I was eighteen I came here to Barcelona, which was when my life became resolved [...] When I came here I began to see how I was a person. I had a position in a house in which, although I worked as a servant, which was then quite normal [for young migrant women], they treated me very well [...] I renounced my pueblo because they exploited me more and they treated me badly. There you were virtually a slave of the *señorial* families. Here I was much more protected and at ease as a person.[51]

Another woman, 'Antonia', from rural Granada, who had led the PCE-inspired Mujeres Antifascistas in her economically polarised pueblo, was imprisoned in Málaga after the city's occupation by the Francoists. She remained in gaol until 1942 and did not return to her home village thereafter, declaring that she would prefer even to stay in prison than to go back.[52] The daughter of a shepherd from rural Córdoba who had been executed by the rebel authorities during the war, migrated to Madrid at about the same time to escape from the village where her father's property had been taken from the family in spite of the wishes expressed in his final letter.[53] Another migrant declared that 'when the Nationalists entered the village [her father] had to sell his olive trees and an embargo was placed on his property'. She and her husband resorted to illegal black market labour in order to survive, collecting esparto grass in the countryside, exchanging it for olive oil and selling this to those who could afford to pay.[54] Ruin through forced eviction or confiscation of a plot of land was frequently brought about because of a denunciation within the community, and it left migration as virtually the only choice.[55]

Politics and economics were thus closely interwoven, as we can see from the conditions which produced migration from the olive-producing latifundia province of Jaén. Here the model of the agro-town dominated,

---

[51] Personal testimony, Elordi (ed.), *Años difíciles*, pp. 187–9. See Chapter 2. For similar: Mercedes Vilanova, 'Las fronteras interiores en la sociedad de Barcelona, 1900–1975', in *Historia, Antropología y Fuentes Orales*, 1, 16 (1996), 133. Not all migrant domestics were treated well: e.g., Botey Vallès, *Relats*, pp. 108, 114. On women and domestic service, generationally, in Barcelona, see Cristina Borderías, 'Las mujeres, autoras de sus trayectorias personales y familiares: A través del servicio doméstico', *Historia y Fuente Oral*, 6 (1991), 105–21.

[52] Angelina Puig i Valls, 'La guerra civil española: una causa de l'emigració andalusa en la dècada dels anys cinquanta?', *Recerques*, 31 (1995), 65.

[53] Personal testimony, Elordi (ed.), *Años difíciles*, pp. 196–7.

[54] Testimony, Puig i Valls, 'La guerra civil', p. 57. Also, Botey Vallès, *Relats*, p. 78; Siguán, *Del campo*, p. 89.

[55] E.g. Botey Vallès, *Relats*, pp. 71–2.

and the community was defined by labour on the great estates: very few people who lived in Jaén did so in communities of less than a thousand inhabitants, and the fields were like factories in the open air.[56] This monocultural dependency with an in-built precipitous fall in labour demand after the harvest each January and February created great social problems. In 1939, power in the pueblos of Jaén fell into the hands of the military and paramilitary 'forces of liberation' who became the associates of pre-war elites to whom they offered loyalty and protection. In return, those with newly acquired authority were able to requisition livestock from locals for resale and take control of flour supplies and benefited from corrupt practices in the supply of olive oil, the area's main product, and of bread, the staple of the calorific intake of the labouring family.[57] With the black market dominant, food and clothing prices in Jaén by the beginning of the 1950s had increased by a factor of 6 compared to 1936, according to official estimates.[58] In the spring of 1951, unemployment in the region was catastrophic, as described by local Falangists, with 20,000 families blighted by permanent unemployment, living in 'utter wretchedness' and permanently in desperation for lack of 'a scrap of bread and oil' in order to live: 'clothing, shoes, housing no longer worry them since these are completely out of reach; they are dressed in rags, the majority barefoot, many having to live in caves'.[59] A further 60,000 families were dependent on the olive harvest and therefore lived in the same state, close to starvation, for five or six months of the year.

This complex of socio-economic and political conditions, combined with the polarisation of the war, formed the basis of the migratory impulse. A migrant who arrived in Barcelona in 1965, aged nineteen, remembered how even as a sickly child of six he had worked at gathering olives in the early 1950s.[60] There was an 'intuitive' sense amongst the ordinary people that catastrophe loomed, because they understood how

[56] *Anuario Estadístico, 1943* (Madrid, 1944), pp. 62–3.
[57] Undated report (1939–40), 'Provincia de Jaén', AGA, SP, 17.02, sig. 52/46, caja 228; Fidel Fernández Martínez, 'El jugo gástrico del soldado andaluz', *Semana Médica Española*, 14 January 1939, pp. 50–3. Also Francisco Cobo Romero, *Conflicto rural y violencia política* (Jaen, 1999), pp. 303–7. As well as the local black market, large quantities were sold to the state for exportation to Germany and Italy to help pay off civil war debts: see Richards, *Time of Silence*, p. 137; for similar in Seville, see internal Movimiento report of 1950, AGA, SP, 17.02, sig. 52/46, caja.71. The situation hardly improved throughout the 1940s. See, e.g., Arco Blanco, *Hambre de siglos*, pp. 134–9; Cobo Romero and Ortega López, *Franquismo*, p. 372. Also, opposition bulletins cited in Eiroa, *Viva Franco*, p. 118.
[58] *Anuario Estadístico, 1950* (Madrid, 1951), p. 592.
[59] Letter, Jefe Provincial, Jaén, 27 March 1951, AGA, SP, 17.02, sig. 52/46, caja 72.
[60] Botey Vallès, *Relats*, pp. 54–5.

their lives were dependent on a minimal supply of basic necessities. In 1946 some 25 per cent of all deaths in the province were brought about because of a deficiency disease.[61] While food supply was in chaos the new authorities' political *asesorías* ('offices of guidance'), dominated by the Falange and the Church, which advised local institutions of power on moral policy, religion, and pedagogy, honed in on doctrinal orthodoxy and the prominence of Francoist symbols of victory rather than sustenance for the population.[62]

The civil war transformed Jaén demographically into a condition of depopulation because of hunger, political repression (including executions), and the inability of the regime born of the war to encourage reconciliation. Population increase had oscillated between 11 per cent and 13 per cent each decade from 1900 to 1936, largely because of the high birth rate.[63] The lack of transport, education and communications in the south before the war meant that emigration had hardly existed then; after the war it would become the most important feature of the social landscape.[64] The province had already lost more than 75,000 inhabitants during the war and the 1940s, some 10 per cent of the total, and in the period 1950–5 depopulation continued; in spite of a high birth rate, which was typical of Andalucía, the number of inhabitants decreased by a further 20,000.[65] It can be estimated that some 20 per cent of the provincial population migrated during the period 1940–55, and the rate of departure would only increase after 1955.[66] By then very few municipalities could claim a stable population and these were centred on the incipient commercial areas or mining districts, such as Andújar and Linares.

Migration in the 1950s was generally a phenomenon of the younger generation. The majority of those who left Jaén in the 1940s and 1950s were in the 20–45 age group, and most migrant families included children. Several reported that their parents, belonging to the civil war

---

[61] Letter of the Civil Governor to the Ministry of Industry and Commerce, Juan Antonio Suanzes, dated 21 April 1951, and that of the National Sindical Delegate, Fermín Sanz-Orrio to the Jefe Provincial del Movimiento in Jaén, 2 April 1951, both AGA, Pres, SGM, caja 72.

[62] 'Informe', 29 January 1940, AGA, SP, 17.02, sig. 52/46, caja 228.

[63] The total population in 1900 was 474,490, rising to 765,697 by 1950, an increase of 291,207 inhabitants.

[64] Joaquín Arias Quintana, 'Una investigación sobre las causas y remedios del paro agrícola y otros problemas de la economía de Jaén', *Cuadernos de Información Económico Social*, 1951, 1.

[65] Antonia Muñóz Fernández, 'La emigración en la provincia de Jaén 1900–1955', in *Estudios geográficos*, 81 (November 1960), 455–96 (464). The total population reduced from 765,697 in 1950 to 746,718 in 1955.

[66] For the migrant shift from Jaén to Madrid, see Ramón Nieto's novel *La patria y el pan*.

generation, had died or that they had been looked after by grandparents.[67] Apart from establishing some form of shelter for the family, the primary objective was finding work with regular payment. Information about employment in construction or in the factories was often passed on by word of mouth. Most migrants were unskilled, as well as being considered uncultured. It was common that they did poorly in intelligence tests and medico-anthropological examinations and were taken on at first as labourers on hazardous urban construction sites rather than in industry.[68] Once work was found, however, a chain of communication could be established between the metropolis and the pueblo, smoothing the path to some extent for later migrants. In many cases the family left for the city one at a time, and it was not unusual for the mother to act as a bridgehead, often by finding employment as a domestic servant in the city.[69] The rural migrant family was typically large, and children usually lacked education and adequate health. Most adults had worked as day labourers for low wages since the age of nine or ten. During the 1940s some rural families survived by keeping a few animals, pilfering crops or poaching, and most collected firewood or pieces of coal, in areas where this could be found, to keep warm or to sell, or burned charcoal as fuel. One husband and wife from Córdoba who left for Madrid in 1954 had resorted to such measures because their wage was not enough to feed their children.[70]

Infant mortality was one of the symptoms of the daily reality and Jaén, as well as having the highest birth rate, also had one of the highest levels of perinatal and infant death. One Madrid migrant, a woman of 35 from Linares, had nine children, the eldest of 22 years, and a tenth on the way. Whilst priests were often helpful, the Church worried equivocally about 'Malthusian' responses to overcrowding. In this case, as in a great many, the family *chabola* had only one room with several mattresses strewn on the ground. The children were described as having enlarged heads, distended stomachs and thin legs.[71] With this environment and background, it was not unusual for children to succumb to the harsh conditions of the migrant *chabolas*. One mother explained that 'we experienced such scarcity then that I'm convinced the sickness of my children came from that time'.[72] In an urban setting it was also likely

---

[67] E.g. Siguán, *Del campo*, p. 106.

[68] José Basabé, 'Inmigrante'; Siguán, *Del campo*, p. 248.

[69] E.g. Puig i Valls, 'La guerra civil', 64–7; Siguán, *Del campo*, pp. 98, 116, 251–2.

[70] Siguán, *Del campo*, p. 55.

[71] Siguán, *Del campo*, pp. 70, 105, 118. On 'Malthusianism' see, e.g., Jesús María Vázquez, *Así viven y mueren: problemas religiosos de un sector de Madrid* (Madrid, 1958).

[72] On steep rises in 1941, 1946 and 1950 in the province of Jaén, Miguel Benedicto Fernández, *Estudio bio-demográfico-sanitario de Jaén* (Jaén, 1953), p. 387.

that mothers would have to face accusations of neglect because of their alleged 'lack of culture'.[73] The rudimentary social security and health provision of the city nonetheless became a significant element of the myth of migration which was conveyed back from the cities to rural places of origin. One mother who came with her family to the capital from Cáceres in 1952, for example, did so, like others, to send her children to the state tuberculosis centre.[74] Another, who had worked in the olive harvest in Jaén since childhood, decided to bring her family to Madrid when she heard how urban employment allowed for the accumulation of credits towards sickness insurance. Her brothers, already in the city, suggested she come to El Pozo del Tío Raimundo, the growing working-class suburb on the periphery of the capital. She had complained for years about having to carry water for miles each day to her home in the countryside, though 'home' in the city was little more than four bare brick walls without windows and a frequently rain-soaked bare-earth floor. Still, although she was a frequent visitor to the local dispensary and the paediatric consulting room, this did not prevent the loss of a child. The sociologist who recorded her testimony suggested the scale of the difficulty: 'we cannot know whether María did not take on board what they said to her or whether her lack of means prevented her from putting such advice into practice'.[75]

Typically, migrants, individually or in small family units, would stay at first with a family from the same pueblo or with other family members, creating a foothold towards which others would gravitate.[76] Alternatives were often desperate and isolated. Some resorted even to living in caves, such as those close to Madrid's eastern cemetery, an unpopular location where wartime and post-war executions had been common.[77] The process of securing a more acceptable dwelling was often exploitative. A sum of money would be sought, sometimes borrowed from an urban employer, to make a down payment on a small plot of land in one of the burgeoning city suburbs, such as Madrid's Puente de Vallecas where large numbers of labouring families from Jaén settled in the 1950s. A small dwelling would be built by the family, often in just a few days, consisting usually of two rooms for sleeping and an area around a chimney for food preparation and eating. There might also have been a space outside, a small patio. Only rarely was there electricity or a water supply, and there was no sanitary provision; the first

---

[73] E.g. Siguan, *Del campo*, pp. 57, 61, 69, 74–5, 94, 106.
[74] Siguan, *Del campo*, p. 54. Also, pp. 57, 61, 67, 90–1; Solé, *Inmigrantes*, pp. 75–6.
[75] Siguan, *Del campo*, p. 58.   [76] See, e.g., Collier, *Socialists*, p. 193.
[77] Siguan, *Del campo*, p. 56.

associational protest movements of the late 1960s would originate in campaigns for basic facilities.[78]

Women and girls often worked outside the home in addition to the daily grind of making ends meet, though they did so frequently against the wishes of their husbands or fathers. Many became domestic servants, some beginning when still children.[79] Men had no alternative but to hire themselves out as unskilled labour to fuel the speculative construction boom of the era. The typical daily wage for a seasonal building labourer by the second half of the 1950s was 36 pesetas. This made an average monthly wage of 1,080 pesetas to which could be added the state's provision to families (the *plus familiar* and *subsidio familiar*: something between 400 and 500 pesetas per month together), and small bonuses at Christmas and, on 18 July, to commemorate the start of the civil war. In Jaén, as in other places, local employers avoided making these extra payments though they were legally supposed to comply.[80] Average monthly income for an immigrant family with just a single wage amounted therefore to some 1,630 pesetas which was reduced to something under 1,000 once rent, fuel and travel to work were paid. Disposable daily income for basic food and clothing was therefore some 30 pesetas, an exiguous sum for a family which might typically include four or five children and when a loaf of bread cost 10 pesetas or more. Compared with the irregular subsistence wage of the day labourer on the olive estates, however, this represented a relative improvement.[81]

It was natural that migrant families from the south should attempt to band together in defence against discrimination. They shared obvious outward signs of identity, like the 'dark skins', 'strong accents' and 'semi-savage' children noted by reticent middle-class observers who frequently found the migrant families to fall short of the ideal 'prototype family in a Christian home'.[82] Whilst neighbours helped one another, traditional pueblo customs, particularly religious festivals, were gradually drained of collective meaning in the new environment. Group identity became more functional. Urban entertainment went far beyond the rural celebration (*romería*) of saints' days experienced as a rural community, and it was frequently claimed by judgemental observers that rural families were

---

[78] E.g. Botey Vallès, *Relats*, p. 145–59; Mayoral, *Vallecas*, p. 37. On lack of water supplies, *Mundo Obrero*, Año XXIX, no. 19, 1 October 1959, 2; 'Queremos viviendas y no bases militares', *Mujeres Antifascistas*, 38, 1 July 1950.

[79] E.g. Botey Vallès, *Relats*, pp. 64, 116. Borderías, 'Las mujeres'.

[80] 'Provincia de Jaén', AGA, SP, 17.02, sig. 52/46, caja 228.

[81] The necessary daily family amount in Madrid was calculated in 1957 as 102.82 pesetas, more than five times the Spanish average: *Orientaciones* (August–September 1957).

[82] E.g. Siguán, *Del campo*, p. 130.

drawn to the city lights by the diversions and materialism of modern urban life. During the 1940s and 1950s, many of the urban middle class and, to a degree, of the established working class in the cities evaded the monotony of post-war existence by frequenting the cinemas. First-generation migrant families would rarely have afforded such diversions, however, though their children would gradually adopt the practice. The focus of life was the family; the struggle for survival reduced engagement, moreover, with other collective endeavours which might formerly have been political. Few migrants in the 1950s appear to have had the time, inclination, money or ability to read newspapers though, in contrast to the countryside, a broader range of reading matter was available.[83] Immigrant men in the 1950s declared themselves to be struggling for their families and little else. This spirit of sacrifice suggests that migrant objectives were fixed upon establishing a foothold, and the priority was a regular wage and children's education.[84] Self-sacrifice, 'prospects' and opportunities were paramount. Learning to read and write, for example, was a prerequisite for children so far as their uneducated migrant parents were concerned. According to one father, 'if God wills it, I intend that the children should learn a trade to make men of them; I don't want them to experience the labours and hardships that I had to'.[85] Whilst the lives of first-generation migrants were circumscribed, restricted to the narrow confines of family, survival and passive adaptation (not unlike the disciplining effects of rural life), it was natural that the next generation would more actively integrate themselves as they became part of the life of the city.

Rural–urban convergence: charity and memory

As we have seen in earlier chapters, many men and women who had been public supporters of the Republic and its war effort were reluctant to return to their home towns and villages because they wanted to avoid possible imprisonment or other punishment, sometimes because they were implicated in violence but more often because their legal political affiliations had been retrospectively criminalised by the victors. In the early post-war years cities offered a refuge because it was possible in urban centres to remain relatively anonymous. In contrast to much of

---

[83] Aceves, *Social Change*, p. 17; Siguán, *Del campo*, p. 99.

[84] On education as motive for migration: e.g., Botey Vallès, *Relats*, p. 105. On the *paseo*, Catholic mass, and organised dances as more morally productive than the cinema: Pérez, 'Trabajo doméstico', p. 97.

[85] Siguan, *Del campo*, p. 55.

rural society, communities based at least on equality of treatment in daily life, if not on political rights, could be established and, ultimately, a new group identity could be forged to replace what had been lost.[86]

Catholic lay organisations and the Church, in part absorbed in the process of mourning after 1939, saw the post-war defeat of the Republican lower classes as an opportunity for conversions. As migration cut the popular classes free of rural Catholic culture, the Church would struggle to provide a religious context for assimilation of the urban influx.[87] Amongst the hungry urban and rural working class of the 1940s and 1950s there was little time for devotional ceremony, though many felt pressure to attend mass.[88] Few migrants in Madrid questioned by sociologists in the 1950s mentioned religion or admitted to church attendance, though some spoke of assistance offered to them by parish priests, and a child's baptism or first communion remained a significant event. For the Church, migration was seen as a threat as well as an opportunity, however, one which was perceived as originating with the war and revolution. In conservative Burgos, the local president of the Catholic lay organisation Acción Católica (AC), which took some responsibility for charitable provision for migrants, reported on the difficulties of the situation in the city in April 1954, in an account shaped by memories of the conflict:

what has been most noticed and has produced bitter reflections is the migratory movement within the nation, the exodus from the countryside to the city [...] I can confidently say that 90 per cent of the families which we visit and give assistance to are not from Burgos, but people attracted by the mirage of the city, who have sold off whatever possessions they had and, without any preparation at all, have implanted themselves in the city in search of employment which they cannot find and today constitute a dead weight which is a burden on the place making its housing, food, health and schooling problems even worse [...] The prison is another problem because it has attracted a considerable number of families of convicts, particularly during the years of the judicial settlement of the civil war. All or almost all of these families have been aided by our institutions (certainly without bearing much fruit) and now, perhaps scared of returning to their own regions where they committed their crimes, have been settled here, compounding our suffering.[89]

---

[86] Domènech Sampere, 'La otra cara del milagro'.

[87] Rogelio Duocastella (Director of the Social Section of Cáritas Española), 'La inmigración interior', Semanas Sociales, *Problemas*, pp. 171–203.

[88] On the Church pointing to parlous effects of black market, see Bishop Tarancón's pastoral letter of 1950: 'El pan nuestro de cada día' ('Our daily bread'): José Luis Martín Descalzo, *Tarancón, el cardenal del cambio* (Madrid, 1982), pp. 84–7. The bishop had received more than 5,000 letters from working-class people saying that they could not afford to live (p. 94).

[89] AAC, caja 93, 'Secretariado de migración – propuestas (1952–1954)', carpeta 93–1–2, report, 27 April 1954.

These fears of the social and cultural effects of migration in the wake of the war were not new. The women's section of AC prepared itself at an early stage to supplement hard-pressed priests through spiritual and material apostleship in the Madrid slums, albeit from a position dependent on the ACNP-dominated hierarchy and of 'Christianity victorious'.[90] Already, in 1942, middle-class women, who would form the majority of AC's members by the mid 1950s, were attending courses to train health visitors, nurses and auxiliaries to priests. Beyond their apostolic mission, and in response to migrant demands, they were to become expert in social legislation, welfare allowances and care of the sick.[91] In the aftermath of civil war, when accepted notions of criminality had been widened and distorted politically, the relationship between giver and receiver was tense. In 1946, the diocesan report on social conditions in Málaga, for example, reported that assistance to transient 'criminals or vagrants' had been withdrawn because such elements were 'wild' and 'uncontrollable'.[92] Such fears existed simultaneously, however, with a commitment to charity based on conscience and faith in the public pronouncements of the Church. Help for the weakest in society was indeed justified within AC in the provinces by reference to 'the requirements of *convivencia* (living together)' and of 'social solidarity'.[93] The Church had obviously been prominent amongst the elites favoured by Franco's war effort, but the social conditions which were the legacy of his victory troubled Catholic consciences and reinforced the Church's suspicions of 'materialism'. The Archbishop of Córdoba lamented in 1951, for instance, that 'we are living in an era of injustice, of all against all'.[94]

Memory of the war and of martyrdom formed a significant part of the context of Catholic charity. Local and regional branches of AC dispensed time and resources in recalling civil war martyrs who had been active within the organisation.[95] In Valencia there was considerable

---

[90] On the importance of the specialised branches of AC, as distinct in purpose and conception from AC in general, see Feliciano Montero García, *La Acción Católica y el franquismo* (Madrid, 2000).

[91] E.g. *Ecclesia*, 10 January 1942, p. 10. AC female membership: Rafael Prieto-Lacaci, 'Asociaciones voluntarias', in Salustino del Campo (ed.), *Tendencias sociales en España, 1960–1990*, vol. I (Bilbao, 1993), p. 199.

[92] AC, Memoria, November 1946, AAC, caja 208, carpeta 208-1-2.

[93] *Extremadura: diario regional de Acción Católica*, 6 July 1951, p. 1. See, e.g., Pius XII's message on significance of the home to XIV Semana Social Española, *La Vanguardia Española*, 11 July 1954.

[94] *Ya*, 22 May 1951; AAC, caja 95, 95-1-1.

[95] E.g., process of beatification of Antonio Rivera, 'el Ángel del Alcázar', Toledo, *Ecclesia*, 17 February 1951, p. 17.

commemorative activity in 1958 related to nineteen of the women of AC, secular 'servants of God', murdered between August and December 1936 in various parts of the diocese. Memorial activities included the commissioning of portraits of the women to be printed for distribution as reproductions – 57,000 were printed – to support the long process of examination of the case for elevation of the victims towards sainthood by an ecclesiastical tribunal and by Rome in consideration of their lives of sanctity and virtue. This required the collection of testimonies about their deaths and identification of remains and places of burial.[96] Many of the young women of AC, who formed, in effect, a community of memory based on martyrdom, attended the process of the transferral and burial of the mortal remains of two of the women to their places of birth; the anniversary of the deaths of other women was celebrated with a dedicated holy communion.[97] By 1958 three visits to Rome had been made in pursuit of their objective. The process, which was seen in the 1950s in part as an 'instrument of evangelisation', would culminate many years later, in March 2001, with beatification by John Paul II as part of the phenomenal sanctification of more than two hundred other Catholic martyrs of the Spanish war.[98]

Alongside commemoration of the 'crusade' and recognition of martyrdom there was also Catholic self-criticism. One significant focus of this was to be found in the specialist movements of AC. Self-examination was motivated in part by a sense of responsibility for the forced exile of the defeated after the war. This consciousness of a country split apart did not, of course, penetrate as deeply or in the same way within those who remained in the country as it did those who had been forced to leave, but was discernible all the same, along with a conflation of war exiles with economic emigrants, in speaking, for example, of 'the tragic problem of our exiles, above all those who live in France, in their majority not adapted to their new environment and abandoned materially and spiritually, above all by us'.[99] Many young Catholic activists felt compelled to verify their faith through direct action. As some of their predecessors before 1931 had done, they intended to pursue apostolic activity in communities beyond direct Church control. Although the immediate effects of this desire to bear witness through social action were limited, transformation of various '*ambientes*', including particularly

<hr />

[96] See also 'Proceso de beatificación de los ocho mártires claretianos de Sabadell', *Ecclesia*, 13 January 1951, p. 20. On the evidence-gathering process of beatification of lay martyrs of AC in Valencia, see *Ecclesia*, 955, 31 October 1959, p. 27. Also Montero, *Persecución*, p. 544.

[97] AAC, Mujeres, 1958–9, caja 4, carpeta 4–1–5.   [98] See Chapter 12.

[99] Report, 18 March 1952, AAC, carpeta 93–1–2.

the burgeoning slums of the city peripheries, formed a part of lay Catholic imagination and faith as much as it aligned with political and economic imperatives. The Church's influence with respect to political activity and public life was regulated and limited, however, according to the conditions of the Franco regime's Concordat signed with the Vatican in 1953. Later, the reforming Second Vatican Council in the early 1960s, because it opened up the possibility of greater freedom of action, meant that reform-minded activists of AC would clash openly with the more politically influential and resistant mainstream Church which accused them of 'temporalism', leading ultimately to a schism within the organisation in 1968.[100]

At the beginning of the 1950s, AC addressed the question of population movement directly by creating a Comisión Católica de Migración, though there were few illusions about the intractability of the problems of proselytism and social reconciliation. The consensus view was that the 'cancerous belt' around the modernising cities was 'bigger than ever before' and certainly too great to be addressed effectively through charity alone. In many dioceses the arrival 'en masse' of migrants 'searching in the big city for a remedy to very real needs which cannot be satisfied in their place of origin' created conditions where inhumanity and sin were rife: 'in their urge to flee from the countryside they install themselves in subhuman and deplorable conditions'.[101] Apprehension was aroused in 1950, for example, when comparing the children of the centre of Madrid with those of the periphery: the two groups, or types, were so different that it was 'difficult to believe them not to be constantly at war'.[102]

Mobilisation of the lay apostolate throughout the 1950s and into the 1960s was not based on a critique of the socio-economic system as such, but was aimed directly at alleviation of these social ills, a consequence of the prevailing 'distribution of varying standards of living in the

---

[100] Monsignor Antonio Palenzuela, Bishop of Segovia, 'Meditación urgente sobre la iglesia en España', *Perspectiva España* (Madrid, 1972), p. 145. Also Mónica Moreno Seco, 'De la caridad al compromiso: las mujeres de acción católica (1958–1968)', *Historia Contemporánea*, 26, 1 (2003), 239–65; Frances Lannon, *Privilege, Persecution and Prophecy: The Catholic Church in Spain, 1875–1975* (Oxford, 1987) pp. 236–8.

[101] Report, 18 March 1952, AAC, Secretariado Social y de Caridad de la Junta Técnica Nacional de la ACE, caja 93, carpeta 93–1–2. On the Church's own Comisión Episcopal de Migración in the 1950s, see, e.g., Cárcel Ortí, *Actas de las conferencias*, pp. 492, 514, 543.

[102] AAC, report of Junta Técnica Nacional de ACE, March 1952, carpeta 93–1–1; 'Apostolado de limpieza en los suburbios', *Ecclesia*, 13 January 1951, p. 15. On 'them and us' division and fear of an 'invasion' or a 'Red wave', and the need to avoid response of *Reconquista* 'reminiscent of the expulsion of the *moriscos*': Valle, 'Inmigración', pp. 378–9.

country'.[103] This work involved material assistance as well as evangelising to address the moral and religious consequences. AC's Casa Social in Badajoz, essentially run by and for women, provided limited facilities for finding work for the poor, for instance, and organised hospitalisation for the sick and care for orphans. Some forty poor women visited each day in 1956, but the office closed during the summer and was only operative in the city and not in the rest of the largely rural province.[104] By 1961, most dioceses had a women's section of the Secretariado de Migración.[105] There was a tension, of course, because material and moral assistance was always surrounded to some degree by doctrine. According to AC activists' bourgeois condemnation of popular religiosity, migrants 'normally suffered from "religious infantilism"'. Those who arrived in the marginal city suburbs possessed 'a faith which is adequate in their own environment', but the radical transplantation of the migrant provoked a spiritual 'crisis': 'Their weak religious life must be rebuilt upon firm foundations which they rarely possess. They have broken with tradition, with their surroundings and with their accustomed practices.'[106] Drawing on what seemed a natural similarity between the image of 'the defeated' and that of the migrant, the itinerant seeker after work and home was equated in internal communications amongst lay Catholic leaders with the familiar figure of the 'war cripple' whose 'soul has been torn away from everything which was formerly his life. The transplanted individual must be cared for with affection. It is a slow, vital and delicate process.'

This concern with souls uprooted from supposedly harmonious communities and from the family, which affected much of southern Europe in the first post-war decades, was a problem addressed by Pope John XXIII, but it had a particular significance in Spanish society because the country was still overcoming the divisions of the civil war and lived under a regime born out of bloody conflict. Threatening practices and creeds were on offer to the vulnerable, particularly if the family had been fragmented. For those who migrated for work to northern Europe these included 'protestantismo'; for those who made their way to the great urban centres of Spain the danger was an unregulated way of life which could become merely an 'all-absorbing struggle for existence and desire for profit; a materialist and corrupted atmosphere [...] All of this is the

---

[103] AAC, 'I Jornadas Nacionales sobre migraciones', 1960, 93–1–4.
[104] Memoria diocesana, 1955–56, AACM, caja 4, 4–1–2.
[105] 'Cuestionario de estadísticas, 1960–61', AAC, 'Mujeres', carpeta 4–1–7.
[106] AAC, 'Migración y evangelización: problemas religiosos y morales que se plantean al emigrante' (1960), 93–1–4.

pernicious and efficient work of enemies of the faith: [the] complex of difficulties irremediably provokes an almost complete apostasy.'[107] The same threat was present in the isolated regions of intensive industrial exploitation. Rural migrants heading north to work in the coal mines of León, for example, were said to be devoid of religious ideas and unlikely to be impregnated with them without intervention.[108]

Catholic concerns about female migrants who moved either to Spanish cities or to northern Europe were focused on two groups: the married and the unmarried. For the latter, loneliness in a new environment was viewed as a great danger, and psychological problems amongst domestic servants were expected, backed up by a substantial psychiatric literature.[109] More tangibly, moral consequences of threats from malicious organisations and individuals were debated, a reflection of an obsession with pregnancy outside of marriage and 'illegitimacy'. Plans for assistance to women who were in need were inevitably shaped by papal teaching which imagined all women as mothers who represented 'the voice of tradition'. The mother, 'as in the *patria*', brought about 'the cohesion of the family: she is guardian of faith and of moral values' and it was believed that this role, performed well, would mean that husbands and sons would integrate better as they confronted problems in their own proper place within the public realm and within 'the *life* of the region'. Thus, finding work for the 'head of the family' was the basis of all religious, social and economic integration. For women, in this urban context, integration would therefore be especially problematic, it was felt.[110] Nevertheless, although there existed material, psychological and cultural difficulties to overcome, many women would not have agreed. As AC apostolates admitted, it was often women who took the lead in migration and who were the first to find employment in the city, belying the prevalent view that women were likely to act as a restraint on social change and also fuelling fears that women would end up neglecting the family, the 'original nucleus of human society'.[111]

[107] AAC, 'Migración y evangelización'. On the role of Spanish priests in host countries, e.g., Botey Vallès, *Relats*, pp. 107–8; Lara, *Emigración andaluza*, p. 198.

[108] E.g., 'Misiones generales en la zona minera norte de la diócesis de León', *Ecclesia*, 957, 14 November 1959, p. 25.

[109] E.g., Dr Ricardo Horno Alcorta, *Humanización y cristianización del matrimonio* (Madrid, 1940), p. 8; Francisco de Echalecu y Canino, *Contestaciones al programa de psicología criminal* (Madrid, 1943), p. 164.

[110] 'Misión, problemas, peligros y necesidades de la mujer emigrante: casada o soltera', AAC, 93–1–4 (1960).

[111] Encyclical of Pius XI, *Ubi Arcano dei Consilio*, On the Peace of Christ in the Kingdom of Christ, December 1922. Women taking initiative in migration: e.g., Díaz Sánchez,

AC missions were therefore based on training to give assistance in preparing for migration, particularly in cases where women were following their husbands and found themselves 'leaderless' ('*acéfala*': literally 'headless'). This involved spiritual and moral guidance, advice about selling off possessions, defence against opportunists who aimed at exploitation, providing information about contacts (especially the parish priest) in the new urban or foreign community, pointing out the responsibilities to be faced, and preparing for the inevitable hardship which was to come. Anecdotes were used to suggest the potential problems of lack of preparation when dealing with 'uncultured' rural people. Of a group of 186 women migrants questioned in the early 1960s, it was claimed, for example, 26 were unable to read and write and 25 had never seen a train or a car.[112] Once *in situ* the challenges of moral safety and material well-being multiplied, and Catholic volunteers became involved in discussion groups, vocational training and intervening in the transmission and mediation of 'public opinion' to migrants by supplying books, newspapers and magazines. Only certain publications were considered to be useful: 'we must teach them what to preserve of the past and what to abandon in order to adapt to the new conditions of life [. . .] and put them in contact with people of their own region who look after themselves well and might be able to help them'.[113] There were limits, however, to what could be done. In the huge diocese of Madrid-Alcalá in 1954–5 the women *visitadoras* of AC numbered only 14 and the total number of visits they made in the year to working-class slums in the city was 236. Much time was spent in arranging baptisms, first communion for 'children of the Republic', the legalisation by the Church of marriages which had been contracted during the 1930s in civil ceremonies (a postwar process necessary in moral terms to avoid the Church's reprimand for living in 'concubinage' and materially to claim the state family subsidy), spiritual exercises, and escorting individuals to weekly mass, although there were also donations of money, clothing, blankets, food and medicine, as well as workshop-schools for 150 women making clothes.[114]

*

Trabajo de las mujeres, pp. 68–9; Solé, *Inmigrantes*, p. 66; Siguan, *Del campo*, pp. 93–8; Morales and Pereira, *Memoria*, p. 38; Botey Vallès, *Relats*, p. 57.

[112] AAC, Secretariado Social, 'Circulares años 1960–1965', report of meeting at Centro de Estudios Sociales del Valle de los Caídos, caja 95, carpeta 95-1-7.

[113] 'Misión, problemas, peligros'.

[114] 'Memoria del curso', 1954–5, Madrid-Alcalá, Mujeres de Acción Católica, AAC, caja 4, carpeta 4-1-1. The *memoria* for 1957–8 reveals a similar programme of action (4-1-4). On civil marriage, seen as valueless in eyes of God, e.g., *Hoja Parroquial*, Santa Cruz (Madrid), 14 November 1943.

For many ordinary Spaniards, the majority who were outside the orbit of Francoist power, the 1950s were lived amidst a profound sense of incertitude. Deep ambivalence about the recent and conflictive past was rooted in the simultaneity of painful memories of the war and the imperative to make a life which would be materially and powerfully shaped by the conflict itself. Reconstruction of broad pre-war social relations in the post-war context was impossible in such a fluid and unevenly changing environment. For those who had been socially and politically defeated, the outcome of the war signified a violent end to hopes of land reform and of revolutionary myths of *el reparto*: 'the land for those who work it'.[115] Memory was displaced. New collective grievances would emerge in the urban neighbourhoods and amid factory production which would become the basis of solidarity and protest in the 1960s. With migration, begun in the 1940s and growing in the 1950s, came a gradually changing relationship of the lower classes to the state, a change which shaped class attitudes and politics and the responses of institutions of authority and charity. To the urban middle classes, many of whom consented to Francoist power, migrants were not only potential antagonists – 'enemies', as far as memories of recent events were concerned – but also a burden on institutions and, increasingly, a responsibility. Ultimately, in the 1970s, and after a long struggle, they would have the status of citizens conferred upon them.

The moral categories voiced by Catholic volunteers in dealing with marginal urban incomers have been instructive in gauging the responses of established urban society. Commentary ranged widely from the expression of Catholic doubts about the pervasive 'all-against-all' reality of materialism and consumerism – and the need somehow to combat it – to evangelising through programmes of baptism of 'Republican children' and hurling accusations about migrants 'fleeing from their crimes'. Alongside campaigns in favour of the beatification of wartime martyrs, Catholic 'memory activists' pursued charity and campaigns to instruct migrants about what ought to be preserved from the past. For all their doubts, Catholic paternalists, though they usually held to the supreme benefits of Christian love, would begin to admit that urban consumerism itself was a key potential route to reconciliation and 'forgetting'.

---

[115] Juliá, 'Obreros y sacerdotes'; Víctor Pérez Díaz, *Pueblos y clases sociales en el campo español* (Madrid, 1974), p. 37.

7 Commemorating 'Franco's peace': the 25th anniversary of the Victory

> For us, the fact of the war produces instinctive reactions, whether we like it or not; for those who are 25 or younger, reactions are 'historical'. Because the war has not really been 'assimilated' or 'absorbed' by them, they think independently about it, on their own account, whether 'liberals' or 'reactionaries', and for motives which have nothing to do with memory of the conflict which they cannot have. It is a much more important rupture between generations than is normally produced in any country or at any time.[1]

Official commemoration in 1964 of the twenty-fifth anniversary of Franco's victory depicted 1939 as 'Year Zero' by conspicuously comparing the era 'before', compressed into a series of images of the Second Republic, with that which came after, crystallised as an epoch of peace and prosperity. Regime legitimacy continued to emanate from the civil war (a 'necessary' war, in the official view) and denigration of democracy and the Republic. The quarter-century since the end of the civil war was thus seen as a uniquely 'compact' and 'homogeneous' period of 'respect for authority and of political calm', the significance of which would be difficult to explain 'to a foreigner'.[2] The 1960s saw an uneasy convergence of socio-economic imperatives, various strands of monarchist opposition, and the political interests of the regime around technocratic change which did not discard the past, but identified certain 'facts', acceptable to reforming insiders and, at the same time, surmountable, 'making them unrepeatable'.[3] New forward-looking myths, founded on the idea of the war as a 'fratricidal conflict' (a war between brothers) and of an 'economic miracle', replaced symbols and memories encapsulated in the crusade narrative. One instance was the self-proclaimed 'objectivity' and even-handedness of José María Gironella's popular novel *Un millón de muertos*, published in 1961, which problematically 'explained' the war and its violence by reference to a

---

[1] 'Futuro: de cara al porvenir', *ABC*, 1 April 1964, p. 105.   [2] *Ecclesia*, 4 April 1964.
[3] Elías Díaz, *Pensamiento español en la era de Franco (1939–1975)* (Madrid, 1983), p. 88.

form of collective madness.[4] In spite of the myth of peace and prosperity, however, the regime was not as solid as it seemed. It was clear, for example, that criticism from conservative groups of the slow pace of change was a threat. To the outrage of Franco loyalists, internal opponents who had once been supporters of the regime convened with members of the exiled opposition in Munich in 1962 to discuss political strategies and the country's future. Reconciling the conflictive past with the demands of the modern world would therefore become the fundamental question of the 1960s.

Contemplating memory and modernity

As the twenty-fifth anniversary of Franco's victory dawned, the editorial of Acción Católica's weekly *Ecclesia* at the end of March 1964 suggested that Spaniards, whatever their affiliations or backgrounds, should pause for an 'honourable meditation' on 1 April 'to look towards the past and towards the future'.[5] When invited in 1964 as one of 'the combatant generation' to comment on the country's future as it appeared a quarter of a century after the end of the civil war, the liberal and Catalan monarchist Santiago Nadal, whose words open this chapter, identified what he saw as a 'colossal problem': the generation which lived through the war as a direct personal experience required earnestly that it not be forgotten by post-war generations, because of the sacrifices and the potential lessons to be learned, but at the same time many who fought and suffered did not want those who came after to be burdened by the past.[6] This would become a particular problem during the 1960s when deep social change and the opportunity for material improvement threatened to widen the gap between those who remembered and those who did not, and in an era when political protest would reach a new

---

[4] *Un millón de muertos* (Madrid, 1961). Some ex-combatants refused to have the Alzamiento Nacional 'downgraded' to a 'demented outburst of an entire people'. See, e.g., Orlandis Rovira, 'Veinticinco años', pp. 12–14. The concept of 'economic miracle' was first noted in Spain with reference to the impressive German case in the mid 1950s; the possibility of a similar 'miracle' in Spain dates from comments of the US Secretary of Trade in 1961, impressed on his visit by the country's 'stability', in the lead-up to a World Bank report the following year. Discussing 'miracles', José María Pemán maintained that rationalisation could be reconciled with Spanish traditions, because (a) even the Battle of Lepanto (1571) had been planned rationally, and (b) economic development would 'diminish the clientele for Communism': *ABC*, 10 May 1962.

[5] 'Ante una fecha histórica', *Ecclesia*, 28 March 1964, p. 1.

[6] See 'Futuro: de cara al porvenir', *ABC*, 1 April 1964, p. 105. Nadal was born in Lérida in 1909 and had an anti-Francoist past: in 1944 he was arrested and detained in a concentration camp for publishing an article obliquely critical of Francoist post-war executions of the defeated.

intensity. Post-war generations, both middle class and working class, had complex social desires, vocations, collective interests and appetites, which the dictatorial system and culture could not accommodate easily. The central theme of this chapter and the next will be the extent to which the country's much-delayed integration into post-1945 global capitalist growth, based on mass consumerism, absorbed the social-psychological effects of the civil war and its harsh aftermath. Whilst the suffering could not really be forgotten, there was a reshaping of the meaning of war-related cultural trauma, an evolving process inevitably tied to growing (though uneven) prosperity and accelerated change.

The ex-Falangist Pedro Laín Entralgo, who by the early 1960s had become a public critic of the regime, would also meditate on the link between the civil war and the 'boom' of the 1960s, enquiring specifically what the sacrifices of the war had produced. In 1962 he penned an extended response to the repressive measures of the Franco authorities against the liberal opposition, though his protest was not in the end submitted to the government or made public.[7] Modernity and development could certainly be measured in material terms, in the number of new cars on the road and in per capita income, Laín argued, but, although material progress was a condition of social harmony (*convivencia*), it was not sufficient of itself. There had, after all, been unprecedented material development during the period 1900–30, and greater intellectual development, but civil war had not been avoided.[8] There had to be a greater emphasis on the habits of collective life, including 'civil liberty': those who disagreed with each other living in peace. However great economic resurgence and the growth in the standard of living of many Spaniards might have been, could 'an even half-solid Spanish political future be imagined if we do not move towards it through a genuine overcoming of our atrocious civil war – genuine in words, sentiments, ideas, conduct and acts?'[9]

There remained a strong element of political continuity in the maintenance of the constitutional Fundamental Laws of the Franco state, promulgated in May 1958, which based its legitimacy on the idea of a national community defined by blood spilt in the name of the 'crusade' and which denied the political claims of regional nationalist identities. The 'national community' was constituted by 'past, present and future

---

[7] The letter remained unpublished until 1976: Laín Entralgo, *Descargo*, pp. 306, 463.
[8] For analysis of the Second Republic as a failure because of raising social expectations which could not be fulfilled, see Payne, *Spain's First Democracy*. The 1930s' weaknesses of the state were equally damaging.
[9] While correct, Laín probably underestimates the political significance that unprecedented comparative prosperity would have.

generations [...] subordinated to the common good of the nation' (article 5), whose interests were assured through 'organic representation'. Article 1 declared that the 'Unity of Spain' and of Spaniards was a 'sacred duty'. All political organisation outside this framework was considered illegal (article 8) and, although the Fundamental Laws did not explicitly distinguish between winners and losers, this concession was compromised by the dubious proposition that 'constitutional evolution' since 1939 amounted to the formation of a 'nation'.[10] The crusade narrative would indeed remain fundamental to those sections of the Francoist elite which viewed government as the administration of the victory, even into the 1960s. Notorious members of the Francoist 'bunker' reacted aggressively to modernisers who wanted to 'forget'. It was all very well to love your enemies, as Christians were obliged to do, but quite another thing to mistake them for your friends or confuse the two sets of values which had been fought over.[11] A feeling of 'oblivion' had been discerned which was to be used, according to hardliners, as a weapon to negate Spain's historical identity. Franco's doggedly loyal political Chief of Staff, Admiral Luis Carrero Blanco, standing in for the Caudillo at the ceremony to mark the visit of the Papal Secretary of State, Cardinal Cicognani, to the memorial temple and crypt at the Valley of the Fallen in January 1964, reflected this resistance:

this great monument commemorates a victory; not a victory over political adversaries, as certain twisted and fake interpretations have sought to have us believe, but a victory of Spain against the enemies of her independence and of her faith, the only ideals whose defence justifies the greatest sacrifice of life, because the war which the Spanish people had to sustain from 1936 to 1939 was in no sense a civil war, but a war of liberation of the patriotic soil from its domination by a foreign power and, at the same time, a crusade in defence of the Catholic faith which this atheist power sought to eradicate.[12]

Modernising pressures were nonetheless irresistible. The liberalising Decree of Economic Stabilisation, introduced in 1959, would dismantle autarky as the economic basis of post-war internal colonisation and thus contradicted any moves to breathe new life into the 'crusade'. The Stabilisation Plan was effectively the much-delayed Spanish equivalent

---

[10] The sacred political texts of the state were: the Fuero del Trabajo (March 1938), the Ley Constitutiva de las Cortes (July 1942), the Fuero de los Españoles (July 1945), the Ley de Sucesión (March 1947); the Ley de Principios Fundamentales (May 1958); the Ley Orgánica del Estado (November 1966), etc. See *La constitución española: leyes fundamentales del estado* (Madrid, 1971).

[11] E.g., Hermandad de Alféreces Provisionales, *Generación del 36*, pp. 8–9, 14. Also Calzada Rodríguez, 'El espíritu del 18 de julio', pp. 601–43.

[12] Luis Carrero Blanco, *Discursos y escritos, 1943–1973* (Madrid, 1974), p. 102.

of Marshall Aid which would herald the unprecedented socio-economic change of the 1960s. The 'economic miracle' myth would soon supersede that of the 'crusade' completely, a pivotal collective social and psychological turning point based on real social change, and 1964 would see a major propaganda effort by the regime which officially celebrated not the victory of Franco but 'twenty-five years of peace'.

Increasingly, social problems and tensions could not be papered over with myths and mysticism which were narrowly political and failed to resonate either publicly or privately. The grandest symbol of the 'crusade', the Valle de los Caídos, where Carrero had spoken in January 1964, had been inaugurated only five years before, and, though the stated intention was to ensure that sacrifices would not be 'lost in the silence of the past', the monument would never become a genuinely national focus of memory. The 'triumph of the Cross' was always a partisan and ideological proposition in post-war Spain. Franco's pantheon to the 'crusade' was to be largely ignored in the 1960s and 1970s except for the egotistical ceremonies of officialdom, the popular perception being that it sanctified Franco's victory rather than the sacrifice of thousands of lives.[13] Only reluctantly, and somewhat in contradiction with the triumphalist rhetoric, were Republican dead permitted a resting place there, although many families, on both sides, were resistant. In towns and villages across the country there were many other monuments to those 'Fallen for God and for the *patria*'. Over time, these had become part of the public 'furniture' of communities where memory was occasionally acted out in sporadic performance rather than deserving of repetitive ritual. At the same time, 'forgetting' was not merely due to the passage of time. Recording the names of 'los Caídos' (the Fallen) was part of defining the indelible nature of the war's collective trauma, but it had been a profoundly selective process: every traumatised collective is always delimited. Some children in the early post-war decades remembered years later how one group of friends whose fathers had been lost in the war could read their names inscribed on memorial stones and plaques, while others had left no trace.[14]

Pragmatic modernisers within the government, including Manuel Fraga, Minister of Information and Tourism from 1962 to 1969, became the forerunners of the technocratic ministers to come in the 1970s. Fraga

[13] Daniel Sueiro, *La verdadera historia del Valle de los Caídos* (Madrid, 1976); Fernando Olmeda, *El Valle de los Caídos* (Barcelona, 2009).

[14] E.g., Pedro Altares to Borràs, *Los que no hicimos*, p. 387. See, e.g., the cemetery in Lora del Río, discussed in Chapter 10. On names and remembering, Avishai Margalit, *The Ethics of Memory* (Harvard, 2002), p. 25.

was born in 1922 and narrowly missed wartime service. Constructing a personal biography with which to assert his place in history, he would depict himself as a symbol of what in 1961 he called 'la generación-puente' ('the bridge generation'), situated between war and division on the one hand, and peace and development on the other. He had risen to prominence as an associate of the liberal Catholic Joaquín Ruiz-Giménez, and, whilst believing resolutely in the conflict's legitimacy as the founding moment of the regime, he looked ahead towards downgrading crusade mysticism in favour of a socially grounded analysis of modernity.[15] He had already, towards the end of the 1950s, assessed Spanish society as 'on the move', and during the 1960s, migration and mass tourism would sweep away traces of the past, both culturally and physically, giving modernisers added momentum. Disregarding Francoist orthodoxy which saw the entire 'liberal' nineteenth century as a catastrophe, Fraga's position was that the country had become modern 150 years before 1958, thus staking a sociological rather than symbolic claim on 1808. Although it may have been more agreeable to study the glorious times of the Catholic monarchs, and although the process initiated with the Napoleonic invasion was not 'gratifying' for patriotic Spaniards, the modern era needed to be faced.[16] Fraga and those like him, who accepted the need for authoritarian government and maintaining traditions but also wished to embrace the modern, were essential to Franco. The Generalísimo reluctantly accepted the idea of progress, though he persisted in the belief that modernisation and industrialisation threatened perpetual conflict. In June 1968, in Asturias, where he was inaugurating the new airport, he would reiterate the need for authority amid the change:

the policy that we have developed during these thirty years has not been a policy of victors, but a policy of peace, of order and of progress [...] But we cannot rest on our laurels: life is struggle and we must prepare ourselves for this struggle, the struggle of markets, the struggle of production. You all know that during these thirty years you have not been without military command [*la voz de mando*] and you will not be without it as long as I live.[17]

This was grudging acceptance that time moved forward. Fraga, implicitly critical of the epic and heroic version of historical memory, would

---

[15] Fraga was a more political and pragmatic figure than Laín Entralgo, but there is nonetheless a degree of convergence between Fraga and the 'new humanism' of ambivalent civil war Falangists. See, for example, Fraga's favourable view of Pedro Laín Entralgo's essay *España como problema* (1949, later published Madrid, 1956), in his *Las transformaciones de la sociedad española contemporánea* (Madrid, 1959), p. 12.

[16] Fraga, *Las transformaciones*, pp. 7, 8.   [17] *La Vanguardia Española*, 18 June 1968.

therefore establish a dedicated department within the Ministry of Information to work on renovating the history of the civil war and to wrest what was viewed as its historiographical control away from non-Spaniards. This office would be directed by Ricardo de la Cierva, an aspiring historian whose father had been executed in 1936 at Paracuellos. A major organ of this propaganda would be the *Boletín de Orientación Bibliográfica*, produced by the ministry between 1963 and 1976, which targeted particularly the works of the Paris-based oppositionist publishing house Ruedo Ibérico.[18] The government-inspired rewriting of the history of the war was, it would be claimed, 'scientific' and 'objective': there would certainly be less frequent reference to the conflict as *la guerra de liberación* or *la Cruzada* and more consistent use of the term *guerra civil*.[19] The regime continued to control access to state records, however, and there were no publicly accessible archives, as such, which held material on the war. While the mythical tone was thus diluted, there remained a propaganda mission behind the reforms. The entire exercise required that the extent and nature of the violence be played down or, at least, that an equivalence of responsibility be apportioned between the two contending forces.[20]

During the second half of the 1960s, therefore, subtle changes in official representation of the past became noticeable, a shift ultimately eased a little by Fraga's new Press Law introduced in 1966. Gradually, the still-censored newspapers would refrain, for instance, from lurid references to Republicans as 'the Red horde' when marking significant occasions relating to the conflict. The tentative veering towards *apertura* represented by the new law would be supported by sections of the media, including the Catholic newspaper *Ya*, which was seen as having a Christian-Democratic bent, and even Falangist organs such as *Pueblo*. There were limits to the process, however, and controls remained, so that cases against the press actually increased after the new law came into

---

[18] For a list of historians who contributed to this process of 'clarification', according to a polemical exchange with Gabriel Jackson, who was accused as an 'outsider' of displaying resistance to change heralded by those listed, many of whom enjoyed privileged access to official documents, see Ramón Salas Larrazábal, 'El mito del millón de muertos: demografía contra leyenda', in Hugh Thomas (ed.), *La guerra civil española* (6 vols.) (Madrid, 1979), vol. V, p. 258. For the polemics over Jackson's *Breve historia de la guerra civil española* (Paris, 1974), see *Boletín de Orientación Bibliográfica*, 100 (December 1974), 7–29. See also Salas, *Pérdidas*, p. 23.

[19] For bolstering the new claims of 'scientific' method and 'truth' in regime historiography in the 1960s, see, e.g., Ricardo de la Cierva, *Cien libros básicos sobre la guerra de España* (Madrid, 1966); *Los documentos de la primavera trágica* (Madrid, 1967); *Bibliografía general sobre la guerra de España y sus antecedentes* (Madrid, 1968).

[20] The implicit purpose behind Salas Larrazábal, *Pérdidas de la guerra*, appearing somewhat later in 1977.

force.[21] Amid an increase in arrests also for illicit association, in January 1968 Fraga's ministry, invoking article 64 of the press legislation, referred the book *La URSS hoy* ('The Soviet Union Today') to the judicial authorities for prosecution. Written by a supporter of the Spanish Association of European Cooperation and edited by the liberal opposi-tionist publishing house Cuadernos Para el Diálogo which published an influential monthly review of the same name, the book had aimed to assess the reality of life behind the Iron Curtain fifty years after the Russian Revolution without taking an anti-Moscow position. It particu-larly stressed what the author saw as the drawbacks in the international sphere of Spain's anti-communism, which derived from positions adopted at a time 'now forgotten'.[22] There was some irony in the fact that only a few weeks after the case was opened, the press was celebrating how trade with the Soviet Union and other states of the Communist Eastern bloc had increased at an almost vertiginous rate during the period 1965-7.[23] Weeks later, at the beginning of March 1968, agents of the Ministry of information seized all copies of February's issue of *Cuadernos* because it included material which 'might constitute a crime'.[24] The law was also used to curtail expressions of regional identity. In June 1969 the ministry ordered judicial proceedings to be initiated against two newspapers in Navarra because they had published the details of speeches made in May at the annual Carlist rally at Montejurra by two of the region's 'family representatives' elected via restricted suffrage to the Francoist Cortes. *El Pensamiento Navarro* and *Diario de Navarra* were guilty of reporting that Auxilio Goñi and José Ángel Zubiaur, two leaders of the Carlist movement, by this time more socially radical than in the 1930s, had been heavily fined by the Civil Governor because they had called for a law granting a degree of regional autonomy and had criticised a proposed official secrets act which threatened to limit press freedom even more.[25] Significantly, the vast majority of active adherents of Carlism by the 1960s had been born after 1939.[26]

[21] See Carlos Barrera, *Periodismo y franquismo: de la censura a la apertura* (Barcelona, 1995), p. 154.
[22] Antonio Menchaca, *La URSS hoy* (Madrid, 1967).
[23] E.g., *La Vanguardia Española*, 24 January 1968, p. 9.
[24] *La Vanguardia Española*, 2 March 1968, p. 7. There were many other confiscations and prosecutions under the notorious provisions of article 64 of the Press Law; for example: the Catholic *Signo* (for an article by Víctor Manuel Arbeloa, 'Progresismo e iglesia'); an issue of the collection 'Criterion' (including an article by Pedro Altares on 'public opinion in the Church').
[25] Francisco Miranda Rubio, 'Los procuradores de representación familiar en la novena legislativa franquista (1967–1971)', *Príncipe de Viana*, 203 (1994), 615–37; *La Vanguardia Española*, 10 July 1969, p. 5.
[26] Josep Carles Clemente, *El carlismo en su prensa* (Madrid, 1999), p. 110.

Although the government was able to claim that it was overseeing a level of socio-economic progress, its record on keeping pace with the technocratic and political requirements of modernity was habitually tarnished. Making consumer goods more available to *the masses* had the benefit of distracting the attention of potential *citizens* from claims for democratisation; the regime had, of course, depicted democracy as 'discredited' since the civil war. In his New Year message, delivered at the end of December 1967, the Head of State emphasised the uniqueness of Spain, declaring that 'we will continue perfecting our political system without compromising the principle of authority'. He sought legitimation not in the principles of democracy but in those elements of the Catholic Church's reforming programme which were most convenient, recalling tendentiously the Papal Encyclical *Populorum Progressio* of March 1967 (on the socio-economic development of peoples) which, according to Franco, 'endorsed with its doctrine all that we have been practising during these last thirty years'.[27] By 1970 one of Fraga's leading lieutenants was able to place this sense of depoliticised contentment, as perceived by the regime, within a historical context: 'economic development and demythologisation [...] produce citizens [who are] enormously sensitised (*'sensibilizados'*) to the value of peace and respectful of divergent attitudes'. Nevertheless, the system still lacked any institutional machinery necessary for modern democracy.[28]

The reforming direction taken by the Catholic Church led by Pope John XXIII at the Second Vatican Council (1962–5) had already contributed to refocusing the politics of war memories. This was reflected in the convoluted declarations at this time of some Spanish Catholics and the Church. In 1964, *Ecclesia* wished to interpret 1 April 1939 'as the beginning of a Christian embrace which will become closer year after year'. Succumbing to temptation to replay old antagonisms would 'betray the blood of the dead' since 'they would have wished to carry such enmities with them to their graves'.[29] The 'Día de la Victoria' (1 April) was always close to Eastertide, offering opportunities for analogies of sacrifice to be drawn. Gradually, and especially from the 1960s, there would be less public meditation on the suffering of the war and more on Calvary understood as the birth of Christian peace. Catholic reforms would be viewed by the Christian Democratic opposition

---

[27] *ABC*, 31 December 1967; 29 March 1967, p. 39; 'Frente al hambre y la opulencia', *La Vanguardia Española*, 30 March 1967, p. 5.

[28] Jesús Unciti Urniza, the director of Editora Nacional del Ministerio de Información y Turismo. Borràs, *Los que no hicimos*, pp. 98–9. Also pp. 27–8.

[29] 'Ocasión propia para el perdón', *Ecclesia*, 4 April 1964, p. 4.

movement, especially, and sections of the clandestine left, as central to hopes for change. Around the country, small groups of progressive Catholics would begin to hold meetings with the opposition to debate social issues. In Córdoba the association of this kind was called the Club Juan XXIII and had been founded by the editors of the Catholic journal of mental health, *Praxis*.[30] The challenge to established Church–state relations represented by the Vatican Council thus amounted to a potential political earthquake. The associated tremors would gradually undermine relations between the Church and the regime and their common objectives.[31] Although many of the bishops accepted that Vatican II called for a reassessment of the conceptual bases of the Church, others were profoundly resistant.[32] Leading the reformers, Vicente Enrique y Tarancón, the Bishop of Madrid, looking back in 1978 at the reception of the reforms, focused significantly on generational divisions: 'the Church had a history behind it, both recent and more distant, which did not permit an easy assimilation of the Council; the generational distances within our country and within our Church were very great; and we had lived through a long epoch marked by lack of communication and even of rejection of ways of thinking which were already current in other parts of the world'.[33] Political conservatives were wary, cleaving ever more to the regime's key symbols of legitimacy. In his end-of-year speech in 1964, Franco addressed calls for religious freedom and, indirectly, the direction of the Vatican Council, suggesting some need for mobility – in some senses, indeed, disavowing all that the triumphal regime had preached for twenty years – but also reasserting the anti-communism which had welded the nascent wartime state to the Church almost three decades earlier and which he perhaps hoped would become the new spirit of the times:

Our tradition, so often intentionally impaired, is that of a people tolerant and respectful of individual rights. In our *patria*, history has meant that men of different races and creeds have lived together for several centuries [...] Spain has always marched at the head in the expansion of the Gospel [...] How could we contribute to this expansion of the Catholic faith if we remain unyielding, fortified in egotism and in our peace and religious renaissance? [...] Can we ignore the cruel and bloody persecution which communism unleashes against

---

[30] Castilla del Pino, *Casa del olivo*, pp. 124, 181.
[31] Olegario González de Cardedal, 'Iglesia y política', in González de Cardedal (ed.), *Iglesia y política en España* (Salamanca, 1980), p. 34.
[32] As discussed in, e.g., Cardenal Narciso Jubany, 'Neutralidad política de la iglesia', in González de Cardedal (ed.), *Iglesia y política en España*. p. 121.
[33] Enrique y Tarancón, 'La Iglesia en España hoy', in González de Cardedal (ed.), *Iglesia y política en España*. p. 66. Also Martín Descalzo, *Tarancón*, pp. 101–13.

members of the Church [in Eastern Europe]? [...] The Church always emerges from martyrdom with greater honour and ennobled, and Spaniards know from experience that there is nothing as fertile as the blood spilt by martyrs.[34]

The inward-looking Spanish Church was ill-prepared for the challenge, and its Episcopal Conference mounted resistance even to the Second Vatican Council's basic postulates. In effect, the Council provoked a division of the Spanish bishops between 'the crusading Church' and the 'Church of peace' which would be maintained throughout the Franco years and beyond.[35] In justifying their position on Church expressions of opinion on temporal matters, the conservatives within the hierarchy resorted to the precedents of the 1930s. The collective document on 'the Church and the temporal order in the light of the Council', issued by the Permanent Commission of the Conference on 29 June 1966, for example, aimed to circumscribe the social activities of Acción Católica and invoked a number of earlier pronouncements by the Church, including the civil war collective letter of 1 July 1937 in support of Franco, pointing out that the Church's collective position had been confirmed by the earlier papal encyclicals of Pius XII: *Dilectissima nobis*, decrying state secularising measures under the Second Republic (3 June 1933), and the subsequent anti-communist *Divini Redemptoris* (19 March 1937) and radio broadcast on 16 April 1939, following the Caudillo's victory.[36] The Commission also defended the political concept of 'organic representation', in effect, Francoism's euphemism for dictatorship, and the state union system.[37] A shift towards reform was made possible, however, when Cardinal Pla y Deniel, Primate of Spain since 1941, died at the age of 92 in early July 1968 and Tarancón, then Archbishop of Oviedo, was named as his successor by Paul VI.[38] Tarancón declared his policy to be one of equilibrium, although at the same moment he insisted on the need to place the past within history and move forward in step with generational evolution: 'there is no area of life where exact agreement is found. A diversity of viewpoints exists amongst the bishops and this is natural. They are marked by their age, by the distinct

---

[34] *Ecclesia*, 1,226, 9 January 1965, p. 31.

[35] José María Llanos, 'Tensión entre dos cleros', *El Ciervo*, October 1966, cited in Blázquez, *Traición*, p. 164.

[36] See José Andrés-Gallego and Antón M. Pazos, *La iglesia en la España contemporánea* (Madrid, 1999), pp. 179–80. On reception of the June 1933 encyclical, see letter of Vidal i Barraquer to Cardinal Pacelli, 23 June 1933, *Arxiu Vidal i Barraquer: Església i estat durant la segona República espanyola, 1931–1936*, vol. III (Barcelona, 1981), pp. 867–8.

[37] See, e.g., D. A. González Madrid and Manuel Ortiz Heras, '"Camilo, no te comas a los curas, que la carne de cura indigesta": la influencia de la Iglesia en la crisis del franquismo', in *La Transició de la dictadura a la democràcia* (Barcelona, 2005).

[38] See front page of Seville edition of *ABC*, 7 July 1968.

education received by each of them, and by many other complex reasons.'[39] Some four years earlier, of course, the ceremonial Church had played an important part in commemorating the twenty-fifth anniversary of the end of the civil war.

Commemoration

In many respects official commemoration of '25 years of peace' in 1964 marked a pivotal moment. While in 1959 the twentieth anniversary of the end of the war had been clearly focused on Franco's victory, the tone five years later was different. The front-page editorial comment in *La Vanguardia Española* referred on 1 April 1959 to 'the Illimitable Victory', while on the same day in 1964 the headline ran 'Peace as a requirement'.[40] All over the country in 1964 there were commemorative activities during the first week of April which combined religious acts with political symbolism. With the Minister of Information and Tourism at its head, an interministerial commission which reported directly to the Head of State was established to organise the ceremonies and publicity celebrating '25 years of peace', including production of a documentary film depicting the Generalísimo as a man of the people: *Franco, ese hombre*.[41] At the beginning of July, a grand exhibition was inaugurated in Madrid, and similar events were held in other cities and in ambassadorial locations abroad, several lasting until the end of the year.[42] In December the commemorations were brought to a close when Fraga, as Minister of Information, laid the first stone of the new Palacio de Congresos y Exposiciones in Madrid. 'We Spaniards', he declared, 'have recognised the value of peace and also the difficulties of maintaining it.'[43] In the Basilica of the Valley of the Fallen, a Te Deum of thanksgiving and commemoration was officiated by the Cardinal Primate, Pla y Deniel, in the presence of state dignitaries. Memorial services had also been held on 1 April at the cemetery of Paracuellos and at the Cross of the Montaña barracks, a significant site of Francoist memory where many rebels had been killed as the 1936 military coup was suppressed

---

[39] *Perspectiva España 1969* (Madrid, 1969), p. 288. On Tarancón and ecclesiastical generations: Martín Descalzo, *Tarancón*, pp. 169–70.

[40] *La Vanguardia Española*, 1 April 1959; 1 April 1964.

[41] The script, by José Luis Sáenz de Heredia, was published: *Franco, ese hombre* (Madrid, 1964). See also Ángel Quintana, 'Y el Caudillo quiso hacerse hombre: la retórica épica e iconográfica en Franco, ese hombre', *Archivos de la Filmoteca*, 42–3 (2002), 174–89.

[42] E.g. *La Vanguardia Española*, 2 July 1964, p. 1; 9 September 1964; 1 October 1964, p. 1; 2 December 1964, p. 1; 17 December 1964.

[43] *La Vanguardia Española*, 22 December 1964, p. 7.

in Madrid. By 1966, the thirtieth anniversary of these deaths, coverage of their commemoration continued to evoke the sacrifice but ceased to focus on the perpetrators or to use such terms as 'horda roja'.[44] In a world which was moving too fast for many, the guardians of crusade memories, including the *alféreces provisonales'* association, had begun to turn towards the future as well as recalling the past.[45] A national competition for essays on the subject of 'España 64' elicited work dedicated to veteran groups and to ideas based on religion, sacrifice, the Caudillo, and *la Cruzada*, but also included paeans to economic development.[46] It was easy to compare such signs of progress with the tragedies of the past, especially if many of the darker realities of post-war progress were overlooked. Ignoring the reality of the shanty towns which continued to grow on the city's margins, the Madrid of 1964 was compared tendentiously, for instance, with that of 1939:

the capital city of today has nothing to do with that starving and trembling city which received the troops of the Army of the Centre [...] The city of today has tripled its population and doubled its perimeter. Where once there were miserable crowded shacks, avenues have been opened [...] Madrid, then, was fearful darkness; today it glitters at night-time without fear. All that was uncertainty has been transformed into confidence.[47]

In Barcelona, a solemn open-air mass was held at the beginning of February in the Plaza de Cataluña in replication of the ceremony held to mark 'liberation' in 1939, and the main public thoroughfare of the city was used to stage an exhibition celebrating economic achievements since the war.[48] The editorial on the front page of the city's most important newspaper offered its congratulations and gratitude to all who had made recuperation possible. Catalonia needed to outdo Madrid in its effusiveness at what had been achieved since 1939. Neglecting previous eras of cultural and scientific achievement, the hyperbole claimed the post-war period as

an unprecedented era in the annals of a history charged with glories and heroism but temperate in its peacefulness, of coexistence and of dedication to

[44] *La Vanguardia Española*, 8 November 1966, p. 10.
[45] E.g., Antonio García Pablos of Acción Católica to Hermandad, *ABC*, 30 January 1963, p. 51; Borràs, *Los que no hicimos*, p. 129. Also, Hermandad de Alféreces Provisionales, *Generación del 36*.
[46] 'Premios de Prensa, Radio y Televisión', *ABC*, 31 March 1964. On peace and the economy, see *25 aniversario de la paz española: el gobierno informa* (Madrid, 1964).
[47] Manuel Pombo Ángulo, in *La Vanguardia Española*, 2 April 1964, p. 7.
[48] *La Vanguardia Española*, 1 February 1964, p. 1; 4 February 1964; 2 April 1964, p. 1; 2 May 1964; 17 May 1964, p. 3; 26 May 1964, p. 1.

technological and scientific tasks, of discovery of sources of wealth and well-being, which have given us prestige and power, collective stature among the concert of peoples and an enviable standard of living in the eyes of other countries of the Christian West in whose orbit we lived for too long as picturesque and poor relatives [...] We have left behind the anarchistic and crazed, tumultuous and bloody, caste-based traditions (*casticismo*), which for more than two centuries was the breeding ground of our decadence, our mediocrity and our ruin.[49]

The Civil Governor of Barcelona, Antonio Ibáñez Freiré, a civil war veteran of the Regimiento de Flandes, who would briefly serve as Interior Minister in Adolfo Suárez's post-Franco government in 1979–80, recalled what the price of peace had been and maintained that 'neither the old nor the young can remain ignorant of the past because history is entirely present'. Catalan suffering, he declared, had not been due to the 'crusade', but because of revolutionary 'persecution' and 'the broken economy' under the 'atheist-Marxist Republic', which engendered 'class struggle' and 'utopian separatism'.[50] Recalling the wartime killing of Bishop Manuel Irurita, the Governor turned to forgiveness, arguing that the Church followed Franco in pardoning crimes of the past and 'proclaiming the brotherhood of all Spaniards'.[51] Many believed silently and conversely that the Church owed an apology to society.

Generally in 1964, commemoration meant recollection and, to some extent, celebration of the war. The corollary of this was selective forgetting. There would be no mention of those killed on the other side or of the violent aftermath of the conflict. Regions and cities, especially those historically aligned with the 'crusade', paid homage in a surge of public monuments to the Caudillo. In Salamanca the General was made honorary and perpetual mayor of the city in gratitude. In Burgos, from where the declaration of victory in 1939 had been announced, a solemn Te Deum was attended by local office-holders.[52] In the Canary Islands, where Franco had been in command in 1936, the proclamation of war and the final communiqué of 1 April 1939 were rebroadcast again over the radio. The Spanish community of Tetuán in Morocco commemorated with a mass attended by the Consul General, where a wreath was laid beneath the commemorative

---

[49] *La Vanguardia Española*, 1 April 1964, p. 5.
[50] *La Vanguardia Española*, 3 April, 1964, p. 24. For the Governor's personal memoir, see *La Vanguardia Española*, 18 July 1964, p. 8.
[51] For Irurita killing, Montero, *Persecución*, pp. 416–21. For the later process of beatification, *El País*, 3 January 2000.
[52] *La Vanguardia Española*, 2 April 1964, p. 7.

stone to 'the first of those fallen in the Crusade'.[53] Statues were erected in Barcelona (1963), Santander (1964) and El Ferrol del Caudillo, the birthplace of Franco (1967).[54] The ceremonial unveiling of the grand equestrian sculpture of Franco in the main square of the city of Valencia, officially the Plaza del Caudillo, was presided over by the popularly venerated image of the Virgen de los Desamparados (Virgin of the Abandoned) which had been carried aloft by occupying Nationalist forces in 1939.[55] The archbishop of the diocese, Marcelino Olaechea, led the open-air mass and lauded Franco: 'the Caudillo of Victory has become during these twenty-five years the Caudillo of the peace which we enjoy'. Ex-captives and ex-combatants were prominent as the mayor unveiled the bronze creation mounted on an inscribed 4-metre-high granite pedestal: 'To Francisco Franco, Caudillo of Spain. Valencia is grateful for your twenty-five years of bountiful peace.'[56] Monuments to peace which were not focused on Franco were few.[57] In Zaragoza, a Te Deum in the Basilica of the Virgin of the Pillar and a floral offering before the monument to the Fallen formed the basis of the ceremony. Though his ultimate prescriptions were imprecise, Bishop Casimiro Morcillo, in carefully chosen words, preached about a future of development and *convivencia*. Recognition of the defeated was avoided, though 'victors' were not explicitly praised either: the divide was conceived as one not between winners and losers but one between those who died and those who survived:

We have come together here to give thanks for these twenty-five years of peace. I call on you to pray for the eternal peace of all those who died and opened the way of peace [. . .] These years have been centred upon the unswerving exercise of peace, the sacrifice of those who generously gave everything, in their [personal] holocaust and also upon that of the Spaniards who wanted peace, prosperity, elevation in all respects for Spain [. . .] These twenty-five years of peace, fruit of a generation determined upon sacrifice, obliges the new generations to serve Spain through another twenty-five years of peace. And this must be established upon work, justice and charity.[58]

---

[53] *La Vanguardia Española*, 1 April 1964, p. 6.

[54] Jesús de Andrés Sanz, 'Las estatuas de Franco, la memoria del franquismo y la transición Política española', *Historia y Política*, 12 (2004). A monument 'to 18 July' was proposed by the authorities in Seville.

[55] See Chapter 10 for campaign to have it removed after 1975. The main square would also be renamed: the Plaza del País Valenciana. Later, the statue was moved to the military barracks (Capitanía General) and, in 2010, it was finally removed.

[56] *La Vanguardia Española*, 2 April 1964, p. 7.

[57] The monolith depicting Angels of Peace installed in the Avenida de Bruselas (Madrid) in 1964 was a rare exception. *ABC*, 11 June 1964.

[58] *La Vanguardia Española*, 2 April 1964, p. 8.

Elite perceptions of the past and the future in 1964

Beside symbolic representation there was significant public comment on the meaning of the anniversary, some of it from tolerated oppositionists. Much of the commentary from staunch loyalists and regime insiders reflected the regime-scripted public history of the Second Republic and the war appearing in the newspapers, which revealed the limits of historical 'renovation'. The focus on 'anarchy' during the period of the Popular Front permitted chaos to appear as the essence of the Republic. It also divested conservatives who had obstructed reform or plotted with the army rebels of any responsibility and made any positive reflection on the period from 1931 to 1936 impossible.[59] Though he had been unwelcome in Franco's Spain after the civil war because of his gradualist approach to discrediting the Republic, the leader of the CEDA, José María Gil Robles, was in effect rehabilitated in the early 1960s. The Cortes intervention he had made on 15 July 1936 following the assassination of the monarchist José Calvo Sotelo two days earlier would be reproduced in full in the state-controlled press in 1964. The assassination had become a hugely important legitimating moment for the rebels and the post-war Franco regime. In the principal conservative-monarchist newspaper, *ABC*, a section entitled 'Assassinated by Agents of the Authorities' reported how the CEDA leader had blamed the Republican government of prime minister Casares Quiroga for the murder. Calvo Sotelo became known as the 'pro-mártir' of the crusade – a model of sacrifice for those who would follow during the war – and a memorial plaque stating that he had been 'vilely murdered in compliance with the threats made in the Congress by the Prime Minister' had been unveiled in July 1954 on the building from where he had been taken away eighteen years earlier. When the building was pulled down, a new plaque was installed in 1974 with less incendiary phraseology.[60] The point in 1964 was to celebrate and renew simultaneously the 'moderate' Gil Robles and the martyred Calvo Sotelo as fundamental to the regime's heritage and basis of its legitimacy.

Images of damage inflicted by 'the horde' upon churches and ecclesiastical buildings accompanied such newspaper reports, as did reproduction of the 1936 death notice of Calvo Sotelo, photographs of the funeral, and an extract from the tribute given by fellow monarchist

---

[59] *ABC*, 1 April 1964.
[60] E.g., *Recuerdo Calvo Sotelo, pro-mártir* (Madrid, 1956). For similarly altered memorials see, e.g., Izquierdo Martín and Sánchez León, *Guerra que nos han contado*, pp. 39–42; Fernández Delgado et al., *Memoria impuesta*, pp. 242–3. See also Ian Gibson, *La noche en que mataron a Calvo Sotelo* (Barcelona, 1982).

and habitual plotter against the Republic Antonio Goicoechea, which called for revenge and for Spain to be saved. In 1964 there was generally less direct demonisation of specific Republican 'enemies within' who had been targets of officially whipped-up public hatred in the 1940s and 1950s. *ABC*'s souvenir issue included no direct reference to Manuel Azaña, for example. The name of the President of the Republic from May 1936 and former bête noir of Francoism appeared only at the foot of several of the more controversial decrees of his reforming government, reproduced in extract though largely without commentary. More attention was paid to Azaña's predecessor as President, Niceto Alcalá Zamora, who appeared on the cover, described as 'not anti-patriotic' but, fatally, as 'a bridge between order and chaos', an implicit warning of where leniency towards democracy might lead and to the moderate opposition which had met with exiles in Munich in 1962 to discuss the Spanish situation and which preached mediation and reconciliation. Although *ABC* was pro-monarchist, its judgement upon Alcalá Zamora counselled caution: 'May God free us in the future from such leaders who would lead the country towards shores where they never thought nor wished to go.'[61]

The image of a white-haired Alcalá Zamora contrasted with the photograph of a nameless but apparently optimistic and dynamic young man on the next page designed to represent all those Spaniards 'born on the Día de la Victoria' twenty-five years earlier, whose gaze seemed to be resolutely fixed on the future. The peace was thus portrayed, from the mid 1960s, as a social phenomenon. There remained heroism in the Victory – Franco, pictured full-page with field glasses assessing military objectives, remained its architect, and the peace brought was essentially won by him. But whereas previous public coverage of the war focused almost exclusively on the charismatic rule of the Caudillo, the Victory had become in 1964 'the work of all', including 'priests' (whose martyrdom was now somewhat skated over), 'mothers' and 'workers', and those 'intellectuals who defended the truth of Spain', indicating that the Republican intelligentsia remained tainted and excluded.

The attempt to associate the regime with youth and with a unified society embracing the future as one was contradicted, however, by much of the rest of the content of the three special editions published by *ABC*, as well as by the political, generational and social tensions of the 1960s which are not difficult to find and which will be explored in the next

[61] For narrative effect, in order to suggest that the 'bridge' to 'chaos' had purposely been crossed, the removal of Alcalá Zamora as President in April 1936 was magnified in this account.

chapter. In ambiguous language which reflects this difficulty, it was maintained that the young knew of the war only through 'intimate' stories, as related within families, which was certainly true, or 'through a culture of what now is history' ('*por cultura de lo que ya es historia*'), as though the confusion wrought by twenty-five years of the imposition of the official narrative of 'the crusade against foreign invaders' had rendered even grammatical sense impossible. The pages of the souvenir editions, just as many of the school texts produced since 1939 and still in use in the 1960s, were consciously offered to the young, not merely to inform them about what had happened in the past, but to impress lessons upon them and to exact respect from them on contemplating 'the sacrifice of the preceding generation'. The problem was that many readers, and not only those belonging to Republican families, understood that they were being presented with a highly partial truth.[62] In terms of international participation, for example, the claim as late as 1964 that the International Brigades represented 'the first foreign intervention' of the conflict, especially when viewed alongside the complete absence of Hitler and Mussolini from the story, was to stretch credibility too far. Nazi and Fascist aid to Franco from the beginning was the most inconvenient truth of all since it fitted neither the narrative of Holy War nor that of National Liberation, nor even that of fratricidal struggle.[63] Connections to the Axis powers could be covered over by accentuating the imprimatur on victory offered to Franco in 1939 by Pope Pius XII in his radio message which was reproduced by the newspapers in 1964. This also allowed the anti-clerical violence of the revolution in the Republican zone to be recalled.[64] The Pope had also made particular mention of Spanish children which 'the Reds sent to Russia', providing an additional emotive edge to memories.[65] The Republican wartime zone was thus represented only by brief texts about events selected for their notoriety, with no commentary: the closure of religious institutions, the arming of trade union militias, the creation of Popular Courts, collectivisation, and regional autonomy.[66] There was coverage of the murder of prisoners in the Modelo prison in Madrid in August 1936 but in spite of references to

---

[62] Richard Evans has noted similar effects of generational evolution on interpreting the past in Germany in the 1960s: 'Redesigning the Past', *Journal of Contemporary History*, 38, 1 (2003), 9–10.

[63] *ABC* suggested implicitly ('Del gorro frigio', p. 22) that the Spanish gunboat the *Dato* had been the only means of transport of Franco's forces from North Africa and, indeed, 'the first great achievement of the war'.

[64] Pius XI, cited in *La Vanguardia Española*, 1 April 1964, p. 6.   [65] See Chapter 4.

[66] The programme of the POUM is included under a headline suggesting that it represented the potential precursor of '*Chinese* Communism' because, presumably, of the party's inconvenient wartime *anti*-Stalinism (see *ABC*, 1 April 1964, p. 27).

'blood flowing amongst the contending forces', no direct mention of Paracuellos, as though to discuss the mass murder of political enemies might provoke thoughts of the killing of thousands of Republican civilians, over which a blanket of silence continued to be laid.

Viewed from 1964, the end of the civil war was seen as the beginning of the contemporary era, not because the tragedy of the war had provoked a spontaneous demographic shift to escape the past, but because it marked the beginning of the regime's programme of reconstruction which could be propagandised as an unalloyed success. The notion of 'Franco's peace' was reinforced by setting the Caudillo's 'resistance to Hitler' in 1940 alongside his victory in 1939. *Ecclesia* emphasised 'continuity' and 'cohesion' in celebrating the 'firmness' of the General in keeping Spain out of the world war, though much of the historical evidence suggests his instincts and ideological preference to fight alongside the Führer had been thwarted by circumstances beyond his control.[67] In the constructed images, the General would be celebrated for his military prowess and for his generosity and statesmanship. Maintaining the image of resolve tempered by magnanimity, Franco conceded a reprieve (*indulto*) to selected political prisoners in celebration of the peace. The prerogative of granting mercy was claimed as inherent to 'the moral force and Christian spirit of state power', a highly personalised concept of political power encapsulated by use of the term *caudillaje*.[68] The previous *indulto* had been in June 1963 to coincide with the accession of Pope Paul VI and, before that, in October 1961, for prisoners who had served more than twenty uninterrupted years in gaol, to mark the twenty-fifth anniversary of Franco becoming head of state (the origin, according to the legal disposition, of the country's post-war 'moral and material prosperity'). Of 465 political prisoners in Burgos in 1961, only one qualified for release.[69]

Priorities in the present were related to administrative efficiency and international standing, upon which economic modernisation depended. The entire front page of the main national newspaper published in business-oriented Barcelona was taken up with an image of a besuited (not uniformed) Head of State consulting a substantial tome beside heavily laden bookcases. The efficacy of administration, as well as the legitimacy which went with it, was implied by extensive coverage of

[67] 28 March 1964, p. 1. On myths and reality, see Preston, *Franco*, pp. 374–400.

[68] Decree 786, 1 April 1964, *BOE*, 84; *ABC*, 1 April 1964, p. 61. That Franco's monarchical pretension originated in civil war rather than inheritance was the problem for the monarchist opposition. See, e.g., Joaquín Satrústegui, cited in José María Toquero, *Franco y Don Juan* (Barcelona, 1989), pp. 298–9.

[69] Ana, *Decidme*, p. 17. Also, Decree 1,824, 11 October 1961, *BOE*, 244; Decree 1,504, 24 June 1963, *BOE*, 157, 2 July 1963.

the evolution of ministerial portfolios: *ABC* carried no less than fourteen pages of photographs of every one of the ministers of Franco's successive governments, beginning with the wartime Junta de Defensa Nacional. A strong sense of continuity, of the war being present, was accentuated by the ranks of uniforms, military and Falangist, until the roll-call reached the government put in place in July 1962, when the militaristic livery disappeared. The continuity was never more evident than when the Caudillo himself proffered an opinion on constitutional evolution. For Franco, in an interview with *ABC*'s editor, Torcuato Luca de Tena, the war remained 'nuestra Cruzada de Liberación'. When asked about revision of the Fundamental Principles of the Movimiento, he insisted that there was no need 'in our time' (meaning 'his'), since 'they are of great contemporary importance [...] The fruit of great sacrifices, they will be immovable while the current generations are still living.'[70] His monarchist interviewer then referred to the General's own wartime declarations about a future monarch having to be 'a pacifier', a figure not 'from among the victors or the defeated', to which Franco retorted that a 'demo-liberal monarchy' would not be countenanced.[71]

In retrospective 1960s sketches of the economy since 1939, the evident failings of autarky and the hunger in the 1940s were brushed aside.[72] The state syndicates which were devised initially to lead economic organisation had been largely reduced by the 1960s to sponsoring folkloric and gymnastic displays. Attention in 1964 had shifted towards depiction of a new economic master plan begun in 1939 and developing in stages: industrialisation had come first (1940s autarky and mythical 'wealth creators', rather than large-scale black market operators aided by the state); stabilisation was next (through the liberalising economic measures of 1959); followed, apparently seamlessly, by the so-called 'development plans' targeted at specific priorities. The symbolic importance of the reconstruction of war-damaged towns was evident, as was that of new towns, such as those in the Vegas de Guadiana, produced as a by-product of vast irrigation projects, several of which were named in honour of Franco. In 1964 many became sites of celebration involving ex-combatant groups, ex-prisoner associations and the Falange. The social costs were little discussed.[73] Making a point of crediting the best-known Catalan

---

[70] *ABC*, 1 April 1964, p. 60.
[71] Wartime interviews with *ABC*, 19 July 1937, and *Jornal do Brasil*, January 1938. Francisco Franco, *Palabras del Caudillo* (Madrid, 1939), pp. 169, 227.
[72] In *ABC*, food consumption published data began in 1952–3 rather than drawing attention to the years of hunger in the 1940s, and ended in 1959 to avoid showing that the improvement between 1960 and 1964 was not dramatic.
[73] Loss of land and livelihood: Botey Vallès, *Relats*, pp. 61, 106.

conservative of the past, Francesc Cambó, for good ideas about regional development, the architect of plans for growth Laureano López Rodó, a contemporary of Fraga, portrayed development as an 'instrument of solidarity', both between Madrid and Barcelona as well as between producers and consumers.[74] The less positive picture of rural decline and urban housing crisis were debated only at the margins of decision making, usually at a local level. In *ABC*'s '25 años de paz' souvenir, claims that the standard of living had improved, by reference for example to the ratio of motor cars to population (1:30 in 1964; roughly equivalent to Portugal) were interspersed with extracts from José Calvo Sotelo's speeches as a way of comparing 1936 accusations of 'anarchy' and economic crisis under democracy with the post-war 'prosperity' under authoritarian government.[75]

A final and fascinating part of the 1964 commemorative edition of *ABC* was composed largely of visions of the war and predictions for the future solicited from a number of prominent commentators, none of them military men, whose observations were grouped according to generations: those who had reached 'full political maturity' before the civil war or during it; those forming the 'combatant generation' who fought in the conflict; and those who reached maturity after 1939.[76] The monarchist editorial position was clearly evident: the political future, as viewed from 1964, was based implicitly here on Franco's designated successor, Prince Juan Carlos. The monarchy would represent a form of political *continuismo*, it was argued: 'like it or not, the new Spanish monarchy will always have its origins in national history crystallised by 18 July'.[77] The canvassing of views was preceded by extracts from Franco's speeches, largely made in the 1940s, making the immutability of the Fundamental Principles abundantly clear. By stating his own '*recuerdos*' of the Second Republic, the General, according to the editorial, defined the 'quintessence' of what had to be learned from that experience of 'blood, mire and tears'.[78] The hand of Manuel Fraga can be discerned in the argument that the Principios Fundamentales (which were reproduced in full over six pages) were not in any way fascist, but

---

[74] On development and state administration, see López Rodó, *Desarrollo y política* (Madrid, 1970).

[75] Extracts were also included from *Autopsia de la República* (1961) by Joaquín Calvo Sotelo (1905–93), the younger brother of the murdered monarchist leader.

[76] No women were consulted.

[77] Juan Claudio Güell y Churruca, 'Lealtad, continuidad, y configuración del futuro', *ABC*, 11 June 1957, cited in 'Futuro', *ABC*, 1 April 1964, p. 90.

[78] On Franco's post-1956 thoughts, see also Fundación Nacional Francisco Franco (ed. LuisSuárez), '*Apuntes*' *personales del Generalísimo sobre la República y la guerra civil* (Madrid, 1989).

had a similar constitutional meaning as the principles of 1789 had for the modern French state, or the Declaration of Independence in the US, Spain's most important ally in the 1960s. The socio-economic future depended, meanwhile, on 'transformation', to be achieved with the help of technology, governmental action and financial orthodoxy, anchored by general European prosperity, without 'radicalism'.[79]

All of the group which were of Franco's own generation were focused firmly on 14 April 1931 and the Republic as pernicious, a way of remembering which was essentially self-serving and justificatory. Several insisted on using the term 'Cruzada' and emphasised political continuity. Amongst them was José de Yanguas Messía (born in 1890), the General's wartime ambassador to the Holy See, who had played a role in justifying to the Vatican the war as a 'crusade'. During and after the civil war Yanguas participated in drawing up the Law for the Protection of the State and other measures of repression; he continued, in 1964, to see the conflict as having prevented the country becoming 'a satellite of the Soviet Union'. The sacrifices achieved could not be compromised, he insisted, although recollection of the war should not be the cause of 'an indefinite Cold War between Spaniards'.[80] The civil war diplomat José Antonio Sangróniz also made reference to the shaping of generational attitudes, though (unlike Ortega y Gasset, the theorist of history as generational succession) his focus was on the influence of events experienced in childhood. He maintained that for a young man of his generation, that of Franco, contemporary history began with the loss of Cuba in 1898, while for young men in 1964 the contemporary era began with the fall of the monarchy in 1931.[81] Others, such as José Múgica, were more Orteguian and pointed to the contradictions between wartime and post-war generations which were now reaching critical maturity.[82] Sangróniz was certainly not alone in his preoccupation with the legacy of war understood as part of a national essence and heritage which already by the 1960s seemed to belong to a different age. The lesson as he saw it was to search for 'a common denominator amongst Spaniards to achieve the continuity of our historical destiny'. The writer Joaquín Calvo Sotelo (younger brother of José, born in 1905), claimed that 'only through war'

---

[79] Carlos Ollero, 'El futuro de las estructuras sociales', pp. 94–5; Juan Sardá, 'El futuro de la recuperación económica', pp. 97–8, both in 'Futuro', *ABC*, 1 April 1964.

[80] 'Futuro', *ABC*, 1 April 1964, p. 99. Yanguas Messía had been demoted as Professor of Law with the arrival of the Republic in 1931.

[81] Sangróniz was born a year after the Spanish-US war, though the influence of 'el Desastre' was strongly felt for several years. See, e.g., also Joaquín Bau (b.1897); Raimundo Fernández Cuesta (b.1897); Alberto Martín Artajo (b.1905).

[82] On Ortega and generations, see Chapter 1.

had it been possible for Spain to be 'saved': 'those who made the war are always looked upon by their children in a special way. Sometimes as heroes, sometimes as barbarians; sometimes with understanding, sometimes without [. . .] I would dare to suggest that we deserve not only their approval but also their own children's gratitude [. . .] The peace of these twenty-five years and those which are to come was paid for with the same blood that runs through their veins.'[83] Joaquín's nephew Luis Emilio Calvo Sotelo, son of the monarchist leader murdered in July 1936, had recently and publicly celebrated the state execution of Julián Grimau (in Carabanchel prison on 20 April 1963) for 'crimes' emanating from the civil war. *ABC* and Manuel Fraga had publicly defended Grimau's torture and execution.[84]

Commentary from 'the combatant generation', of which the liberal monarchist Santiago Nadal, quoted at the beginning of this chapter, was a member, tended towards a more searching, and belated, critique of the war's legacy. Nadal maintained, for example, that because they had lived in the shadow of war, those who reached the age of twenty-five on 1 April 1964 ought not to be thought of as 'young' at all. The young, he suggested, were those instead who were born into 'the world of the teenager' in the 1950s, an era freer of the war, focused on sport, physically better developed 'with vitamins', an implicit contrast with the effects of hunger on infants in the early 1940s: 'for those born on 1 April 1939 our civil war carries with it no living confrontation. At most it is about their first memories, in which appear the reactions of their parents to the recently ended civil conflict. But for the teenagers there is not even this.' Other monarchists of this generation, including Joaquín Satrústegui (also born in 1909), who had played a pivotal role in the Munich meeting of oppositionists in 1962 and spent a year in forced internal exile as a result, focused on overcoming the war and integrating the country within Europe. Some who were more compromised by association with the regime were less outspoken. Florentino Pérez-Embid (b.1918), in control of censorship as Director General of Information for much of the 1950s, viewed the civil war as an armed plebiscite which decided on a monarchist future. From the pages of the Opus Dei-inspired journal *Arbor*, Pérez-Embid had been a critic of Laín Entralgo's diagnosis of Spain's 'problem' as a historic resistance to plurality; he now supported the new orthodoxy which reduced the country's problems to technical

---

[83] 'Futuro', *ABC*, 1 April 1964, p. 100.

[84] Nicolás Sartorius and Javier Alfaya, *La memoria insumisa* (Madrid, 1999), pp. 241–4. On newspapers and state police, see, e.g., José Ignacio San Martín, *Servicio especial: a las órdenes de Carrero Blanco* (Barcelona, 1983), pp. 231–2.

and economic, rather than ideological, questions.[85] Laín's most prominent critic, Rafael Calvo Serer, was similarly forward-thinking, not prepared to look back at a fragmented pre-war history, but to see the conflict as marking a starting point in Spanish history. The leading academic psychiatrist Juan José López Ibor (b.1908) saw this form of '*progresismo*' as a sign of confidence in the future, although he warned that it could also take 'ideological' form. Gregorio Marañón Moya (b.1914), a wealthy lawyer and son of the internationally renowned, formerly Republican, academic and doctor, focused on the wartime sacrifices of the junior officers, the *alféreces provisionales*, with whom he had served, as many middle-class youths of his generation had, and on remaining 'alert' during the 'natural evolution' of the state.

There were also decidedly more retrograde interpretations of the relationship of the past to the future. The Carlist Bernardo de Salazar was content to laud the role of the Requeté, the Carlist militia, in suppressing 'the Bolshevik horde'. Eugenio Vegas Latapié (b.1907), a leading figure of Acción Española (AE) in the 1930s, plotter against the Second Republic and, later, close adviser of the exiled Juan de Borbón in the 1940s, warned that if 'the victors rest on their laurels they may awake to catastrophe'; the aristocratic Francisco Moreno y Herrera (Marqués de Eliseda, b.1909), pre-war financial backer of the Falange and supporter of AE, saw the Republic simply as 'a heresy', remaining fixated on 'contemptible separatists', insisting on the need for the 'repetition of the truths' of what the war signified for national unity.[86] Beyond this intransigence and the contrasting conservative monarchism already discussed, there was a diversity of other emphases about the meaning of the civil war twenty-five years afterwards. Figures related to the Falange, such as Pedro Gamero del Castillo (b.1910), a one-time protégé of the pro-Axis Foreign and Interior Minister Serrano Suñer, struck radical poses. Gamero was critical of monarchism and concentrated on the development of institutions, the need for an 'authentic' public sphere, and was critical of 'restorationist impatience'.[87] Gamero had become a wealthy businessman by this time. Rafael García Serrano (b.1917), a writer whose novels of the 1940s and 1950s contained a level of critique of the privileged and who had fought on the Nationalist side and been injured during the war, advocated greater recognition of 'those motives

---

[85] Díaz, *Pensamiento*, pp. 55–7.
[86] For background about Vegas Latapié and Moreno y Herrera, see Pedro Carlos González Cuevas, *Acción Española: teología, política y nacionalismo autoritario en España (1913–1936)* (Madrid, 1998), especially (on Moreno), pp. 271–6.
[87] Emilio Romero, *El futuro de España* (Madrid, 1958), p. 47.

of the enemy which had been valid', arguing that both sides had fought in what was 'a revolution', from which the post-war reality was realised. The gap between society and politics was also a preoccupation of another journalist, the editor of *Pueblo* Emilio Romero (b.1917), who perceived 1964 as marking a 'frontier' between a 1950s' 'decline of ideologies' and growing calls for prosperity.[88] The less thoughtful José María Sánchez-Silva (b.1911), a Falangist writer whose Republican father had been exiled in 1939, ventured no further than seeing Franco himself as the very personification of Spain's past, present and future. Like many in the 1960s, the novelist Ignacio Agustí, one-time Catalan nationalist who later joined the Falange, affirmed that peace had prepared the country for alignment with Europe. The writer Pedro de Lorenzo (b.1917) called for a form of solidarity 'in which all Spaniards could find a place', and Juan Manuel Fanjul (b.1914), son of the famously executed rebel general and also an *alférez* (reserve officer) during the war, believed that a 'new social formula' in defence against 'the Marxist east' required a juridical order to safeguard 'public peace' and, in the aftermath of the execution of Julián Grimau, the protection of 'human rights': 'the generation of '36 will not be frightened of the world which approaches as long as it is genuinely more just'.[89] The architect Miguel Fisac (b.1914) argued that there had not really been peace since 1939 because peace required more than a simple absence of war; it consisted of 'equality of respect and consideration'. He did not wish Spain to forget the war, he said, but there should remain no trace of the categories of 'victors and vanquished', drawing attention to the social effects of urban marginalisation of migrants. He was also critical of the concentration of power which he felt had been a necessity at the end of the war but which was now unrepresentative (to say the least).[90] The dissident Catholic lawyer Jaime Miralles (b.1921) was a civil war hero (also an *alférez provisional*) who had nonetheless been condemned and sanctioned, like Satrústegui, for attending the conciliatory meeting of internal oppositionists and exiled Republicans in Munich in 1962. The regime, fearful that memories of the civil war might be weakened by 'neutralists' and their attempts at reconciliation, condemned Munich as a replaying of the Republic which

---

[88] Alongside eulogies to Franco and the system of which he was a part, for the theme of economic modernisation based on a more radical political change than most monarchists desired, see Romero, *Cartas a un príncipe* (Madrid, 1964); and *Cartas al pueblo soberano* (Madrid, 1965). Like other Falangist writers, Romero also acted as a state censor. On the significance of new, post-war generations: *Futuro de España*, pp. 44–5.

[89] His brother had also been killed, at the Montaña barracks in Madrid in 1936. 'Futuro', *ABC*, 1 April 1964, p. 105.

[90] Fisac, 'Urbanismo suicida', *CPED*, January 1964.

212 Memories of war during the Franco years

'had led to revolts and murders' and, like Satrústegui, Miralles and others were exiled for a year.[91] In 1964, he would invoke the papal encyclical *Pacem in terris* in maintaining that peace involved 'the healing of wounds' more than merely 'the silence which follows the battle'; the basis of legitimacy, moreover, was evolution since history did not belong to a single generation.[92] Later, during the regime's crisis years of the early 1970s, Miralles would be gaoled for his role in the campaign for judicial reform.

The first post-conflict generation, those who were 'children of the war', too young for wartime combat, also presented contrasting images. These ranged from the dour reflections of Federico Silva Muñoz (b.1923), shortly to become Franco's Minister of Public Works, to personal reflections on childhood loss. Pedro Muñoz-Seca, whose rightist father had been executed at Paracuellos in November 1936, provided a tribute to the mothers, widows and orphans, on both sides, who had lost loved ones: they were a 'living testament to the sacrifice'. The Conde de Zumalacarregui distinguished between the childhood experiences of those old enough to have lived through the war and those born after it.[93] The future-oriented position adopted by the nephew of the monarchist leader killed in July 1936, Leopoldo Calvo Sotelo (b.1926), who would become prime minister in 1981, had no time for a critique of the war and its repressive aftermath, as such, but was based on fear that the conflict's legacy threatened to hold back economic opportunities and development. Calvo Sotelo maintained that 'memory of violence is neither the only nor the best antidote to violence'; other means to peace, advocated in a paternalistic way and somewhat belatedly, consisted of 'greater culture and wealth, better distributed, little by little' and contacts with other states which were 'experts in peaceful coexistence'.[94] In similar terms, the constitutional lawyer Jesús Fueyo Álvarez, head of the Instituto de Estudios Políticos, implied that periodic states of emergency and martial law were hardly optimal for capitalism: modernity (and by this he meant 'social democracy [...] without ideologies') was desirable because it would be capable of 'normalising and concretising economic and social tensions'.[95] Alfonso Osorio, Under-Secretary of Trade

---

[91] Joaquín Satrústegui, *Cuando la transición se hizo posible: el contubernio de Munich* (Madrid, 1993), pp. 15–17, 36–7. Miralles would intervene in favour of the censored author Antonio Menchaca in 1968. Javier Muñoz Soro, *Cuadernos para el Diálogo (1963–1976)* (Madrid, 2005), p. 44. For attacks on 'neutralists', see Hermandad de Alféreces Provisionales, *Generación del 36*, pp. 12, 20, 89–93; Marrero, *Trust de cerebros*; Jorge Vigón, 'Meditación', *ABC*, 17 July 1956.

[92] 'Futuro', *ABC*, 1 April 1964, p. 109.   [93] 'Futuro', *ABC*, 1 April 1964, pp. 110–11.

[94] 'Futuro', *ABC*, 1 April 1964, p. 110.

[95] See also Jesús Fueyo Álvarez, *Desarrollo político y orden constitucional* (Madrid, 1964), pp. 22–3, 35–6, 49–56.

in 1965 and later a founding member of the Christian Democratic Tácito group during the transition to democracy, focused on the significance of youth as the impulse behind 'economic take-off'.

Economic development entailed social mobilisation, however. As universities grew, higher education would represent an opportunity to escape from stultifying provincial life which seemed to be stuck in the past.[96] The consequent tensions, within an authoritarian system, were understood by those with power as a 'crisis of obedience'. Those born during the civil war and its aftermath matured between the ages of eighteen and twenty-five during the period from 1954 to 1964, as it became evident that social change in Spain had accelerated. Whilst they were too young to have participated in the plebiscite of March 1947 on the Law of Succession (confirming the state as non-democratic), they were expected to celebrate the anniversary of peace in 1964.[97] Barely tolerated opposition groups maintained that there was a consequent individual and collective resentment, 'fruit of the bloody upheavals of recent years, as in other societies at the time: totalitarian systems, bloody repression, world war, defeat in war, penury and distress of the post-war years', which was felt particularly by the young and especially in Spain where defeat had led directly to Franco's rule.[98] The 1960s would became an era of political protest and struggle for a minority of the young who already felt some freedom as a result of Vatican II and were increasingly engaging with critical thought associated, not least, with the movement against the Vietnam war. University, for some, was a first opportunity to learn that it had not only been the Francoist side which had suffered the consequences of the civil war. A more adventurous and critical literature played a part: Miguel Delibes' dissection of provincial conservatism in his novel *Cinco horas con Mario* and Juan Goytisolo's autobiographically informed meditation on the problem of Spanishness, *Señas de identidad*, both appeared in 1966.[99] A new perspective on the past was also opened for the younger generation by meeting Spanish emigrants, both migrant workers and political exiles.[100]

[96] University places expanded in the 1960s from a low level in comparative European terms: graduating students rose from 63,000 in 1959 to over 115,000 in 1967–8.

[97] 'Explicación de un voto', *CPED*, January 1964, pp. 20–1.

[98] '¿Crisis de obediencia o crisis de confianza?', *CPED*, 2, November 1963, p. 5.

[99] Miguel Delibes' *Cinco horas con Mario* (Barcelona, 1966) and Juan Goytisolo's *Señas de identidad* (Mexico, 1966). On opening up for new generation, see also Goytisolo, *Disidencias*, p. 304.

[100] E.g., Piñero Valverde, 'Mi viejo álbum', pp. 72, 75.

A key moment in this politicisation was the 1965 dismissal by the regime of three Madrid University professors because they had accompanied students in a peaceful protest for reform of student representation, until then monopolised by the Falangist SEU.[101] The academic tribunal which heard the case of Aranguren, García Calvo and Tierno Galván was headed by the former CEDA deputy for Valladolid and postwar professor of history at Murcia University, Luciano de la Calzada, who was also provincial President of the Hermandad de Alféreces Provisionales.[102] He had accepted the task which others had declined to carry out, though, at the time, most professors also remained silent. In 1970 he would be awarded the Gran Cruz del Orden de Cisneros al Mérito Político.[103]

The war memories of those who would entrench the bunker mentality exemplified by Calzada remained unswerving and would be publicly aired increasingly as the regime was threatened by popular mobilisation and by radical Basque nationalism. Following the requiem mass in Vitoria for the Chief Inspector of the Guipúzcoa Brigada Social, assassinated by a combat unit of the radical Basque nationalist movement ETA on 3 August 1968, a rightist demonstration was mounted of several hundred people with Spanish flags and banners which read: 'Viva la unidad de España'.[104] The persistence and heightened display of crusade memories, which foreshadowed repression and threats to democratisation to come, was typified by the Captain-General of Catalonia, Alfonso Pérez Viñeta, during a commemorative speech on 1 April 1968, the twenty-ninth anniversary of the end of the civil war, when military decorations were awarded to members of the Hermandad de Alféreces

---

[101] Miguel A. Ruiz Carnicer, *El Sindicato Español Universitario (SEU), 1939–1965* (Madrid, 1996), pp. 374–9; Pedrero Sánchez, 'Las cartas', pp. 117, 121; Castilla del Pino, *Casa del olivo*, pp. 332–3, 366–9.

[102] On his determination to keep the war alive: Calzada, 'El espíritu del 18 de Julio'. For his 1934 political views: 'Derogación de la legislación sectaria y antiespañola' (1934), cited in Antonio Elorza, 'El nacionalismo conservador de Gil Robles', in Elorza, *La utopía anarquista, procedido de otros trabajos* (Madrid, 1973), pp. 262–3: 'All the rest – Jews, arch-heretics, Protestants, communists, Moors [*moriscos*], encyclopedists, francophiles, Masons, Krausists, liberals, marxists – were and are a dissenting minority outside [our] nationality, and outside and against the *patria* is the anti-*patria*.'

[103] Laín Entralgo, *Descargo*, pp. 465–6; Antonio Martínez Sarrión, *Una juventud* (Madrid, 1997), p. 28; José Álvarez Cobelas, *Envenenados de cuerpo y alma* (Madrid, 2004), pp. 150, 156; *La Vanguardia Española*, 18 July 1970.

[104] In 1999, as victims of the wartime military rebels were beginning to be publicly remembered, the Inspector's remaining family would be awarded compensation by the state. Critics felt that some victims of political violence were deemed to be deserving and others not. *El País*, 19 November 2002; Francisco Espinosa, *Contra el olvido: Historia y memoria de la guerra civil* (Barcelona, 2006), pp. 190–1.

Provisionales, in which an 'orden extraordinaria' was issued to troops to 'ensure that the Victory does not lose its validity':

the army is here, safeguard of all that is permanent, backbone and military arm of the nation, vigilant, disciplined, well-instructed. Now, as then, should the moment arrive, it is ready to destroy those who would attempt to turn away from Spain's essence and prepared to die for the ideals for which the greatest part of our youth fell to the cry of '¡Viva España!' or '¡Arriba España!'[105]

Despite extreme pronouncements such as these, official memory during the 1960s was generally less catastrophist than this vision of the past. Commemoration in 1964 of the twenty-fifth anniversary of the end of the civil war, used to celebrate twenty-five years of 'Franco's peace', would be a pivotal moment. As far as representatives of new generations of privileged élites were concerned, war memories could be lived with provided that their prescriptions for safeguarding the viability of state and economy in the future were heeded. Memory would, in theory, not be permitted to become an obstacle to social and economic development. The key idea of the decade was 'normalisation': of memory, history and economy. Since the idea was constructed upon efforts by regime loyalists within the state administration and at a local level to play down and distort the history of the war, its violence and the painful aftermath, 'normalisation' was not, however, the same thing as reconciliation. Some Francoists maintained that life had returned to normal rapidly after 1939 and that the effects of the conflict had been 'liquidated' quickly and effectively. This was belied by the efforts made from the early 1960s to peddle a new myth of the conflict as a war between brothers, a reconfiguration and broadening of the cultural trauma of the war, but an image profoundly contradicted by the selective historical narrative publicised by the regime which continued to exclude 'the defeated'. The process of normalising memory was therefore little more than a pragmatic makeover. These limits to the process did not prevent the protestations of Francoist interest groups and influential 'meaning makers' who coalesced around what they guarded jealously as their exclusive possession of the trauma and sacrifices of the war, fearing the possible negative effects of 'forgetting'.

For now, ties between the Church, the army and the state strengthened the political status quo. As well as use of the military and the judicial apparatus to suppress dissent, Francoist power was wielded in the form of the theocratic, confessional state which formally defined national identity. Catholic vows continued to be sworn by all those becoming members of legal public institutions, including those of

[105] *La Vanguardia Española*, 2 April 1968.

the state itself. It was assumed that Christian principles would be constituent elements of all civil legislation. Any proposals in contravention of
Catholic dogma or Christian morality would, in effect, be anti-
constitutional. Religious freedom was still read through the categories
of heresy and a threat to the unity and historical idiosyncrasy of the
Spanish people and state. Social change had accelerated at the same time
through burgeoning urbanisation and the gradual modernisation of the
Church. Denial of reconciliation began to be reassessed. Institutional
resistance to political and constitutional reform continued – a resistance
fuelled by the legacy of the civil war – and would lead ultimately, in the
early 1970s, to a crisis-fuelled end to the Franco regime.

8 Contesting 'Franco's peace': transformation from below in the 1960s

> Fear had been assumed and dealt with, not through withdrawal, but through a form of complicity, resulting in a kind of fleeing forwards in order to achieve things deserving of praise; later this fear demanded an often impossible payment in return, in a manner which thrust deeply into a person for the rest of his or her life.[1]

'Normalisation' and society

As Chapter 7 suggested, when significant dates in the life of a people previously in conflict with itself come to be celebrated, questions related to coexistence are reopened, often with great intensity. The Franco regime's solution was to 'normalise' history and memory by replacing the crusade narrative with the mask of 'fratricidal conflict', supposedly confirmed by 'objective' consideration of the past. Neither the new narrative of the war nor state-sponsored history writing permitted the story of the defeated to emerge. Having explored in Chapter 7 the public politics of the past and of memory in 1964, in this chapter I focus on society and social change. Even more than the 1940s and 1950s, the social 'story' of the 1960s is of migration. In 1964 alone, according to the Instituto Español de Emigración, some half a million individuals in Spain left their province of residence to live in another.[2] As we have seen, migration presented a possible alternative to the 'silence' of reimposed normality in daily life after 1939, especially in rural communities torn apart by wartime conflict. Beginning with 'Year Zero' the victors defined what was meant by 'normality'. The Francoist mayor of a small town in Huelva ignored the bitter local violence of the civil war when he explained in 1963 how 'once the military passed through, order was restored and little by little things have returned to normal since then'.[3]

---

[1] Castilla del Pino, *Casa del olivo*, p. 317.
[2] Salustiano del Campo, 'Los procesos ecológicos y sociales en la inmigración a Barcelona', *Conversaciones sobre inmigración interior* (Barcelona, 1966), p. 65.
[3] Collier, *Socialists*, p. 165. Also p. 210.

This continuity between the 1940s and 1960s is important. The psychiatrist Carlos Castilla del Pino, whose words are cited above, argued in the 1960s that both the suppression of memories originating in the violence and imposed socio-cultural marginalisation had deeply damaging effects, in part because one way of repressing a painful past was to submit oneself to the strict moral code of social norms which was reimposed after 1939. This conclusion was based on his own clinical practice and on Marxist and Freudian theory, a potent mix in thinking about the interaction of repressed memories, exploitative economic development, and pathology.[4] Castilla del Pino had become active in the underground opposition of the PCE, and because his classes held in his Córdoba clinic in the late 1950s and 1960s were considered to be political they would be raided by the Brigada Político Social.[5] The collective silence of the 1940s was not a political myth invented retrospectively by anti-Francoists; it was maintained long afterwards as a form of complicity even within families.[6] When, in the 1960s, Sabina de la Cruz returned to her family's pueblo in Valladolid to locate the burial site of her father who, along with others, in August 1936 had been taken away by Falangists and shot, nobody would speak to her about the war; it was as though her father had left no trace whatever.[7]

In October 1955, Castilla del Pino had made an entry in his diary which seemed to relate to this silence, a 'consciousness of complicity' beneath the surface, within the psyche of many of the troubled patients who visited his consulting room and had witnessed communal violence: 'There are many people who allow things to happen. What they don't realise is that they also "kill" when they let others do the killing.'[8] People on both sides, in other words, had painful memories to deal with and not only because some were the direct perpetrators or victims of violence. In the 1960s, economic liberalism and the free market had a 'unifying' effect, seeming to smooth over differences of social class. For many across the social and wartime divisions, the consumer society

---

[4] See Freud on repression of memories and 'normalisation': 'we may imagine that what is repressed exercises a continuous straining in the direction of consciousness, so that the balance has to be kept by means of a steady counter-pressure'. Sigmund Freud, 'Repression' (Die Verdrängung) (1915), *Standard Edition of the Complete Psychological Works of Sigmund Freud*, 24 vols. (London, 1924–50), vol. XIV, p. 143. See also José Luis Abellán, 'La antropología dialéctica de Carlos Castilla del Pino', in Abellán, *La cultura en España* (Madrid, 1971), pp. 143–52.

[5] Castilla del Pino, *Casa del olivo*, pp. 307–8, 312.

[6] E.g. Goytisolo, *Coto vedado*, pp. 63–5.

[7] Gustavo Martín Garzo, 'Las enseñanzas de Antígona', *El País*, 24 August 2009; Cruz, 'Una familia rota', pp. 79–84.

[8] Castilla del Pino, *Casa del olivo*, p. 317.

became a form of refuge; with the satisfaction or pursuit of modern desires within a repressively traditional environment, however, came the threat of guilt.[9] Behaviour against post-war norms which had been considered as dissent in the 1940s, was by the 1960s seen as 'failure to adapt', leading to self-marginalisation or 'abnormality'.[10] This, according to Castilla del Pino's argument, was fundamental to understanding life during the dictatorship, and his case notes, published in 1966, will inform elements of this chapter.

The violent past followed people as they moved from place to place. The memory of a migrant who left his home town in Seville in 1963, where more than three hundred were killed in the post-war Francoist repression and whose father was imprisoned for three and a half years, leaves little doubt about the extent of the destruction:[11] 'it was complete annihilation'. Physical violence made other forms of coercion and repression possible. Property and economic resources, as we have seen, were monopolised by the victors: 'We lost everything: the rooms we had, the few pieces of furniture we possessed, clothes, and family mementos [...] We had to remake our lives [...] without knowing why [...] And I remember my trembling mother telling us: "Don't say anything outside, in the street, they'll kill us. You keep quiet."' The father, once released, also kept silent, though some nights he would listen to the Communist Party's clandestine station known as Radio Pirenaica.[12] For many migrants to urban centres of population and production, year zero was not 1939, as the Franco regime itself claimed, because with the end of the war they were plunged 'backwards' into conditions not seen for many years before the war. The new starting point would be the moment of leaving rural life behind. What followed for most was a life of material and political – and, for some, emotional – difficulty and sacrifice. These challenges formed the crucial 'micro' ingredients which made possible the macro 'miracle' of economic development.[13]

Integration with the booming global economy of the 1960s and the possibility of mass consumerism was compared by many with the dearth of the 1930s which were recalled as an era when 'consumer goods' meant

[9] Piñero Valverde, 'Mi viejo álbum', p. 64. Also Vázquez Montalbán, 'Para una nueva conciencia nacional catalana', in Solé, *Inmigrantes*, pp. 9–13.

[10] Castilla del Pino, *Estudio sobre la depresión*, which sold surprisingly well.

[11] Botey Vallès, *Relats*, pp. 70, 72–3, 81. Similar despair in rural Catalonia, p. 74; hunger and misery at end of war in Barcelona, p. 75.

[12] The name popularly given to the PCE's Radio España Independiente (founded in July 1941 and broadcast from Moscow) was designed to create an impression of proximity to the Pyrenees, symbolic of the north, of Catalonia, and of escape.

[13] See, for example, the testimonies in Botey Vallès, *Relats*, pp. 111–29. Also Castilla del Pino, *Estudio sobre la depresión*, pp. 98–103.

only food and, at best, adequate clothing too.[14] Rural strikes, like the bitter anti-state actions of the 1930s, were no longer possible after 1939. Working-class consciousness in the shadow of defeat and of military government would coalesce gradually around new objectives and a collective identity based increasingly on urban existence. This gradual homogeneity would contribute to social integration from the late 1950s; during the 1960s there would be industrial strikes over pay and working conditions and, in the 1970s, collective struggle for democratisation of the state rather than its overthrow.[15] Industrialism, based on large, increasingly rationalised, factories and mines, would produce a democratic political culture of militancy based on factory elections and organised collective bargaining with employers. Material expectations also increased amongst a new, growing, and more technocratic middle class; at the same time, dissatisfied sections of the 'old middle class', including lower-ranking military officers, state functionaries, municipal civil servants, and small traders, began to feel that opportunities for upward mobility were ever more restricted.[16] While graduations from the military academies slumped in the 1960s, the managerial stratum became more influential as rational organisation and technology were accepted and applied across ever wider sectors of industry and service.[17] This technocratic 'class' was imbued with a post-war cult of education and pressed for investment in learning, swelling the growing body of university students who increasingly protested against the regime which they saw as 'stagnant'.

Expansion of higher education made it more difficult for the state to control information. Franco's Minister of Information, Manuel Fraga, maintained in 1961 that in the early stages of any period of 'historical acceleration', with society becoming rapidly urbanised, control through the family and the school was inevitably more difficult.[18] This was to do with not only mass society but also generational attitudes. In some of its first issues during the early 1960s, the oppositionist *Cuadernos para el Diálogo* published a series of imagined conversations between a conservative father who had experienced the civil war and his son, born after

---

[14] Fraser, *Blood*, p. 243. Statistically, there was no mass consumer society until the end of the 1960s. See José María Marín, Carme Molinero and Pere Ysàs, *Historia política, 1939–2000* (Madrid, 2001), p. 160. See also Fundación FOESSA, *Informe . . . 1970*.

[15] Juliá, 'Obreros y sacerdotes', p. 153; Domènech Sampere, 'La otra cara del milagro'; Botey Vallès, *Relats*, pp. 131–2. On Madrid, 1951–77, Babiano Mora, *Emigrantes*.

[16] On the 'old middle class', see, e.g., Semanas Sociales, *Problemas de la clase media* (Madrid, 1951).

[17] Military graduations had stood at 3,787 in 1961–2 but at only 1,378 by 1967–8. See Manuel Cabeza Calahorra, *Ideología militar hoy* (Madrid, 1973).

[18] Manuel Fraga Iribarne, 'El 18 de julio y la juventud', in Cátedra "General Palafox" de Cultura Militar, *La guerra de liberación nacional* (Zaragoza, 1961), pp. 669–92.

1939, appearing under the title 'Don José y Pepe' ('José Senior and José Junior'), written by the novelist José Luis Martín-Vigil, who had volunteered for the rebel army during the war and afterwards studied for the priesthood.[19] Some of these conversations were broadcast by Catholic radio stations even though they pushed at the censorship boundaries when they were critical of the attitudes of the older generation about the civil war. In one such conversation, for instance, 'Pepe' claimed that his father constantly used the word 'intellectual' as an insult directed at the intelligentsia of the early 1960s, because they were critics of the Franco system just as many of their predecessors had supported the Republican reforms of the 1930s. This particular dialogue began typically with an exchange about responsibility for the vehemence of their conversations.[20] The young are always too passionate, according to the father, to which the son agreed except where the war was concerned: 'in terms of the war, it is your generation which made it, who made it possible [. . .] In that sense, it could be said that you have all remained young.' The father's response reflects a dialogue that would have been possible within many Spanish families, while also highlighting important, recurrent themes in how the recent past was conceived and discussed:

DON JOSÉ: I'll ignore what might be the irony of what you say, a lamentable irony if you think of the deaths and the suffering which the war brought about [. . .] Anyway, I don't know what intellectuals have to do with the war.

PEPE: That's exactly what I say; but it's precisely you (and those like you) who mix the two things.

DON JOSÉ: I don't agree. And besides, there were intellectuals on both sides.

PEPE: [. . .] If one listens to your lot, it would seem that there were only intellectuals amongst the Republicans [. . .]

DON JOSÉ: (*With seriousness.*) I don't like the way you use that language. You say "your lot" as if you were apart from it, as if the conflict that scarred the nation for several generations did not affect you.

PEPE: I was born in 1944, don't forget, father.

DON JOSÉ: But you are my son, you are . . .

PEPE: Heredity does not necessarily condition politics.

DON JOSÉ: What do you mean?

PEPE: That we've reached an age at which we have personal opinions and must choose for ourselves.

DON JOSÉ: (*A little angry.*) Do you want to choose Communism?

---

[19] Martín-Vigil was born in Oviedo in 1919 and had therefore been seventeen in 1936.
[20] 'Don José y Pepe: Paliques con treinta años por medio', *CPED*, 3, December 1963, p. 9.

PEPE: (*With insistence*). [...] Nobody's talking about Communism. But, in any case, if we have to be anti-Communist, surely it's only worth it if we do it out of conviction. [...]

In spite of Pepe's claim that 'the future belongs to us', his father believes his son's generation to be too immature to safeguard the political system and the hierarchical and ordered society which were the achievement of the war and for which a heavy price was paid. He claims, at the same time, that the sacrifices were made for the sake of future generations.

Generational estrangement was but one problem. In the 1960s the regime would have to contend with an epochal shift away from ideology and constrained politics towards the social sphere because of mass urbanisation, the Church's increasing divisions over questions of social justice, and mounting protest.[21] Francoism understood peace as social stasis; those who contested the official celebration of 'Franco's peace' would maintain, however, that peace meant not merely the absence of war but rather the reign of social justice.[22] The essence of the social order was growth and development, evolving relations, and even instability, though it would take a great deal to persuade those who saw Franco as their saviour that conflict could be creative. An important distinction was nonetheless being made within society, at times implicitly, between what in the past might have satisfied 'the *masses*' and that which ought now to be demanded by *citizens*, responsible individuals capable of judgement based on broad dissemination of objective knowledge and public communication, suggesting an important linguistic and conceptual change compared to the 1930s, at least on the part of intellectual critics of the regime.[23] This distinction was borne out by the dynamics of change. Rates of mobility were radically different from one generation to the next. When a sample of Madrid housewives was asked in 1969, for example, what social classes existed in Spain, 57 per cent referred to a tripartite classification, equivalent to 'high, middle and low', and only 26 per cent preferred the dual schema typical of the 1930s and 1940s: 'rich' and 'poor'.[24] War memories and the articulation of cultural trauma would be reshaped by all of these changes.

---

[21] By the early 1960s, opposition to regime brutality (including notorious executions) would emanate from a more developed (though still constrained) civil society. See, e.g., Nicolás Sartorius and Javier Alfaya, *La memoria insumisa* (Madrid, 1999), pp. 243–9.

[22] See Alfonso Ruiz Miguel, 'Paz y guerra', in Elias Díaz and Ruiz Miguel (eds.), *Teoría del estado* (Madrid, 1996), p. 246.

[23] José María Setién, 'Sobre la verdadera paz', *CPED*, 1 (extraordinario), 1963, 13; 'España es diferente', *CPED*, 4, January 1964, 30. See also *Pacem in terris*, paragraph 74.

[24] Fundación FOESSA, *Informe . . . 1970*, pp. 166, 174.

Migration and *chabolismo*

During the 1950s, thirty thousand new migrants arrived in Madrid each year. The population, which had been 1.3 million in 1940, doubled to reach 2.6 million by 1964. In 1956, 20 per cent of inhabitants were living in self-assembled dwellings (*chabolas*) or caves on the margins of the city. Towards the end of 1968 there were 18,000 *chabolas* in the capital and more than 60,000 sublet rooms into which whole migrant families were squeezed.[25] By 1970 the number of *chabolas* in the country as a whole stood at some 110,000, where 600,000 people resided, and the number in the capital by 1973 had risen to between 26,000 and 35,000.[26] By the 1970s, 47 per cent of all Madrid *chabolas* were to be found in the area of Vallecas, the total population of which in 1976 was more than 300,000, more than the entire cities of Córdoba, Murcia or Valladolid.[27] The self-made shacks were vulnerable in bad weather, and the heavy rain in December 1958 led to flooding, forcing hundreds of people from the barrios of Vallecas, Pozo del Tío Raimundo, Carabanchel and Peña Grande to flee to emergency shelters.[28] Even the censored newspapers maintained that the migrant suburbs constituted a 'belt of poverty, abandonment, promiscuity and desperation'. A medical doctor, who had been one of the young mobilised generation of the war and amongst the advancing Nationalists in the Casa del Campo, on the outskirts of Madrid, employed a metaphor of disease in 1964 to express the intractability of the problem of the *chabolas*: 'it is the clearest case of resistance ever known'. He recalled that after the fighting was over in 1939 many of the people of the city without a roof over their heads had 'invaded' the many shacks which had acted as shelters around the battle trenches, used first by Republican forces and then by the rebels. In the end they were burned down: 'it was not pleasant. With the flames went the imprint of our youth which at least had known how to fight.'[29] The authorities frequently announced the end of the *chabola*, but resolution of the 'aesthetic and moral problem', which, according to the general view, originated in the war itself, was beyond the capacity of the regime

---

[25] Pedro Montoliú, *Madrid, villa y corte* (Madrid, 1996), pp. 275–6; Manuel Castells, *The City and the Grassroots* (Berkeley, 1983), p. 218.

[26] Fundación FOESSA, *Estudios sociológicos*, pp. 71, 421; Santos Juliá, David R. Ringrose and Cristina Segura, *Madrid: historia de una capital* (Madrid, 1995), p. 564.

[27] Mayoral, *Vallecas: Las razones*, p. 13.

[28] *La Vanguardia Española*, 24 December 1958, p. 9.

[29] Manuel Pombo Angulo, medical doctor, born 1914: *La Vanguardia Española*, 14 January 1964, p. 9. Also 'Nuestra solidaridad con el pueblo español', *Nuestra Bandera*, 31 May 1944, pp. 69–70; Marañón Moya, 'El alférez definitivo', in Hermandad de Alféreces Provisionales, *Generación del 36*, pp. 97–8.

and the Madrid slums would become 'a never-ending story' as the city perimeter broadened and migrants became consolidated through employment, marriage and the bearing of children.[30] The next generation would be properly *madrileña*, adapted by force of circumstances with relatively few ties to rural life which, in many cases, had brutalised their parents.[31]

Perception of the difference between rural and urban worlds is multifaceted in the memoir of José López Bulla, a trade union leader of Andalusian origins, born in 1943 in the small town of Santafé (Granada), who emigrated in 1965 as a young man to the textile, construction and metalworking town of Mataró, in the north-eastern area of Greater Barcelona, where the rate of migration was if anything even more vertiginous than in Madrid.[32] López Bulla's working-class consciousness was effectively born in the urban setting, although he would explain his cultural and political roots by reference to the pueblo, his Republican father and uncle and his reading of the Andalusian poet Federico García Lorca. In the city, he would embrace urban culture in all its forms, and for his activism in the PSUC-led Comisiones Obreras he would be arrested and imprisoned in 1967. Like thousands of other rural migrants, many of them born during the first fifteen years or so after the civil war, he saw the city as 'a promised land'.[33] Population growth in Santafé had been halted by the civil war, remaining around 10,000 throughout the 1940s. In an area with a diverse landholding structure, the Guardia Civil had taken control in July 1936, supporting the rebellion, with some popular support, and meeting minimum resistance. The socialist and anarchist trade unions were suppressed and the Republican mayor and councillors were executed by the rebels.[34] *Latifundismo* was not the issue in Santafé, something PCE activists tended to forget when it made

---

[30] See, e.g., *Nueva Alcarria*, 16 November 1968; *Hoja de Lunes*, 23 June 1958, p. 16. On the wartime origins of the 'towns without law', e.g. *ABC*, 14 July 1954, p. 16.

[31] For intergenerational relations in leftist families, see, e.g., Molina, *Los otros madrileños*, pp. 15, 26; Martha Ackelsberg, *Mujeres Libres*: The Preservation of Memory under the Politics of Repression in Spain', in Luisa Passerini (ed.), *Memory and Totalitarianism* (Oxford, 1992), pp. 125–43; Gina Herrmann, 'Voices of the Vanquished: Leftist Women and the Spanish Civil War', *Journal of Spanish Cultural Studies*, 4, 1 (March 2003), 11–29.

[32] López Bulla, *Cuando hice*. Immigration to Barcelona in 1961–4 totalled 443,222: *Conversaciones sobre inmigración*, p. 40.

[33] López Bulla, *Cuando hice*, p. 21. See also Solé, *Inmigrantes*, p. 103; Botey Vallès, *Relats*, p. 99; Candel, *Otros*, p. 118. On the sixth 'cohort' since the generation of '98: see Chapter 1. Also Marías, 'Actitud religiosa', pp. 331–2. At thirty-three in 1976, when he became General Secretary of the Workers' National Commission of Catalonia, López Bulla had entered into the phase of life described by Ortega as 'initiation'.

[34] Arco Blanco, *Hambre de siglos*, pp. 40, 60, 84.

strategic sense later to simplify the country's social conflicts as a clash between 'feudalism' and modernity. In many other areas of Andalucía migration was indeed triggered by crises of monocultural production, as we saw in Chapter 6. Civil war violence had often been much greater in these areas, as, for example, in Lora del Río (Seville), where 3,000 families were dependent on the seasonal and declining olive harvest in 1965 and where the wartime violence had been horrific.[35] In regions with more diverse landholding structures, as in the pasturelands of Granada, the problem was the dearth of land: in 1962, 50 per cent of farming in Santafé was based on holdings of less than a hectare.[36] During the 1960s, one in eight inhabitants of Andalucía would migrate either to urban areas or beyond Spain; in Badajoz, another largely latifundia zone, in the south-west (Extremadura), the proportion was one in three.[37]

Following the general trend in the industrial towns of Barcelona during the post-war period, the population of Mataró, where López Bulla arrived in 1965, grew by 20 per cent in the period 1955–60 and by more than 40 per cent from 1960 to 1965, to almost 60,000. The 77 per cent growth between 1960 and 1970 would be twice the rate of increase in Barcelona as a whole.[38] Some 44 per cent of residents of Mataró in the mid 1960s were born outside Catalonia and almost half the total migrants in the year 1966 were from Andalucía. Even so, the influx to Mataró was relatively small compared to other burgeoning manufacturing towns around Barcelona, such as the industrial suburb of Hospitalet de Llobregat. Some 50,000 people arrived there during the five years from 1961 to 1965; from 50,000 in 1940, the population of Hospitalet was to expand to 240,000 by 1970.[39] Social marginality was an inevitable

---

[35] Juan Manuel Lozano Nieto, *A sangre y fuego: los años treinta en un pueblo anadaluz* (Seville, 2006). See also Chapter 10.

[36] Arco Blanco, *Hambre de siglos*, p. 89. As in other regions: e.g. Botey Vallès, *Relats*, pp. 91, 99.

[37] Luis Pascual Estevill, '¿Estamos tratando a los andaluces como animales de cría y carga?', *ABC*, 16 September 1973.

[38] Rogelio Duocastella, *Mataró: estudio socio-económico y de planificación de servicios sociales*, 2 vols. (Barcelona, 1967), vol. I, p. 0.11; Raimon Bonal, *Mataró 1974* (Barcelona, 1974), pp. 13–14. Mataró had four hundred textile firms in 1966, with some 8,000 employees. The majority produced knitwear; most had fewer than five employees and many relied on women home workers. Duocastella, *Mataró*, vol. I, pp. 2.14, 2.15. There is some evidence that integration was easier in the smaller industrial towns around Barcelona than in centres with an even more accelerated growth. See Lara, *Emigración andaluza*, p. 196.

[39] The years 1950–80 saw a 423 per cent rise in population (from 70,000 to 300,000). See Clara Carme Parramón, 'Polític cultural i migracions, l'Hospitalet, 1960–1980', in Carles Santacana (ed.), *El franquisme al Baix Llobregat* (Barcelona, 2001), pp. 483–505 (p. 484). On similar levels in Sabadell, Solé, *Inmigrantes*, p. 79; on the vast influx to Badalona: *Conversaciones sobre inmigración*, p. 141.

structural consequence of this rapid expansion: the most recent arrivals, mainly from Andalucía, lived furthest from the centre. The 'natural population', established in the nineteenth century, identified with local traditions, attended the Centro Católico, and conversed in Catalan. The first workers' barrios, from where participation in political and union life had sprung before the war, had formerly acted as a force for social cohesion and were the basis of the class-based political identity which was destroyed by the war. Under the dictatorship, the dynamism and specificity of these barrios and the old associations gradually disappeared: 'Gradually, a style of life associated with a consumer society and mass culture became generalised.'[40]

Neither factory life, earning a living in the construction industry, nor social integration were easy, and migrants would report that it took time to be sure about definitively leaving the pueblo, of which, inevitably, there were memories which recurred, even in dreams, decades later. These migrants did not feel quite the same way as many political exiles did that their souls had been split in two or the similar pressures experienced by 'economic migrants' beyond Spain, but when they returned to the pueblo to visit, they felt that they no longer belonged there.[41] Urban economic and social relationships were different to the countryside, though there were also continuities. Work and income in the city were based on the 'clocking' of daily life and depended on the labour power not only of men but also of women and children, both of whom earned less than men.[42] There was also discrimination against migrants; racist attitudes meant that 'outsiders' had frequently been blamed, at times, for the revolutionary violence in Barcelona.[43] The established Catalan population did not live in the shanty dwellings, nor later in migrant barrios, of course, and the derogatory term *charnego*, used by some to describe those from rural society outside Catalonia, marked the

---

[40] Angels Pascual, 'El impacto de la inmigración en una ciudad de la comarca de Barcelona: Hospitalet', in Antoni Jutglar (ed.), *La inmigración en Cataluña* (Barcelona, 1968), p. 74.

[41] López Bulla, *Cuando hice*, pp. 47, 52. On forced migration within Spain as 'exilio', Armando López Salinas, *La Mina* (Barcelona, 1960), p. 39. On dreams, a woman born in Ávila in 1903, migrating to Barcelona in 1950 and speaking in 1979, in Botey, *Relats*, p. 49. On a 'schizophrenic' sense of exile beyond Spain, see, e.g., Plá Brugat, 'La experiencia del regreso', pp. 71–91; Jesús J. Alonso Carballés, 'La construcción de una memoria colectiva del éxodo infantil vasco', in Josefina Cuesta Bustillo (ed.), *Memoria e historia*, special edition of *Ayer*, 32 (1998), 163–93.

[42] López Bulla, *Cuando hice*, pp. 49, 50–3. Also, for Madrid, Díaz Sánchez, *Trabajo de las mujeres*; Babiano Mora, *Emigrantes*. On child and female labour in Mataró, see Duocastella, *Mataró*, vol. II, p. 8.27.

[43] E.g. Fraser, *Blood*, pp. 141, 149.

difference between insiders and outsiders.[44] There was also economic exploitation: immigrants took on the jobs many Catalans did not want.[45] A counterbalance to this was the often positive feeling migrants had about Catalans and Catalonia, sometimes based on an appreciation of a common work ethic, migrants' willingness to adapt, and the sense of hope for the future represented by perceived cultural advancement and even the great geographic distance placed between the old life and the new.[46] Moreover, in the new urban landscape it became possible to express a common class identity and consciousness, something impossible in the rural south since the war. The early post-war migrants arrived in Catalonia at a time when the region was being repressively 'castilianised'.[47] Knowing that many Catalans had also suffered grievously the effects of the civil war, although it was rarely spoken about, contributed to solidarity.[48] One of the young men who fled the south, finding work and solidarity in Mataró, and who became acquainted with López Bulla, was the son of a leftist shot by Falangists in Perchel, a working-class neighbourhood of Málaga which had been devastated by the conflict.[49] Catalonia had witnessed similar social convulsions. One son of Mataró, for example, was the anarchist wartime minister Joan Peiró, who had worked in the town's glass-making cooperative and, as a member of the wartime Comité de Salud Pública, had resolutely criticised Republican violent excesses. At the end of the war he fled to France but was handed back to Franco's authorities by the Nazis, executed in 1942, and buried in Mataró's cemetery.[50]

---

[44] Many believed the post-war influx was politically provoked by the state to dilute Catalan (and Basque) identity. Candel, *Otros*, pp. 120–1; 'Emigración, un tema para denuncia', *Boletín HOAC*, no. 705, cited in Lara, *Emigración andaluza*, pp. 202–3.

[45] Botey Vallès, *Relats*, pp. 114–15, 143; Candel, *Otros*, pp. 89–90; Lara, *Emigración andaluza*, pp. 195–6.

[46] Duocastella, *Mataró*, vol. I, pp. 5.19, 5.29; Solé, *Inmigrantes*, pp. 66, 78, 86; Botey Vallès, *Relats*, p. 122.

[47] Candel, *Otros*, p. 79. The civil war formed a political, social and cultural barrier: 'the Catalonia of before was distinct from that of now [1964]': p. 84.

[48] López Bulla, *Cuando hice*, pp. 115–16, 125–6, 130–3 (urban leftist solidarity); pp. 127–9 (silence in Catalonia).

[49] López Bulla, *Cuando hice*, p. 141. On wartime Perchel, see Richards, 'Biology and Morality'; J. J. Piquer y Jover, 'Consideración etiológica sobre algunas fallas del juicio moral en la disciplina del niño abandonado de la postguerra española', *Actas Españolas de Neurología y Psiquiatría*, 4, 2–3 (1943), 166.

[50] See 'Proyecto de ley por la que se reconocen y amplían derechos y se establecen medidas en favor de quienes padecieron persecución o violencia durante la guerra civil y la dictadura', Número de expediente 121/000099, Congreso de los Diputados, 14 December 2006. Also, Margarida Colomer, *La guerra civil a Mataró, 1936–1939* (Barcelona, 2006), pp. 66, 78, 93–4, 136–8.

Immigrants were on average younger than those born in the town and more than 60 per cent of the active immigrant population were unskilled labourers who had known only deficient schooling, normally until the age of nine or ten because they were needed for work: 'we were not children as they are now' (1979).[51] Many migrants recalled how Catalonia offered the prospect of cultural development and the possibility of aspiring to a life that was more than mere material struggle to survive. In the city, people dressed every day 'as though it were Sunday': 'everyone wore shoes'.[52] In the countryside, status was largely conferred through land ownership, while in the city it could be gained in more diverse ways, through professional qualifications, commercial success or union activism.[53] Social mobility was possible because of higher and steadier wages. As long as the wage could be stretched far enough, consumer goods could be purchased beyond the constrained relations of paternalist dependency on an elite of dominant rural families. In contrast to the rural black market economy and politics of the 1940s and 50s, the law functioned more impartially in the city, alongside an increasingly liberalised and free market, rather than at the behest of the prerogative powers of landowners' agents.[54] In the socially complex city, there were also by the late 1960s the roots of an associational culture which functioned between family and state, including (formally illegal and often suppressed) trade unions, labour lawyers and sections of the Church, inculcating a level of human respect towards migrants and also increasing their sense of their own worth.[55] In industrial Barcelona López Bulla would meet Catholic-Marxist activists and experience a Church very different to that which he had known in the rural south.[56] Although the relative anonymity and facelessness of urban existence were daunting, they were also liberating. In the pueblo 'we looked at each other,

---

[51] 'Gracia', born Zamora, 1933: Botey Vallès, *Relats*, p. 61. See also pp. 53–8; Duocastella, *Mataró*, vol. I, pp. 1.12, 1.14–15, 1.18; Candel, *Otros*, p. 31; López Bulla, *Cuando hice*, pp. 34–5, 119.

[52] On *alpargatas* (rope sandals) hung around the neck in the countryside to save them from wear and put on the feet when entering the village at the end of the working day, see López Salinas's novel, *La Mina*, pp. 12–13. Also, Botey Vallès, *Relats*, pp. 56, 59–60, 64.

[53] Miguel Siguan, 'Actitudes y perspectivas de la inmigración', in *Conversaciones sobre inmigración interior* (Barcelona, 1966) p. 144.

[54] Botey Vallès, *Relats*, p. 71.

[55] López Bulla, *Cuando hice*, pp. 20, 70–5; Botey Vallès, *Relats*, pp. 97, 141. On migrants' own sense of inferiority: e.g. Siguan, 'Actitudes y perspectivas', p. 143.

[56] On the rural influence of the Church, see J. Sánchez Jiménez, 'La jerarquía eclesiástica y el estado franquista: las prestaciones mutuas', *Ayer*, 33 (1999). On the shared social aims of Communists and, increasingly, many Catholics: Castilla del Pino, *Casa del olivo*, pp. 180, 350.

one group at another, in a very distinct way to Mataró'.[57] Rural communities were intimate; the look, gazing at each other, killed time, but glances and expressions also carried their own subtexts related to rigid understandings of power and subordination.

Compared to the city, where time very obviously moved forward (people wore wristwatches, and women dressed in mourning were rarely seen), the repressive weight of tradition was heavy. In rural society, young women, once married, seemed rapidly to age, though the process at times began with a father's death: 'I began to dress in mourning when I was 18 [1951] and didn't cease to until I married at 25.'[58] Tensions within families were thus, in part, a function of surrounding social, economic and political influences; one indirect effect of the civil war was a reassertion of the notion of paternal authority.[59] In rural areas, young people lived rather isolated lives, reliant on family since there was no youth culture as such, with a distinct public identity. Frustrations were at times manifested in a sense of guilt, self-reproach and moral disparagement.[60] For women, the difficulty of reconciling the demands of Catholic family life with an existence beyond domesticity was often manifest. Nevertheless, by the 1960s the family was changing; the take up of state 'marriage dowries' – awarded to men whose wives gave up paid employment on getting married – was in decline. Displacement of the morally constructed traditional family, functioning as a unit of agrarian production, was resisted, however, by paternal authority which was normally unquestioned. The widely accepted role of young women in small-town rural society was to marry or, failing that, to take over the domestic duties of the mother when she became elderly. In many families there were two distinct codes of conduct and morality, one for men and one for women. It was 'bad – simply bad, without rationale' – that a woman might go for a walk on her own, or read works of literature, or stray from the traditional norm, however slightly. Woman was 'for the home and the kitchen, at the service of the husband and the children; the husband has no reason to expose his problems to her'.[61] Such attitudes were part of the legacy of the civil war which had reflected in part

---

[57] López Bulla, *Cuando hice*, pp. 25–7, 45. Also, Botey Vallès, *Relats*, p. 119.

[58] Botey Vallès, *Relats*, p. 89.

[59] Carlos Castilla del Pino, *Estudio sobre la depresión*, p. 63; *Casa del olivo*, pp. 314–17.

[60] See also Castilla del Pino, *La culpa: un estudio sobre la depresión y teoría de los sentimientos* (Madrid, 1968).

[61] Castilla, *Estudio sobre la depresión*, p. 95. Also, Folguera, 'Construcción de lo cotidiano'; Carme Molinero, 'Mujer, franquismo, fascismo: la clausura forzada en un "mundo pequeño"', *Historia Social*, 30 (1998), 97–117.

a violent reaction against the Republic's alleged 'disordering' of sexual-social relations, as Castilla del Pino's case notes illustrate.

'Carmen M.', for example, was a 38-year-old single woman and teacher who lived in a small community in the province of Córdoba. Her teaching position in a lay Catholic school – which she took up secretly at first because her father disapproved – would allow her some limited social position as long as she remained 'chaste' and carried out the tasks before her with 'exemplary virtue'.[62] At the same time she was talented in artisanal crafts which she also taught when she could. It was noted how she was 'rigid with herself', resigned to family and community constraints and incapacitated by depression each spring, dreaming intensely of *'impurezas'* ('unchaste things'), even harming herself physically. In one dream, as related during therapy, General Franco came to the pueblo: 'I managed to get as close to him as I could and an offering from our artisan school was presented to him for the good of the pueblo. And he seemed to be pleased with it. Then I woke up.'[63]

Another patient, 'María R.', a single woman of 49 years, harboured a desire to become a teacher. Her father insisted that this was improper and put a stop to her studies. She did not suppress her resistance; though ambivalent, her hostility was openly expressed. A sense of guilt remained, particularly after her father's death, which is when her depressive condition began: 'our father was an egotist, a man of former times [...] It is so sad to have to talk of a father in such terms, but it is true [...] We always lived with fear.'[64] 'Carmen F.' represented a similar case: a married woman of 42 years, born into a well-off farming family and the only daughter among five brothers who all worked in the family business, she was prevented from going to university and confided that her parents were 'cold' and 'hard': 'my father has always been very authoritarian; his only preoccupation is with money [...] He never gave reasons.'[65] Gradually, she became colder herself, in her attitude towards religion, practising through obligation rather than desire, and she felt a sense of failure.

The intimacy of rural communities and the fear of denunciation (moral as well as political), imposed shame on those who acted outside previously accepted norms. This sense of shame could induce feelings of claustrophobia and desperation which are redolent of the violence of the war and its aftermath. 'Dolores T. R.' was a married woman of 53 years who became psychologically ill to the extent of attempting suicide

---

[62] Castilla del Pino, *Estudio sobre la depresión*, pp. 65–8. On the memory of daughters restricted to home: Botey Vallès, *Relats*, p. 90.
[63] Castilla del Pino, *Estudio sobre la depresión*, pp. 65–7.
[64] Ibid., pp. 70–2.   [65] Ibid., pp. 91–3.

because of feeling shameful after writing to the presenter of a local radio station to express her enjoyment of the 'love songs' played on a programme dedicated to housewives. The radio held a broadening appeal commensurate with consumerism's rise, and there was wider ownership of radio sets. These changes meant that the state was less able to control the private sphere, though subverting the old conventions could create anxiety. 'Dolores' began to worry that the letter she had sent might be read on air and that it could be interpreted for something other than it was and she would incur sanctions from the community: 'I imagined that I would be denounced; that they would make an announcement to warn people that there was a bad woman in this street at this house.'[66] So anxious did she become that she disappeared from home, ran away, and attempted suicide: 'I wanted to kill myself outside the pueblo, so that nobody would know who I was.' She fled to the city of Málaga, where, thinking she had been followed by somebody from the community and was being watched, and that this person was intent on making the reasons for her death public, she escaped to Seville where she attempted suicide and was detained.[67]

Compared to the atmosphere of stasis and claustrophobia which could produce such desperate responses, Catalonia seemed to be all movement. There the public space meant activity and diversity, instead of symbolising dependency, as it did in the pueblo, where in the village square men and women congregated in the early hours hoping to be hired for a day's work.[68] Some traced the age-old rural routines all the way back to the expulsion of Muslim forebears (moriscos or nazarís) and claimed it was not easy to 'say goodbye to five hundred years of history'. In the suburbanised shanty towns many age-old popular traditions of the pueblo quickly died out.[69] If you arrived from outside in Santafé, you remained an outsider for ever, whereas in Mataró, although establishing a way of life was difficult, there were strong integrating forces.[70] According to López Bulla, instead of sterile migrant resentment at the single dominant landowner and the Guardia Civil, the sound and fury of the factory was, in effect, an ally of the workers, pushing society onwards, and by the late 1960s it was possible to declare oneself a leftist, although organising or publishing leftist ideas would still land you in prison.

---

[66] Ibid., pp. 115–17.
[67] On extreme wartime and post-war communal violence in rural Córdoba, see, e.g., Francisco Moreno Gómez, *La guerra civil en Córdoba, 1936–1939* (Madrid, 1985); and his *Córdoba en la posguerra*.
[68] Memories: Morales and Pereira, *Memoria*, pp. 130–1; Botey Vallès, *Relats*, p. 90.
[69] López Bulla, *Cuando hice*, p. 122. See also pp. 29, 36, 123; Candel, *Otros*, pp. 27–9; Vázquez Montalbán, 'Para una nueva conciencia'; Botey Vallès, *Relats*, p. 141.
[70] López Bulla, *Cuando hice*, p. 29.

In a fast-changing society, the family was becoming increasingly a unit of consumption. Relations within the family were also evolving. The image of the urban middle-class housewife as a social actor, albeit within the limited sphere of consuming goods, gradually reflected a more common reality. When a national newspaper advertisement in 1962 invited entrants to a 'housewife of the year' competition, the ideal woman was constructed according to many of the traditional criteria, but the advert appeared amongst others appealing to women to become equipped with fridges, cookers, cosmetics and fashion, adverts which depicted women as modern and glamourised and independent, at least to the extent of intervening directly in the public economic sphere.[71] This zone of 'freedom' did not extend to all social classes, however, or to other spheres of life. Distribution of the contraceptive pill, for example, was actively repressed by the police into the 1970s, though technical and medical advice existed in some non-specialist publications; one such report reminded readers in rather secular language that 'any medical intervention destroys something of nature's essence'.[72] As the consumerist gaze fixed on neon lights and the headlamps of newly produced cars and motorcycles, other things were lost, for both good and ill: children lost their connection to older generations who knew the countryside, nature, and farming implements; also gradually lost was a common sense of identity as southerners, this partly based on the ancestral experience of hunger – although few expressed doubts that either their move to the city or the extreme poverty they had experienced would have been necessary had the agrarian reform of the 1930s been allowed to happen. Migrants and some historians have wondered whether mass migration would have occurred in the same painful way if the many families from the south who had lost breadwinners on the Republican side as a result of the civil war had received war pensions or compensation immediately after the conflict instead of four decades later.[73]

The concentration of population in Greater Barcelona was still creating a major housing problem towards the end of the 1960s, as was clear from the petition for urgent financial subsidies made to the Francoist Cortes by the regime's official union organisation.[74] One strategy had been to develop rapidly constructed urban settlements: the so-called *poblados dirigidos* and *unidades de absorción*, devised from 1957 and into

---

[71] *ABC*, 1 May 1962.

[72] 'Anovulatorios, estado de la cuestión', *Ondas*, 15 January 1967, p. 51. On repression: Castilla del Pino, *Casa del olivo*, pp. 428–9.

[73] E.g. Botey Vallès, *Relats*, pp. 69, 91, 120; Espinosa Maestre, *Columna de la muerte*, p. 238.

[74] *La Vanguardia Española*, 1 August 1968, p. 18.

the 1960s and run by the municipality as temporary measures. Critics of the regime saw these 'concentration camps' as no solution, viewing the vulnerable migrant as a historical legacy, 'a plaything of circumstances, not really a person [...] an inferior being without an awareness of his destiny'. The threat posed by the migrant was also viewed historically: 'it cannot seem strange that, in certain moments, this type of individual produces revolutionary situations, bloody and destructive, because the deformation which structures his life brings him towards moments of desperation'.[75] Various further housing plans produced high-rise solutions – poorly constructed *chabolas verticales*, as they were called, insufficient to tackle the problem – so that the national housing deficit was calculated as 3.7 million in 1972, and 52 per cent of the country was badly housed.[76] A report from the Instituto Nacional de Estadística in early 1969 claimed that there had been a marked improvement in satisfying the material necessities, 'which has much to do with the current consumer society', but that 34 per cent of homes in Spain still had no running water and 68 per cent of rural families had no need of a refrigerator because they had no electricity.[77] The refusal of the local and central state when it came to remedying these deficiencies would become a primary motive behind the urban neighbourhood associations of the 1960s, whose protests would gradually develop into campaigns in the 1970s in favour of democracy and a political amnesty.[78]

Catholicism and social justice

López Bulla's first sight of the Mataró shanty community of Cirera reminded him of the pueblos of Granada, although the inhabitants were from many of the southern latifundia regions of Andalucía, Extremadura and Murcia. Viewing the conditions in the slums he would realise that the 'fantasies' imagined in his village about life in Catalonia, based on stories from those who had already migrated, obscured a grim reality.[79]

---

[75] See 'El fin del suburbio', *CPED*, no. 4, January 1964, 4.

[76] Mario Gómez-Morán y Cima, *Sociedad sin vivienda* (Madrid, 1972), cited in Fundación FOESSA, *Estudios sociologicos sobre la situación social de España: 1975* (Madrid, 1976), p. 421; Ramón Tamames, *Estructura económica de España* (Madrid, 1980), pp. 572–3, 578; Jaume Fabre and Josep M. Huertas, 'Crònica d'una suburbialització', *L'Avenç*, 88 (1985), 45–9.

[77] *La Vanguardia Española*, 18 January 1969, p. 7.

[78] E.g. Mayoral, *Vallecas: Las razones*, pp. 36, 97–112.

[79] López Bulla, *Cuando hice*, p. 79. On the peripheral migrant suburbs, see Duocastella *Mataró*, vol. I, pp. 11; 5.1–5.3, 6.5–6.6 and vol. II, pp. 9.21–2. On lack of education, as in other industrial towns of the region, such as Terrassa, Sabadell, and Hospitalet del Llobregat, I, pp. 5.15 and II, pp. 8.3, 8.7.

Cirera was in the north of the town, formed entirely from post-1953 migration, and the residents, numbering some 4,450 in 1965, had largely been abandoned by the municipality.[80] Later López Bulla would become involved in running the Social Centre in the neighbourhood, similar to that in the Madrid slums pioneered by Father José María Llanos, a Jesuit priest and clandestine Communist Party affiliate. Several leading radical priests, such as Llanos and Cardinal Tarancón's right-hand man, Alberto Iniesta, were former Francoists who felt they had been indoctrinated against 'Reds', a process which had seemed to have a logical basis in the purge of priests during the war. Father Llanos, for example, had published an account of the martyrdom of priests in Toledo during the 'National Crusade'.[81] By the 1960s, however, he had turned against the notion of Holy War and become an advocate of 'mundialismo' (or 'world government'), an internationalist movement sponsored by leading humanists, which believed that the abstract frontiers of nations led to atavistic aggression, idolatry, martyrdom and war. The movement had support from a growing number of Spanish exiles of the civil war.[82] In terms of daily witness to poverty, the urban social centres were the result of collaborative efforts between priests and self-educated migrant workers, in alliance with young middle-class lay Catholics, many influenced, like Alfonso Comín, by the French theologian Emmanuel Mounier. The worker priest 'philosophy of engagement' was utterly different to the outlook of the priest in López Bulla's rural pueblo of Santafé who had been closely allied to those with economic power.[83]

There were already Catholic lay movements of working-class men and women, such as the HOAC, formally controlled by the Church, concerned with questions of citizenship, which had been active in making claims for greater social justice since the second half of the 1940s. This was at a time when political Catholics had begun to displace Falangists in government, though the authorities were troubled by 'communist

[80] López Bulla, *Cuando hice*, pp. 79–80, 106. On the vertiginous growth of the self-built barrio of Cirera in early 1960s, Duocastella, *Mataró*, vol. I, p. 0.15; vol. II, pp. 7.7, 7.9, 7.17; Bonal, *Mataró 1974*, p. 21.

[81] For Llanos on the 'crusade', see his *Nuestra ofrenda: los jesuitas de la provincia de Toledo en la Cruzada Nacional* (Barcelona, 1942). Also Alberto Iniesta, *Recuerdos de la Transición* (Madrid, 2002). For a seminarist of the 'crusade years', later 'with the defeated': Josep Vilaró, in Borràs, *Los que no hicimas*, pp. 284–7.

[82] *La Vanguardia Española*, 25 June 1967, p. 13.

[83] López Bulla, *Cuando hice*, pp. 87–94. Also, on priests dissociated from power, Botey Vallès, *Relats*, p. 86; Solé, *Inmigrantes*, p. 76. The social centres were not state-run social services but venues for discussion groups about religion and social justice and, specifically, about *Pacem in terris* (López Bulla, *Cuando hice*, p. 136). Also *Documentación Social: los Centros Sociales* (Madrid, 1958), p. 5.

infiltration' into HOAC.[84] Increasingly, and particularly from the
1950s, the focus of younger priests and lay reformists was on religion
not as tradition, custom or adornment but as belief and practice lived
in the world; progressive priests practised evangelical values ascetic-
ally by discarding the inheritance of the Church's history and old
ways in favour of social dynamism and Christian communitarianism.[85]
The message of apostolic mission and prophetic ministry would be
summed up in May 1970 by the Jesuit leader Father Pedro Arrupe,
who had been a participant of the Vatican Council, in celebration of
mass for five hundred young members of the Vanguardias Obreras
Católicas (Catholic Workers' Vanguard) who were urged to bear witness through their Christian lives in the world: 'You will understand
the language of today's world [...] We are not and cannot be outside
of history.'[86]

The Catholic Church, once essential to the notion and legitimacy
of the 'crusade' thesis, partly because of its own sacrifice in blood,
would thus become divided as some sections of the hierarchy responded
positively to the reforms emanating from the Vatican Council and many
priests would come to view the poverty of migrant existence itself as, in
effect, an extension of wartime collective trauma. These internal tensions
were echoed by lay institutions such as Acción Católica. The National
Women's Council of AC had established a Civic-Social Commission
in 1962, and in 1966 a questionnaire about 'forming citizenship' was
distributed to its various sections. Responses focused on social conscience and 'worldly commitment'. The respondents of the Movimiento
Urbano de Mujeres (Urban Women's Movement), for example, defined
'social-civic education' as 'preparation of the individual to be an active
and responsible member of temporal society'.[87] These groups worked
alongside autonomous oppositionist and neighbourhood associations in

---

[84] Basilisa López García, *Aproximación a la historia de la HOAC, 1946–1981* (Madrid,
1995), pp. 49–60; Tusell, *Franco y los católicos*, pp. 214–25.

[85] José María Llanos, *Ser católico y obrar como tal* (Bilbao, 1968), pp. 20–1, 31–8, 175–98.
Also Ramón Echarren Ysturiz, 'Los nuevos curas', in Ruiz-Giménez, *Iglesia, estado y
sociedad*, pp. 284–5.

[86] 'Una eficacia del apostolado seglar está en razón directa de su inserción en el mundo y de
su inserción en Cristo', *La Vanguardia Española*, 17 May 1970, p. 1. On radicalism of the
Vanguardias Obreras, founded as early as 1949 and subjected to state suppression, see
Blázquez, *Traición*, p. 167; Javier Domínguez, *Organizaciones obreras cristianas en la
oposición al franquismo, 1951–75* (Bilbao, 1985), p. 213. On worker priests, Xavier
Corrales Ortega, *De la misa al tajo* (Valencia, 2008). See also Ángel Alcázar, 'Carta de
un militante obrero a unos posibles sacerdotes obreros', *Apostolado Seglar*, 200 (1966),
8–10.

[87] 'Resumen de las contestaciones recibidas al cuestionario sobre formación cívico-social'
(1966), AACM, caja 95, carpeta 95–1–7.

the 1960s.[88] A 1964 issue of AC's publication *Ecclesia*, agreeing that 'fraternity' was the most imperious collective duty and that peace depended on 'purifying ever more the hearts of Spaniards', was barely keeping pace, however, with some urban parish priests who believed that fraternity depended as much on social justice and institutional reform as it did on Christian love. Socially conservative Catholics meanwhile recalled the civil war in fearing what they described as 'the subsoil of social rebellion'. Institutional 'normalisation', they felt, might better prepare the system to absorb social threats. Certain axioms of 'natural law', 'civilisation' and 'culture' had to be accepted by all, permitting peaceful disagreement about less fundamental questions. In the end, a more equitable designation of civil and military responsibilities and the separation of powers would not become a reality for another decade and a half.[89]

The Second Vatican Council had thus given impetus to grassroots Catholic movements which were in tension with the hierarchy of the Church and with the civil authorities, although the 'urban revolution' (mass migration) produced an ultimately unmanageable challenge for pastoral and evangelical work on the periphery of the city.[90] The difficulties of Church and regime were clear in responses to several papal declarations relating to human rights, political action and economic policy: *Mater et magistra* (May 1961, on Christianity and social progress); *Pacem in terris* (April 1963); and *Populorum progressio* (1967), all of which placed renewed emphasis on such concepts as truth, justice, and peace.[91] As far as the regime was concerned, the Second Vatican Council's decrees on religious freedom encouraged 'subversion', while for radicals they were 'safe conducts for some to defend themselves with religious arguments against a state which legitimated itself religiously'.[92] Conversely, other significant figures within the hierarchy would come to consider Catholic opposition to Francoism as a betrayal of a regime which had saved the Church during the war and protected and enriched it since 1939.

---

[88] See, e.g., Pamela Beth Radcliff, *Making Democratic Citizens in Spain: Civil Society and the Popular Origins of the Transition, 1960–78* (Basingstoke, 2011); Joan Camós and Clara C. Parramón, 'The Associational Movement and Popular Mobilizations in L'Hospitalet, 1960–80', in Ángel Smith (ed.), *Red Barcelona* (London, 2002), pp. 206–22. Migrant women were often at the forefront of protest: e.g., Morales and Pereira, *Memoria*, p. 109; Solé, *Inmigrantes*, pp. 65, 68, 70, 77, 86–7.

[89] 'Ante una fecha histórica', *Ecclesia*, 28 March 1964, p. 4.

[90] *Ecclesia*, 23 January 1965, p. 16; 6 February 1965, pp. 19–20.

[91] Dionisio Ridruejo, 'El santo y su milagro' (1964), in Ridruejo, *Entre literatura y política* (Madrid, 1973), p. 153. See also Joaquín Ruiz-Giménez, in *Vida Nueva*, reprinted in *Apostolado Seglar*, 205, 1966.

[92] González de Cardedal, 'Introducción', in his *Iglesia y política*, p. 35. Also *CPED*, 1, October 1963, 26–7.

Whether they were Catholics or not, critics of the regime who wrote for the Christian Democractic political review *Cuadernos Para el Diálogo* drew heavily on *Pacem in terris* and complained that the regime's considerations on peace were motivated purely by politics rather than the requirements of truth.[93] The Catholic Church's broader desire to overcome the past would lead to an emphasis on apology and forgiveness from the Vatican, although the Spanish Church's own plea for forgiveness for its support of the Franco cause during the civil war was still a decade in the future. At the initiation of the second phase of the Council, John XXIII's successor, Paul VI, would ask other Christian Churches for forgiveness for historical offences, and in January 1964 he would make a pilgrimage to Palestine and specifically to Bethlehem, suggesting to liberal Catholics in Spain, through the symbolism of baptism, how the weight of the past might be overcome and that life could be renewed in the process of redemption, even in the face of rapid economic development.[94] Amongst liberal Catholics there was a clamour for the past to be 'transcended', a need not merely for a negation of what went before but for new ways which would be 'faithful to the historical requirements of the moment'.[95] According to *CPED*, treating entire sectors of the population as too psychologically or spiritually immature for active political intervention amounted to a form of 'political eugenics'.[96] The leading Christian Democrat and former Franco minister Joaquín Ruiz-Giménez called for informed dialogue about the relationship of peace to justice and liberty: '[S]o that past conflicts, clashes between classes, races, or political groups, can be overcome, an authentic conversion in the most radical sense is required; becoming aware of reciprocal wrongs, of sins of hatred and cruelty, of incomprehensions and injustices, committed by one group and by others.'[97]

There was thus a continuity between the civil war and its repressive aftermath, mass migration, and consequent calls for toleration and reform. Looking back from 1978 at the response of the Church in Spain

---

[93] The special edition in October 1963 was devoted to the encyclical. Also Lannon, *Privilege, Persecution and Prophecy*, p. 244.

[94] 'Hoy es siempre todavía', *CPED*, 4, January 1964, 1–2.

[95] Setién, 'Sobre la verdadera paz', *Cuadernos Para el Diálogo*, 1 (extraordinario), 1963. Also José María Setién, *La iglesia y lo social: ¿intromisión o mandato?* (Madrid, 1963), especially pp. 259–65, 280–6, and, on HOAC, 293–311. Setién, a young Basque priest who had taught in the Seminary of Vitoria and the Pontifical University of Salamanca, would in 1979 become Bishop of the diocese of San Sebastián and be publicly accused of 'separatism' by the regime's official historian Ricardo de la Cierva for supporting Basque nationalism: Blázquez, *Traición*, p. 215.

[96] 'Eugenesia política', *CPED*, 2, November 1963, 5.

[97] 'La fuerza del perdón', *CPED*, 2, November 1963, 3.

to the reforms of the Second Vatican Council in the 1960s, Cardinal Tarancón would note as an important factor the extent of the migration of working-class people towards the cities:

Large sections of the working population, notably enlarged by industrial expansion, profoundly jolted in their consciences by the cultural consequences of migration and uprooting, explicitly demonstrate their lack of confidence and distance with respect to a Church which since the time of the civil war, without looking for origins longer ago, they viewed as indifferent to their problems, spiritually and materially removed from their ways of living and even in opposition to their aspirations.[98]

Politics and protest

Official ceremonies aimed at relieving the crisis of migration offered opportunities for political propaganda and remembering. When Franco, accompanied by the Housing Minister José Luis de Arrese and other members of the government, visited an emergency housing project in Madrid on 18 July 1958, for example, it was reported that he was greeted with cheers and applause.[99] In April 1959 the Minister of Education, Jesús Rubio, accompanied by a retinue of other state and Party functionaries, visited the Madrid shanty town of El Pozo del Tío Raimundo to assess the role of the so-called 'rural schoolrooms' built there. They were received by the deputy mayor of Vallecas, where underground opposition was active, and by Father Llanos, who blessed the new classrooms as the national flag was raised.[100] Measures of social justice were invariably linked to Franco's victory. The 1962 First National Assembly of the Falangist social security agency, for example, presented the Minister of Labour with a plaque commemorating Franco's 'victory for social justice' during his twenty-five years of 'Caudillaje'.[101]

Alongside the agencies of the state Movimiento, Catholic charitable work, directed at children and mothers particularly, was carried on in the urban slums by various boards and missionary congregations under the banner of the Comisión Católica Española de la Infancia. The Marian

---

[98] Enrique y Tarancón, 'La iglesia en España hoy', p. 72.
[99] *La Vanguardia Española*, 19 July 1958, p. 4.
[100] *La Vanguardia Española*, 28 April 1959, p. 9. Also *La Vanguardia Española*, 15 December 1965. For Vallecas opposition, see International Commission of Jurists, *Spain and the Rule of Law*, p. 119.
[101] *ABC*, 2 May 1962. For 1964 plaques commemorating Franco at the Ciudad Sanitaria 'La Paz' in the Paseo de la Castellana, Madrid, see Fernández Delgado et al., *Memoria impuesta*, pp. 239–41, 392.

congregation, for example, had centres in Carabanchel Bajo, Vallecas, Palomeras, El Pozo, Vicálvaro, and La Elipa, amongst others, where Acción Católica was also at work.[102] The effects of state action were generally limited. Although educational development gradually became less overtly ideological over the years, it was held back by lack of funding because fiscal policy had hardly changed since 1939, even though most social groups in the 1960s believed that the tax system as it existed was unjust.[103] In February 1968, the Director General of Primary Education admitted that the deficit of school places was some 600,000 and a large percentage of children did not proceed to the secondary level, affirming that only by 1972 would all children from 6 to 14 years have a place. On the Día de la Victoria in April 1968, the XXVII Semana Social de España, organised by lay associations of the Catholic Church, concluded that: 'in the exercise of their legitimate freedoms of association and expression', the interests of young people had to be promoted. Besides calling for generational dialogue, it also maintained that, 'as the basis for living together socially, free and equal primary education for all Spaniards' was a necessity.[104] Within a year, the principle of the right to free primary education, one inspired by 'the Christian concept of life' and the tenets of the Movimiento Nacional, as well as the interests of economic development, would be accepted, in theory, by the government.[105]

As critical voices rose in the 1960s, moments of political conflict prompted memories of the war. Parents of young detained strikers recalled the violence and imprisonment of the civil war and its aftermath, only fifteen or twenty years before, for example, and relived those experiences in the fear felt by their sons and daughters.[106] Once protesters or strikers were arrested, access to justice was severely limited. The imprisonment of one group invariably provoked further protests calling for their release or an amnesty. In Córdoba in 1962, a group of six labourers had been incarcerated without trial for distributing leaflets calling for an amnesty for political prisoners, but two years later their case still had not been heard and there seemed little prospect of their release.[107] The confusion between justice, politics and the state attracted international criticism, including a 1962 report by the Geneva-based Commission of Jurists which questioned the status of the Franco regime

---

[102] *La Vanguardia Española*, 5 May 1960, p. 7.
[103] Fundación FOESSA, *Informe ... 1970*, pp. 147, 169.
[104] For a full list of conclusions: *La Vanguardia Española*, 2 April 1968, p. 4.
[105] 'La reforma de la enseñanza', *ABC*, 13 February 1969.
[106] E.g. Castilla del Pino, *Casa del olivo*, pp. 185, 270.
[107] For memory of PCE organisation repressed in rural Córdoba: Botey Vallès, *Relats*, pp. 94–5.

as a modern state of law. The July 1959 Law of Public Order and penal legislation for the Protection of the State and Defence of the Regime were employed frequently against Catholic workers' groups. In December 1959, a group of seventeen individuals who were linked to the HOAC and JOC and who coalesced around the concept of a 'Nueva Generación Ibérica' had been sentenced to long prison sentences for 'military rebellion' after they organised an opposition movement marking twenty years of the regime. Most of the accused, who had been caught distributing a newsletter called *Libertad* (Freedom) amongst university students, had been born in the 1930s and were part of the first post-war generation. The Captain-General of Madrid, Tomás García Rebull, previously president of the Delegación de Ex-Combatientes, intervened to insist on longer prison sentences than those originally handed down. The examining judge, Enrique Eymar Fernández, President of the Special Military Court for the Suppression of Extremist Activities, was also an army colonel of the wartime veteran association the Benemérito Cuerpo de Mutilados por la Patria. Whilst the opposition thus recognised that the post-war generation was, in effect, being punished by those who had fought the war, the official press claimed the Commission of Jurists to be unduly influenced by 'exiles' and Fraga declared it part of an 'orchestrated Communist campaign'.[108] Also in reaction to this international pressure, the Córdoba labourers' case was finally heard under civil jurisdiction. The attitude of state officials was complex; memories of the civil war were still alive, but there was also a countervailing recognition of injustice and backwardness. Carlos Castilla del Pino, who had assisted the wives of the prisoners to press for a hearing, remembered how the appointed state defender addressed the accused in private: 'I know that you are communists; if one day communism triumphed in Spain, it wouldn't seem strange to me that you'd shoot me. But I will still defend you because I believe in justice and am a man of law.' Fortunately, the judge and the prosecutor, whose father had been executed by those on the Republican side during the war, also felt obliged to act within the law and, given the length of time already served, the men were given their liberty.[109]

---

[108] International Commission of Jurists, *Spain and the Rule of Law*, pp. 60–74, 111–43. For Fraga: *ABC*, 7 December 1962 (p. 129). On Eymar, see José Ignacio Álvarez-Fernández, *Memoria y trauma en los testimonios de la represión franquista* (Barcelona, 2007), pp. 244–5. The defence lawyer of the group's leader was José María Gil Robles, leader of the CEDA in the 1930s. The leading oppositionist Christian Democrat, Joaquín Ruiz-Giménez, also acted for those arrested for political crimes.

[109] Castilla del Pino, *Casa del olivo*, pp. 189–92.

A much more publicised protest was the Asturian miners' strike of April 1962, which was triggered by the government programme of economic restructuring leading to unemployment, and which was rapidly supported by similar action in the Basque Country. The repressive reaction of the state in its aftermath produced widespread protests both within the country and internationally.[110] A long list of dissenting intellectuals signed a petition against what was believed to be a programme of torture of detained miners.[111] In turn the authorities opened a file on those who had signed. Fraga announced that they had been duped by 'Communists' and invoked 'los mártires del pueblo' but was pressured into admitting that the police might have shaved the heads of two of the wives of the strikers, a form of punishment frequently employed during and after the civil war and symbolic of the apparently fossilised condition of the state apparatus and culture of public order.[112] The 1967 Ley Orgánica del Estado proposed some measures to make the law more independent, and in September 1968 the Minister of Justice, Antonio María de Oriol y Urquijo (a wartime captain in the Carlist Requeté), declared that 'a thorough, general, total and coordinated reform of the justice system was needed', but that it would proceed 'with great caution'.[113]

The Catholic-Marxist writer and activist Alfonso Carlos Comín would also be arrested and imprisoned towards the end of the decade for publishing an article in a French journal critical of the referendum of December 1966 on the so-called Ley Orgánica. The article had declared that the Spanish people were 'waiting for a peace which is not the peace of prison cells'.[114] In January 1969, he would also be detained

---

[110] Rubén Vega García (ed.), *Las huelgas de 1962 en Asturias* (Gijón, 2002). In the Basque Country, there had already been veiled protests against arbitrary authority and repression of Basque identity, as, for example, in the letter signed by 339 Basque priests to the bishops of the region (30 May 1960); Blázquez, *Traición*, pp. 141–4.

[111] On the Amnesty International report into treatment of Asturian prisoners by the Civil Guard, see, e.g., *Guardian*, 1 April 1964, p. 7. For Fraga's misrepresentation of the Amnesty report: *Guardian*, 5 May 1964, p. 6. Rubén Vega García (ed.), *Las huelgas de 1962 en España y su repercusión internacional* (Gijón, 2002).

[112] *ABC*, 13 October 1963. For women's active participation in and support for the strike, see Claudia Cabrero Blanco, 'Asturias: Las mujeres y las huelgas', in Babiano (ed.), *Del hogar*, pp. 196–202.

[113] *ABC*, 17 September 1968, pp. 35–6.

[114] Alfonso Comín, 'Aprés le référendum, la répression', in *Obras*, vol. V (Barcelona, 1987), pp. 735–7 (originally *Témoignage Chrétien* (January 1967)). The case against him was initiated in May 1967. Comín, 'Fe en la tierra', in *Obras*, vol. II, p. 449. The Tribunal de Orden Público pronounced a sentence of 16 months for 'illegal propaganda'. *ABC*, 8 September 1967; 17 January 1968; 24 January 1968. Later, copies of the Catholic *Dirigentes* (January 1968, no. 220), were confiscated by the censor because of Comín's article 'Los costes sociales de la austeridad'. *ABC*, 5 March 1968; Comín, *Obras*, vol. V, pp. 791–6.

with others by agents of the Brigada Político for holding a small gathering with the widow of Emmanuel Mounier during the 'state of exception' introduced following the assassination of a state security police officer in San Sebastián. Other activists of this generation included the Barcelona publishers José María Castellet (like Comín from a Carlist background) and Carlos Barral (also from a decidedly middle-class family), and the writer Manuel Sacristán (who had gravitated from the Falange), all concerned, in various ways, with the notion of peace as social justice and consideration of 'the defeated', which Comín encapsulated in the question: 'Cain, where is your brother?'[115] Several Barcelona activists of the organisation Cristianos por el Socialismo, ordained priests amongst them, had it noted in their police files when they had associated with Comín. One such, a priest in the parish of Nuestra Señora del Puerto in Barcelona, was described by the Brigada as a 'progressive Catalanist' with 'Marxist tendencies' and a 'declared enemy of the regime', whose telephone was duly tapped in the early 1970s. Amongst other acts considered by the police to be dubious, he had attended the Assembly of the National Commission for Peace and Justice and supported the 'line of [reformist] cardinals Enrique Tarancón and Narciso Jubany', the recently appointed, popular – and Catalan – Bishop of Barcelona.[116]

Churchmen were prominent amongst the groups detailed in the state police's 'Red Book of Subversion', produced at the end of the 1960s, where a survey was cited which claimed that 63 per cent of priests disagreed with the Church hierarchy on social and political issues and that almost as many favoured 'socialism'.[117] In 1963, civil jurisidiction over political crimes had been introduced (through the so-called Tribunales del Órden Público (Public Order Courts – TOP)), though military jurisidiction also remained in parallel. Five years later, the Madrid College of Lawyers, led by Joaquín Ruiz-Giménez and others, proposed that all penal jurisdictions be unified and that the penal regime for political prisoners be reformed. The response of the state counsel present was to argue that such 'improvised' measures 'remind us of past historical events', a clear reference to the Second Republic and one which provoked certain 'incidents' to ensue.[118] The system of TOPs

---

[115] José María Gironella, *Cien españoles* (Barcelona, 1969), cited in Comín, 'Fe en la tierra', in *Obras*, vol. II, p. 292.

[116] Antoni Batista, *La Brigada Social* (Barcelona, 1995), pp. 202–3.

[117] See (Lieutenant Colonel) José Ignacio San Martín, *Servicio especial*, p. 137. The author, head of Franco's counter-subversion organisation, was later gaoled for his involvement in the attempted coup against the democratic government in February 1981.

[118] *ABC*, 17 January 1969, p. 41. On covert state influence over the College: San Martín, *Servicio especial*, pp. 88–90, 241.

was virtually as draconian as the military courts. In the same month a court martial sentenced four students to long prison sentences for 'terrorism' for starting fires on the Madrid University campus as part of a political protest.[119] In early March, four Catalan priests were sentenced to a year's imprisonment for their part in a demonstration in May 1966 which involved delivering a letter of protest to the Archbishop of Barcelona (at that time the traditionalist Marcelo González Martín) and the city's police chief.[120] Mounting rejection of the anachronistic judicial system would come to a head in December 1970 during the televised court martial in Burgos of Basque nationalists accused of terrorist acts.

By the end of the 1960s there were calls from some close to the regime for symbolic acts of reconciliation to end the stigma of the civil war. In April 1968, *Ecclesia*, the weekly publication of Acción Católica, which had assumed a mildly critical position for much of the decade, supported a motion to Franco's pseudo-parliament the Cortes for recognition of the rights of wounded men who had been mobilised for the Republic during the war. It argued that classifying sympathisers of one or other set of ideas through the disposition of battle lines and trenches was 'simplistic'; and yet, 'on no few occasions it has been, and perhaps continues to be, a discriminatory element with political, social and even religious significance, as much inappropriate as it is unjust and hazardous in practice'.[121] The issue had to be looked at with 'Christian eyes' rather than exclusively through the lens of what constituted 'political health'.

In July 1968, the Barcelona *procurador* (member of the Cortes) Eduardo Tarragona, newly elected under the provisions of 'family representation' (by which some male 'heads of household' were able to vote for members who could attempt to influence the government), called in the press for the national day's holiday commemorating the 1936 rebellion (18 July) henceforth to be known as 'el día de la Concordia nacional'.[122] This was not an argument against remembrance, but for depoliticisation of memory. On 18 July 1968, for instance, Tarragona attended the religious acts of remembering with members of the families of those killed in Barcelona during the revolution, a less public act of commemoration

---

[119] *ABC*, 23 January 1969, p. 23.   [120] *La Vanguardia Española*, 6 March 1969, p. 6.

[121] 'También los "otros" mutilados', *Ecclesia*, 20 April 1968, p. 4. The motion was put by the procurador José María del Moral y Pérez de Zayas, formerly Civil Governor in Guipúzcoa and certainly no radical. A few years before, on Victory Day in 1964, he had received from the Caudillo the Gran Cruz de la Orden Imperial del Yugo y las Flechas. Decree of 1 April 1964, *BOE*, 79, 1 April 1964.

[122] On Tarragona (b.1927) see Aguilar, *Memoria*, pp. 140, 143–4.

than the triumphalist military parade which had preceded it.[123] It was also proposed that public employees who had been dismissed from service as a result of the war should be recognised officially as 'retired' and thus become eligible to receive a pension, as should the Republican war wounded, and that 'illicit' political antecedents should be eliminated from official records since thirty years had now passed.[124] A proposal for legislation to repeal the February 1939 Law of Political Responsibilities, which had been used to purge public employment, was presented in September 1968, but came up against the lack of any properly laid down legislative functions of the Cortes. Genuine power to make policy had never been part of its remit because this would have smacked of the importation of 'foreign doctrines' or the 'resuscitation of *parliamentarisms* from our past'. Voices calling for reconciliation, even when they came from within the old guard, were always blocked by an immutable politics born of the Francoism of the first hour.

Other channels of reform were also sealed off. The Liga de Mutilados e Inválidos de la Guerra de España, which represented Republican veterans and became active in 1967, would not be legalised until ten years later, and a law granting pensions to wounded ex-combatants in the Republican zone who could demonstrate permanent physical or psychological damage would not be passed until June 1980.[125] Although Cortes proposals were not directly successful, they applied pressure, and on 28 March 1969 the Council of Ministers approved a government decree by which 'criminal responsibilities' related to actions committed before 1 April 1939 would at last be considered spent in the eyes of the law. This was the long-awaited signal for many civil war leftists who in 1939 had feared execution or imprisonment to emerge into the open.[126] The decree did not include recognition of the conditions of Republican war disabled, as was pointed out in the communiqué sent by the Liga de Mutilados to the Bishops' Conference (Conferencia Episcopal) in July 1969 invoking the words of Paul VI which called on Catholics to fight injustice.[127] Neither was it free of Francoist rhetoric or linguistic

---

[123] *ABC*, 19 July 1968, p. 51.

[124] See proposals by Manuel María Escudero Rueda and José María Adán García in Ángel Garrorena Morales, *Autoritarismo y control parlamentario en las Cortes de Franco* (Murcia, 1977), pp. 383, 417.

[125] 'Ley sobre pensiones a los mutilados ex-combatientes de la zona republicana' (35/80): *BOE*, 165, 10 July 1980. See Chapter 11. Also, Antonio Sánchez-Bravo and Antonio Tellado, *Los mutilados del ejército de la República* (Madrid, 1976), p. 81; Vega, *Historia de la Liga*; *La Vanguardia Española*, 9 January 1969.

[126] See Jesús Torbado and Manuel Leguineche, *Los topos* (Barcelona, 1977); Ronald Fraser, *In Hiding* (Houndsmills, 1972).

[127] Sánchez-Bravo and Tellado, *Mutilados*, pp. 21, 80.

confusion: imagining the war as both a 'War of Liberation' and a fratricidal conflict, it inevitably, though paradoxically, denied that the anomaly being addressed had ever arisen:

the peaceful living together of Spaniards for the last thirty years has consolidated the legitimacy of our Movement, which has been able to give to our generation three decades of peace, development and juridical liberty, only achieved with difficulty in other historical epochs [. . .] On the occasion of reaching, on 1 April 1969, thirty years since the end of the War of Liberation [Guerra de Liberación], it is opportune to recognise expressly the extinguishing of possible criminal responsibilities which derived from any act committed in relation to that crusade, remaining juridically inoperative, therefore, any consequence from what was at the time a struggle between brothers, united today in the affirmation of a common Spain, more representative, and disposed as never before to work towards its greatness.[128]

This chapter has explored from a social perspective the concept of 'normalisation', discussed previously in Chapter 7 from the point of view of a state-inspired strategy for economic development and a modernised version of the history of the civil war. This analysis of the social dimensions of normalisation has developed key themes from the 1950s, such as migration and marginal urbanisation (see Chapter 6), as they inter-acted with the renovated official memory of the war constructed by the regime. The scale of migration in the 1960s was greater even than that of the 1950s and the problem of marginal urbanisation was therefore also greater, as was the psychological burden of memory registered amongst sections of society left behind by the changes, particularly women in rural communities. The phenomenon of *chabolismo* produced a complex of responses and effects, including changes in the bases of collective identity, expectations and fears of the social consequences of materialism and consumerism, a greater emphasis amongst lay Catholics and many priests upon social justice, and, ultimately, new forms of political protest. Although much of this change had been initiated by the civil war and its outcome (something which was understood by many migrants and social commentators), the doctrinal foundations of 'Franco's peace', as formulated through the 'fratricidal conflict' thesis, remained irrelevant to the new society being shaped largely from below. Social conformity was determined less by parameters set by the ideology of the dictatorship than by the pressure felt to flee from the past towards a better way of life, as consuming 'masses', but with the hope of becoming citizens.

---

[128] *ABC*, 29 March 1969.

9   Transition and reconciliation: politics and the Church in the 1970s

> Wishing to be mediator and pacifier, the Church had in the end been on the side of the victors, supporting its repression, piling silence and religious marginalisation upon those who had been defeated politically [. . .] This externally victorious Church was in reality internally defeated. It owed its life and continued existence to the victorious side and felt obliged to repay this debt with fidelity or silence.[1]

Virtually the entirety of the Spanish episcopate supported the Franco regime during and after the war because it represented continuation of a traditional way of understanding Spain's history. One critical member of the hierarchy commented in 1979 how ideological and political clashes had 'shattered the life of the country and the conscience of many during the last few centuries; we have still not yet emerged from these'.[2] The remote and recent past would weigh heavily on Catholic conscience during post-war social and political change. Stimulated by currents within society and searching for an appropriate role in a changed world, reformists began to adopt a position of self-examination, humility, and what one described as 'active political neutrality', during which the history of the *patria* and the association of Spanish identity with wars against 'invaders' were reconceived.[3] A reformer of the post-'crusade' generation, the priest and theologian Olegario González de Cardedal, born in 1934, reflected on the troubled past and on the new era ahead at the end of the 1970s and was both critical of the hierarchy's political compromises in the past and empathetic in appreciating the devastating effect on the Church's collective consciousness of the wartime revolutionary purge of priests. But, as the passage quoted at the beginning suggests, compromise with the Franco regime came with significant costs to the Church, though González de Cardedal overstated the extent of the Church's

---

[1] González de Cardedal, 'Introducción', in González de Cardedal (ed.), *Iglesia y política*, p. 31.
[2] Cardenal Jubany, 'Neutralidad política', pp. 119–20. On 'corrientes populares, desde zonas pre-políticas', see p. 128.
[3] González de Cardedal, 'Introducción', pp. 42, 45–6. On political neutrality, see especially Tarancón, 'Iglesia en España' (28 June 1978), pp. 63–82 (p. 75).

'defeat'. There had certainly been an element of self-censorship, but many important figures had believed in the Holy War narrative without much question. There was also, however, a process of ideological change from the 1950s onwards within Spanish Catholicism, largely initiated from the grassroots and lay associations in response to migration and social change, a conversion which would gain considerably from the Second Vatican Council in the early 1960s in which several leading Spanish reformers participated. The Church's encouragement of the democratising process, including making a critical reassessment of its civil war record and divesting the former ecclesiastical elite of control of the Church's official position on the past, would crystallise around the President of the Bishops' Conference (Conferencia Episcopal) from 1971 to 1981 and Archbishop of Madrid, Cardinal Vicente Enrique y Tarancón, described by one colleague as 'a man with historical instinct'.[4]

At the end of the 1960s, attitudes of the laity towards the Church's position vis-à-vis the Second Republic in the 1930s remained separated into two broad groups, particularly if exiles were included: first, those who believed that the Church and Catholics in general had done all that was possible to coexist with the Republic but that religion had been systematically persecuted from the beginning; and, second, those who maintained that the Republic had begun without any intention to persecute the Church and that it was the latter which had sabotaged the new regime. In 1968 the liberal Basque priest Víctor Manuel Arbeloa produced a study of these attitudes, with a prologue by the Bishop of Salamanca, Mauro Rubio, which created controversy when the entire edition was confiscated by the state censors.[5] Those questioned in the study belonged overwhelmingly to the 'generación rectora' of the 1930s and the 'mobilised generation' of the war (born during the broad period 1879–1915), so that the division of opinion was based largely on wartime ideologies. Those who depicted the Church as victim included Francoist ministers, philosophers, historians and journalists, such as Esteban Bilbao, Ernesto Giménez Caballero, Joaquín Arrarás and Manuel Aznar. Those who saw the Church as belligerent included Republican politicians and party leaders and those who fought in the Republican ranks: Manuel de Irujo, Luis Jiménez de Asúa, José Peirats, Eduardo de Guzmán and Manuel Tuñón de Lara. This political divide, seemingly frozen in time, can be symbolised by the fact that the ex-CEDA leader José María Gil Robles and the socially conservative Minister of Interior of

---

[4] See Juan María Laboa, 'El cardenal Tarancón, testigo del cambio', *Cuenta y Razón*, 12, July–August 1983.
[5] Víctor Manuel Arbeloa, *La Iglesia en España, ayer y mañana* (Barcelona, 1968).

the first Republican government, Miguel Maura, who had clashed over responsibility for the anti-clerical violence of May 1931, would again be found on opposing sides in the 1968 survey, even though both had gone into exile during the civil war.[6] The Jesuit José María de Llanos, one of the most famous 'worker priests' of the 1960s and 1970s, was something of an exception because, though he had actively supported the 'crusade' in the 1940s, he aligned himself in 1968 with supporters of the Republic. The reasoning behind both broad positions was decidedly unsophisticated in historical method, since both, in effect, projected ideas about the Church and the Republic (1931–6) forward into the period of the civil war: while those who were 'pro-Church' essentially based their judgement on the wartime anti-clerical violence, the pro-Republicans did so by focusing on the July 1937 collective letter of the bishops in support of General Franco, a way in both cases of avoiding the real causes of the conflict. Few of those questioned adopted a middle position, that of the tolerant Arbeloa himself, by suggesting a more complex reality and focusing specifically on the pre-war era between 1931 and 1936. Several who did were Catalans who insisted on a distinction between the tendency of the Spanish Church during the Republic and war and the nuanced criticisms made by such relatively liberal Catalans as Cardinal Vidal i Barraquer.

Discussions about the role of the Church during the Republic would implicitly form a backdrop to debates about the nature of a new democratic constitution for the post-Franco era. Manuel Azaña's claim in October 1931 that Spain had 'ceased to be Catholic' had been repeated for decades by Francoists to support the claim that democracy had in effect traumatised Catholics. A more subtle analysis, supported from within the highest level of the Church, would become possible by the early 1970s. Bishop Tarancón was certain, for example, that 'the Church and civil society are two fundamentally distinct realities. One does not begin to form part of the Church by birth, nor as a requirement of citizenship or nationality, nor in virtue of particular social behaviour [. . .] The necessary criticism of our own historical tradition had to be faced' and faith had proved to be 'stronger than historical idiosyncrasies'.[7] There was also recognition that new generations which had not experienced the war had become painfully aware of

---

[6] See Hilari Raguer, *La unió democràtica de Catalunya i el seu temps (1931–1939)* (Barcelona, 1976), pp. 22–4. Another figure questioned was Salvador de Madariaga: although he had been a Republican minister, he was repulsed by the anti-clerical violence and aligned himself with the Republic's critics in 1968.

[7] Tarancón, 'Iglesia en España' (1978), pp. 76, 67. On the essential Church–civil society distinction, in origins, objectives and procedures, see also Jubany, 'Neutralidad política', p. 123. Azaña's words had been explicit in maintaining that society had become

the collaborative role played by the Church in the divisions between Spaniards. If the key word of Church–society relations in the 1960s had therefore been *concilio*, a decade later, the conciliar impulse had evolved into the notion of *reconciliación*, the coming together of 'las dos Españas', the reuniting of 'separated brothers', expressed in part by the general clamour for a political amnesty and idealisation of a society reborn. Church reformers insisted that this would involve remembering as well as forgetting. The Church would have to accept that it constituted a community in coexistence with other communities. Its values, images, and models of conduct could no longer function as an ideology to be proclaimed as an individual and collective obligation. The hierarchy's intransigents were bound to baulk at what seemed to be a willingness to negotiate over Catholic doctrine; they also disagreed when liberals argued that political freedom was the prerequisite for religious freedom and vice versa. Ecclesiastical reformers sidestepped these criticisms from the right by reminding the left (those 'distanced from faith') to leave behind historical myths about the Church and religion (as exemplified by the Catholic intransigents) and to accept a Church which was 'culturally up to date' instead of resurrecting outdated anti-clericalism.[8]

From the Burgos Trial to the assassination of Carrero Blanco (1970–1973)

In 1971, shortly before he was appointed by the Caudillo as prime minister, Franco's ultra-loyal lieutenant Admiral Luis Carrero Blanco was to be found maintaining the outdated litany of commemorative slogans of the narrative of the war established during and after its fighting. In a speech celebrating the victory of the papal forces over the Turks at Lepanto in 1571, Carrero insinuated that the triumph over 'the infidel' was essentially a precursor of Franco's victory over liberalism, a victory, he declared, which had still to be carefully guarded even after three decades. One of several commemorative tomes published to celebrate Lepanto maintained the same argument: 'if we pass from then [1571] to now [1971], instead of the Turk we see Asiatic communism. The

---

extensively secular by the 1930s. See, e.g., Carlos Seco Serrano, '¿Era católica España en 1930?', in Ruíz-Giménez, *Iglesia, estado y sociedad*, pp. 25–6. There remained ambiguities about the extent of Catholicism in Spain at end of the 1970s, however, even for liberals (e.g. Jubany, p. 131: 'Spain – a country where a large Catholic majority exists').

[8] E.g., González de Cardedal, 'Introducción', p. 16.

situation is the same and Spain, as then, struggled in a crusade – that is, the War of Liberation [Guerra de Liberación] – to achieve victory.'[9]

Beside the badly resuscitated myths, however, the regime was entering into decline and, as is not uncommon in the final stages of repressive regimes, the security apparatus went into overdrive, as if it could somehow compensate for Francoism's ever-diminishing real control in dealing with protests mounted in favour of liberty. Three events in the early 1970s would crystallise particularly the opposition to and the vulnerability of the Franco regime: the so-called Burgos Trial at the end of 1970; the Assembly of Spanish Bishops and Priests in September 1971, and the assassination by ETA of Carrero Blanco himself in December 1973.

In Burgos, throughout December 1970, the military trial of sixteen individuals, including two priests and two women, charged with being members of the radical Basque nationalist organisation ETA and of involvement in the murder of a police chief at Irún in 1968, was to be fundamental in focusing domestic and foreign opposition to Francoism largely because, in what seemed a throwback to the past, the prosecution was calling for death penalties to be imposed.[10] The ensuing internal crisis faced by the regime also drew attention to divisions within Spanish Catholicism, especially when Pope Paul VI interceded on behalf of the accused, much to the fury of the right-wing press in Spain which questioned his right to do so and used the occasion to criticise progressives within the Church. The bishops of Bilbao and San Sebastián petitioned Franco to end the death penalty and to hold the trial publicly in a civil court. Amid student and worker protests and mass arrests of dissidents in the Basque Country, Catalonia and beyond, the Episcopal Conference issued a statement asking for clemency. When the court went ahead in handing down death sentences for several of the accused, a number of foreign governments protested and Franco was compelled to commute the sentences to long terms of imprisonment.[11]

The politics of Basque identity had long constituted a faultline in society which had been much deepened by the civil war and its aftermath. Part of the impetus behind the post-war liberalising movement within the Church, even as early as the 1940s, had been Basque nationalism. Traditionally this was strongly Catholic but anti-centralist in political terms, and priests, in spite of close Church–state relations, had long been

---

[9] Antonio Macio Serrano, *Lepanto* (Madrid, 1971), p. 54. Also Luis Carrero Blanco, *Años cruciales en la historia del Mediterraneo: 1570–1574* (Madrid, 1971); Luis Carrero Blanco, *La Victoria del Cristo del Lepanto* (Madrid, 1948).

[10] See, e.g., Castilla del Pino, *Casa del olivo*, p. 272.

[11] For sentences, see María Carmen García-Nieto, *La España de Franco* (Madrid, 1975), pp. 634–6.

at the forefront of manifestations of this regional difference. Critical priests pressed for freedom to express their 'denuncia profética' of the socio-political situation and structure which, as they argued, violated common understanding of basic justice and the rights of the individual.[12] As early as July 1970, the Church had published a communication addressing what was described as the 'political, cultural and social poverty of Spain', and in June 1971 the Bishops' Conference pronounced critically on 'the moral life of our people'.[13] In spite of inevitable conflicts with the bishops, many priests had chosen to adopt class struggle as an instrument to end injustice through socialism, and by 1973 there were more than five hundred worker priests in Spain, some seventy in large factories and the rest in construction or smaller workshops or services. The largest numbers were in Madrid (especially the marginal zones of Carabanchel, Barajas, Leganés, Moratalaz, and El Pozo del Tío Raimundo), Barcelona and Valencia, but they could also be found in the north, particularly in the Basque Country and, to a lesser extent, Asturias.[14] In April 1973 the work of Father Llanos was recognised with the Juan XXIII Memorial Award, instituted by the organisation Pax Christi, for his book *Un plan de paz*, which in effect called for a new social settlement.[15]

The Burgos Trial and the movement for reform within the Church thus coincided with and formed the background to the Assembly of Bishops and Priests (Asamblea Conjunta) held in September 1971 under the presidency of Cardinal Tarancón and with the participation of the hierarchy and 171 priests elected by more than 1,500 diocesan groups. According to the reformers who had pressed for this combined assembly, it would open 'a period of hope' in addressing the rapidly, irregularly, and sometimes brutally changing world.[16] The aim was to 'take the pulse of the country', to orientate priestly action and assist the Church to become 'dynamically present within society'.[17] The associated

---

[12] Lannon, *Privilege, Persecution and Prophecy*, p. 5. On Tarancón, e.g. *La Vanguardia Española*, 24 October 1971, p. 24.

[13] Tarancón, 'Iglesia en España', p. 69.

[14] There were fewer in Castile and in the south of the country. *La Vanguardia Española*, 27 May 1973, p. 22; Morales and Pereira, *Memoria*, p. 122.

[15] *La Vanguardia Española*, 5 April 1973, p. 29; José María de Llanos, *Un plan de paz* (Madrid, 1972).

[16] Asamblea Conjunta Obispos-Sacerdotes, *Historia de la Asamblea* (Madrid, 1971), pp. 34–5.

[17] González de Cardedal, 'Introducción', p. 37. Also Feliciano Montero García, 'El taranconismo: La transición de la Iglesia antes de la Transición', in Rafael Quirosa-Cheyrouze y Muñoz (ed.), *Historia de la Transición en España: los inicios del proceso democratizador* (Madrid, 2007), pp. 195–210; Martín Descalzo, *Tarancón*, pp. 165–85; Jesús Infiesta, *Tarancón: el cardenal de la reconciliación* (Madrid, 1995).

manifesto, 'Iglesia y Mundo en la España de hoy', set out ideas for a radical revision of the Concordat of 1953 and, therefore, of the relation between the monolithic state and Church. Areas for reform supported particularly strongly by younger priests at a time of a 'vertiginous transit between generations' included state participation in the election of bishops, the presence of civil authorities and representatives of economic elites at religious acts, and the lack of a framework of 'human rights'.[18] The proposed withdrawal of the Church from political power was accompanied by controversial calls for reconciliation and for past failings to be recognised, but these proposals narrowly failed to obtain the required two-thirds of votes and the planned apology was therefore not included in the final document, though the significance of the resolution could not be ignored: 'we humbly recognise and ask forgiveness because, when it was required, we did not always know how to become true ministers of reconciliation within the heart of our people, brothers divided by war'.[19] Though Tarancón had been in favour of the basis of the statement, he later expressed reservations about alluding to the war, which he thought 'a great risk' because it touched upon an emotional area and provided an opportunity for the document to be attacked.[20]

The deliberations and proposals of the Assembly provoked hostility from conservatives within the hierarchy who enjoyed some support from television and press; in a document in February 1972, apparently emanating from Rome (though without papal authority) and drawn up with the intervention of numerous members of Opus Dei (the so-called 'Documento de la Congregación del Clero'), the liberals were accused of 'temporalism' and 'democratism'. A collective letter from resistant conservative priests had already been published immediately after the Assembly; this protested 'against the manoeuvre of those who seek time and again to have the Assembly condemn the attitude of the Church in Spain's war'.[21] In a replaying of the liturgy of memory of the 1940s, the religious martyrs of the 'crusade' were conjured up to criticise the reformers; the conclusions of the Assembly were 'an affront to the bishops and the thousands of priests who, together with innumerable religious laymen and women, gave their lives for the love of Christ and cast the light of their pastoral charity upon us'. The reformers were

---

[18] 'Iglesia y Mundo en la España de hoy', in Asamblea Conjunta, *Historia de la Asamblea*, especially on the Church–state relation, pp. 57–8, 134–6, and need for intergenerational dialogue, pp. 35, 73–5, 652–3; and Enrique y Tarancón, *Confesiones*, p. 470.
[19] The word 'always' was added following an amendment. Asamblea Conjunta, *Historia de la Asamblea*, pp. 170–1. On migrants' view of the Church as culpable: e.g. Botey Vallès, *Relats*, pp. 76, 87.
[20] Martín Descalzo, *Tarancón*, p. 176.   [21] *ABC*, 11 November 1971, pp. 23–4.

criticised for daring 'to judge the consciences of their elders [whilst] systematically refusing to confess their own failings in the current situation of the Church'. Moreover, critics argued that moral assessment of the clergy during 'the great test [*prueba*]' of the war had already been made 'by those who had authority and knowledge of the case'. In turn, conservatives' accusations were refuted by reformists, amongst them an important group in Salamanca, including González de Cardedal, Antonio Rouco, Fernando Sebastián and José María Setién, which posed the choice as one between 'a Church of Peace' and 'a Crusading Church'.[22] As Tarancón attempted to make clear at the time, the intention had never been to repudiate the actions of the Church during the war but rather to enable priests to direct themselves 'with authority to all Spaniards, including the defeated'.[23] The intransigence of conservatives would nonetheless form the germ of a breakaway faction departing from the ethos of the Second Vatican Council which would gather pace in the 1980s. The reaction of the Franco regime at the time to the reformist movement can be summed up in the attitude of Carrero Blanco who bluntly accused the Church of disloyalty and ingratitude and threatened to withdraw the state's religious subsidy.[24] But this did not for the moment halt the reform movement, and 'Taranconismo' would produce a further statement, in January 1973, in the document entitled *La Iglesia y La Comunidad Política*, to be welcomed by the Vatican, in which political pluralism and the separation of Church and state would be advocated in the interests of 'the common good'.[25]

The faultline within the Church would be replicated in the political world. Shortly after the staging of a national homage to Franco in Madrid on the Día del Caudillo (1 October) in 1971, a group of clandestine trade union leaders was arrested amid much publicity. Much later, at the end of December 1973, they would be sentenced to periods of imprisonment ranging from 12 to 20 years. ETA's attack against Carrero Blanco would be timed to coincide with the court's sentencing of these trade union leaders. There had been further clashes between students and police at Madrid University in January 1972 and soon afterwards riots amongst

---

[22] 'Estudio teológico-jurídico sobre el Documento de la Congregación del Clero', *Iglesia Viva*, 38 (1972), 133–61. See also, in the same edition of *Iglesia Viva*, Rafael Belda, 'La clave del proceso a la Asamblea Conjunta', 111–32.

[23] Enrique y Tarancón, *Confesiones*, p. 470. For the controversy behind the scenes, Martín Descalzo, *Tarancón*, pp. 176–80.

[24] Tarancón, 'Iglesia en España', p. 69; Blázquez, *Traición*.

[25] Monseñor Cirarda (Córdoba), 'Por primera vez la Iglesia de España toma la iniciativa de separarse del Estado', *La Vanguardia Española*, 28 March 1973, p. 27; *ABC*, 1 February 1973.

workers in Franco's city of birth, El Ferrol. The unintended consequence of the clampdown on students and trade unionist protesters was to heighten politicisation. The effects of a beating from the police or a short spell in a prison cell, at the order of the notorious Tribunal del Orden Público, were considerable in legitimating the claims and increasing the popularity of anti-regime movements.[26] After Carrero Blanco was assassinated by ETA in December 1973, events at the funeral revealed how tensions could easily surface, on this occasion in the macabre form of right-wing anti-clericalism, which made a connection between the reformist strands in the Church and public disorder and provoked memories of the civil war by resorting to the slogan 'Tarancón al Paredón!': 'a firing squad for Tarancón'.[27] Some years later the Cardinal would express the personal feelings provoked: 'I had lived through the era of the Republic and had been insulted many times with similar words, but then I knew that those insults came from enemies of the Church. To see myself now insulted by people who believed themselves to be more Catholic than I produced a very deep sorrow in me.'[28]

After much prevarication, the reaction of the government to the assassination of Carrero Blanco was given on national television, first by the Vice-President of the government, Torcuato Fernández Miranda, assuming the functions of prime minister, who asserted the legitimacy of the state, the government's 'serenity' and 'fortitude', and its determination to prevail. He also referred back to the state's origins in the conflict of the 1930s, but also warned against 'useless revenge': 'we wish to forget the war but we will never forget the victory'.[29] Fernández Miranda seemed the most logical choice as permanent successor to Carrero but was mistrusted by Franco hardliners who were suspicious of his close relations with Prince Juan Carlos. Under pressure from his closest advisers, the Caudillo appointed Carlos Arias Navarro, the Minister of Interior at the moment of the assassination, widely seen as the hardest man in Carrero's cabinet having carried out a major offensive against ETA and the illegal Communist-affiliated trade union, several leaders of which had been languishing in gaol in 1973 awaiting their much-anticipated trial. The governmental team headed by Arias Navarro and

---

[26] E.g. Piñero Valverde, 'Mi viejo álbum', p. 70; Feixa and Agustí, 'Discursos', pp. 210–11.

[27] See San Martín, *Servicio especial*, pp. 96–101; Piñero Valverde, 'Mi viejo álbum', p. 88; González de Cardedal, 'Introducción', p. 36; Antonio Jiménez Blanco, *Los niños de la guerra ya somos viejos* (Madrid, 1994), p. 73; Juliá et al., *Memoria*, p. 115. For politicking behind the scenes, Martín Descalzo, *Tarancón*, pp. 186–202.

[28] Martín Descalzo, *Tarancón*, p. 196.

[29] TVE documentary *La Transición* (1995), episode 1. See also José Luis Alcocer, *Fernández-Miranda: Agonía de un estado* (Barcelona, 1986).

announced in January 1974 was profoundly anti-reform.[30] Years earlier, Arias himself had been a state prosecutor in summary hearings against Republican prisoners in Málaga and elsewhere, and the sobriquet 'the butcher of Málaga' would become attached to him, partly as a means to critique the much-lamented sense of political *continuismo* represented by his appointment after Carrero.[31] In any event, the assassination had provoked a widespread concern that disorder would follow and considerable fear amongst the leftist opposition that there would be repression and a clampdown. Right-wing *ultras* harked back to the violent purges of the civil war, using the North African term *razzia*, as the rebels had in 1936, to threaten punitive raids against the oppositionists in prison.[32] Many leftists went into hiding, though in the end there was little violence.[33]

Within a few months of the assassination a new regime strategy of *apertura* ('openness') would be announced, though the contradiction with the repressive public order strategy was clear when in February 1974 the Bishop of Bilbao, Antonio Añoveros, who had long preached the need for Catholic action in favour of social justice, was placed under house arrest by the police (in the name of the Interior Ministry) for issuing a homily to be read at Mass throughout the diocese calling for recognition of Basque cultural identity. The government claimed that the detention was to protect the Bishop from possible attack by extremist elements, but a major crisis in Church–state relations ensued. When the Minister of Justice, Ruiz Jarabo, telephoned Tarancón to demand that the homily be withdrawn immediately to resolve what he perceived to be a matter of national security, he was not much placated by the Cardinal's assurances that the patriotism of Añoveros, as a wartime volunteer chaplain to a *tercio* (division) of the Carlist militia (Requeté), could not be in doubt. The strongly integrist Catholic economic elite of Vizcaya, powerful in government, applied much pressure, however, and the Bishop came close to expulsion from the country. Nevertheless, the homily could not be withdrawn for fear that there would be a revolt in the Basque Country, at least amongst

[30] Paul Preston, *The Triumph of Democracy in Spain* (London, 1986), pp. 51–2.
[31] Arias Navarro seems to have been unable to save at least one person from execution who had given him refuge during the bloody revolution in Málaga. See *Interviú*, 8 June 1977. When accused as 'el carnicerito de Málaga' in the 1970s, he brought court cases against several publications: *El País*, 15 June 1977; 14 July 1977; Javier Tusell, *Tiempo de incertidumbre* (Barcelona, 2003), pp. 39–42.
[32] San Martín, *Servicio especial*, p. 91; Alberto Reig Tapia, *Violencia y terror* (Madrid, 1991), p. 55.
[33] E.g. Castilla del Pino, *Casa del olivo*, pp. 194, 408–9; Victoria Prego, *Así se hizo la Transición* (Barcelona, 1995), pp. 17–19, 24.

priests.[34] The *apertura* was further compromised by the execution in March of the Catalan anarchist Salvador Puig Antich, found guilty by a military court of killing a Guardia Civil officer in a shoot-out in Barcelona. According to one view, the Church was in a 'traumatised' condition, but its reforming direction had a momentum which would be maintained by wider events as the regime entered a period of acute crisis.[35]

'The bunker': the death throes of Francoism (1974–1976)

In July 1974 Franco was taken seriously ill and power was delegated to his designated successor Juan Carlos in accordance with article 11 of the Ley Orgánica del Estado.[36] But by September, the General was deemed well enough to take up the reins again as Head of State, and in late December a new Law of Political Associations was introduced.[37] The new year saw increased militancy with a fresh wave of strikes in February and in April a reversion to government limitations on freedoms, including declaration of a 'state of exception' in much of the Basque Country, where state counter-insurgency forces were concentrated following actions by ETA. Attempting in vain to keep pace with the dynamics of socio-economic change, the government in May 1975, would announce a framework for broadening the legal requirements for labour disputes, liberalising the 1962 Law of Collective Disputes.[38] Economic protests went hand in hand with organised political dissent, and in July the newly formed moderate opposition coalition Plataforma de Convergencia Democrática, uniting the PSOE with social democrats, the Christian Democrats of Ruiz-Giménez, and regionalist groups, published its manifesto.[39] Later, in March 1976, the Plataforma would merge with the Junta Democrática to become Coordinación Democrática, including the PCE, once the latter had dropped its commitment to a complete 'rupture' with the old regime, by which it meant exclusion of all Francoist public servants from office.[40] Within the armed forces too there was some level

---

[34] Enrique y Tarancón, *Confesiones*, pp. 629–37. Also Tarancón, 'Iglesia en España', p. 69. For Añoveros (b.1909) and social policy in Cádiz, e.g. 'Crece el sentido social cristiano, pero con excesiva lentitud', *Ecclesia*, no. 944, 15 August 1959, pp. 19–20; 'Apatía en lo social', *Ecclesia*, no. 963, 26 December 1959, p. 13.

[35] Comín, 'Fe en la tierra', *Obras*, vol. II, p. 295.

[36] Paul Preston *Juan Carlos* (London, 2004), pp. 345–55. On events, see Juliá et al., *Memoria de la Transición*.

[37] Estatuto jurídico del Derecho de Asociaciones Políticas (Madrid, 1975).

[38] Decree, 22 May 1975, *BOE*, 127, 28 May 1975.

[39] Juliá et al., *Memoria de la Transición*, p. 46; Prego, *Así se hizo*, p. 225.

[40] Preston, *Triumph*, pp. 74–5, 85.

of support for modernisation emanating from the younger generation of officers. In July 1975 nine serving military officers, inspired by the role of the military in the fall of the Portuguese dictatorship the previous year, had been arrested as 'rebels' for organising the pro-reform Unión Militar Democrática (UMD). They would be sentenced to imprisonment in March 1976 and later excluded from the Amnesty Law of October 1977, their anomalous position only being settled in 1986 with their reincorporation into the army in spite of the reservations of some PSOE ministers.[41]

In August 1975 a new law against terrorism was instituted in the face of renewed ETA attacks against the armed forces. Notoriously, on 27 September 1975, five ETA and FRAP militants convicted of terrorist acts would be executed in spite of a wave of domestic protest and foreign abhorrence against the death sentences.[42] There were further anti-Franco demonstrations and official condemnations throughout Europe, including a protest at the Spanish embassy in London. While several European states recalled their ambassadors, a public mobilisation in support of the government was mounted in the Plaza de Oriente in Madrid (recalling similar mobilisations in the late 1940s), where Franco, in what would be his last public appearance, declared, as he had three decades before, that foreign interference was part of a 'leftist–Masonic conspiracy'. In October 1975 the General would suffer a heart attack and Juan Carlos would succeed him as Head of State.

Faced with the political crisis, the Church took up recent papal pronouncements on peace. Warning against those who hold the 'elimination of adversaries' as a primary principle, in April 1975 the Spanish bishops had issued a collective letter on the theme of reconciliation, which reignited the tensions following the 1971 Assembly, though, since political change now seemed inevitable, with less vehemence than before. Many within the hierarchy remained reluctant to mention the role of priests in legitimating the civil war repression, though some Catholics were more forthcoming. Pedro Laín Entralgo maintained that because of the political violence the rebel side had not been justified in calling itself 'Christian', though he clearly had believed otherwise during the conflict.

---

[41] José Fortes and Luis Otero, *Proceso a nueve militares demócratas* (Barcelona, 1983). *El País*, 16 September 1986. See open letter of Luis Otero Fernández to Narcís Serra, Minister of Defence, on sense of desertion by PSOE, *El País*, 6 January 1986. In February 2010, fourteen UMD officers were to be awarded the Cruz al Mérito Militar by the Spanish government – three of them posthumously – in recognition of their democratic stance. *El País*, 16 February 2010.

[42] Miguel Ángel Aguilar, 'El prestigio del terror', in Juliá et al., *Memoria de la Transición*, pp. 61–2.

Even though the rebels had 'raised Christ's cross above their heads', the 'original sin' of the repression rendered the victors incapable of adequately resolving post-war problems.[43] With the country in 1975 again blighted by political violence, Church reformists saw the moment as decisive and believed the Church had a responsibility to contribute to peace as it had not done in 1936; this view was reflected in the section of the 1975 collective letter which criticised those within the Church who attempted to argue from ideological positions against change. An explicit call was made to support reconciliation between generations. Though the Church 'abstained' from all direct political action, this did not mean that it would advocate 'evasive abstentionism'. The letter also condemned dictatorship as a form of government and defended the heritage of 'ethnic minorities' within the state. The legacy of civil war was explicitly recalled as a vital element of reconciliation:

In our *patria*, the progressive effort for the creation of appropriate political structures and institutions has to be sustained by the will to overcome the harmful effects of the civil conflict which in those days divided citizens into victors and defeated and which still constitutes a serious obstacle to a full reconciliation between brothers. Fidelity to Christ's mandate, which urges us towards mutual forgiveness, must make possible, in private and public life, that which is so hard and so difficult for the hearts of men. The new generations which did not live through that conflict ask us, and with good reason, for sufficient generosity to construct, united in hope, a more just and more fraternal future.[44]

Traditionalists remained sceptical and damped down hopes of reform. Franco had not yet disappeared from the scene, though it was not expected that he would see the year out. The conservative newspaper *ABC* commented acerbically that the year 1975 seemed to have been designated significant in varying ways according to taste: 'women's year', 'year of change', 'electoral year' and 'year of reconciliation', which 'almost everyone' was talking about.[45] Arguing that a 'just order' and 'prosperity for all' had been created by 'the men who won', ultra-conservatives rejected the idea that a programme for reconciliation, as such, was needed at all. So insignificant was the past that ex-minister Gonzalo Fernández de la Mora celebrated what he believed to be

---

[43] Laín Entralgo, *Descargo*, p. 225. Retrospectively he maintained that he had always found the crusading Catholicism of the 1940s 'infantile' (p. 175).

[44] *La reconciliación en la iglesia y en la sociedad* (17 April 1975), *La Vanguardia*, 20 April 1975, pp. 4–8. See also José Manuel Cuenca Toribio, 'Las relaciones entre la Iglesia y el Estado en la España democrática', in Paul Aubert (ed.), *Religión y sociedad en España (siglos XIX y XX)* (Madrid, 2002), p. 58; Tarancón, 'Iglesia en España', p. 69.

[45] 'La reconciliación', *ABC*, 18 April 1975, p. 29.

Spaniards' ignorance about the war.[46] Linked to foreign ideas peddled by 'new, ideological, international brigades', those who were exiled and who were leading party political opposition to the Franco regime had, he insisted, an understanding of the war which was 'anchored in the waters of the past'. Diehard Francoists refused to recognise that a multitude of organisations and social groups inside the country had long called for a policy of reconciliation and that this had been rejected by the regime. In September 1975 the Permanent Commission of the Spanish Episcopate condemned both terrorist violence and governmental repression and called for the commuting of further death sentences. Part of the transition process, indeed, would be the emergence of the concept of human rights, and a Spanish Association against the Death Penalty was founded in late 1976.[47] For the first time since the Second Republic, the Constitution of 1978 (in article 15) would abolish the death penalty in all circumstances other than war.[48]

Following Franco's death, on 20 November 1975, as a posthumous message to the nation was broadcast on state television by the prime minister, Arias Navarro, there was a surge of demonstrations in many cities demanding democratic reform. These were met with police violence.[49] At the same time, in various parts of the country, a number of priests who had been imprisoned for preaching 'conflictive' sermons were given their freedom as 'a mark of respect for the memory of Franco and his spiritual testament'.[50] Members of the Madrid College of Lawyers and a number of prisoners' wives were detained near Carabanchel prison, however, for protesting against the limited nature of the political amnesty decreed on 25 November which made no provision for the return of those in political exile.

There would be some fear that the funeral of the Caudillo would present an opportunity for extremist paraphernalia, uniforms and gestures to be displayed, and Cardinal Tarancón worried that his participation would see him involved in controversy.[51] Ideologically, Arias Navarro favoured the conservative Primate of Spain, Cardinal Marcelo González Martín. Tarancón, however, presented the homily during the *misa de corpore in*

---

[46] Gonzalo Fernández de la Mora, 'Reconciliación', *ABC*, 13 November 1975. See also Borrás, *Los que no hicimos*.

[47] *El País*, 16 January 1977.

[48] *Constitución Española, 1978–88*, 3 vols. (Madrid, 1988), vol. I, pp. 91–3. The death penalty had been reintroduced in October 1934 and formalised as part of the Penal Code by Franco in 1938. It would not be fully abolished in all circumstances until 1995.

[49] E.g., Castilla del Pino, *Casa del olivo*, p. 414.

[50] *La Vanguardia Española*, 25 November 1975, p. 16.

[51] Francisco G. Basterra, 'España vuelve a tener rey', in Juliá et al., *Memoria de la Transición*, pp. 96–7.

sepulto at the Pardo palace (Madrid) on 20 November in which he paid tribute by recognising the emotions aroused by the passing of a figure who had been a defining symbol of an era, though, for many, a malign presence during what Laín described as forty years of 'never-ending provisionality':[52]

I, who as a priest, have pronounced these words so many times, feel a special emotion on repeating them before the body of a man who for almost forty years, with total dedication, governed the destinies of our country. At this time we all feel distressed by the disappearance of this truly historical figure [. . .] I am sure that God will pardon his mistakes, reward his successes, and recognise his endeavours.[53]

Infuriated by the notion that the Caudillo might have erred, Arias declined to shake the hand of Madrid's archbishop after the proceedings.[54] He had desired a grandiose funeral as a re-creation of the atmosphere of the past, applying pressure to hold the ceremony in the Plaza de Oriente with all bishops present and with Tarancón officiating. These belated plans, hatched in the mind of the Prime Minister, were thwarted by the preparations already put in place during the previous weeks by departments designated according to protocol and by the Church. The widespread feeling, not least amongst priests, was that resurrecting the pomp of Imperial Spain was inappropriate. Tarancón would anyway excuse himself from officiating at the funeral itself, in favour of González Martín.[55]

Having excluded himself from public association with the regime and its past glories, Tarancón would pronounce a further homily a week after the General's death on 'the obligations of the Church before the country'. Presented in the church of San Jerónimo el Real in Madrid, the homily was addressed to King Juan Carlos on becoming Head of State, but was also aimed at society in general, and the sentiments expressed were oriented towards the future. This was a form of sanctification of what was to become the post-Franco state, but one which made the subordinate role of the Church clear. The contrast with the crusading Church of the 1930s was obvious enough, and the homily marked, in a sense, the end of the era of the civil war, in its almost obsessive reference to inclusiveness, concord and consensus:[56]

You take the reins of the state at a moment of transition, after many years in which an exceptional and now historical figure assumed power in a way and in

[52] Laín Entralgo, *Descargo*, p. 376.
[53] Ricardo de la Cierva, *La historia se confiesa* (Madrid, 1976).
[54] Juliá et al., *Memoria de la Transición*, pp. 73, 93. For the complex delicacy of the arrangements, see also Martín Descalzo, *Tarancón*, pp. 220–4.
[55] Prego, *Así se hizo*, pp. 327–30.
[56] On the homily, specifically, Santo Juliá, 'Homilía para el fin de una guerra', in Juliá et al., *Memoria de la Transición*, pp. 114–15. On 'consenso', Rafael del Aguila and Ricardo Montoro, *El discurso político de la transición española* (Madrid, 1984), pp. 127, 134–5.

circumstances which were extraordinary. Spain, with the participation of *all* and under your care, advances on its way, and the collaboration of *everyone* will be necessary, the prudence of *all*, the talent and the judgement of *all*, so that it might be a way towards peace and progress, the way of liberty and of mutual respect [...] I ask that you be the king of *all* Spaniards, of *all* those who feel themselves to be children of the maternal *patria*, of *all* those who desire to live together, without privileges or distinctions, in mutual respect and love. A love which, as the [Second Vatican] Council taught us, must be extended to those who think in a different way to us [...][57]

The hierarchy of the Church and the political elite would be reminded very specifically of this focus on 'everyone' in a number of campaigns, including by such neglected groups as the Republican war wounded.[58]

Nonetheless, in a concession to hardliners, Catholic intellectuals and ex-combatant groups, Tarancón would be very clear during his address to the Plenary Assembly of the Episcopacy, in December 1975, that the 'crusade' of the 1930s had possessed social roots. He declared that he was not attempting to revise history but to adapt the Church's teaching to the present. Referring explicitly to the Bishops' collective letter of July 1937, he maintained that

the Spanish ecclesiastical hierarchy did not put the name of Crusade artificially on the so-called war of liberation: it was the Catholic people of *then*, which, already, from the first days of the Republic, had confronted the government and which, precisely for religious reasons, had united faith and *patria* in those decisive moments [...] But this watchword, which had airs of the warrior's cry and served undoubtedly to defend substantial and permanent Spanish and Catholic values, does not now serve the new relations between the Church and the world, between religion and the *patria*, or between faith and politics.[59]

Though it quickly became clear how little had been done by the old regime to fill the political vacuum left by the personal authority of the Caudillo, the anti-Franco opposition would have little choice but to accept a negotiated transition to democracy which would compromise some of the aims of 1931. With the handover of formal power to Juan Carlos imminent, the Republican government in exile declared that there was no other legitimate regime than that emanating from the Republican Constitution of 1931, restating, in effect, that Francoism had rested upon the violent overthrow of a legally constituted government. This was indisputable, but the opposition would have to take account of the social transformation which had occurred since the war. In early

---

[57] Tarancón, *Confesiones*, pp. 864–8. Emphasis added.
[58] See Sánchez-Bravo and Tellado, *Mutilados*, pp. 15–16.
[59] Chao Rego, *Iglesia*, pp. 83–4.

December, Arias Navarro had been confirmed as Prime Minister and a new government was formed with the support of several cautious and pragmatic reformers, including Manuel Fraga, José María Areilza and Joaquín Garrigues. There was a widespread desire for constitutional reform and social advance, but also a fear of a return to the atmosphere and dangers of the 1930s, particularly because of the mindset of the officer corps which was overwhelmingly loyal to Francoist principles, and because of the violence of ETA.[60]

Following Franco's demise, manifestations of the memory of wartime martyrs were more obviously ideological than ever but were also becoming marginal to mainstream political and cultural life. The annual remembrance ceremony at Paracuellos had been infiltrated – if not taken over completely – by the extreme right-wing grouping Fuerza Nueva, led by Blas Piñar.[61] Myths and propaganda about the principal hate figures of the Second Republic did not, of course, cease overnight. On 12 August 1976, a religious service was held in Madrid at the Church of the Sacred Heart in suffrage of the souls of sixty-four individuals executed in 1938 in the Castle of Montjuich (Barcelona), in pursuance of death sentences 'approved in the Council of Ministers presided over by Juan Negrín'.[62] The PSOE wartime premier would be particularly tarred by the anti-Communist opprobrium heaped upon the leaders of the Republic because, it was widely believed (including by liberals and sections of the left) that he had been 'hoisted to power by extraneous [that is, Communist] forces'.[63] With the demise of Franco, however, important archival records would now gradually become available for historical scrutiny.[64] Negrín would be partially vindicated by the

---

[60] The legal case for high treason and mutiny, brought by the Karamanlis government against the Greek junta which ruled during the years 1967–74 and heard from July to December 1975, received little coverage in Spain.

[61] *La Vanguardia*, 1 November 1977, p. 9; 8 November 1977, p. 11. Also Ferran Gallego, *El mito de la Transición* (Barcelona, 2008), p. 788.

[62] *ABC*, 12 August 1976, p. 19. On the use of the death penalty by the besieged Republican government, see Solé i Sabaté and Villarroya, *Repressió a la reraguarda*, pp. 274–6.

[63] Salvador de Madariaga, *Victors, Beware* (London, 1946), p. 32. See also Bolloten, *El gran engaño*.

[64] For need of an objective history of PSOE and socialism, and gradual appearance of fruits of research, largely published in Mexico, see, e.g., Elías Díaz in *CPED*, 76, January 1970, 47. On the social history of the Second Republic, reception of Edward Malefakis's *Reforma agraria y revolución campesina en la España del siglo XX*, in *CPED*, 92, May 1971, 47–8. See Antonio Elorza, *La utopía anarquista bajo la Segunda República* (Madrid, 1973); Francesc Bonamusa, *El Bloc Obrer i Camperol: els primers anys, 1930–1932* (Barcelona, 1974); Xavier Cuadrat, *Socialismo y anarquismo en Cataluña (1899–1911): los orígenes de la CNT* (Madrid, 1976); *Catalunya sota el règim franquista: informe sobre la persecució de la llengua i la cultura de Catalunya pel règim del General Franco* (Paris, 1973); Beltza, *El nacionalismo vasco, 1876–1936* (San Sebastián, 1976).

historian Ángel Viñas in his 1977 study of the Prime Minister's role in the financing of Soviet imports of war material. The book, because of its alleged sensitivity, had initially been held back from distribution by the first post-Franco foreign ministry.[65]

Attempts through ceremonial acts to resurrect the 'crusade' in the aftermath of Franco's death were muted, sporadic and took place away from the centre-stage of politics. In early January 1976, in one of the final ceremonial occasions hosted at El Pardo by Doña Carmen, the General's devout widow, a commission of the devotional confraternity of el Santísimo Cristo Mutilado de Málaga, founded in 1939, was received in order to express sympathy.[66] The Pardo palace had to be vacated at the end of the month and, at the express wish of the King, was opened to the public for guided tours at the beginning of August.[67] Part of the building became a museum, and casts of the Caudillo's face in death and of his hands were included amongst the displays.[68] The main attraction was the interior of Franco's residence where the faithful and others came and were awed.[69] Hardliners upheld the charismatic status of the Caudillo, but the fate of the palace was symbolic: it ceased to be a place of power, becoming instead a heritage site. The writer and dramatist Joaquín Calvo Sotelo, brother of the monarchist leader assassinated in July 1936, was resigned to the fact that 'everything to do with Francoism is now, through biological imperative, merely material for a museum'.[70]

In the aftermath of the dictator's death, there was little appetite more broadly for recriminations. Laín Entralgo's note in his memoir summed up the general mood: 'most Spaniards under 45 see any prospect at all of [another] civil war with great hostility – they do not want to repeat the past and have seen what their parents suffered. In a few months we will know if the war has been a truly corrective lesson.'[71] Many actively feared that there would be campaigns for judicial retribution against the officials, public servants and political class of Francoism, and conservatives

---

[65] Ángel Viñas, *El oro de Moscú: alfa y omega de un mito franquista* (Barcelona, 1977).

[66] *ABC*, 10 January 1976, p. 26. On the symbolism of the mutilated image of Christ, see Richards, 'Presenting Arms', pp. 199–200.

[67] 'El Palacio de El Pardo vuelve a ser historia', *ABC*, 6 August 1976, p. 26.

[68] *ABC*, 5 August 1976, p. 1.

[69] *ABC*, 1 February 1976, p. 44. For the 'austera y total entrega al servicio de España', see, e.g., p. 14. Satirical commentary about the museum was censored because it was 'disrespectful': e.g., in August 1976 the satirical review *Por Favor*, no. 111, had relevant pages removed at the order of the Ministry of Information.

[70] Calvo Sotelo, 'Del franquismo sin Franco', *ABC*, 29 February 1976, p. 3. Nonetheless, when in November 1976 the psychiatrist Carlos Castilla del Pino published an article entitled 'Psicoanálisis de Franco' it provoked threats from the so-called Guerrilleros de Cristo Rey. Castilla del Pino, *Casa del olivo*, p. 415. The article: *CPED*, 186, 20–26 November 1976.

[71] Laín Entralgo, *Descargo*, p. 477.

particularly fretted about the growth of political organisations without, as they saw it, a concomitant popular sense of responsibility. Looking back, some have wondered long afterwards at the generally peaceful way in which the transition to democracy was achieved.[72]

The Amnesty Law and the democratic constitution (1977–1979)

As critics of the regime had argued since the 1960s, a modern democratic society required freedom of movement, dynamism and even instability, and 1976 would see the eruption of pent-up economic and political demands. Whereas in 1966 some 1.5 million labour hours were lost through strikes, ten years later the figure would be 150 million. In January there was a strike of 500,000 employees in Madrid. State authorities reacted with the force to which they had been accustomed; in March 1976 five demonstrators were killed in clashes with police in Vitoria. The newly united leftist parties preached restraint, even though at the first PSOE Congress to be held in Spain for forty years Marxism had apparently been confirmed as a guide to action and there was a continued stress on the need for a rupture with the past. At the beginning of July the outdated Arias Navarro, one of the 'crusade' generation (born in 1908), resigned, and two days later Adolfo Suárez, previously a regime bureaucrat and Director General of RTE (state radio and television), though decidedly a representative of the new generation (born in 1932), was appointed as Prime Minister, largely as a result of the wishes of Juan Carlos.[73] The programme of Suárez would be based on dismantling the institutions of Francoism and the Movimiento, introducing far-reaching measures of political reform (including free elections as soon as possible and a new constitution), and ending remaining and significant elements of legal discrimination arising from the civil war. He would do so essentially through a process of political deal-brokering that sought to avoid alienating those groups most tied to the old regime, particularly the army, thus hoping to defuse the threat of a backlash. The Church, as we have seen, was already moving towards a reformed position. Incipient democracy required a process of learning democratic practices and new ways of thinking. The Church would be a part of this. The volume dedicated to religion in the series of widely disseminated short guides called the Biblioteca de Divulgación Política (entitled 'What the Church Thinks with Respect to Politics') was written by the progressive Bishop of

---

[72] E.g. Morales and Pereira, *Memoria*, p. 127.   [73] Preston, *Juan Carlos*, pp. 352–3.

Segovia, Antonio Palenzuela, and attempted to explain how the transition within the Church was linked to the broader process of political and social change occurring in the country:

reaction against past situations, or the need to lend a voice and action to those who could not previously speak or act, has led us quite suddenly to discover new social and political arenas, terrain upon which the authenticity of our faith and its future will be played out.[74]

One of the first decisions of Suárez's new government at the end of July 1976 was to grant a partial political amnesty – something which had been campaigned for by the left and by social Catholic groups such as Justicia y Paz, established by the Bishops' Conference and headed by Joaquín Ruiz-Giménez.[75] The organisation's general secretary, the Basque priest Juan José Rodríguez Ugarte, was to be instrumental in several further campaigns, in spite of being suspected by the security police of being a leader of the PCE, and the HOAC would also play a significant role in pro-amnesty demonstrations.[76]

Government overtures were soon being made to the PSOE leader Felipe González, on the one hand, and the military, on the other. In September 1976 a law of political reform was announced and in December Suárez's 'reform from above' was given 94 per cent support in a referendum. In April 1977 the Francoist single party and state bureaucracy (el Movimiento) was legislated out of existence and, most controversially, the PCE was accorded legal status by the government.[77] The logic of democratic pluralism was that it could not exclude from the system even those groups perceived as its enemies and against which the civil war had been fought. Even though to Francoists the PCE had symbolised the 'Anti-España', the party would reject Leninism at its congress held a year later. Times had changed; the ex-Falangist Laín Entralgo confessed that 'for reasons of principle and of experience I am no Marxist; but neither can I deny the intellectual toughness and historical justification of Marxism – without it, would the continual advance of social justice for more than a century have been possible?'[78] Recognition of the PCE, nonetheless, signified a collision with everything which Francoist history had taught and, for a minority, it represented a blow even to 'their own sense of dignity as Spaniards'.[79] The extremist

---

[74] *Cuál es el pensamiento de la Iglesia respecto a la política* (Barcelona, 1976).
[75] For reception and critique, see *El País*, 5 August 1976.
[76] E.g. *El País*, 10 August 1976; *La Vanguardia*, 13 July 1976, p. 7.
[77] M. A. Bastenier, 'El camino hacia las urnas', in Juliá et al., *Memoria de la Transición*, pp. 197–216.
[78] Laín Entralgo, *Descargo*, p. 472.   [79] González de Cardedal, 'Introducción', p. 44.

backlash included death threats levelled at the PCE leader, Santiago Carrillo, accusing him of signing the death warrants of those killed at Paracuellos in 1936; his own role during *la Transición*, as the period was known, would be conciliatory, however, and, like Tarancón's, was essential to its success.[80] The past continued to intrude during the 1970s, however, most brutally on 24 January 1977, when five young labour lawyers linked to the PCE were savagely murdered by Falangist gunmen while in their office in the Calle de Atocha, central Madrid. The effect of what became known as 'the Tragic Week' was to make the Communists more acceptable in society, not less, and to encourage political compromise.[81] There was indeed something of a backlash against decades of Franco's anti-Communist propaganda, registered in mildly favourable social attitudes towards Communism, although this would not go as far as electoral support. The funeral of the murdered lawyers would become the focus of a huge demonstration in Madrid of some two hundred thousand people, led by Carrillo.

The violent outbursts were terrible, but the debt to the past was owed as much in terms of retrospective legal recognition of the state's covenant with citizens as it was in terms of avoiding a return to violence. The claims of disabled Republican war veterans, both within Spain – between 5,000 and 10,000 individuals in 1976 – and in exile, to be granted equal status with Nationalist ex-combatants as 'sons of Spain', who fought for the *patria*, were urgent, and the case was intimately bound up with democratisation, it was argued, because 'the state can never be sectarian'.[82] The Franco government had put a stop to pensions for Republican veterans and their widows after 1 April 1939 and it was estimated that fifty thousand men had died whilst waiting for the regime to grant material assistance. As Rodríguez Ugarte wrote in January 1976, 'nobody denies that this is a delicate and complex problem which rubs up against the sacrosanct myths of this country in the last few years'.[83] Discrimination against ex-Republican soldiers had been particularly senseless because many had been conscripted into the army or had merely responded to the call from the constituted government of the time. Thousands had been unable to join the officially recognised

---

[80] See Alfonso Guerra, interview with Soledad Alameda, in Juliá et al., *Memoria de la Transición*, p. 234. *La Vanguardia*, 30 June 1977, p. 9. The PCE was prevented by the government from holding a demonstration in Paracuellos in May 1978 which the Falange and Fuerza Nueva had promised to disrupt. *La Vanguardia*, 12 May 1978, p. 7.

[81] Juliá, 'La estrategía de la tensión', in Juliá et al., *Memoria de la Transición*, p. 187.

[82] Joaquín Ruiz-Giménez, 'La mutilación de la guerra', in Sánchez-Bravo and Tellado, *Los mutilados*, p. 112; Florencio Martínez Durán, in *El País*, 18 May 1976.

[83] Sánchez-Bravo and Tellado, *Los mutilados*, p. 85.

and state-privileged Cuerpo de Caballeros Mutilados por la Patria, for Nationalist veterans, and spent years making ends meet by becoming itinerant street vendors catering for tourists or by selling lottery tickets. Their organisation called for adequate economic compensation, as, for example, in Italy where Mussolini's war-wounded had been awarded pensions by the post-Fascist state.[84] The hierarchy of the Church was criticised for delaying any public pronouncement on the question, and Rodríguez Ugarte maintained that it too owed a debt of responsibility because of the Church's 'belligerent position' during the war and 'many years of peace'.[85] The depth of the suffering caused by the war was expressed by Ruiz-Giménez in support of the campaign, arguing that civil wars 'mutilated the spirit' of individuals and societies, 'which remain broken for decades and transmit wounds to children and grand-children'.[86] The culmination of the campaign came in March 1976 when, to circumvent persistent resistance in parliament, the King signed a decree granting pensions (graded according to level of disability) to those who had suffered some disability as a result of the war but who 'cannot join the public body of war-wounded gentlemen [caballeros] in the name of the patria'.[87] Not only had the equivalence of honourable civic status conferred by the title of caballero been denied to Republic-ans, but the new pension was non-retroactive and offered nothing to widows and families.[88] Applicants were given six months from the publication of the decree to undergo the necessary process, including a medical examination.

A law enacting Republican war widows' pensions would materialise only in September 1979 following a campaign by the Asociación de Viudas de Guerra de la República which pressured the PSOE to chal-lenge limited earlier proposals made by Suárez's UCD government.[89] Little mention was made of the unequal treatment of war widows – the dependants of those who died on the other side had received pensions for many years – though there were complaints that the new benefits were insufficient: 'some are still considered Nationalists while the others are "Reds"'.[90] Some provision was made for the children and dependants of

---

[84] Sánchez-Bravo and Tellado, *Los mutilados*, pp. 17, 23. Also, Vega, *Historia de la Liga*.

[85] Cited in Sánchez-Bravo and Tellado, *Los mutilados*, p. 85.

[86] In 'La mutilación de la guerra', p. 111; *CPED*, 76, January 1970, 21.

[87] Decree 670/1976, 5 March, *BOE*, 84, 7 April 1976. The decree made no mention of the Republic or of the status of the government in 1936.

[88] On campaign for equivalence in one single veteran association for Nationalists and Republicans, *Boletín Oficial de las Cortes Generales, Senado*, 61, 5 September 1980. Bullón and Diego, *Historias*, p. 46.

[89] *BOE*, no. 233, 28 September 1979.   [90] *El País*, 2 December 1980.

those killed as a result of violent actions during the war, whether they were combatants or not, and included dependants of those who died in prison, either during or after the formal end of the conflict, including those condemned for 'political opinions'. The vast majority were the families of victims of rebel violence; most of those on the other side had already been compensated. Other social groups discriminated against since the civil war, such as Republican teachers, ejected from their profession, were gradually and unevenly rehabilitated in the 1970s, although not without great difficulties and often only partially. One teacher, a socialist, and his wife, also a teacher, had spent much of the post-war years working in a local flour factory as a result of the ideological 'purge' of schools, until they saved enough eventually to move to Madrid so that their children could go to university.[91]

The first free elections since before the civil war were held on 15 June 1977 and attracted virtually 100 per cent voter participation. It was a highly significant moment and those who had been implicated in political opposition to the dictatorship began gradually to feel less tense: 'The tone of caution in speaking, and even in looking at one another, which had been a characteristic of life for the last forty years, ceased.' Nevertheless, vestiges of the 'Liberation Crusade' as a continuing 'struggle against Marxism' remained in pre-election publicity of ex-combatant groups and the extreme right.[92] Some on the left expressed the view that the elections signified that the war was at last over, a sentiment expressed during the final address of the Madrid PSOE campaign of Felipe González in the stadium at Vallecas, centre of urban migration since the 1940s. The Socialists would not win the elections, however; voters were cautious – perhaps even fearful – and many flocked to the centre as the best guarantor of a peaceful transition.

With a new elected government under Suárez the business of making up for lost time was given impetus. In July 1977, as the new parliament opened, the government requested full membership of the European Economic Community, and in September the Catalan government (the Generalitat), which had been declared illegal by Franco in 1938, was re-established and Josep Tarradellas returned from exile as Catalan president. Most significant of the new Spanish parliament's actions was the Amnesty Law (Ley de Amnistía), passed on 15 October 1977, which went further than the partial concession of March 1976 and wiped the slate clean of responsibilities for all politically motivated acts of both regime and opposition since 1936. This meant that opposing the

---

[91] See, e.g., 'Los mutilados de la paz', *CPED*, 20 November 1976, 23.
[92] Castilla del Pino, *Casa del olivo*, p. 434; *El Alcázar*, 27 April 1977.

dictatorship on the basis of democratic conscience was in effect equated with the institutional violence of the military regime, a prescriptive form of forgetting resorted to in other post-civil-conflict situations. Unusually in the Spanish case, it came some four decades after the end of the war, an intervening period which saw repressive erasure of memory (by the state) and a humiliated silencing (with some level of complicity within emerging civil society) during the first twenty years, followed by another two decades of rebuffed calls for reconciliation.

Although seen at the time by politicians of most political groups as a fundamental document of the democratic state – which could not be overturned – the Amnesty Law would later, especially from the late 1990s, be seen by proponents of the recuperation of war memories as instrumental to a damaging 'pact of forgetting'.[93] The right had been reluctant to agree from the beginning, although, during the period from 1996 to the present (as we will see in Chapter 12) the conservative Partido Popular (PP) has been the most insistent in maintaining that the law must not be amended in any way. A week before the parliamentary debate on the amnesty, a leading politician in the Basque Country and his bodyguards were assassinated by ETA, and the deputies of the conservative Alianza Popular (predecessor of the PP), founded by Manuel Fraga in 1976, abstained in the vote, arguing that an amnesty placed state authority in jeopardy.[94] The 'disorder' of the Second Republic was invoked in support of a contention which saw the state as essentially repressive: 'the only medicine that the most genuine and consolidated democracies apply is a strict application of the law and of justice'.[95] All other parliamentary groups favoured a broad amnesty, and the spokesmen of the left were explicit in wanting to 'bury the past'. In an impassioned and moving address, Marcelino Camacho of the PCE-PSUC, who had only been released from prison months earlier under the provisions of Suárez's partial amnesty, generously articulated the consensus: 'that which seemed impossible a year ago, almost a miracle – to emerge from the dictatorship without serious traumas – is being realised before our eyes'.[96] The sentiments expressed during the amnesty debate in October 1977

---

[93] Ley 46/1977, 17 October 1977, *BOE*, 248.

[94] For funerals of policemen as opportunity for anti-democratic protest, see, e.g., *El País*, 11 February 1977.

[95] Antonio Carro Martínez, in *Diario de Sesiones del Congreso de los Diputados* (*DSCD*), 14 October 1977, p. 959.

[96] *DSCD*, 14 October 1977, p. 961. For the PSOE, see speech of Txiki Benegas: p. 966. In 1973, Joaquín Ruiz-Giménez had acted as defence lawyer in the case (known as 'sumario 1001') against Camacho and other clandestine union leaders, when the defendants received sentences of between 12 and 20 years.

would be extended to austerity measures to tackle the economic crisis in the so-called Moncloa Pacts agreed by capital and labour at the end of October. As a result, inflation was halved, but unemployment was doubled.[97] Two months later, the Council of Ministers would ratify a further symbolically important move: abolition of 18 July as a national public holiday. At the end of December a preliminary level of autonomy was granted to the Basque Country.

The Church would have to overcome institutional inertia and philosophical divisions to keep pace and remain relevant. Although Tarancón's position, more or less articulated at the Asamblea Conjunta in 1971, had the support of a narrow majority of bishops, the Cardinal Primate, González Martín, remained resistant, holding to the dogma that priests must be obedient and not take up political causes. According to his counter-argument to the reformers, typified in his 1979 address entitled 'What Remains of Catholic Spain?', certain historical and often-cited historical moments – the consecration of Spain to the Sacred Heart (1919); the burning of churches during the Republic; Azaña's 1931 claim in parliament that Spain had 'ceased to be Catholic'; the collective letter of the Spanish Bishops (1 July 1937); the Second Vatican Council – were all peripheral when compared to 'the soul of the people'. In effect, he wished to place faith and 'culture' together as the constituent elements of 'la España Católica', thereby implicitly, at least, denying validity to Azaña's position and, by extension, to that of Tarancón at the end of the 1970s.[98] Maintaining that the 'painful drama' of the civil war had been many things, including a 'crusade', a 'war with social causes', and a political confrontation, he evoked the trauma and professed himself unwilling to discuss it: 'I cannot refer to it, or even to other aspects of Catholicism in Spain during the twentieth century, because many things impede me: sadness which is stirred by memories, a lack of political serenity in which we live today, the magnitude of so dense a theme with so many implications [...] events of such spiritual, cultural, social and political profundity.'[99] The effect of his paralysis, however, was to return to the debates of the past and, particularly, to turn the clock back to the philosophical and religious clash which occurred under the Second Republic:

religion does not merely live within the interior of the conscience [...] It has constituted the most creative cultural and political enterprise of Spain throughout

---

[97] In March 1978 the Communist-influenced Comisiones Obreras was most popular in the national trade union elections.

[98] For Tarancón: 'La iglesia en España hoy' (28 June 1978), pp. 63–82.

[99] Marcelo González Martín, '¿Qué queda de la España Católica? ¿Qué puede quedar a final de siglo?' pp. 93–4.

the centuries [...] A religious way of being and living [...] Acceptance of a moral praxis and generalised customs, inspired by the commandments of God and the Church, with an understanding of the family as sacred nucleus for many [...] Popular religiosity manifested in a thousand diverse forms of expression and participation in common in religious sentiments.[100]

In the process, Ramiro de Maeztu, who had become a civil war martyr of the 'crusade' in 1936, was recalled. A highly controversial figure, Maeztu had been the inspiration behind the anti-democratic review *Acción Española* during the Republic and author of a famous and influential tract in 1934 on Catholic conservative nationalism with the confessional state at its heart.[101]

Conservatives were essentially addressing what they felt to be the trauma of modernity; indeed, they may have deliberately conjured up images of the more widely felt cultural trauma and threat to collective Catholic identity of the 1930s in order to play on the latterday reformers' own doubts about modernity.[102] As was clear from the process of social mobility undergone since the late 1950s, community ties had been weakened thereby and, in the absence of timeless values, were incapable of withstanding the 'new rhythms of history'.[103] But the conservative Cardinal Primate went much further towards an almost apocalyptic image of modernity than any reformer would have done. In a situation where 'man depends solely on man, on what in a given moment is judged most pragmatic and efficient, cities can be destroyed, populations eradicated with radiation and bacteria, acts of terrorism, abortion, sterilisation of women and men can all be carried out [...] if some specialists or technicians consider it "necessary" or "convenient" ', an image of the world which would gain resonance more widely amongst the Catholic community again in the globalised and culturally uncertain era from the 1980s during the papacy of John Paul II. This was also a warning, however (and, again, it locked into memories of the 1930s), that democracy 'could not prevail' if it meant merely that the most popular opinion became the motive force behind state action. There had to be control of 'idolatrous' appetites arising from 'materialist doctrines': consumerism, 'pleasure', 'comfort', 'atheism' and 'Marxism'.[104]

---

[100] González Martín, '¿Qué queda de la España Católica?', pp. 85, 87–8, 93–4.
[101] Ramiro de Maeztu, *Defensa de la Hispanidad* (Madrid, 1934). The Cardinal's position in 1978 was essentially 'España católica sin problema'. See the earlier intellectual controversy, e.g., Laín Entralgo, *España como problema* (Madrid, 1962) (1949)), pp. 639–84; Rafael Calvo Serer, *España sin problema* (Madrid, 1949).
[102] On 'value erosion' under dictatorship, see, e.g., Ilie, *Literature and Inner Exile*, p. 24.
[103] González Martín, '¿Qué queda de la España Católica?', p. 103. The Cardinal expressed little confidence in sociology – a 'vehículo de ideologías' (p. 94).
[104] González Martín, '¿Qué queda de la España Católica?', pp. 102–3. See also Chapter 12.

The reformers' counterposition was that the Church could not stand outside the process of democratisation, precisely because the end of the regime ran the risk of society 'emptying itself ethically' during modernisation and falling irretrievably into directionless consumerism, indifference and 'moral insensibility'.[105]

While some conservatives argued that confessionality of the state ought to have been put to a vote, the drive towards democratic ways of thinking caused reformists to question whether it was right for the Church to be mentioned at all when the content of the new constitution began to be discussed in the autumn of 1978.[106] Radical criticisms were deflected by the Church hierarchy's willingness to accept, and even to take a lead in, the process of change, and it was also convenient to recall in the 1970s, as the regime ended, that the Church had been obliged at certain moments to conform to the dictatorial state against its own will. Cardinal Gomá's pastoral letter 'Lecciones de la guerra y deberes de la paz', written in August 1939, the publication of which was prohibited in the Francoist newspapers of the time, was recalled to reinforce the point, somewhat tendentiously, that the objective of bringing about reconciliation in the aftermath of the war had been tried and failed and that the Church then, as now, could not be a belligerent in politics.[107] The constitutional settlement was therefore only possible because it was not the fruit of the old attitude of one Spain against the other, although the place of Catalonia and the Basque Country within the democratic state provoked some difficulties for the parliamentary commission established to frame the founding document, remaining the most intractable problem thereafter. When the civil war and the repression were brought into the constitutional debates it was invariably the Basques and Catalans who introduced them, largely to bolster the demands of nation building. The worst ETA offensive yet and an aborted military coup, projected to be staged in November 1978, coincided with the referendum on the constitutional settlement in December; fears were heightened, though neither was able to derail the process.[108] The attempted military coup of February 1981, discussed in Chapter 11, would create a broader sense of fear which, in effect, would place limits upon post-transition reforms and

[105] Jubany, 'Neutralidad política', p. 129.
[106] González Martín, '¿Qué queda de la España católica?', p. 98; José María González Ruiz, 'Reconciliación nacional y confesionalismo', El País, 1 August 1976. See also El País, 2 July 1978.
[107] Jubany, 'Neutralidad política', pp. 126–7; González de Cardedal, 'Introducción', pp. 28, 30, citing the Spanish Bishops' collective letter to the faithful, 1 July 1937. For Gomá's 1939 pastoral, see Granados, El cardenal Gomá, pp. 387–429.
[108] On 'Operación Galaxia', see Preston, Triumph, pp. 146–9.

the recovery of war memories. For now, the new constitution would open the way for regional autonomy statutes and the elections of May 1979, again won by Suárez, though with PSOE gains, confirmed the left's drift towards the centre and the party's dropping of Marxism as the basis of its political theory.

This chapter has sought to demonstrate the nature of the political and social basis of reconciliation as the Franco era drew to a close and democracy dawned. The approach has deliberately been chronological to enable the course of political events to be mapped with some precision onto the cultural assumptions of the 1970s. These assumptions were largely about the conflictive past and the aim here has been to show how potentially divisive events (particularly the Burgos Trial and the assassination of Carrero Blanco) were socially assimilated – with an important contribution from the Catholic Church – in the interests of reconciliation. Bringing the Church (as a conduit of broader social opinion) back into the story of the transition to democracy represents one facet of a critique of the notion of a homogeneous and blanket 'pact of silence' in the aftermath of Franco. Silence was, in fact, partial and selective; in terms of justice, the Amnesty Law hugely favoured the victors. If the ever-present and tragic image of the civil war was to serve as a warning, however, an avoidance of the most sensitive questions about the war and its aftermath – the intimate violence of the war, which, as earlier chapters have shown, had been silenced for complex reasons over decades, and the suppression of public memories of the Republican dead – was tacitly deemed a necessity.

Part III

Memories of war after Franco

10 Transition and consent: the presence of the past, 1975–1980

Those of us born after 1939 have had to clear the undergrowth away from our recent past, a past which has left us with too many defects to reconstitute our historical health. We are consciously or unconsciously ignorant. If we are conscious of it we suffer resentment and anger.[1]

History and the democratic state

Precisely a year after Franco's death, the Nationalist ex-combatants' confederation sent a letter to all those holding mayoral office in Spain with a reminder to commemorate the occasion. On the same day, 20 November 1976, the editorial in the liberal newspaper *El País* invoked the 1930 command of the country's most eminent philosopher of modernity, José Ortega y Gasset, made in the aftermath of the fall of General Primo's earlier military regime: 'the state does not exist. Spaniards: reconstruct your state!'[2] Ortega had been calling for a republic and for the monarchy of Alfonso XIII to be toppled, and there is some irony in the fact that his call should be remembered when the hopes for democratisation in 1976 depended on the legitimacy of another monarch, King Juan Carlos. The fact remained, however, that in the turbulent wake of the dictatorship's demise, powerbrokers nationally and internationally perceived that the new political order had to be seen to be based on explicit social consent if its stability was not to be compromised.

The role of memory in processes of political legitimation is never more important than during transitions to democracy. Hence, the enthusiastic sponsorship across the political spectrum of the Amnesty Law of 1977, as

---

[1] Montserrat Roig, *Els catalans als camps nazis* (Barcelona, 1977). Quotation from Spanish version: *Noche y niebla: los catalanes en los campos nazis* (Barcelona, 1978), p. 19.

[2] *Ya*, 19 November 1976; *El País*, 20 November 1976. Originally, Ortega y Gasset, *El Sol*, 15 November 1930.

discussed in Chapter 9.[3] Though politically rational, consigning the conflictive past to 'oblivion' through a tacit 'pact of forgetting' seemed, nonetheless, to some observers at the time and many others since to have favoured those who had supported and participated in the Franco system. A strong sense of the past was rarely far from the surface of public life during the post-Franco transition to democracy and a perception of the threat that history might carry with it. To remember one thing, especially in political state-building, is consciously to forget something else.[4] Political activists appreciated this by avoiding conflictive language and radical demands. If rhetoric redolent of the 1930s did surface during the transition it was quickly criticised, though the pent-up pressures of the past were considerable: 'class resentment was of such magnitude that it made me think about how fearsome individuals such as these could become in turbulent moments'.[5] Any suggestion of a settling of accounts could be depicted as returning to the days of the purges of the past, as Julián Marías's defence of Laín Entralgo in 1976 suggests:

Labelling as guilty during four decades anyone who was on the side of the defeated is morally and politically monstrous [...] as is the supposed contrary position: that one is culpable simply for having been on the side of the victors [...] Is it that the spirit of the 'purges' ['depuraciones'] of 1939, whose contribution to national debasement is beyond measure, is about to be reborn? [...] If a great, general, confession is to be considered necessary, then make it – [and if so] I consider that it should be done secretly and in accord with each conscience; but, it must be [a confession] of all Spaniards. For forty years it was obligatory only for half [the population]; if now we are obliging exclusively the other half to do so we will perpetuate the coercion, the violence, and to be quite correct, the lies [...][6]

This was also true in relation to the seemingly intractable problem of regional identities. When a Basque representative to the Constitutional Commission in 1978 declared that the state police in the Basque Country

---

[3] On amnesty, W. James Booth, 'The Unforgotten: Memories of Justice', *American Political Science Review*, 95, 4 (December 2001), pp. 783–6; on Europe-wide form of amnesia after 1945: Hans Magnus Enzensberger, *Civil Wars: From LA to Bosnia* (New York, 1990); Judt, 'The Past Is Another Country', in Deák et al. (eds.), *Politics of Retribution*; Pieter Lagrou, *The Legacy of Nazi Occupation: Patriotic Memory and National Recovery in Western Europe, 1945–1965* (Cambridge, 2000).

[4] Maja Zehfuss, 'Remembering to Forget/Forgetting to Remember', in Duncan Bell (ed.), *Memory, Trauma, and World Politics* (London, 2006), pp. 213–30. The dialectic of remembering and forgetting in transitional Spain is explored in political terms in Aguilar, *Memoria*.

[5] Castilla del Pino, *Casa del olivo*, p. 196.

[6] Julián Marías, 'Los supuestos', *La Vanguardia Española*, 27 June 1976, p. 15.

represented a 'force of repression' he was chastised by other members for looking backwards, for failing to recognise the difference between an authoritarian regime and democracy, and for attempting to provoke a divisive reaction or even for sabotaging proceedings.[7]

The political 'pact of forgetting' has come to be understood as a much broader 'pact of silence' than was really the case during the transitional process, though it is true that many people's memories of the civil war and broad consciousness of the past clashed with the dominant, highly rationalised and constrained political memory constructed from above. As we have seen throughout the period since 1939, remembering and forgetting did not develop in isolation from social change, and Spanish society in the 1960s and 1970s was not trapped in a condition of stasis. A danger of relying on a simple discourse of 'forgetting' to analyse attitudes to the past in the aftermath of the dictatorship is that society can seem homogeneous and passive, as mere recipient of a political *diktat*. In fact, social actors were active participants in the dynamic and variegated process of constructing a democratic constitutional state.

The policy of 'forgetting' had been justified by figures associated with the Franco regime, in effect by internalising the 'black legend' of Spain, constructed over centuries by foreigners, a myth which regime ultras claimed to detest while at the same time projecting it as a justification of 'necessary' authoritarianism.[8] This politically driven, strategic manipulation of a powerful myth posited that Spaniards were uncontrollable and too politically immature to govern themselves – a notion exemplified in Carrero Blanco's intervention in April 1970 against importation of the 'demo-liberal system', warning of the addiction of society to a lack of self-control which was only encouraged by democracy. Since the civil war, the country had thus benefited from the 'treatment' provided by the dictatorship. To support his case, Carrero recalled a litany of the 'sins' of the Popular Front: 'endless revolts, assaults, church burnings, killings of the religious, reprisals and cruel persecutions'.[9] So often was it repeated that collective 'amnesia' was the best medicine for Spain that it became widely accepted: 'it has been said over and over again that in Spain we cannot enjoy the freedoms that they have in other countries because we are ungovernable, because we have "fire in our veins", because we are uncultured, because, because [...]'[10] A 'fratricidal'

---

[7] Comisión de Asuntos Constitucionales y Libertades Públicas, *DSCD*, 90, 15 June 1978.
[8] E.g., Fernández de la Mora, *ABC*, 13 November 1975.
[9] Ginés de Buitrago (pseudonym), '¡Un poco de formalidad!', *ABC*, 2 April 1970.
[10] Enrique Meneses (b.1929), in Borràs, *Los que no hicimos*, pp. 248–9.

explanation or narrative of the civil war – that it had been a senseless and tragic act of collective madness of which all Spaniards were to some degree culpable – had obvious appeal after nearly four decades of Francoist propaganda. As was pointed out, however, this obscured the real dynamics of the wartime violence: 'the fanatic' in the so-called 'zona nacional' and 'the fanatic' in the 'zona roja' had much in common but could hardly be described as 'brothers'.[11] Moreover, there was nothing simple about the heterogeneous social support for the fratricidal thesis. The constructed cultural trauma of the conflict as a 'war between brothers' seemed to confirm the Francoist hardliners' blunt and oppressive vision of the congenital defects of Spain and of Spaniards. Its imposition created another form of trauma. Acceptance of an equally shared sense of responsibility for the war implied that the 'baptism of blood' and the 'purification' and 'purge' of dictatorship were somehow justified.[12] While the 1940s required the expiation of guilt through suffering, therefore, the transition to democracy seemed to call for a sharing of guilt and responsibility and only grudgingly allowed an uncovering of the more complex historical realities.[13] In 1977 the Catalan novelist Montserrat Roig (1946–91), a brilliant early advocate of a recuperation of historical memory – specifically of the deaths en masse of Catalan Republican prisoners in Mauthausen concentration camp during the Second World War – related the consequent sense of historical deficit and distress to a legacy of conscious or unconscious ignorance.[14] Meeting the claims of the so-called 'parenthetical generation', born between the suffering of war and its aftermath and the 'boom' of the 1960s (those between 24 and 38 in 1977, including Roig), would be limited, therefore, first by the politics of the Transition, the theme of this chapter, and later by the race towards post-Franco modernisation (see Chapter 11).

The control of history during the dictatorship meant that there was indeed public ignorance, which could only be rectified over time. For many people the association of the Franco regime with Nazism had more to do with the pioneering work of writers such as Roig than it did with Hitler's aid to Franco's war effort in 1936. The longevity of Francoism by the 1970s and its control of history from above meant that there was

---

[11] Laín Entralgo, *Descargo*, pp. 191, 243.

[12] Arturo Pardos Batiste to Borràs, *Los que no hicimos*, pp. 541–2.

[13] See Víctor M. Pérez Díaz, *The Return of Civil Society: The Emergence of Democratic Spain* (Cambridge, MA, 1993), p. 24.

[14] See epigraph. Republican victims who volunteered to fight against Nazi Germany and were captured were not only from Catalonia. Some nine hundred of the dead, for example, were from Andalucía. See, e.g., the motion for a monument in *Boletín Oficial del Parlamento de Andalucía*, 330, 29 November 2005.

something of a temporal slippage in distinguishing the past from the present. The veil on the past was being cautiously lifted at a time when repressive outbursts from the declining regime under attack were becoming more common. While some brutal episodes from the civil war and early 1940s were beginning to be known about in the 1970s, historical consciousness was limited. The degree of change in the social and political context of the 1970s since the 1940s was not necessarily understood. It was natural later that some interpretations of the past would also be shaped at this time in part by attempts in Germany to confront and master a shameful past which remained present. The sense of belated revelation and unburdening of an 'evil', though ill-defined, 'something' can be sensed in recent testimony: 'I lived my time enthusiastically in the Sección Femenina, believing faithfully in everything they taught me there [...] People had little idea what was happening behind the smokescreen.'[15]

Richard Evans has argued that 'in political transitions, historians can never be sure that their voice will be heard, because what they say is not always what people want to hear'.[16] The problem in the period 1975–80 was that, although there was a broad range of discussion about the past, the extent of the historical narrative's complexity could not be controlled or channelled. There was a strong likelihood that a range of fragmented and contradictory stories would burst forth as democracy flowered, but drawing 'lessons' for the present from this process would be difficult. This was the case particularly with the violence of the war. In 1974, the liberal American historian Gabriel Jackson, whose books were still prohibited in Spain, summarised the position: 'historians of the regime have spent thirty-five years hypnotised by the version of the war given by the victors. The exiles took few documents with them, and the most aware sections of the people in the interior know that it is better for their own security not to speak publicly or write about the massive killings of their political opponents by the Nationalists.'[17] A decade or more before regional and local studies based on newly available municipal archives appeared in the 1980s and 1990s, the nature of the violence of occupation in such places as Zaragoza, Valladolid, Seville, Zamora or La Coruña was part of the collective subconscious of those who had lived through the war, but was not spoken about, and its precise extent could not been calculated. Neither had there been public

[15] Buendía Gómez, 'Peinando recuerdos', pp. 169–70.
[16] Evans: 'Redesigning the Past', 12.
[17] *Boletín de Orientación Bibliográfica*, 100, December 1974, 7–29.

recognition or identification of the victims.[18] In his 1975 memoir, the one-time Falangist Laín Entralgo examined his own conscience about silencing the truth, but this kind of public self-questioning was rare, even in the 1970s.[19] Those who were not as conscious of having played a part in history – 'ordinary people' – did not generally record their memories and feelings about the past, though they have done so increasingly since the 1990s. For one thing, remembering was often painful, and the context was not favourable to recollection. Typical responses in the late 1970s suggest reluctance: 'I don't want to remember all that'; 'just remembering it makes me fearful'.[20] Until the 1990s there seems to have been no coherently and collectively formulated purpose behind remembering; nor was there an easy mechanism for dealing with, understanding, or acting upon the traces of the past that might have been uncovered. The February 1981 attempted military coup also acted as a warning. This is the ambivalence of cultural trauma. First, there was the question of whether reliving the pain was worthwhile. Second, there was uncertainty about the extent to which this reluctance might be overcome at a broad social level after Franco by rejecting forty years of imposed limits on the claims of 'the defeated'. And, third, there was insecurity about possible reactions to the challenging of the previous Catholic and conservative monopoly of collective trauma.

Social memory and democracy

In the aftermath of the dictator's demise it was argued that those who governed, as well as those constituting the opposition, were largely 'niños de la guerra civil' and, therefore, that 'they would never be able to forget the conflict'. The hope was that those childhood memories would serve to avoid a new civil war, 'the worst kind of war'.[21] We naturally consider the public figures of the Franco era and the Transition as primarily political actors, but there is a case for analysis of the socialisation and cultural conditioning of such individuals in order to understand the origins and functions of remembering. This is true of opponents of the regime and reformers as well of those who took refuge in the bunker mentality of Franco's last years. The tension between the needs of the

---

[18] Regime insiders produced some of the first research, though their privileged access to sources meant that their methods and findings could not be scrutinised for some years. See, e.g., Salas, *Pérdidas* (1977).

[19] Laín Entralgo, *Descargo*, pp. 263, 275.

[20] Testimony in 1979: Botey Vallès, *Relats*, pp. 75, 82.

[21] Pàmies, *Niños de la guerra*, pp. 9–10. Also Alicia Alted Vigil, 'Los niños de la guerra civil', *Anales de Historia Contemporánea*, 19 (2003), pp. 43–58. See also Chapter 6.

moment for 'official memory' to overcome the past and refusal to relinquish the essential emotional investment in the war possessed by all those still constituted as 'the victors' was clear. One representative of the politically immobile tendency was the belligerent Opus Dei minister of education (for a short spell in 1973) Julio Rodríguez Martínez, a former Rector of Madrid University, who stressed the continuity of past, present and future and, at the funeral of his political mentor, Carrero Blanco, in December 1973, had notoriously declined to shake the hand of the reforming Archbishop of Madrid, Cardinal Tarancón, who he perceived to be in league with the opposition.[22] Rodríguez Martínez was born in 1928 and was therefore fifteen to twenty years younger than three of the emblematic figures of the post-1940s turn towards tolerance and reconciliation who have figured throughout these pages: Enrique y Tarancón himself, Laín Entralgo and Joaquín Ruiz-Giménez. In 1975, Rodríguez would attempt to appropriate the term 'war child' in a way which was politically manipulative, certainly, but which also indicated a particular interpretation of the effects of post-war social change on war memories. This was a view not of child victims brought up in Republican families but of those whose memories were coloured by stories of the 'crusade' and the 'heroic gestures' of the Alcázar of Toledo, the red berets of the Navarrese *tercios* which weekly filled the 'indelible pages of vivid colour' of children's comic books in the rebel zone and in the aftermath of the war, and the Republican 'checas', the clandestine prisons which became symbolic of the tyrannical enemy.[23]

In a short series of essays in 1973–5, Rodríguez Martínez would reflect on the concept of 'war children', understood as if it had been something exclusive to the victors' side: a generation which was 'expert in living on the home front, in bombardments, in hunger [. . .] Of those who never knew if a kiss from a father who was a pilot of the Crusade would be the last.'[24] Rather as with backward-looking Falangist ex-combatants who had fought for Franco and considered themselves 'a generation which refused to grow old', this background, it was obdurately supposed, would prepare the men of his generation to face up to the challenges of the regime's decline.[25]

Other *niños* of the war had experienced similar wartime emotions, but their post-war lives would be shaped very differently by the conflict.

[22] Enrique y Tarancón, *Confesiones*, pp. 619–20.
[23] 'Omisiones', *ABC*, 8 January 1975. See also, e.g., Luis Otero, *Flechas y pelayos* (Madrid, 2000).
[24] 'Dos fronteras', *ABC*, 7 November 1973, p. 3.
[25] Diego Salas Pombo (b.1918), Consejero Nacional del Movimiento, *Arriba*, 18 March 1973.

In 1977, Pedro González Juarranz, one of the ninety thousand children evacuated from wartime Madrid by the Junta Provincial de Protección de Menores, sat down to record his bittersweet memories of the school-children's colony for refugees in Arbúcies, Catalonia, where he discovered the countryside – 'the equivalent of being born again' – only later to be overtaken by the advancing privations of war as the Republican resistance was pushed back and to suffer 'the calamities, perils and horrors of the war':

Until then our infantile nervous systems had withstood fifty-five bombardments by artillery and fascist aviation, together with the piercing separation from our families, and, in addition, for my brother Higinio and I, with the lacerating and heart-rending loss of our eighteen-year-old brother César, volunteer militiaman fallen in the defence of Madrid.[26]

The only explicit concession to Republican experience made by Rodríguez Martínez, however, was his reference to the 'sorrowful boarding of a boat on the way to Russia' of evacuee children in the government zone, a stock ideological reflex when Francoists made reference to childhood experience on the Republican side, which figured often in post-war state propaganda. Wartime hunger, according to his analysis, affected both home fronts equally, though the reality was more complex and privations were far greater in the overcrowded and besieged loyalist zone. On 'liberation', according to Rodríguez, the physical characteristics of children were restored, a version of the past which forgot the effects of economic discrimination in the aftermath and the famine conditions of 1941.[27] The psychological damage done to children of the war was recognised; again, however, this was reduced to one wartime zone, and the continued post-war plight of the defeated was ignored. According to this narrative, it was as though the post-war social rebuilding of Spain had indeed been based on a single community of the victors: 'we knew that the parents of some schoolfriends had been murdered and we felt particularly close to them, seeking to distract them and mitigate their sorrow. We understood, up to a point, death at the front, in combat, but not the shootings on the home front for political reasons.'[28] For diehard Francoists such as Rodríguez Martínez, the killing of José Calvo Sotelo, carried out by Republican police on 13 July 1936, continued to be seen as the first of these murders, that which had provided

---

[26] Testimony in Elordi (ed.), *Años difíciles*, pp. 130–1. On Madrid evacuations, *El Socialista*, 15 December 1936, p. 2; 9 January 1937, p. 2.
[27] Rodríguez Martínez, 'La generación de la paz', *ABC*, 24 November 1974, p. 21.
[28] 'Omisiones', *ABC*, 8 January 1975.

justification for the military rebellion.[29] In sum, there is a strong sense in these reflections that the 'fratricidal' thesis allowed the victors to usurp the suffering of the defeated and counter the latter's sense of collective trauma which had begun to be expressed as the regime drew to a close:

> the generation of war children [...] is configured by a coming together of circumstances that, although with geographic and personal differences, had some level of homogeneity throughout Spain. The bellicose spirit, the bombing, the killings, the personal vengeance, the hatreds, the patriotism, the patriotic acts, the war hymns [...] All these circumstances formed our character [...] We were obliged to mature rapidly [...] Peace imposed certain requirements. We had to struggle for it [...] It was necessary to analyse the causes of the war so that it would not be repeated. A million dead and three years of conflict cannot, must not, be forgotten.[30]

The sharing of the blame was, however, uneven. The middle classes had sinned in allowing economic inequalities and religious hypocrisy to prevail in the pre-war era but, according to this intransigent analysis, political liberals and revolutionaries bore most responsibility for leading the country astray. The war had been a form of punishment demonstrating that apoliticism and sacrifice were preferable to protest. This was shown by the hard-working, 'austere' generation born during and immediately after the conflict, those conservative families who would pause and stand over a paltry meal during the 1940s and 1950s to pay heed collectively to the Himno Nacional broadcast daily on the radio, as Rodríguez remembered his family always did, though, in fact, most of the post-war sacrifice had been forced from the lower classes who had fought for the Republic.[31] Those born during the 1920s and 1930s – growing up between 'los campos de batalla' and, borrowing a phrase from Charles de Gaulle, the 'génération de la commodité' (the 'generation of convenience') – had been pressed socially and politically. They were part neither of the 'generation of the 1930s' (which we have called the 'generación rectora' – those who were publicly active in the lead-up to the civil war), nor of the protesting, 'unquiet' 'generation of the 1950s', the university students and sons and daughters of the wartime victors who, according to Rodríguez Martínez, should have been obedient but who took to the streets to demonstrate since 1956. The minister's resentment, in recalling nostalgically his own university days, of an 'apolitical and patriotic generation', 'without strikes', was aimed at those who had betrayed the

---

[29] E.g. Buitrago (Carrero Blanco), 'Formalidad', *ABC*, 2 April 1970.
[30] Rodríguez Martínez, 'La generación de la paz', *ABC*, 24 November 1974.
[31] See also Chapter 4, p. 108.

memory of the war, including reformists who had positions in Franco's Cortes and who did not feel as his generation did:

I refer to my period as a student, and although things have changed and the consumer society imposes its laws, we are capable of any sacrifice, compared to later generations which did not experience the war. The war left an imprint which it is difficult to forget [. . .] We have the bad memory of the fratricidal struggle, of something which we must not repeat, but also of a new resurgence out of the ashes [of the war].[32]

For the Republican side, cultural trauma across generations was shaped not by resentment at perceived betrayal but by exile and denial of access to justice. Republican traumatised identity originated in the discourse and social practices of the regime years and of the experience of war itself. Again, it is worth viewing one illustrative case in contrast to that of Rodríguez Martínez. In early January 1973 Francisco León Trejo, a military aeronautical engineer and Spanish Republican veteran, died in exile in Bay City, Michigan, at the age of 83, the last of his familial generation. The exile of professional military personnel who remained loyal to the Republic was not officially considered by the Franco state to have been motivated politically, an anomaly confirmed by the Amnesty Law of October 1977. Affected individuals had been formally discharged from service by the regime on the grounds of desertion and unknown whereabouts. This interpretation was somewhat in contradiction with the decree of the rebel authorities on 5 December 1936, signed by General Franco, by which state civilian and military personnel who continued to serve the government of the Republic were dismissed precisely for remaining loyal to the political regime of the time. Judged for 'rebellion', according to articles 237 and 238 of the Code of Military Justice, when they lost the war, therefore, these men also lost their military careers.[33] At the end of the war, many professional military men thus chose exile. Two decades after the Amnesty Law, a judicial case was initiated in October 1997 by Francisco León's son, Alexander Sáenz León, which was heard in the Spanish Supreme Court where the sanction imposed on his mother and father by the Spanish High Commission in Morocco in May 1937 that they were 'traitors to their *patria*' would be officially revoked.[34]

---

[32] *ABC*, 2 April 1974, on publication of his memoir *Impresiones de un ministro de Carrero Blanco* (Barcelona, 1974).

[33] See *Boletín Oficial de las Cortes Generales*, 61, 5 September 1980, pp. 1,537–8; 17 October 1980, 67, pp. 1,733–5; 71, p. 1,955. The Amnesty Law of 15 October discriminated against professional soldiers loyal to the Republic because it offered, in effect, a reprieve rather than annulling Francoist sentences against them. See, e.g., Javier Paulino Pérez, *El País*, 25 July 1980.

[34] *BOE*, 7 November 1997.

Other relatives had drawn attention to the case before. Francisco León's nephew was the journalist Joaquín León Fernández who arranged for an announcement of the death of his uncle in 1973 to be sent to the newspaper *ABC*. The short notice, aimed at notifying acquaintances and leaving a simple record of his passing, did not appear, however, and shortly afterwards Joaquín León published an open letter to the editor of the newspaper in the opposition periodical *Cuadernos para el Diálogo* protesting at the rejection of the notice because, presumably, it had mentioned that Francisco León had died 'in exile'. The more politically loaded term *destierro* (banishment) had deliberately not been used, but there remained great reluctance to publish announcements of the deaths of Republican exiles.[35] *ABC*'s uncharitable decision left the family feeling that, in spite of the passage of many years, society was 'still not on the right track'.[36] In his letter, Joaquín León had drawn attention to far-reaching questions which related war memories to the future, reminding the newspaper's editor that 'neither your children nor my own are affected by the sounding of anthems which once moved us', songs produced by an 'inept generation' which had been 'incapable of resolving its problems without a barbaric war'. Nevertheless, the dead, for good or ill, had 'written history' and 'nobody [had] the right to erase a single name from those pages which are written for ever'.[37] Although the pages of the newspapers spoke increasingly about 'harmony' and 'openness', they failed to go beyond 'sophistry', León argued, when they lacked a sincere sense of conscience which was acted upon in practice. His desire was that those who were implicated in the war, even though they might not have fought in it, 'disappear' quickly from the decision-making process.

For the Republican León Trejo family, which had actively supported political and social reform in Seville in the 1930s, the civil war had been a great tragedy.[38] Three brothers, all members of Unión Republicana, would be executed by the rebels during the early months: Manuel, Joaquín and José, the latter being the father of the author of the 1973 open letter, Joaquín León.[39] His uncle, who shared the name Joaquín,

---

[35] Official resistance to use of the term 'exiliado' was gradually overcome, though rarely in conservative publications. See testimonial: 'El exilio de Jiménez de Asúa', *CPED*, 87, December 1970, 33–9. Also Ramón Gómez Molina, *Qué son los exiliados* (Barcelona, 1977), which recuperated the term after Franco, placing the exile of 1939 in the context of a long history reaching back to the expulsion of the Jews and of the *moriscos*, but also even-handedly including the Republican dissolution of the Jesuits in 1932.

[36] 'Carta abierta al Director de *ABC*', *CPED*, 113, February 1973, 41. As with the death notice, this open letter seems also not to have appeared in *ABC*.

[37] On names and memory, see Margalit, *Ethics*, p. 25 (and Chapter 12).

[38] See *ABC* (Madrid), 18 April 1937.   [39] Ortiz Villalba, *Sevilla '36*, pp. 172, 245–6.

had been the school teacher in the small town of Castilleja del Campo where he led efforts to end illiteracy and offended traditionalists because of his modernising and anti-clerical ideas. When the military rebellion took place in July 1936 he had gone to Seville to aid the defence but was arrested. The headlines of the rebel-supporting newspapers of the city fuelled the purge: 'Denounce and detain the traitors'.[40] Joaquín would be executed in a few weeks, shot against the wall of the cemetery in Castilblanco de los Arroyos on 22 August 1936.[41] His brother José, also a teacher, had been Civil Governor in Guadalajara during the first year of the Republic and was also arrested and executed, on 17 October 1936. The third brother, Manuel, had fled the repression and went into hiding but was later captured and met the same fate. Francisco, the military aviator and engineer, had joined no political organisation because he believed that the military should not be involved in politics. As a Lieutenant Colonel, he was made military commander of the Cuatro Vientos aerodrome in Madrid only days before the military coup and remained loyal to the Republic, helping successfully to defend the capital.[42]

José León Trejo, executed in October 1936, had been the father of nine children, and Joaquín León, who had written to *ABC* in 1973, was one of these *niños de la guerra* and would live with the personal trauma of the conflict ever after. In 1971, some two years prior to the death of his uncle Manuel in the United States, he had felt compelled to broach publicly his personal past in the light of the political situation. Motivated by political and family stimuli, he had published an article in the pages of *Cuadernos para el Diálogo* – 'Rojos al paredón' ('Shoot the Reds'; or, more literally, 'Reds up against the wall') – which reflected on his memories.[43] He began by acknowledging a modest political critique written six months earlier by Pedro Laín Entralgo, at the time of the Burgos trials, which the daily press would not print, calling for an end to bloodshed.[44] León in fact dedicated his own article to the wife of Laín, Milagros Martínez Prieto, whose father, Jesús Martínez, a moderate member of Acción Republicana, had also been shot by the rebels in Seville, with no judicial process; his body had been deposited in a

---

[40] See the Carlist newspaper *La Unión*, 9 December 1936, cited in Ortiz Villalba, *Sevilla '36*, p. 172.

[41] Barker, *Largo trauma*, pp. 43, 137–8.

[42] The name Francisco León Trejo is today immortalised as part of a display at the Museo del Aire de Cuatro Vientos, the only military museum created in Spain during the period since Franco's death.

[43] 'Rojos al paredón', *CPED*, 93, June 1971, 11–12.

[44] Laín Entralgo, 'Entre el temor y la esperanza', *CPED*, 87, December 1970. Also, later and similarly Laín, 'Sangre en la calle', *CPED*, 117, June 1973, 21–2.

common grave.[45] Many years later Laín would write that for his wife 'imagining this act was until the end of her days a permanent and grievous wound'.[46] More immediately, Joaquín León had been emotionally moved by a question from his six-year-old son on seeing the slogan 'Rojos al paredón' on a wall during a Sunday morning walk: 'Papá, ¿Qué es paredón?' ('What is a firing squad?') More or less defining what inherited conflict-related personal trauma is, León reports how he had long meditated inwardly, in 'dark silence', about being an orphan of the war and how the motivation finally for outwardly expressing the memory had come from such an innocent and deeply intimate source as his own son.

More graffiti later appeared in the same place: '¡Viva Franco!'; '¡1st Abril Victoria!'; '¡Arriba España!' The past was intruding on daily life, as it frequently did during the 1970s, largely because of the prospect of political change and because change, in some quarters, was resisted. The savage execution against the wall of their office of five labour lawyers linked to the PCE by Falange supporters in Madrid in January 1977 was perhaps the most public example.[47] At the subsequent trial of the Atocha killers in February 1980 one of the gunmen would testify how 'ever since I was small the history books had taught that communists were murderers who maintained the war for three years'.[48]

Whilst an objective of wartime bombardment had been the deliberate intimidation of civilians, victims were not singled out as they were for execution, as the León Trejo brothers had been, in a premeditated and

---

[45] Laín Entralgo, *Descargo*, pp. 185–6. For a ceremony of remembrance fifty years later, in which Milagros Martínez and Laín Entralgo played a leading role in unveiling a plaque at the site of the common grave in the cemetery of San Pedro, see *ABC*, Seville, 24 August 1986, p. 3.

[46] Laín Entralgo, Prólogo to Ortiz Villalba, *Sevilla '36*. Juan Ortiz's 1998 study of the repression in Seville was also dedicated to Milagros Martínez, for whom the book allowed the name of her father to be recorded: on Jesús Martínez, his imprisonment and murder, and the culpability of Queipo de Llano, see Ortiz Villalba, *Sevilla '36*, pp. 271–5. On the narrow line between political collaboration and complicity with violence in civil wars, see, e.g., Laín's unfortunate competition entry in early 1937 in the form of a dedicatory article on the Seville Falangist, *torero* and landowner José García Carranza ('El Algabeño') and his death (29 December 1936) at the front, which appeared in *Arriba España* (5 January 1937) entitled 'Redención de lo castizo: a la muerte del Algabeño en acto de servicio'. García Carranza was well known as an extremist, was close to Queipo de Llano, and had been heavily implicated in 'paseando' ('Taking for a ride') Republicans in Seville. Queipo broadcast, *ABC*, 4 August 1936, p. 4; Francisco Moreno Gómez, *1936: El genocidio franquista en Córdoba* (Barcelona, 2008), p. 51. Laín, in Pamplona, did not know about the killing, although he had gone to Seville to try to find out what had happened to his Republican father-in-law: Laín Entralgo, *Descargo*, p. 196. On the death of El Algabeño, *ABC* (Seville), 31 December 1936.

[47] See also Chapter 9.   [48] *El País*, 19 February 1980.

often ritualised way, aimed at utter humiliation of particular individuals.[49] In formulating an answer in 1971 to his son's question, Joaquín
León felt a strong desire to confront those who were responsible for
re-creating the image of the firing squad and the shadow of the cemetery
wall: 'I'd ask them about my father and my uncles and above all, I'd
ask them about the hundreds and even thousands of anonymous victims,
of whatever ideology [...] I'd ask them if they have children and if
they hoped and desired that those children live in peace and [have a
chance] to work for their future.' He had in time come to see that his own
'intimate wall' did not have to 'drain away the sources of enthusiasm
and hope of my own children' and that he could contribute to 'the
demolition of *los paredones*', even if 'forgetting' them represented 'the
greatest renunciation that a man can offer'.[50]

The effects of becoming a wartime orphan were profound and long-
lasting. The trauma of loss in aerial bombardment was also considerable,
as the memoir written by the novelist Juan Goytisolo, whose mother
had been killed in a bombing raid in Barcelona in March 1938, during
the period of the Francoist saturation bombing of the Catalan capital,
confirms. Goytisolo considered that rather than being merely the 'son of
a woman who is and always will be unknown to you, one is a son of
the civil war, its messianism, cruelty and anger'.[51] Deaths at the front
perhaps leave a different legacy again: the father of the radical priest
Víctor Manuel Arbeloa, for example, was killed on the Bilbao front and
his son expressed his memories less traumatically once it became possible
to speak publicly about the war: 'we do not have memories. And this is
quite poor. But neither do we have bitterness. And this is a gift.'[52] The
force of memory across generations remains clear, however.

The story of the León Trejo family also encapsulates the relationship
of the civil war, and memories related to it, to migration and accelerated
transgenerational change. Even into the 1970s, this relationship can
be approached through the dialectic of the rural and the urban. One
woman who had left her village for Barcelona as soon as she was able
after suffering taunts as the daughter of 'rojos' killed during the civil
war felt 'protected by the city' and its relative sense of freedom. After
Franco's death she would attend political meetings with her children

---

[49] On intimidatory intentions of bombing, see, e.g., Joan Villaroya i Font, *Els bombardeigs de Barcelona durant la guerra civil (1936–1939)* (Barcelona, 1999).
[50] 'Rojos al paredón'.
[51] Goytisolo, *Coto vedado*, p. 66. Also his brother, José Agustín Goytisolo, in Marsal, *Pensar bajo el franquismo*, p. 161. On aerial bombardment, death and memory, see also Ana, *Decidme*, pp. 48–9; Cava Mesa, *Memoria colectiva*, pp. 265–8 (on Guernica).
[52] 'Recuerdo de Julián Besteiro', *CPED*, 32, May 1966, 17.

where discussion was about liberty, associated explicitly for her with the city itself and the escape from rural life: 'There, where there was freedom, were my children and I.'[53] The Spanish case confirms that women's memories – whether of war, authoritarianism or social change – are invariably related to and framed by family. Franco's tenure unavoidably structured Spain's twentieth century, marking the 'before' and the 'after' of public life. His death allowed a circle which had begun in 1936, encompassing the public and the private, to be closed: 'At last the dictator had died, just three days after the birth of my first grandchild.'[54] For many people who would previously not have spoken openly about relatives killed during the war, there was an opening up. One widow of an executed coalminer from Asturias broke her silence on the eve of the first democratic elections in 1977: 'I am going to vote for the Socialist Party even if they kill me for it.'[55] Though there would be some level of disillusion, even leftists would later recognise that Adolfo Suárez, the conservative ex-regime bureaucrat and leader of the UCD, who became the country's first post-war elected prime minister, had been instrumental in making the process of transition peaceful.[56] After 1975, there would also be a surge in registrations of civil war deaths, partly in the hope that a war widow's pension law for Republicans, denied for decades after the war, would be introduced.[57] Women who had worked to compensate for the loss of income and bring up children had received little help from the state even when they were too old to work. When it was finally legislated that the families of war victims should have a pension it represented something materially and symbolically important, even though it was considered by most people to be long overdue.[58]

In rural society, silence had been no simple sign of forgetting, and the greater sense of freedom began to be registered as the regime declined. In the town of Mijas (Málaga) the businessman who in the 1940s had been granted a state monopoly over collection of the area's 10,000 hectares of esparto grass used for weaving stood for election in 1971 in the limited 'organic democracy' introduced at municipal level during the last years of the regime. Esparto had formerly been central to a moral peasant economy based on common access to land and exploitation of the resource as a basic form of income. Villagers had not forgotten how the war had made his economic power possible and, on the day of the

---

[53] Testimony in Elordi (ed.), *Años difíciles*, p. 189.   [54] Testimony in ibid., p. 316.
[55] Testimony in ibid., p. 190.   [56] E.g., Morales and Pereira, *Memoria*, p. 127.
[57] E.g., Espinosa, *Contra el olvido*; Collier, *Socialists*, p. 161.
[58] See, e.g., Elordi (ed.), *Anos difíciles*, p. 269.

poll, he received only 200 of the 3,000 votes cast. Some people went as far as tearing up his propaganda leaflets in public.[59] Similarly, when the funeral was held in the early 1970s of the long-standing mayor of a small village who had come to power as a result of the war and been involved in identifying women 'with Republican ideas' to undergo ritual head shaving as punishment, not a single villager could be found who was willing to help carry his coffin to the cemetery for burial. The shame of the women, imposed by parading them through the streets in the aftermath of suppression of the Republic, had never since been spoken about openly in the village. This was before the death of Franco and was not a case of collective opinion shifting with the political transition to democracy, but a new consciousness of freedom on the horizon: 'That day, in silence, the village avenged itself on one who in former times had been all-powerful.'[60]

There were further, more direct, attempts to break the tacitly agreed silence within communities concerning the intimate violence of the past, including action to have some of the neglected remains of victims of Francoist violence who still lay in common graves dignified by reburial. Many communities were aware of ravines or gullies in the local landscape where the bodies of victims had been disposed of. In the province of Soria (Castile), between 1977 and 1981, exhumations of war graves were carried out at sixteen different sites.[61] That the mortal remains of the dead became the subject of disinterring and proper reburial in the aftermath of Franco's demise suggests that the era of the war, for many people, had not yet been symbolically ended.[62]

One of the first sites of disinterment was in the hamlet of Fonelas (Granada), where many people in the 1970s continued to live in dwellings which were essentially caves, as their forebears had in the 1930s,

---

[59] Fraser, *Pueblo*, p. 73.

[60] E.g. Piñero Valverde, 'Mi viejo álbum', p. 90; Buendía Gómez, 'Peinando recuerdos', pp. 168, 173.

[61] See Gregorio Herrero Balsa and Antonio Hernández García, *La represión en Soria durante la guerra civil* (Soria, 1982). See attempts by isolated PSOE deputies to make the process easier: Espinosa, *Contra el olvido*, p. 161.

[62] See, for example, 'Jinámar: La sima de los "caídos". Matanza de "rojos" en Canarias', *Interviú*, 66 (August 1977), 24–8; 'El cementario güanche', *Interviú*, 67 (September 1977), pp. 24–7; 'Otro "Valle de los Caídos" sin cruz. "La Barranca" fosa común para 2,000 riojanos', *Interviú*, 74 (October 1977), 88–90; 'Matanzas franquistas en Sevilla', *Interviú*, 86 (5–11 January 1978); 'Solo dejaron los huesos. Albatera (Alicante), ensayo general para el exterminio', *Interviú*, 105 (May 1978), 40–2; 'El pueblo desentierra a sus muertos. Casas de Don Pedro, 39 años después de la matanza', *Interviú*, 109 (June 1978), 86–8; Dionisio Giménez Plaza, 'Navarra, 1936', *Interviú*, 136 (Nov.–Dec. 1978) 136–7; Silva and Macías, *Fosas*, pp. 184–95, 259, 314, 322–5. For Burgos, in 1979, see Luis Castro, *Capital de la cruzada* (Barcelona, 2006), p. 333.

without many of the necessities of modern life. On 1 April 1976 (Día de la Victoria), having received permission from both the mayor and the commander of the local Guardia Civil, a group of some sixty locals, including at least one recently returned from abroad as a labour migrant, proceeded to the place only a kilometre or so from the village where three Republicans had been shot and hastily buried together in April 1939. The deaths had never been officially registered, and nobody had dared talk about the tragic deed for almost forty years although gradually it had become normal for villagers to say a prayer when passing and to tie a knot of ribbon in the bushes which grew around the burial site, gradually obscuring it over the years.[63] The collective remembering began with excavation of the bones of the three men and their transferral to the cemetery. This was a cautious process, the participants preferring to remain anonymous and expressing a sense of the act being illegal. No officials were present. The fear was not simply of reprisals from the authorities. The resentments and pain of intimate violence ran deeply, seeming in some instances to paralyse those affected within the community, so that in several cases initiatives to rebury victims would come from villagers or townsfolk returning to the community from outside after years spent elsewhere, usually as migrant workers. During 1976, some eighty thousand Spanish emigrants returned, though almost 3.5 million remained abroad, one-third of them in Europe.[64]

In January 1978, some two thousand people gathered at the cemetery at Aranjuez, south of Madrid, for the inauguration of two burial vaults, financed through public collection and funds sent from migrants in France, Switzerland and Mexico, to house the mortal remains of two hundred victims killed in the repression and disposed of in burial pits between 25 May 1939 and 17 December 1942. Newspaper reports announced briefly that 'the bodies of these persons, who fought on the side of the Republican Popular Army, belonged to locals of Aranjuez, Villarejo de Salvanés, Belmonte del Tajo and other pueblos of the area'. One of them was the uncle of the leftist militant and Republican heroine of the war Rosario Sánchez Mora, whose father, a prisoner in the Almendros concentration camp in Alicante, had himself been executed, though his body was never found.[65] The Aranjuez vaults were to be inscribed in a way which made an implicit connection between the meaning and

---

[63] Eduardo Castro, 'Muertos sin sepultura', *CPED*, 6 November 1976, 32–3; 'Granada: Las matanzas no se olvidan', *Interviú*, 81 (July 1977), 32–5.

[64] *Ya*, 28 November 1976, pp. 4–5.

[65] Julio Rodríguez Puértolas (ed.), *La República y la cultura: paz, guerra y exilio* (Madrid, 2009), p. 181. Rosario Sánchez was born in Villarejo de Salvanés in 1919 where her father was later leader of Izquierda Republicana.

defence of the Republic and the new-born democracy after 1975: 'In gratitude for your dedication to defending liberty. We will always remember you. Comrades [*compañeros*] and Family.'[66]

In the municipality of Siero (Asturias), where one of the first anti-regime guerrilla campaigns of the 1940s had emerged, an inspection was carried out in November 1979 by a judge, forensic scientist, lawyer, the mayor and other local officials to confirm the existence of a large common burial pit close to the parish of Lugones. A mass of human remains was found which belonged to 'individuals shot by the victorious side at the end of the civil war'. On All Saints' Day (1 November), traditionally since the war the date when Francoist families had openly remembered their dead, a cross and placard had appeared at the site with the inscription: 'Hijos del pueblo asesinados por los fascistas'.[67] In November 2006, after considerable debate, the establishment of a more prominent and permanent memorial to the victims of the civil war and the post-war in Siero would be approved. The stone monument aroused controversy and opposition because of its prominence and because it 're-awoke' what to some were 'almost forgotten arguments'.[68]

In Lora del Río (Seville), to cite another typical case, anarchism had been strong long before the heightened class conflict of the 1930s, and there had been imprisonment and subsequent killing of some rightists when the revolution began following the military coup in 1936. When the pueblo was 'liberated' by the rebels soon after, however, the counter-violence was devastating: the executions of 623 individuals between 1936 and 1943 have been documented in recent years.[69] As was common across Spain – and as we have seen in Aranjuez – many of the townsfolk had moved away after the war and its bloody aftermath. The writer Juan Goytisolo met one migrant from Lora del Río in Paris in the 1950s.[70] An American woman, Maria Corrales, reported many years later how her father had witnessed as a five-year-old boy the killing of his Republican mother in the town.[71] Following the practice across the country after

---

[66] 'Aranjuez: traslado de los restos mortales de 200 personas', *La Vanguardia*, 7 January 1978, p. 4.

[67] 'Fosa común de fusilados en la guerra civil', *El País*, 11 November 1979.

[68] *El Comercio Digital*, 18 January 2007. For the guerrilla campaign, see Juan Antonio Sacaluga, *La resistencia socialista en Asturias* (Madrid, 1986).

[69] As of 2005 by the Asociación Andaluza de Memoria Histórica y Justicia. See also Lezcano Nieto, *Sangre y fuego*; Ronald Fraser, 'El comienzo: la "liberación" de Lora del Río (1936)', *Cuadernos del Ruedo Ibérico*, 46–8 (June–December 1975), pp. 81–94; Espinosa, *Columna*, p. 89. On pre-'liberation' anti-clerical killing: Montero, *Persecución*, pp. 776, 798.

[70] Goytisolo, *En los reinos de taifa* (Barcelona, 1986), p. 184.

[71] *The Volunteer*, September 2002, pp. 17, 20.

1 April 1939, a substantial commemorative monument to those killed by
Republican supporters was erected in the cemetery soon after Franco's
declaration of victory. But it was not until after Franco, and the initiative
of a local PSOE councillor, Manuel Vázquez Guillén, that a commemorative plaque was placed at the site of the common burial pit of those
killed by the rebels.[72]

The contrasting treatment of the remains of the war's victims had
thus been a significant source of the division of the country, a problem
brought out into the open tentatively and sporadically in the era between
the death of Franco and the attempted military coup in February 1981
(see Chapter 11). In Yeste (Albacete), the site of armed political conflict
in May 1936, the repression in 1939 had been ferocious, leaving the
inhabitants isolated, circumspect and in silence.[73] Juan Goytisolo had
first visited the pueblo in 1963, and when he returned eighteen years
later people still spoke in murmurs of what had happened and said
nothing when asked questions about the violence. He had narrated the
events in Yeste in his novel *Señas de identidad*, first published in Paris in
1966, the central character of which is the son of a Republican killed in
the town during the war returning to the country from exile.[74] In 1981,
the area was still politically backward-looking and fearful; one resident
feared that the democratically elected authorities might deprive him
of his pension if he talked about the past.[75] A similar fear was expressed
in former anarchist strongholds in Bajo Aragón, a region which had been
fiercely repressed during the war. After Franco there was no longer a
CNT presence in the area and the communities in general had shrunk.
Los Molinos (Teruel), for example, had been a pueblo of 1,500 residents
in the 1930s, but the population had dwindled to around 400 by the early
1980s. One resident explained by associating migration with a sense of
reticence about the past: 'the youngsters have all migrated to Zaragoza,
Barcelona or abroad. Nobody wants problems.'[76] Goytisolo, in Yeste,
took note of the commemorative cross by the road entering the pueblo
recording the deaths of Civil Guard officers in the May 1936 violence,
with the inscription 'murdered by the Red mob', but no mention of
the several local peasants who had died in the same outbreak of class
conflict. He also noted the memorial tablets in the churchyard and

---

[72] Julio Ponce Alberca, *La ilusión de una reforma: Lora del Río durante la Segunda República*
(Seville, 1991). For Republican killings, see Espinosa, *Columna*, pp. 89, 340. Also
Preliminary Report of Atrocities, pp. 48, 58.
[73] Manuel Requena Gallego, *Los sucesos de Yeste* (Albacete, 1983).
[74] *Señas de identidad* (Barcelona, 1986), pp. 108–16.
[75] Juan Goytisolo, 'Los cruces de Yeste', *El País*, 17 November 1981.
[76] 'Nos queda el miedo pegado a las entrañas', *El País*, 22 August 1982.

inscriptions to 'the glorious fallen for God and Spain', which abounded whilst those who fell 'for rebelling against hunger, abandonment and age-old oppression' were left to languish, anonymously, in a common grave. His summation lamented how at the end of the 1970s, fear of the past seemed to prevent expression of any latent collective traumatic identity: 'Heaven, prayers, posthumous glory, all continue to be the exclusive patrimony of those upon whom fortune smiled since their birth. Our society prolongs into the future life its unshakable desire for stratification.'

The tentative moves of the late 1970s to unearth the past were not widely welcomed; in some cases they met with hostility, just as the broader process since the late 1990s was to provoke criticism and anger from some quarters. With the attempted military coup of February 1981, the process would be abandoned rapidly, even before the PSOE government was elected in 1982 with its dominant ethos of 'moving forward'. In one case, in Extremadura, in the south-west of the country, the recently elected leftist mayor of the town of Torremejía in Badajoz was brought before the courts of Mérida in the summer of 1979 and threatened with removal from office by conservative councillors for misappropriation of funds which had been used, at the behest of the municipality, to pay those who had carried out the work of recovering the remains of thirty-three local Republicans executed in September 1936 and transferring them to the new cemetery.[77] The families had petitioned several previous mayors in vain to authorise removal of the remains from the common burial pit of the old cemetery and rebury them in a more dignified place and with some formal process of remembering. Although the process had been carried out publicly and with complete probity, the council was split politically after the elections and a leftist pact allowed it to hold power; in a move perceived as redolent of the politics of Francoism, the mayor had been denounced to the authorities by a UCD official.[78] One of those widowed forty-three years earlier, a woman of 79 in 1980, testified how she had lived for forty years opposite one of the men who had shot her husband:

In that time I've never opened my mouth to call him a criminal or anything [...] Yes, yes, I saw how they shot them and I know who they were, who went in the lorry which took them to the cemetery. I know them [...] When they shot my

---

[77] 'Alcalde del PTE, juzgado por supuesta malversación', El País, 17 June 1980; José María Baviano, 'El juicio contra el alcalde de Torremejía el recuerdo de los fusilamientos de 1936', El País, 22 June 1980. See also Silva and Macías, Fosas.

[78] Torremejía was famous as the setting of Camilo José Cela's novel La familia de Pascual Duarte (1942), in which a local aristocrat is murdered. In fact, the town had been the site of a bloody purge of civil war leftists.

husband they left me with two children, one of two years and the other of eight months, and I was three months pregnant. I've never told my children who shot their father because one of them especially has a bad temper.

Since the day of the killing she had not wished to return to the old cemetery and had not gone back even to escort her mother and father there when they had died. She had never been the same, and since the remains had been moved she had been unwell.[79] The effects of uncovering and acknowledging the truth about the past were, and remain, unpredictable. Many of those who became involved had lost relatives but had been reluctant to return to the past because the sense of obligation to seek redress conflicted in rural society with social pressure to avoid discord. The lack of political encouragement or legal precedent and structure to facilitate truth, justice and reconciliation at a community level were further impediments. Beyond achieving the dignity of reburial, there were also disagreements about what was to be done with the truth once it had been uncovered.[80] During the decades intervening between the conflict and the coming of democracy, moreover, politics and culture had recrystallised in an urban setting far from the sites of rural intra-community terror.

Whilst consent to govern was necessary throughout society, the politics of the state were largely enacted in the environment of cities where much collective protest also took place and representations of social and political demands were made. This was where the future seemed to be – not least because post-war generations had migrated over the decades since 1939 – and where a civic culture of dissent had arisen by the 1970s. A new press would gradually play a vital role in this process. After many years of censorship, Spain lacked experience of press freedom, a problem which was partially addressed by the founding of a new independent national newspaper, to be called *El País* ('The Country'), widely supported, initially in 1973, across the political spectrum, including by a number of regime insiders, and designed to be strong enough to resist economic and political influence, although the first edition would not appear for another three years, on 4 May 1976, six months after Franco's death.[81] The first editorial made the intention clear: 'the attitude and tone of the daily press has to change in order to assist in the construction of democracy in our country'. The newspaper's 'Tribuna

---

[79] Baviano, 'El juicio'.

[80] See, e.g., the documentary made by C. M. Hardt on 1948 killing in Bembibre, León: *Death in el Valle*. This is a further example where an 'outsider' was instrumental in enquiring into the past.

[81] *ABC*, 12 May 1973.

Libre' ('Open Forum') would allow discussion amongst all individuals and ideologies, the only condition being that 'their arguments [...] are always respectful towards contrary viewpoints and that they propose solutions towards harmonious coexistence amongst Spaniards'. Perhaps inevitably, the opinions expressed would be overwhelmingly those of intellectuals and politicians, but the 'Tribuna Libre' would become a key space where discussion of the Transition's relationship to the civil war would take place.[82]

A notable additional effort to offer democratic political education was made by the publishing house La Gaya Ciencia, founded in 1970 by the writer Rosa Regàs Pagés, most prominently through its series of pocket-sized introductory texts to key political themes, produced from 1976 by leading authors from across the political spectrum, which formed the so-called Biblioteca de Divulgación Política ('Library of Political Dissemination'). The simple title of each book – begun each time with an interrogative pronoun: 'Qué es' or 'Qué son' or 'Cuál es' – and the colourful and attractive covers reinforced the point that these were popularising works, though they offered serious introductions to the themes in question. A new addition to the series appeared virtually each week and included such titles as *Qué son las izquierdas* ('What Is the Left?'),[83] *Qué son las derechas* ('What Is the Right?'),[84] *Qué es la democracia* ('What Is Democracy?'),[85] and *Qué es la monarquía* ('What Is the monarchy?').[86] Other significant volumes included those dedicated to Christian Democracy (by Joaquín Ruiz-Giménez) and the Falange (by Miguel Primo de Rivera), and another entitled *Qué fue la guerra civil*, written by Juan Benet, aiming succinctly to explain to a projected hundred thousand readers what the war had been, concentrating on the facts as 'accepted with almost complete unanimity', which admittedly left much unexplored.[87] This opening of critical space, broadening the sources of reference for popular participation in democratic change, was also reflected in the development of television after Franco with similar news programmes such as *¿Quién es?, ¿Qué es?, Opinión Pública, España Hoy* and *Informe Especial*.[88]

---

[82] Juan Luis Cebrián, 'El país que queremos', *El País*, 4 May 1976.

[83] By the leading leftist intellectual Enrique Tierno Galván.

[84] By the prominent conservative historian Ricardo de la Cierva (1976).

[85] By Manuel Jiménez de Parga, Rector of Barcelona University (1976–7) and later Labour Minister in the first Suárez UCD administration.

[86] By the veteran political monarchist who had been a linchpin of the 1962 meeting of internal and external opposition in Munich, Joaquín Satrústegui.

[87] Juan Benet, *Qué fue la guerra civil* (Barcelona, 1976). See also *El País*, 20 November 1976.

[88] See José Ramón Pérez Ornia, *La televisión y los socialistas: actividades del PSOE respecto a TVE durante la transición (1976–1981)* (Madrid, 1988), p. 91; Manuel Palacio, *La historia de la televisión en España* (Barcelona, 2001), pp. 103–8; Joaquín de Aguilera and Josep C. Vergés (eds.), *La televisión libre en la nueva democracia española* (Barcelona, 1980).

Sensitive questions, such as legalisation of the PCE, were debated during the Transition on the programme *La Clave*, for example. As with writing for *El País*, participating in these discussions (many transcribed in the published review *Triunfo*) was an expression of the new-found symbolic authority of the intellectual, and the series included appearances by such illustrious figures as Ruiz-Giménez and Tierno Galván.[89] At the same time, there were limits to raking over the past publicly. In September 1980 a two-part TV programme about foreign correspondents during the civil war, featuring a discussion with Basilio Martín Patino (who had made a controversial documentary film called *Caudillo* in 1977), included images which some considered so disturbing that there were subsequent calls to avoid too close an examination of the past. There remained little indication, however, of how incendiary the issue would become a generation later in the 1990s.[90]

Both the limited excavation of burials and this reticence about discussing the conflictive past coincided with reports of political 'disappearances' at the hands of military dictatorships in Argentina and Chile, of civil war violence in Guatemala, and the discovery in these places of unmarked common graves.[91] The military coup in Chile in 1973 had already had a radicalising effect on the tolerated anti-Francoist opposition, as was witnessed by coverage in such publications as *Cuadernos Para el Diálogo*. The first edition to appear after the military coup in Santiago was fronted by a full-page photograph of President Allende and was suggestively subtitled 'the snares of the right'.[92] Inside, several of the leading articles discussed the possibility of a civil war erupting in Chile, a debate inevitably conducted in the light of Spain's own 1930s' experience and the prospects for democracy. For many observers the options in Chile were reduced, indeed, to a choice between civil war or definitive consolidation of the military, and the Spanish censors were sensitive to analogies. The Ministry of Culture intervened, for instance, to prevent distribution of a book on the Chilean coup by Manuel Vázquez Montalbán, who had covered the situation for the Barcelona evening newspaper *Tele/exprés*, because, though it did not mention Spain, in its chapter on 'Philosophy

---

[89] This important series was broadcast from January 1976 until 1985. See Juan Pecourt, *Los intelectuales y la transición política* (Madrid, 2008), pp. 249–55.

[90] 'La guerra civil española sigue siendo motivo de polémica entre políticos, historiadores, y periodistas', *ABC*, 3 September 1980, p. 13.

[91] E.g., 'Morir en Argentina', *El País*, 8 October 1978; 'Más cadáveres de chilenos descubiertos en una fosa común', *El País*, 21 October 1979; 'Juan Pablo II denuncia las "desapariciones" en Argentina y Chile', *El País*, 30 October 1979; 'Hallazgo de nuevos restos de "desaparecidos" chilenos', *El País*, 30 December 1979; Pedro Ramírez, 'El porqué de la violencia en Guatemala', *El País*, 2 February 1980.

[92] *CPED*, 121, October 1973.

and the Military Coup' (with a section on 'the ideological purge of the masses') it was perceived as drawing critical attention to the similarities with the Spanish rebellion of 1936.[93] One of the founders of *Cuadernos*, the PSOE lawyer and intellectual Gregorio Peces-Barba, who would later play a significant role in drawing up the democratic constitution of 1978, produced a forthright critique of Spanish conservative opinion and particularly of the newspapers *ABC* and *Ya* which both approved of the Chilean coup, 'demonstrating the mentality of some, or of many, of our compatriots'.[94] Attempts to legitimate the violent overthrow of democracy in Chile were based on the same arguments as those made by the military rebels ('saviours of the *patria*') in 1936: the lack of legitimacy of the Popular Front government and, by extension, of Allende's Unidad Popular regime. Spanish critics argued that ideas which are silenced through arms return inexorably, 'fertilised by the blood of martyrs', so that they grow and are spread; Allende had already become 'mythical', just as Julián Besteiro had before him.[95]

The events in Chile did expose faultlines, however, amongst the Spanish opposition. The Socialist Peces-Barba placed himself at odds with some Christian Democrats, for example, when he argued that Chilean Catholic democrats had been ambivalent both about Allende and the military coup. There was a fierce debate, indeed, amongst the editorial board of *Cuadernos*, as witnessed in the letters page the following month. José María Gil Robles, son of the leader of what some have seen as the 'proto-Christian Democratic' CEDA during the Second Republic, wrote to the editor taking issue with the philosopher José Luis Aranguren for his 'short memory' because he had maintained that 'Christian Democracy, in all countries, at the moment of truth, always turns towards the right'.[96] Gil Robles, avoiding mention of his father and of the CEDA, used the civil war cases of the Catholic Republican and Catalan Manuel Carrasco i Formiguera and the Basque President during the 1930s, José Antonio

---

[93] Vázquez Montalbán, *La vía chilena al golpe de estado* (Barcelona, 1973), pp. 159–61; *La Vanguardia Española*, 24 January 1974, p. 9; José-Carlos Mainer and Santos Juliá, *El aprendizaje de la libertad* (Madrid, 2000), p. 114. See also Preston, *Coming of the Spanish Civil War*, p. xiii.

[94] 'A la memoria de Allende, con dolor y esperanza', *CPED*, 121, 28–9. For a more cautious critique of the conservative press, Pablo Álvarez, 'La preocupación que no cesa', *CPED*, 121, 38.

[95] Besteiro, the moderate Socialist (and anti-Communist), was an interesting choice for rehabilitation, an ongoing process before, during and after the Transition, beginning well before the centenary of his birth in 1970. See, e.g., Víctor Manuel Arbeloa, 'Recuerdo de Julián Besteiro', *CPED*, 32 (May 1966), 16–17. For an account of his death in Carmona prison in 1940: *CPED*, suplemento, 16 (1970), 15–16.

[96] *CPED*, 122, November 1973, 45. The CEDA in fact veered closer to fascism than what would become Christian Democracy in other parts of Europe after 1945.

Aguirre, both figures from parts of the country shaped by a notably liberal form of Catholicism, to counter Aranguren.[97] The tragic example of Carrasco was powerful since he had been imprisoned and executed by the Franco state in 1938. On hearing of his death and underlining his religious ethics, Carrasco's colleagues in the Unió Democràtica de Catalunya had published an obituary in the newspapers with a Christian cross at the top.[98] In the face of the criticism in 1973, however, the leading Christian Democratic figure of *Cuadernos*, Joaquín Ruiz-Giménez, wrote in the clearest terms to condemn both the military action and the behaviour of a section of the Christian Democratic Party in Chile. Raúl Morodo, co-founder with Tierno Galván of the Partido Socialista Popular, reflected the times when he argued in support that it was possible in the Spain of the 1970s to be a socialist without being anti-Catholic. Ruiz-Giménez, in his condemnation of the Chilean repression which had already begun – what he termed 'the hunting down of men' – was speaking with the benefit of his own Spanish wartime experience: 'the lesson of Chile must not be forgotten in any sense. And Chile is too close to Spain's heart for us not to feel for it with more intensity than in any other country.'[99]

These discussions reflected the development of a democratic culture. During the urban protests as the old regime declined, working-class activists interacted with intellectuals and university students in calling for change. Activism within the urban public sphere became in fact the primary channel for changing ideas about the past. Juan Goytisolo had maintained that the 'silent complicity of home' was disrupted only at university, with politicisation, public association, and the reading of gradually available objective historical accounts of the war. The adults of the closed, conservative circle of family and friends during his childhood, partly because they were made impotent by events, remained silent about the contradictions: that his father had been imprisoned by the 'Reds' and his mother had been killed by those of the 'crusade': 'Franco's bombs – not the innate evil of the Republicans – were directly responsible for the

---

[97] On the problems of Christian Democracy in 1930s Spain see Javier Tusell, 'La democracia cristiana catalana', *CPED*, 112, January 1973, 46; Tusell, *Historia de la democracia cristiana en España* (Madrid, 1974), especially, pp. 131–2.

[98] Hilari Raguer, *La pólvora y el incienso* (Barcelona, 2001), pp. 220–34 (p. 233). In September 2005, the CiU put forward a motion which was passed in the Spanish Congress for the annulment of the sentence of execution pronounced by the Summary Military Court against Manuel Carrasco i Formiguera in 1937. See Chapter 12.

[99] See *CPED*, no. 121, pp. 46–7; editorial, p. 5. On the violence, especially on 'denuncias', 'delaciones' and 'fosas comunes', see 'Represión en Chile'; 'Informe sobre Chile', *CPED*, no. 122, November 1973, 18 and 43.

break-up of [my] family'.[100] This public remembering of the painful past as a way of giving greater impulse to reform was also channelled through the cinema, in spite of the state censor, in a number of hard-hitting films of the early 1970s, many of them productions, in effect, about the modern city reflecting on rural society.[101] Two examples made by Carlos Saura in the early 1970s, *La prima Angélica* (1974) and *Cría cuervos* (1975), had an important impact in universities and amongst intellectuals, as did Víctor Erice's *El espíritu de la colmena* (1973) and José Luis Borau's *Furtivos* (1975), in conjuring up the sense of uncertainty during the last years of the dictatorship: 'Going to the cinema in those years became an act of complicity with those who wanted political change.'[102] A woman who had grown up in a provincial town recalled the time when she first met student members of the PCE at university in Valencia:

I had always heard negative things about these people; in my imagination they were bad – devils – and suddenly, I found myself with one of them and it turned out that he was a normal person, pleasant, sensitive to the suffering of others [...] It was as though a great storm had swept through everything I had learned previously at home, at school, in the Sección Femenina, in books [...] I never commented on this experience to anyone; I kept it to myself.[103]

This chapter has explored the relationship of social memory to the reconstitution of the state democratically after Franco. Remaking the state and securing political legitimacy required a tacit agreement about history and memory which extended beyond political elites. Although the political imperative to accept the 'fratricidal' thesis and even to 'forget the past' was in some ways persuasive in order to see an end to four decades of dictatorship, this conflicted with social memory of the war's violence, a memory which began to coalesce and be expressed and conveyed as the Franco era drew to a close. By the early 1970s the regime seemed less invulnerable than before, and a developing public and urban culture (centred on universities, literature, press and cinema) produced a critique of constrained historical consciousness, in part informed by publication of the first objective histories, by the influence of returning migrants and by the lessons of conflict in South and Central America. The case studies in this chapter have shown that the political and moral legacy of Spain's civil war was understood, however, in essentially two divergent ways. First, political resistance from within the

---

[100] Goytisolo, *Coto vedado*, p. 65.
[101] Peter William Evans (ed.), *Spanish Cinema* (Oxford, 1999), pp. 115–18.
[102] E.g. Piñero, 'Mi viejo álbum', p. 79; On catharsis in *La Prima Angelica*, see Marvin D'Lugo in *The Films of Carlos Saura: The Practice of Seeing* (Princeton, 1991), pp. 115–17.
[103] Buendía Gómez, 'Peinando recuerdos', pp. 167–8.

regime attempted to utilise the constructed fratricidal narrative of the war to 'equalise' the suffering and trauma of Spain's civil war. This was, in effect, a project to maintain the post-war culture of silence and to argue that the dictatorship had successfully paved the way for democracy because, particularly since the 1960s, it had gradually incorporated sections of society into the orbit of an agreed constructed vision of the cultural trauma related to the 'war between brothers'. Thus, it was maintained, the state could be remade legitimately on this basis. For many critics who had Republican backgrounds, however, the moral legacy of the war was quite different: as the history of the León Trejo family demonstrates, the war wrought devastation from which a great many had not recovered by the 1970s. Although, as earlier chapters have argued, millions of Spaniards adapted to the aftermath of civil war by making great sacrifices, the past intruded painfully into the lives of those for whom collective expression of an identity based on shared traumatic experiences had been made impossible. With the death of Franco there was an inevitable return to thinking about the past. Without being in favour of 'silencing' or 'forgetting', many Republicans and enemies or critics of his regime felt some ambivalence about this. After 1975, as the first attempts to disinter the remains of victims and responses to political violence show, the urgent need to call on the past and have sacrifices recognised and validated conflicted with an overwhelming desire for freedom and the building of a modern, legitimate and constituted state. Consummation of this leap towards modernity and representation, as well as subsequent disillusionment and a turn back to war memories sacrificed during the 1970s, are explored in turn in the final two chapters.

11 'The level of our times': memory and modernisation, 1981–1996

The man who lives completely and pleasurably in accord with current ways is conscious of the relationship between the level of our time and that of various past times.[1]

Consolidating democracy

In May 1982 the influential Catalan businessman and liberal politician José María Figueras summarised both the inherent progress and the dangers of the political situation as he viewed it: 'there is a great difference between the Spain of today and that of yesterday: Spain today is moderate'.[2] Figueras, a child of the war, born in 1928, who had founded the Centro de Estudios de Historia Contemporánea in Barcelona in the 1960s to encourage study of the civil war, supported a broad movement to disseminate information about the difficult past and its relationship to the present. The Centro, possessing a library which included many works donated by Republican exiles, was opened to the public only in 1976 and, in the same year, a pocket book entitled *What Is Capitalism?* had been published by him in the series Biblioteca de Divulgación Política.[3] The country's 'moderation' at the start of the 1980s was 'as novel a phenomenon as it is fundamental', according to Figueras, and originated in both 'the great lesson of the civil war' and the economic development of the 1960s: 'certainly a materialist phenomenon, but also a pacifying one'. Spain, he went on, was enjoying a 'consensus within the body social and amongst its political parties'. Like others, he was also conscious of a continued threat, however: 'we cannot yet be sure that this [democracy] is firmly

---

[1] Ortega y Gasset's 1929 work *Rebelión de las masas*, where the concept of modernity as the '*altura de los tiempos*' is developed: pp. 78–86 (p. 79).
[2] *El País*, 17 May 1982.
[3] José María Figueras, *Qué es el capitalismo* (Barcelona, 1976). See also Chapter 10.

consolidated; traditions, mental habits, genuine political forces, are lacking and there is economic crisis and will be again'.

War-related memories and images from the years 1939 to 1975 have been explored in previous chapters through a duality of state-controlled, public representations of the past, on the one hand, and those which emerged within society and in the private sphere, on the other. After Franco, as we have seen, the role of civil society associations, institutions and organisations became a central element of democratisation and this had obvious effects on the way in which the past was recalled. While the state continued, of course, to have a role in regulating archives and sponsoring public history, the mass media and, especially at this time, the printed press and television were no longer strictly controlled, though there would be much criticism that TV towed the line of whichever party happened to be in government, whether the UCD (1976–81), the PSOE (1982–96) or the PP (1996–2004).[4] There was also increasing freedom for historians to research into and publish on contemporary history, though the phenomenal overlap between burgeoning academic history and more public representations of the past would not occur until the 1990s.[5] Equally gradually, individuals felt able to talk about the conflictive past, even to journalists or historians who were motivated by a desire to compensate for the deficit in historical consciousness which had built up through the years of dictatorship, although, again, there was no journalistic 'boom' in covering war-related themes as there would be two decades later. That these efforts were not met by a widespread and profound public resonance is indeed an important feature of the 1980s.

The effects of the repression upon the generation of the left which had made the Republic in the 1930s were long-lasting, however. The son of the leftist mayor of a small town in rural Burgos reported in 1979 that his father, 'in spite of being a strong man, even now at 87, remained broken'.[6] There was a reluctance to speak about the war and often a refusal to implicate specific individuals.[7] One woman from a small

[4] See, e.g., Justino Sinova, 'El acoso a la libertad de información en una sociedad pluralista', in Bernhard Hagemayer and Javier Tusell (eds.), *Diez cuestiones del panorama español* (Madrid, 1987), pp. 55–65.

[5] On historiography, see Santos Juliá, 'Historiografía de la Segunda República', and Paul Preston, 'La historiografía de la guerra civil española: de Franco a la democracia', in José Luis de la Granja, Alberto Reig Tapia and Ricardo Miralles, *Tuñón de Lara y la historiografía española* (Madrid, 1999), pp. 143–59; 161–74.

[6] Botey Vallès, *Relats*, p. 75.

[7] On the difficulty of recalling painful memories and the interpretation of silences, see Mark Klempner, 'Navigating Life Review Interviews with Survivors of Trauma', in Robert Perks and Alistair Thomson (eds.), *The Oral History Reader* (Abingdon, 2006), pp. 198–210.

community in Huelva refused to tell her daughters that their father had been executed; their aunt revealed the truth to them many years later.[8] When the writer Eduardo Pons Prades ventured out to collect testimonies from around Spain about the war and its aftermath in 1984 and 1985 he concluded that 'the same fears as ever ran in the veins of the people'.[9] A fear of retribution, ostracism, and reopening wounds persuaded many people to maintain the silence and even to destroy evidence from the family's past: 'my brothers tore up the letters he wrote from prison. They did not want those memories to endure.'[10]

Many of the families of those considered as 'the defeated' who had fled the hunger and discrimination of rural life for the anonymity and a future in the city had, over the course of a couple of generations, found success and prospered. They were able to return to the pueblo of their parents and grandparents by the early 1980s and verify its decline and the relative fall of many of 'the victors' who had remained.[11] Some of the latter had been generous and refused to denounce those for whom the authorities searched during the war; they would be recalled with gratitude. Those who had denounced villagers were ever after seen by some of the victims' families as objects of resentment, as villains who personified the suffering of the wartime and post-war purge. Some were openly cursed for years after by relatives, but in many cases there was silence. Confronting those who were responsible remained difficult. In many cases the turning point was October 1982, the election of the government of the PSOE.

In 1984, in San Roque, Cádiz, where political control in 1936 had switched violently from left to right in the first days following the military rebellion, the daughter of a leftist father killed by occupying rebels, and complicit neighbours, determined to find the individual she knew to be responsible, a rare documented instance from this period of such direct confrontation with the past. Making sense of what had happened and assimilating the memories had been made acutely difficult because the violence was linked to a family which had been close to that of the victim. The intimacy of the violence seemed to be heightened because the daughter had herself opened the door to those who would be the killers. Her feeling of responsibility and need to confront the past was compounded because she had also publicly supported the Republic and spent six years in prison after the war. Her family had never discovered where the body of her father had been buried. She had recounted the story to a neighbour, Carlos Castilla del Pino, whose own family had been victims

[8] Collier, *Socialists*, pp. 148, 179.

[9] Eduardo Pons Prades, *Crónica negro de la transición española* (Barcelona, 1987), p. 16.

[10] E.g. Elordi (ed.), *Años difíciles*, p. 267.   [11] E.g. Collier, *Socialists*, pp. 20, 163–4.

of the violence of 'the other side', leftist revolutionaries arriving from Málaga shortly before on the same day in late July 1936.[12] On the appointed day, accompanied by her husband and an official of the mayor's office and having attended mass, she went to the house of the perpetrator, though without success. When confronted with the story the individual in question claimed to know nothing about it, and the search for meaning and resolution, as in other cases, met with frustration. Although a narrative of events could in some cases be constructed, though always with considerable emotional effort because of the reluctance from within the community to 'open old wounds', or indeed open hostility, the meeting itself ultimately came to little, leaving a sense of disillusionment.[13]

At state level, the veil of silence drawn specifically over wartime and post-war violence after 1975 remained in place, as though throwing off the shackles of dictatorship was sufficient achievement in itself without attempting to tackle the contentious problems of the past. The immediate objectives were multiple. Many political activists of course based their sense of self-identity on anti-Francoism, perhaps more than on deeply rooted ideology, and some found it difficult to find a political home after the dictatorship. In some cases the political discourse employed began to sound dated.[14] Freedom and modernity called for much to be done in material and civic terms, and the achievement of establishing democracy could perhaps be savoured best without spending time looking back.

The latter stages of the political transition, which had seen the conservative UCD heading the government, were accompanied therefore by a widely recognised sense of political disenchantment.[15] Two events would partially, and perhaps temporarily, put an end to this feeling of disengagement: the attempted military coup in early 1981, known as the Tejerazo, after Colonel Antonio Tejero, who on 23 February had led a group of civil guards which took armed control of the chamber of parliament, and, in October 1982, the election of the first socialist government in Spain since the civil war. The arrival of the Socialists to power had considerable symbolic as well as direct political significance.[16] Both the Tejerazo and the 1982 elections provoked a temporary moment

---

[12] See Castilla del Pino, *Casa del olivo*, pp. 504–8; Fraser, *Blood*, pp. 155–7.

[13] For a later confrontation with the perpetrator of a post-war killing (1948), see Hardt's film *Death in el Valle* (1996).

[14] Castilla del Pino, *Casa del olivo*, p. 373.

[15] See, e.g., Elías Díaz, 'Ideologies in the Making of the Spanish Transition', in Paul Heywood (ed.), *Politics and Policy in Democratic Spain* (London, 1999), pp. 26–39.

[16] E.g. Morales and Pereira, *Memoria*, p. 129; Barker, *Largo trauma*, p. 329. On both the attempted coup and the 1982 election: Preston, *Triumph*, pp. 195–202, 221–5.

of looking back, though the dominant feeling during what would become the fourteen-year PSOE tenure in government would be forward-looking as politics became almost obsessively focused on modernisation. At the beginning of the 1930s, the philosopher José Ortega y Gasset had conceived modernity as social alignment with what was possible in each era in cultural, economic and political terms, what he called 'the level of our time'. By the 1980s, modernity was therefore perceived widely as a process of making up for lost time and relieving the backwardness of Spain which was the legacy of protracted authoritarian government since the civil war, in spite of the economic changes and experiments of the 1960s. Ortega, the intellectual reference-point of the Second Republic in 1931, was seen across the political spectrum after Franco as the country's primary theorist of modernity. His conception of a civilised Spain had been taken up by Manuel Azaña in the 1930s, and during the 1980s and early 1990s the erstwhile President of the Republic would be reinvented at election time as a political model even for conservatives.[17]

Threats remained, however. The collective state of mind of the army, in considerable part shaped by memories of the civil war or, at least, its legacy, and the extent to which sections of the military might respond both to democratisation itself and the terrorist acts of radical Basque nationalism by adopting direct action, were crucial to the transition process. The PSOE general secretary, Felipe González, who would become President of the government in 1982 and win three further general elections, recalled twenty years later how during the previous administration of Adolfo Suárez (1976–81), General Manuel Gutiérrez Mellado, at that moment Chief of Staff of the army and Suárez's deputy, had warned him personally that if the Socialist Party ever came to power 'it would be wise not to dig up the civil war because "beneath the ashes, burning embers remained"'.[18]

Some army officers, including Manuel Cabeza Calahorra, who acted as defence lawyer at the trial of General Milans del Bosch, the leader behind the plot of February 1981, lamented the passing of the moralising effects of military thinking on society, while others saw the necessity of a symbolic break with the past.[19] In February 1980, amid the threat to the transition to democracy represented by the direct action of ETA, the

---

[17] E.g. Francisco Umbral, El País, 30 July 1982. Umbral adds a third figure, the dramatist Valle-Inclán. On Azaña as Aznar's model, El País, 28 April 1993; 3 June 1993. Marta Ruiz Contreras, La imagen de los partidos políticos: el comportamiento electoral en España durante las Elecciones Generales de 1993 y 1996 (Madrid, 2007).

[18] El País, 24 February 2001. Also Felipe González and Juan Luis Cebrián, El futuro no es lo que era: una conversación (Madrid, 2001), pp. 37–8, 45–6.

[19] For the traditionalist way of thinking, see Cabeza Calahorra, Ideología militar.

twenty-fifth anniversary of the graduating intake of 1955 of the Academia General Militar in Zaragoza was celebrated. The academy had been headed by General Franco from 1928 until 1931 when it was controversially closed as part of the military reforms introduced by Manuel Azaña as Minister of War, and had an almost mythical status as the military cradle of Franco's crusade. Some fifty years later, the celebrants of the anniversary in 1980 would pay homage to the Caudillo as the 'historical glory of our armed services, permanent reminder and example of military virtues', invoking his memory in rallying fortitude for the struggle, and proclaiming that 'terrorism is as nothing compared with our history'. The director of the academy, General Luis Pinilla Soliveres, however, was a supporter of the reformist Unión Militar Democrática, and whilst affirming that the country needed, 'now more than ever, a magnificent armed service', he believed this required a younger force, more technically up to date in its methods, and 'in permanent union with all those who identify themselves and feel themselves to be Spaniards; an army reticent with respect to politics and political parties because it represents all of Spain'.[20] Pinilla, born in 1921, was a child of the civil war, the son of one of the military rebels of 1936, and had fought in the last stages of the conflict. After the war, he became associated with 'liberal' elements of the Falange which gradually departed from the Francoist political line, and he was thus a somewhat untypical army officer. In 1940, he had taken part in a Catholic catechising mission in Ventas, at that time a marginal barrio of Madrid, and in 1945 he underwent a course of spiritual exercises with Father José María Llanos and was drawn gradually towards radical psychological ideas and techniques in work with young people. The modernisers would not have things all their own way after Franco, however, and Pinilla would later resign his commission citing as cause the resistance he encountered in carrying through modernising ideas.[21] A year after his address to the Academia General Militar, the ultras within the army would stage their rebellion which would see the entire democratising project placed in jeopardy.

It is doubtful that there was a real possibility of renewed war following the attempted coup in 1981; that the perception at the time was of a very real threat and that it resurrected painful memories of 1936 is much clearer. Encarnación Plaza, married to the radical psychiatrist Carlos Castilla del Pino, telephoned in tears on the evening of 23 February to

---

[20] *El País*, 24 February 1980.
[21] See Javier Fernández López, 'Los militares en la transición', in Pelai Pagès i Blanch (ed.), *La transició democràtica als Països Catalans: història i memòria* (Valencia, 2005), pp. 187–8.

give him the news, fearing a return to 18 July 1936.[22] Her father, a lifelong republican, had been arrested and imprisoned at the end of the civil war and condemned to death, although the sentence was later commuted. She still remembered as a child seeing the middle-class women of Madrid on the day the Nationalist army entered the city in 1939 – 'on all their faces I saw not joy but hatred and rage' – and these memories were suddenly made present again.[23] Spaniards spent the rest of the evening and much of the night waiting for news, and those who were at all active politically did so in groups to discuss what might happen. Women in particular recalled the fear intimately, through stories about the whereabouts and safety of family members. Many did not feel able to go to bed until the King broadcast in the early hours of the morning.[24] Some twenty years later one woman remembered the effect that the threat from the military had: 'we were filled with fear and were scared of what might happen. There were many anxious hours. The King appeared on TV to ask for calm and to affirm that the democratic process would not be altered and that he had issued the appropriate orders.'[25] The following day, approximately one million people marched in solidarity for democracy through the Madrid streets.

In its moderate response to the aborted coup, the PSOE leadership, both before it came to power and afterwards, was following the example of Juan Carlos, linchpin of resistance to the conspirators, making sure that the entirety of the armed and security services were not blamed for the plot. Felipe González would later explain his government's avoidance of dwelling on the past in part by reference to such warnings as that given by Gutiérrez Mellado and by the attempted coup in 1981. There would be no very notable public commemoration either of the fiftieth anniversary of the beginning of the war in 1986 or of its end in 1989, and the PSOE leader would later recall that there had been no widespread social resurgence of war memories in the 1980s as there was to be towards the end of the 1990s. There was also a generational dimension to this: PSOE activists and leaders of the 1970s and 1980s, including González and Alfonso Guerra, were born after 1939. They were neither part of the mobilised generation nor 'war children', and their politics of memory, while shaped by the legacy of civil war, was really a function of the profound social changes, combined with political constraints, of the 1960s and 1970s. There would, for example, be relatively little moral or political recognition in the first years of democracy by the PSOE

---

[22] Castilla del Pino, *Casa del olivo*, p. 399.   [23] Fraser, *Blood*, p. 502.

[24] E.g. Morales and Pereira, *Memoria*, p. 128; Castilla del Pino, *Casa del olivo*, p. 434.

[25] Elordi (ed.), *Años difíciles*, p. 316.

leadership of its own exiles as victims of Francoism.[26] The mood in 1982 was, in short, of a new democratic political culture transcending the dialectic of 'the two Spains'.[27]

The limits of memory: popular culture

In some senses, there was a veritable surge of nostalgia for the past in the 1980s, though much of the war-related literary, film and television production in this era tended to avoid sensitive questions related to the violence. Spanish national TV, for example, during the period from 1982 to 1990 made ten series of historical drama set in the 1930s. The public appetite was reckoned to be for nostalgic treatment of the past rather than hard-hitting critique. Though TV historical documentaries were generally aimed at educating their audiences – the 1984 docu-drama *El balcón abierto*, which begins with schoolchildren discovering about the history of the death of Lorca, was a case in point – the re-creation of conflictive historical events for TV and cinema frequently perpetuated popular myths which reduced or ignored the violence.[28] Documentaries were outnumbered by drama series set during the years of the Republic. Although most were only tangentially about the war, the sense of a counterweight to years of Francoist portrayal was noteworthy in depictions of Republicans, destined to be defeated, and their actions, as heroic rather than malign, and not necessarily tragic, with a modernist framework of idealism rather than the current, twenty-first-century tone shaped by human rights. This tendency towards a 'colonisation of the past with the present'[29] can be seen in a whole series of such dramatisations, including the earliest, *Los gozos y las sombras* ('Pleasures and Shadows'), broadcast in 1982 and based on a 1957 novel by Gonzalo Torrente Ballester, about personal conflicts within a small community in Galicia during the period 1934–6, and the most lavish, based on Arturo Barea's novel in three parts *La forja de un rebelde*, shown in six 90-minute episodes in 1990 and described by the conservative press as both expensive and 'interminable'. An editorial in the perennially gloomy *ABC* did not wait for the series to reach the 1930s before accusing it of 'insulting

---

[26] Mateos, 'La política de la memoria de los socialistas', pp. 66–7.

[27] Juan Luis Cebrián, 'Para una nueva cultura política', in Edward Malefakis (ed.), *La guerra de España, 1936–1939* (Madrid, 1986).

[28] Fernando Trueba's period sex comedy the Oscar-winning *Belle Époque* (1992), set during the Second Republic, is the best-known example.

[29] Barry Jordan and Rikki Morgan-Tamosunas, *Contemporary Spanish Cinema* (Manchester, 2001), p. 58. Also Manuel Palacio, 'La historia en la televisión', *Cuadernos de la Academia*, 6, 1999, 141–50.

the armed services' in the episode devoted to the Moroccan wars and predicted that it would cause ill feeling, though, in general, the programme was much praised.[30] Other examples included *Crónica del alba* (1983), based on a novel by Ramón Sender; *Vida privada* (1987), an adaptation of a story by Josep María de Sagarra about an aristocratic family in the Barcelona of the late 1920s and 1930s; *Lorca, muerte de un poeta* (1987); *Vísperas* (1987), a version of Manuel Andújar's narrative trilogy set in rural Andalucía; *El olivar de Atocha* (1989), set in Madrid; and *Los jinetes del Alba* (1990), about the Asturian rebellion of 1934. The literary works selected for adaptation reflected in part the geographic variety of the autonomous communities, a policy of cultural inclusion which became particularly significant after 1982.[31] Many of these productions had little ambition beyond entertainment and tended to have a distancing effect rather than developing and deepening historical consciousness and an appreciation of the complexity of the past.

There were also several documentary series dedicated to other contemporary historical themes.[32] *La Víspera de Nuestro Tiempo* ('On the Eve of Our Times'), directed by Luis Ignacio Seco, consisted in large part of over a hundred 15-minute biographical presentations broadcast between 1981 and 1985, about historical figures of the recent past who had shaped the country's modern condition. The selected subjects reflected a desire for political inclusiveness, within limits, including Joaquín Costa, Francesc Cambó, Julián Besteiro, Francisco Largo Caballero, Ramiro de Maeztu, Indalecio Prieto, Angel Pestaña, Miguel de Unamuno and Ortega y Gasset. Other editions were more thematic, including the Carlist wars of the nineteenth century, anarchism in Spain, the 1931 constitution and the law of agrarian reform, the Popular Front during the civil war, and, leaping forward, the post-war US–Spain pacts, thus broadening contemporary history chronologically and implicitly critiquing the dictatorship's obsessive focus on the Republic and war. Following the example set by the format of the successful discussion slot *La Clave*, begun in 1976, a spirit of open dialogue was fostered by a broadcast discussion after each edition between scholars, experts and, in some cases, witnesses.[33]

---

[30] 'La forja del rencor', *ABC*, 22 April 1990.
[31] See Francisca López, 'La guerra civil en la TVE de los ochenta', in López, Elena Cueto Asín and David R. George (eds.), *Historias de la pequeña pantalla* (Madrid, 2009), p. 95.
[32] Palacio, 'La historia en la televisión', pp. 141–4.
[33] Sira Hernández Corchete, 'La voluntad democratizadora de las series documentales históricas producidas por televisión española en los años ochenta', in Elsa Moreno (ed.), *Los desafíos de la televisión pública en Europa* (Pamplona, 2007), pp. 569–79.

The eighteen-part television series *Memoria de España: Medio siglo de crisis*, shown from April to September 1983, explored the period leading up to the civil war, reaching back beyond 1931 and the Republic to the last years of the nineteenth century, looking at the Cuban defeat of 1898, the First World War, and the rise of fascism, a broad focus inspired by the scholarly work of the historian Manuel Tuñón de Lara (a wartime Republican soldier and former exile) and again in contrast to the reductionist official history of the Franco era which heaped blame upon the Republic.[34] According to the director, the aim was to 'reclaim for Spaniards, in the most objective way, the memory of their most recent past'.[35] A year later, the series *España, historia inmediata* covered the period from before the civil war until 1948, including 'the untold story' of the 1940s and, according to its producer, offering 'a progressive interpretation of Spain's history, without offending anyone'. In justification, he maintained that a more academic series could have been made, 'but we have chosen one which everyone can understand'.[36] The episode topics included 'la guerra civil'; the 'año de la victoria'; 'los vencidos' ('the defeated'); 'La División Azul'; 'La guerrilla'; 'Hijo de rey, padre de rey' ('Son of the King, Father of the King', about Juan de Borbón and narrated by José María de Areilza); 'Los católicos' (narrated by José Luis Aranguren); 'Los falangistas' (narrated by Carmen Werner); 'Los anarquistas'; 'Los socialistas'; and 'Los comunistas'. The material of the series was presented according to three points of view: that of protagonists and witnesses to the events (both well-known personalities and others); the official version emitted during the Franco years, particularly through state newsreel footage; and the view of the programme, synthesising the facts objectively with the help of judgements of historians, a similar method to that used in Granada Television's 1982 series *The Spanish Civil War*, for which historical guidance had been provided by Ronald Fraser, Hugh Thomas and Javier Tusell.[37] It would not be until 1987 that a Spanish-produced series dedicated solely to the civil war was shown. *España en guerra* was aimed at

a generation which does not know the horrors of war, either directly or through their parents [and] also to those who have some knowledge gained from the experience transmitted by their parents during the Franco era. We have sought to offer them a clear narrative, wanting to stimulate them to ponder their own position and, in any event, to improve their knowledge of a period over which the previous regime drew a heavy veil of myths, distortions and half-truths.

[34] Tuñón de Lara, *La crisis del estado español, 1898–1936* (Madrid, 1978).
[35] *El País*, 17 April 1983.   [36] *El País*, 8 January 1984.
[37] A Spanish version was produced in 1983. There were many historical assessors for *España, historia inmediata*, suggesting, perhaps, that pains were taken to include all viewpoints, though possibly with a consequent loss of focus.

Historical documentaries made during the 1980s about Spain's war were viewed, of course, in the context of other contemporary imagery. Children growing up after Franco saw violence on the television screen, produced as a result of conflicts, even dead bodies, in coverage of civil wars in such places as El Salvador or in Lebanon and they saw the effects of hunger and famine. The radio often presided over family life in the 1930s, and the children of that era were not used to seeing violent images. When those who had been children in 1936 viewed televised brutality from around the world decades later it brought back the frightful events of the past which were rarely included in the wave of documentary and drama produced in the 1980s about the war.[38]

The limits of memory: politics

The PSOE's 1982 manifesto promised reform of the civil service, a progressive foreign policy, the creation of 800,000 jobs through public investment, and expenditure on social security, health, education, and housing. Ultimately, the PSOE would fail to deliver on many of the promises, but the mere fact of the left being in power seemed to offer hope and, in a sense, to rectify the past. In 1979, during the final years of the UCD, several rural migrants to Barcelona who had been born in the 1930s reflected with a mixture of resignation and hope about their own personal trajectories through war, dictatorship, urbanisation and economic recession and on perceptions of the future: 'We were born into this, and this is how we have to live; what else can we do?' 'This has to change. We of this generation will have to put up with these things, but the next generation cannot do so.'[39] One woman, who as a child had not been close to her socialist father because, after release from prison in the 1940s, he had become distant towards his family, later, on discovering more about the country's conflictive past, felt she understood him better: 'the day that Felipe González was elected I wept bitterly because he [her father] had died before [witnessing it]'.[40] People felt more able to speak about the past, but there was also a degree of disillusion and disappointment. The ethnologist George Collier, who was studying the legacy of the civil war in a small town in Huelva, was asked by one resident, 'Why have the Socialists not sent someone to investigate what happened in this town, as you are doing?'[41] The grandson of a socialist woman from

---

[38] Rodríguez Aldecoa, *Niños*, pp. 13–14.   [39] Botey Vallès, *Relats*, p. 61.
[40] See Elordi (ed.), *Años difíciles*, pp. 231–2.
[41] Collier, *Socialists*, pp. 9, 184. Also Espinosa, *Contra el olvido*, p. 161; Herrero Balsa and Hernández García, *La represión en Soria*; Morales and Pereira, *Memoria*, p. 129.

Madrid who had been executed after the civil war spoke of the long-lasting sense of fear which passed from generation to generation: 'when I decided by myself in 1980 to join the Socialist youth movement I had the biggest row of my life with my parents and they almost prevented me from doing it'.[42]

In real policy terms, there would be a strong element of continuity after October 1982 and conciliatory overtures by the PSOE government towards the army. As Javier Solana, one of the prime minister's closest advisers had declared in January, 'democracy and its consolidation come first, before our political programmes'. There would be no official unburdening of the past and, of course, no return to a republic.[43] Quietly and tacitly it was accepted that financial orthodoxy and foreign policy conservatism – ratification of Spain's joining of NATO following a referendum in March 1986, for example – and the general avoidance of dwelling on the past, were the price paid for modernising. Acceptance of the monarchy was generalised, not least because the King himself had become a symbol of democracy following his vital stabilising role on 23 February 1981, and, even more significant, the PSOE could not overturn the constitutional arrangements agreed during the Transition without risking conflict. One journalist asked rhetorically in April 1982, 'Who are the most loyal subjects today of His Majesty than we who would once have been republican citizens?'[44] Progressives could take comfort from the fact that there were certain parallels between the new democratic parties, including the smallest, such as Acción Democrática, led by Francisco Fernández Ordóñez, and the democratic parties of the Second Republic, and from the fact that its emblematic figures and their writings, which had been virtually unknown in the 1960s and early 1970s, could be rehabilitated. In 1980, on the centenary of Azaña's birth, a modest plaque dedicated to him, with a wartime quotation, was unveiled high on the wall of what was once his residence in Calle Serrano in Madrid, in spite of UCD votes against the local authority's gesture.[45] Thus, by necessity, there was no violent institutional rupture; one way of not dwelling on this simple fact was to avoid mention of the past and to focus on images of the future.

The key achievements in the drive forwards at all costs after 1982 are easily itemised. Symbolically and economically, EEC membership in January 1986 marked the country's incorporation into Europe, which

---

[42] See Elordi (ed.), *Años difíciles*, p. 227.
[43] See, e.g., on street naming: J. Carlos González Faraco and Michael Dean Murphy, 'Street Names and Political Regimes in an Andalusian Town', *Ethnology*, 36, 2 (Spring 1997), 123–48.
[44] 'Acción Republicana, '¿Antecedente de Acción Democrática?', *El País*, 8 April 1982.
[45] Fernández Delgado et al., *Memoria impuesta*, p. 215.

had been denied to Franco for more than two decades by the democratic governments of Europe. Drawing the country towards European cultural life had been a guiding principle of 'regenerationists' since 1898, and Republicans such as Azaña in the pre-war era had viewed democratisation as the prerequisite of this.[46] The Socialists would be victorious again in the fourth democratic elections in June 1986, just weeks before the fiftieth anniversary of the 1936 military coup which had led to the civil war.

The government's 1986 declaration on the occasion of the anniversary constituted, in effect, a summation of this ordering of political priorities, as well as recognition of the intrinsic difficulty of national commemoration of civil wars and, in particular, a rationalised statement of reconciliation and *convivencia* as essential to the future:

> a civil war is not an event which can be commemorated, much as it may have been a determinant episode of the biographical trajectory of those who lived through and suffered it [...] The government wishes to honour and praise the memory of all those who gave their lives in defence of freedom and democracy [and to] record also with respect those, from positions distinct from those of democratic Spain, who fought for a different society for which they also sacrificed their very existence.[47]

Given the umbilical link of political conservatism to Franco's war and dictatorship, it is not surprising that the centre-right also declined to look enquiringly towards the past. At the beginning of January 1986, in a form of pre-emptive strike, the monarchist newspaper *ABC* had devoted several pages to the forthcoming fiftieth anniversary. Superficially, the tone was very different to that adopted twenty-two years earlier in April 1964. On the front cover there was an image of the moderate socialist Julián Besteiro, a useful figure of moderation who had rejected and criticised the 'communism' which for Francoists lay behind the leftist governments of the Republic during the civil war. There was no real attempt to explain the conflict, however; rather, the war was reduced to 'a failure of *convivencia*'.[48] Spaniards had, in the past, allowed their passions to run away with them, it was argued, and been unable to live harmoniously together. The best that could be hoped for was reconciliation and a 'complete transcending of the civil war', though fifty years might not suffice. Because of 'the powerful affective complexes associated with the

---

[46] See, e.g., Santos Juliá, *Vida y tiempo de Manuel Azaña, 1880–1940* (Madrid, 2008), p. 70, citing Azaña's *El problema español* (1911).

[47] Cited in Julio Aróstegui, 'Traumas colectivos y memorias generacionales', in Aróstegui and François Godicheau (eds.), *Guerra civil: mito y memoria* (Madrid, 2006), pp. 85–6.

[48] *ABC*, 5 January 1986, especially, pp. 1, 15.

trauma of civil war', it might be necessary for a hundred years to pass.[49] This line – argued as a 'liberal' mouthpiece, according to *ABC* itself – contrasted with what the editorial line perceived to be the 'revanchism' of other commentators, though, in reality, calls from the left for revenge were extremely rare. *ABC*'s 'liberalism' involved the recycling of myths about communism, based, for example, on La Pasionaria, hardly a dominant topic of discussion nor a theme of historical consciousness in 1986, with the help of Besteiro's own anti-communist statements. The socialist professor's death in a Francoist prison in September 1940 was meanwhile skirted around.

Later, on 18 July 1986, *ABC*'s front page was dominated by images of the horrors of the war, largely from the Republican zone, including one of religious desecration, a construction of the cultural trauma suffered by Catholics and conservatives, all under the heading 'Never Again Civil War'. The accompanying editorial, recalling the murder of Calvo Sotelo and defending the paper's own anti-government position in 1936, focused again on the failure of the Republic and on looking forward in peace.[50] Somewhat in contradiction with its own reductionism, the historian Manuel Tuñón de Lara's call for reasoned historical method rather than refighting the war, made in a commemorative volume published a few months before, was 'borrowed' by the right (without naming Tuñón): 'it is about time that facts whose evocation has been polemical up to now, and which have even been used (metaphorically) as missiles, become converted into historical facts; that is, documented, admitted and inserted into a historical totality'.[51] Tuñón's point was that it was easy in the wake of forty years of censorship for all groups to fetishise 'facts' whilst simultaneously being highly selective.

Viewed amid the 'memory boom' in Spain begun in the second half of the 1990s, the urge of the González government in 1986 to move forward and to forget seems precipitate. It was argued by figures close to the government that because more than two-thirds of the population in 1986 had not been born in 1936, those who had played an active part in the conflict had become a 'marginal' section of society (a view seeming to disregard the effects of the war on children) and that, 'in these times', it

---

[49] This prediction had been made by the erstwhile Republican (and subsequently rehabilitated) medical doctor Gregorio Marañón.

[50] *ABC*, 18 July 1986, p. 3. For controversy over Ian Gibson's book *La noche en que mataron a Calvo Sotelo* (Madrid, 1982), see Joaquín Calvo Sotelo, 'Sobre el diagnóstico del doctor Vega Díaz', *El País*, 18 March 1982; Francisco Vega Díaz, 'Aclaraciones para don Joaquín Calvo Sotelo', *El País*, 2 April 1982.

[51] Manuel Tuñón de Lara et al., *La guerra civil española 50 años después* (Barcelona, 1985), p. 433.

was difficult to find 'anything new to say' about the war: 'it has all been written and possibly too much'.[52] This position, somewhat contradicted by the veritable avalanche of published research on the war produced since the 1980s, has recently been much criticised, though the critique has in turn tended to overstate the pervasiveness of the Transition's 'pact of forgetting'.[53] Historiographically, the war had not been ignored during the anniversary year; the Socialist UGT sponsored two symposiums on the war, through its Fundación Pablo Iglesias, in Madrid, and a historical congress was held in Salamanca. Two sets of collectible histories were produced; one published via the pro-PSOE newspaper *El País*.[54] A 1986 editorial in the same newspaper, entitled 'Nunca más', which appeared alongside an article suggesting that the war had been written about too much, was nonetheless unequivocal in condemning the 1936 rebels and admitted that the fear engendered still remained.[55]

More perhaps than at other times, the daily realities of fast-moving political life could easily obscure thoughts of the past. Madrid's hosting of the Arab-Israeli peace conference in 1991 appeared to confirm Spain's arrival as a significant participant in peace-building on the world stage. Barcelona's staging of the 1992 Olympic Games signalled the arrival of Catalonia as a modernising force in its own right, and the high-velocity train (AVE – declared by the prime minister to be 'the train to modernity'), unveiled in the same year, would link Madrid (1992's European Cultural Capital) to Seville, largest city of the historically underdeveloped south, whence masses of migrants had come to provide labour power to fuel the 'miracle' of the 1960s and, three decades later, host city of the Universal Exhibition (Expo).[56] A broad historical circle could be drawn linking these achievements with the national past, especially the discovery of America five hundred years earlier. Little was said officially about the expulsion of the Moors and the Jews from Spain which coincided in 1492 with what some in Spain thought of as a genocide in America but what in 1992, officially and ambiguously, was termed not a conquest but an 'encounter'. Domestically, in spite of the effects of a rising international profile, the government was weakened by a series of corruption scandals which embittered the political contest between the PSOE and the PP during the final period of PSOE government from

---

[52] Juan Luis Cebrián, 'La memoria histórica', *El País*, 18 July 1986.
[53] For the critique, see, e.g., Espinosa, *Contra el olvido*.
[54] Both with the collective title *La guerra de España*. See, e.g., Antonio Muñoz Molina, 'Desmemorias', *El País*, 6 September 2008.
[55] 'Nunca más', *El País*, 18 July 1986.
[56] On the significance of 1992 summed up: '1992: El año de España en el mundo', *ABC*, 31 December 1992.

1991 to 1996. Increasingly beleaguered, the socialists began for the first time, during the 1993 electoral campaign, to point regularly to the PP's links to the Francoist past, and this would affect the nature of political debate once the latter won power three years later.[57]

Memory and the public sphere: a democratic deficit

Despite the limitations imposed by a rapidly moving cultural and political landscape, war-related memories which went beyond nostalgia were kept alive during the 1980s and early 1990s. In the aftermath of the attempted military coup of February 1981, a forum on *convivencia* took place, organised as an arena for political discussion by members of the short-lived Partido Izquierda Democrática, with the participation of Joaquín Ruiz-Giménez, Pedro Laín Entralgo, Enrique Tierno Galván and Federico Sainz de Robles. In his 1976 'unburdening of conscience', Laín had noted how during the civil war he had been culpable in fixating on the brutality committed by 'the other side' to the exclusion of the barbarity of his own, and how there had always been Republican voices willing to denounce the violence in that zone, whilst the Nationalist leadership had remained silent about its own sins.[58] He believed in 1981 that a better understanding across the divide left by the war had become essential: 'quite a few more influential Spaniards than is desirable' continued to view society as composed simply of 'victors' and 'defeated'. Motivated by the attempted coup in late February, Laín maintained that 'if our civil harmony is to be authentic and robust, it cannot be settled through simulated and irresponsible forgetting. A way of thinking that on the night of 23 February [. . .] acquired a renewed vigour and outline for me.'[59] His summary in the aftermath of the military grasp for power is worth citing at length:

For almost forty years, public consideration of the defeated as 'anti-Spaniards', 'murderers', 'Red horde', etcetera, has been the general rule amongst the victors [. . .] A General Cause [*causa general*] was published, there were memorials to the fallen on the home front, the name of Paracuellos was made into a symbol, a doctoral thesis on the murdered priests and other religious was meticulously elaborated [. . .] All of this [wartime violence] is fact. All of it is horrible. And even though there were, from an early stage, authoritative voices amongst the Republicans and socialists which denounced this horror and protested against it [. . .] it would not be inappropriate if the current socialists and communists would say 'No more to this; never again.' But, at the same time, other equivalent things were going on on the 'National' home front [. . .] in so many towns and villages

---

[57] See, e.g., *El País*, 21 February 1993; 24 May 1993.
[58] Laín Entralgo, *Descargo*, p. 187.
[59] Laín Entralgo, *El País*, 6 May 1981, 7 May 1981, pp. 11–12.

behind the lines. As counterpart of the vilely killed priests and rightists, how many Republicans, socialists and freemasons fell, murdered no less vilely, for the simple fact of being honourably what they were? They have had no 'causa general', and since 1975 [. . .], apart from the case of Federico García Lorca, they have been mentioned only sporadically and in a fragmented way, and on occasion not with the dignity which the theme required. And which voices have come out from the social and political groups most representative of the victors, recognising this cruel reality, in repentance saying 'No more to this; never again' or faithfully confessing that it was 'also us'? This is a painful story of what ought to have happened and has not [. . .] It has not been forgotten within the hidden interior of real life in Spain, especially in rural society, and if anyone doubts it they should carry out a detailed and sensitive examination of comparative reactions in the interior to the criminal plot of 23 February.

Laín also made prominent mention of the 'hard repression' following the war. Largely because of the strictly limited access during the dictatorship to state records for the war and post-war period, quantification of the Francoist repression rested solely on the work of the regime historian and ex-army officer Ramón Salas Larrazábal, published in 1977 as *Pérdidas de guerra* ('Losses of the War'), which has been discussed in previous chapters. The purpose of the study carried out by Salas was to calculate total population loss as a result of the war rather than to identify and recognise the victims of the violence and place their deaths within a historical context.[60] Only gradually would the deficient official record, constituted by civil registries, be crucially supplemented by research carried out by individuals and small groups without official support in the few scattered and newly accessible local and municipal archives.[61] Laín would be critical of the prevalence of 'half-truths' about the war which had been maintained; he recognised in 1986, whilst many others did not, the progress represented by regional and local (and often marginalised) studies of the violence and called for a much fuller examination of the ways in which the conflict affected life in Spain.[62]

[60] Salas, *Pérdidas de guerra*. The title can be compared with Juliá (ed.), *Víctimas de la guerra*, a revealing change of focus by 1999.
[61] Several of the published results of this process are cited in chapters 2 and 4. Those based on archival research and, to some degree, on oral sources include Herrero Balsa and Hernández García, *Represión en Soria*; Carlos Fernández, *El alzamiento de 1936 en Galicia* (La Coruña, 1982); Solé i Sabaté and Villarroya, *La repressió*; Hernández García, *Represión en La Rioja*; Nadal, *Guerra civil en Málaga*; *Fosa común del cementerio de Oviedo* (Oviedo, 1984); Josep María Solé i Sabaté, *La represió franquista a Catalunya 1938–1953* (Barcelona, 1985); Altaffaylla Kultur Taldea, *Navarra, 1936*; Moreno Gómez, *Guerra civil en Córdoba*; Álvarez Oblanca, *Represión de postguerra en León*; Asociación de Viudas de los Defensores de la República y del Frente Popular de Asturias, *Represión de los tribunales militares franquista en Oviedo. Fosa común del cementerio civil de Oviedo* (Oviedo, 1988).
[62] Laín Entralgo, 'La verdad y el sentido', *El País*, 18 July 1986.

Some of the research was done in conjunction with tentative exhumations of wartime burial pits, though these efforts went largely unsupported by the PSOE, and quantification was aided by a surge of registration of civil war deaths during the consolidation of the democratic transition.[63] This remained no easy process because individuals had been executed without legal proceedings taking place, a fact which undermined Salas's faith in the civil registries. As was pointed out in parliament in 1980, putting prisoners of war in front of a firing squad violated the Geneva Convention, but the problem in obtaining recognition decades later was that though widows and other dependants may have been informed of executions by other prisoners, in many cases no such cause of death was recorded.[64] Republican soldiers frequently destroyed their own official documents which might have incriminated them, making later claims to receive a pension when the possibility was granted in the 1980s difficult to substantiate.[65] Nonetheless, the grandchildren of civil war victims, although living in urban centres and raised in very different surroundings to their grandparents, would frequently from the late 1990s become linked again to the family pueblo partly through the process of recuperating painful memories.

Against Laín, who had related the February 1981 *golpe del estado* to the mentality of the civil war, Salas Larrazábal insisted that the possibility of a praetorian solution to the country's problems was 'extremely remote', though this probably represented little comfort to many observers.[66] Undaunted, Laín went on to define what he perceived the objectives of democratisation to be by restating the meaning of *convivencia*: 'the sincere acceptance of a public life in which the *razón de ser (raison d'être)* of those with divergent views, their opinions, their right to express them freely, and the possibility of their access to power, if they convince the majority through peaceful means to share their views, are all genuinely recognised'.[67] Although he relied on the less-than-persuasive myth that Spaniards suffered from a 'psycho-social habit' of bloody violence to explain both the war of the 1930s and the events of 23 February (a myth, in relation to the 1930s, at least, shared by many of the intransigent Francoist 'bunker'), he nonetheless identified three vital means necessary

---

[63] E.g. Herrero Balsa and Hernández García, *La represión en Soria*. This book was largely ignored; news coverage was focused more on the treatment of Basque prisoners, the 'disappeared' under the military junta in Argentina, and the political situation in Catholic Poland. See also Chapter 10. Also, Collier, *Socialists*, p. 32.

[64] *Boletín Oficial de las Cortes Generales*, 72, 28 November 1980, p. 2,000; 86, 23 March 1981.

[65] 'Las penurias de los perdedores', *El País*, 18 July 1986.   [66] *El País*, 9 April 1981.

[67] Laín Entralgo, *El País*, 6 May 1981, pp. 11–12.

to *convivencia*: 'conciliation' (falling short, if necessary and *in extremis*, of the more difficult re-conciliation), 'example' (*ejemplaridad* – in the exercise of civil liberties in the broadest sense), and 'education' (in overcoming the 'scars' of the past on public life, developing science and culture, for example, and bilingualism in the regions).

In fact, the problem of recognition of the discrimination against and neglect of those who became 'the defeated' had not disappeared during the transition process. Public campaigns were under way, even though their claims for recognition of rights were not yet articulated and represented coherently as cultural trauma to the same extent as would become possible almost two decades later. Although the question of disabled Republican ex-combatants had been addressed in June 1980, the budgetary committee of parliament was also forced to debate a law of pensions for civilians injured or disabled during the war. This debate would take place in February 1982 in the presence of representatives of those directly affected.[68] Several senators supporting the proposal were members of the 'mobilised generation' and had direct experience as wartime protagonists, airing their own personal memories. The former journalist José Subirats Piñana, for example, a member of the parliamentary group Catalunya, Democracia i Socialisme, had been called up by the Republican army and was later subjected to a war trial and detained in a labour camp after 1939 from which he was not released until the Allied victory in 1945. Subirats professed his memories to be live decades afterwards: 'I have never been able to forget the horror and panic of the first bombings I witnessed.' Nor had he been able to erase from his memory the succession of other tragedies, including executions during the political repression.[69] The terms of the debate prefigured those which would be taken up more broadly and popularly in the 1990s: the abandonment throughout the Franco years of civilians who had suffered irreparable trauma during the war. Satisfaction of the aspirations of disabled groups would, it was argued, allow a sense of liberation from the past and would emphasise that assenting to democracy signified also an acceptance of justice as a defining principle.

This sense of demonstrating a shared consciousness of a past which was 'still being lived' and use of the law to bring about reconciliation

---

[68] 'Proposición de ley de pensiones a los mutilados civiles de guerra', *Diario de Sesiones del Senado*, 140, 24 February 1982, pp. 7,010–30. The new provisions became law on 29 March 1982.

[69] Subirats (b.1920) authored several historical works, including the autobiographical *Pilatos, 1939–1941: Prisión de Tarragona* (Madrid, 1993). See also Joan Ventura Solé, *Presó de Pilats: Apunts sobre la repressió de la postguerra a les comarques tarragonines* (Tarragona, 1993); Feixa and Agustí, 'Discursos', p. 206.

were echoed by Javier Paulino Pérez, PSOE senator for Ciudad Real, born in 1913, who had been a medical doctor in the wartime Republican forces and would be a vocal advocate of the rights of professional soldiers who had remained loyal to the government in 1936. Some months before the debate he had pressed the government to investigate a scandal involving subsidised housing in the centre of Madrid for leading Francoist military officers, including some of those implicated in the February 1981 coup attempt. Now, returning to 1936, he brought up the question of the responsibility of foreign governments for the wartime bombing of civilians, mentioning the examples of the Ebro, Guernica, Almería, Alicante, Valencia and Barcelona:[70] 'more than the pensions, this is about granting [the victims] the honour of [recognition] that they are as much Spaniards as the others, even though their disabilities were inflicted in a different zone to that of the victors'.[71]

The consolidation of democracy in the post-transition period was viewed by UCD senators on the budgetary commission, however, less as an issue of recognition of suffering and responsibility for past acts than as avoiding a 'reopening of old wounds'. This rationale would become a constant element of the discourse of the Partido Popular from the mid 1990s. In 1982 its predecessor the UCD was exercised by the potential financial costs of the recognition of victims through the broadening of war pensions. In arguing for placing a limit on costs, however, the right unwittingly resurrected a fundamental question which had tended to be played down by Francoists but which ran through discussion of the war's legacy: the range of social and human effects of the conflict, which extended long after 1939. Manuel Tisaire Buil (b.1924) and Julio Nieves Borrego (b.1932), both 'children of the war', typified this response. Nieves Borrego maintained that the UCD had been at the forefront of 'laws of reconciliation' since 1977, though this was in part because his party had happened to be in power in this period and had acted under the pressure applied by other groups. A more significant point, however, was that the proposal under discussion included civilians disabled in both wartime zones and, therefore, was potentially conciliatory and, by implication, that collective trauma and the terms of reconciliation could not be 'owned' by 'the defeated', a claim which would become highly controversial in more recent years. It was also insisted that any policy of compensation had to be realised 'without demagoguery' and 'without

---

[70] See *Boletín Oficial de las Cortes Generales*, 67, pp. 1,735–6. On Guernica, see Manuel Tuñón de Lara (ed.), *Gernika: 50 años después (1937–1987)* (San Sebastián, 1987). For the housing scandal, *Diario 16*, 30 September 1981.

[71] *Diario de Sesiones del Senado*, 140, 24 February 1982.

electoralism', a warning to the left not to attempt to associate the UCD with the Francoist past of many of its affiliates and senators. The difficulty was that virtually any reference to the war having produced winners and losers was liable to be depicted as demagogic posturing. Tisaire justified the UCD position by maintaining that 'all Spaniards suffered the damage of the war in some way and they could not all become beneficiaries [of the law]'. The irony of this should be noted: at the moment of calculating the financial costs of compensation, many of the arguments made for decades by opponents of Francoism and rejected by supporters of the dictatorship who played down the human effects of the war were now articulated by those who defended Franco's regime in order to reduce potential costs:

everyone who was Spanish in 1936, those born between 1936 and 1939, and some of those born afterwards [...] could adduce direct or indirect consequences of the civil war [...] Hunger, for example; the hunger suffered by many Spaniards which, of course, altered their metabolism and might have produced some serious effects and consequences [...] Consider a pregnant woman during the conflict who might suffer serious consequences as a result of the upset and shocks of the war [including] the birth of a deformed child or abnormal birth.

The long-lasting and traumatic effects of the war were now admitted by the right, albeit as a means to deter a possible wave of claims for financial compensation. Several issues had thus come together: the reluctance of UCD representatives to attach blame or responsibility at the moment of calculating the costs and providing compensation; the difficulty of defining who precisely the victims of the collective trauma born out of the war and its aftermath were; and conservatives' concern with balancing the budget. As was argued during the debate, in these circumstances it was not possible to know precisely which social groups in fact constituted the collective which was making the claim in question. This was an issue, in other words, of memory's intimate relation to collective identity, a question which ran through all manifestations of and discussions about war-related memories since 1939 and which would become paramount at the end of the 1990s.[72]

Compared with the stormy return of memory a generation later, critical responses to public representations of the civil war were thus less dramatic in the early 1980s, but situating the conflict in the past was by no means a politically uncontested process. It had not gone unnoticed, for example, that the word 'rojo' was still used in displays in the Army

---

[72] On construction of cultural trauma dependent on coherence of collective identity, see, e.g., Alexander, 'Toward a Theory of Cultural Trauma', in Alexander (ed.), *Cultural Trauma*.

Museum in Madrid to label that section of the army which had defended the government, and protests in parliament were made.[73] Other public manifestations of memory of the war were intended to be conciliatory. In September 1981, the return to Spain from New York of Pablo Picasso's *Guernica* would be successfully negotiated by the historian Javier Tusell, Director General de Bellas Artes y Archivos, a section of the Ministry of Culture. According to Tusell, also a UCD councillor in Madrid, the painting formed part of 'the imagination of all Spaniards' and principally of the 'dissident' imagination, and its recovery became one of the most significant moments of the cultural transition, although controversy over its 'ownership' did not end in 1981.[74]

Earlier, in October 1980, four months before the Tejero coup, an exhibition on the civil war had been mounted under the auspices of Bellas Artes in the Palacio de Cristal at the Retiro Park in the centre of Madrid. It was called simply La Guerra Civil Española, and both left and right of the political spectrum were represented in its content and design by the appointment as consultants of the historians Ángel Viñas, later an adviser to the PSOE Foreign Minister Fernando Morán, and Ramón Salas Larrazábal.[75] Based on material from the civil war section of the state archive, which had come under the control of the Ministry of Culture in May 1979, the event was symbolic of the process by which documentary traces of the war would come to be considered not as evidence to support state claims of political criminality but as source material for public perusal, investigation and verification. This already complex transition in use and purpose would be complicated further by Catalan nationalist claims upon the section of the archive which had been seized by Francoist forces in occupying Catalonia during the war.[76] The question of archiving the past – of making it accessible as the raw material of history – would clearly be important for historians, though it was not always a key social demand or a priority of government in the 1980s. José María Areilza, an ex-minister of the Franco regime, would nonetheless declare that 'no democratic country can exist by closing its archives to the public', though access particularly to military archives, which have proved during the last ten years or so to be a rich source of historical

[73] *Boletín Oficial de las Cortes Generales*, no. 61, 5 September 1980, p. 1,538; 71, 21 November 1980, p. 1,959.

[74] On *Guernica*, see Tusell, 'El Guernica y la administración española', in Museo del Prado, *Guernica: Legado Picasso* (catalogue, Madrid, 1981) pp. 32–78.

[75] Salas Larrazábal (b.1916) had fought for the rebels in the civil war and volunteered for the Blue Division in 1941.

[76] La Comissió de la Dignitat, *Volem els papers: la lluita de la Comissió de la Dignitat per la repatriació dels papers de Salamanca* (Lleida, 2004).

material, was a particularly delicate matter and, as the old regime drew to a close, there was much destruction of documents.[77]

Public exhibitions of documents and objects to be treated as traces of a past event are, however, rarely the place for intricate historical analysis. By the beginning of the 1980s, historians had begun to show how the rupture of society in 1936 had led to the creation of two opposing states which clashed not only in the trenches but also within communities; this sense of rupture could only be evident, however, by displaying and discussing the communal violence. This would prove to be too sensitive in 1980.

The displays, which also included material lent by military museums and individuals, were arranged according to a typology of object or artefact, in this case, posters, paintings and drawings, film, the press, photographs, flags, uniforms and armaments, and coins, stamps and notes of exchange. This objectification, thus categorised and arranged, accentuated a sense of impartiality in order to emphasise what were claimed as the shared values of the time. They formed a unified and 'whole' picture, an aim determined by a perceived need of the organisers to demonstrate 'loyalty to both the forced and voluntary participants [of] this period of history, so intensely experienced'. The two sides were neither good nor bad, though they had 'two different ways of understanding what Spain is'.[78] The defects of each of the contestant forces had already been exploited by historians, perhaps overly so, it was argued, a telling observation in the light of the later rush of research on the war. The view was that the 'wounds' were so recent that they might not have been 'completely healed'; the descendants of protagonists needed to be considered.[79] Although many of the displayed objects related to the social revolution within the Republican zone during the war – stamps, coins, notes of exchange, etc. – collectively they represented daily life drained of any sense of conflict or of political commitment. The sense conveyed was of an intensification of distance, of other-worldliness, of a

---

[77] 'Ángel Viñas revela la depredación de los archivos de El Pardo', *ABC*, 22 May 1981. Masses of state papers were said to have gone up in smoke when there was a mysterious fire in February 1978. Preston, *Franco*, p. 781. On Barcelona, see 'Memoria que quema', *El País*, 1 November 1992. During four days in early April 1977, a caravan of vehicles made continuous journeys from the building of the state party's provincial headquarters to a disused factory where the furnace burned constantly for eight hours a day. On questions to the Minister of Interior, Rodolfo Martín Villa, *El País*, 16 December 1977; *ABC*, 19 January 1978, p. 8; and, in parliament, Josep Benet and Fernández Viagas, *Diario de Sesiones del Senado*, 4, 18 January 1978, pp. 203–11.

[78] See Ángel Viñas interview, *ABC*, 23 October 1980.

[79] See Ministerio de Cultura, *La guerra civil española: exposición organizada por la Dirección General de Bellas Artes y Archivos* (Madrid, 1983) (citation, p. 7).

nostalgic view of a world left behind, making the contrast with the modern reality of Spain after Franco all the greater. The conflict had been 'recent in time' but was simultaneously firmly in the past because of the subsequent 'unprecedented historical acceleration'. So distant was the past as conceived by the curators that the term 'archaeology' was used, albeit metaphorically, to describe the recovery of the objects displayed and used to tell stories about the 'humble existence' of Spaniards two generations before. Evocative items, including food products sent by families to soldiers at the front and the tobacco consumed, had a domesticating and even idealising effect on the imagination, bestowing a sense of innocence upon the conflict and situating it within a bygone age to be consigned unproblematically to 'history' and rightfully, therefore, belonging in a museum.

Regional differences, the basis of the most complex and threatening political issue in 1980, were avoided altogether in the discourse surrounding the exhibition. Avoidance of the wartime communal violence is also suggested by the choice of the relatively non-controversial theme of foreign intervention in the war as basis of the concurrent cycle of academic conferences. The interviews with individuals who remembered the war which were printed in the catalogue were based not on politics but on 'the human aspects' of the conflict, though these were the reminiscences not of popular experience but largely of celebrities and individuals from the artistic world.[80]

The intention of the civil war exhibition was to satisfy a yearning to 'recuperate a collective memory claimed as their own' amongst those not born in 1939. Viewed from the vantage point of the 'memory boom', seventy years or more since the conflict, however, the aim of its designers to achieve this by avoiding explicit references to the political ideas of those who were fighting and by eschewing any 'thesis about causes and consequences' appears naïve. In 1980, however, this purpose was justified because the exhibition was viewed as contributing to a necessary sense of 'closure' which benefited the political process of transition.[81] Then, as now, this was a conservative social project which, naturally, was supported by political conservatives. The newspaper *ABC* placed its hope in those 'who neither know nor want to know who was on each side and if their father belonged to the side opposed to that of their grandfather'.[82]

---

[80] See particularly the interview with Nini Montián in Ministerio de Cultura, *Guerra civil*, pp. 101–5.

[81] *ABC*, 12 September 1980, p. 29; 21 October 1980, p. 37.

[82] *ABC*, 23 October 1980. Some on the right regretted, however, that the exhibition was 'aseptic' and 'neutralist', and that crusading nostalgia was displaced by nostalgia for the revolution.

The grandchildren of the war – those born in the late 1950s and early 1960s – have affirmed a different need during the recent resurgence of war memories which, in part, has been precisely to discover these truths. A more nuanced picture of the recent past has thereby become possible.

The 1980 exhibition depicted a simple and determining logic to the outcome of the civil war: a facile dichotomy between victory and exile, denying the reality for millions of people who, though they remained, were by no means 'victors' and who struggled long and hard with the far-reaching political, social and economic consequences of the civil war. This depiction again consigned the war 'safely' to the past in the interests of the present, a position compounded by the claim that 'no other outcome was possible, unless it were reconciliation [...] Has not this other outcome now arrived?' The answer to the rhetorical question was evident 'merely by going out into Spain's streets'.[83] The initial aim for the Madrid exhibition to be followed by others did not in the end materialise, as more local and regional research gradually complicated the historical picture. With Franco gone, the message of the exhibition had been that the promise of modernisation offered during the last decade of his reign could at last be fulfilled; the new political system had been legitimated and the technocratic discourse accompanying the displays was of its time.[84]

In 1996, marking the sixtieth anniversary of the war, the historian Santos Juliá argued that a civil war, because it violently divides society in two, is in fact 'uncelebratable' except as a form of repression. This is what the Franco regime had done for almost forty years. The only possible achievement worthy of celebration would be reconciliation.[85] The largely peaceful transition to democracy was thus a genuine cause for celebration, and not for sentimental reasons. The problem, however, was that in so arguing it became difficult not to argue also against remembering. By the 1990s there remained an implicit sense that historians had obsessed too much – and too dispassionately – about the history of political parties, about decision making at the level of the state, and about causation, to the detriment of the daily experience and the sorrow of the conflict and its aftermath, so that recognition and commemoration of the suffering had been neglected.

---

[83] Introduction, Ministerio de Cultura, *Guerra civil*, pp. 9–11. On Tusell's directing role, see *ABC*, 22 October 1980.

[84] See Ricard Vinyes, 'La memòria com a metàfora', in Jordi Font Agulló (ed.), *Història i memòria: el franquisme i els seus efectes als Països Catalans* (Valencia, 2007), pp. 382–3.

[85] See the article by Santos Juliá coinciding with the week of the sixtieth anniversary of July 1936: 'Saturados de memoria', *El País*, 21 July 1996.

The Socialist government was guilty of not broaching difficult questions related to the violence of Francoism, much in contrast to the PSOE's response at the end of the 1990s and after the turn of the millennium to the surge of memory related to the cultural trauma of the war and dictatorship.[86]

---

[86] E.g. Espinosa, *Contra el olvido*, pp. 177–84. For later reflections of Felipe González, 'Chile, Argentina y las Comisiones de la Verdad', *El País*, 22 April 2001.

12   Collective identity and the ethics of memory, 1996–2007

This is not about exhuming bodies, or generating hatred or animating vengeance, but reaffirming the values of freedom, the superiority of democracy, the magnificence of pluralism, the importance of a balanced, functioning, state of law.[1]

Unearthing the past

In late October 2000 a team of forensic archaeologists began excavating an anonymous ditch in the town of Priaranza del Bierzo in León, northern Spain, thought to be the site of the disposal of the body of Emilio Silva Faba, a member of Manuel Azaña's moderate liberal Izquierda Republicana party of the 1930s, who, with twelve others, had been shot by anti-Republican rebels on 16 October 1936, at the age of 44, leaving a wife and six children. Silva Faba's grandson, also called Emilio, had been researching the history of his grandfather and the location of his remains for some time. The case was by no means unique. It has been estimated that the bodies of some 30,000 unidentified men and women, killed by armed groups supporting the rebels of 1936, remained to be recovered from similar burial pits at the end of the 1990s.[2] For Silva, born in 1965, and many other Spaniards of his generation – the 'grandchildren of the war' – it was morally wrong that victims of political violence who in the 1930s had 'dreamed of and worked for public freedoms and universal social rights' should remain buried in unmarked pits and forgotten as the twenty-fifth anniversary of Franco's death and burial in the Pharaonic tomb at the Valle de los Caídos was commemorated.[3] This application of

---

[1] Luis Yáñez-Barnuevo, 'Habla, memoria, habla' ('Speak, memory, speak'), *El País*, 3 December 1997.

[2] Silva and Macías, *Fosas*; Montse Armengou and Ricard Belis, *Las fosas del silencio: ¿hay un holocausto español?* (Barcelona, 2004).

[3] Letter of Emilio Silva Barrera, 'No muere la memoria', *El País*, 7 November 2000. See also Rodolfo Serrano, 'La memoria exhumada', *El País*, 8 September 2001.

a universalist conception of rights and justice, both retrospectively (to the original violent act) and currently (to the subsequent failure to remember), was manifested within a globalised environment which was different to that of the ethos of the government-sponsored modernity of the 1970s and 1980s and would play a significant role in the politics and culture of memory in Spain from the late 1990s onwards.[4]

At the same time that Emilio Silva was researching his grandfather's history, judicial authorities in Spain were attempting to have General Pinochet of Chile extradited from Britain to face trial for heinous acts while President from 1973 to 1990, including the sequestration and murder of hundreds of young leftists, some of whom were Spanish citizens. It was partly this which prompted Silva to publish an article in a León newspaper entitled 'my grandfather was also one of the disappeared'.[5] Applying the principle of universal jurisdiction and overriding local amnesty laws (in Chile's case, passed by Pinochet himself in 1978), the General had been indicted in October 1998 by the Spanish magistrate Baltasar Garzón for human rights violations against Spanish citizens in Chile.[6] Pinochet had been arrested soon after in London, being released finally by the British government in early March 2000 and returned to Santiago, where he was received with military honours, although non-state agencies there were emboldened by the case to make greater demands on the state to confront impunity.[7] Emilio Silva had decided to act on 7 March amid a widespread sense of disgust amongst the left at

---

[4] See, e.g., Felipe Gómez Isa (ed.), *El derecho a la memoria* (Guipúzcoa, 2006).

[5] *La Crónica de León*, 8 October 2000. A copy can be found at www.derechos.net/esp/ algomas/silva.html. In 1997, at the time of the fall of Mobutu, dictator in the Congo, who had supported Hutu unrest in Rwanda, there had been calls for internationally sanctioned justice to make him accountable and comparisons with Pinochet. See, e.g., Rosa Regàs, '¿Para qué olvidar?', *El País*, 15 November 1997.

[6] Stephanie R. Golob, 'The Pinochet Case: Forced to Be Free, Abroad and at Home', *Democratization*, 9, 4 (Winter 2002), 22–57. On other high-profile human rights cases lodged in Spain with universal jurisdiction bases, relating to Guatemala and Argentina, see Golob, 'Volver: The Return of/to Transitional Justice Politics in Spain', *Journal of Spanish Cultural Studies*, 9, 2 (July 2008), 133. On the authority of laws based on supranational principles to redress past wrongs: David Hirsch, *Law Against Genocide* (London, 2003). One of the several results of the relative insecurity of the Socialist government from 2007 to 2011, in terms of politics of memory, was the closing of the legal 'window' through which Spanish lawyers were able to gain access to 'universal justice' and a rightist backlash including indictment of Garzón in 2010, in effect for having probed into rebel civil war violence.

[7] Though, like Spain, Chile has been characterised as a divided 'nation of enemies', unlike Franco, Pinochet's memory was not widely honoured and his stock of political capital had already been diminished between 1990 and 1998. When he died in December 2006, many prominent conservatives were absent from the funeral; there was no monument and the body was cremated, in contrast to the return of Salvador Allende's body to Santiago and its ceremonial reburial.

Pinochet's release, not least in Spain, where it was believed that the conservative government of José María Aznar – the PP had defeated the PSOE in March 1996 – had intervened in the General's favour.[8]

The exhumation at Priaranza del Bierzo was the first of many; during the next two years there would be nineteen further excavations, all of them accompanied by a sense of fear and trepidation amongst those who had experienced the war, but spurred by a belief in the need to recuperate historical memory. At Priaranza, there was financial and political support for the operation, in contrast to the few, somewhat circumspect, excavations during the late 1970s and early 1980s which lacked official encouragement and means of gaining publicity, mobilising support, and seeking scientific assistance.[9] In 2000, the León regional administration had granted funds to cover the costs of investigation, exhumation and identification of the remains found in the common graves; a modest conference on the debt owed by society to democracy, the Republic and the guerrilla resistance was also organised by the local section of the PSOE youth movement. Transferral of remains to a cemetery for dignified reburial and the placing of public monuments were called for to record the place of rest of the victims and publicly to restate the circumstances of their deaths. Although there was a sense of unease and some resistance, people began to talk openly of a past about which they had kept silent for decades. The process represented the emergence into the public sphere of a number of intergenerational civil society movements, such as Silva's broadly pro-Republican Asociación para la Recuperación de la Memoria Histórica (ARMH), which has many provincial branches and is motivated primarily by a humanitarian ethic, and the similar Foro por la Memoria, linked to the PCE and with a more pronounced ideological position.[10] The ARMH was, and is, motivated by a social critique and a sense of critical ambivalence about capitalist modernisation and consumer culture; in an interview with Victoria Ginzberg, the daughter of two of 'the disappeared' seized by the Argentine junta of the late 1970s, Silva argued that Spain's transition to democracy represented not only a silencing but a 'pact for consumerism and economic development' and had 'assumed that [the grandchildren of the victims of the war] would be content with this'.[11]

---

[8] See, e.g., Juanjo García del Moral, 'Pinochet', *El País*, 7 March 2000.

[9] See Chapter 10.

[10] Asociación para la Recuperación de la Memoria Histórica: www.memoriahistorica.org. es/; Foro por la Memoria: www.foroporlamemoria.es/.

[11] Interview in January 2003, found at www.foroporlamemoria.info/documentos/ victoria_ginzberg.htm.

These organisations to recuperate historical memory connect the communities which were torn apart by the intimate violence of the civil war (see Chapter 2) and its aftermath (Chapter 4), on the one hand, and, on the other, a globally articulated ethic and culture of remembering. This culture of memory has emerged through the sharing of recollections, representations and ideas about the past via the media of television and the internet in the interests of 'rescuing those who had been forgotten'. This has been viewed as the prerequisite of reconciliation. Several of the objectives required claims upon the state to be made, to establish, for instance, a 'truth commission' in the style of that established in South Africa by an act of the post-apartheid parliament in 1995, and the regularising of access to archives which held previously declassified material because they were under military jurisdiction.[12] These claims on the state – on the 'rule of law' – hark back to the legality of the Second Republic which was rent asunder by the military coup on 18 July 1936, as well as to Francoism's own contention to have constituted a legitimised state. These submissions, in part, call on the state to act to make up for the sense of disorientation brought about by the transnational diffusion of political authority since the 1980s.[13] In a rapidly changing world, this disorientation is also temporal; historical representation by the civil society memory forums of the post-war era has been highly fragmented. They have generally failed, for example, to point to commonalities between their own objectives and the strands of tolerance and calls for reconciliation in Spain since the 1950s (including from sections of the Catholic Church), as discussed in earlier chapters.

The main focus instead has been on the notion of a 'pact of silence' about the past which was agreed to during and after the transition to democracy. The tacit agreement to such a 'pact' has been disputed, most prominently by the historian Santos Juliá, who was close to the PSOE in the 1980s and helped shape and rationalise the Socialist government's muted approach to the fiftieth anniversary of 1936, as discussed in Chapter 11. Juliá has emphasised the broadening foundation of fact-based historical knowledge during the late 1970s and 1980s, whilst also maintaining that there had indeed been a simultaneous, conscious and rational *decision to forget* collectively, as distinct from silence or actual personal and private forgetting.[14] Other historians have argued similarly, including Juan Pablo Fusi, generally from a

---

[12] On denial of access to state archives, see, e.g., *El País*, 11 July 1999.

[13] On the postmodern waning of the nation-state: David Held et al., *Global Transformations: Politics, Economics and Culture* (London, 1999); Susan Strange, *The Retreat of the State: The Diffusion of Power in the World Economy* (Cambridge, 1996), part 1.

[14] See also Juliá, 'Echar al olvido: Memoria y amnistía en la transición', *Claves de Razón Práctica*, 129 (2003), 14–24.

position closer to the PP.[15] Counter to this position, it may be said that in recounting the production of history and memory during the process of the transition to democracy, both Juliá and Fusi have failed to distinguish adequately between the relatively limited social significance of specifically historiographical recuperation, within a circumscribed sphere, and the importance of commemoration, justice, or moral reparation, though accurate and objective knowledge of past events is of course necessary for both forms of recollection and reconstruction.

Clearly, by the late 1990s, a groundswell of social memory, formed from direct recollection of the painful past and from memories passed on generationally, which people were willing and prepared to relate, had gathered momentum. The liberal media called on the PP government to help with the costs of locating and identifying those who were 'our own disappeared', again in reference to the ongoing campaigns for recognition and remembering of the victims of military regimes in Chile and Argentina, and in order to 'help heal the wounds' of the war.[16] Between September 2001 and June 2002, Spain's most popular radio programme, the award-winning *Hoy por hoy* ('Today' or 'Our Times'), produced by the network Cadena SER and largely devoted to political news and discussion, began to invite listeners' memories of the past for broadcast, requesting stories in general, although, in the end, some eight out of ten of the resulting testimonies received were related to the civil war and its aftermath. At the time, the programme had some 2.5 million listeners and this sizeable market share has since grown even larger.[17] A book, *Los años difíciles*, collected together many of these moving and revealing stories which were arranged in three sections: 'war', 'defeat' and 'post-war'.[18] Several TV documentaries were produced which related to memories of the war and its repressive aftermath, including *Les fosses del silenci* (on Catalan television in March 2003) and *Las fosas del olvido* (TVE, January 2004), about the killing and the exhumations in Badajoz, Catalonia and León, and *Els nens perduts del franquisme* (Catalan TV-3), about the forced adoption of the children of executed, imprisoned and exiled Republican parents, first shown in 2002.[19]

---

[15] E.g. *ABC*, 8 December 2002, p. 9.

[16] 'Desaparecidos nuestros', *El País*, 8 August 2002.

[17] *El País*, 12 December 2001. For awards: 29 November 2001. The presenter of *Hoy por hoy*, Iñaki Gabilondo, recorded that radio constitutes 'a service to society, not an organ of propaganda': *El País*, 7 November 2001.

[18] The resulting published volume is Elordi (ed.), *Años difíciles*. (For background, see *Años difíciles*, p. 14.)

[19] The Catalan films were also shown more widely in Spanish versions. See Montse Armengou Martín, 'Investigative Journalism as a Tool for Recovering Historical Memory'; and Gina Herrmann, 'Mass Graves on Spanish TV', both in Carlos

At the same time, the excavation of wartime human remains continued. In July 2002 the mortal remains of nine men, mostly with cranial damage resulting from the impact of gunshots, were exhumed as burial pits were unearthed at Piedrafita de Babia, in León. Again, most of the villagers knew how these men had died and came to be buried there but few had dared to speak about the terrible events of November 1937.[20] In October 2002 the excavation took place of an anonymous site containing the remains of three women in the pueblo of Poyales del Hoyo (Ávila) killed by local Falangists. The local authorities, some with familial links to the Franco regime, refused to allow their reburial in the local cemetery and only relented after a campaign in the local press. As the church bells rang, the three small caskets were paraded around the village's narrow streets and the local politicians, mainly of the PP, showed their disapproval merely by staying away as a commemorative plaque was positioned.[21] In early October 2004 the remains of five republican councillors in Sepúlveda (Segovia), including a 68-year-old schoolteacher, were exhumed from a burial pit which had been fenced and marked anonymously with a cross as early as 1952. This revivified local activity would be framed by the global perspective in appeals made to international human rights agencies. In August 2002 the ARMH, for example, presented its case for recognition and support to the United Nations Working Group on Forced Disappearances based on the recognised duty of all states to investigate serious and systematic violations of fundamental rights.

There were dozens more excavations of war victims during the decade after 2000 in a process which was intertwined with the tense politics of memory. In September 2002, several opposition parties, including the PSOE and Izquierda Unida (IU), presented a number of motions for discussion by the Constitutional Commission of the Spanish parliament calling for the collaboration of public institutions, including the judiciary, to resolve outstanding questions related to the war and the dictatorship, and for state assistance with resources to carry out the unearthing process. This culminated on 20 November 2002, the anniversary of Franco's death, with a unanimously supported declaration by the Congress which affirmed that no group or individual 'may be legitimated, as happened

---

Jerez-Ferrán and Samuel Amago (eds.), *Unearthing Franco's Legacy* (Notre Dame, 2010), pp. 156–67 and 168–91 respectively.

[20] *El País*, 9 July 2002.

[21] Giles Tremlett, *Ghosts of Spain* (London, 2006), pp. 3–17. Conflict between members of the memory associations and some locals over the reburial flared again in August 2011 when the current PP mayor authorised removal of the remains to an unmarked common grave in the cemetery on grounds of 'hygiene': *El País*, 7 August 2011.

in the past, in employing violence with the aim of imposing their political convictions and establishing totalitarian regimes, contrary to the freedom and liberty of any citizens', though, significantly, it did not condemn the *coup d'état* of July 1936.[22] The declaration also reaffirmed the duty of government and society to recognise morally (though not legally) the sacrifices of the victims of the war and the dictatorship. Initiatives in this direction, particularly at a local level, would receive institutional support, although participants were required to avoid 'reopening old wounds' or provoking confrontation. Furthermore, a governmental and legislative duty was recognised towards the political, economic and social rights of exiles – with particular mention of the 'war children', including those who had suffered evacuation in order to escape the war and repression – allowing for recuperation of Spanish nationality and the right to vote upon application.

The Congress's November 2002 declaration was to be liberally scattered with quotes on the desire to 'bury the past' made by participants in the debate on the Amnesty Law twenty-five years earlier, in 1977, the vote on which the PP's predecessor, Alianza Popular, had abstained.[23] The domestic circumstances on that occasion, only two years after Franco's death and nine months after the bloody murder by fascist gunmen of five communist lawyers at Atocha, followed by the mass mourning of two hundred thousand sympathisers during the funeral, had been quite different.[24] In 2002, under pressure from protest groups and the UN, the Congress, now including PP deputies, approved a declaration which many conservatives believed would again draw a line under the past. The condition for the PP's support had been that, more than two decades after the re-establishment of democracy, the civil war thesis which viewed society as split between 'two Spains' be henceforth 'left out of political argument', in essence, the same hope of the political right in 1977.[25] For reasons which will be explored, this was not to happen and many more conflicts over collective memory were to follow. These have included conflict over the failure of government to fulfil several of the key terms of the November accord (and later undertakings) – to assign resources and make documentation more accessible, for example – and, more fundamentally, the declaration's avoidance of assigning responsibilities for the 1936 rebellion. Before exploring legal

---

[22] Whether the PP had, in effect, condemned the rebellion of 18 July 1936 was left ambiguous; no such condemnation appears in the declaration.

[23] See, e.g., Santos Juliá, 'Acuerdo sobre el pasado', *El País*, 24 November 2002.

[24] Patxo Unzueta, 'Euskadi: amnistía y vuelta a empezar', in Juliá et al. (eds.), *Memoria de la transición*, p. 281.

[25] *El País*, 21 November 2002.

measures, however, it is necessary to look at the background of the politics of memory and identity as power shifted from left to right after 1996.[26]

The politics of memory and identity

Only once it had lost power in 1996 did the PSOE begin to turn back in earnest towards the troubled, pre-democratic, past. The emergence of socio-civic movements for the recuperation of historical memory thus coincided with a new political focus on history. As we have seen, these movements were focused primarily not on the historical past of the Republic and the war *in general*, but on the victims of the terror and the trauma left behind. Moral reparation and repentance on the part of the institutions of Francoism, including those who were seen as the dictatorship's ideological and political heirs, were part of the objective of this memorial activity. Regional nationalist political groups and the left were encouraged by this renewed interest in memories related to the war and dictatorship, a motive for political agitation, particularly since the avowedly centralist PP was reluctant to condemn the military rebellion and properly honour the memory of the defeated.

Towards the end of the second year of the Aznar government, in November 1997, the PSOE member of Congress from Seville, Luis Yáñez-Barnuevo, whose words are cited at the beginning of this chapter, justified his exhortation that memory should 'speak' by invoking democratic ideals within a state of law. While suspension of memory had been necessary during the transition in the late 1970s and early 1980s, it was now time to 'recuperate it to preserve democracy from its enemies'. Another writer, the Catalan Josep Ramoneda, maintained that, without reference to the pluralist tradition of the 1930s, a 'myth of reconciliation' was possible which would allow Francoism to appear unjustly as the antechamber of democracy.[27] The making of this historically unsophisticated plea is interesting in itself. It failed, however, to distinguish between the dictatorship, as regime, and society during the Franco years, and it did not appreciate that the leftist principles of the 1930s, though recoverable as a 'tradition', were not easily applicable to the functioning of a late-capitalist democratic state of the twenty-first

---

[26] For critique of the parliamentary accord, see Espinosa, *Contra el olvido*, p. 193. The damaging cycle of assigning responsibilities for perceived national failure and conflict goes back to the Moroccan wars, the Primo dictatorship, the Republic and the civil war and its aftermath.

[27] Josep Ramoneda 'Memoria, amnesia, perdón', *El País*, 7 November 1997.

century. These arguments were made, we should remember, in the fraught political atmosphere created by the former government's fall from grace amid corruption scandals and, in the light of this, resentment at the PP's own political opportunism.

The PP government had in fact signalled at an early stage that it would resist opening up the Francoist past to scrutiny. There were signs indeed that the government would do whatever it could to influence the media which disseminated public historical debate beyond the world of academia. As a counter to the PSOE-oriented *El País*, the PP enjoyed the support of the national daily *El Mundo*, founded in 1989, at the same time that the party, based partly on Manuel Fraga's AP, was itself reconstituted. State television was to be run by a PP appointee, Fernando López-Amor, who was soon criticised for presenting tendentious historical programming. The edition of the TV series *Debate* (TVE1) entitled 'Lo que queda del franquismo' ('What Remains of Francoism'), broadcast in November 1997 to coincide with the twenty-second anniversary of Franco's death, for example, featured the respected historian Juan Pablo Fusi surrounded by figures from the extremes, including the former Franco minister Gonzalo Fernández de la Mora, propagandist-cum-historian Ricardo de la Cierva, and two journalists from *El Mundo*, one of whom was criticised for belittling democracy by claiming that Francoism and 'Felipismo' were 'the same thing'.[28] A similar position was taken by Fraga who had intervened during the regional elections in Galicia in 1997 alluding to the previous PSOE government as a paradigm of corruption, an accusation seen as hypocritical by the left since it came from a leading ex-minister of the democratically unaccountable Franco regime. Luis Yáñez-Barnuevo had called for the pasts of key political figures of the right to be investigated, a call which was met with some ambivalence by the PSOE leadership in the aftermath of its defeat in March 1996. The Secretary General of the party, Joaquín Almunia, considered it 'a duty to reflect upon the recent past [...] to make a robust and critical judgement of what happened to avoid the risk of repetition', though he felt it improper to talk of overturning the judicial terms of the 1977 amnesty.[29]

The politics of memory have therefore been shaped by party allegiances and strategies. But resurgence of memories of the war and dictatorship (in which, in spite of Yáñez-Barnuevo's claim cited at the start of this chapter,

[28] See *ABC*, 21 November 1997. For a critique: Javier Tusell, *El País*, 22 December 1997.
[29] *El País*, 14 October 1997. Yáñez-Barnuevo referred specifically to Fraga's involvement in covering up the physical punishment of the wives of Asturian workers on strike in the 1960s. See Chapter 8.

the exhumation of human remains would indeed play a vitally symbolic role) was encouraged by other, specifically social and cultural, influences. The decline of the nation-state and the end of the Cold War (and the ideological structures which accompanied them), coupled with cultural and economic globalisation, have made the search for meaning and identity in a turbulent world of seemingly constant change all the more significant.[30] Collective identities are always complex compositions of myth, memory and (often) political convenience, and Yáñez-Barnuevo would cite the sociologist José Vidal-Beneyto in support of his contention that 'there is no identity without memory'.[31] Although politicians regularly deploy memory, however, they do not need to engage with its complexity and ambiguities. The construction of cultural trauma, based initially on episodes of intra-community violence, and subsequently on the social agency of 'memory makers', is ambivalent because it depends on the ability and motives of competing collectives to lay claim to 'ownership' of the suffering. Hence the ambiguities in Spain of a situation where one section of society feels that the violence of the war is intimately present while, simultaneously, another views the suffering and terror as belonging to the distant past, in part because they belong to a tradition which formerly monopolised representation of the collective trauma. Recognition of this ambivalence – a product of the particular global 'moment', historical evolution (change over time), and limited knowledge of the past – rarely registers in the rhetoric of political debate. What Yáñez-Barnuevo saw as the 'fragility' of Spanish democracy, derived from the 'absence of historical roots to legitimise it and from the nonexistence in individual and collective memory of the subject matter of the past', was, in part, a search for a secure sense of collective identity. The sense of disorientation, brought about not least by the retreat of the state itself, was palpable in claims for collective memory as a right. Ramoneda and Yáñez-Barnuevo were thus merely exemplars of a broader perception that

---

[30] On intimations of the cultural effects of post-industrial society, see the US sociologist Daniel Bell: e.g., *The Cultural Contradictions of Capitalism* (New York, 1996 (1976)) and, specifically on 'the victory of culture over class', 'El mapa que surgió del frío', *El País: 20 años*, 5 May 1996, pp. 105–6.

[31] On memory and identity, Tony Judt, 'The Past Is Another Country', in Deák et al. (eds.), *Politics of Retribution*. José Vidal-Beneyto was a founder of the group of intellectuals and artists Memoria Democrática, which aimed to keep alive for new generations the anti-Franco cultural dissidence of the 1960s and 1970s, arguing that 'democracy was not granted but obtained': *El País*, 14 November 1997. See José Vidal-Beneyto (ed.), *Memoria democrática* (Madrid, 2007). His recent work has been largely devoted to questions of global identity. E.g. *Ventana global: ciberespacio, esfera pública mundial y universo mediático* (Madrid, 2002); *Hacia una sociedad civil global* (Madrid, 2003); *Poder global y ciudadanía mundial* (Madrid, 2004); *Derechos humanos y diversidad cultural* (Barcelona, 2006).

the twentieth century constituted a repository of memories from which moral and political lessons could and should be learned:

Nobody has the right to place obstacles in the way of the citizen's exercise of memory. It is memory from which the social texture is constructed. Out of unremembering [*desmemoria*] only the uncontrolled struggle of all against all, amongst subjects without history, can ensue. Memory is one of the few resources that we have to defend ourselves against history, which is always written by the victors.[32]

Group memories, especially those of war and conflict, are therefore bound up with a striving after identity, authenticity and a point of anchorage; questions of values and beliefs are a response to this striving.[33] As in other post-conflict settings, the surge of memory in Spain has had cathartic and theological or sacred overtones, evidenced in the moving responses of those who have given testimony at gravesides and in the language used by the 'makers' or 'carriers' of cultural trauma in the public sphere, as exemplified in the exhortatory title of Yáñez-Barnuevo's article: 'Speak, memory, speak'. The blocked access to historical truth in the past, it is argued, created a collective sense of trauma: 'those of us who practised oral history in the 1980s know that the political climate of the Transition did not set "traces of the past" free. Fear persisted, and this was because a failure to be definitive about the past [*indefinición del pasado*] impeded catharsis', though, as we have seen, this feeling only began to be expressed as such during the 1990s.[34] There can be little doubt about this fear in the past, though it had more complex roots than has often been suggested, relating as much to reluctance to breach community taboos and the personal problems and pain of reviving old feelings as to fear of sanction or retribution. The emotional shock of wartime experiences caused some of those who suffered them, in effect, to make a pact of silence with themselves and to adopt forgetting as a defence mechanism.[35] If catharsis requires retribution, then many historians are wary of creating

---

[32] Ramoneda, 'Memoria, amnesia, perdón'. On the 'moral memory palace', see Tony Judt, 'The World We Have Lost', in Judt, *Reappraisals: Reflections on the Forgotten Twentieth Century* (London, 2009), pp. 3–4. On historical memory as educative in the Spanish case, see Espinosa, *Contra el olvido*, pp. 184–6.

[33] Duncan S. A. Bell, 'Mythscapes: Memory, Mythology and National Identity', *British Journal of Sociology*, 54, 1 (2003), 63–81, 65.

[34] Espinosa, *Contra el olvido*, p. 197.

[35] Anna Miñarro and Teresa Morandi, 'Trauma y trasmissió. Efectes en la subjectivitat dels ciutadans de Catalunya de la guerra del 36, la postguerra, el franquisme y la transició', *Intercanvis*, 19 (2007), 37–52. See also Ignacio Fernández de Mata, 'La memoria y la escucha, la ruptura del mundo y el conflicto de memorias', in Aróstegui and Gálvez (eds.), *Generaciones*, pp. 891–913.

historical knowledge to be used as an instrument of justice, however. Henry Rousso, in analysing the politics of memory related to Vichy France – of collaboration and resistance – has maintained that the historian should not be 'an agitator of collective memory'; nor, of course, are historians primarily witnesses to past events.[36]

The relation with other conflicts is essential: technologies of global communication and dissemination of news have fuelled the new civic movements upholding universal rights in a world of conflict fought out rhetorically and often simplistically between 'good' and 'evil', a model with religious connotations. Commentators have noted a form of 'pan-continental collective memory', of reparation and apology exercised by a 'world citizenry' and based on generalised symbols of human suffering.[37] We have seen in an earlier chapter how the Chilean example had political influence in Spain in the 1970s as the repression meted out by Pinochet was viewed with trepidation by Franco's domestic opponents. The moral potency of memories of the Chilean violence and claims for reparation has been important again since the late 1990s in Spain. Other cases, including Argentina, South Africa and the Balkans, have similarly been instrumental in stirring traumatic memories. Luis Yáñez-Barnuevo has been prominent in calling for violations of human rights in Latin America to be recognised through reparations.[38] This has been recognised and encouraged at a global level through the establishment of the International Criminal Court in The Hague in July 2002. Lawyers had already petitioned the government in 2001 for the Spanish Penal Code to incorporate the concept of crimes against humanity, in accordance

[36] Henry Rousso, *The Haunting Past: History, Memory, and Justice in Contemporary France* (Philadelphia, PA, 2002): a critique of what he saw as an obsessive culture and politics of public memory in France (p. 86). Rousso argues that the internal divisions in France during the period 1940–5 were so numerous that it is 'not unreasonable to refer to them collectively as a civil war [though] in France there was nothing comparable to what took place in Spain'. Rousso, *Vichy Syndrome*, p. 7. The violent repression after this 'civil war' (some 800–1,500 executions) paled in comparison with what happened in Spain from 1939. See, e.g., Javier Tusell, 'Los muertos de Franco', *El País*, 22 December 1997.

[37] Espinosa cites the book series Memorias de la Represión, based on Latin America and published in Madrid, as an influence in his claims 'against forgetting' (*Contra el olvido*, p. 312). See, e.g., Claudia Feld, *Del estrado a la pantalla: Las imágenes del juicio a los excomandantes en Argentina* (Madrid, 2002), p. 59. Also Elizabeth Jelin, *Los trabajos de la memoria* (Madrid, 2002); Jelin (ed.), *Las conmemoraciones: las disputas en las fechas 'in-felices'* (Madrid, 2002); Ludmila da Silva Catela and Jelin, *Los archivos de la represión: documentos, memoria y verdad* (Madrid, 2002). For critique, see Alexander, 'On the Social Construction of Moral Universals', in Alexander (ed.), *Cultural Trauma*, pp. 196–262. Conversely, e.g., Daniel Levy and Natan Sznaider, 'Sovereignty Transformed: A Sociology of Human Rights', *British Journal of Sociology*, 57, 4 (2006), 657–76.

[38] Yáñez-Barnuevo referred to the ongoing investigations of the Spanish judge Baltasar Garzón into members of the Argentine military junta in Spain. *El País*, 14 October 1997.

with the Rome Statute.[39] The sense of a duty to remember crimes as a source of state legitimacy developed in two post-war phases, focused first on Germany and Japan in the 1940s, and from which Spanish society was crucially excluded, and second on conflicts in the 1990s, particularly Yugoslavia, Rwanda and East Timor, and subsequent processes of reconciliation where a 'confessional space' was created, the paradigm being the Truth and Reconciliation Commission in post-apartheid South Africa.[40] The 'debt' to remember and dignify the victims through rituals of recognition and acknowledgement is powerful in all these cases. Because of Franco's longevity, resolution of cultural trauma in Spain is caught temporally between the post-1945 era and that of the 1990s, so that the perception that crimes were allowed to slip into oblivion is all the stronger.[41]

Former prime minister Felipe González, during a visit to Chile in April 2001 to observe the proceedings of the ongoing National Commission on Political Imprisonment and Torture, took a different view on this point. Whilst certainly not criticising the Argentinian, Chilean and South African procedure of reconciliation *without* forgetting (by contrast, it may be said, with Spain's transition), González commented that the 'memory of horrors' was 'more alive' in these other societies than in Spain because they were closer in time.[42] Carlos Castresana Fernández, one of the Spanish lawyers who had initiated the case against General Pinochet, agreed that 'democracy without justice' had been possible in Spain because 'there had not been thousands of missing persons who had been victims of the state' – an idea disputed by the ARMH and other groups carrying out excavations of burial sites – 'and because almost all of those responsible for the systematic crimes during our civil war and its aftermath have already died'.[43] He nevertheless maintained

---

[39] *El País*, 12 June 2001. More generally: Richard Evans, 'History, Memory and the Law', *History and Theory*, 41, 3 (October 2002), 331.

[40] See David Beetham (ed.), *Politics and Human Rights* (Oxford, 1995). The Eichmann trial in Jerusalem in 1961 played a clearer and largely uncontested role in educating Israelis about national consciousness than recent putative proceedings against Francoists might in Spain (as the uproar caused by the Baltasar Garzón case suggests). Though the moral basis is quite different, in terms of the function of state building, the use of Holocaust memory in Israel is perhaps closer to Franco's use of memory after 1939.

[41] On 'remembrance of past wrongs' as 'one of the faces of justice' (an 'ethics of remembrance') in transitions to democracy, see W. James Booth, 'The Unforgotten'. Memories of Justice', *American Political Science Review*, 95, 4 (December 2001). See also Booth, *Communities of Memory: On Witness, Identity and Justice* (Ithaca, NY, 2006).

[42] *El País*, 22 April 2001. He also confirmed his belief that the Spanish transition was carried out well, 'in our circumstances, but in no way better than the Chileans and Argentinians in theirs'.

[43] *El País*, 1 May 2001.

critically that General Franco had never been brought before 'the court of memory'. Lamenting the disjunction between past and present brought about by the drive for modernity, Castresana argued that there had been little interest in 'recuperating the human, civic and democratic heritage of the defeated, of the exiled, squandered in an absurd manner'. His lament in fact echoed that of several reformers who had argued during the Franco years for greater tolerance of 'the defeated' and those in exile: 'Chileans can begin to view their transition as completed [. . .] We cannot say the same [. . .] They can visit the Palacio de la Moneda [seat of the President of Chile] and, in front of it, contemplate the monument erected to the last constitutional president, Salvador Allende. There will be no triumphal arches and equestrian statues for the dictator [in Chile].'[44]

At the same time as the articles of Luis Yáñez-Barnuevo and Josep Ramoneda appeared, another writer, Antonio Muñoz Molina, produced an extended defence of the academic discipline of history, focusing particularly on its dilution, as evidenced in certain pedagogic failings in Spanish schools. The humanities curriculum, he maintained, was problematic in understanding both the relation of the past to the present and the relation of the regions to the state. First, according to the analysis of Muñoz Molina, the 1980s had been shaped by 'a precipitate Socialist catechism of modernity' which had 'added a new dimension to the abolition of the past and of its memory'.[45] A more critical sense of the past was therefore needed. In education, because concentration had been shifted to confirming collective identities, children, it was widely (though not logically) believed, no longer needed 'to know about anything which might be beyond their own field of direct experience'.[46] Second, and more directly calling for a reconstitution of the central state as a democratic arena, Muñoz was highly critical of the regionalist, fragmenting and distorting direction of history, arguing that rigorous and fact-based knowledge was overlooked as a result, in some measure, of the 'colossal mess' which was the system of regional governance.[47] The state of autonomies, as the post-1978 constituted regional settlement is

---

[44] See also Vicenç Navarro, 'Los costes de la desmemoria histórica', El País, 16 June 2001.

[45] Antonio Muñoz Molina, 'La historia y el olvido', El País, 9 November 1997. He would return to the theme, including a critique of claims that the civil war had not been written about in literature before the current memory boom: Muñoz Molina, 'Desmemorias', El País, 6 September 2008.

[46] On the global dimension, see, e.g., Allan Megill, 'History, Memory, Identity', History of the Human Sciences, 11, 3 (1998), 47.

[47] See also Aurora Rivière Gómez, 'Envejecimiento del presente y dramatización del pasado', in Juan Sisinio Pérez Garzón (ed.), La gestión de la memoria: la historia de España al servicio del poder (Barcelona, 2000), pp. 161–219.

known, produced an ambiguous territorial pluralism which was the result of party strategies and bargaining.[48] The notion that there existed no politics 'outside of the narrowest and always oppressed nationalist identity', whether Catalan, Basque or Andalusian, had consequently and mistakenly been encouraged. Compounding this, for the left, since 1975, 'the idea and even the name of Spain [...] were inventions of the Francoist right'. According to this analysis, therefore, particular memories were hallowed, but this was not the same thing as history. Muñoz went so far, indeed, as to maintain that, whilst the dictatorship had concealed and falsified the history of Spain, democracy, instead of recovering it, had 'confirmed its prohibition'. The question was whether 'we choose to bother to investigate what really happened or prefer the comfort of myths'.

Memory, ethics and the Catholic Church

The interventions made by Luis Yáñez-Barnuevo, Muñoz Molina and others had come amid the minor storm which erupted in October 1997 when an article in the form of a survey of bishops, theologians and historians was published in *El País* on the question of the need for the Spanish Church to ask forgiveness for, in effect, blessing the rebellion of July 1936 as a 'crusade'.[49] Yáñez-Barnuevo had made public calls for the Church to ask forgiveness, the immediate context of which was the French Catholic hierarchy's own plea to French society – made on 30 September 1997 – for forgiveness for its silence at the time of anti-Jewish measures which had devastating consequences during the Vichy regime: the trial of Maurice Papon had begun in 1995, though media reports about his role in deportations of Jews from Bordeaux to the Drancy internment camp from 1942 to 1944 had first appeared during the presidential campaign in 1981.[50] The trial in France, which raised many questions about law and ethics and their relationship to history and memory, was drawing towards its close and Papon would ultimately be found guilty of crimes against humanity. The historian Pierre Nora, renowned for his theorisation of the crisis of 'traditional memory', would comment on the way the proceedings had demonstrated the 'sacrality' of modern memory and the generalisation of a 'human rights ideology'

---

[48] See Josep M. Colomer, 'The Spanish "State of Autonomies": Non-Institutional Federalism', in Heywood (ed.), *Politics and Policy*, pp. 40–52.

[49] Inmaculada de la Fuente, 'La Iglesia española no se arrepiente', *El País*, 12 October 1997.

[50] Rousso, *Vichy Syndrome*, p. 180.

which he perceived as originating in the 1970s, though, of course, he was not arguing in defence of Papon. Henry Rousso, meanwhile, saw the trial as a 'commemorative ritual' which explained much about the present but not about history.[51] Such subtle inflexions did not occur to many commentators in Spain, though the left's anxiety that Spanish democracy was in danger if there was not to be a fuller and franker examination of conscience seems in part to have been motivated by the trial. According to one critic, Vichy was viewed as the antechamber to De Gaulle's democracy, which in part explained the later Algerian conflict – Papon was, after all, accused of participation in torture in the Algerian war (1954–62) – implying that Spain's democracy might be similarly degraded by failure to deal with the Francoist legacy.[52] Later, as reparations cases and involvement of the state in dealing with the legacy of the civil war increased, the complexities and ambiguities seen in France's struggle with the past would be broadly replicated in Spain. This would mean that the apparently less ambiguous cases of political violence in Argentina and Chile would become the main moral exemplars of injustice for public declarations of memory activists in Spain by 2000, leading ultimately to the establishment by the new PSOE government in 2004 of an interministerial commission on 'the study of the situation of the victims of the civil war and Francoism'.

Returning to the Church in 1997, the ecclesiastical hierarchy, faced with calls to make amends, insisted that it, and Catholics generally, had been primarily *victims* of the war. This position was exemplified by Ramón Echarren Ystúriz, archbishop of the Canary Islands, who argued that the Spanish Church had agreed to ask forgiveness in September 1971 when a survey of priests on this question had been discussed at the Bishops' and Priests' Assembly in Madrid and a majority decided that such a course was necessary.[53] Critics pointed out that because there had been no two-thirds majority, there was in the end no such resolution in the public communiqué of the Assembly. Other priests rallied to the defence of the Church, rejecting what they viewed as attempts to put it on trial for supporting Franco.[54] Francisco Gil Delgado, for instance, maintained that the bishops had been ahead of other social groups and

---

[51] Richard J. Golsan (ed.), *The Papon Affair: Memory and Justice on Trial* (New York, 2000), including commentary of Pierre Nora (pp. 171–7) and Henry Rousso (pp. 205–10).

[52] Ramoneda, 'Memoria, amnesia, perdón'. On the interaction of Papon, Algeria and domestic repression: Jim House and Neil MacMaster, *Paris 1961: Algerians, State Terror and Memory* (Oxford, 2006).

[53] Ystúriz, '¿Debe pedir perdón la Iglesia por la guerra civil?', *El País*, 26 October 1997. See fuller discussion in Chapter 9.

[54] *ABC*, 26 October 1997, p. 62.

institutions because, during the 'hard era of Carrero Blanco', the conclusions of the Assembly had been so liberal that they were later incorporated more or less wholesale into the first three chapters of the democratic constitution of 1978. He did not mention that the conclusions relating to the war had been formulated by parish priests rather than bishops and that they in fact caused outrage from elements within the Church hierarchy. Echarren's argument strayed more directly (and crudely) into the political realm – a rather different environment in the late 1990s to that of the early 1970s – by insisting that leftist organisations had not apologised for the killing of priests during the civil war; moreover, in a manner which had long before become mechanical on the political right, he maintained that discussing such things caused 'sadness' and kept the 'rupture' of the past 'alive'.

For many observers, however, the significance of a formal recognition of the Church's responsibilities in the past was less to do with condemnation or assigning blame, as such, than with establishing and accepting a more strictly historical picture of the past. One such observer was the publisher and writer Rosa Regàs, a child of the war, born in 1933, whose Republican parents had been exiled without her. In the 1970s Regàs had initiated a ground-breaking and popular series of educational booklets on politics and contemporary history, commissioned from intellectuals across the political spectrum, including priests. Twenty years later, in 1997, she insisted on this need for a less fallible historical consciousness: 'we want to know what happened, we must know, not only with the Church during the war and Francoism, but with the right and the left, with the Communists and with the capitalists, with the dictators and with the liberals'.[55] This inclusive reading of the problem, in the name of objectivity, balance and accuracy, was complicated, however, by the very present political and cultural power the Church exercised, which seemed to be growing after the arrival to power of the PP in 1996. Apology for aligning the Church with political power in the 1930s clearly ran the risk of it accepting that such alignment with the nonconfessional state of the 1990s ought also to be questioned. Many on the left were critical, more broadly, of the Church's post-war role in maintaining nonconciliatory social policies and traditionalist education and failing to foster social and cultural reconciliation.[56] The participation

---

[55] Rosa Regàs, '¿Para qué olvidar?', El País, 15 November 1997. See her contribution to the ARHM conference in 2003: 'El pozo del miedo', in Silva (ed.), Memoria de los olvidos, pp. 71–2. On the booklet series Biblioteca de Divulgación Política, see Chapter 10.

[56] E.g., the wife of a Republican army officer, the exiled socialist Carmen Parga, El País, 2 November 1997. See her memoir, Antes que sea tarde (Madrid, 1996).

of politicians who were members of the conservative and secretive lay organisation Opus Dei in matters of the laic state, and at ministerial level, had become controversial, for example.

Religion continued, therefore, to be an important element of the political and cultural identities which constituted a primary motive of public memory and of denial of the past. One example, the response of the Catholic right and Franco apologists to publication in 1999 of the collective synthesis of historical research on the extent of civil war and post-war violence, *Víctimas de la guerra*, illustrates this point.[57] In 1974, the historian Gabriel Jackson had expressed a hope that the moment might soon arrive 'when a group of Nationalist and Republican historians will be capable of evaluating freely and completely all the available evidence and make a mutually acceptable calculation of the total number of political executions'.[58] Coverage in the conservative newspaper *ABC* in March 1999 in response to the *Víctimas* book revealed how distant the prospect of such mutual acceptance had become.[59] Against all of the historiography of the 1980s and 1990s, *ABC* maintained that the 1977 study by the Francoist former military officer Ramón Salas Larrazábal constituted the definitive quantitative accounting of the wartime killings. This judgement was made on the basis of the imprimatur granted by such 'specialists' as the historian Luis Suárez Fernández, director of the archive of the Fundación Nacional Francisco Franco, a staunchly pro-Caudillo private institute, to which access was denied to historians who were deemed to be unsympathetic and which, controversially, was to gain state funding under the PP administration.[60] Another supporter of the Salas account was the some-what bizarre ex-terrorist, turned revisionist polemicist, Pío Moa, who was interviewed by the newspaper for a response. Typical of coverage of the violence in politically conservative publications since 1975, *ABC* placed its scanty report on *Víctimas de la guerra* amongst more extensive coverage of anti-clerical violence in the Republican zone, in this case a horrendous recounting, redolent of the narratives related for many years in dozens of publications during the Franco years, of the martyrdom of Augustinians in Motril (Granada) in 1936. One of the victims of the violence had been beatified by John Paul II

---

[57] Juliá (ed.), *Víctimas de la guerra*. Its findings could not yet be considered definitive as primary research had only been completed in approximately half of the country's provinces.

[58] *Boletín de Orientación Bibliográfica*, 100, December 1974, pp. 7–29.

[59] *ABC*, 14 March 1999.

[60] E.g., *El País*, 20 September 2002. State funding was withdrawn soon after the election of the PSOE in 2004.

some days before.[61] This seemed to be a declaration that if the dead were not to 'be allowed to rest in peace', the price of bringing up rebel violence would always be more discussion of leftist wartime atrocities.[62] The religious dimension of violence in the Republican zone was then filtered into the brief treatment given by *ABC*'s report on the volume under discussion. Noteworthy in Moa's contribution was the crude re-imagining of the Spanish 'fratricidal' conflict as a 'war of placentas torn in two' (*'guerra de placentas rotas'*), thereby entangling objective history with emotively charged questions of religious identity at a moment when there had been papal condemnation, during a pastoral visit to the United States, of war, racism, abortion and euthanasia, as equivalent forms of violence.[63] Meanwhile, the portrayal of Pío Moa at home, a model of familial harmony, playing with his young daughter, seemed integral to the ideological argument.

Gradually, some leading Catholics would question reliance on the by now somewhat obscure proceedings of the Bishops' Assembly in 1971, some thirty years before, and began openly to return to the era of the reformist Primate of the 1970s, Enrique y Tarancón, in condemning uncritical religious legitimation of the war and dictatorship. In December 1999 a group of ten priests protested openly at the decision of the Bishops' Conference (Conferencia Episcopal) to exclude specific mention of the Church in asking 'forgiveness for all those implicated in actions which the gospel would reprove'.[64] They expressly recognised that, though many Spaniards had not lived through the war and, strictly speaking, had nothing to repent, its influence had been passed on generationally and that 'no easy exculpation was possible'. Later, in 2003, the regional parliament in Navarra, prompted by the families of wartime victims, passed a resolution calling for the 'moral reparation' of the three thousand Republicans killed in the region by the rebels in the first weeks of the war, and

---

[61] See Ángel Martínez Cuesta and Jesús Berdonces, *Una comunidad mártir: el beato Vicente Soler y los otros mártires de Motril* (Madrid 1999).

[62] The article was based on the 1999 re-edition of Bishop Antonio Montero's 1961 study *Historia de la persecución religiosa*. The doyen of post-war Spanish liberalism, Salvador de Madariaga, was cited by *ABC* in support of the notion that killing priests 'for political reasons' (as the rebels did in the Basque Country) was different to 'a systematic persecution and wholesale murder of priests *qua* priests'. See Madariaga, *Spain* (London, 1961 (1942)), p. 494. Madariaga was not, presumably, justifying killing for political reasons. That the purge of priests in Republican territory, however, was 'systematic' is a moot point. There is a good case for historical analysis of the religious killing (on both sides) which focuses on non-class-based 'purification'. See, e.g., Delgado, 'Anticlericalismo, espacio y poder'; Cueva, 'Religious Persecution'.

[63] *ABC*, 27 January 1999.

[64] 'Diez teólogos piden perdón para la Iglesia española por su "implicación evidente" en la guerra civil', *El País*, 13 December 1999.

the archbishop of Pamplona was petitioned publicly to make an apology for the 'connivance of the Church'. In so doing, he reiterated that 'in a strict sense' the claim that the Church was 'co-responsible' for the killing was 'untrue' and 'offensive to believers of then and now'.[65]

In a global sense, the Catholic Church would in fact contribute substantially to the millennial cult of apology. Cardinal Joseph Ratzinger had asked in 1997 for the violence of the Holy Inquisition (forerunner of the Congregation of the Doctrine of the Faith, of which he was head) to be forgiven and this was followed by John Paul's apology, early in the holy year 2000, for sins committed against Jews, heretics, women, 'gypsies' and native peoples. According to critics, the significance of these acts was diminished by the Church's tacit support for the death penalty in some states and in Spain by the PP's tampering with the autonomy of the private sphere of religious faith and sexual life, seen as defining elements of modern democratic society and culture. Critical voices were raised in protest at the focus during 2000, the twenty-fifth anniversary year of Franco's death, on celebrating the Transition and the constitutional monarchy rather than drawing attention to the perceived limitations of the democratic process since 1975 and the failure to revivify the democratic memory of the early 1930s.[66] Controversy also raged when TVE decided at short notice to prevent broadcast of the documentary *La sombra del caudillo*, which explored vestiges of the regime through images of the dictator in public statuary and street names.[67] At Easter 2000, the conservative archbishop of Madrid, Antonio Rouco, when asked whether papal apology ought to extend to the Church's blessing of the military rebellion as a 'crusade', rejected the notion that the Church was culpable, arguing that such an admission would 'hurt many people'. He also shifted attention by suggesting that, 'tragically', there remained 'a seed of war' in Spanish society. In effect, he maintained the 'crusading' position by distinguishing between the Pope asking forgiveness for offence to God and the settling of political accounts.[68]

Since the aftershock of the Second Vatican Council's radicalism there has been a general hardening of the Church's position as victim.

---

[65] *El País*, 20 March 2003.
[66] E.g., Vicenç Navarro, 'La democracia incompleta', *El País*, 19 December 2000. Also Espinosa, *Contra el olvido*, p. 197. On the trope of the Republic as a 'paradise lost', particularly in film and literature, see José F. Colmeiro, *Memoria histórica e identidad cultural* (Barcelona, 2005).
[67] *El País*, 14 November 2000. The issue had been broached before at the time of the fiftieth anniversary of the war, without causing much of a stir: 'Vestigios mudos del pasado', *El País*, 18 July 1986.
[68] *El País*, 13 April 2000.

With the accession of John Paul II in 1978, the papacy became devoted to reconquest and to breaking with Paul VI's acquiescence in modernity, secularism, and compromise. Beatification and sanctification were the key to popular mobilisation, and John Paul recast the history of his Church in a hagiographic and martyrological vein.[69] Papal blessing of many of the priests and other men and women of religion killed during the civil war appeared to reach its apogee in March 2001 with the beatification of 233 victims, but was intensified by his successor who would beatify some five hundred Spanish Catholic victims in October 2007. In putting them on the path to sainthood, Pope Benedict paid tribute to the martyrs, while addressing thirty thousand pilgrims in St Peter's Square: 'their forgiveness towards their persecutors should enable us to work towards reconciliation and peaceful coexistence'. The sense of inequality in honouring the dead belonging to the Church while appearing to forget other affected groups, particularly Spanish Republicans in general, was widely registered. Basque nationalist priests who had been loyal to the Republic and were killed by the rebels were not recognised as martyrs by the Church. A month later, however, in a somewhat exceptional move which coincided with the thirty-second anniversary of Franco's death, the head of Spain's Bishops' Conference, Ricardo Blázquez, Bishop of Bilbao, surprised many of his colleagues by issuing an unprecedented apology for the Church's 'specific acts' during the conflict and recalling Tarancón as 'providential' and as 'an efficient instrument of reconciliation'. In part motivated by his own efforts to bring about an end to the violence of ETA, and directly referring to the mass beatification in October, he maintained that 'on many occasions we have reasons to thank God for what was done and for the people who acted, [but] probably in other moments we should ask for forgiveness and change direction'.[70] He also addressed and upheld the functions of collective memory in confirming a sense of identity: 'each human group – a particular society, the Catholic Church in a given geographic space, a religious congregation, a political party, a trade union, an academic institution – has the right to remember its history, to cultivate its collective memory, because in this way they penetrate their identity more deeply [. . .] We look to the past in a desire to purify memory, to correct possible failings, in search of peace.'[71]

[69] Tony Judt, 'A "Pope of Ideas"? John Paul II and the Modern World', *New York Review of Books*, October 1996, reproduced in Judt, *Reappraisals* (p. 151).
[70] *El País*, 20 November 2007.
[71] On Basque nationalism and religion, see Antonio Elorza, *Un pueblo escogido: génesis, definición y desarrollo del nacionalismo vasco* (Barcelona, 2001).

National identity and the state

The Bishop's summation on memory and identity reminds us that reparation was sought not only from the Church but from the state, through legal measures, and in the name of regional and national identity. At the same time as exchanges amongst commentators in the press, a fragmented array of collective memory claims was articulated. For example, following the return of Basque war children from Russia after the collapse of the Soviet Union at the beginning of the 1990s, the Basque regional parliament approved a proposal to recognise the forced nature of their expatriation to Russia and the Ukraine in 1937, necessitated by the advance of rebel troops and German bombers following the destruction of the town of Guernica.[72] Since 2000, more generally, many regional authorities have granted some form of compensation to those deprived of their liberty during the Franco years. By 2005, only two Spanish regions, Galicia and Extremadura, had not introduced a process of indemnification in favour of those who had been imprisoned, often in labour detachments, for political reasons.[73] Historical research conferences and symposiums about the war and dictatorship, and memory and reparation, were organised in many areas, more often than not funded by regional governments, especially those with a particularly strong collective cultural and political identity, and focused on looking back on the twentieth century in order to count the human cost of the conflict.[74]

The politics of memory, frequently expressed through the symbolism of national martyrdom, has been particularly important in Catalonia, partly in reaction against the vestiges of traditionalist Spanish nationalism which came to be associated with the government of José María Aznar and its foreign policy.[75] If one of the key moments in provoking an eruption of collective memory claims in the late 1990s had been the Pinochet case, the devastating terrorist attack in Madrid on 11 March

---

[72] Carmen González Martínez, 'El retorno a España de los "niños de la guerra civil"', *Anales de Historia Contemporánea*, 19 (2003), 75–100.

[73] E.g., Defensor del pueblo Andaluz, *Informe al parlamento 2002* (Seville, 2003), pp. 74–80.

[74] E.g., the Catalan research group linked to the Autonomous University of Barcelona, November 2000, conference 'El franquismo: un balance desde el fin de siglo' and 'Los campos de concentración y el mundo penitenciario durante la guerra civil y el franquismo', held at the Museu de l'Historia de Catalunya (October 2002). See Molinero et al. (eds.), *Inmensa prisión*.

[75] On projection of Catalan identity and the battle for control of civil war archival material seized by Franco in 1938, see (aside from much press coverage), Joan B. Culla and Borja de Riquer, 'Sobre el archivo de Salamanca'; Antonio Morales Moya and Carlos Dardé, 'Razón de un archivo'; both in *Ayer*, 47 (2002), 279–93, 295–303.

2004 heightened political tension such that the ongoing 'memory wars' were reignited. Widely seen as the worst terrorist attack in European history and as a crime against humanity, ten bombs in all were detonated on four trains during the morning rush hour, killing 191 *madrileños* of 14 different nationalities and causing injury to more than 1,500 others.[76] Although the PP government attempted to lay the blame on ETA, it quickly became obvious that the attack, perpetrated on the eve of Spain's general election, had been the work of an Islamic fundamentalist group. Aznar's government had supported the United States-led war in Iraq and had sent military support, although parliament had not been consulted and polls showed that 90 per cent of Spaniards opposed the war, a higher proportion than in any other European society. The PSOE leader, José-Luis Rodríguez Zapatero, of the same generation as the founders of the principal civic memory groups, whose grandfather, a Republican military officer, had been executed during the civil war, was opposed to Spain's involvement. Those who were active supporters of the ARMH were usually also actively opposed to the war.[77] The very idea of the war was associated with the horrors of the country's own conflict of the 1930s, and Aznar's yearning for a more prominent international role, through resurrection of a heroic form of nation-statehood and a pro-Atlanticism which entailed alliance with what some viewed as the totalitarian ethos of the Bush administration, conflicted with Spanish society's long-standing pro-Europeanism. In its disregard for the consensus and cultural variety which was believed to have brought about democratisation, Spain's role harked back to the days of Franco.[78] The brutal shock of the Madrid bombing produced a coordination of leftist support and electoral victory in a similar way to that produced by the failed *coup d'état* in February 1981.[79] The banners and placards of the mass anti-terrorism demonstrations in the aftermath of the bombs focused on the democratic constitution of 1978 and the rule of law.[80]

Political relations were embittered by the election, first, because the PP believed it had been decided by outside influence and that the new

[76] José Antonio Martín Pallín, magistrate of the Tribunal Supremo, *El País*, 26 March 2004.

[77] E.g., Regàs, 'Pozo del miedo', pp. 69, 73; Dulce Chacón, 'La mujer y la construcción del olvido', p. 75, both in Silva (ed.), *Memoria de los olvidos*.

[78] E.g., Pedro Ruiz Torres, *El País*, 12 March 2004. On policy, see, e.g., José María Aznar, *Ocho años en el gobierno* (Barcelona, 2004).

[79] Josep M. Colomer, 'The General Election in Spain, March 2004', *Electoral Studies*, 24 (2005), 149–56.

[80] E.g., communiqué of anti-racist organisations, *El País*, 13 March 2004; Mustafá Al Mirabet, president of Moroccan Migrant Labour Association in Spain, *El País*, 7 April 2004.

government lacked legitimacy, and, second, because the commission of inquiry into the bombing was damning in its criticisms of the Aznar government's unpreparedness and subsequent manipulation of information. One highly respected commentator concluded that 'the process of the construction of a system of democratic coexistence (*convivencia democrática*) has not yet finished'.[81] The new PSOE government came to power promising to tell the truth about responsibility for the bombings and began to set forth a project redefining citizenship and the 'common good' through policies which resonated with the social norms embedded in what has been called 'transitional justice culture', constituted by the righting of past wrongs, by rejecting impunity, prioritising the search for truth and accountability, and shaping a more tolerant democratic culture, against what was widely perceived as the PP's narrow faith in a single cultural identity.[82]

Debates over historical memory took place between 2004 and 2007 in this environment of largely two-party polarisation, with added tension created by regional questions. In late September 2004, for instance, the left-of-centre Catalan nationalist party Esquerra Republicana de Catalunya (ERC) presented a proposal to the Spanish parliament calling on the PSOE government to annul the death sentence of the Francoist military court of 1940 against the President of Catalonia during the Second Republic, Lluís Companys, who had been captured in France and returned to Spain by the Nazi authorities and executed.[83] The proposal was symbolic both of broad Catalan nationalism and of the memory claims of many other, more anonymous, victims of those who, as the text put it, had 'rebelled against legality'. For Catalan nationalists and sections of the left, the move was intentionally against the 'impunity' provided by the Amnesty Law of 1977, a law which the right saw as fundamental to the post-Franco constitutional arrangements.[84] The matter was put to the session by the historian and member of parliament Joan Tardá, who began, speaking in Catalan, by declaring that 'the entire Catalan nation awaits the historical reparation which is proposed', a contention supported by a short resumé of international human rights law since 1945. The extreme wartime violence in

---

[81] José Álvarez Junco, 'Patriotismo y cultura democrática', *El País*, 5 April 2004.

[82] Golob, 'Volver', p. 133. Particular policy priorities included: reinvigorating European identity; immigration reform; legalising gay marriage; the ETA peace process; and renegotiating the Catalan statute.

[83] Generalitat de Catalunya, *Consejo de guerra y condena a muerte de Lluís Companys* (Barcelona, 1999); Josep Benet, *Lluís Companys, presidente de Cataluña, fusilado* (Barcelona, 2005).

[84] *Diario de Sesiones del Congreso de Diputados*, no. 34, 28 September 2004, pp. 1,451–71.

Catalonia and the Basque Country 'exemplified the extent to which fascist elements and the Spanish army which rebelled [...] were in thrall to hatred of national communities distinct from that of the Spanish state' (though, in fact, the number of victims, in proportional and numerical terms, was no greater in these regions than in other strongly Republican regions, such as Andalucía or Aragón).[85] The declarations of the PP during the debate implicitly (and at times explicitly) reflected the belief that the resolution on reconciliation issued in November 2002 by the all-party Constitutional Commission, supported by the PP, had drawn a definitive line under further claims related to war memories. In this belief the party betrayed a tendency to hark back to Franco-style rhetoric of the kind discussed in previous chapters. One of its spokespersons maintained during the debate on the rehabilitation of Companys, for example, that, rather than speak specifically of the tragedy of the civil war of 1936–9, the country needed to put behind it 'the tragedy which was the nineteenth century and a substantial part of the twentieth'.[86] Although the proposal was accepted in a parliamentary vote, the annulment remained unfulfilled in 2011.

A year after the Companys proposal, on 27 September 2005, a similar petition was made, this time initiated by the Catalan nationalists of the centre, the CiU, about the execution in Burgos in 1938 of the Republican and Catholic founder of Unió Democràtica de Catalunya (UDC), Manuel Carrasco i Formiguera, a moderate by any standards, who had defended the Church from political attack during the 1930s. In the early part of the war Carrasco, as an official of the Catalan Generalitat's finance department, had been in danger of being liquidated by revolutionary militias in Barcelona. While Companys had been leader of the Esquerra, Carrasco's more centrist UDC was one of the predecessors of the CiU, which had been unified as a new party in 1978.[87] Carrasco was therefore representative of 'the Third Spain', that section of society which recoiled at the violence but was caught between the contending forces.[88] The objective of the proposal was much the same as in the Companys case: restitution of the subject's 'historical memory' (in other

[85] *DSCD*, 114, 27 September 2005. The term 'genocide' was employed to mean destruction or attempted destruction of cultural/national identity. On physical repression in Catalonia and the Basque Country, see, respectively, Solé i Sabaté, *Repressió franquista a Catalunya*; Iñaki Egaña, *Los crímenes de Franco en Euskal Herria* (Tafalla, 2009).

[86] Fernández-Díaz, in the parliamentary debate, 28 September 2004, p. 1,455. Also, on the 1978 Constitution as a 'seal' on the recent past: *Diario de Sesiones de la Asamblea de la Comunidad de Madrid*, 11 April 2002.

[87] Two of Carrasco's children, both very young when he was killed, were present in the Congress during the debate. On Carrasco, see also Chapter 10.

[88] See Preston, *Las tres Españas*.

words, that he be properly remembered by history), though not restitution of his honour – since this had never been in doubt – or a pardon since he had committed no crime, although 'the official truth' recorded otherwise.[89]

Between the two debates, the interministerial commission on war victims had begun to meet, though it had rejected arguments from the ERC and the United Left (IU) that it focus on cataloguing Republican victims, in a manner similar, in this respect, to the Franco state's Causa General in 1940. This proposed 'libro blanco' would, it was argued, have represented a form of monument of 'anti-fascist memory' at a moment when 'totalitarian horrors' were being 'trivialised' by Franco apologists.[90] Those who spoke most enthusiastically in support of the proposal complained, at the same time, of the government's inactivity in the case of Companys, which had become bogged down in disputes over legal jurisdiction, as had happened in other such cases, including the one opened in 1994 in support of the anarchist Salvador Puig Antich who had been executed by the Francoist state in 1974, accused of having killed a policeman.

In supporting the proposal, the PSOE emphasised Carrasco's defence of Republican legality, rather than his Catalanism, and justified its own former government's position during the later stages of the transition to democracy: 'a widely shared decision' had been taken 'to turn the page', to not look back, in order that 'we might safeguard the still uncertain future'. Parliament was reminded that Socialists had been prominent amongst the victims of the war: of the 99 Socialist parliamentarians elected in 1936, one-third of them had been executed or had died in prison, including the moderate Julián Besteiro, another representative of 'the Third Spain', who had died precisely 65 years before, on 27 September 1940, in Carmona prison. The equivalent symbolic figure for the Galician nationalist deputies who contributed to the debate was Alexandre Bóveda, like Carrasco a Catholic, who was executed following a summary trial on 17 August 1936 (commemorated today in Galicia as the Día da Galiza Mártir). For the parliamentary group of IU and Greens, the emphasis was on the inhumanity of the death penalty: 27 September was also the day, 30 years before, of the last executions carried out by the Franco regime in 1975.

On behalf of the Basque nationalists, Margarita Uría emphasised how the Transition had 'robbed us of our immediate past', making reference to the recent report produced by the Spanish section of the global human rights organisation Amnesty International, published on 18 July 2005, on the theme of the 'unsettled debt' which the country owed to the

---

[89] *Diario de Sesiones del Congreso de Diputados*, 114, 27 September 2005.
[90] Summarised in proposed law formulated shortly afterwards: *Diario de Sesiones del Congreso de Diputados*, no. 219–1, 2 December 2005.

victims of war and dictatorship, and which upheld the necessity of collective memory, the right to truth and justice, and access via the state to adequate resources to achieve these ends.[91] Daniel Fernández-González, speaking for the government, referred to the interministerial commission on the situation of the victims, established in 2004, maintaining that although the war had been 'a tragic aberration', Spanish society was now 'prepared and wishes to be protagonist of a consensual recuperation of our most immediate past', pointing out that a law for compensation of 'war children' (those who had been displaced from Spain) had already been passed.[92] The main opposition party, the PP, was more reticent and more embarrassed. Manuel Atencia skirted around Carrasco's Catholic faith and felt the need to articulate that which other parties already assumed: that the execution of Carrasco had 'without doubt' been 'unjust'. Citing the PSOE representative in the Companys debate a year before, Atencia repeated the legal position which upheld the principle of 'the juridical security of the Constitution', making annulment of sentences impossible. The PP also went further than rejecting legal revision, however, declaring, as it had several times before, that neither was it in favour of '*historical* revisionism'. According to this idealisation of a history apparently frozen in time, revision would be 'reckless', leading, in the end, to upsetting the post-Franco transitional settlement. After a PSOE amendment, the PP nonetheless voted to support the proposal in principle and to refer the matter to the new interministerial commission. A remaining problem, however, was that the PSOE had already recognised in June 2004, when debating the remit of the commission, that the courts had ruled it 'juridically impossible' to revise the 1977 Amnesty Law or judicial acts of the dictatorship.[93] Such revision would, in effect, be anti-constitutional, and these constraints would be reflected in both the commission report (July 2006) and the subsequent Law of Historical Memory, approved at the end of October 2007, in which, although it was declared that Francoist military courts had been 'illegitimate', the possibility of vacating judicial sentences passed down by these courts was dropped.[94]

*

[91] Amnistía Internacional, Sección Española, *Poner fin al silencio y a la injusticia: la deuda pendiente con las víctimas de la guerra civil española y del régimen franquista* (Madrid, 2005).

[92] Ley 3/2005, 18 March 2005, *BOE*, 68, 21 March 2005. The historian Pierre Vidal was cited in defence of the Socialist government's position prior to 1996.

[93] See comments of Ramón Jáuregui, PSOE member of the parliamentary Constitutional Committee: *Diario de Sesiones del Congreso de Diputados*, 13, 1 June 2004, p. 488.

[94] *El País*, 1 November 2007. On the illegitimacy of the Franco courts (as repressive organs rather than judicial bodies): 'Jiménez Villarejo exige que se anulen los juicios sumarísimos de Franco', *El País*, 6 October 2006. The report of the commission is: *Informe general de la Comisión Interministerial para el Estudio de la Situación de las Víctimas*

The resurgence of war-related memories in Spain since the late 1990s has been explained here by the conjunction of domestic political tensions, which came to a head with the fall of the PSOE government in 1996, and several other conditions: a propitious global environment of law and ethics; a broad context of often bewildering economic and cultural change related to post-modernity; and, not least, the legacy of a struggle within Spain since 1939 to claim 'ownership' of collective trauma related to the civil war in the light of almost four decades of political dominance by the victors. The prominence of this contest over memory had much to do superficially with party politics. The change of government in 1996, after the previous PSOE administration had become embroiled in corruption scandals, represented the first election of a conservative government with links to the Francoist past since the transition to democracy. The corruption, on the left, and these historical associations, on the right, as well as the foreign policy inclinations of the conservative PP government, lent a belligerent ethos to politics at the close of the millennium. The sense of settling accounts was encouraged by a global scene shaped by an increasingly universal juridical framework for the claims of victim groups against those guilty of 'crimes against humanity'. This globalisation of justice ran parallel to a more general decline in authority of the nation-state as the well-spring of collective identity and responses to social demands, and concurrent advances in communications technology which facilitated the development of identities based in part on shared legacies of suffering. The unearthing of the past in Spain, most graphically symbolised by the excavation of anonymous wartime burial pits, has been linked to these combined influences, as have the responses of regional governments within the Spanish state and institutions such as the Catholic Church which have an interest in the ways in which historical memory is 'recuperated'.

A number of recurrent features are clear. First, there has developed a perception of the desirability of historical memory (which has been led by a particular generation), as well as the creation of means to legitimate, sustain and disseminate this desire. Second, a generally weak sense of historiographical consciousness and fallibility of historical knowledge within society have been notable, even amid the ubiquitous discourse on historical memory. And, third, it has been clear that collective or cultural memory is contingent, heavily dependent on the demands and pressures of the present. All three conclusions reinforce a highly

de la Guerra Civil y del Franquismo (28 July 2006), available at www1.mpr.es/uploads/media/pdf/6/informegeneral2_1232475655.pdf.

significant absence of any sense of the processes of social change in much public discourse about the past. These processes saw the country 'remade', in effect, from the ground up, after the catastrophe of war and during subsequent decades. This 'remaking' of Spain affected social relations fundamentally and, in turn, influenced the complex and changing ways in which the war was remembered.

Conclusion: the history of war memories in Spain

In the light of debates since the death of Franco about the legacy of war and dictatorship, the redressing of past wrongs, and the role of public history, this study has sought to explain the relationship between multiple memory narratives of the Spanish civil war. An understanding of the aftermath of the civil war and the regime to which it gave rise has been outlined which delineates the connections between the devastation and dislocation of the conflict and later processes of change. The objective has been to integrate the phases of Francoism more effectively than has previously been achieved by exploring social change and social memory decade by decade, from the ground up (in the even-numbered chapters, 2–10), interspersed – again, chronologically – with the politics and practices of memory of the victors (in the odd-numbered chapters, 3–9). Collective articulation of war memories depended primarily on the violence of the conflict but was also in large measure contingent, shaped by post-war events and changing social circumstances. Memory corresponded to present political and social requirements and collectively constructed ways of explaining the relation between 'then' and 'now'. This extended account of changes in memory over time during Franco's dictatorship serves as the essential context for analysis in the final two chapters, 11 and 12, of recent debates about the recuperation of historical memory. Current concerns are placed alongside the modernisation of society after Franco, the retreat of the nation-state, and uncertainties about collective identity.

The intimate violence of the civil war, taking place within the confined space of village, town and community, as a destructive breach of cultural norms, has often been misleadingly represented. Violence has usually been framed within the legitimating narratives of either the wartime Republic (narratives of 'class war' and 'democracy') or the rebel – later Francoist – state (the 'crusade', followed by the fratricidal thesis – a 'war between brothers'). Family stories have personalised the war and its pain and suffering, as human beings naturally do, drawing on the grand legitimating narratives at the same time. Competing post-war collective constructions of cultural trauma have implicitly recognised that the violence and the war itself had a broader meaning than the sum of individual suffering. The differential experience of violence between the rebel and loyalist zones has usually been restricted to comment upon the more coordinated nature of rebel violence than that employed by Republicans, though in both cases the level of coordination depended on the evolution of institutions of authority. While in the Republican zone, the coalescence of a relatively solid and coherent system of authority during the war led to a sharp diminution of violence, in the rebel zone state-building involved a continuation of violence, placing a brutal stamp of permanence on the new order, throughout the war and beyond. The intention here has been to explore the diversity of the experience of violence and terror in ways which have been less commented on. The passage from war to post-war was complex in temporal, political and social terms. The micro level of rebel conquest was crucial. Fragmentation of the state and of its multi-level structure of authority wrought by the military rebellion created pressure to impose power in communities by co-opting civilians willing to denounce 'enemies'. Reconstituting communities thus permitted a fierce sanctioning of the defeated and the instilling of fear, eliciting collusion and corruption, and using a sense of shame as the motive force behind silence and selective forgetting. This rupture of social relations motivated large numbers of rural Spaniards to migrate to urban centres, seeking the shelter of anonymity. Aside from this multi-level remaking of power, a distinction and a relationship have therefore been established between rural and urban settings. The complex experience of violence at the micro level, and discrimination against the defeated once villages and towns were 'liberated' by rebel forces, undermined previous social ties and former political aims and practices, indirectly influencing social responses and memory in the aftermath of the war and later economic 'take-off' through post-war migration.

Migration, in part a form of resistance to hunger, exclusion and segregation, formed the basis of the subsequent unprecedented change which began in the 1940s and gathered momentum during the 1950s. Remaining silent, fleeing from the past, and 'forgetting' had already become rationalised. The war and its aftermath thus saw both the punishment of the defeated and an uneasy convergence of rural and urban worlds in the form of burgeoning marginal shanty towns on the perimeter of many cities. This would require a response from the authorities – a state more centralised since the civil war – and from the regime's natural support base amongst the Catholic middle classes. These responses were naturally shaped by memories of the war. After the horror and exhaustion of the conflict, Spaniards of all social classes (unless they formed part of the public political elite of the New State) turned inwards to focus on the domestic sphere of the family and yearned for 'normality'. Passive acceptance of a return to peace and order – rather than mobilised active support – coincided with the imagined 'natural order' of Francoists and the Catholic Church and formed the basis of the meagre, though vital, social consensus of the 1940s and 1950s.

The rural–urban convergence would ultimately fuel a halting process of reconciliation, though this would be fraught with contradictions, not least, those accentuated by the dictatorship's reluctance to let go of the war and victory as its primary myth of legitimation as it consolidated its control. Notable individuals and some groups once internal to the regime, including Catholics who had supported the rebels' wartime 'crusade', developed attitudes which demonstrated greater tolerance towards those they continued to call 'the defeated' and became critics of the dictatorship and its public monopoly of war memories. Reform of the Catholic Church according to the radical 'updating' signalled by the Second Vatican Council in the early 1960s confirmed the direction already taken by worker priests who were active in the sprawling migrant slums of the late 1940s and 1950s. Development of a public sphere, though heavily circumscribed politically, would permit a gradual but broad shift of mentality from the designation and imposition of shame, associated with rural society, towards a heightened sense of conscience encouraged by intersocial mixing and greater public discussion. From the 1960s there would be less talk of 'the masses' and 'the multitude' and increasing emphasis on consumption of goods by 'citizens', though civil society remained paradoxically shackled by poverty, censorship, arbitrary imprisonment, and military justice.

It has been necessary to engage with the violence of both the rebel wartime zone and that of the Republic because subsequent collective representations of 'the memory of the victors' and of 'the defeated' during the dictatorship depended on mutual interaction. The construction of collective memory claims (especially those of 'the victors') depended on denying the claims of 'the other' and always on the mediating action, for good or ill, of institutions which held power or controlled access to the constrained public sphere, whether these were religious, aesthetic, legal, state-bureaucratic, scientific (especially the academic historical world), or those of the mass media. With a backdrop of vertiginous social change, the construction of memory was also significantly mediated by generational succession. Events were of such magnitude and changes so radical that the experience of each successive generation was often fundamentally different to the last. What each cohort chose to explain to the next – and the means found to confer meaning upon these narratives – forms a significant part of the post-war social history.

From 1939 until 1975, the process of constructing claims to have suffered collective trauma took place within spaces circumscribed by and reserved for the victors. In the 1960s and 1970s, a new 'modernised' official narrative employing the integrative vocabulary of 'fratricidal struggle' accompanied urbanisation and economic liberalisation. The aim was to replace the language of crusade and martyrdom through which the rebel war had been depicted by officially encouraged memory activists until then as glorious and through which its shameful aspects had been deflected entirely onto the Republic and its supporters. Though successful to the extent of contributing to the largely peaceful transition after Franco, the 'fratricidal struggle' thesis ultimately amounted to a government-inspired form of forgetting which resurrected the 'two Spains' myth in order to obscure the real causes of the war and responsibilities for it. Later, especially from the late 1990s on, the contest over memory took place within a cultural and political arena shaped by domestic and global influences which were favourable to the long-overdue public representation of memories of the defeated. In between, the articulation of war memories, though publicly present in several ways, was more muted, placed in the shade by the political and social imperatives of democratisation (which was still under threat in the early 1980s) and social and cultural modernity. The final two chapters have explained how this consensual narrative prevailed in relative terms for much of the modernising 1980s and how it broke down after 1996.

During this last period, the disorienting effects of the decline of ideological certainties, the retreat of the state, and the rise of globalisation have shaped the confluence of identity formation, history, justice and widely supported calls for 'catharsis'. There has been an evident (and stimulating) tension between seeking redress, reparation, and assigning responsibilities for crimes, on the one hand, and the writing of history, on the other. This has been accentuated by the trend of the mass media and emergent global judicial agencies (aided by the wide scope and accessibility of global communications) to pursue forms of 'performative purification' in relation to painful national pasts.[1] A quasi-psychoanalytical framework of unassimilated collective pain and the need to throw off the burden of the past has been part of the recent growth of memory of war and dictatorship, not only in Spain but in other parts of Europe and the wider world. Often influenced by advocate literature produced within the

---

[1] Jeffrey C. Alexander, 'The Social Construction of Moral Universals', in Alexander (ed.), *Remembering the Holocaust: A Debate* (Oxford, 2009), p. 51.

orbit of disciplines such as Holocaust and Literary Studies, this framework of analysis assumes that the natural and inherent legacy of brutal collective experiences will be collective trauma. This is often done without any reference to the ways in which the associated cases are in part expressions of politically and/or culturally constituted collective identity claims, whether encouraged or repressed by the state – in Spain, respectively, memory of 'the victors' and of 'the defeated'. In isolation, the psychoanalytic metaphor which argues for the collectively harmful effects of the suppression of painful memories in the aftermath of violent conflict is too static an image of a 'collective mind' at work to account for variations of public memory over time. The flowering of war-related personal testimony of recent years has acted as a positive spur to historians in complicating previous interpretative frameworks, but memory coexists for historians with other theorised and fact-based ways of knowing. Trusting in objective truth, honed with care by setting such testimony alongside other evidence, arguably remains the best contribution that history can make to ensuring that appalling violence does not recur.[2]

Several points can therefore be made in summary. First, collective memories of cataclysmic social and political events are constructed (or 'made') cumulatively and in complex ways. The complexity becomes evident when group memories are shown to change over time (and are 'remade'), partly in response to political power and the changing parameters of social relationships. Memory is therefore social to the extent that it is both processual and relational.

Second, the nature of this making and remaking of social memory of collectively life-shattering events is dependent on the degree to which such a 'happening' constitutes a watershed 'moment', the essential origin of subsequent state evolution or fundamental and often forced societal changes of direction. The dynamics of the violence of the originating 'event' and the shape that reconstruction, recovery and reconciliation take, both through top-down initiatives and action from the ground up, are thus highly significant. It follows that making memory is also closely related to post-cataclysm processes of state building and political strategies to gain and sustain legitimacy. This is particularly noteworthy in cases such as Spain where the salience of civil war, as with revolutions, is profound and where the victors crystallised and retained power for decades thereafter.

Third, making memory is also intimately bound up with the construction of collective political and cultural identities. Investigating post-war

---

[2] For a critique of subjectivity which is valuable because it explicitly does not discard trauma as a proper theme for historians, see Megill, 'History, Memory, Identity', 51, 53.

memory allows the experiential and the representational to be brought together in mapping political attitudes and processes onto often unspoken assumptions about the past and the social meanings attached to daily life. Much of the personal testimony in Spain recorded during the 'memory boom' since the late 1990s reinforces the contention that memory after the civil war depended on and formed a central element of such assumptions.

Fourth, an important component of identity building based on past experience of collective victimisation and violence is the composition and dissemination of evidence- and discourse-based cultural trauma claims.[3] The active construction and mediation of these claims in Spain – their rise and fall over seven decades and the relationship between the claims of 'victors' and 'defeated' as they struggle for 'possession' of collective trauma – has formed a thread throughout this study. Restricting analysis of war memories to 'the defeated' is unsatisfactory because the shape of collective traumatic memory is in part determined by the content of the counterclaims and strategies of denials adopted by other collective groups. The contest over cultural trauma constitutes, indeed, one of the many ways in which social memory is profoundly relational, not least in the responses to appeals made by key 'carriers' or agents of memory from the rest of a rapidly changing society.

Finally, the intention of this study has not been to call for or contribute to 'closure'; instead, it has been interested in the conditions under which identified social groups, for a variety of reasons, consider resolution, reparation and recognition of violent events in the past to be necessary, pending and urgent. It has reconstructed the motives behind collective actions which articulate, convey and sustain memory claims as they have evolved since the civil war. Whilst the affirmation of memory is often concerned with recuperation or pardoning, history is about interrogation and evidence-based explanation. The aim has been to record past conflicts and tensions over memory and to explain them historically without resurrecting the claims of one side or the other; only in this sense has it attempted to draw a line under the past.[4] In the end, when investigating life-shattering civil violence committed in the past – particularly if the conflict remains within living memory – the state remains the only body which can be petitioned to prosecute or pardon. Post-war memory since 1939 can indeed only be understood in relation to the making and remaking of power. The state in Spain during the dictatorship was

---

[3] See also my Introduction, pp. 1–5.

[4] Gabrielle Spiegel, 'Memory and History: Liturgical Time and Historical Time', *History and Theory*, 41 (2002).

ultimately the primary historical product of the war, of its divisions and its repressive aftermath. In terms of sovereignty, the post-Franco state remains the heir and descendant of *both* the wartime contending forces. As is suggested by the 2007 Law of Historical Memory and the recent trial of the magistrate and human rights investigator Baltasar Garzón, in part for opening a case against those responsible for Francoist repression, the state will continue to be the crucial arena for negotiation with society about the connection of the past to the present. The rationale behind collective memory claims emanating from society and institutionalised power's degree of responsiveness to them will continue to be analysed by historians and others. This analysis will have to relate the state's response to social memory to the contingencies of politics, socio-economic conditions, technology, collective identity, and the stories handed down from generation to generation in explaining the painful past.

Glossary and abbreviations

AC: Acción Católica (Catholic lay organisation)
ACNP: Asociación Católica Nacional de Propagandistas (secular political organisation of Catholic social elites)
AE: Acción Española (conservative political group which published an anti-Republican journal of the same name)
alféreces provisionales: volunteer provisional officers (second lieutenants) of wartime rebel forces largely composed of middle-class university students
apertura: political reform in 1970s (literally, 'opening up')
ARMH: Asociación para la Recuperación de la Memoria Histórica
barraca: self-made shanty dwelling and community of same in Barcelona/Catalonia from 1940s to 1970s
cacique/caciquismo: local political 'boss' and pre-war clientelist political system based on election rigging and economic control; it continued after the civil war by incorporating Falangists
Casa del Pueblo: literally 'House of the People': a local meeting place and/or branch office of the socialist PSOE and trade union or anarcho-syndicalist CNT
casticismo: the Spanish 'essence', found in a pure 'caste' or 'race', the search for this essence, and the exclusion of foreign elements
caudillaje: theory of authority founded on the prestige of the Caudillo
caudillo: leader, usually with military connotations; Caudillo was the title assumed by Franco, the equivalent of Duce or Führer (i.e. supreme political leader)
Causa General (General Cause): Collective lawsuit brought by the Franco state in early 1940 against wartime actions carried out in the Republican Zone
CEDA: Confederación Española de Derechas Autónomas (Confederation of Spanish Autonomous Rightist Groups)
cedistas: members or activists of the Catholic mass political organisation, the CEDA

chabola: self-made shanty dwelling and community of same in Madrid and much of Spain from 1940s to 1970s

checa: term based on Soviet word *tcheka*, used to describe the secret police organisations of the Popular Front during the war, particularly their clandestine prisons, symbolising political tyranny

CiU: Convergencia i Unió (centre-right Catalan nationalist party founded in 1978)

CNT: Confederación Nacional del Trabajo (National Confederation of Labour): anarcho-syndicalist union confederation founded in 1909

convivencia: living together harmoniously

Cortes: parliament (used in relation to the constituted law-making body of the Second Republic; later used under Franco for a body which was a direct emanation of executive power)

CSIC: Consejo Superior de Investigaciones Científicas (Higher Scientific Research Council, founded in 1939 to further Francoist cultural policy)

ETA: Euskadi Ta Askatasuna (Basque Homeland and Freedom, radical armed nationalist movement of the Basque Country, particularly active since late 1960s)

FAI: Federación Anarquista Ibérica (radical Iberian Anarchist Federation of the 1930s)

Falange: Spanish fascist party founded in 1933 by José Antonio Primo de Rivera, son of former military dictator from 1923 to 1930. Basis of Franco's single party FET-JONS

FET-JONS (also FET): Franco's single state political organisation formed by merging the Falange and Carlists in April 1937. Often known as the Movimiento.

FRAP: Frente Revolucionario Antifascista y Patriota (anti-Francoist Marxist-Leninist organisation of the 1970s)

HOAC: Hermandad Obrera de Acción Católica (Catholic workers' organisation founded in 1946)

Institución Libre de Enseñanza: liberal and progressive education movement founded in 1876, independent of the state-controlled and Catholic-influenced university system

IU: Izquierda Unida (United Left, formed in 1986, a coalition of leftist groups, including the PCE)

JAP: Juventud de Acción Popular (uniformed youth movement of the CEDA)

JOC: Juventud Obrera Cristiana (young workers' section of Acción Católica, AC)

JONS: Juntas de Ofensiva Nacional Sindicalista (fascist organisation founded in 1931 and fused with the Falange in 1934)

JSU: Juventudes Socialistas Unificadas (Socialist–Communist youth movement unified in 1936)

latifundismo: predominant land-holding system of much of southern Spain based on large estates, monocultural production, low-cost labour, and social injustice

moriscos: Muslims (often of European descent) converted forcibly to Christianity and repressed as heretics following the expulsion of Islam at the end of the fifteenth century

Movimiento: *see* FET-JONS

NKVD: Stalinist secret police (People's Commissariat of Internal Affairs)

PCE: Partido Comunista de España (Spanish Communist Party)

POUM: Partido Obrero de Unificación Marxista (Workers' Party for Marxist Unity)

PP: Partido Popular (conservative People's Party, founded 1989 and based on Alianza Popular)

PSOE: Partido Socialista Obrero Español (Spanish Socialist Party)

PSUC: Partit Socialista Unificat de Catalunya (Catalan Unified Socialist Party, the Catalan wing of the PCE)

RE: Renovación Española (monarchist elite political organisation of the 1930s)

requeté: member of the Carlist militia unit, the Requeté

SEU: Sindicato Español Universitario (Francoist-Falangist University Students' Union)

tercio: military division, often used with reference to the Foreign Legion or Carlist *Requeté*

UCD: Unión de Centro Democrático (conservative political party elected in 1977)

UGT: Unión General de Trabajadores (socialist General Workers' Union)

ultras: frequently used term for extremist or diehard rightists

vergüenza: shame

Sources and select bibliography

Primary sources
Archives
Archivo de Acción Católica General de Adultos de Madrid (AAC)
Archivo de la Cámara de Comercio de Bilbao (ACCB)
Archivo General de la Administración, Alcalá de Henares (AGA)

Sección Presidencia: Secretaría General del Movimiento (SGM)
Delegación Nacional Provincias (Correspondencia) (DNPC)

Barcelona	Guipúzcoa	Santander	Vizcaya
Córdoba	Jaén	Seville	
Granada	Madrid	Valencia	

Secretaría Política (SP)
Correspondencia
Vicesecretaria General (VCG)

Boletines Información Ambiente	Correspondencia	Proyectos de Ley
(Delegación Nacional de Información e	Informes	
Investigación – DNII)		

Archivo del Ministerio de Asuntos Exteriores, Madrid (MAE)
Archivo Municipal de Málaga (AMM)
Archivo de la Prisión Provincial de Málaga (APPM)
Arxiu General del 'Tribunal de Responsabilidades Polítiques' del Tribunal
Superior de Justicia de Catalunya, Barcelona (ATRP)
Centro Documental de la Memoria Histórica, Salamanca (CDMH)
The National Archives, Kew (TNA)

*Newspapers, periodicals and official publications (published in Madrid unless
otherwise stated)*

ABC (Madrid and Seville)	Arriba
Alcázar	La Batalla (Barcelona)
Anuario Estadístico	Blanco y Negro
Apostolado seglar	Boletín Minero e Industrial (Bilbao)

370   Sources and select bibliography

Boletín Oficial del Estado (BOE)
El Correo de Andalucía (Seville)
Cuadernos Para el Diálogo (CPED)
Diario de Burgos (Burgos)
Diario de Navarra (Pamplona)
Diario 16
Ecclesia
Fuego: Órgano de Acción Católica de Málaga (Málaga)
Gaceta de Madrid
Gaceta Médica Española
Hechos
Heraldo de Aragón (Zaragoza)
Hoja de Lunes
El Ideal Gallego (La Coruña)
Imperio (Zamora)
Información (Bilbao)
Informaciones
Interviú

Julio (Málaga)
Juventud
Libertad Española (Paris)
Mundo Obrero
Nuestra Bandera (Paris)
El País
El Popular (Málaga)
La Publicitat (Barcelona)
Pueblo
El Pueblo Gallego (Vigo)
Reconstrucción
Revista de Occidente
Semana Médica Española
El Socialista
Sur-¡Arriba! (Málaga)
La Vanguardia Española (Barcelona)
Vértice
Vida Nueva (Málaga)
Ya

Published documents
Congreso de los Diputados. *Diario de Sesiones del Congreso de los Diputados (DSCD)*
La Constitución Española (Madrid, 1971)
Dictamen de la comisión sobre ilegitimidad de poderes actuantes en 18 de julio de 1936 (Barcelona, 1939)
Ministerio de Justicia. *Causa general: La dominación roja en España. Avance de la información instruída por el Ministerio público* (Madrid, 1943)
La obra penitenciaria durante el año 1941 – El Patronato Central de Nuestra Señora de la merced para la redención de penas por el trabajo (Madrid, 1942, 1946, 1947)
Senado de las Cortes Generales. *Boletín Oficial de las Cortes Generales*

Published contemporary accounts, memoirs and testimony
Ana, Marcos. *Decidme cómo es un árbol* (Barcelona, 2007)
Arrarás Iribarren, Joaquín. *Historia de la cruzada española*, 6 vols. (Madrid, 1939–41)
Asamblea Conjunta Obispos-Sacerdotes. *Historia de la Asamblea* (Madrid, 1971)
Azaña, Manuel. *Obras completas* (ed. Juan Marichal), 3 vols. (Mexico City, 1966–7)
Barral, Carlos. *Años de penitencia* (Madrid, 1975)
Benet, Juan. *Qué fue la guerra civil* (Barcelona, 1976)
Bonal, Raimon. *Mataró 1974* (Barcelona, 1974)
Borràs Betriu, Rafael. *Los que no hicimos la guerra* (Barcelona, 1971)
Botey Vallès, Jaume. *Cinquanta-quatre relats d'immigració* (Barcelona, 1986)
Brenan, Gerald. *The Face of Spain* (Harmondsworth, 1965 [1950])
Buendía Gómez, Josefa. 'Peinando recuerdos', in María Guadalupe Pedrero and Concha Piñero (eds.), *Tejiendo recuerdos de la España de ayer* (Madrid, 2006)

Bullón de Mendoza, Alfonso and Álvaro de Diego. *Historias orales de la guerra civil* (Barcelona, 2000)

Caballero Giménez, Ernesto. *La matanza de Katyn (Visión sobre Rusia)* (Madrid, 1945)

Cabeza Calahorra, Manuel. *Ideología militar hoy* (Madrid, 1973)

Calvo Serer, Rafael. *España sin problema* (Madrid, 1949)

Calzada Rodríguez, Luciano de la. 'El espíritu del 18 de julio, como realidad histórica y proyección hacia el futuro', in Cátedra 'General Palafox' de Cultura Militar, *La guerra de liberación nacional* (Zaragoza, 1961)

Campo, Salustiano del. 'Los procesos ecológicos y sociales en la inmigración a Barcelona', in *Conversaciones sobre inmigración interior* (Barcelona, 1966)

Candel, Francisco. *Los otros catalanes* (Barcelona, 1965)

Careaga de Lequerica, Pilar. 'El advenimiento de la república', in *De la Regencia al día de la victoria* (Bilbao, 1956)

Castilla del Pino, Carlos. *Casa del olivo* (Barcelona, 2004)
La culpa: un estudio sobre la depresión y teoría de los sentimientos (Madrid, 1968)
Un estudio sobre la depresión: fundamentos de antropología dialéctica (Barcelona, 1966)

Cierva, Ricardo de la. *Cien libros básicos sobre la guerra de España* (Madrid, 1966)
Los documentos de la primavera trágica (Madrid, 1967)

Comín, Carlos Alfonso. *Obras*, 7 vols. (Barcelona, 1986–94)

Comissió de la Dignitat, La. *Volem els papers: la lluita de la Comissió de la Dignitat per la repatriació dels papers de Salamanca* (Lleida, 2004)

Conversaciones sobre inmigración interior (Barcelona, 1966)

Cruz, Sabina de la. 'Una familia rota; una sociedad truncada', in Emilio Silva (ed.), *La memoria de los olvidados* (Valladolid, 2004), pp. 79–84.

Domínguez Marroquín, Xavier. 'La Falange y sus caídos', in *De la Regencia al día de la victoria* (Bilbao, 1956)

Duocastella, Rogelio. *Análisis sociológico del catolicismo español* (Barcelona, 1967)
Mataró: estudio socio-económico y de planificación de servicios sociales, 2 vols. (Barcelona, 1967)

Elordi, Carlos (ed.). *Los años difíciles* (Madrid, 2002)

Enrique y Tarancón, Vicente. *Confesiones* (Madrid, 1996)
'La Iglesia en España hoy', in Olegario González de Cardedal (ed.), *Iglesia y política en España* (Salamanca, 1980), pp. 61–82
Recuerdos de juventud (Barcelona, 1984)

Esteva Fabregat, Claudio. *Industrialización e integración social* (Madrid, 1960)

Fraga Iribarne, Manuel. 'El 18 de julio y la juventud', in Cátedra 'General Palafox' de Cultura Militar, *La guerra de liberación nacional* (Zaragoza, 1961), pp. 669–92
Las transformaciones de la sociedad española contemporánea (Madrid, 1959)

Franco, Francisco. *Palabras del Caudillo* (Madrid, 1943)

Fraser, Ronald. *Blood of Spain: The Experience of Civil War, 1936–1939* (Harmondsworth, 1979)
In Hiding: The Life of Manuel Cortes (London, 1972)
The Pueblo: A Mountain Village on the Costa del Sol (London, 1973)

Fueyo Álvarez, Jesús. *Desarrollo político y orden constitucional* (Madrid, 1964)
Fundación FOESSA. *Informe sociológico sobre el cambio social en España,
    1975–1983* (Madrid, 1983)
    Informe sociológico sobre la situación social de España: 1970 (Madrid, 1972)
Fundación Nacional Francisco Franco (FNFF). *Documentos inéditos para la
    historia del Generalísimo Franco*, 3 vols. (Madrid, 1991–4)
Galinsoga, Luis and Francisco Franco-Salgado. *Centinela del occidente:
    semblanza biográfica de Francisco Franco* (Barcelona, 1956)
García Alonso, Francisco. *Flores de heroísmo* (Seville, 1939)
    Oración fúnebre predicada en la Santa Iglesia Catedral de Málaga (Cádiz, 1942)
García Arias, Luis. 'Sobre la mediación o la denominada tercera España',
    in Hermandad de Alféreces Provisionales, *Generación del 36* (Zaragoza,
    1962)
García Valcárcel, Jesús. 'Causas de la emigración española, interior y exterior', in
    Semanas Sociales, *Los problemas de la migración*, pp. 89–112
Gil Robles, José María. *No fue posible la paz* (Barcelona, 1968)
Gironella, José María. *Un millón de muertos* (Madrid, 1961)
González de Cardedal, Olegario. 'Iglesia y política', in González de Cardedal
    (ed.), *Iglesia y política en España* (Salamanca, 1980), pp. 23–60.
González Martín, Marcelo. '¿Qué queda de la España Católica? ¿Qué puede
    quedar a final de siglo?' in Olegario González de Cardedal (ed.), *Iglesia y
    política en España* (Salamanca, 1980), pp. 83–112.
González Posada, Carlos. *Diario de la revolución y de la guerra (1936–1939)*
    (ed. Miguel Ángel del Arco Blanco). (Granada, 2011)
Goytisolo, Juan. *Coto vedado* (Barcelona, 1985)
    Señas de identidad (Mexico, 1966)
Hardt, C. M. *Death in el Valle* (film: 1996): www.deathinelvalle.com/.
Iniesta, Alfonso. *Garra marxista en la infancia* (Burgos, 1939)
International Commission of Jurists. *Spain and the Rule of Law* (Geneva, 1962)
Jubany, Narciso. 'Neutralidad política de la iglesia', in Olegario González de
    Cardedal (ed.), *Iglesia y política en España* (Salamanca, 1980), pp. 113–34.
Laín Entralgo, Pedro. *Descargo de conciencia* (Barcelona, 1976)
    España como problema (Madrid, 1962 [1949])
Lara Sánchez, Francisco. *Emigración andaluza* (Madrid, 1977)
López Bulla, José. *Cuando hice las maletas: un paseo por el ayer* (Barcelona, 1997)
López Salinas, Armando. *La Mina* (Barcelona, 1960)
Llanos, José María. *Ser católico y obrar como tal* (Bilbao, 1968)
Marañón Moya, Gregorio. 'El alférez definitivo', in Hermandad de Alféreces
    Provisionales, *Generación del 36* (Zaragoza, 1962)
Marcos Hernández, Francisco. *La generación perdida: Murcia, Valencia y
    Barcelona (1926–1950)* (Barcelona, 2005)
Marías, Julián. 'La actitud religiosa de siete generaciones españolas', in Joaquín
    Ruiz-Giménez (ed.), *Iglesia, estado y sociedad en España, 1930–1982*
    (Barcelona, 1984), pp. 325–33.
    Una vida presente: memorias, 2 vols. (Madrid, 1989)
Marrero Suárez, Vicente. *La guerra española y el trust de cerebros* (Madrid, 1961)
Marsal, Juan F. *Pensar bajo el franquismo* (Barcelona, 1979)

Martín Gaite, Carmen. *Esperando el porvenir: homenaje a Ignacio Aldecoa* (Madrid, 1994)

Martínez-Alier, Juan. *Labourers and Landowners in Southern Spain* (London, 1971)

Mayoral, Juan. *Vallecas: las razones de una lucha popular* (Madrid, 1976)

Menchaca, Antonio. *La URSS hoy* (Madrid, 1967)

Mesa, Roberto (ed.). *Jaraneros y alborotadores: documentos sobre los sucesos estudiantiles de febrero de 1956 en la Universidad Complutense de Madrid* (Madrid, 1982)

Ministerio de Cultura. *La guerra civil española: exposición organizada por la Dirección General de Bellas Artes y Archivos* (Madrid, 1983)

Ministerio de Información. *25 aniversario de la paz española: el gobierno informa* (Madrid, 1964)

Molina, Esperanza. *Los otros madrileños* (Madrid, 1984)

Montero Moreno, Antonio. *Historia de la persecución religiosa en España, 1936–1939* (Madrid, 1961)

Morales Lezcano, Víctor and Teresa Pereira Rodríguez. *Memoria oral de una transformación social: percepciones de Madrid y sus pueblos a través de la senectud (1940–1992)* (Madrid, 1997)

Moreno Torres, José. *La reconstrucción urbana en España* (Madrid, 1945)

Muñóz Fernández, Antonia. 'La emigración en la provincia de Jaén 1900–1955', *Estudios geográficos*, 81 (November 1960), 455–96.

Orlandis Rovira, José. 'Veinticinco años después', in Hermandad Provincial de Alféreces Provisionales, *Generación del 36* (Zaragoza, 1962)

Oriol y Urquijo, Lucas María de. 'Los horizontes abiertos en 1936', in Hermandad de Alféreces Provisionales, *Generación del 36* (Zaragoza, 1962)

Ortega y Gasset, José. *Obras completas*, 12 vols. (Madrid, 1962–83)
  La rebelión de las masas (Madrid, 1976 [1929])

Pàmies, Teresa. *Los niños de guerra* (Barcelona, 1977)

Pedrero Sánchez, María Guadalupe. 'Las cartas de tío Eusebio', in Pedrero and Piñero, *Tejiendo recuerdos*

Pedrero Sánchez, María Guadalupe and Concha Piñero Valverde. *Tejiendo recuerdos de la España de ayer* (Madrid, 2006)

Pérez Díaz, Víctor. *Emigración y cambio social: procesos migratorios y vida rural en Castilla* (Barcelona, 1971)
  Estructura social del campo y éxodo rural: estudio de un pueblo de Castilla (Madrid, 1966)

Piñero Valverde, Concha. 'Mi Viejo album', in Pedrero and Piñero, *Tejiendo recuerdos*, pp. 55–91

Piquer y Jover, José J. *El niño abandonado y delincuente: consideración etiológica y estadística* (Madrid, 1946)

Reñones, Ángela. 'Un crisol para mis recuerdos', in Pedrero and Piñero (eds.), *Tejiendo recuerdos*, pp. 127–49

Ridruejo, Dionisio. *Escrito en España* (Buenos Aires, 1962)

Rodríguez Aldecoa, Josefina. *Los niños de la guerra* (Madrid, 1983)

Romero, Emilio. *El futuro de España* (Madrid, 1958)

Ruiz-Giménez, Joaquín. *Del ser de España* (Madrid, 1963)
  (ed.). *Iglesia, estado y sociedad en España, 1930–1982* (Barcelona, 1984)

San Martín, José Ignacio. *Servicio especial: a las órdenes de Carrero Blanco* (Barcelona, 1983)

Satrústegui, Joaquín. *Cuando la transición se hizo posible: el contubernio de Munich* (Madrid, 1993)

Sección Femenina de FET y de las JONS. *Formación familiar y social* (Madrid, n.d.)
Formación política: lecciones para las flechas (Madrid, n.d.)

Semanas Sociales de España. *Problemas de la clase media* (Madrid, 1951)
Los problemas de la migración española (Madrid, 1959)

Setién, José María. *La iglesia y lo social: ¿intromisión o mandato?* (Madrid, 1963)

Siguán, Miguel. *Del campo al suburbio: un estudio sobre la inmigración interior en España* (Madrid, 1959)

Valle, Florentino del. 'La inmigración en Madrid', in Semanas Sociales, *Los problemas de la migración*, pp. 375–92.

Vallejo Nágera, Antonio. *Divagaciones intrascendentes* (Valladolid, 1938)

Vidarte, Juan-Simeón. *Todos fuimos culpables* (Madrid, 1978)

Werner Bolín, Carmen. *Convivencia social: formación familiar y social* (Madrid, 1958)

Zugazagoitia, Julián. *Guerra y vicisitudes de los españoles*, (ed. Juliá, Santos). (Barcelona, 2001 [1940])

Secondary sources

Aceves, Joseph. *Social Change in a Spanish Village* (Cambridge, MA, 1971)

Aceves, Joseph and William Douglass (eds.). *The Changing Faces of Rural Spain* (Cambridge, MA, 1976)

Aguado, Ana and María Dolores Ramos. *La modernización de España (1917–1939): cultura y vida cotidiana* (Madrid, 2002)

Aguilar Fernández, Paloma. *Memoria y olvido de la guerra civil española* (Madrid, 1996)

Alexander, Jeffrey C. (ed.). *Cultural Trauma and Collective Identity* (Berkeley, CA, 2004)

Alonso Carballés, Jesús J. 'La construcción de una memoria colectiva del éxodo infantil vasco', in *Memoria e historia*, special edition of *Ayer* 32 (1998), ed. Cuesta Bustillo, pp. 163–93.

Altaffaylla Kultur Taldea. *Navarra, 1936: de la esperanza al terror* (Tafalla, 1986 (2nd edn, 2003))

Alted, Alicia (ed.). *Entre el pasado y el presente: historia y memoria* (Madrid, 1996)

Álvarez Oblanca, Wenceslao. *La represión de postguerra en León: depuración de la enseñanza, 1936–1943* (León, 1986)

Anderson, Peter. *The Francoist Military Trials: Terror and Complicity, 1939–1945* (London, 2010)
'In the Interests of Justice? Grass-roots Prosecution and Collaboration in Francoist Military Trials, 1939–1945', *Contemporary European History*, 18, 1, (2009), 25–44.

Arco Blanco, Miguel Ángel del. *Hambre de siglos: mundo rural y apoyos sociales del franquismo en Andalucía oriental (1936–1951)* (Granada, 2007)

Aróstegui, Julio (ed.). *España en la memoria de tres generaciones* (Madrid, 2007)
Historia y memoria de la guerra civil, 3 vols. (Valladolid, 1988)

Aróstegui, Julio and Sergio Gálvez (eds.). *Generaciones y memoria de la represión franquista* (Valencia, 2010)

Aróstegui, Julio and François Godicheau (eds.). *Guerra civil: mito y memoria* (Madrid, 2006)

Babiano Mora, José. *Emigrantes, cronómetros y huelgas: un estudio sobre el trabajo y los trabajadores durante el franquismo* (Madrid, 1995)

(ed.). *Del hogar a la huelga* (Madrid, 2007)

Balfour, Sebastian. *Dictatorship, Workers and the City: Labour in Greater Barcelona since 1939* (Oxford, 1989)

Barciela, Carlos. 'El mercado negro de productos agrarios en la posguerra 1939–1953', in Josep Fontana, (ed.), *España bajo el franquismo* (Barcelona, 1986)

Barker, Richard. *El largo trauma de un pueblo andaluz* (Seville, 2007)

Barranquero Texeira, Encarnación. *Málaga entre la guerra y la posguerra* (Málaga, 1994)

Barranquero Texeira, Encarnación, Matilde Eiroa San Francisco and Paloma Navarro Jiménez. *Mujer, cárcel, franquismo* (Málaga, 1994)

Barrull Pelegrí, Jaume. *Violència política i ruptura social a Espanya, 1936–1945* (Lleida, 1994)

Batista, Antoni. *La Brigada Social* (Barcelona, 1995)

Bell, Daniel. *The Cultural Contradictions of Capitalism* (New York, 1996 (1976))

Bell, Duncan S. A. 'Mythscapes: Memory, Mythology and National Identity', *British Journal of Sociology*, 54, 1 (March 2003), 63–81

Bernal, Antonio-Miguel. 'Resignación de los campesinos andaluces: la resistencia pasiva durante el franquismo', in Sánchez et al. (eds.), *España franquista*

Bessel, Richard and Dirk Schumann (eds.). *Life After Death: Approaches to a Cultural and Social History of Europe during the 1940s and 1950s* (Cambridge, 2003)

Blázquez, Feliciano. *La traición de los clérigos en la España de Franco: crónica de una tolerancia, 1936–1975* (Madrid, 1991)

Bolloten, Burnett. *The Grand Camouflage: The Communist Conspiracy in the Spanish Civil War* (London, 1961). Spanish edition: *El gran engaño* (Barcelona, 1961)

Bonet Correa, Antonio. *Arte del franquismo* (Madrid, 1981)

Borderías, Cristina. 'Las mujeres, autoras de sus trayectorias personales y familiares: a través del servicio doméstico', *Historia y Fuente Oral*, 6 (1991), 105–21

Brandes, Stanley H. *Migration, Kinship, and Community: Tradition and Transition in a Spanish Village* (New York, 1975)

Cámara Villar, Gregorio. *Nacional-catolicismo y escuela: la socialización política del franquismo (1936–1951)* (Jaén, 1984)

Campo Urbano, Salustiano del. *Análisis de la población de España* (Barcelona, 1972) *Tendencias sociales en España (1960–1990)*, 3 vols. (Madrid, 1994)

Campo, Salustiano del and Manuel Navarro. *Nuevo ánalisis de la poblacion espanola* (Barcelona, 1987)

Casanova, Julián. *República y guerra civil* (Barcelona, 2007)

Casanova, Julián, Angela Cenarro, Julita Cifuente, María del Pilar Maluenda, and María del Pilar Salomón. *El pasado oculto: fascismo y violencia en Aragón (1936–1939)* (Madrid, 1992)

Castro Berrojo, Luís. *Capital de la cruzada: Burgos durante la guerra civil* (Barcelona, 2006)

Cava Mesa, María Jesús. *Memoria colectiva del bombardeo de Gernika* (Bilbao, 1996).

Cazorla Sánchez, Antonio. *Fear and Progress: Ordinary Lives in Franco's Spain, 1939–1975* (Chichester, 2010)

Cervera, Javier. *Madrid en guerra: la ciudad clandestina* (Madrid, 2006)

Chao Rego, Xosé. *Iglesia y franquismo* (La Coruña, 2007)

Chaves Palacios, Julián. *La represión en la provincia de Cáceres durante la guerra civil (1936–1939)* (Cáceres, 1995)

Cobo Romero, Francisco. *Conflicto rural y violencia política* (Jaén, 1999)

Cobo Romero, Francisco and Teresa María Ortega López. *Franquismo y posguerra en Andalucía oriental* (Granada, 2005)

Collier, George A. *Socialists of Rural Andalusia: Unacknowledged Revolutionaries of the Second Republic* (Stanford, CA, 1987)

Conde, Rosa (ed.). *Familia y cambio social en España* (Madrid, 1982)

Confino, Alon. 'Collective Memory and Cultural History: Problems of Method', *American Historical Review*, 55, 3 (1997), 1,386–403

Connerton, Paul. *How Societies Remember* (Cambridge, 1989)

Crespo Redondo, Jesús, José Luis Sáinz Casado, José Crespo Redondo and Carlos Pérez Manrique. *Purga de maestros en la guerra civil: la depuración del magisterio nacional de la provincia de Burgos* (Valladolid, 1987)

Cruz, Rafael. *En el nombre del pueblo* (Madrid, 2006)

Cuesta Bustillo, Josefina (ed.). *Memoria e historia*, special edition of *Ayer*, 32 (1998)

Cueva, Julio de la. 'Religious Persecution, Anticlerical Tradition and Revolution: On Atrocities against the Clergy during the Spanish Civil War', *Journal of Contemporary History*, 33, 3 (1998), 355–69

Deák, István, Jan T. Gross and Tony Judt (eds.). *The Politics of Retribution in Europe* (Princeton, NJ, 2000)

Delgado, Manuel. 'Anticlericalismo, espacio y poder: la destrucción de los rituales católicos, 1931–39', *Ayer*, 27 (1997), 149–80

Díaz, Elías. *Pensamiento español en la era de Franco (1939–1975)* (Madrid, 1983)

Díaz Sánchez, Pilar. *El trabajo de las mujeres en el textil madrileño* (Málaga, 2001)

Díez Nicolás, Juan. 'La mortalidad en la guerra civil española', *Boletín de Demografía Histórica*, 3, 1 (March 1985), 41–55.

'La transición demográfica en España, 1900–1960', *Revista de Estudios Sociales*, 1, 89–158.

Domènech Sampere, Xavier. 'La otra cara del milagro español: clase obrera y movimiento obrero en los años del desarrollismo', *Historia Contemporánea*, 26 (2003), 91–112.

Eiroa San Francisco, Matilde. *Viva Franco: Hambre, racionamiento, falangismo. Málaga 1939–1942* (Málaga, 1995)

Elorza, Antonio. *Un pueblo escogido: génesis, definición y desarrollo del nacionalismo vasco* (Barcelona, 2001)

Escudero Andújar, Fuensanta. *Dictadura y oposición al franquismo en Murcia* (Murcia, 2007)

Espinosa Maestre, Francisco. *La columna de la muerte: el avance del ejército franquista de Sevilla a Badajoz* (Barcelona, 2003)

Contra el olvido: historia y memoria de la guerra civil (Barcelona, 2006)
Guerra civil en Huelva (Huelva, 1996)
La justicia de Queipo (Seville, 2000)
Evans, Richard. 'Redesigning the Past', *Journal of Contemporary History*, 38, 1 (2003), 5–12
Febo, Giuliana Di. *Resistencia y movimiento de mujeres en España, 1936–76* (Barcelona, 1979)
Feixa, Carles and Carme Agustí. 'Discursos autobiográficos de la prisión política', in Molinero et al. (eds.), *Una inmensa prisión* (Barcelona, 2003)
Fentress, James and Chris Wickham. *Social Memory* (Oxford, 1992)
Fernández Delgado, Javier, Mercedes Miguel Pasamontes and María Jesús Vega González. *La memoria impuesta: estudio y catálogo de los monumentos conmemorativos de Madrid (1939–1980)* (Madrid, 1982)
Fernández de Mata, Ignacio. 'El surgimiento de la memoria histórica: sentidos, malentendidos y disputas', in L. Díaz Viana and P. Tomé Martín (eds.), *La tradición como reclamo: antropología en Castilla y León* (Salamanca, 2007), pp. 195–208.
Folguera, Pilar. 'La construcción de lo cotidiano durante los primeros años del franquismo', *Ayer*, 19 (1995), 165–87.
Fontana, Josep (ed.). *España bajo el franquismo* (Barcelona, 1986)
Gabarda Ceballán, Vicente. *Els afusellaments al País Valencià (1938–1956)* (Valencia, 1993)
Gallego Méndez, María Teresa. *Mujer, falange y franquismo* (Madrid, 1983)
Garate, José María. *Alféreces provisionales: la improvisación de oficiales en la guerra del '36* (Madrid, 1976)
García-Nieto, María Carmen. *La España de Franco* (Madrid, 1975)
Garrabou, R., J. Lleixà and O. Pellissa. *Franquisme: sobre resistència i consens a Catalunya (1939–1959)* (Barcelona, 1990)
Gibson, Ian. *The Assassination of Federico García Lorca* (London, 1979)
Gil Andrés, Carlos. *Lejos del frente: la guerra civil en la Rioja Alta* (Barcelona, 2006)
Giner, Salvador. *España: sociedad y política* (Madrid, 1990)
Religión y sociedad en España (Madrid, 1993)
Gómez Benito, Cristóbal. *Políticos, burócratas y expertos: un estudio de la política agraria y la sociología rural en España (1936–1959)* (Madrid, 1996)
González Martínez, Carmen. *Guerra civil en Murcia* (Murcia, 1999)
Goytisolo, Juan. *Disidencias* (Barcelona, 1977)
Gracia, Jordi. *Estado y cultura: el despertar de una conciencia crítica bajo el franquismo, 1940–1962*, 2nd edn (Barcelona, 2006)
Graham, Helen. *The Spanish Republic at War, 1936–1939* (Cambridge, 2002)
The War and Its Shadow: Spain's Civil War in Europe's Long Twentieth Century (Eastbourne, 2012)
Gross, Jan T. *Revolution from Abroad: The Soviet Conquest of Poland's Western Ukraine and Western Belorussia* (Princeton, 1988)
Gutiérrez Flores, Jesús. *Guerra civil en Cantabria y pueblos de Castilla* (Buenos Aires, 2006)
Halbwachs, Maurice. *On Collective Memory* (ed. and trans. Lewis Coser) (Chicago, 1992 (1941, 1952))
Hansen, E. C. *Rural Catalonia under the Franco Regime* (Cambridge, 1977)

Hernández García, Antonio. *La represión en La Rioja durante la guerra civil*, 2 vols. (Logroño, 1984)

Herrero Balsa, Gregorio and Antonio Hernández García. *La represión en Soria durante la guerra civil* (Soria, 1982)

Heywood, Paul (ed.). *Politics and Policy in Democratic Spain* (London, 1999)

Holo, Selma Reuben. *Museums and Identity in Democratic Spain* (Liverpool, 1999)

Iglesia y sociedad en España, 1939–1975 (Madrid, 1977)

Ilie, Paul. *Literature and Inner Exile* (Baltimore, 1980)

Izquierdo Martín, Jesús and Pablo Sánchez León. *La guerra que nos han contado* (Madrid, 2006)

Jarne i Mòdol, Antonieta. *La secció femenina a Lleida* (Lleida, 1991)

Jerez-Ferrán, Carlos and Samuel Amago (eds.). *Unearthing Franco's Legacy* (Notre Dame, 2010)

Judt, Tony. *Reappraisals: Reflections on the Forgotten Twentieth Century* (London, 2009)

Juliá, Santos. 'El fracaso de la República', *Revista de Occidente*, 7–8 (November 1981), 196–211

'Obreros y sacerdotes: cultura democrática y movimientos sociales de oposición', in Tusell et al. (eds.), *La oposición al régimen de Franco*, 3 vols. (Madrid, 1990), vol. II, pp. 147–59

(ed.). *Víctimas de la guerra* (Madrid, 1999)

Juliá, Santos, Javier Pradera and Joaquín Prieto (eds.). *Memoria de la Transición* (Madrid, 1996)

Jutglar, Antoni (ed.). *La inmigración en Cataluña* (Barcelona, 1968)

Kalyvas, Stathis. *The Logic of Violence in Civil Wars* (Cambridge, 2006)

Kenny, Michael. *A Spanish Tapestry: Town and Country in Castile* (Bloomington, 1962)

King, Charles. *Ending Civil Wars* (Oxford, 1997)

Koselleck, Reinhart, *Futures Past: On the Semantics of Historical Time* (Columbia, 2004 (1979))

Lagrou, Pieter. *The Legacy of Nazi Occupation: Patriotic Memory and National Recovery in Western Europe, 1945–1965* (Cambridge, 2000)

Lannon, Frances. *Privilege, Persecution and Prophecy: The Catholic Church in Spain, 1875–1975* (Oxford, 1987)

Lazo, Alfonso. *Retrato del fascismo rural en Sevilla* (Seville, 1998)

Lebow, Richard Ned, Wulf Kansteiner and Claudio Fogu. *The Politics of Memory in Postwar Europe* (Durham, NC, 2006)

Ledesma, José Luis. *Los días de llamas de la revolución: violencia y política en la retaguardia republicana de Zaragoza durante la guerra civil* (Zaragoza, 2003)

Le Goff, Jacques. *History and Memory* (Columbia, 1992 (1977))

Lisón Tolosana, Carmelo. *Belmonte de los Caballeros: A Sociological Study of a Spanish Town* (Oxford, 1966)

Lizcano, Pablo. *La generación del 56: la universidad contra Franco* (Barcelona, 1981)

Losada Malvárez, Juan Carlos. *Ideología del ejército franquista, 1939–1959* (Madrid, 1990)

Lozano Nieto, Juan Manuel. *A sangre y fuego: los años treinta en un pueblo andaluz* (Seville, 2006)

Lucea Ayala, Víctor. *Dispuestos a intervenir. Antonio Plano Aznárez: socialismo y republicanismo en Uncastillo (1900–1939)* (Zaragoza, 2008)

Madalena Calvo, José, María Carmen Escudero, Alfredo Prieto Altamira and José Francisco Reguillo. 'Los lugares de la memoria de la guerra civil en un centro de poder: Salamanca 1936–39', in Aróstegui, *Historia y memoria*

Mann, Michael. *Fascists* (Cambridge, 2004)

Mannheim, Karl. 'The Problem of Generations' [1928], in *From Karl Mannheim*, ed. Kurt H. Wolff, 2nd edn (New Jersey, 1993)

Margalit, Avishai. *The Ethics of Memory* (Harvard, 2002)

Martín Descalzo, José Luis. *Tarancón, el cardenal del cambio* (Madrid, 1982)

Martín Gaite, Carmen. *Usos amorosos de la posguerra española* (Barcelona, 1987)

Martín Jiménez, Ignacio. *Guerra civil en Valladolid* (Valladolid, 2000)

Martínez Reverte, Jorge. *La batalla de Madrid* (Barcelona, 2004)

Martínez Tórtola, Esther. *La enseñanza de la historia en el primer bachillerato franquista (1938–1953)* (Madrid, 1996)

Mayordomo Pérez, Alejandro. *Nacional-catolicismo y educación en la España de posguerra* (Madrid, 1990)

Megill, Allan. 'History, Memory, Identity', *History of the Human Sciences*, 11, 3 (1998), 37–62.

Miguel, Amando de. *España cíclica: ciclos económicos y generaciones demográficas en la sociedad española contemporánea* (Madrid, 1986)

Ministerio de Cultura. *Justicia en guerra: jornadas sobre la administración de Justicia durante la guerra civil española* (Madrid, 1990)

Las mujeres y la guerra civil española, II Jornadas de estudios monográficos, Salamanca, October 1989 (Madrid, 1991)

Mir, Conxita. *Vivir es sobrevivir: justicia, orden y marginación en la Cataluña rural de la postguerra (1939–1951)* (Lleida, 2000)

Molinero, Carme, Margarida Sala and Jaume Sobrequés (eds.). *Una inmensa prisión* (Barcelona, 2003)

Molinero, Carme and Pere Ysàs. *'Patria, Justicia y Pan': la repressió franquista a Catalunya, 1939–1951* (Barcelona, 1985)

Monasterio Baldor, Agustina. 'Cuando los árboles caminan: memoria oral y guerra civil en el valle del Miera', unpublished paper, New York University, 2010

Montero García, Feliciano. *La Acción Católica y el franquismo* (Madrid, 2000)

Montoliú Camps, Pedro. *Madrid en la guerra civil* (Madrid, 1999)

Moral Roncal, Antonio Manuel. *Diplomacia, humanitarismo y espionaje en la guerra civil española* (Madrid, 2008)

Moreno Gómez, Francisco. *Córdoba en la posguerra* (Córdoba, 1987)

La guerra civil en Córdoba 1936–1939 (Madrid, 1985)

Moreno Juliá, Xavier. *La División Azul: sangre española en Rusia, 1941–1945* (Barcelona, 2005)

Moreno Seco, Mónica. 'De la caridad al compromiso: las mujeres de Acción Católica (1958–1968)', *Historia Contemporánea*, 26, 1 (2003), 239–65

Morente Valero, Francisco. *La escuela y el estado nuevo: la depuración del magisterio nacional (1936–1943)* (Valladolid, 1997)

Müller, Jan-Werner (ed.). *Memory and Power in Post-War Europe* (Cambridge, 2002)

Muñoz Cidad, Cándido and Laureano Lázaro Araújo. 'El desarrollo desigual en España', in Roberto Carballo, Antonio González Temprano and José Antonio Moral Santín (eds.), *Crecimiento económico y crisis estructural en España, 1959–1980* (Madrid, 1980)

Muñoz Soro, Javier. 'Joaquín Ruiz-Giménez o el católico total (Apuntes para una biografía política e intelectual hasta 1963)', *Pasado y Memoria: Revista de Historia Contemporánea*, 5 (2006), 259–88.

Nadal, Antonio. *Guerra civil en Málaga* (Málaga, 1984)

Naredo, José Manuel. *La evolución de la agricultura en España (1940–1990)* (Granada, 1996)

Núñez Seixas, Xosé Manoel. 'Los vencedores vencidos: la peculiar memoria de la División Azul, 1945–2005', *Pasado y Memoria*, 4, 2005

Olick, Jeffrey. *The Politics of Regret* (London, 2007)

Olmeda, Fernando. *El Valle de los Caídos* (Barcelona, 2009)

Ortiz Heras, Manuel. *Violencia política en la II República y el primer franquismo: Albacete, 1936–1950* (Madrid, 1996)

Ortiz Villalba, Juan. *Sevilla '36: del golpe militar a la guerra civil* (Córdoba, 1998)

Payne, Stanley. *Falange* (Stanford, 1961)

   The Franco Regime, 1936–1975 (Wisconsin, 1987)

   Spain's First Democracy: The Second Republic, 1931–1936 (Madison, 1993)

Pérez, José Antonio. 'Trabajo doméstico y economías sumergidas en el gran Bilbao a lo largo del desarrollismo', in José Babiano (ed.), *Del hogar a la huelga*, pp. 77–136.

Pérez Díaz, Víctor. *Pueblos y clases sociales en el campo español* (Madrid, 1974)

Pérez Díaz, Victor M. *The Return of Civil Society: The Emergence of Democratic Spain* (Cambridge, MA, 1993)

Pitt-Rivers, J. A. *The People of the Sierra* (London, 1954)

Plá Brugat, Dolores. 'La experiencia del regreso: el caso de los exiliados republicanos catalanes', in Trujillano and Gago, *Historia y memoria*, pp. 84–7

Prego, Victoria. *Así se hizo la Transición* (Barcelona, 1995)

Preston, Paul. *The Coming of the Spanish Civil War: Reform, Reaction and Revolution in the Second Republic* (London, 1978)

   Franco: A Biography (London, 1993)

   The Politics of Revenge: Fascism and the Military in Twentieth-Century Spain (London, 1990)

   The Spanish Holocaust (London, 2012)

   Las tres españas del '36 (Barcelona, 1998)

   The Triumph of Democracy in Spain (London, 1986)

Puig i Valls, Angelina. 'La guerra civil espanyola, una causa de l'emigració andalusa en la dècada dels anys cinquanta?' *Recerques*, 31 (1995), 53–69

Radcliff, Pamela Beth. *Making Democratic Citizens in Spain: Civil Society and the Popular Origins of the Transition, 1960–78* (Basingstoke, 2011)

Raguer, Hilari. *La pólvora y el incienso* (Barcelona, 2001)

   La unió democràtica de Catalunya i el seu temps (1931–1939) (Barcelona, 1976)

Richards, Michael. 'Between Memory and History: Social Relationships and Ways of Remembering the Spanish Civil War', *International Journal of Iberian Studies*, 19, 1 (2006), 85–94

'Biology and Morality in the Spanish Civil War: Psychiatrists, Revolution and Women Prisoners in Málaga', *Contemporary European History*, 14, 1 (2001), 395–421.

'Falange, Autarky and Crisis: The Barcelona General Strike of 1951', *European History Quarterly*, 29 (4) (1999), 543–85.

'From War Culture to Civil Society: Francoism, Social Change and Memories of the Spanish Civil War', *History and Memory*, 14, 1/2 (Fall 2002), 93–120.

'Ideology and the Psychology of War Children in Franco's Spain, 1936–45', in Kjersti Ericsson and Eva Simonsen (eds.), *Children of World War II: The Hidden Enemy Legacy* (Oxford, 2005), pp. 73–101

'The Limits of Quantification: Francoist Repression and Historical Methodology', in Aróstegui and Gálvez (eds.), *Generaciones*, pp. 787–820.

'Presenting Arms to the Blessed Sacrament: Civil War and Semana Santa in the City of Málaga, 1936–1939', in C. Ealham and Michael Richards (eds.), *The Splintering of Spain: Cultural History and the Spanish Civil War* (Cambridge, 2005)

A Time of Silence: Civil War and the Culture of Repression in Franco's Spain, 1936–1945 (Cambridge, 1998)

Rilova Pérez, Isaac. *Guerra civil y violencia política en Burgos (1936–1939)* (Burgos, 2001)

Riquer, Borja de and Joan Culla. *El franquisme i la transicio democratica (1939–1988), Historia de Catalunya*, vol. VII (Barcelona, 1989)

Roca i Girona, Jordi. *De la pureza a la maternidad: la construcción del género femenino en la postguerra española* (Madrid, 1996)

Rodrigo, Javier. *Cautivos: campos de concentración en la España franquista, 1936–1947* (Barcelona, 2005)

Rodríguez, José Luis. *Reaccionarios y golpistas: la extrema derecha en España* (Madrid, 1994)

Roig, Montserrat. *Noche y niebla: los catalanes en los campos nazis* (Barcelona, 1978)

Romero Salvadó, Francisco J. *The Spanish Civil War* (Houndmills, 2005)

Rousso, Henry. *The Vichy Syndrome: History and Memory in France since 1944* (Cambridge, MA, 1991)

Ruiz, Julius. *Franco's Justice* (Oxford, 2005)

Saíz Marín, J. *El Frente de Juventudes: política de juventud en la España de la postguerra (1937–1960)* (Madrid, 1988)

Salas Larrazábal, Ramón. *Pérdidas de la guerra* (Barcelona, 1977)

Sánchez, Isidro, Manuel Ortiz and David Ruiz (eds.). *España franquista: Causa General y actitudes sociales ante la dictadura* (Castilla-La Mancha, 1993)

Sánchez-Bravo, Antonio and Antonio Tellado. *Los mutilados del ejército de la República* (Madrid, 1976)

Sánchez Jiménez, José. *Vida rural y mundo contemporáneo* (Barcelona, 1976)

Sánchez Tostado, Luis Miguel. *La guerra no acabó en el 39* (Jaén, 2001)

Santacana i Torres, Carles. *Victoriosos i derrotats: el franquisme a L'Hospitalet, 1939–1951* (Barcelona, 1994)

Saz, I. and J. A. Gómez Roda (eds.). *El franquismo en Valencia: formas de vida y actitudes sociales en la posguerra* (Valencia, 1999)

Seidman, Michael. *Republic of Egos: A Social History of the Spanish Civil War* (Madison, 2002)

Sevilla Guzmán, Eduardo. 'El campesinado en el desarrollo capitalista español (1939–1975)', in Paul Preston (ed.), *España en crisis* (Madrid, 1978), pp. 183–215

La evolución del campesinado en España (Barcelona, 1979)

Sevilla Guzmán, Eduardo and Manuel González de Molina. 'Política social agraria del primer franquismo', in J. L. García Delgado (ed.), *El primer franquismo* (Madrid, 1989), pp. 135–87.

Shubert, Adrian. *A Social History of Modern Spain* (London, 1990)

Silva, Emilio (ed.). *La memoria de los olvidados* (Valladolid, 2004)

Silva, Emilio and Santiago Macías. *Las fosas de Franco: los republicanos que el dictador dejó en las cunetas* (Madrid, 2003)

Sivan, Emmanuel and Jay Winter. *War and Remembrance in the Twentieth Century* (Cambridge, 1999)

Smelser, Neil J. 'Psychological Trauma and Cultural Trauma', in Alexander (ed.), *Cultural Trauma*

Solé, Carlota. *Los inmigrantes en la sociedad y en la cultura catalanas* (Barcelona, 1982)

Solé i Sabaté, Josep María. *La repressió franquista a Catalunya 1938–1953* (Barcelona, 1985)

Solé i Sabaté, Josep María and Joan Villaroya. *La repressió a la reraguarda de Catalunya (1936–1939)* (Barcelona, 1989)

Southworth, Herbert. *Antifalange* (Paris, 1967)

Souto Blanco, María Jesús. *La represión franquista en la provincia de Lugo (1936–1940)* (La Coruña, 1998)

Souto Kustrín, Sandra. '*Y ¿Madrid? ¿Qué hace Madrid?'* Movimiento revolucionario y acción colectiva (1933–1936)* (Madrid, 2004)

Sueiro, Daniel. *La verdadera historia del Valle de los Caídos* (Madrid, 1976)

Tortella, Gabriel. 'Sobre el significado histórico del franquismo', *Revista de Occidente*, 59 (1986), 104–14.

Townson, Nigel (ed.). *Spain Transformed: The Late Franco Dictatorship, 1959–75* (Basingstoke, 2007)

Trujillano Sánchez, José Manuel (ed.). *Historia y fuentes orales: memoria y sociedad en la Espana contemporánea* (Ávila, 1993)

Trujillano Sánchez, José Manuel and Pilar Díaz Sánchez (eds.). *Historia y fuentes orales: Testimonios orales y escritos. España, 1936–1996* (Ávila, 1998)

Trujillano Sánchez, José Manuel and José María Gago (eds.). *Historia y fuentes orales: historia y memoria del franquismo* (Ávila, 1997)

Tuñón de Lara, Manuel, Julío Aróstegui, Ángel Viñas, Gabriel Cardona and Josep M. Bricall. *La guerra civil española 50 años después* (Barcelona, 1985)

Tusell, Javier. *Franco y los católicos: la política interior española entre 1945 y 1957* (Madrid, 1984)

(ed.). *El régimen de Franco (1936–1975)* (Madrid, 1993)

Tusell, Javier, Alicia Alted Vigil and Abdón Mateos López (eds.). *La oposición al régimen de Franco* (Madrid, 1990)

Ugarte Tellería, Javier. *La nueva Covadonga insurgente: orígenes sociales y culturales de la sublevación de 1936 en Navarra y el País Vasco* (Madrid, 1998)

Ureña, Gabriel. *Arquitectura y urbanística civil y militar en el período de la autarquía (1936–1945)* (Madrid, 1979)

Vázquez Montalbán, Manuel. 'Para una nueva conciencia nacional catalana', in Solé, *Inmigrantes*, pp. 9–13.

Vega, Pedro. *Historia de la Liga de Mutilados* (Madrid, 1981)

Vega Sombría, Santiago. *De la esperanza a la persecución: la represión franquista en la provincia de Segovia* (Barcelona, 2005)

Vilanova, Mercedes (ed.). *El poder en la sociedad* (Barcelona, 1986)

Vincent, Mary. *Catholicism and the Second Spanish Republic: Religion and Politics in Salamanca, 1930–1936* (Oxford, 1996)

'The Keys of the Kingdom: Religious Violence in the Spanish Civil War, July–August 1936', in C. Ealham and M. Richards (eds.), *The Splintering of Spain: Cultural History and the Spanish Civil War* (Cambridge, 2005), pp.68–89.

'"The Martyrs and the Saints": Masculinity and the Construction of the Francoist Crusade', *History Workshop Journal*, 47 (1999), 69–98.

Spain, 1833–2002: People and State (Oxford, 2007)

Vinyes, Ricard, Montse Armengou and Ricard Belis. *Los niños perdidos del franquismo* (Barcelona, 2002)

Viñas, Ángel. *El Escudo de la República* (Barcelona, 2007)

Winter, Jay. *Remembering War* (New Haven, 2006)

Index